T0137751

Lecture Notes in Computer Science 13321

More information about this series at https://link.springer.com/bookseries/558

Marcelo M. Soares · Elizabeth Rosenzweig ·
Aaron Marcus (Eds.)

Design, User Experience, and Usability

UX Research, Design, and Assessment

11th International Conference, DUXU 2022
Held as Part of the 24th HCI International Conference, HCII 2022
Virtual Event, June 26 – July 1, 2022
Proceedings, Part I

Springer

Editors
Marcelo M. Soares
Southern University of Science
and Technology – SUSTech
Shenzhen, China

Elizabeth Rosenzweig
World Usability Day and Bubble Mountain
Consulting
Newton Center, MA, USA

Aaron Marcus
Aaron Marcus and Associates
Berkeley, CA, USA

ISSN 0302-9743 ISSN 1611-3349 (electronic)
Lecture Notes in Computer Science
ISBN 978-3-031-05896-7 ISBN 978-3-031-05897-4 (eBook)
https://doi.org/10.1007/978-3-031-05897-4

This Springer imprint is published by the registered company Springer Nature Switzerland AG
The registered company address is: Gewerbestrasse 11, 6330 Cham, Switzerland

Foreword

Human-computer interaction (HCI) is acquiring an ever-increasing scientific and industrial importance, as well as having more impact on people's everyday life, as an ever-growing number of human activities are progressively moving from the physical to the digital world. This process, which has been ongoing for some time now, has been dramatically accelerated by the COVID-19 pandemic. The HCI International (HCII) conference series, held yearly, aims to respond to the compelling need to advance the exchange of knowledge and research and development efforts on the human aspects of design and use of computing systems.

The 24th International Conference on Human-Computer Interaction, HCI International 2022 (HCII 2022), was planned to be held at the Gothia Towers Hotel and Swedish Exhibition & Congress Centre, Göteborg, Sweden, during June 26 to July 1, 2022. Due to the COVID-19 pandemic and with everyone's health and safety in mind, HCII 2022 was organized and run as a virtual conference. It incorporated the 21 thematic areas and affiliated conferences listed on the following page.

A total of 5583 individuals from academia, research institutes, industry, and governmental agencies from 88 countries submitted contributions, and 1276 papers and 275 posters were included in the proceedings to appear just before the start of the conference. The contributions thoroughly cover the entire field of human-computer interaction, addressing major advances in knowledge and effective use of computers in a variety of application areas. These papers provide academics, researchers, engineers, scientists, practitioners, and students with state-of-the-art information on the most recent advances in HCI. The volumes constituting the set of proceedings to appear before the start of the conference are listed in the following pages.

The HCI International (HCII) conference also offers the option of 'Late Breaking Work' which applies both for papers and posters, and the corresponding volume(s) of the proceedings will appear after the conference. Full papers will be included in the 'HCII 2022 - Late Breaking Papers' volumes of the proceedings to be published in the Springer LNCS series, while 'Poster Extended Abstracts' will be included as short research papers in the 'HCII 2022 - Late Breaking Posters' volumes to be published in the Springer CCIS series.

I would like to thank the Program Board Chairs and the members of the Program Boards of all thematic areas and affiliated conferences for their contribution and support towards the highest scientific quality and overall success of the HCI International 2022 conference; they have helped in so many ways, including session organization, paper reviewing (single-blind review process, with a minimum of two reviews per submission) and, more generally, acting as goodwill ambassadors for the HCII conference.

This conference would not have been possible without the continuous and unwavering support and advice of Gavriel Salvendy, founder, General Chair Emeritus, and Scientific Advisor. For his outstanding efforts, I would like to express my appreciation to Abbas Moallem, Communications Chair and Editor of HCI International News.

June 2022   Constantine Stephanidis

HCI International 2022 Thematic Areas and Affiliated Conferences

Thematic Areas

- HCI: Human-Computer Interaction
- HIMI: Human Interface and the Management of Information

Affiliated Conferences

- EPCE: 19th International Conference on Engineering Psychology and Cognitive Ergonomics
- AC: 16th International Conference on Augmented Cognition
- UAHCI: 16th International Conference on Universal Access in Human-Computer Interaction
- CCD: 14th International Conference on Cross-Cultural Design
- SCSM: 14th International Conference on Social Computing and Social Media
- VAMR: 14th International Conference on Virtual, Augmented and Mixed Reality
- DHM: 13th International Conference on Digital Human Modeling and Applications in Health, Safety, Ergonomics and Risk Management
- DUXU: 11th International Conference on Design, User Experience and Usability
- C&C: 10th International Conference on Culture and Computing
- DAPI: 10th International Conference on Distributed, Ambient and Pervasive Interactions
- HCIBGO: 9th International Conference on HCI in Business, Government and Organizations
- LCT: 9th International Conference on Learning and Collaboration Technologies
- ITAP: 8th International Conference on Human Aspects of IT for the Aged Population
- AIS: 4th International Conference on Adaptive Instructional Systems
- HCI-CPT: 4th International Conference on HCI for Cybersecurity, Privacy and Trust
- HCI-Games: 4th International Conference on HCI in Games
- MobiTAS: 4th International Conference on HCI in Mobility, Transport and Automotive Systems
- AI-HCI: 3rd International Conference on Artificial Intelligence in HCI
- MOBILE: 3rd International Conference on Design, Operation and Evaluation of Mobile Communications

List of Conference Proceedings Volumes Appearing Before the Conference

39. CCIS 1582, HCI International 2022 Posters - Part III, edited by Constantine Stephanidis, Margherita Antona and Stavroula Ntoa
40. CCIS 1583, HCI International 2022 Posters - Part IV, edited by Constantine Stephanidis, Margherita Antona and Stavroula Ntoa

http://2022.hci.international/proceedings

Preface

User experience (UX) refers to a person's thoughts, feelings, and behavior when using interactive systems. UX design becomes fundamentally important for new and emerging mobile, ubiquitous, and omnipresent computer-based contexts. The scope of design, user experience and usability (DUXU) extends to all aspects of the user's interaction with a product or service, how it is perceived, learned, and used. DUXU also addresses design knowledge, methods and practices, with a focus on deeply human-centered processes. Usability, usefulness, and appeal are fundamental requirements for effective user-experience design.

The 11th Design, User Experience, and Usability (DUXU) Conference 2022, an affiliated conference of the HCI International Conference, encouraged papers from professionals, academics, and researchers that report results and cover a broad range of research and development activities on a variety of related topics. Professionals include designers, software engineers, scientists, marketers, business leaders, and practitioners infields such as AI, architecture, financial and wealth management, game design, graphic design, finance, healthcare, industrial design, mobile, psychology, travel, and vehicles.

This year's submissions covered a wide range of content across the spectrum of design, user-experience, and usability. The latest trends and technologies are represented, as well as contributions from professionals, academics, and researchers across the globe. The breadth of their work is indicated in the following topics covered in the proceedings.

Three volumes of the HCII 2022 proceedings are dedicated to this year's edition of the DUXU Conference:

- Design, User Experience, and Usability: UX Research, Design, and Assessment (Part I), which addresses topics related to processes, methods, and tools for UX design and evaluation; user requirements, preferences and UX influential factors; as well as usability, acceptance, and user experience assessment.
- Design, User Experience, and Usability: Design for Emotion, Well-being and Health, Learning, and Culture (Part II), which addresses topics related to emotion, motivation, and persuasion design; design for well-being and health; learning experience-design; as well as globalization, localization, and culture issues.
- Design, User Experience, and Usability: Design Thinking and Practice in Contemporary and Emerging Technologies (Part III), which addresses topics related to design thinking and philosophy, analysis of case studies, as well as design and user experience in emerging technologies.

Papers of these volumes are included for publication after a minimum of two single–blind reviews from the members of the DUXU Program Board or, in some cases, from members of the Program Boards of other affiliated conferences. We would like to thank all of them for their invaluable contribution, support, and efforts.

June 2022   Marcelo M. Soares
                                        Elizabeth Rosenzweig
                                              Aaron Marcus

11th International Conference on Design, User Experience and Usability (DUXU 2022)

Program Board Chairs: **Marcelo M. Soares**, Southern University of Science and Technology – SUSTech, China, **Elizabeth Rosenzweig**, World Usability Day and Bubble Mountain Consulting, USA, and **Aaron Marcus**, Aaron Marcus and Associates, USA

- Sisira Adikari, University of Canberra, Australia
- Ahmad Alhuwwari, Orange Jordan, Jordan
- Claire Ancient, University of Winchester, UK
- Roger Ball, Georgia Institute of Technology, USA
- Eric Brangier, Université de Lorraine, France
- Tian Cao, Nanjing University of Science & Technology, China
- Silvia De los Rios, Indra, Spain
- Romi Dey, Solved By Design, India
- Marc Fabri, Leeds Beckett University, UK
- Wei Liu, Beijing Normal University, China
- Zhen Liu, South China University of Technology, China
- Martin Maguire, Loughborough University, UK
- Judith Moldenhauer, Wayne State University, USA
- Gunther Paul, James Cook University, Australia
- Francisco Rebelo, University of Lisbon, Portugal
- Christine Riedmann-Streitz, MarkenFactory GmbH, Germany
- Patricia Search, Rensselaer Polytechnic Institute, USA
- Dorothy Shamonsky, Brandeis University, USA
- David Sless, Communication Research Institute, Australia
- Elisangela Vilar, Universidade de Lisboa, Portugal
- Wei Wang, Hunan University, China
- Haining Wang, Hunan University, China

The full list with the Program Board Chairs and the members of the Program Boards of all thematic areas and affiliated conferences is available online at

http://www.hci.international/board-members-2022.php

HCI International 2023

The 25th International Conference on Human-Computer Interaction, HCI International 2023, will be held jointly with the affiliated conferences at the AC Bella Sky Hotel and Bella Center, Copenhagen, Denmark, 23–28 July 2023. It will cover a broad spectrum of themes related to human-computer interaction, including theoretical issues, methods, tools, processes, and case studies in HCI design, as well as novel interaction techniques, interfaces, and applications. The proceedings will be published by Springer. More information will be available on the conference website: http://2023.hci.international/.

General Chair
Constantine Stephanidis
University of Crete and ICS-FORTH
Heraklion, Crete, Greece
Email: general_chair@hcii2023.org

http://2023.hci.international/

Contents – Part I

User Requirements, Preferences, and UX Influential Factors

Usability, Acceptance, and User Experience Assessment

Contents – Part II

Contents – Part III

Design and User Experience in Emerging Technologies

Processes, Methods, and Tools for UX Design and Evaluation

Customer Hierarchy of Needs: Customer Centric Approach to Agile Product Development

Paige Dysert$^{(\boxtimes)}$ and Sasanka Prabhala

Design Research, Crown Equipment Corporation, 44 S Washington St.,
New Bremen, OH 45869, USA
`{paige.dysert,sasanka.prabhala}@crown.com`

Abstract. Oftentimes in Agile product development, the MVP (minimum viable product) is defined and agreed upon for development to release product quickly to learn directly from customers. As the team develops and works through the requirements for MVP, scope creep can happen; requirements change; or new customer requests come in which may change the direction of the work. When this occurs, the instinct of the team is to "react" to the changing demands and can cause the team to lose focus of what the original customer need was. To ensure that the development team is keeping the customer at the focal point of the work, the Customer Hierarchy of Needs was developed. The Customer Hierarchy of Needs method is an effective way to define and prioritize features and functionality for a product through the lens of what the customer may need or want based on their existing level of need. In this paper, we will explain the customer hierarchy of needs method, how it was applied to a project at Crown Equipment Corporation, lessons learned by the development team, and the benefits of utilizing this method.

Keywords: Agile · MVP · Customer Value · Hierarchy of Needs · Design research

1 Introduction

Agile is an iterative approach to software development that allows companies to deliver value to their customers fast [1]. Agile has many advantages; like being able to release product quickly to the market with less documentation, getting product in the hands of customers to learn directly from them to continually improve the product, and being lean in processes to be able to pivot at any time as customer needs evolve. When creating a new product for the market, defining the minimum viable product (MVP) based on the minimal amount of work that can be done that adds value to the product is the main objective. But as the team works on the agreed upon MVP, scope creep can happen; requirements can change; and customer needs can shift which will change the direction of the project. This leads to teams getting sidetracked, which then makes it difficult to measure the progress of the MVP solution leading to teams feeling that they are on projects that never end. Furthermore, there are very few tools or methods that are in place today to help management keep track of requirements as they come in and help

© The Author(s), under exclusive license to Springer Nature Switzerland AG 2022
M. M. Soares et al. (Eds.): HCII 2022, LNCS 13321, pp. 3–11, 2022.
https://doi.org/10.1007/978-3-031-05897-4_1

with evaluating whether those requirements will ultimately meet the needs of customers and at what level [2]. Such requirements can come from various sources including the project sponsor, stakeholders, executives, and end-users. The lack of documentation for projects and the nature of Agile to not fully define the vision of a solution also leads to potential confusion if requirements and features change over time due to customer feedback and requests. This can also lead to difficulties onboarding new developers if the background of why decisions were made are not documented or the vision of the solution beyond MVP [3].

To ensure that the development team is keeping the customer at the focal point of the work and to reduce the likelihood of the previous challenges being introduced to a project, this Customer Hierarchy of Needs was created.

2   What Is the Customer Hierarchy of Needs

The Customer Hierarchy of Needs method is an effective way to define and prioritize features and functionality of a solution through the lens of what the customer may need (see Fig. 1). Also, it can be used as a checkpoint to ensure that the final solution fulfills the customer's need and to validate that it doesn't inhibit the customer from being able to progress to the next level of need. The framework helps to define the functionality, in other words, the "what" and "how" behind a solution. The inspiration for the Customer Hierarchy of Needs method is Maslow's hierarchy of needs, "…a motivational theory in psychology comprising a five-tier model of human needs, often depicted as hierarchical levels within a pyramid" [4]. Just as humans progress in their personal lives, customers also have basic (or functional) and complex needs that products or services must fulfill before they are able to experience the full potential of the product or service. Also, like Maslow's hierarchy, customers can face challenges or set-backs which may move them to a different level of need [4]. So, it is important to ensure that the solution developed meets the customer with wherever they are professionally or personally.

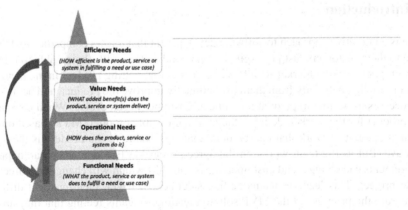

Fig. 1. Customer hierarchy of needs template.

This method can be used once preliminary research has been completed, and the perceived value of the solution has been defined and understood. This method can be applied to both create a vision and, in an Agile development process, to evaluate changes in requirements. It should be used to facilitate conversations around defining and validating the product vision, as well as MVP features and functionality of a solution in the development process, with the understanding that the customers level of experience and expectations can determine their beginning level within the hierarchy. Lastly, this method can be utilized by design teams, development teams, and other business groups that may interface with customers and influence solution requirements. Now we will walk through the method in detail, starting with Functional Needs.

2.1 Functional Needs

The first level is Functional Needs. They are the most basic needs that are practical and needed for the market. In other words, what should the solution do to help customers address their business challenge. Functional needs can also be foundational aspects that are needed for the solution being developed. Like physiological needs that must be met at the foundation of Maslow's hierarchy, the functional needs of a technical product must include the functionality and feature(s) that are foundational to the final solution [4].

To further explain how this method can be applied with a consumer product we will use the example of a digital watch. The functional purpose of a watch is to tell the time. Why consumers purchase a watch is to be able to tell time whenever and wherever they need to. There are options for analog or digital watches, providing different preferences for consumers, but the basic goal is for consumers to be able to quickly check the time from anywhere directly on their wrist (Fig. 2).

Fig. 2. Customer Hierarchy of Needs: Functional Needs.

2.2 Operational Needs

The second level within the hierarchy is Operational Needs. These are the routine obligations required of customers to run their business operations. In other words, how can
the solution help customers improve their business operations or personal lives. The fea-
ture(s) and functionality that are discussed for the operational needs should build upon
the concepts for the functional needs and may still be basic by nature, but ultimately
should progress the customer to be more efficient and/or enhance their lives further.

To reference the example of a digital watch, it is important to think through what
else could a watch do to help individuals either stay on time or maintain order in their
lives. Examples of what could then be added to meet the operational need are improving
the battery life (e.g., adding a battery that lasts over 24 h and can be recharged at any
time) and adding more features that can be customized by the individual via the user
interface to help them stay on track with their daily activities (e.g., the brightness of the
screen, alarms, and reminders) (Fig. 3).

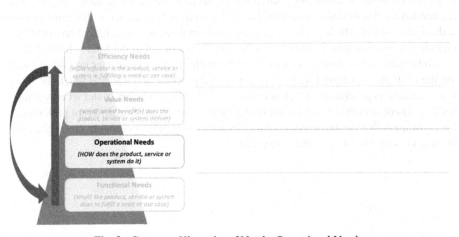

Fig. 3. Customer Hierarchy of Needs: Operational Needs.

2.3 Value Needs

The third level within the hierarchy is Value Needs. They are the higher-level benefits
that are provided to the customer. In other words, what added benefit(s) can the solution
deliver to the customer. As a customer moves up the hierarchy, the needs do shift to
being more complex. Similar to Maslow's hierarchy, the feeling of accomplishment or
more value obtained from a solution becomes the focus [4]. One may even ask, what
more could technology provide for me? As the bottom needs are met, users are able to
think beyond their basic, immediate needs and can expand their imagination to what
other benefits the solution can potentially provide to them (e.g., time savings, efficiency
improvements, cost savings, etc.). Again, the value need should build from what has

been discussed for the operational and functional needs but should deliver value that is obvious to the customer and that the customer is striving to obtain.

Again, to use the example of a digital watch, with building upon the idea of what other benefits could a watch provide a consumer with the understanding that the watch will be on their wrist throughout the day and is connected to their devices. An example of a value need could be the ability for the watch to track the individual's fitness activity throughout the day. For example, the ability to track steps, stairs climbed, total calories vs active calories burned, miles walked, heartrate, etc. This not only provides visibility to the end-user of their activity, but potentially keeps them accountable to their health and may change their lifestyle for the better (Fig. 4).

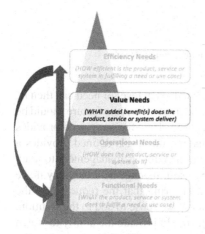

Fig. 4. Customer Hierarchy of Needs: Value Needs.

2.4 Efficiency Needs

The fourth and final level is the Efficiency Needs. This level is the peak performance that customers want to reach. In other words, how the solution can improve the efficiency in customers business operations or personal lives. Like Maslow's hierarchy, this is the point at which either the company or consumer needs the solution to assist them in fulfilling their full potential.

At this point, we have reviewed how a digital watch can transition from simply telling time to helping consumers maintain order throughout their day, and to ultimately improve their lifestyles by being more conscious of their daily activity. For this final need, it is important to think how a device on an individual's wrist can help the end-user further strive to be healthy and productive in their day-to-day activities. Examples of efficiency needs could be motivational reminders to stay active to meet one's goals, and the ability to connect with others building a community to remain accountable with their fitness and health goals (Fig. 5).

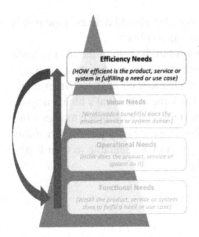

Fig. 5. Customer Hierarchy of Needs: Efficiency Needs.

Once the Customer Hierarchy of Needs is completed, each level of need can then be designed and critiqued by the development team to understand how the feature should be built into the solution, and what functionality is required. The efficiency need provides a north star for the team to work towards. Also, having the levels defined provides a vision that the development team can work from and then allows management to track progress. As new requests are funneled through the team, management can now make prioritization decisions against the hierarchy. First ensuring that the request gets the solution closer to the vision defined, if not it may not make sense to add to the solution. For example, if a consumer suggests that the watch should provide the ability to watch videos or stream movies, that does not fit within the vision. If it does align, then the team can critically think through the need that the request may fit and when it can be delivered. For example, if a consumer provides feedback that the watch should provide the ability to track specific workouts. This does fit the vision and delivers on the value need.

To see how this method would be applicable to real problems, we applied the method to a project at Crown Equipment Corporation. Specifically, the method was implemented to define the vision for APIs (application programming interface) to be integrated within Crown's fleet management solution. Now we will walk through exactly how the method was applied and considerations that should be made at each step.

3   Customer Hierarchy of Needs Creation

The product development team utilized the Customer Hierarchy of Needs method at Crown Equipment Corporation to understand and prioritize the features and functionality of a solution that must be built to ensure that the product delivers on customers' expected outcome(s) and value. For this specific exercise, the solution's features are as follows:

1. Ability for customers to integrate with a system to pull data relevant to their forklifts on-demand.

2. Ability for the solution to integrate with customers' business systems to automatically port data relevant to their forklifts directly into their own systems.

As always in product development, it is important to start with the customer need before defining the solution. The research team at Crown first facilitated a jobs-to-be-done (JTBD) workshop with individuals in product development to help define what the customers expected outcome would be for this solution. Within the workshop, we first introduced the theory and then applied it to the project. Jobs-to-be-done (JTBD) theory is that customers "hire" products or services to fulfill a job or need. People buy products or services to make progress in their lives essentially to make their lives better. "We call this progress the "job" they are trying to get done and understanding this opens a world of innovation possibilities." [5] For example, one JTBD statement that the team created for this solution was "I want to quickly access and consume data when needed to improve my operations". Past ethnographic research and customer requests were referenced to fully understand the customer's expected outcome.

Next, the research team at Crown facilitated a second workshop to introduce and apply the Customer Hierarchy of Needs method (see Fig. 1). Within this session, the development team created the hierarchy of features and functionality of the solution that will deliver on the expected outcome and meet the needs of customers no matter the level of need they are at or will transition to in the future. Also discussed was what the vision could be for this specific project, again giving the team a "north star" to work towards. Now we will dive deeper into how the development team applied the Customer Hierarchy of Needs method to an active project. For the APIs project, the solution was broken down and analyzed by each level of need of the hierarchy: functional, operational, value, and efficiency.

3.1 Functional Needs

For the project at Crown, the functional need that the solution must deliver on is the ability for end-users to pull data from the system via CSV reports on-demand. The development team is able to then discuss how the end-user should access the report through the user interface, what data should be displayed, and how the data will then need to be stored.

3.2 Operational Needs

Moving up the hierarchy to operational needs, the team then discussed what if the end-user wants a more advanced feature beyond pulling CSV reports on-demand to retrieve data out of Crown's fleet management solution. It was determined that the solution should provide different ways for end-users to pull data from the fleet management solution based on their preferences (e.g., ability to schedule reports to be sent automatically on a specified cadence, and ability to pull data in different formats like Excel).

3.3 Value Needs

At this point, the team had a very good understanding of the basic needs that the solution must meet to fulfill customers' expectations. Next, the team transitioned into value needs and thinking through how the solution can make the customer's life simpler and easier to retrieve data out of Crown's system. In other words, how can the solution require less steps and human intervention to pull the data. The feature decided on for this level was the ability to provide APIs for customers to integrate with to pull data either on-demand or scheduled on a specified cadence.

3.4 Efficiency Needs

Lastly, for the customer to obtain their peak performance for this solution, the efficiency need identified for this solution is to provide a digital platform for customers to quickly see what data can be provided and how the customer can integrate with each. This not only allows customers to see all potential data that they can pull and the APIs that they have integrated with, but they can also get updates as new data becomes available electronically that they may be able to utilize to inform business decisions.

Once the Customer Hierarchy of Needs is created, the perceived value of the solution is then understood in terms of the customer's expectations, which then allows the team to take a data-driven approach to measuring whether it delivers the perceived value. A method that can be utilized to measure value is Value Equations, more information can be found in the following paper "Understanding Customer Value Propositions Through the Lens of Value Equations Methods: A Systematic Approach" [6].

4   Implications of Customer Hierarchy of Needs

This Customer Hierarchy of Needs has many advantages that other prioritization methods do not inherently have. It helps to ensure that the solution delivers a holistic user experience at each level of customer need. It assists in defining and validating a vision for a solution, with the features and functionality that should be a part of that vision. Also, it encourages differentiation and innovation to think out of the box on what feature or functionality can help customers or consumers reach their full potential. Lastly, it is a tool to help development teams think through what may be expected in the market (basic needs) for the solution and what are market differentiators (complex needs).

Once the JTBD is defined and the Customer Hierarchy of Needs is developed, it is much easier for the team to understand what value should be delivered to the customer. As features are completed and MVP is reached, the solution can be released to customers and the team can then measure whether the solution is delivering the value to customers that was anticipated. If the solution is falling short, the team then has a hierarchy to follow that not only provides structure for their internal development conversations but provides a way to communicate what needs to be done next to ensure that the solution delivers the expected value to customers.

5   Lessons Learned

This method is to be used as a facilitation tool with identifying and prioritizing features and functionality. It is important to not take it literally but to use it as a tool to facilitate creative ideation and discussion. For example, the method will not tell the development team exactly what they need to build. But rather provides critical questions and a structured exercise for the team to follow to ideate on the solution. When used appropriately, it is very effective in guiding development teams into having a strong dialogue about what the building blocks of a solution should be and why.

Also, it is important to understand what the customer's problem is and how they want to improve upon it before defining the solution. It is easy for teams to jump to defining the solution (the "What" and "How") before fully understanding the overall need or problem that the customer faces (the "Why"). This allows the team to test and validate that the final solution solves the customer's problem.

Lastly, the method can be altered to fit the needs of the active project, as each project is slightly different with the size of work, resources available, and timeline. Maintain flexibility in applying the method to ensure that the use fits the need of the project. For example, if the vision (or efficiency need) is defined already and the team needs to discuss the features that should be a part of it, the team can potentially work from the top of the hierarchy down.

References

1. ATLASSIAN Agile Coach: https://www.atlassian.com/agile
2. Lucid Chart: https://www.lucidchart.com/blog/3-disadvantages-of-agile-methodology
3. Sharma, S., Sarkar, D., Gupta, D.: Agile processes and methodologies: a conceptual Study. Int. J. Comput. Sci. Eng. (IJCSE) **4**(5), 892 (2012)
4. McLeod, S.: Maslow's Hierarchy of Needs. Simply Psychology (2018)
5. Christensen Institute Jobs to Be Done: https://www.christenseninstitute.org/jobs-to-be-done
6. Drapp, J., Prabhala, S.: Understanding customer value propositions through the lens of value equations method: a systematic approach. In: Soares, M.M., Rosenzweig, E., Marcus, A. (eds) Design, User Experience, and Usability: UX Research and Design. HCII 2021. LNCS, vol. 12779. Springer, Cham (2021). https://doi.org/10.1007/978-3-030-78221-4_15

Context is Key: Mining Social Signals for Automatic Task Detection in Design Thinking Meetings

Steffi Kohl[1,2]([⊠]) [iD], Mark Graus[1,3] [iD], and Jos G.A.M. Lemmink[1]

[1] Maastricht University, Maastricht, Netherlands
`stefanie.kohl@maastrichtuniversity.nl`
[2] Human Data Interaction Lab, Zuyd University of Applied Sciences, Heerlen, Netherlands
[3] Obvion, Heerlen, Netherlands

Abstract. Despite the importance of team communication for successful collaborative problem solving, automated solutions for teams are notably absent from the literature. One promising avenue of research has been the development and integration of speech-based technology for team meetings. However, these technologies often fall short of meeting the needs of the teams as they do not take meeting context into consideration. In this paper, we demonstrate the efficacy of context detection with data collected during real team meetings. By capturing and analyzing social signals of rotation in team dynamics, we can demonstrate that different stages of collaborative problem solving using the design thinking methodology differ in their dynamics. Using supervised machine learning, we successfully predict design thinking mode with an overall F1 score of 0.68 and a best-performing sub-class model of 0.94. We believe this to be an essential step towards improving speech-based technology that aims to assist teams during meetings. Making these automated systems context-aware will enable them to provide teams with relevant information, such as resources or guidance.

Keywords: Social signals · Context detection · Predictive modeling

1 Introduction

Collaborative problem solving (CPS) has become an essential skill critical to efficiency, effectiveness and innovation in the modern workforce. This has placed an increasing amount of attention on teams. Understanding team needs and supporting them while creating minimal disruption to their workflow has been a prominent focus point of team researchers in the last decade [38]. One promising avenue of research has been the development and integration of speech-based technology during team meetings [7,16,18,34]. While the idea of integrating speech-based support tools into team meetings satisfies the requirement of minimal disruption to the workflow, these technologies often fall short of meeting the

M. M. Soares et al. (Eds.): HCII 2022, LNCS 13321, pp. 12–27, 2022.
https://doi.org/10.1007/978-3-031-05897-4_2

needs of the teams [21]. Past studies indicate that to generate value from these tools, future research needs to focus on understanding meeting context. Making these automated systems context-aware will enable them to provide teams with relevant information, such as resources or guidance [13].

This paper contributes to the literature on speech-based support tools by demonstrating the efficacy of context detection during CPS episodes within teams based on social signals alone. We use predictive modeling of proxemic and paralinguistic signals in face-to-face conversational interactions captured through sociometric badges. Research demonstrates the feasibility and utility of leveraging these signals to capture behavioral patterns [29]. We aim to demonstrate the value of using these multi-modal signals to detect high-level collaborative patterns such as design thinking contexts. Specifically, we use the proxemic feature, rotating leadership, and the paralinguistic features, rotating contribution, turn-taking, successful interruption and unsuccessful interruption.

2 Related Work and Hypothesis Development

We rely on existing literature when investigating the feasibility of context detection for design thinking modes. The first section highlights theoretical work on convergent and divergent thinking in design thinking that is relevant for the development of the hypotheses. The second section introduces multimodal features collected from sociometric badges, followed by a review of existing speech-based technology approaches that aim to support teams and how context detection poses a challenge to them.

2.1 Collaborative Problem Solving Through Design Thinking

CPS is a critical skill in modern teamwork. It involves two or more people engaged in a coordinated attempt to find a joint solution to a problem by establishing common ground that pertains to the problem space and jointly developing a solution that accommodates multiple perspectives [33, 38].

While there are many methods used to facilitate CPS, Design Thinking (DT) is one of the most popular methods used today, with applications ranging from New Product Development (NPD) to education [8]. This human-centered problem-solving method relies heavily on communication and is used by many companies aiming to foster innovation and generate a competitive advantage [10]. While there are different governable elements of DT depending on the underlying school of thought, three macro stages can be identified, namely need finding, ideation and prototyping [1,9]. Need finding is the definition of a problem. Ideation is the process of generating ideas and solutions. Prototyping encompasses building models to facilitate the development and selection of concepts [20,35]. As argued by Kohl et al. [19], research should differentiate between tasks when evaluating communication in teams during CPS to account for the underlying cognitive operations utilized by the team members. As such, this paper will use the term "mode" to differentiate interactions for different tasks within teams during the individual DT stages.

In all DT modes, there are two main types of thinking: divergent and convergent. While divergent thinking aims to find many possible answers or options to a particular problem, convergent thinking narrows down multiple ideas into a single solution [14]. During the DT process, teams use convergent and divergent thinking to explore the problem and the solution space in order to successfully apply CPS. Need finding inhabits the problem space, and ideation and prototyping share the solution space. This process can be visualized as a double diamond as shown in Fig. 1. Teams working on CPS with the DT methodology will go through this double diamond process iteratively, meaning they will move forwards and backward [9].

In a similar manner, existing research on CPS suggests that distinct phases exist in group problem solving. Each of these phases requires different relational and structural elements [32]. Phases are identified with distinct primary needs. Some relational and structural elements, such as the number of interruptions or frequency of taking turns, are beneficial for one phase but detrimental to another. Similarly, Stempfle and Badke-Schaub [37] identify four cognitive operations that DT teams utilize at different stages and for different tasks. Prior studies have not included differentiation of interaction modes [25] or have assumed that all modes will benefit from the same signals.

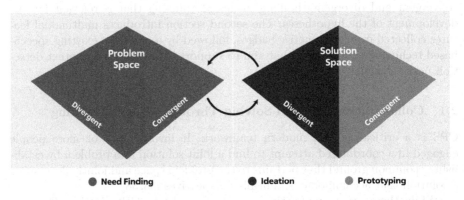

Fig. 1. The double diamond maps the divergent and convergent stages of a design process to the team modes. Need finding consists of both convergent and divergent thinking, while ideation consists only of divergent and prototyping of convergent thinking.

Given these elemental properties, this paper will quantitatively measure the theoretically proposed elements of convergent and divergent thinking with respect to the impact on context detection for the DT mode.

2.2   Modeling Behavioral Patterns During Collaborations

While early work for data-driven modeling on collaboration behavior patterns has mainly aimed to model lower-level behavioral dimensions, such as turn-taking [31], recent efforts go beyond low-level signals to model high-level collaborative behavioral patterns. For example, postural markers have been used in human activity recognition to differentiate team member group functions [6], and proxemic features have been shown to be indicators of knowledge-sharing dynamics and affect group creativity [12,17].

As unimodal features often cannot richly capture complex social interactions, multimodal signals have been increasingly used in modeling high-level collaborative patterns. An example of this is the study by Murray and Oertel [23] that modeled task performance on a team problem-solving task. They trained a random forest classifier to predict task performance from vocal and linguistic features. The multimodal feature set outperformed the unimodal feature set, demonstrating the added value of multimodal data collection.

Utilizing these signals in successful machine learning models requires theoretical foundations drawn from human–computer interaction (HCI) and organizational science literature with regards to team dynamics. Until recently, these dynamics have remained elusive due to their complexity and lack of quantitative measures. However, wearable electronic devices have made it affordable to collect detailed information on team communication. Research indicates that there is predictive power in social signals collected with these devices [29]. This is particularly applicable to colocated collaboration settings because face-to-face teamwork remains the dominant mode for solving complex problems despite the increase of virtual teams. Furthermore, colocated collaboration provides unique benefits that are not easy to achieve in digitally mediated forms of teamwork [28], such as increasing creativity [12] and performance [25]. While preliminary work has demonstrated the feasibility and utility of leveraging multimodal signals to predict behavioral patterns during collaboration activities, more research is needed to understand which data sources work best to predict certain activities.

This paper addresses this gap in the literature by combining proxemic and paralinguistic features. These features have proven to be robust in previous studies in nonverbal communication. They stem from a diverse set of domains such as sociology, psychology [15] and, most recently, human–robot interaction [22]. Scholars in these domains have investigated human proxemic and paralinguistic behavior since the 1920s. Proxemic behavior relates to how people use space when communicating. Paralinguistic behavior relates to all aspects of spoken communication, except for the semantic content.

We are collecting these quantitative, non-verbal features using a wearable sensor called the sociometric badge that has been successfully deployed in a variety of organizational contexts with a variety of predictor variables. The badges have been used to predict organizationally relevant outcomes, such as job attitudes and performance [27], job satisfaction [26], network cohesion [40], creativity [39], group performance [25], and group collaboration [18]. This study introduces the novel context of predicting DT as a context for the sociometric badge.

The current paper is one of the first investigations using proxemics and paralinguistics multimodal models to understand DT collaboration dynamics. We aim thereby to show the value of using these multimodal signals when modeling high-level collaborative patterns.

2.3   Context Detection for Speech-based Technology

Past research has produced many forms of speech-based technology to support meetings for online [2,11,34] and colocated collaboration [4,7,16,18,24]. However, these approaches have exclusively conducted data collection in lab settings with short term study setups. In the case of the Meeter study [16], data were only captured for a duration of 10 min per meeting. While these studies demonstrate the potential of speech-based technology, their limitations also negatively affect ecological validity and limit the extent to which the findings can be generalized. Studies investigating speech-based technology in real team meetings, similar to the data presented in this paper, are still uncommon. Further, these studies do not consider context and are, therefore, unable to provide differentiated guidance or feedback. A severe shortcoming when it comes to the perceived usefulness of such tools is noted by McGregor and Tang [21]. Their study aimed to investigate if speech-based agent systems could support teams by proactively detecting useful actions that could be presented to a team for improved performance. Their results highlight difficulties in applying automated technology to team meetings, concluding that future research needs to focus on detecting meeting context to produce helpful recommendations from automated systems. Automated context detection in meetings can be challenging. Research within the domain of context detection focuses on (1) the difficulties associated with defining the set of potential contexts and (2) the feature selection to accurately determine the correct state [5,13], among other elements. As Greenberg states, "Determining an appropriate set of canonical contextual states may be difficult or impossible" [13]. However, if designers can a priori determine a limited set of likely contexts and what describes them, application building becomes significantly easier. Within the specific context of DT, the contextual states are known. This research focuses on determining features for context detection for this limited set of known contexts.

2.4   Hypothesis Development

The literature review outlines the gap of knowledge about the dynamics of team communication during CPS. It further indicates a need to understand the various patterns of communication dynamics that exist among teams working in different modes to provide useful guidance to them. It follows that context detection is essential for the development of speech-based technology. Given this, we will evaluate the research questions: Can the DT mode of an individual in a team be predicted using team rotation features? To answer this research question, this study tests four hypotheses.

H1: Design thinking modes can be predicted from the selected features with above-baseline performance of the F1 score.

Meetings can have more or less focus on a single DT mode. Certain meetings may be dedicated to only ideation, while other meetings may go back and forth between ideation and prototyping. Meetings with more focus on a single DT mode are expected to have more distinct interactions characteristics and thus are expected to be easier to predict.

H2: Meetings with a higher percentage of a single design thinking mode have better predictability.

We expect to find unique interaction characteristics for each mode, given the elemental properties of the modes. The predictive models developed to answer H1 are often black-box and do not show the properties of the features in the feature space. We expect a class analysis to better illustrate the properties of the features, demonstrating how each mode has a unique dynamic between the selected features.

H3: Design thinking modes have different dynamics.

As highlighted in Sect. 2.1, we expect to find differences between the predictability of the different modes given the theoretical literature as need finding shares divergent and convergent properties that are also found in ideation and prototyping.

H4: Need finding is harder to distinguish than the other two modes.

3   Methods

3.1   Study Set up

To investigate the research question, we collected social signals from a group of young professionals (N = 18) engaging in an NPD sprint exercise at a large consultancy. The data set was collected during the 4-week sprint lasting from idea generation to prototype development. In total, for the duration of the sprint, four groups with either five or four members were observed on 13 days in an open-space office floor. All teams worked autonomously without direct supervision by consultants, so each team structured their workdays and scheduled team meetings or requested support from consultants as necessary.

Participants wore sociometric badges during working hours whenever engaged in potentially work-related activities but not during lunch breaks. The badge is an unobtrusive device originally developed by the MIT Media Laboratory and later commercialized by Sociometric Solutions (now Humanyze). This sensor was specifically selected due to its ability to collect multimodal data streams with minimal disruption to the workflow. The sociometric badge is worn around the neck and is the approximate size and shape of an ID tag. It records data via a microphone, an infrared sensor, a Bluetooth detector, and an accelerometer. These four sensors are used to capture individual data about the wearer's voice, body motion, dyadic data of face-to-face interactions, and proximity to other wearers. After undergoing a series of computations, the raw data from these sensors are used to create measures of lower-level behavioral dimensions, such as body movement, colocation, and verbal activity. While the collected data can be considered raw, they are generated using the badge firmware. As such, the data do not necessarily reflect the true values for the external stimuli observed [36]. In addition, the Sociometric Solutions software can enrich the data set by generating additional variables.

Printed questionnaires were also used to collect daily information on DT activities. The participants were asked to fill in the questionnaire once a day after finishing all work-related activities. The questionnaire assessed how much time in percentages participants spent on need finding, ideation or prototyping on a given day. The response rate to this question was 100% (222 responses).

Figure 2 illustrates the data flow. The manual data collection consists of questionnaires capturing the percentages of time spent in different modes on a given day. These data are used to generate thresholds that create labels. The automated data collection consists of the raw data from the sociometric badges, processed by the Sociometric Solution software, which provides low-level measurements of team activity. The mode prediction model calculates highly predictive features from these low-level measurements. The labels and features are combined with machine learning algorithms to predict the DT mode.

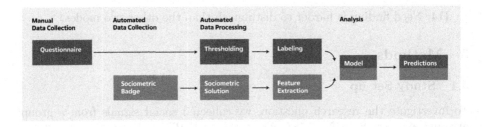

Fig. 2. Pipeline of data

3.2 Thresholding the Outcome Variable

The outcome variables, ground truth, or labels are determined by thresholding the percentages reported by participants. For example, at a threshold of 90%, the positive class for need finding is participants who reported need finding at least 90% on a given day. The negative class is those participants who reported less than 90% need finding. Multiple thresholds have been used for comparison to understand the impact the focus on a single mode has on predictability. While most meetings will use a single mode, that is, a meeting will focus on prototyping only, some meetings will be more diverse and include a mix of, for example, ideation and need finding. Thresholds of 50%, 60%, 70%, 80%, and 90% have been used. The relevant threshold is indicated in the respective tables.

3.3   Features

This study uses rotation features to predict the DT mode as described in Sect. 2.2. All signals are collected using the sociometric badges. The conversation characteristics used as features in this study are derived from the speech conditions as provided by the Sociometric Solutions software [36]. The features are defined in the following sections.

Rotating Leadership. Rotating leadership measures how frequently people change their network position in the team. In order to calculate how often people change from a central position to a peripheral one, we count the number of local maxima and minima in the betweenness centrality curve of a person. This is described in Eq. 1 and visualized in Fig. 3. Higher numbers indicate more rotation of leadership. The figure shows a hypothetical betweenness centrality curve of a person over time. The red Xs mark instances of local minima and maxima as described in Eq. 1, where the superscript BC indicates that they are for the betweenness centrality curve, and i indicates the person.

$$RL_i = \#localMinima_i^{BC} + \#localMaxima_i^{BC} \tag{1}$$

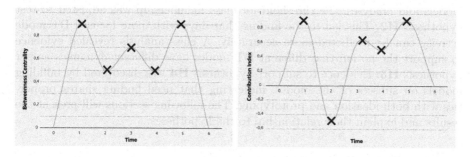

Fig. 3. Rotating leadership (left) and rotating contribution (right)

Rotating Contribution. Rotating contribution measures how frequently people change the amount of time they spend listening vs. speaking. We calculate the contribution index (CI) of each person (speaking − listening/speaking + listening) and count the number of local maxima and minima in the CI curve of a person. This is described in Eq. 2 and visualized in Fig. 3. Lower numbers indicate fewer changes in the level of contribution for an individual person. The figure shows a hypothetical CI curve of a person over time. The red Xs mark instances of local minima and maxima as described in Eq. 2, where the superscript CI indicates that they are for the CI curve, and i indicates the person.

$$RC_i = \#localMinima_i^{CI} + \#localMaxima_i^{CI} \tag{2}$$

Turns. Turns are speaking segments that occur after and within 10 s of another speaking segment. By default, a speech segment must be made within 10 s after the previous one ended in order to be considered a turn. Note that the two speech segments need not be from two different people to count as a turn—a person can pause and then start speaking again. This would count as two speech segments and one "self-turn."

Interruptions. Interruptions in speech can be successful and unsuccessful. Interruptions are defined as a situation during which Person A is talking, and Person B starts talking over Person A. If Person A talks for less than 5 of the next 10 s, then Person B successfully interrupted Person A. If Person A instead talks for more than 5 of the next 10 s, then Person B unsuccessfully interrupted Person A.

4   Results

Multiple models were trained, and DT modes were analyzed. The results support our hypotheses. First, single and multiclass models were trained. These models outperformed the F1 score of the random baseline models, demonstrating that the DT mode can be predicted as stated in hypothesis **H1**. Throughout all of the models and analyses, the threshold for class membership was adjusted to test hypothesis **H2**. This led to the finding that days with more focused DT mode activity can be predicted more accurately. A class analysis revealed evidence to support the notion that different DT modes have different dynamics as per hypothesis **H3**. Evidence to support hypothesis **H4** was discovered by building models on subsets of the modes, indicating that need finding shares properties with both ideation and prototyping. The following sections will present the results and explain their relationship to the hypotheses.

4.1   Predicting Design Thinking Mode

DT mode was predicted for different values of the threshold for class membership. Single class and multiclass models were trained in sci-kit learn using a non-linear Support Vector Machine (SVM) with a radial basis function kernel [30]. This model showed a greater increase over the random baseline than other models tested, including random forest, logistic regression, AdaBoost, KNN and naive Bayes when comparing F1 scores to a stratified random baseline F1 score where the probability of a label occurring is proportional to the occurrence in the original data set.

While a single class model can be used to demonstrate the feasibility of the approach, a multiclass model is more practical for use in a context aware system. In a single class model, for each input observation, the output describes whether a single DT mode is relevant. A single class model would have to be constructed for each of the DT modes of interest. Consequently, for an observation, more than one model might indicate their corresponding DT mode to be active, requiring additional logic to make the final decision about which DT mode is active.

The results of the trained models are shown in Tables 1 and 2. All scores are evaluated using leave-one-out cross-validation, which is known to be an almost unbiased estimator of model generalization performance on unseen examples [3]. One hundred experiments were conducted to measure the variability of the models and oversampling. All models showed low variation to initialization with standard deviations between 0.01 and 0.02.

Table 1. Single class model, where the subscripts of b, p and n correspond to the baseline, the positive and the negative class. The metrics along which the models are compared are F1, accuracy (Acc), precision (P), and recall (R). In addition, F1 and support (S) for the negative and positive class are reported.

Cut Off	Mode	$F1_b$	Acc	F1	P	R	$F1_n$	$F1_p$	S_p	S_n
50	NF	0.64	0.78	0.76	0.76	0.78	0.86	0.49	50	172
60	NF	0.61	0.76	0.74	0.74	0.76	0.85	0.46	49	173
70	NF	0.72	0.76	0.74	0.74	0.76	0.85	0.43	40	182
80	NF	0.66	0.53	0.57	0.71	0.53	0.62	0.39	27	195
90	NF	0.68	0.67	0.69	0.71	0.67	0.78	0.37	16	206
50	ID	0.58	0.67	0.67	0.67	0.67	0.76	0.48	79	143
60	ID	0.53	0.67	0.67	0.67	0.67	0.76	0.49	56	166
70	ID	0.53	0.68	0.68	0.7	0.68	0.75	0.53	47	175
80	ID	0.66	0.76	0.77	0.78	0.76	0.83	0.61	33	189
90	ID	0.77	0.88	0.87	0.87	0.88	0.93	0.61	12	210
50	PR	0.48	0.68	0.68	0.72	0.68	0.67	0.68	82	140
60	PR	0.54	0.69	0.69	0.74	0.69	0.68	0.69	74	148
70	PR	0.45	0.7	0.7	0.74	0.7	0.69	0.71	68	149
80	PR	0.62	0.75	0.74	0.77	0.75	0.71	0.78	59	163
90	PR	0.46	0.77	0.76	0.77	0.77	0.65	0.82	45	177

Single Class Model. Table 1 shows the results of 1 versus all models at the different thresholds for the three modes. When comparing the baseline to the model performance, different thresholds have higher F1 scores for the different DT modes, showing different underlying dynamics supporting **H3**. For need finding, the F1 score peaks at a threshold of 50% with an improvement over the baseline of 0.12. In contrast to this, ideation peaks at 70% with an improvement of 0.15, whereas prototyping peaks at 90% with an improvement of 0.3.

Multiclass Model. The performance of a multiclass model in predicting DT mode can be seen in Table 2. The table also displays the predictive performance for different threshold values. The F1 score of the model peaks at 0.68 when the threshold is at 90%.

The best performing model has a 0.25 increase over the baseline model and an F1 score of 0.68. A model with a 70% threshold provides an F1 increase of 0.23 over the baseline model, whereas models with a threshold of 60%, 80% or 50% lead to improvements of 0.2, 0.18 and 0.18, respectively. The 90% threshold model also shows the highest F1 score for the ideation and the prototyping class with 0.63 and 0.84, respectively, indicating that these classes are identified well by the model. However, the model does not perform as well for the need-finding class, as it only shows an F1 score of 0.27. What stands out in the table is that the need-finding class overall performs worst among all cut-off values. This provides partial support for hypothesis **H4**, indicating that need finding can not be separated as well as the other classes as suggested by the theoretical framework of convergent and divergent thinking. The following section investigates this problem in more detail by conducting a sub-class analysis.

Table 2. Multiclass analysis, where the subscripts of b, nf, id and pr correspond to baseline, need finding, ideation and prototyping. S indicates the support for a class.

Cut Off	$F1_b$	Acc	F1	P	R	$F1_{nf}$	$F1_{id}$	$F1_{pr}$	S_{nf}	S_{id}	S_{pr}
50	0.33	0.54	0.51	0.55	0.54	0.32	0.51	0.64	50	79	82
60	0.35	0.58	0.55	0.6	0.58	**0.43**	0.5	0.67	49	56	74
70	0.34	0.6	0.57	0.61	0.6	0.33	0.56	0.71	40	47	68
80	0.38	0.62	0.60	0.59	0.62	0.3	0.58	0.75	27	33	59
90	0.43	0.73	**0.68**	0.7	0.73	0.27	**0.63**	**0.84**	16	12	45

Model and Threshold Conclusions. In conclusion, we are able to predict DT modes with F1 scores above the baseline models, supporting **H1**. Further, increasing the threshold has a positive effect on the ideation and prototyping classes in single class models. When used in the multiclass model, the overall predictability increases even though the need-finding predictability suffers. These observations provide partial support for **H2** and indicate that further work is needed to better differentiate need finding.

4.2 Understanding Design Thinking Modes

In the previous section, different DT modes could be successfully predicted, outperforming random baseline models. This suggests that the modes are distinguishably different from each other with regard to the underlying feature dynamics. This led us to investigate hypothesis **H3** by analyzing the relationship between the features and the DT modes. Specifically, we conducted a class analysis using three different approaches to understand the structure of the features in the feature space.

For approach 1, a mean was produced for every mode by taking the average of all features for all examples in the class: a class centroid. A mean was created to reduce the effect of outliers. The Euclidean distance between these class centroids was measured as shown in Table 3. A smaller number indicates the modes are more similar. As the threshold is increased, the modes become more separated where the effects between need finding and prototyping and between need finding and ideation do not always increase; that is, they are non-monotonic. This indicates that the modes have different dynamics with respect to the rotation features. If they were similar, the numbers would be close to zero as there would be a minimal distance between the features in the feature space.

In approach 2, we calculated the average Euclidean distance between all pairs of points in two modes. In contrast to approach 1, this approach is more sensitive to outliers as the mean of the features was not taken first. The outliers are directly compared and added to the average distance. This is reflected in the results. Similar to approach 1, a higher number indicates a larger distance between the modes. As shown in Table 3 the between-class similarity scores indicate that all modes have different underlying dynamics. Unlike approach 1, the between-class similarity shows that at most thresholds, all modes are equally separated.

Approach 3 highlights the density of a given mode in the feature space. The average Euclidean distance between all pairs of points in each mode was calculated. The results in Table 3 show that prototyping is the most dense mode with the lowest average Euclidean distance between all pairs of points at any threshold. As the threshold is increased, the modes become more dense by removing less-focused meetings from the data set.

All three approaches indicate that the underlying features for the individual DT modes are different and show different dynamics. Especially, prototyping shows different dynamics of the features compared to the other modes, as the numbers in Table 3 indicate that it is better separated and more compact. In contrast, need finding shows more similarity to the other modes overall. We find support for **H3**, as all measures show differences between the modes.

Table 3. Results of class analysis with three approaches: distance between class means (Approach 1), average distance metween class observations (Approach 2) and class density (Approach 3)

Cut off	Distance between class means			Average distance between classes			Class density		
	NF-ID	NF-P	ID-P	NF-ID	NF-P	ID-P	NF	ID	P
50	0.1	0.28	0.25	0.48	0.41	0.41	0.46	0.49	0.23
60	0.11	0.31	0.27	0.51	0.45	0.43	0.5	0.51	0.24
70	0.1	0.26	0.31	0.48	0.41	0.45	0.45	0.5	0.24
80	0.17	0.26	0.4	0.54	0.39	0.53	0.45	0.6	0.22
90	0.29	0.32	0.56	0.78	0.67	0.78	0.77	0.71	0.46

4.3   Evidence for Convergent and Divergent Thinking in Design Thinking Modes

The previous section showed that prototyping is better separated, more compact, and is easier to predict. Need finding tends to be more similar to ideation and prototyping. In the theoretical framework of convergent and divergent thinking [9], need finding consists of convergent and divergent thinking, whereas ideation is convergent thinking, and prototyping is divergent thinking. While this overlap of elemental properties can be observed in the class analysis, it becomes clearer in a sub-class analysis where all combinations of models were built using only two of the three modes. The results are shown in Table 4. The best ideation and prototyping model outperforms the other two best models with an improvement over the random baseline of 0.3. The improvements for the other two models are 0.16 (NF-I, 90%) and 0.17 (NF-P, 80%). Furthermore, an F1 score of 0.94 is reached for the ideation and prototyping model, which approaches a perfect F1 score of 1.0. In other words, these findings show that while ideation and prototyping can be distinguished almost perfectly, it is more difficult to identify the difference between need finding on the one hand and ideation and prototyping on the other. This supports hypothesis **H4**, indicating that need finding shares divergent thinking with ideation and convergent thinking with prototyping.

Table 4. Subclass analysis, where the subscripts of b, nf, id and pr correspond to baseline, need finding, ideation and prototyping.

Cut off	Model	$F1_b$	F1	P	R	$F1_{nf}$	$F1_{id}$	$F1_{pr}$
50	NF-I	0.51	0.57	0.62	0.63	0.29	0.75	–
60	NF-I	0.5	0.58	0.66	0.62	0.41	0.72	–
70	NF-I	0.5	0.52	0.52	0.53	0.39	0.62	–
80	NF-I	0.51	0.54	0.54	0.55	0.45	0.62	–
90	NF-I	0.54	0.7	0.72	0.71	0.78	0.6	–
50	NF-P	0.5	0.67	0.72	0.69	0.57	–	0.76
60	NF-P	0.51	0.71	0.75	0.73	0.56	–	0.81
70	NF-P	0.53	0.71	0.76	0.74	0.52	–	0.82
80	NF-P	0.55	0.72	0.75	0.76	0.46	–	0.84
90	NF-P	0.63	0.74	0.79	0.79	0.38	–	0.87
50	I-P	0.50	0.67	0.68	0.68	–	0.63	0.71
60	I-P	0.49	0.72	0.72	0.72	–	0.64	0.77
70	I-P	0.51	0.76	0.76	0.77	–	0.69	0.81
80	I-P	0.52	0.84	0.85	0.85	–	0.77	0.89
90	I-P	0.64	0.94	0.95	0.95	–	0.86	0.97

5   Conclusion

Our research set out to answer the question: Can the DT mode of an individual in a team be predicted using team rotation features? Using proxemic and paralinguistic signals in face-to-face conversational interactions captured through sociometric badges, we introduce novel predictive models of the DT mode. We analyzed a data set of NPD teams using design thinking, and we found that the DT mode can be predicted well above random chance by the predictive models, thus reproducing the self-reported labeling of the recordings on previously unseen examples.

We answered our research question to what extent DT modes can be predicted from social signals. With an overall F1 score of 0.68 and a best-performing sub-class model of 0.94, the analysis demonstrated the efficacy of context detection during CPS episodes within teams based on social signals alone. The analysis shows the potential and challenges involved in detecting context during DT meetings and thus supports the idea of further studying context-aware systems which can provide teams with relevant information, such as resources or guidance.

However, our findings should be interpreted in consideration of the small sample size. Future research should focus on increasing the sample size, expanding the set of contexts detected, and revisiting the selected featured to optimize model performance.

References

1. Brown, T., et al.: Design thinking. Harvard Bus. Rev. **86**(6), 84 (2008)
2. Calacci, D., Lederman, O., Shrier, D., Pentland, A.: Breakout: An open measurement and intervention tool for distributed peer learning groups. arXiv preprint arXiv:1607.01443 (2016)
3. Cawley, G.C., Talbot, N.L.: On over-fitting in model selection and subsequent selection bias in performance evaluation. J. Mach. Learn. Res. **11**, 2079–2107 (2010)
4. Chandrasegaran, S., Bryan, C., Shidara, H., Chuang, T.Y., Ma, K.L.: Talktraces: Real-time capture and visualization of verbal content in meetings. In: Proceedings of the 2019 CHI Conference on Human Factors in Computing Systems, pp. 1–14 (2019)
5. Coutaz, J., Crowley, J.L., Dobson, S., Garlan, D.: Context is key. Comm. ACM **48**(3), 49–53 (2005)
6. Dietzel, J., Francu, R.E., Lucas, B., Zaki, M.: Contextually defined postural markers reveal who's in charge: Evidence from small teams collected with wearable sensors (2018)
7. DiMicco, J.M., Pandolfo, A., Bender, W.: Influencing group participation with a shared display. In: Proceedings of the 2004 ACM Conference on Computer Supported Cooperative Work, pp. 614–623 (2004)
8. Dorst, K.: The core of 'design thinking' and its application. Des. Stud. **32**(6), 521–532 (2011)
9. Efeoglu, A., Møller, C., Sérié, M., Boer, H.: Design thinking: Characteristics and promises. In: Proceedings of 14th International CINet Conference on Business Development and Co-creation, pp. 241–256 (2013)

10. Elsbach, K.D., Stigliani, I.: Design thinking and organizational culture: A review and framework for future research. J. Manage. **44**(6), 2274–2306 (2018)
11. Faucett, H.A., Lee, M.L., Carter, S.: I should listen more: Real-time sensing and feedback of non-verbal communication in video telehealth. Proceedings of the ACM on Human-Computer Interaction 1(CSCW), pp. 1–19 (2017)
12. Gloor, P.A., Almozlino, A., Inbar, O., Lo, W., Provost, S.: Measuring team creativity through longitudinal social signals. arXiv preprint arXiv:1407.0440 (2014)
13. Greenberg, S.: Context as a dynamic construct. Hum. Comput. Interact. **16**(2–4), 257–268 (2001)
14. Guilford, J.P.: Creativity. Am. Psychol. **5**(9), 444–454 (1950). https://doi.org/10.1037/h0063487
15. Harrigan, J.A.: Proxemics, kinesics, and gaze. In: The New Handbook of Methods in Nonverbal Behavior Research, pp. 137–198 (2005)
16. Huber, B., Shieber, S., Gajos, K.Z.: Automatically analyzing brainstorming language behavior with Meeter. In: Proceedings of the ACM on Human-Computer Interaction, vol. 3(CSCW), pp. 1–17 (2019)
17. Kidane, Y.H., Gloor, P.A.: Correlating temporal communication patterns of the eclipse open source community with performance and creativity. Comput. Math. Organ. Theory **13**(1), 17–27 (2007)
18. Kim, T., Chang, A., Holland, L., Pentland, A.S.: Meeting mediator: Enhancing group collaboration using sociometric feedback. In: Proceedings of the 2008 ACM Conference on Computer Supported Cooperative Work, pp. 457–466 (2008)
19. Kohl, S., Graus, M.P., Lemmink, J.G.: Deciphering the code: Evidence for a sociometric DNA in design thinking meetings. In: International Conference on Human-Computer Interaction, pp. 53–61. Springer (2020)
20. Liedtka, J.: Perspective: Linking design thinking with innovation outcomes through cognitive bias reduction. J. Prod. Innov. Manage. **32**(6), 925–938 (2015)
21. McGregor, M., Tang, J.C.: More to meetings: Challenges in using speech-based technology to support meetings. In: Proceedings of the 2017 ACM Conference on Computer Supported Cooperative Work and Social Computing, pp. 2208–2220 (2017)
22. Mumm, J., Mutlu, B.: Human-robot proxemics: Physical and psychological distancing in human-robot interaction. In: Proceedings of the 6th International Conference on Human-Robot Interaction, pp. 331–338. ACM (2011)
23. Murray, G., Oertel, C.: Predicting group performance in task-based interaction. In: Proceedings of the 20th ACM International Conference on Multimodal Interaction, pp. 14–20 (2018)
24. Nathan, M., et al.: In case you missed it: Benefits of attendee-shared annotations for non-attendees of remote meetings. In: Proceedings of the ACM 2012 Conference on Computer Supported Cooperative Work, pp. 339–348 (2012)
25. Olguin, D.O., Gloor, P.A., Pentland, A.S.: Capturing individual and group behavior with wearable sensors. In: Proceedings of the 2009 AAAI Spring Symposium on Human Behavior Modeling, SSS, vol. 9 (2009)
26. Olguín, D.O., Waber, B.N., Kim, T., Mohan, A., Ara, K., Pentland, A.: Sensible organizations: Technology and methodology for automatically measuring organizational behavior. IEEE Trans. Syst. Man Cybern. Part B (Cybernetics), **39**(1), 43–55 (2008)
27. Olguin Olguin, D.: Sensor-based organizational design and engineering. Ph.D. thesis, Massachusetts Institute of Technology (2011)
28. Olson, J.S., Teasley, S., Covi, L., Olson, G.: The (currently) unique advantages of collocated work. Distributed work, pp. 113–135 (2002)

29. Parker, J.N., Cardenas, E., Dorr, A.N., Hackett, E.J.: Using sociometers to advance small group research. Sociol. Methods Res. 0049124118769091 (2018)
30. Pedregosa, F., et al.: Scikit-learn: Machine learning in python. J. Mach. Learn. Res. **12**, 2825–2830 (2011)
31. Pentland, A.: Honest Signals: How They Shape Our World. MIT Press (2010)
32. Perry-Smith, J.E., Mannucci, P.V.: From creativity to innovation: The social network drivers of the four phases of the idea journey. Acad. Manage. Rev. **42**(1), 53–79 (2017)
33. Roschelle, J., Teasley, S.D.: The construction of shared knowledge in collaborative problem solving. In: Computer Supported Collaborative Learning, pp. 69–97. Springer (1995)
34. Schröder, K., Kohl, S.: Vicon - towards understanding visual support systems in collaborative video conferencing. In: International Conference on Human-Computer Interaction, Springer (2022)
35. Seidel, V.P., Fixson, S.K.: Adopting design thinking in novice multidisciplinary teams: The application and limits of design methods and reflexive practices. J. Prod. Innov. Manage. **30**, 19–33 (2013)
36. Solutions, S.: Sociometric badge 03–02: Preliminary user guide. Boston, MA (2014)
37. Stempfle, J., Badke-Schaub, P.: Thinking in design teams-an analysis of team communication. Des. Stud. **23**(5), 473–496 (2002)
38. Stewart, A.E., et al.: I say, you say, we say: Using spoken language to model sociocognitive processes during computer-supported collaborative problem solving. In: Proceedings of the ACM on Human-Computer Interaction, vol. 3(CSCW), pp. 1–19 (2019)
39. Tripathi, P., Burleson, W.: Predicting creativity in the wild: Experience sample and sociometric modeling of teams. In: Proceedings of the ACM 2012 Conference on Computer Supported Cooperative Work, pp. 1203–1212 (2012)
40. Wu, L., Waber, B.N., Aral, S., Brynjolfsson, E., Pentland, A.: Mining face-to-face interaction networks using sociometric badges: Predicting productivity in an it configuration task. Available at SSRN 1130251 (2008)

Selection and Modeling of a Formal Heuristic Evaluation Process Through Comparative Analysis

Adrian Lecaros$^{(\boxtimes)}$ ⓘ, Arturo Moquillaza ⓘ, Fiorella Falconi ⓘ, Joel Aguirre ⓘ, Alejandro Tapia ⓘ, and Freddy Paz ⓘ

Pontificia Universidad Católica del Perú, Av. Universitaria 1801, San Miguel, Lima 32, Lima, Perú

{adrian.lecaros,ffalconit,aguirre.joel}@pucp.edu.pe,
{amoquillaza,a.tapiat,fpaz}@pucp.pe

Abstract. Due to the importance of usability, multiple usability evaluation methods have been proposed that help Human-Computer Interaction (HCI) specialists determine whether the interfaces of a software product are usable, easy to use, understandable, and attractive. Among these methods, the heuristic evaluation proposed by Jakob Nielsen is the one that stands out. Although Nielsen offers general guidelines for the execution of heuristic evaluations, very few authors of different studies present a formal agreement or process on how the evaluations should be carried out, which leads us to the problem of the absence of a comparative analysis that allows determining the most appropriate formal evaluation process to carry out heuristic inspections. To complement, some proposals found in the literature compare the results of the execution of heuristic evaluations, the definition of new heuristics, qualification forms, and the formalization of the complete process in 5 phases. Although these proposals contribute to the formalization of the heuristic evaluation process, the literature review has not provided a comparative analysis that allows determining which is the most appropriate, which could cause usability evaluators to interpret and carry out their own procedure, which would lead to inaccuracies in the results and increase the probability of improperly executing the inspection. The purpose of this study was to elaborate a comparative table of the formal processes; this allowed the grouping of the various studies found in the literature, to select a process, and thus, and to model by a BPMN tool the whole process. Finally, this process modeled was validated by expert judgement of HCI specialists.

Keywords: Human-Computer Interaction · Usability · Heuristic evaluation · Process · BPMN

1 Introduction

Nowadays, usability is an essential aspect of the User Experience in the context of interaction between users and software products since it establishes a fundamental role in

M. M. Soares et al. (Eds.): HCII 2022, LNCS 13321, pp. 28–46, 2022.
https://doi.org/10.1007/978-3-031-05897-4_3

the use, acceptance, and interaction of users with those software products [1]. Due to the importance of usability, multiple usability evaluation methods have been proposed that help Human-Computer Interaction specialists determine whether the interfaces of a software product are usable, easy to use, understandable, and attractive. Among these methods, the heuristic evaluation proposed by Jakob Nielsen is the one that stands out [2]. Although Nielsen offers general guidelines for the execution of heuristic evaluations, very few authors of different studies present a formal agreement or process on how the evaluations should be carried out, which leads us to the problem of the absence of a comparative analysis that allows determining the most appropriate formal evaluation process to carry out heuristic inspections [3]. To complement, some proposals found in the literature compare the results of the execution of heuristic evaluations, the definition of new heuristics, qualification forms, and the formalization of the complete process in 5 phases: planning, training, evaluation, discussion, and report. Although these proposals contribute to the formalization of the heuristic evaluation process, the literature review has not provided a comparative analysis that allows determining which is the most appropriate, which could cause usability evaluators to interpret and carry out their own procedure, which would lead to inaccuracies in the results and increase the probability of improperly executing the inspection. As the objective of this study, a comparative table of the formal processes was elaborated, and this allowed the grouping of the various studies found in the systematic literature review, which have used protocols or formal processes that contribute, to a certain extent, to the execution of heuristic evaluations. This grouping made it possible to measure and compare the characteristics, the degree of coverage, and the benefits of each one, and the result led to a complete formal process. This result was achieved using a systematic review of the literature, where the question sought to be answered: "what are the characteristics of the protocols or formal processes that are being used to improve the performance of heuristic evaluations of software products?". The comparison of the characteristics gave as a result that the formal process that is part of the category "Formal processes with duly defined steps" obtained the best results by providing a positive response for each of the criteria when contributing to the entire evaluation process heuristics through duly defined steps and by consolidating the different ways in which the evaluations are carried out into one, allowing the interpretations of the usability evaluators to be reduced in how to carry them out.

Additionally, the detailed diagram of the selected process was made with the objective of modeling in detail the steps and tasks that must be followed to carry out the process correctly and without room for different interpretations by the evaluators who use it. In addition, the main process has been divided into the execution of 5 sub-processes that correspond to the steps indicated in the selected formal process: (1) planning, (2) training, (3) evaluation, (4) discussion and (5) report. This result was achieved using the Bizagi BPMN Modeler tool [4], which allowed the design and modeling of the process through the BPMN notation. This modeling consisted of 6 flows that are presented in this research. All these deliverables were validated by expert judgement of HCI specialists.

This paper is structured as follows: In Sect. 2, we describe the main concepts belonging to the Human-Computer Interaction area used in the study. In Sect. 3, we present the result of the systematic literature review that answers the question of the characteristics of the protocols or formal processes that are being used to improve the performance of heuristic evaluations of software products. In Sect. 4, we present the comparative analysis and discussion of the protocols or formal processes and the selected process for this research. In Sect. 5, we present the modeling of the selected formal process using the Bizagi BPMN Modeler tool, and its validation. Finally, in Sect. 6, we present the conclusions of the research and the future works to be done.

2 Background

In this section, we present the main concepts related to this work.

2.1 Usability

Usability, according to ISO 9241-210-2019 [5], is the "extend to which a system, product or service can be used by specified users to achieve specified goals with effectiveness, efficiency, and satisfaction in a specified context of use".

Additionally, Jacob Nielsen [6] defines it as the evaluation of five attributes the user interface of a system must have, which are the following:

- Learnability: The system should be easy to learn so that the user can perform some tasks with the system as quickly as possible.
- Efficiency: The system should be efficient during its use to provide the highest level of productivity possible.
- Memorability: The system should be easy to remember so that the casual user can use it again after a period of leaving it, without the need to relearn how it works.
- Errors: The system should provide a low error rate so that users make as few errors as possible and can quickly recover from them. Errors considered cata-strophic must not occur.
- Satisfaction: The system should be pleasant to use so that users are subjectively satisfied while using it.

2.2 Heuristic Evaluation

According to Andreas Holzinger [7], Heuristic Evaluation (HE) belongs to us-ability inspection methods and is the most common informal method. For its exe-cution, it requires usability experts who can identify if the dialogue elements or other interactive software elements follow the established principles of usability.

According to Jacob Nielsen [6], the heuristic evaluation allows the inspection of what is good and bad in the interface of a system, which could be done through one's own opinion or, ideally, using well-defined guidelines. The author also maintains that the main goal of the evaluation is to find usability problems in the design of an interface that is carried out through a group of evaluators who will inspect and judge it through usability principles called heuristics. Additionally, a single evaluator can find only 35% of the usability problems in an interface; however, each evaluator usually encounters different types of problems; for this reason, he recommends the participation of 3 to 5 evaluators to obtain the best cost-benefit ratio. These evaluations are performed singularly, and then, upon completion, the results are compared for overall usability analysis.

2.3 Systematic Literature Review

According to Barbara Kitchenham and Stuart Charters [8], Systematic Literature Review (SLR) consists of identifying, evaluating, and interpreting the most relevant available studies and answering review questions about an area or phenomenon of interest. Additionally, for this study, we will use the formal protocol proposed by Kitchenham that consists of the review being carried out in three phases: (1) planning, (2) conducting and (3) reporting.

Planning consists of defining stages to identify the need for the review, as well as the specification of research questions, developing and evaluating review protocols. Additionally, the conduction will allow the identification of the review, selection of primary studies, as well as the extraction, monitoring and synthesis of data. Finally, the reporting phase will facilitate the specification of propagation mechanisms, as well as provide formatting and review of the main report generated.

2.4 Heuristic Evaluation Formal Process

According to Freddy Paz [9], it consists of a framework that has a base in the analysis of case studies that will provide a structured way to execute of the heuristic evaluation to reduce the different interpretations that arise now of its use. An example of the formal process is the one defined by the author, who establishes five phases for its execution: (1) planning, (2) training, (3) evaluation, (4) discussion and (5) report.

3 Characteristics of Protocols or Formal Processes Used to Improve the Performance of Heuristic Evaluations

According to our previous research's systematic literature review [3], the answer to the research question of "what are the characteristics of the formal protocols or processes that are being used to improve the performance of heuristic evaluations in software products?" was divided by grouping the information obtained by 33 studies into 6 main protocols. Table 1 shows the selected primary studies to answer the review question.

Table 1. Selected primary studies

ID	Study	Quote	Search engine
S01	Usability Problem Areas on Key International and Key Arab E-commerce Websites	[10]	Scopus
S02	Usability evaluation of web-based interfaces for Type2 Diabetes Mellitus	[11]	Scopus
S03	Heuristic Evaluations of Cultural Heritage Websites	[12]	Scopus
S04	PROMETHEUS: Procedural Methodology for Developing Heuristics of Usability	[13]	Scopus
S05	A formal protocol to conduct usability heuristic evaluations in the context of the software development process	[14]	Scopus

(continued)

Table 1. (*continued*)

ID	Study	Quote	Search engine
S08	Observation and heuristics evaluation of student web-based application of SIPADU-STIS	[15]	Scopus
S09	Usabilidad en sitios web oficiales de las universidades del ecuador	[16]	Scopus
S10	The E-health Literacy Demands of Australia's My Health Record: A Heuristic Evaluation of Usability	[17]	Scopus
S11	Experimental validation of a set of cultural-oriented usability heuristics: e-Commerce websites evaluation	[18]	Scopus
S12	A heuristic evaluation on the usability of health information websites	[19]	Scopus
S13	Websites with multimedia content: A heuristic evaluation of the medical/anatomical museums	[20]	Scopus
S14	A Heuristic Evaluation for Deaf Web User Experience (HE4DWUX)	[21]	Scopus
S15	A comparative study of video content user interfaces based on heuristic evaluation	[22]	Scopus
S16	Heuristic evaluation for Virtual Museum on smartphone	[23]	Scopus
S17	A User-Centered Design for Redesigning E-Government Website in Public Health Sector	[24]	Scopus
S18	Developing Usability Heuristics: A Formal or Informal Process?	[25]	Scopus
S20	Método para la evaluación de usabilidad de sitios web transaccionales basado en el proceso de inspección heurística	[9]	Alicia Concytec
S21	Usability testing of conferences websites: A case study of practical teaching	[26]	Scopus
S22	Evaluating the usability of the information architecture of academic library websites	[27]	Scopus
S23	A perception study of a new set of usability heuristics for transactional websites	[28]	Scopus
S24	Comparing the effectiveness and accuracy of new usability heuristics	[29]	Scopus
S26	Quantifying the usability through a variant of the traditional heuristic evaluation process	[30]	Scopus
S27	University students' heuristic usability inspection of the national library of Turkey website	[31]	Scopus
S28	Usability heuristics evaluation in search engine	[32]	Scopus
S29	A collaborative RESTful cloud-based tool for management of chromatic pupillometry in a clinical trial	[33]	Scopus

(*continued*)

Table 1. (*continued*)

ID	Study	Quote	Search engine
S30	Heuristic Evaluation of eGLU-Box: A Semi-automatic Usability Evaluation Tool for Public Administrations	[34]	Scopus
S31	The Relationship of the Studies of Ergonomic and Human Computer Interfaces – A Case Study of Graphical Interfaces in E-Commerce Websites	[35]	Scopus
S32	Evaluation of usability heuristics for transactional web sites: A comparative study	[36]	Scopus
S33	Heuristics for grid and typography evaluation of art magazines websites	[37]	Scopus
S34	Usability of tourism websites: a case study of heuristic evaluation	[38]	Scopus
S35	Programmer experience: a set of heuristics for programming environments	[39]	Scopus
S36	Exploring the usability of the central library websites of medical sciences universities	[40]	Scopus
S37	Heuristic Usability Evaluation of University of Hong Kong Libraries' Mobile Website	[41]	Scopus

Also, Table 2 shows the protocols or formal processes and the studies in which they were found.

Table 2. Studies that include protocols or formal processes used for heuristic evaluations

Protocol or formal process	Research studies	# Studies
Definition of new heuristics	S01, S03, S04, S11, S14, S18, S22, S23, S24, S29, S31, S32, S33, S35	14
Nielsen derived evaluation items	S12, S13, S15, S21, S27, S28, S30, S34, S36, S37	10
Comparison and grouping between evaluations	S01, S08, S10, S17, S18, S23, S24, S32	8
Qualification methods	S02, S16, S34	3
Methodologies applied to heuristic evaluation	S09, S22, S26	3
Formal processes with properly defined steps	S05, S20	2

Descriptions of formal protocols or processes and their benefits are presented below.

1. Definition of new heuristics: Definition of new heuristics is a fundamental protocol applied in the execution of heuristic evaluations since, despite having the Nielsen heuristics, these will not always be able to cover what is required for the usability evaluation of a particular software [S01 & S03], as well as relate to the object of study [S04]. For this reason, the benefits obtained with the definition of new heuristics are the best representation of the case study [S01] that could not be performed using only Nielsen heuristics [S03] and obtaining usability problems that are desired to be found in a particular system [S04, S11, S14, S22, S23, S24, S29, S31, S32, S33 & S35]. Additionally, methodologies applied to the generation of new heuristics [S18] such as PROMETHEUS are presented, which will allow dividing the process into stages that validate that the heuristics are being properly constructed, iterating through a refinement step if necessary [S04].

2. Nielsen derived evaluation items: One of the protocols used for the evaluation that is derived from Nielsen is the use of its ten heuristics in conjunction with the eight Schneiderman golden rules for grouping them into evaluation elements [S12]. Additionally, in another protocol, phases are used for the application of the evaluation, which consist of the initial navigation on the website to judge the flow, perception and dynamics of the interaction, and then, in the second phase, use the metrics of Nielsen usability heuristics [S13]. Other studies show that Nielsen heuristics could be used in conjunction with metrics to enrich the collected data [S27], with attributes defined in ISO / IEC 25023 [S28] and in conjunction with case study-specific heuristics [S34]. Finally, the ten Nielsen heuristics could also be applied by themselves to perform usability evaluations [S15, S21, S30, S36 & S37].

3. Comparison and grouping between evaluations: Comparison of results of the execution of heuristic evaluations between the country to be evaluated versus key international pages allows providing improvement indicators and recommendations of good practices [S01]. Likewise, evaluation questions grouping allows comparisons between the generated groups to be made, in order to obtain more precise answers [S08]. Additionally, dividing heuristic evaluations into groups by used heuristics allows comparisons to be made of how many usability problems have been found with each one [S10]. Complementarily, if a heuristic evaluation is made to a website and then an additional one is made to the improved site as a result of the first evaluation, it will be possible to quantitatively compare how much the score has improved [S17]. Finally, comparing test execution with Nielsen heuristics in contrast to newly designed heuristics allows the measurement of their effectiveness [S18, S23, S24 & S32].

4. Qualification methods: The use of Nielsen severity rating and Olson's ease of fix will allow providing a quantitative assessment according to the severity of the usability problem encountered and how easy or difficult it will be to fix it [S02]. Likewise, another form of rating is the use of a heuristic evaluation questionnaire that consists of assigning a score of five points on the Likert scale for the evaluation of prototypes [S16], as well as adding structured sub-elements to the defined heuristics whose questions can be used by evaluators. [S34].

5. Methodologies applied to heuristic evaluation: The protocols oriented to heuristic evaluation methodologies show the proposal for the use of a heuristic method based on ISO-9241–151 standard that consists of the execution of a heuristic evaluation by applying indicators divided into criteria that allow each indicator to be assessed, which facilitates the evaluation of results by the criterion as well as in general [S09]. In addition, a framework is defined for the evaluation of dialogue elements in web pages so that the evaluators consider the same previously defined elements to be evaluated, as well as a definition of a workflow that allows its applicability in other types of software [S22]. Finally, the definition of a quantitative evaluation procedure of the results of a heuristic evaluation is proposed to obtain consistent and quantifiable results without the need for user participation [S26].

6. Formal processes with properly defined steps: The heuristic inspection process can be fully formalized through five duly defined steps: (1) planning, (2) training, (3) evaluation, (4) discussion, and (5) report [S05 & S20]. In this way, this formalization consolidates the different ways in which evaluations are carried out into a single one, allowing interpretations on how to carry them out to be reduced [S05 & S20].

4 Comparative Analysis and Discussion

After grouping the studies according to their main characteristics, a comparative table was made that allowed the comparison of said protocols or formal processes, in general criteria such as the level of coverage, which consisted of qualifying the contribution to the heuristic evaluation process to classify them in one of the following levels as appropriate: Low, Medium and High. In addition, the benefits found and the types of software evaluated by each one were shown. Finally, the definition of new heuristics protocol was not taken into consideration, since, although it is a formal process, the direct contribution to the heuristic evaluation process is not as significant as it only results in new heuristics for inspection. Table 3 shows the characteristics mentioned.

Table 3. Characteristics of the protocols or formal processes

Protocol or formal process	Coverage level of the heuristic evaluation process	Found benefits	Application
Nielsen derived evaluation items	Medium: They contribute mainly to the execution of the heuristic evaluation by using the Nielsen heuristics to carry out the evaluation together with additional elements that allow improving the inspection	(1) They allow for quantitative results when using metrics related to Nielsen's heuristics (2) They allow the heuristic evaluation to be carried out, covering the demands proposed by conventional professional standards (3) They allow adding additional heuristics in conjunction with the Nielsen heuristics	Health information websites, medical museums, conferences, libraries, and tourism, as well as video content interfaces

(*continued*)

Table 3. (*continued*)

Protocol or formal process	Coverage level of the heuristic evaluation process	Found benefits	Application
Comparison and grouping between evaluations	Low: They contribute mainly to the comparison of results of heuristic evaluations by proposing more than one form of execution to finally evaluate which is the best	(1) They allow usability evaluation results to be compared to generate good practice recommendations (2) They allow us to compare how much the results of a new system have improved compared to the initial one (3) They allow to measure the effectiveness between groups of heuristics	E-commerce, student, health, and transactional websites
Qualification methods	Medium: They contribute mainly to the execution of the heuristic evaluation by providing protocols that allow formalizing the qualification during the inspection	(1) They allow determining and prioritizing which are the usability problems that must be solved as soon as possible (2) They allow the structuring of questions for the evaluators and that their answers are acquired quickly	Diabetes screening and tourism websites as well as virtual museum mobile apps
Methodologies applied to heuristic evaluation	Medium: They contribute mainly to the execution of the heuristic evaluation through indicators and the inspection of dialogue elements. In addition, they contribute to the results as they are considered procedures for obtaining quantitative results	(1) They allow assessments to be given through indicators that will facilitate the evaluation of the result by criteria and in total (2) They allow all evaluations to consider the same navigation elements (3) They allow obtaining consistent and quantifiable results of the evaluation carried out	University and library websites
Formal processes with properly defined steps	High: They contribute to the entire heuristic evaluation process through duly defined steps: planning, training, evaluation, discussion and reporting	Consolidates the various ways in which evaluations are carried out into one, allowing the interpretations of usability evaluators in how to carry them out to be reduced	Transactional websites

Additionally, to carry out the comparative analysis, a comparative analysis matrix was prepared and it allowed the characteristics of each process to be compared through the following criteria:

- Applied contexts: It is verified if it has been applied in an academic or industrial context or in both.
- Types of software evaluated: These are the types of software present in the various studies
- Does it divide the evaluation into duly defined steps?: It is verified if the studies present the protocol or formal process with indications of steps that must be followed to carry out the inspection.
- Is it a complement or a new proposal to the evaluation process proposed by Nielsen?: It is verified if the way of carrying out the evaluation is an adaptation of the process proposed by Nielsen that includes additional characteristics, or if a new process has been proposed.
- Does it include previous training for evaluators?: It is verified if the previous training for evaluators is included as part of the protocol or formal process.
- The validation of the submitted proposal is evidenced: It is verified if the protocol or formal process used in the studies has been validated.
- Result of the evidence: Detail of the evidence of the validation of the proposal, if any.
- Coverage level of the Heuristic Evaluation: Measurement of the coverage of the evaluation, which can be (1) Low, (2) Medium or partial, (3) High or total.
- Description of coverage: Justification of the level of coverage of the evaluation.
- Benefits found: Detail of the benefits found by the use of the protocol or formal process.

Table 4 shows a summary of the comparative analysis matrix with the result of its five measurable criteria that were considered because they were the ones that allowed a comparative analysis between the protocols and formal processes to give a measurable answer in how much was contributed in the heuristic evaluation process.

Table 4. Summary of the comparative analysis matrix

Protocol or formal process	Does it divide the evaluation into duly defined steps?	Is it a complement or a new proposal to the evaluation process proposed by Nielsen?	Does it include prior training for evaluators?	The validation of the submitted proposal is evidenced	Coverage level of the Heuristic Evaluation
Nielsen derived evaluation items	No	Complement	No	No	Medium or partial
Comparison and grouping between evaluations	No	Complement	No	No	Low

(continued)

Table 4. (*continued*)

Protocol or formal process	Does it divide the evaluation into duly defined steps?	Is it a complement or a new proposal to the evaluation process proposed by Nielsen?	Does it include prior training for evaluators?	The validation of the submitted proposal is evidenced	Coverage level of the Heuristic Evaluation
Qualification methods	**Yes** (one study)	Complement	No	No	Medium or partial
Methodologies applied to heuristic evaluation	No	Complement	No	No	Medium or partial
Formal processes with properly defined steps	**Yes**	**New proposal**	**Yes**	**Yes**	**High or total**

The comparison of the characteristics gave as a result that the formal process that is part of the category "Formal processes with properly defined steps" obtained the best results by providing a positive response for each of the criteria by contributing to the entire heuristic evaluation process through duly defined steps and by consolidating the different ways in which evaluations are carried out in one, allowing the interpretations of usability evaluators on how to carry them out to be reduced. For this reason, this formal process was selected as the basis of this research project.

5 Selected Formal Process BPMN Model

The detailed diagram of the selected process was made with the aim of modeling in detail the steps and tasks that must be followed to carry out the process properly, and that there is no room for different interpretations by the evaluators who use it. In addition, the process has been divided into the main flow that consists of the execution of 5 sub-processes that correspond to the steps indicated in the selected formal process [9]: (1) planning, (2) training, (3) evaluation, (4) discussion and (5) report.

This result was achieved using the Bizagi BPMN Modeler tool, which allowed the design and modeling of the process through the BPMN notation which consisted of 6 flows that are detailed below:

- General: Flow in which all the threads that must be followed to carry out the process in its entirety are described. Figure 1 shows the BPMN diagram of said process flow.

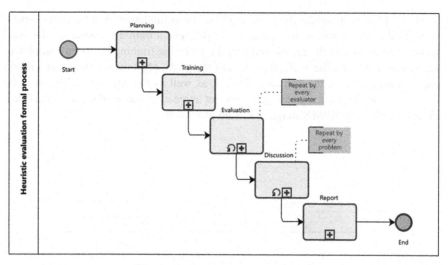

Fig. 1. General process flow diagram

- Planning: Flow that defines the initial phase related to the preparation of the heuristic evaluation. In this phase, the evaluation manager carries out the preliminary steps to carry out the evaluation. Likewise, the objective and scope of the evaluation, the software product to be evaluated, the profiles and the number of evaluators that will make up the team, the set of heuristics and the evaluation template to be used are defined. Once the above has been defined, the professionals who will form part of the evaluation team are recruited. Figure 2 shows the BPMN diagram of said process flow.

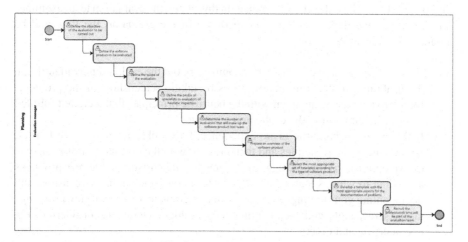

Fig. 2. Planning flow diagram

- Training: Flow that defines the training phase for evaluators with little or no experience. In this phase, the evaluation manager prepares a training session for the evaluators who belong to the mentioned criteria. Once the training has been completed, the manager informs the evaluation team of the goals, objectives, framework criteria and a general idea of the software product, as well as the type of evaluation to be carried out, so that the team can then carry out a free exploration of system interfaces. Figure 3 shows the BPMN diagram of said process flow.

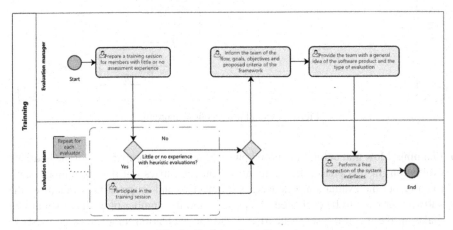

Fig. 3. Training flow diagram

- Evaluation: Flow that defines the execution phase of the heuristic evaluation of the interfaces of the selected software product. In this phase, the evaluation team examines the interfaces and depending on the experience of the evaluator; the flow will be continued in one of two ways:

(1) If the evaluator has experience, he should carry out the evaluation by identifying the usability problems in the interfaces by taking screenshots of the problems found, to later associate them with the heuristic principles that were not fulfilled and document them in the evaluation template.

(2) If the evaluator has little or no experience, he should first familiarize himself with the heuristic principles and then proceed with the evaluation following one of two options: (a) Reviewing the complete list of heuristics to identify problems according to what is learned and remember at the time, taking screenshots and documenting your findings in the assessment template. (b) Identifying problems, taking screenshots, and documenting in the evaluation template considering only one heuristic at a time.

Figure 4 shows the BPMN diagram of said process flow.

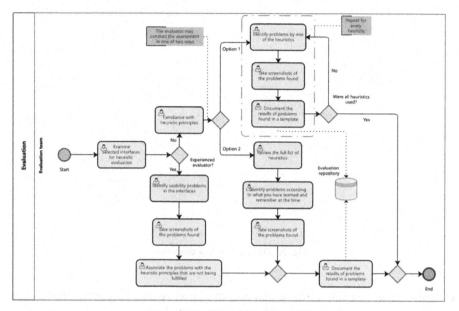

Fig. 4. Evaluation flow diagram

- Discussion: Flow that defines the elaboration phase of the final list of usability problems by determining if the problem has been found by more than one evaluator or if it really refers to a usability problem. In this phase, the evaluation manager verbalizes each of the problems so that the evaluator who identified the problem can provide more details and evidence of each one. Then, the team determines if the identified aspect really refers to a usability problem, if it is not considered so, the evaluator will determine if it still considers that it is a usability problem, otherwise, it is discarded.

  If it is a relevant aspect and the problem was identified by more than one evaluator, it must be determined whether it is the same incident or different usability aspects. If it is the same incidence, a definition and description of the problem is prepared collaboratively, otherwise, it is classified as a usability problem to be discussed later.

  Then, if the identified aspect was classified as a usability problem, it must be determined if it clearly expresses the incident to which it refers. If not, a definition and description of the identified problem is prepared. Finally, this problem is included in the final list.

Figure 5 shows the BPMN diagram of said process flow.

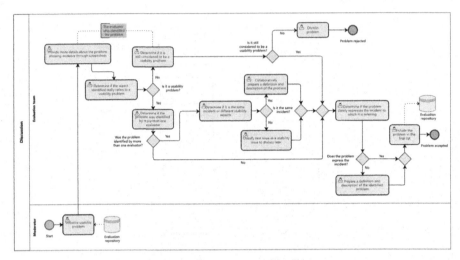

Fig. 5. Discussion flow diagram

- Report: Flow that defines the assignment of a severity and frequency value to each problem, to determine which are the problems that should be solved most urgently. In this phase, the assessment manager sends the consolidated list to each member of the team. Then, each evaluator must rate the severity and frequency of each problem and then average the scores assigned individually and calculate the standard deviation together with the ratings made by the entire team. In case the standard deviation value is high, the reasons for assigning the severity and frequency values should be discussed, to later reach a consensus on the criticality.

Finally, the evaluation team must offer possible solutions for each of the problems, also highlighting the positive aspects of the proposed interfaces, to prepare a final report that describes all the results of the heuristic evaluation process. Figure 6 shows the BPMN diagram of said process flow.

For the validation of the modeling realized, an HCI specialist was interviewed who validated 100% of the result by confirming that all the criteria were successfully met, as presented in the interview. These criteria were the following:

- The detailed diagram of the formal heuristic evaluation process selected in BPMN format was presented using the Bizagi BPMN Modeler tool.
- The flow of the process was clearly understood with no room for it to be interpreted in more than one way.
- The process was correctly modeled using standard BPMN notations for process modeling.
- The process was adequately explained, and the questions asked about it were clearly answered.

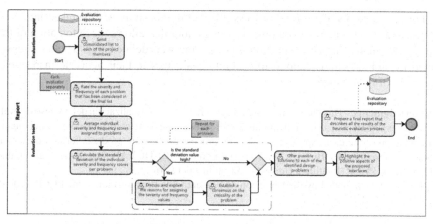

Fig. 6. Report flow diagram

6 Conclusions and Future Works

The objective of this research was to select and model a formal process of heuristic evaluation applicable to the usability inspection process of software products through a comparative analysis, whose results were the following: (1) a comparative table of the formal processes documented in the literature to carry out a heuristic evaluation and (2) a detailed diagram of the selected process modeled in BPMN.

The first result of this objective was achieved by developing a comparative table with the formal processes obtained as part of the systematic review of the literature, where five protocols or formal processes were evidenced that were compared through 5 measurable criteria. After analyzing all the process proposals, it was possible to conclude that the formal process "Formal processes with duly defined steps" was the most appropriate, because it fully covered the heuristic evaluation process, complied with dividing the evaluation into duly defined steps and because it included prior training for evaluators unlike the others.

Additionally, it was presented as a new proposal to the evaluation process proposed by Nielsen, where its validation was evidenced through case studies that allowed to find a greater number of severe and critical problems, as well as that the evaluators tend to make fewer errors compared to the Nielsen process.

The second result of this objective was achieved by modeling the process through the BPMN notation, where the flow that must be followed to carry out the process properly was presented in detail. The process modeled was validated by expert judgement.

By complying with the two mentioned results, it is concluded that the objective has been met, since a solution has been given to the problem caused by the absence of a comparative analysis of the formal processes documented in the literature, having prepared a table with criteria that allowed to quantitatively and qualitatively evaluate the formal processes found in the systematic review of the literature, and to be able to recommend the process with the best indicators after reviewing the results obtained.

For future works, the formal process selected in this study will be taken into consideration as the basis for developing a software tool that allows the automation of the heuristic evaluation process, since, in this way, the well-defined steps could be represented in said system as support to usability evaluators in their heuristic inspections regardless of their experience level.

Acknowledgments. This work is part of the research project "Virtualización del proceso de evaluación de experiencia de usuario de productos de software para escenarios de no presencialidad" (virtualization of the user experience evaluation process of software products for non-presential scenarios), developed by HCI-DUXAIT research group. HCI-DUXAIT is a research group that belongs to the PUCP (Pontificia Universidad Católica del Perú).

This work was funded by the Dirección de Fomento a la Investigación at the PUCP through grant 2021-C-0023.

References

1. Li, Y., Liu, C.: User experience research and analysis based on usability testing methods. In: Zhao, P., Ye, Z., Xu, M., Yang, Li., Zhang, L., Zhu, R. (eds.) Advances in Graphic Communication, Printing and Packaging Technology and Materials. LNEE, vol. 754, pp. 263–267. Springer, Singapore (2021). https://doi.org/10.1007/978-981-16-0503-1_39
2. Nielsen, J.: Usability inspection methods. In: Conference Companion on Human Factors in Computing Systems. pp. 413–414 (1994). DOI: https://doi.org/10.1145/259963.260531
3. Lecaros, A., Paz, F., Moquillaza, A.: Challenges and opportunities on the application of heuristic evaluations: a systematic literature review. In: Soares, M.M., Rosenzweig, E., Marcus, A. (eds.) HCII 2021. LNCS, vol. 12779, pp. 242–261. Springer, Cham (2021). https://doi.org/10.1007/978-3-030-78221-4_17
4. Goetz, M.: Modeling Workflow Patterns through a Control-flow perspective using BPMN and the BPM Modeler BizAgi. Bpmn. (2009)
5. International Organization for Standardization: ISO 9241–210–2019: (2019)
6. Nielsen, J.: Usability Engineering. Morgan Kaufmann Publishers Inc., San Francisco, CA, USA (1993)
7. Holzinger, A.: Usability engineering methods for software developers. Commun. ACM. **48**, 71–74 (2005). https://doi.org/10.1145/1039539.1039541
8. Kitchenham, B., Charters, S.: Guidelines for performing Systematic Literature Reviews in Software Engineering (2007)
9. Paz Espinoza, F.A.: Método para la evaluación de usabilidad de sitios web transaccionales basado en el proceso de inspección heurística [Doctoral Thesis]. Pontif. Univ. Católica del Perú. 275 (2018). http://hdl.handle.net/20.500.12404/9903
10. Hasan, L., Morris, A.: Usability problem areas on key international and key arab e-commerce websites. J. Internet Commer. **16**, 80–103 (2017). https://doi.org/10.1080/15332861.2017.1281706
11. Davis, D., Jiang, S.: Usability evaluation of web-based interfaces for Type2 Diabetes Mellitus. In: IEOM 2015 - 5th International Conference Industrial Engineering Operations Management Proceeding (2015). https://doi.org/10.1109/IEOM.2015.7093713
12. Lam, D., Sajjanhar, A.: Heuristic evaluations of cultural heritage websites. In: 2018 International Conference Digital Image Computing Techniques Appllications DICTA 2018 (2019). https://doi.org/10.1109/DICTA.2018.8615847

13. Jiménez, C., Cid, H.A., Figueroa, I.: PROMETHEUS: procedural methodology for developing heuristics of usability. IEEE Lat. Am. Trans. **15**, 541–549 (2017). https://doi.org/10.1109/TLA.2017.7867606
14. Paz, F., Paz, F.A., Pow-Sang, J.A., Collazos, C.: A formal protocol to conduct usability heuristic evaluations in the context of the software development process. Int. J. Eng. Technol. **7**(2.28), 10–19 (2018). https://doi.org/10.14419/ijet.v7i2.28.12874
15. Maghfiroh, L.R.: Observation and heuristics evaluation of student web-based application of SIPADU-STIS. J. Phys. Conf. Ser. **1511**, 0–10 (2020) https://doi.org/10.1088/1742-6596/1511/1/012019
16. Pincay-Ponce, J., Caicedo-Ávila, V., Herrera-Tapia, J., Delgado-Muentes, W., Delgado-Franco, P.: Usabilidad en sitios web oficiales de las universidades del ecuador. Rev. Ibérica Sist. e Tecnol. Informação. 106–120 (2020)
17. Walsh, L., Hemsley, B., Allan, M., Adams, N., Balandin, S., Georgiou, A., Higgins, I., McCarthy, S., Hill, S.: The e-health literacy demands of Australia's my health record: a heuristic evaluation of usability. Perspect. Heal. Inf. Manag. **14** (2017)
18. Díaz, J., Rusu, C., Collazos, C.A.: Experimental validation of a set of cultural-oriented usability heuristics: e-Commerce websites evaluation. Comput. Stand. Interfaces. **50**, 160–178 (2017). https://doi.org/10.1016/j.csi.2016.09.013
19. Chen, Y.N., Hwang, S.L.: A heuristic evaluation on the usability of health information websites. In: Bridging Research and Good Practices towards Patient Welfare - Proceedings of the 4th International Conference on HealthCare Systems Ergonomics and Patient Safety, HEPS 2014, pp. 109–116 (2015)
20. Kiourexidou, M., Antonopoulos, N., Kiourexidou, E., Piagkou, M., Kotsakis, R., Natsis, K.: Websites with multimedia content: A heuristic evaluation of the medical/anatomical museums. Multimodal Technol. Interact. 3(2), 42 (2019). https://doi.org/10.3390/mti3020042
21. Yeratziotis, A., Zaphiris, P.: A Heuristic Evaluation for Deaf Web User Experience (HE4DWUX). Int. J. Hum. Comput. Interact. **34**, 195–217 (2018). https://doi.org/10.1080/10447318.2017.1339940
22. Eliseo, M.A., Casac, B.S., Gentil, G.R.: A comparative study of video content user interfaces based on heuristic evaluation. In: Iberian Conference Information Systems Technologies CISTI, pp. 1-6 (2017). https://doi.org/10.23919/CISTI.2017.7975820
23. Motlagh Tehrani, S.E., Zainuddin, N.M.M., Takavar, T.: Heuristic evaluation for Virtual Museum on smartphone. In: Proceeding - 2014 3rd International Conference User Science Engineering Experimental Engineering Engag. i-USEr 2014, pp. 227–231 (2015) https://doi.org/10.1109/IUSER.2014.7002707
24. Puspitasari, I., Indah Cahyani, D.: Taufik: a user-centered design for redesigning e-government website in public health sector. In: Proceeding - 2018 International Seminar Application Technology Information Communication Creat. Technology Human Life, iSemantic 2018, pp. 219–224 (2018) https://doi.org/10.1109/ISEMANTIC.2018.8549726
25. Quinones, D., Rusu, C., Roncagliolo, S., Rusu, V., Collazos, C.A.: Developing usability heuristics: a formal or informal process? IEEE Lat. Am. Trans. **14**, 3400–3409 (2016). https://doi.org/10.1109/TLA.2016.7587648
26. Halaweh, M.: Usability testing of conferences websites: a case study of practical teaching. In: Uden, L., Hadzima, B., Ting, I.-H. (eds.) KMO 2018. CCIS, vol. 877, pp. 380–389. Springer, Cham (2018). https://doi.org/10.1007/978-3-319-95204-8_32
27. Silvis, I.M., Bothma, T.J.D., de Beer, K.J.W.: Evaluating the usability of the information architecture of academic library websites. Libr. Hi Tech. **37**, 566–590 (2019). https://doi.org/10.1108/LHT-07-2017-0151
28. Paz, F., Paz, F.A., Arenas, J.J., Rosas, C.: A Perception study of a new set of usability heuristics for transactional web sites. In: Karwowski, W., Ahram, T. (eds.) IHSI 2018. AISC, vol. 722, pp. 620–625. Springer, Cham (2018). https://doi.org/10.1007/978-3-319-73888-8_96

29. Paz, F., Paz, F.A., Pow-Sang, J.A.: Comparing the effectiveness and accuracy of new usability heuristics. Adv. Intell. Syst. Comput. **497**, 163–175 (2017). https://doi.org/10.1007/978-3-319-41956-5_16

30. Paz, F., Paz, F.A., Sánchez, M., Moquillaza, A., Collantes, L.: Quantifying the usability through a variant of the traditional heuristic evaluation process. In: Marcus, A., Wang, W. (eds.) DUXU 2018. LNCS, vol. 10918, pp. 496–508. Springer, Cham (2018). https://doi.org/10.1007/978-3-319-91797-9_36

31. Inal, Y.: University students' heuristic usability inspection of the national library of Turkey website. Aslib J. Inf. Manag. **70**, 66–77 (2018). https://doi.org/10.1108/AJIM-09-2017-0216

32. dos Santos Pergentino, A.C., Canedo, E.D., Lima, F., de Mendonça, F.L.L.: Usability heuristics evaluation in search engine. In: Marcus, A., Rosenzweig, E. (eds.) HCII 2020. LNCS, vol. 12200, pp. 351–369. Springer, Cham (2020). https://doi.org/10.1007/978-3-030-49713-2_25

33. Iadanza, E., Fabbri, R., Luschi, A., Melillo, P., Simonelli, F.: A collaborative RESTful cloud-based tool for management of chromatic pupillometry in a clinical trial. Heal. Technol. **10**(1), 25–38 (2019). https://doi.org/10.1007/s12553-019-00362-z

34. Federici, S., et al.: Heuristic evaluation of eglu-box: a semi-automatic usability evaluation tool for public administrations. In: Kurosu, M. (ed.) HCII 2019. LNCS, vol. 11566, pp. 75–86. Springer, Cham (2019). https://doi.org/10.1007/978-3-030-22646-6_6

35. de Menezes, M., Falco, M.: The relationship of the studies of ergonomic and human computer interfaces – a case study of graphical interfaces in e-commerce websites. In: Marcus, A., Wang, W. (eds.) HCII 2019. LNCS, vol. 11586, pp. 474–484. Springer, Cham (2019). https://doi.org/10.1007/978-3-030-23535-2_35

36. Paz, F., Paz, F.A., Pow-Sang, J.A.: Evaluation of usability heuristics for transactionalweb sites: a comparative study. Adv. Intell. Syst. Comput. **448**, 1063–1073 (2016) https://doi.org/10.1007/978-3-319-32467-8_92

37. Retore, A.P., Guimarães, C., Leite, M.K.: Heuristics for grid and typography evaluation of art magazines websites. In: Kurosu, M. (ed.) HCI 2016. LNCS, vol. 9731, pp. 408–416. Springer, Cham (2016). https://doi.org/10.1007/978-3-319-39510-4_38

38. Huang, Z.: Usability of tourism websites: a case study of heuristic evaluation. New Rev. Hypermedia Multimed. **26**, 55–91 (2020). https://doi.org/10.1080/13614568.2020.1771436

39. Morales, J., Rusu, C., Botella, F., Quiñones, D.: Programmer experience: a set of heuristics for programming environments. In: Meiselwitz, G. (ed.) HCII 2020. LNCS, vol. 12195, pp. 205–216. Springer, Cham (2020). https://doi.org/10.1007/978-3-030-49576-3_15

40. Okhovati, M., Karami, F., Khajouei, R.: Exploring the usability of the central library websites of medical sciences universities. J. Librariansh. Inf. Sci. **49**, 246–255 (2017). https://doi.org/10.1177/0961000616650932

41. Fung, R.H.Y., Chiu, D.K.W., Ko, E.H.T., Ho, K.K.W., Lo, P.: Heuristic usability evaluation of university of hong kong libraries' mobile website. J. Acad. Librariansh. **42**, 581–594 (2016). https://doi.org/10.1016/j.acalib.2016.06.004

Design Trend Analysis and Design Innovation Based on Card Heuristic Method

Li-Jun Liu and Yi Li$^{(\boxtimes)}$

School of Design, Hunan University, Changsha, China
{sallyliu,2012171}@hnu.edu.cn

Abstract. Quickly uncovering innovation opportunities from trends is an important step in the pre-design phase and an essential skill for designers. However, there is no specific and detailed set of methods on how to get design inspiration by analyzing trends. In our research, we designed and validated an innovative approach in using heuristic cards to expand on design trends. The first is the acquisition of trend keywords. Through the collection of relevant trends of a research topic, some keywords are extracted by the method of text summarization. Next, research on trend-based creative stimulation is carried out, using the acquired trend keywords to make physical cards, which are used by designers for brainstorming and design inspiration. This form can assist designers in the divergence of thinking in the early stage of design. The third part describes how to evaluate the effectiveness of the process in stimulating creativity. This method can help designers turn intangible trends into tangible, exploitable design opportunities that can be better utilized.

Keywords: Trend · Trend analysis · Card heuristic · Co-creation

1 Introduction and Motivation

1.1 Trend Analysis

Design as a contemporary material-making activity, design objects act as a mirror of the times, mapping out trends in social change, cultural changes, and lifestyle changes, and fully reflecting current political, cultural and economic forms. A thorough understanding of design trends can help us understand the age and society and reflect them better in design. Evans [1] believes that trend analysis is an integral part of the design process. When designing products, the trends often provide designers with inspiration, material, and motivation. From the vast amount of social and cultural resources, designers can access cultural genes, inspire their designs, make the right market decisions. Finally, they design products that meet people's lifestyles effectively, thus continuously satisfying people's potential needs for material and spiritual aspects and increasing the core value of the products.

As material living standards continue to rise, people devote their attention to chasing fads and enhancing their tastes. Trends are gradually expanding in scope, with the

M. M. Soares et al. (Eds.): HCII 2022, LNCS 13321, pp. 47–56, 2022.
https://doi.org/10.1007/978-3-031-05897-4_4

influence of trends gradually extending from the fashion sector to the home, design, interior, media, advertising, and travel industries, setting the direction for future product and service launches. And as society progresses, product development cycles accelerate, the cycle of integration into mainstream culture becomes shorter, and product homogenization becomes severe. Issues such as global competition, market saturation and rapid product evolution have led companies to rethink the path to developing new products. The ability to understand and stay ahead of trends has become a strategic tool for new product development [2], and many companies have placed new demands on designers: to quickly tap into innovation opportunities from fashion trends and industry trends. In short, the analysis of trends has a positive impact on the translation of designers' knowledge, the development of innovative corporate products and the development of marketing strategies.

Trends potentially influence the development of design, and design also leads the trends. Trends must exist and change alternatively in virtue of the design, production, and circulation of objects. However, it is not enough to study and list the trends in relation to an industry. It is crucial to clarify the meaning and implications of trends into concrete, actionable and implementable ways. We therefore attempt to translate the intangible trends into tangible and exploitable design opportunities through some methods.

1.2 Feature of Trends

A distinctive feature of trends is that they do not form easily overnight, but rather they emerge gradually. Firstly, weak signals of trends appear in seemingly disorganized dots at the edges of society, which at first appear unrelated, irregular, and hardly ever meaningfully connected. As time passes, these dots form patterns that converge and evolve into a dominant trend [3], as shown in Fig. 1.

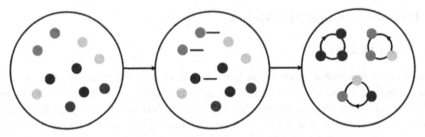

Fig. 1. The Process of trend formation

1.3 Factors Influencing Trends

Design trends are influenced by many factors. Changes in the political landscape, economic developments, technological innovations as well as cultural changes and human needs all influence trends. And these influences can change the macro trends in society, which are often referred to as 'revolution'. Specifically, technology is a passive chooser of design, and design chooses which technology to use, as well as being an active change agent, with technology driving design forward. In the case of design, cultural differences create design diversity, and design diversity further influences and reinforces cultural differences. In terms of human psychological needs, both the search for commonality and the search for difference are constantly driving design trends. In simple terms, the search for common ground drives the acceptance of a new trend, while the search for difference drives the public to tire of a trend and to pursue a different design trend. Vejlgaard [4] sees trends as processes of change that arise because of product development and lead to new products. The emergence of new products also affects design trends.

1.4 Stimulate Creative Ideas

Idea Stimulation. Idea stimulation is the design process of uncovering potential ideas [5], which can lead to early ideas for the styling and functional design of a product. Some of the current challenges to creative stimulation include, design entrenchment, functional entrenchment, the neglect of analogical relationships, and narrow verbal associations [6]. The key to solving these problems lies in providing designers with a sufficiently rich design stimulus. Design stimuli are triggers or springboards for design ideas or concepts, effectively facilitating the generation of design innovation by reducing the cognitive difficulty of accessing design starting points, introducing useful information, and quickly expanding the search space [7].

The purpose of the concept generation stage is to conceive as many creative solutions as possible that meet the requirements of the design problem definition, so that there are enough solutions to be screened during the thinking process. Design heuristics are cognitive strategies applied to design problems that can take designers to different parts of the potential design solution space during the concept generation phase [8]. Design heuristics is a transformational strategy that introduces an existing concept into a changing form to foster a possible design idea. We use methods to extract design heuristics from different trends [9].

Card Heuristic. Card is an effective tool for transferring knowledge between theory and practice, hence the choice of the card format as a tool. The card heuristic we used allows for divergent associations through several random card connections, allowing for an infinite collision of ideas within a limited number of elements to inspire designers, expand the boundaries of their thinking and help to capture a large number of creative ideas. Between the inevitability of the connection and the serendipity, the potential for disruptive innovation can exist.

1.5 Motivation

Based on the characteristics of trends and the factors influencing them, this paper proposes the use of card heuristics for creative stimulation and the search for new design opportunities. We use links between cards to stimulate ideas. The reason is that trends are inherently complex, interactional, and interrelated. Through the connections between trends, insight and inspiration can be gained.

As far as we know, no research has been found that gives a more effective approach to how to use trends, but only some trend keywords for designers to use. We have designed and validated a new approach that addresses this issue in an innovative way. We strive to provide a practical and hands-on approach to trend analysis that can help designers find connections between trends and disperse them. In addition, we aim to gain a deeper understanding of the interaction between individuals in a group creativity process. With the method we have developed, we will provide an effective approach on how to conduct pre-design trend analysis, which can bring new insights to research and practice. It should be noted that our approach is mainly aimed at novice designers, as they lack some experience in getting inspiration than expert designers. And expert designers have enough experience to acquire trends and translate them into concrete designs.

1.6 Introduction

In this section, we focus on the importance of trend analysis and the salient features and influences of trends, as well as specific methods of creative stimulation. Through the combination of trends and stimulating creativity, we have devised a method, based on the card-inspired approach to design trend analysis and innovation. In the next chapters, we present the specific research. The research is divided into two parts, including the acquisition of trend keywords and the stimulation of trend-based ideas. The first study was a collection of relevant trends for a particular research topic, using an extractive text summary method to extract several keywords. The second study was to use the trend keywords obtained in the first part to create physical cards that designers used to brainstorm. This format aids the designer in the early stages of the design process by allowing for a meeting of minds and an exchange of ideas. The third part will be how to evaluate the effectiveness of the process in stimulating creativity.

2 Research

2.1 Study 1

There are many methods of trend analysis, which are mainly divided into qualitative method by analyzing trend influencing factors and quantitative method based on trend representation data analysis. Qualitative analysis methods include PESTLE model [10]. In addition, there are methods based on data analysis, which go through the process of expert information collection and intuitive judgment at the beginning, and then computer technology for prediction and analysis, as shown in Table 1. Through the following comparison, we can know that the trend analysis method using computer can ensure the accuracy and scientific nature of trend analysis. Therefore, we choose to use big data technology for analysis.

First, we need to identify which areas to trend from. Since the PESTLE model is primarily used for corporate strategic planning, we decided to refine the model to analyze six major influencing factors for design. They are economy, culture, technology, society, human needs, and current design. For the four aspects of economy, culture, technology, and society, we mainly look for hot news, national policy documents, etc. These are generally recent or current society, culture, economy, environment, or technological events, especially those expected to have a significant impact on the design in the next 2–5 years. For the design trend, we mainly through the well-known design awards, trend reports, etc. One of our innovations is to capture trends from diverse and heterogeneous data and a vast amount of hot information. Using the method of abstracted text summary [11], several keywords are extracted. More than 70 keywords were obtained by word clustering. The use of advanced big data acquisition technology is more efficient and more comprehensive than the manual collection of designers in the past. The specific technical route is shown in Fig. 2. Some trend keywords are shown in Table 2.

Table 1. Development of data-driven research methods

	Before	Now
Methods	Gather expert information and make intuitive judgments	Predictive analysis using computer technology
Area	Clothing field	Multiple areas
Analyze	It generally relies on experts or professionals to extract and analyze information	Quantitative analysis
Advantages and disadvantages	Completely relying on the insight and intuition of researchers cannot guarantee the accuracy and continuity of prediction	Efficient, relatively accurate, effective information extraction more complex, high cost

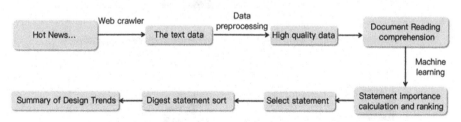

Fig. 2. Step of text summary

Table 2. Keywords of trends

Area	Culture	Technology	Society	Economy	Needs
Trends	Generation Z	New Energy Vehicle	Glass Society	Green wave	Privacy Right
	Metaverse	Artificial Intelligence	Healthy Crazy	Stakeholder Economy	Fairness
	China New Wave	NET ZERO	Elder Society	Common Prosperity	Recognition
	Ancient Customs	Block Chain	Three-child Policy	The Belt and Road	Entertainment

2.2 Study 2

The Design of Card. After obtaining the keywords in the first study, we used physical cards to present them. Physical cards have the following advantages: they can be easily observed by users, they can be randomly placed together for thinking. Users can play them together like playing cards, making research more interesting.

The second study involved using the trend keywords obtained in Study 1 to create physical cards, which were divided into six categories, including social, economic, cultural, technological trends, human needs, and popular design products currently present in the market, as shown in Fig. 3. Each card would display the keyword for that trend, a representative image, and a short introduction. The combination of graphic and text can make designers more intuitive to understand what the trend is.

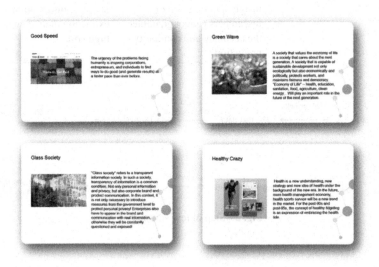

Fig. 3. The design of trend card

In terms of how these cards will be used, here are our assumptions. The experimenter first learns about the cards, and then they can connect the different cards with a line, randomly combining them. After the combination to brainstorm about their causal relationships and how they relate to the research topic, and whether the combination offers better design opportunities. This format can assist designers in the early stages of the design process by allowing for a meeting of minds and an exchange of ideas. In this way it can advance the leap of thinking, where the collision of two or three cards will generate new possibilities with a randomness. The reason we use links between cards to stimulate ideas is that trends are inherently complex, interactional, and interrelated. Through the connections between trends, insight and inspiration can be gained.

Procedure of Experiment. The experiment was conducted as follows: ten designers (four men and six women) with one to two years of design experience were invited to participate in the experiment. All of them have used trend analysis in their designs before. The specific process of this experiment is shown in the Fig. 4.

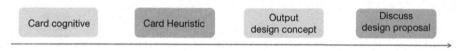

The Design Process

Fig. 4. Procedure of experiment

Stage 1: Self-discovery of Use. In the early stages of the design, some of the cards were given to the experimenter to use. The experimenters were initially unaware of the cards. They were first allowed to browse through the cards to familiarize themselves with their content and freely explore their use to generate new ideas. In general, this takes 1–3 min per card. During this process, participants can discuss the contents of the cards and offer their thoughts on the trend. The card usage process is shown in Fig. 5.

The results showed that experimenters were able to use the cards themselves, relying on their intuition to randomly pick a trend card and associate it with the design theme, without specifying how to use the cards. A lot of ideas come out of this intuitive and simple way of thinking.

Fig. 5. Card browsing process

Stage 2: Explain and Use. The use of the cards is explained to the experimenter, who can choose 2–4 trend cards to connect according to their interests and use the chosen cards for 10 min to think out of the box and then present their design concept as a sketch in 30 min, as shown in Fig. 6. Any number of cards can be combined to create a design concept. The cards are pasted onto poster-sized canvases. Participants are encouraged to write descriptions and brief scenes on the canvas to learn more details.

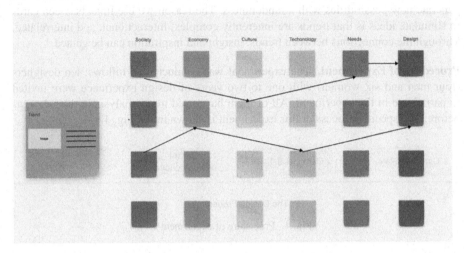

Fig. 6. Schematic diagram of the experiment

During this card linking process, the experimenter may discover that some successful designs stem from an economic or political trend that has become apparent. A cultural trend has a profound impact on the product being sought after. A design trend in one industry may not yet be visible in another but currently seems promising and could lead to new developments and opportunities. All trends are intertwined and influence each other, and the connections made through the cards allow for more collisions and relationships between trends.

Stage 3: Co-creation. The experimenters began to show their canvases and discuss them. In this process, to better support the idea, design criticism of the design concept at this stage is best left to a later stage. Additions to the idea are welcome.

3   Evaluation of the Method and Outlook

Our planned evaluation can be divided into two parts. First, we plan to conduct a set of experiments to specifically assess the effectiveness of the set of cards. We will invite design experts to assess the quality, quantity, novelty, and diversity of the ideas generated by the experimenters [12] and whether the process of brainstorming by the experimenters was successfully executed. In addition, we plan to examine future developments of this method, e.g. whether and how the set of cards can be expanded, and whether the method can be used in other areas, such as business field. Both evaluations can bring valuable insights to research and practice.

In our experiments, we did not address a specific design theme. But through this method, we want to expand the divergent thinking of new designers and help them to explore innovation with processes and mediators. Once they have learned this method, they can conduct theme-specific trend collection and design innovation on any design topic. In a real design project, designers may focus on using trend cards in different fields when working on different projects. For example, when it comes to cultural and creative products, trends in culture and design will be taken into account. For products with high technical content, technical cards are used.

Of course, we also found the drawbacks of using physical cards for design inspiration in our experiments. When a designer is given a certain number of cards, the designer's thinking is limited to a certain extent. In the following research, we want to increase the number of cards by designing them by designers to make up for the deficiency of physical cards themselves.

4 Discussion

We present a research process for trend analysis and design innovation. We use a card heuristic, a method that helps designers to better stimulate creativity and identify market directions and potential design opportunities. Through our methodology, we provide a practical and innovative approach to trend analysis that designers can use and implement when brainstorming. Through our evaluation, we plan to examine the practicality and effectiveness of our approach. In addition, we plan to investigate the expansion of the trend cards, which will allow designers to have more references when using the method in the future. We plan to further investigate the process of interaction between designers when using the method. Overall, we have designed a novel set of cards about trend that can contribute to practice in many ways and change or further develop the theories relevant to designers when brainstorming.

Acknowledgement. This work is supported by the National Natural Science Foundation of China (No. 61772186) and the State Key Laboratory of Advanced Design and Manufacturing for Vehicle Body of Hunan University. Thanks to Niu Wen-jie and Hu Zhe for their contributions to this research.

References

1. Evans, M.: Trend forecasting for design futures. In: European Academy of Design 5th International Conference, Barcelona, 2003. Proceedings. Barcelona, pp. 1-10 (2003)
2. Marseille, J., Roos, I.: Trend analysis: an approach for companies that listen. Design Manag. Rev. **16**(1), 68–72 (2005)
3. Webb, A.: The signals are Talking: Why Today's Fringe is Tomorrow's Mainstream. PublicAffairs (2016)
4. Vejlgaard, H.: Anatomy of a Trend. McGraw-Hill, New York (2008)

5. Hartson, R.: The UX Book: Process and Guidelines for Ensuring a Quality User Experience. Morgan Kaufmann Publishers Inc., San Francisco (2012)
6. Mccaffrey, T., Krishnamurty, S.: The obscure features hypothesis in design innovation. Int. J. Design Creativity Innov. 3(1), 1–28 (2015)
7. Yin, B., Li, Y., Xiong, Y., et al.: Current research situation and development tendency of design thinking. Comput. Intergrated Manuf. Syst. 19(6), 1165–1176 (2013)
8. Yilmaz, S., Seifert, C., Gonzalez, R.: Cognitive heuristics in design: instructional strategies to increase creativity in idea generation. Artif. Intell. Eng. Des. Anal. Manuf. 24(3), 335–355 (2005)
9. Blösch-Paidosh, A., Shea, K.: Design Heuristics for Additive Manufacturing. In: DS 87–5 Proceedings of the 21st International Conference on Engineering Design (ICED 17), 5, Design for X, Design to X, Vancouver, Canada, The Design Society, Glasgow, pp. 91–100 (2017)
10. Kotler, P., Keller, K.L., Brady, M., et al.: Marketing Management. Pearson, UK (2019)
11. Zhou, Q., Yang, N., Wei, F., et al.: Neural document summarization by jointly learning to score and select sentences. In: Proceedings of the 56th Annual Meeting of the Association for Computational Linguistics (Volume 1: Long Papers), (2018)
12. Shah, J.J., Smith, S.M., Vargas-Hernandez, N.: Metrics for measuring ideation effectiveness. Des. Stud. 24(2), 111–134 (2003). https://doi.org/10.1016/s0142-694x(02)00034-0

Reporting the Application of User Experience Tools and Proxy Users in an Industrial Process Based on Double Diamond

George Moreno de Oliveira[✉], Andrine Nascimento Carvalho,
Beatriz Sgobi Lamego, Ingrid Teixeira Monteiro, Enyo José Tavares Gonçalves,
and Alyson Fernandes Basilio

Universidade Federal do Ceará, Campus Quixadá, Quixadá-CE, Brazil
georgemoreno@alu.ufc.br

Abstract. User experience research techniques and tools play a central role in the design of digital solutions. This paper reports the use of proxy users as a source of information about the end users in the discovery, definition and development stages as part of the Double Diamond design process, which offers a structure that diverges and converges between its stages, promoting flexibility to suit the project. The design process of an administrative tool as part of a mobile application to digital commerce is described and discussed. With the support of proxy users and the adoption of design tools such as Service Blueprint, User Journey, Proto-personas and Brainwriting, we arrived at the definition of the initial requirements for this administrative tool. At the end of the process, it was possible to recognize that the application of proxy users in common artifacts for User Experience research enabled the discovery of information about the end users from intermediaries. Unlike a process with direct contact with them, in this case, there was a need to carry out more steps to confirm the data since the user proxy may not represent the real expectations and needs of the end users.

Keywords: User experience · Proxy users · Double diamond · E-commerce

1 Introduction

User-Centered Design (UCD) arises from Human-Computer Interaction (HCI) and is a methodology applied in software systems design [25]. For Norman [30], the UCD means to focus on making products that are understandable and easily usable, corresponding to the users' needs and desires. In this way, it is possible to consider that the UCD, applying HCI and User Experience (UX) concepts, uses design thinking to guide the digital system production to the user's needs.

One way to use digital environments on the rise is e-commerce. Electronic commerce (e-commerce) emerged in 1979 by the Englishman Michael Aldrich

M. M. Soares et al. (Eds.): HCII 2022, LNCS 13321, pp. 57–74, 2022.
https://doi.org/10.1007/978-3-031-05897-4_5

[31] who idealized real-time transactions between different devices. Currently, on the market, several companies produce solutions for this type of trade. In this paper, we will present a project developed at Company X[1], which provides software to support digital commerce for other companies, characterized as a B2B (business to business) relationship.

Among Company X's products available on the market, interest us Application Y, a solution for physical stores that enables the integration of products advertised in the client company's website catalog with products from physical stores, placing its customers at the center of the process. The proposal is to avoid the separation between the physical and virtual entities of the store from the consumer's point of view of the products. Company X understands that the digital world is constantly evolving and recognizes that its products must keep pace with this constant development. For this reason, Application Y is under continuous development, seeking to keep up with market changes and user needs.

Application Y allows the physical store administrator, through a control panel, to configure some system functionalities to adapt them according to the store's needs. However, these settings are applied by editing Javascript programming codes in a text field application's interface. This scenario has made the configuration process difficult and motivated the creation of a solution with a graphical interface, avoiding the insertion and direct alteration of the code and would provide a better user experience through a control panel.

Administrative tools such as control panels [22] are used in systems that involve users who are not experts in the product to be managed. These tools bring greater visibility into the system to maintain control and freedom for the user, allow use flexibility, and help prevent errors. This type of solution can be used for the most diverse purposes, as in the case of building a database interface [5].

This paper presents an experience report of UX techniques usage and tools applied to the Double Diamond design process [11] with proxy users' participation. Proxy users mediate the contact of the project team with the final users when there are restrictions or limitations to directly contact them [32].

This experience took place in an industry project linked to digital solutions for digital commerce to create an administrative module for Application Y. Fourteen (14) design techniques were adopted distributed in four (4) cycles applied in the Double Diamond process. These cycles occurred iteratively and incrementally and adapted to the needs presented in each cycle.

This paper is organized as follows: Sect. 2 presents the theoretical background about Human-Computer Interaction (HCI) and User Experience (UX), proxy users participation and Double Diamond methodology. Next, in Sect. 3 we describe in detail the application of techniques and tools used in each of the cycles applied in the Double Diamond design process. Finally, conclusions and future work are presented in Sect. 4.

---

[1] For industrial confidentiality reasons, the real name of the company and the name of the application brought in this paper will not be revealed. They will be, from now on, referred to as "Company X" and "Application Y". Job and role names have also been changed.

2   Theoretical Background

HCI and UX's focus on the quality of use of systems and their impact on the lives of their users [4]. These areas argue that thinking about the systems' usability from the project's beginning contributes to reducing development costs, as it positively influences the user's perception of the product [4]. In this section, concepts involving the User Experience tools (Sect. 2.1), the participation of Proxy Users (Sect. 2.2), and the Projectual Design Methodology - Double Diamond (Sect. 2.3) are presented.

2.1   HCI and UX Concepts and Tools

UX encompasses a set of users' perceptions, emotions, and responses to a system, product, or service [4]. In this way, UX designers work to build products with better usability, reducing friction and allowing users to complete the desired task in less time, with less noise and obstacles [39].

Another important concept of HCI is usability, which involves understanding how human beings relate to digital products [25], their aspirations, and how certain activities are elaborated and incorporated into people's lives [13]. In the HCI community, in the mid-1990s, UX began to gain space when research, showing that in addition to being functional interactive products also had to be pleasant for the user, emerged [4].

In UX projects, the UCD is usually used as a basis, which allows the designer to design a solution focusing on the users' needs [4]. Studying the interaction phenomena between human beings and computer systems enables us to understand them to improve the design, construction, and insertion of these technologies in people's lives, always looking for a good experience of use [4].

UX, as an HCI practice, applies data collection methods to design a user-centric product and set goals for the project from the identification of requirements. Through UX it is possible to translate the strategy outlined in the planning stage into forms of screens and flows that will be used by users [39]. For this, the use of specific tools supports the product development process.

In this work, popular design tools such as UX Canvas, Service Blueprint, Brainwriting, and others were used, as will be detailed in Sect. 3. The tools used helped in team management and project development, to facilitate the identification of the problem to be solved until the product delivery stage. It is the UX designer's role to use empathy and objectivity skills to create a good experience for users [19], using the appropriate tools to develop solutions by collecting, investigating, and mapping the perceptions of users, or even of proxy users.

2.2   Proxy Users

Proxy user participation is a strategic research alternative when there are difficulties in directly contacting the end-users, and it is possible to count on intermediary people who know them well. Proxy users may be crucial during the development of a project through their knowledge of users, acting as direct representatives of the user.

Proxy users contribute, for example, in works aimed at elderly people who need the daily use of digital technologies. Direct data collection with these users, the elderly, is often unfeasible due to their dependence on others to perform their daily tasks [6]. For this, another agent (a proxy) is consulted who allows the facilitation and description of the use of digital technologies, as shown in [40].

Another example of the proxy users participation is in the usability evaluation of a mobile digital commerce system with geographically distant users [32]. In this case, the work reports that a new evaluation was performed with the users to validate the results obtained in the first evaluation, performed with the proxy users.

It is common knowledge that there are limitations when consulting proxy users since they are not the real application's users being studied, so they do not have the same behaviors and needs as those they represent [38]. However, when working with a product that already has a version in the market, it is possible to learn a lot, for example, by talking to the user support team [4]. These are responsible for constantly interacting with users, more than other company sectors. Thus, support team members can act as proxy users in many cases.

In this project, it was identified that the users of Application Y constantly resorted to Company X's support team to solve errors faced during the Application Y configuration, via Javascript code. As mentioned earlier, the users (store administrators) had to apply the customizations in a non-intuitive interface, for which users did not have the necessary technical knowledge and ended up frustrated due to the compromised autonomy.

In an attempt to configure the system without basic knowledge of programming languages, users caused errors in functionalities that were not notified by the system, causing application malfunction and compromising the flow of buy and sell in the physical store.

From this scenario, it was identified that the participation of proxy users was viable since, in a support position, proxy users understand the customers' needs, what satisfies them, and why they exchange their company for a competitor. Nevertheless, users had an intense customer service routine in physical stores, which made the frequent contact with Application Y support team difficult.

Our project team's contact with proxy users, in contrast to real users, took place more directly because proxy users were Company X employees (mainly people from customer support team) who shared the same online communication channel with us. This facilitated contact allowed us to run interviews, surveys through questionnaires, and faster conversations through direct messages.

2.3   Design Projectual Methodology - Double Diamond

The development of a project takes place through a progressive elaboration, being iterative and incremental, because its conception comes from repetitions and each repetition causes the increase of new information [35]. However, for the estimation and planning of the stages to be developed much later in the project, the designer must seek "the mediation between the technical knowledge and the experiments about the possible idealized solutions" [36].

The design process is formed by the set of relationships that permeate the phases that constitute it and by the actions performed and established in the course of a process [33]. Some classic processes in the area of product design are the Star Life Cycle by Hix and Hartson [20]; Nielsen's Usability Engineering [29] and Garrett's UX design process [16]. There are also academic and experimental processes such as the Disruptive Digital Design Process (D3P) [34]; and others currently more popular such as Double Diamond [11] and Design Thinking [26].

Design Thinking [8] is a design process focused on understanding the user, experimenting with methods and redefining problems in order to generate potential solutions. Specifically, it "is a process that rests on three pillars: empathy (immersion), collaboration (co-creation) and experience (prototyping)". One of the ways to apply Design Thinking to digital solutions is with the application of Double Diamond, a process based on Design Thinking, popularized in 2005 by the Design Council in the United Kingdom, being an adaptation of dynamics of divergence and convergence [11].

This process is graphically represented by two diamonds that divide the process' four phases: discovery, definition, developing and delivery; having two stages of divergence and convergence interspersed with each other [2]. In the first two phases (first diamond), the process of discovering the problem takes place, and in the last two (second diamond), the process of building the solution takes place.

In the discovery phase, the focus is to understand the problem faced, it is a moment of knowledge of the environment where the users are inserted, realizing what challenges they face to carry out their activities. In the definition phase, the focus is on the convergence of ideas for the definition of priorities in relation to the problem. In the development phase, the goal is to explore possible solutions and their technical feasibility. The delivery phase, the last step of the process, is the moment to start putting into practice and validating the solution chosen to solve the identified problem [3].

In industry, Double Diamond is applied in many ways in product development. As an example, we can mention the case study by Clune and Lockrey [9], on the application of the Double Diamond of environmental impact in the care of the elderly. Another application for the process is for solutions in the health area using Inclusive Design [41], in this case the importance of a multidisciplinary team in the development of the design process is highlighted.

Company X has the use of the Double Diamond design process as a culture. Due to it being an iterative process that allows flexibility to move between phases, it is possible to go back and continue when necessary. This flexibility allows for unconventional possibilities and different ways of solving, which increases the options for the repertoire of ideas and solutions for the project [36].

3 Double Diamond Design Method Application

This section presents the experience report of the use of UX methods, techniques and tools, applied to the Double Diamond process [1], in the project to create an administrative configuration tool for Application Y.

The project team is composed of a software development technical leader with a degree in IT and a design technical leader, with a degree in Design. The project team also includes eight scholarship students from the Federal University of Ceará (UFC) - Brazil, five of them software development scholarship students (computer science, software engineering and information systems students) and three design scholarship students (Digital Design students). The project also has the participation of two experienced researchers, working in Software Engineering and HCI, both PhD professors at (UFC).

Due to the COVID-19 pandemic, the team activities took place remotely through the use of the following collaborative tools: Slack[2], Discord[3] and ZOOM[4], for text and video communication; Notion[5], for activity management and documentation; Miro[6], for mind maps and diagrams construction; Figma[7], for building interactive prototypes; Maze[8], for carrying out the prototype remote tests; and Github[9], for storing the project's programming code files.

The activities developed by the design team followed the Double Diamond process and were distributed throughout the project as illustrated in Fig. 1.

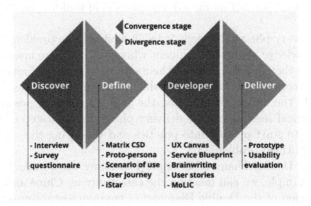

Fig. 1. Methods, techniques and tools applied in the Double Diamond process.

---

[2] https://slack.com.
[3] https://discord.com.
[4] https://zoom.us.
[5] https://notion.so.
[6] https://miro.com.
[7] https://figma.com.
[8] https://maze.co.
[9] https://github.com.

The ideal for the project would be to use interview and observation techniques with the users themselves, however, due to the pandemic and other difficulties to maintain frequent contact with the user, the participation of proxy users was necessary. The proxy users were some Company X's employees who were part of the support or products teams. These teams are responsible for providing a better experience between the company and the customers and for the process of creating and delivering the product and experience to customers and users.

The project, at the time of writing this article, has gone through the four cycles within the design process, as described in 3.1, 3.2, 3.3 and 3.4 sections. The details of the execution cycles and the tools used in each step of Double Diamond are in Fig. 2.

Method	Discover	Define	Developer	Deliver
First cycle				
Interview	✓			
Matrix CSD		✓		
UX Canvas			✓	
Second cycle				
Proto-persona		✓		
Scenario of use		✓		
Service blueprint			✓	
User journey		✓		
Third cycle				
Survey questionnaire	✓			
iStar		✓		
Brainwriting			✓	
Fourth cycle				
User stories			✓	
MoLIC			✓	
Prototype				✓
Usability Evaluation				✓

Fig. 2. Distribution of methods, techniques and tools per cycle in Double Diamond.

3.1   First Cycle - Problem and User Needs Identification

In the design process' first cycle, three steps were performed - discovery, definition and development. To carry out them, interviews, Certainty, Suppositions and Doubts Matrix (CSD Matrix), and UX Canvas were used.

As a first step towards discovery, during this phase, five interviews were carried out, one unstructured and four semi-structured with the objective of gathering information regarding the problem to be solved. The interviewees, proxy users of the project, worked directly with Application Y in the product and support team.

Three semi-structured interviews were carried out with the support team to identify the problems reported by users and how they were reported. Two other interviews were also carried out with the product team, the first unstructured and the second semi-structured, to find out about the system's features.

Interviews with the support team lasted an average of one hour and with the product team, an average of 30 min. The interviews were performed by using video calls. As they were semi- or unstructured, they allowed for a more spontaneous conversation to generate more insights from proxy users during data collection.

After carrying out the first interviews, the construction of a CSD Matrix took place. This tool aims to help each team member classify their thoughts and ideas into "certainties", "suppositions" and "doubts" [12]. As a method of convergence, it allows grouping and generating new ideas.

In this model, in the certainties column, the points on which all team members agree are added, in the suppositions column, the points that have different opinions and, in the doubts column, what is unknown about the project [15]. The CSD matrix was chosen due to the need to analyze the data collected during the interviews and understand the real objectives of the project.

The interview process along with the matrix filling, in an intercalated way, was repeated three times and, in each of them, there was a predominance of a column, as shown below:

- 1st Matrix (D predominant) - More doubts were obtained, since the problem was still unknown to all.
- 2nd Matrix (S predominant) - Resulted in more suppositions due to the increase in data collected and analyzed, and consequently different thoughts about the problem.
- 3rd Matrix (C predominant) - There were more certainties in contrast to the previous ones as it went through two other moments for validation with the proxy users.

According to Barbosa et al. [4], "the data must be valid and reliable, otherwise the risk of causing more harm than good is great, as distorted, corrupted, or invalid data can result in inappropriate design decisions". This repetition in the matrix production process generated maturity and objectivity in the researchers in the way of conducting and modifying the methods. According to Grant [19], this repetition process demonstrates empathy to understand the user's goals and frustrations.

To continue the process of defining the project, the UX Canvas [21] was used, which contributed to visualize all project related aspects, dividing the information into three areas: customer, user and experience.

In the customer area, the more technical aspects regarding the problem, requirements and resources are detailed; in the user area, the user's goals, touchpoints and the idea for the project are specified; and, finally, in the experience area, the mediation between the two previous areas is carried out, focusing on the experience that is desired [21]. At the end of this process, the experience proposal was defined as: "providing freedom and agility for the user in the process of customizing the digital commerce application". Figure 3 brings all the information of the project's UX Canvas.

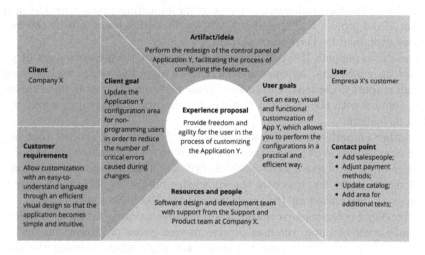

Fig. 3. Project's UX Canvas

After analyzing the results of the first cycle, the need to start a new step in the process was identified to obtain more information, since the researchers were not yet satisfied with the amount of data collected.

3.2 Second Cycle - Empathy Tools

The second cycle started with an inversion of the design process starting from the development and returning to the definition stage. This cycle is mainly focused on empathy tools such as Service Blueprint, Proto-personas, Usage Scenario and User Journey.

The Service Blueprint [24] is a technique used to map the current state of the user experience when using a product or service. From its flows it is possible to identify errors and opportunities for improvement. Its production must be collaborative and, in the case of this project, four steps were carried out.

In the first step, it focused on describing the vision, actions and user experience during each step of the process. In the second, the contact points and feedbacks between the service and the user were described. In the third, the internal processes for the production of the points of contact with the user were build from the company's vision and evidence of the project. As a last step, the use of third parties, infrastructures and other tools that help in supporting the evaluated service was described.

The Service Blueprint contributed to the discovery of the existence of other critical points besides the need to improve the customization process. Among them, the insufficiency of information available for the execution of user activities within the platform stands out, which was characterized by proxy users as one of the reasons for the increase in the frequency of opening calls for technical help.

After understanding the problem and user needs, a Proto-persona was created, which, like the traditional persona, is an important artifact for the development of the project and is used not only by the design team, but by the entire team as explained by Ferreira et al. [14].

The Proto-persona [18] is a fictional character that represents a set of people and their interests. Its construction aims to align knowledge and personify, through empathy, the user. Unlike the classic persona, it is not defined through direct contact with the user, but through information passed on by proxy users and stakeholders.

Another empathy tool used was the Usage Scenario, an artifact that helps in the representation of the context and contributes to the understanding of the influence of the problem on the user's reality [33]. The information collected by the design team so far, specially the knowledge on the Application Y users by Company X, were used for the production of the Usage Scenario.

After defining the usage scenario, it was possible to carry out the user journey, a technique used to map the user process in each phase of interaction with the product or service [26]. Its construction takes place after mapping the needs and characteristics of users, since the creation of innovative solutions based on what the user does, thinks and feels is encouraged. The process begins with the division of the journey into phases, each phase can represent a moment or an objective. After separating the phases, the user's actions, the points of contact with the system, thoughts, feelings and opportunities for improvement in each phase are described. The User Journey is displayed at Fig. 4

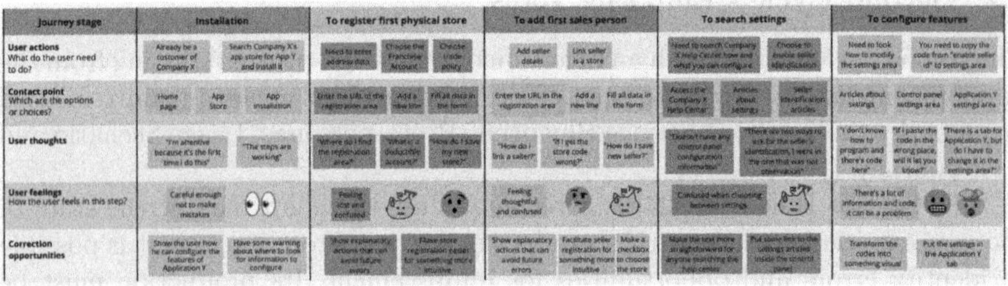

Fig. 4. User journey

This empathy tool helped to identify the user's thoughts and feelings during the setup process. Previously, with the Service Blueprint we discovered the service process and its points of improvement, while with the User Journey, we tried to interpret the feelings of the users in each phase of interaction.

The final version of Service Blueprint, Proto-persona and Usage Scenario are avaliable as supplementary materials[10].

3.3   Third Cycle - Process Requirements Definition

As a first step towards data validation, an investigation was carried out through a questionnaire created with Google Forms[11] and applied to the members of the team responsible for the production and maintenance of the system, also serving as proxy users. According to Barbosa et al. [4], the use of questionnaires allows collecting information from more people and obtaining results that are more representative of the public of interest quickly.

This questionnaire allowed us to validate the information collected about the customizations available in Application Y and to mitigate doubts about the support team's role in the product customization and the user experience during customization. This information helped the researchers to define project priorities based on the customizations reported as the most important and with the highest number of doubts.

Also in third cycle, models were also created with iStar [42], an objective-oriented language to perform organizational and systems requirements modeling. iStar models actors, agents and roles along with their intentional elements (goals, resources, tasks and qualities) and their interconnections (dependence, "is a", "participates in", contribution, qualification, refinement, "is needed by").

The modeling language was initially used in the project as a tool to represent the Company X process, related to Application Y, as it was at the time of the research ("as-is"). The models were built collaboratively by all project members (research, design and software development).

The "as-is" modeling started with the iStar Strategic Dependency (SD) model, a simpler model recommended for the development process early stages. The final version of the "as-is" SD has 2 agents, 12 actors, 3 roles, 26 tasks, 8 goals, 2 resources, 11 participates-in, 12 dependencies and 27 refinements. Then, we move on to modeling the strategic reason (SR) diagram. The final version of the "as-is" SR has 2 agents, 5 actors, 5 participates-in and 1 dependency.

Following, We used SD and SR diagrams "as-is" as the start point of "to-be" modeling, that is, the team's vision of how the process should look after the design solution has been implemented. The final version of the "to-be" SD diagram has 4 agents, 13 actors, 3 roles, 19 participates-in and 8 dependency links. Then, we move on to modeling the SR diagram. The final version of modeling with iStar are avaliable as supplementary materials[12]. More details about the experience with iStar were described in [17].

At this point in the project, the modeling language use leveled the team's knowledge of the objectives, requirements and customizations for the product

---

[10] https://drive.google.com/drive/folders/1V5Vv545-TbUxqzjGPjnTEz9C8g1FAKgw.

[11] https://forms.google.com.

[12] https://drive.google.com/drive/folders/1V5Vv545-TbUxqzjGPjnTEz9C8g1FAKgw.

previously obtained through the questionnaire, Service Blueprint, User Journey, among other tools.

This leveling enabled the team to start the development phase of the design process using Brainwriting?, a co-creation method that seeks to find solutions based on collective intelligence. This method consists of a moment for generating ideas in writing, and another for collective discussion, a necessary moment for the construction of the common product.

To assist in the process' collectivity, Miro was used, where the objective of the activity was presented and some instructions on the dynamics were provided. The next step was to divide the team into two groups, one with five participants and the other with four, with a design team member acting as a mediator in each group. After the division, the individual production of the initial ideas of each participant was carried out. From then on, the ideation process began on the basis of each other's ideas.

Subsequently, the ideas generated were discussed, grouping similar ones and voting on the best ones. Finally, the two groups met and a quantitative analysis took place based on how desirable by the users, technically feasible and economically viable was each idea presented. The multidisciplinary team made it possible to obtain a variety of ideas and discussions.

At the end of the entire process, the main solution ideas for the project were outlined, which would be implemented in the next phases of the project, they are:

- Active error prevention by contextual help during the customization process.
- Enabled customization manager with simple controls.
- Visualization of the effects of customizations before applying to the system.
- Creating a library of default settings.

3.4   Fourth Cycle - Idea Implementation and Test

In the process' last cycle, four tools were used, two in the development stage and two in the delivery stage, respectively in the process steps' order. In the development stage, User Stories were built, which help in defining the system requirements using the user's perspective [37]. In this project, User Stories were created using the information collected in the online questionnaire and interviews with proxy users, and based on the usage scenario and Proto-persona defined in the empathy cycle (Second cycle - Empathy tool), in addition to following decisions consolidated in the iStar models and in Brainwriting.

The formulation of User Stories takes place from the model: "as [user], I want to perform [action] for then [result/goal]", as presented in [37]. This model requires the definition of three elements: the user who will perform the action, the action that needs to be done and the result or goal that will be achieved after performing the action. At the end of the process, five user stories were addressed, as listed below:

- Identify customer
- Text to the order print

- inStore language
- Payments conditions
- Forcing stock availability

After the construction of the User Stories, it was possible to identify the functional requirements of the system, thus facilitating the modeling of interactions and interfaces for the application of customization management of Application Y. The modeling of user interaction was developed using MoLIC (Modeling Language for Interaction as Conversation). It allowed us to define system interaction as a conversation between the designer's deputy (the spokesperson for design decisions) and the user before decide on the interface details [4].

Within the process of defining the interaction with the use of MoLIC, there was a previous training carried out by one of the team's professors, a HCI specialist. This training enabled the entire team to participate in the tool's modeling process, thus maximizing the benefits of the team's multidisciplinarity in defining the interaction[13].

In addition to the professor, the Digital Design course's team members also had previous knowledge of the language, which provided greater agility during the process. This agility was an important factor, because, for each User Story, two scenarios were modeled, that of the customizing user in the customization module and that of the salesperson in the use of Application Y in the physical store, after customization.

For example purposes, Fig. 5 presents the interaction model created with MoLIC for the User Story Configure Customer Identification.

With the interaction modeled and the system requirements defined, it was possible to start the development of the interface for the system. The MoLIC diagrams were the basis for the construction of the prototypes, since the interface is the representation of the interaction in a visual way, and the point of contact between the user and the tool [28].

The interfaces were built based on the Company X's style guide, which aims at guiding and standardizing the company's interfaces' construction. This document, in addition to containing interface guidelines, also contained a design system implemented in Figma.

With the interaction and interface flows defined in the prototype, we started the process of planning usability tests with the navigable prototype, by defining the general context, the users tasks and some metrics to measure the level of user experience and satisfaction. We also decided to apply SUS (System Usability Scale) [7] at the end of the test, in order to quantitatively evaluate the usability of the system.

The prototype test has the objective of evaluating the prototype's functionality and the usability test aims to verify the prototype's usability [4]. Before

---

[13] We analyzed the usage of MoLIC in the process from the point of view of the participants. They highlighted the relevance in the usage of its usage to the creation of the prototypes. The final version of MoLIC is avaliable as supplementary materials [27].

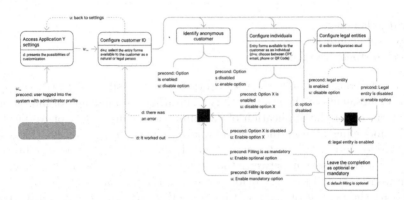

Fig. 5. MoLIC for customer identification

running the usability test with the customizing users, two pilot tests with members of the product team ran in order to validate the script and the planned prototype. After the pilot tests, we modified some messages in the prototype interface to improve the user experience in the digital environment.

With the test script validated and the prototype's necessary updates, we run two types of tests with two groups of users. The first group was formed by 14 internal employees of Company X who had previous knowledge about the customization process of Application Y (proxy users). For this group, the test was used to validate the interface elements and the solutions writing, through a remote and unmoderated test. In the second group, formed by four real customers, divided in tree interviews, of Company X, a remote and moderated usability test was applied in order to validate the information previously collected with proxy users, identify system usability problems and assess the learning curve in the customization management tool. Both tests' types ran remotely with the support of Maze, a platform that allows free prototype tests using the Figma project without needing to implement the system.

From the proxy users feedback on the prototype, we identified improvement opportunities in the consistency of the textual language of the solution. These inconsistencies were identified by product area employees who were linked to the user experience textual design team. During the prototype test, questions also arose about the order of presentation of the information and the degree of severity of each one of them.

At the end of the usability test, a few problems were identified during the customization process. In addition, users reported a significant improvement in the usability of the system compared to the previous method, with Javascript code changes. The biggest gain, according to users, is in the process of adding stores and sales people. In the other five customizations there were no problems regarding the system's usability.

As result of the usability test with users, we highlight the following findings:

- It was observed that the users' background influences the understanding of the system, but even those with a technical background found difficulties in the customization process.
- The implementation time is related to the number of salespeople and stores registered, so the more sellers and stores, the longer the time.
- For some users, there is a need for dashboards as well as the creation of access levels between users, a salesperson should not have access to sensitive sales data in the store.
- Some customers develop internal solutions to resolve issues not answered by Company X, such as: creating a registration manager through the Rest API and a sales manual for sellers.
- Another solution is related to training on the application, there is a transfer of knowledge at scale, the person responsible for installing teaches the manager and the manager teaches the salespeople.

The usability test confirms that the system requirements initially collected with the help of proxy users really represented the demands of the system users regarding the ease and freedom to customize Application Y without the need for help or causing errors.

4   Conclusions and Future Works

This work presented the report of the use of methods, techniques, and design tools applied to the Double Diamond process in an administrative tool software development project to support e-commerce in an ICT company.

Some tools described in the paper correspond to the models and representations commonly used "throughout different HCI design processes, focusing on the design activities of the interactive solution" [4]. Some of these models are used to motivate the designers' reflection, during the HCI design, about alternative strategies for using the system and other details. Furthermore, we present the use of modeling with iStar, still little known in the HCI and UX Design communities, to promote the integration of HCI and Software Engineering processes.

During all stages of the design process, with the participation of proxy users, the researchers managed various technical methods and design tools to collect information about the users needs and preferences in the Application Y configuration process. Proxy users' collaboration helped in the project due to the impossibility of direct contact with the user. However, due to the need for constant validation of the collected data, this strategy increased the research time. Tools like the CSD Matrix, Service Blueprint and Questionnaire provided more qualified directions for the project, allowing the team to define the project requirements and the next steps. During the project, there was a concern in maintaining the existing system's design and adding the new customization features identified.

Thus, as a contribution of this work, we highlight the usage of a wide variety of methods, techniques and tools in a real industry project, helping to strengthen the insertion of user-centred and UX design practices in the professional and not just academic scope. We believe that the report presented can be useful to UX research and design teams by explaining the modes of use and results obtained with each tool.

We also highlight the epistemic value of the methods, techniques and tools, allowing a more comprehensive understanding of the investigated problem, collaborating with decision making design with more property in the search for solutions for the project. The generated artifacts also fulfilled the role of epistemic tools, which according to de Souza [10], do not directly generate an answer or solution to the problem. Instead, they support the designer "in exploring the space and nature of the problem, as well as restrictions on candidate solutions" [10].

As future works, we identify the application of methods, techniques and tools equivalent to those used in this report in the context of other Company X projects. For example, by applying KAOS (Knowledge Acquisition In Automated Specification) [23] instead of iStar. Thus, we will compare the techniques used and identify their advantages and disadvantages in the context of their projects.

References

1. Are behavioural science and design the building blocks of innovation?. Apr 2014, Design Council. https://www.designcouncil.org.uk/news-opinion/are-behavioural-science-and-design-building-blocks-innovation
2. What is the framework for innovation? Design Council's evolved Double Diamond. Mar 2015, Design Council. https://www.designcouncil.org.uk/news-opinion/what-framework-innovation-design-councils-evolved-double-diamond
3. Ball, J.: The Double Diamond: A universally accepted depiction of the design process. Oct 2019, Design Council. https://www.designcouncil.org.uk/news-opinion/double-diamond-universally-accepted-depiction-design-process
4. Barbosa, S.D.J., Silva, B.S.d., Silveira, M.S., Gasparini, I., Darin, T., Barbosa, G.D.J.: Interac ao Humano-Computador e Experiᵉncia do Usuario. Autopublicac ao (2021)
5. Bravo, U., Bohemia, E.: Os papéis dos modelos de processos de design como materiais didácticos, pp. 8–17 (2019)
6. Brazil, Departamento de Atenção Básica: Cadernos de Atenção Básica: programa saúde da família. Ministério da Saúde, Secretaria de Políticas de Saúde, Departamento de Atenção Básica, Brasília (2006)
7. Brooke, J.: Sus: A quick and dirty usability scale. Usability Eval. Ind. **189** (1995)
8. Carvalho, H.: Design Thinking: entenda como funciona o modelo. Nov 2019. https://vidadeproduto.com.br/design-thinking/
9. Clune, S.J., Lockrey, S.: Developing environmental sustainability strategies, the double diamond method of LCA and design thinking: A case study from aged care. J. Cleaner Prod. **85**, 67–82 (2014). Special Volume: Making Progress Towards More Sustainable Societies through Lean and Green Initiatives. https://doi.org/10.1016/j.jclepro.2014.02.003. https://www.sciencedirect.com/science/article/pii/S0959652614001449

10. De Souza, C.S.: The Semiotic Engineering of Human-Computer Interaction. Acting with technology, MIT Press, Cambridge (2005)
11. Drew, C.: The Double Diamond, 15 years on... (Sep 2019). https://medium.com/design-council/the-double-diamond-15-years-on-8c7bc594610e
12. Dutra, R.: Matriz CSD no Processo de UX Design - Certezas, Suposições e Dúvidas, Mar 2018. http://designr.com.br/matriz-csd-no-processo-de-ux-design-certezas-suposicoes-e-duvidas/
13. Ellwanger, C., Rocha, R.A.d., Silva, R.P.d.: Design de Interação, Design Experiencial e Design Thinking: a triângulação da Interação Humano-Computador. Revista de Ciências da Administração, pp. 26–36. Dec 2015. https://doi.org/10.5007/2175-8077.2015v17n43p26. https://periodicos.ufsc.br/index.php/adm/article/view/2175-8077.2015v17n43p26
14. Ferreira, B.M., Conte, T., Barbosa, S.D.J.: Eliciting requirements using personas and empathy map to enhance the user experience. In: 29th Brazilian Symposium on Software Engineering, pp. 80–89 (2015)
15. Fonseca, K.: Matriz CSD: tudo o que você precisa saber, Apr 2021). UX Collective. https://brasil.uxdesign.cc/matriz-csd-tudo-o-que-voc%C3%AA-precisa-saber-897e39c797e7
16. Garrett, J.: The Elements of User Experience: User-Centered Design for the Web, vol. 10, p. 208, Oct 2002
17. Gonçalves, E.J.T., Monteiro, I.T.: Reporting the usage of iStar in a model-based industrial project to evolve an e-commerce application (2021)
18. Gothelf, J.: Using Proto-Personas for Executive Alignment. May 2012, UX Magazine. https://uxmag.com/articles/using-proto-personas-for-executive-alignment
19. Grant, W.: UX Design: Guia definitivo com as melhores práticas de UX. Novatec Editora (2019). https://books.google.com.br/books?id=b5KeDwAAQBAJ
20. Hix, D., Hartson, H.R.: Developing User Interfaces: Ensuring Usability through Product & Process. Wiley, New York (1993)
21. Katekawa, B.: Projeto de Aplicação Mobile para Recarga de Bilhete de Transporte - Parte 6, Jul 2017. https://brunokatekawa.medium.com/projeto-de-aplica%C3%A7%C3%A3o-mobile-para-recarga-de-bilhete-de-transporte-parte-6-de106decdca3
22. Khan, S.: How to Create an Admin Panel — Best Practices & Tips. Oct 2018, Coding Infinite. https://codinginfinite.com/create-admin-panel-best-practices-tips/
23. van Lamsweerde, A.: Goal-oriented requirements engineering: From system objectives to UML models to precise software specifications. In: Proceedings of the 25th International Conference on Software Engineering, ICSE 2003, pp. 744–745. IEEE Computer Society, USA (2003)
24. Lewrick, M., Link, P., Leifer, L.J.: The Design Thinking Toolbox: A Guide to Mastering the Most Popular and Valuable Innovation Methods. Wiley, Hoboken (2020)
25. Lowdermilk, T.: Design Centrado no Usuário. Novatec Editora (2013). https://books.google.com.br/books?id=_XqKDQAAQBAJ
26. Melo, A., Abelheira, R.: Design Thinking & Thinking Design: Metodologia, ferramentas e uma reflexão sobre o tema. Novatec Editora (2015). https://books.google.com.br/books?id=vCyLCgAAQBAJ
27. Monteiro, I., G.E.: Experiência com a molic na indústria: ensino e aplicação em um projeto para o comércio eletrônico. Workshop sobre Educação em Interação Humano-Computador (WEIHC) (2021)
28. Moran, Thomas P..: The command language grammar: A representation for the user interface of interactive computer systems. Int. J. Man-Machine Stud. 15(1), 3–50 (1981). https://doi.org/10.1016/S0020-7373(81)80022-3

29. Nielsen, J.: Usability Engineering. Morgan Kaufmann Publishers Inc., San Francisco (1994)
30. Norman, D., Deiró, A.: O design do dia a dia. Anfiteatro (2018). https://books.google.com.br/books?id=IVRVDwAAQBAJ
31. Norman's, J.: Michael Aldrich Invents Online Shopping. HistoryofInformation.com. https://www.historyofinformation.com/detail.php?entryid=4528
32. Novak, G., Lundberg, L.: Usability evaluation of an m-commerce system using proxy users. In: Stephanidis, C. (ed.) HCI 2015. CCIS, vol. 529, pp. 164–169. Springer, Cham (2015). https://doi.org/10.1007/978-3-319-21383-5_28
33. Pazmino, A.V.: Como se Cria: 40 Métodos Para Design de Produtos. Editora Blucher, Jan 2020
34. Pinheiro, T.S.M., Monteiro, I.T., Felipe, D.A., Sampaio, A.L.: O processo de design digital: endereçando o desafio da multidisciplinaridade. In: Anais Estendidos do XVII Simpósio Brasileiro sobre Fatores Humanos em Sistemas Computacionais. SBC, Porto Alegre, RS, Brasil (2018). https://doi.org/10.5753/ihc.2018.4215. https://sol.sbc.org.br/index.php/ihc_estendido/article/view/4215
35. Silva, F.B.: Gerenciamento de projetos fora da caixa: fique com o que é relevante. Alta Books, 1ª edição edn. Jul 2016
36. Silva, T.B.P.e.: A cognição no processo de design. InfoDesign - Revista Brasileira de Design da Informação 12(3), 318–335, dez 2015. 10.51358/id.v12i3.359. https://www.infodesign.org.br/infodesign/article/view/359
37. Stickdorn, M., Hormess, M., Lawrence, A., Schneider, J. (eds.): This is Service Design Doing: Applying Service Design Thinking in the Real World; A Practitioners' Handbook. O'Reilly, Sebastapol, first edn. (2018)
38. Tate, E.: What's the Problem With Proxy Users?, Jul 2018. https://www.mindtheproduct.com/whats-the-problem-with-proxy-users/
39. Teixeira, F.: Introdução e boas práticas em UX Design. Casa do Código (2014). https://books.google.com.br/books?id=vWuCCwAAQBAJ
40. Toczyski, P., Kowalski, J., Biele, C.: Proxy users enable older people creative writing on the web. Frontiers in Sociology 4 (2019). 10.3389/fsoc.2019.00015. https://www.frontiersin.org/article/10.3389/fsoc.2019.00015
41. West, J., et al.: Developing the double diamond process for implementation. In: Barron, D., Seemann, K. (eds.) Design4Health, Melbourne. In: Proceedings of the Fourth International Conference on Design4Health 2017, 4–7 Dec 2017, Melbourne, Victoria, Australia, vol. 1, pp. 310–312. Sheffield Hallam University and Swinburne University of Technology, June 2018. https://researchonline.rca.ac.uk/3603/
42. Yu, E.S.K.: Modeling strategic relationships for process reengineering. In: Social Modeling for Requirements Engineering (2011)

A Process to Support the Remote Tree Testing Technique for Evaluating the Information Architecture of User Interfaces in Software Projects

Alejandro Tapia[(⊠)] [iD], Arturo Moquillaza[iD], Joel Aguirre[iD], Fiorella Falconi[iD], Adrian Lecaros[iD], and Freddy Paz[iD]

Pontificia Universidad Católica del Perú, Av. Universitaria 1801, San Miguel, Lima 32, Lima, Perú

{atapiat,amoquillaza,fpaz}@pucp.pe, {aguirre.joel,ffalconit, adrian.lecaros}@pucp.edu.pe

Abstract. Nowadays, due to technological advancement, people are bound to use multiple digital tools and interact with them through a User Interface. For this reason, User Experience (UX) is one of the most important keys to success. UX includes the design and evaluation of an adequate Information Architecture. To design Information Architecture, the best-known technique is Card Sorting. For evaluation, there is the Tree Testing or Reverse Card Sorting technique. This technique can be applied in remote or non-remote ways. We identified three main issues: 1. The remote processes to apply Tree Testing are not standardized; 2. the tools were modeled and built after a process defined by the supplier of those tools, most of which are now discontinued. 3. In many development projects these techniques are left aside, the Information Architecture is assessed using other methods and techniques (i.e. User Testing) in later phases of the project. These result in Information Architecture errors and defects found late or not found at all. Hence, this study is focused on developing and validating a standardized remote Tree Testing process with an emphasis on automation. To meet the objectives, we conducted interviews and literature reviews to find out how Tree Testing is currently carried out and what tools are used to support the technique (AS-IS workflow). Subsequently, we proposed a process that can support the technique, considering the pain points found on the current processes, resulting in a TO-BE workflow. As a result, a proposal of this standardized process was modeled using the notation BPMN, and validated by the expert judgment of specialists in Human-Computer Interaction (HCI). Finally, it is important to mention that Tree Testing is useful, practical in its remote application, and should be applied in the early stages of software projects; a tool to support the whole process should be implemented.

Keywords: Architecture Information · User Experience · Human-Computer Interaction · BPMN · Tree Testing

© The Author(s), under exclusive license to Springer Nature Switzerland AG 2022
M. M. Soares et al. (Eds.): HCII 2022, LNCS 13321, pp. 75–92, 2022.
https://doi.org/10.1007/978-3-031-05897-4_6

1 Introduction

In the last years, Information and Communication technologies have advanced so far that are part of our daily activities. Nowadays, due to technological advancement, people are bound to use multiple digital tools offered by various companies and interact with them through a User Interface to fulfill their activities and needs [1]. For this reason, these companies have identified that User Experience (UX) is one of the most important keys to success [2]. UX includes the design and evaluation of an adequate Information Architecture [3]. For the design of the Information Architecture, the best-known technique is Card Sorting [4, 21]. For evaluation, there is the Tree Testing or Reverse Card Sorting technique [4]. This technique can be applied in remote or non-remote ways. However, Information Architecture evaluation techniques are not popular among UX practitioners and specialists.

In addition, specifically on Tree Testing, three main issues have been identified:

1. The remote processes to apply this technique are not standardized, and non-remote processes consume a lot of time to execute [26];
2. Then, the tools were modeled and built after a process defined by the supplier of those tools and most of them are now discontinued, and the few that remain are limited in their free versions and require a license to be used with all their functionalities [3];
3. Thus, in many development projects these techniques are left aside, the Information Architecture is assessed indirectly using other methods and techniques (i.e. User Testing) in later phases of the project [26].

These issues result in Information Architecture errors and defects found late or not found at all. These issues impact the UX, the revenue, the cost and timeline set for the project, and the final product [2, 5]. In this sense, this study focused on modeling and validating a standardized remote Tree Testing process with an emphasis on automation.

This paper is organized as follows: The first section presents an introduction to the matter of study, and the main issues encountered on the application of Tree Testing. The second section details the most relevant concepts related to the research. The third section details the steps followed to carry out the present proposal. The latter section mentioned details the Systematic Literature Review (SLR), the interviews with UX specialists and HCI experts, as well as the review of remote Tree Testing tools that were reviewed. The fourth section details the process modeled in BPMN, as well as the validation that was carried out. Finally, the fifth section details the most important results, as well as future work.

2 Context

This section details the main concepts related to the present work, in the context of the proposed solution.

2.1 Tree Testing

In 2003, Donna Spencer defined the process for manual application of the Card-Based Evaluation Classification technique [4, 24], known by the name of Tree Testing. She is the author who defines the technique as a quick way to evaluate the Information Architecture (IA) without visual elements or development of views.

This technique is being used for the evaluation of the IA. In this sense, it has been evidenced that its use allows early identification of AI issues [26]. However, according to the literature reviewed and the interviews conducted, its use is not yet widespread.

2.2 Information Architecture

Information Architecture (IA) is defined as "the design, integration, and aggregation of information spaces and systems" [11]. According to the interviews conducted, the elaboration of the AI is a typical activity within a UX Design processes.

An effective organization of the information [11] allows the user to navigate the tool and find the content they need [17], reducing the number of errors the user would make and making the system or product much easier to use [16].

Then, the concept of AI is related to UX in the sense that an adequate and well-designed AI allows a software product to have an adequate usability and an adequate findability. As mentioned by Morville, usability and findability are important facets of UX [16, 28].

2.3 UX

According to standard ISO 9241-210:2019 [15], User Experience (UX) is defined as the users' perception and response resulting from the use or anticipated use of the system, product, and service.

From the initial definition, ISO 9241-210:2019, adds that the UX is the consequence of a series of external factors to the user (branding, functionality, presentation, interactivity, behavior, and assistance capacity of the products, services, and systems), and internal factors (past experiences, abilities, personality, attitudes, and aptitudes) and the context of use.

Likewise, Morville proposed in 2004 [16] his honeycomb structure with the different facets of the UX:

- Findable: related to the ease of finding content that the user presumes is within the application [17].
- Usable: related to usability [16] and its 5 components: learnability, memorability, error rate, efficiency, and satisfaction.
- Useful: according to Nielsen [18] is a combination of usability and utility, that defines the product, service or system capacity to provide the functionalities the user needs.
- Desirable: related to the elements of Emotional Design (images, branding, identity) [16].
- Valuable: related to the value of a product, system or service should provide to their stakeholders or interested parties such as the sponsor. Moreover, for nonprofit projects, user satisfaction is the main final value of the project [16].

- Accessible: related to the fact that everyone, including users with disabilities, could use a product, service, or system [19].
- Credible: related to the truth with which the product, system, or service does what it has been said to do [20].

Likewise, Garrett in 2011 identifies five UX planes: Strategy, Score, Structure, Skeleton and Surface. Within them, Garrett places Information Architecture within the Structure plan, along with Interaction Design [29].

As it was mentioned before, using both the User Experience and Information Architecture definitions, it is possible to establish the following: to fulfill a better UX, a good IA needs to be developed.

2.4 Process

A process constitutes a series of steps, tasks, and activities that are executed in an orderly manner to achieve a result, product, or service [14]. In general, a process is made-up of inputs that will transform into results or outputs through the execution of one or more activities.

Based on the above definition, in order to determine the flaws of the Tree Testing process, it is necessary to understand how the technique is applied, what the process is, and what activities it consists of to find opportunities for improvement.

2.5 BPMN

BPMN (Business Process Model and Notation) is a notation that is currently maintained by the Object Management Group (OMG) to provide a process-modeling standard that can be easily understood by various users [13]. Its use extends to both processes and choreographies, and a series of elements, rules, and symbols defined that will help represent them [13].

We used this notation to model the remote application process of the Tree Testing technique with a focus on the automation of manual tasks. In addition, for this, Bizagi Modeler tool was used.

3 Methods

This section presents the sequence of steps that were carried out to obtain the proposed modeled processes as a result.

3.1 Approach

As was mentioned, the main objective of this work was to model and to validate a standardized remote Tree Testing process with an emphasis on automation, that is, a process supported by a software tool.

To carry out this objective, we followed a set of steps in order to obtain a process modeled in BPMN. Figure 1 shows the steps followed as the approach of the present work.

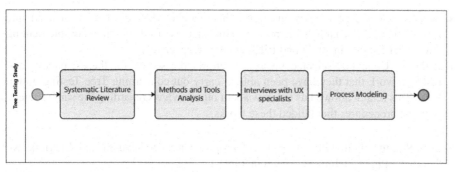

Fig. 1. Research approach

According to Fig. 1, Interviews were conducted with UX practitioners, and the literature was reviewed in order to find out how Tree Testing is currently carried out and what tools are used to support the technique. Subsequently, we proposed a process that can support the technique, considering the pain points found on the current processes.

3.2 Systematic Review

First, a Systematic Literature Review (SLR) was conducted. The main objective was to know the state of the art of the application of the Tree Testing technique. This SLR was performed following the protocol proposed by Kitchenham and Charters [6]. In addition, we used the Parsifal tool [12] as a support tool for the SLR process.

Research Questions. Following the Kitchenham and Charters protocol, three central questions were set for guiding the SLR:

- P1. How did the Tree Testing technique affect, positively or negatively, the improvement of the Information Architecture and projects in general?
- P2. What protocols, processes, and steps were followed to apply the Tree Testing technique, and how were they applied?
- P3. What tools were used to apply the Tree Testing technique, and what were its limitations and strengths?

Search Engines. The search engines used to review the documents were the following:

- ACM Digital Library of ACM (Association for Computing Machinery) was selected because ACM promotes work, innovation, and research in the computational field [8]. Its digital library contains studies from the domains that are useful for the computerized approach of the present work.
- IEEExplore of the IEEE (Institute of Electrical and Electronic Engineering) is among the selected search engines because the institute, as with ACM, makes available high-quality work at a global level on information technology issues, engineering, and computing [9].

- Scopus, selected because is an engine that searches different bodies of academic information [10]. That helps to review many sources of information, complementing what can be found in ACM and IEEE engines respectively.
- Alicia of Concytec, selected because it allows the search for theses, papers, and research work that they have been able to carry out concerning Tree Testing within Peru. This search allowed us to know about other reviews regarding the same subject, with the procedures that guided these works.

Search Strings. Following the protocol proposed by Kitchenman and Charters, we elaborated a PICOC table [7], shown in Table 1.

Table 1. PICOC table

Population	Software product
Intervention	Tree testing, Information architecture
Comparison	-
Outcome	Protocols, tools
Context	User experience

We identified the population as software products since the Tree Testing technique (subject of study or interest) was be applied to evaluate their information architecture. It is intended, with this work, to arrive at the protocols and tools used to apply the technique in the identified population within the academic and industrial fields. Because of this, we used four of the five letters that define the PICOC technique. The first letter C, which corresponds to Comparison, is not used since we did not compare the Tree Testing technique or the Information Architecture with other techniques or concepts of usability or UX.

We used the concepts from the PICOC table to determine synonyms. Table 2 shows both the words used in the PICOC technique and the synonyms in the English language, which will allow the creation of search strings in the selected engines.

Table 2. Keywords for the search string

Keyword	Synonyms	PICOC
Software product	Applications, apps, developments, software, systems, websites	Population
Tree testing	Reverse card sorting, tree test, task test, card-based classification evaluation	Intervention
Information architecture	IA	Intervention
Protocols	Mechanisms, methods, phases, procedures, steps	Outcome
Tools	Software support, support	Outcome
User experience	UX, usability	Context

With the help of the Parsifal tool, it was possible to form four initial conditions generated by the words in Table 2 joined by the logical OR connector (each one represents a letter of PICOC except for the C that represents the comparison).

- C1: ("Software product*" OR "Application*" OR "App*" OR "Development*" OR "Software" OR "System*" OR "Website*")
- C2: ("Information architecture" OR "IA" OR "Tree testing" OR "Reverse card sorting" OR "Task test" OR "Tree test" OR "Card-based Classification Evaluation")
- C3: ("Protocol*" OR "Mechanism*" OR "Method*" OR "Phase*" OR "Procedure*" OR "Step*" OR "Tool*" OR "Software support" OR "Support")
- C4: ("User experience" OR "Usability" OR "UX")

These conditions are then joined by means of the logical AND connector as follows: C1 AND C2 AND C3 AND C4; with which we arrive at the final search string:

```
("Software product*" OR "Application*" OR "App*" OR "De-
velopment*" OR "Software" OR "System*" OR "Website*") AND
("Information architecture" OR "IA" OR "Tree testing" OR
"Reverse card sorting" OR "Task test" OR "Tree test" OR
"Card-based Classification Evaluation") AND ("Protocol*"
OR "Mechanism*" OR "Method*" OR "Phase*" OR "Procedure*"
OR "Step*" OR "Tool*" OR "Software support" OR "Support")
AND ("User experience" OR "Usability" OR "UX")
```

For the search in Alicia, we adapted the search string to be in Spanish language.

Documents Found. The search in the search engines was executed on Sunday, October 19, 2020. Likewise, we added four additional studies that we considered relevant for the solution of the questions and the objectives raised when designing the protocol. These additional studies were found and suggested, in some cases, in the papers previously reviewed. In other cases, the review carried out on tools that use Tree Testing.

Table 3 shows the results of the searches for each of the engines. We reviewed the results with the exclusion and inclusion criteria to determine those studies relevant to the subject of study.

Table 3. Studies found by each search engine

Search engines	Unique studies found	Duplicated	Selected
ACM	263 studies found	17 studies	–
Scopus	240 studies found	20 studies	3 studies
IEEExplore	27 studies found	10 studies	1 studie
Alicia	5 studies found	–	–
Additional	4 studies found	–	4 studies

Inclusion/Exclusion Criteria. Following the Kitchenham and Charters protocol, inclusion and exclusion criteria were also established.

Inclusion Criteria. For the inclusion criteria, we took as a reference the research questions. The three questions reflected the four criteria used. The first criterion answers the question about the tools used. The second criterion answers what application protocol was used in the Tree Testing technique. Finally, the third criterion defines whether the study carried out describes the impact that the application of Tree Testing had on a software product:

- The study presents a tool that supports the Tree Testing technique.
- The study describes a Tree Testing application protocol.
- The study describes the impact on the software product that the Tree Testing application had when it was applied.

Exclusion Criteria. For the exclusion criteria, we considered a general criterion that describes the language of the study: English and Spanish since they are languages dominated by the authors.

On the other hand, the four remaining criteria define the studies we cannot consider due to their content. From this group, the first excludes those studies that do not deal with user experience or information architecture, a technical problem, Tree Testing, seeks to evaluate. The second excludes those studies that speak of protocols other than the application of the technique (communication protocols, network, among others). Moreover, the last one excludes the studies that only list user experience techniques without deepening the Tree Testing technique:

- The language of study is different from English and Spanish.
- The study does not deal with User Experience or Information Architecture issues.
- The study describes protocols that have nothing to do with the application of Tree Testing.
- The study only briefly describes and lists user experience techniques.

Data Extraction Form. We employed an Extraction Form to obtain the necessary information from the literature to be reviewed. The form has general information fields of the selected studies and fields related to the research guiding questions.

Research Results. The result of both reviews resulted in only four selected studies: three studies from Scopus and one from IEEExplore. Due to the small number of studies, we added another four studies found independently. Outside the scope of the review with search engines and in the time range of the other studies found, we added studies from gray literature, considering them very relevant for the present project. Table 4 summarizes the results of the SLR.

Table 4. Selected studies

ID	Title	Author	Type study
S01	Novel bluetooth-enabled tubeless insulin pump: A user experience design approach for a connected digital diabetes management platform	(Pillalamarri et al. 2018) [21]	Paper
S02	Responsive, mobile app, mobile first: Untangling the UX design web in practical experience	(Mullins 2015) [22]	Paper
S03	Tree testing of hierarchical menu structures for health applications	(Le et al. 2014) [23]	Paper
S04	Information architecture assessment of BPS headquarter official website	(Nurcahyanti & Suhardi 2014) [24]	Paper
S05	User experience (UX) in the CIS classroom: Better information architecture with interactive prototypes and UX testing	(White & Kapakos 2017) [25]	Paper
S06	Usability and quality tests in software products to oriented of user experience	(Arslan et al. 2018) [1]	Paper
S07	How should startups evaluate their website's UX? Comparison of UX evaluation methods through evaluation of UX of the prototype of a matching platform for the rental housing market in Finland – Sopia	(Borisova 2019) [26]	Thesis
S08	TreeTest: online tree testing for information hierarchies	(Mehic 2019) [3]	Thesis

With the analysis carried out on these works found, we proceeded to answer the research questions. P1, related to the impact on IA in development and design projects. P2, related to the steps and phases applied to execute Tree Testing, and P3 to review the various support tools used. Both P1, P2 and P3 have served to subsequently propose the process that has been modeled; P1 and P2 have served to obtain information on the current situation and how Tree Testing is applied, while P3 has served to identify Tree Testing remote application tools and how they have implemented this technique, adapting it to their own proposals.

3.3 Tree Testing Tools

Based on the SLR carried out, and following the approach presented, a description of the tools identified that provide or have provided support to the application of Tree Testing is presented.

Regarding the way to apply Tree Testing, every tool presents variations from one another, but all of them maintain the central idea of having three stages on the execution of the mentioned technique [3, 25]:

- An initial preparation stage in which a tree or hierarchy is created, and the tasks to be completed
- An evaluation stage in which end users perform the tasks on the tree created
- An analysis metrics are created for the evaluators

Below is a description of each of the tools identified. As can be seen, most of these tools are proposals that are currently discontinued.

Heurekia. This tool for remote Tree Testing application is currently discontinued and is only mentioned in the case study that corresponds to Mehic's 2019 thesis. Heurekia is allowed to create the hierarchy of information, create the tasks for navigation in the hierarchy, to configure the list of users so that they can perform the test, to configure an introductory message, and to observe the results of the created test [3].

C-Inspector. Like Heurekia, is a discontinued tool that is mentioned in a study by Mehic. It included the same functionalities as the previous tool and, additionally, the evaluator could define multiple responses for a task, choose between English and German as the study language, add a limit of retries for the tests (from 1 to 5 times), and set up instructions and thank you messages [3].

Plainframe. Tool purchased by Optimal Workshop and discontinued on April 3, 2014, and mentioned by Borisova [26] and Mehic [3]. Plainframe had the same functionalities as the other two tools described; however, it implemented improvements for the analysis of results since, apart from the graphs and statistics resulting from user testing, it allowed any user session to be replayed again.

Naview. A tool that only maintains its limited free layer and that is mentioned and described by Mehic [3], as well as the previous tools. Naview adds the functionality of being able to paste a previously created tree, identifying the levels by tabs [3]. It also includes the possibility for the user to skip a task if he/she cannot find a way to complete it. It also complements the analysis of the results by having the information of the number of clicks made per task. The main limitation of the tool is the fact that the free layer only allows creating 2 tests with 2 questions per test for 10 users [27].

Treejack. This tool is the most mentioned in studies. Treejack adds the functionality of being able to import from a file the hierarchy of the tree to be analyzed [3]. A feedback questionnaire can also be created and with the results of the tests, the tool generates graphs and statistics for analysis in conjunction with logs of the user's interaction with Treejack

[3, 25]. It is in White & Kapakos' study that the use to which the tool was put is indicated [25]. In this study, Treejack was used for academic purposes, for teaching information architecture assessment techniques, and not for industrial purposes, obtaining a student approval of 90% or more on five criteria: ease of learning the tool, ease of use, clear and understandable interaction, and ease of mastering the tool.

UserZoom. This is a platform that has several tools including one that supports the Tree Testing application. UserZoom is mentioned in the same studies as Plainframe [3, 25]. The platform's Tree Testing tool allows, in addition to the functionalities presented by the previous tools, to define the type of device to be analyzed (desktop, mobile, or both), place a title to the study, and determine the language to be used (and not only English and German as was the case with C-Inspector). It allows creating a list of users for the test and can be shared with other people as well. Finally, in the analysis section, the tool provides more information about the user: their operating system, screen resolution, and browser used [3].

TreeTest. This tool developed by Mehic in 2019 [3]. This tool combines several functionalities seen in the other tools. It allows configuring introductory messages, instructions, and thank you messages [3]. It evaluates the time to finish tasks, clicks made on the hierarchy, clicks on the skip button to skip tests, and abandons occurring during testing with users. On the other hand, for the analysis of results, it has graphs and general statistics, per participant and task. It also includes graphs to see the clicks made and the paths taken by users when using the tree [3]. In addition, it is worth mentioning that this tool was developed using the thinking aloud technique in order to improve the usability of TreeTest. The main limitation of the tool is that it is not possible to access it since the author did not leave a URL link nor does it work to download the source code from the GitLab repository, since it requires credentials that are not found within the study.

Custom Tool. A tool developed in 2014 by Le, Chauhuri, Chung, Thompson, and Demiris for Health Information Technologies (HIT) because, at that time, the authors found several limitations in the tools for the application of Tree Testing in this type of technology [23]. The instrument, additionally, allows adding three tasks on an example base tree so that users can become familiar with the technique and with the tool before proceeding to the final test with the tree, they were analyzing [23]. On the other hand, for the analysis, the graphs of the paths followed were added, just as TreeTest does [3, 23]. Furthermore, the authors concluded that the remote application through the tool is quite flexible and serves as evidence to evaluate the information architecture in HITs. [23]. However, and as the last point, it should be noted that the tool is not available since the only link left by the authors to use the tool is not currently active.

3.4 Specialists' Interviews

In order to explore how UX practitioners execute the Tree Testing technique, as well as to identify pain points and learn what steps are typically followed when executing this technique, semi-structured interviews were conducted with UX practitioners. These interviews were realized virtually using Google Meet.

Because of these interviews, it was found that the technique is little known, that mainly the form of remote application is known, through the Optimal Workshop tool, and that in general, UX practitioners carry out the steps that the tool itself establishes in its own interaction. Likewise, the interviewees commented that they normally evaluated the Information Architecture as a whole with the entire interface through User Testing. During the interviews, they reflected that this evaluation could be too late, given that since there are already designs, often at a high level, correcting errors in the Information Architecture could take more time than if it had been applied at earlier stages.

4   Process Proposed

Following the defined approach, with the information obtained from the previous steps, mainly the information obtained from the literature, the Tree Testing tools, and the interviews with experts, we proceeded to model the Tree Testing remote application process.

We have used a framework to standardize the remote process using three macro-steps: In the first place: Planning, a step in which we are going to prepare the test and select the target users to execute the Tree Testing technique. In the second place: Execution, that is the step in which Tree Testing is properly executed. And in the third and final place: Analysis, a step that is used to validate and draw conclusions about the Information Architecture Information design and determine whether or not more investigation is required, more redesigns, or if the design is the most adequate for the users selected. As a result, a proposal of this standardized process was modeled using the notation BPMN, and this proposal was validated by the expert judgment of specialists in Human-Computer Interaction (HCI) and UX Practitioners.

4.1   Model Description

Two views were considered for the model: a general view and a detailed view. For the general view, a diagram summarizing the entire process with the identified phases: Planning, Execution, and Analysis was considered. As shown in Fig. 2, the diagram contains the inputs and outputs required for each of the phases.

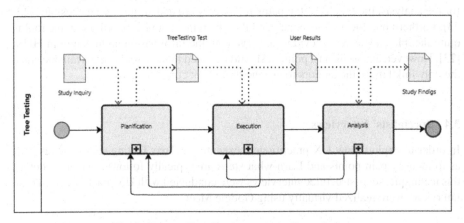

Fig. 2. Remote Tree Testing process. General view.

The detailed view is made up of five diagrams. Two of these make up the complete process due to the performance of two actors: the UX specialist and the User who performs the test. The UX specialist is present in all phases of the process and can return from one phase to another if required. On the other hand, the User only participates in the execution phase and has no control over the other phases, as he/she is limited to completing the tasks that will be of use for the final analysis.

The other three diagrams complement the main process, describing the three sub-processes identified. The first one corresponds to the planning of the study as shown in Fig. 3. The sub-process is carried out in the initial planning phase and in this phase, the purpose of the study is determined, the scope of the study is defined, the people who will participate, the risks, the estimated costs and time, as well as the profile of the users to be evaluated.

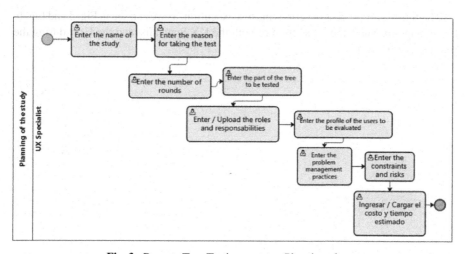

Fig. 3. Remote Tree Testing process. Planning phase.

The second sub-process corresponds to the realization of the pilot. Here, an internal user is considered, which can be the UX specialist himself, a person or several people internal to the organization or from the team of designers. This user can carry out the test and detect errors in terms of the hierarchy tree, the tasks to be performed, the questionnaires and the messages that were written for the user. This sub-process is iterative and several modifications may be made before testing is enabled for end-users.

The third sub-process describes the selection of users based on the profile established in the first sub-process, as we can see in Fig. 4. In this sub-process, the test link is generated and sent to the selected users via email or through social networks.

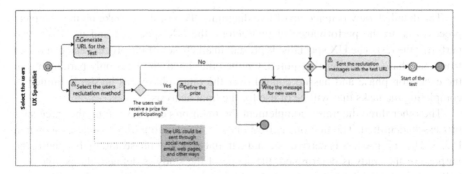

Fig. 4. Remote Tree Testing process. Users' selection.

The fourth sub-process describes the test execution, as we can see in Fig. 5 and Fig. 6. These diagrams show the interaction of both the UX Specialist and the User during the execution of the test.

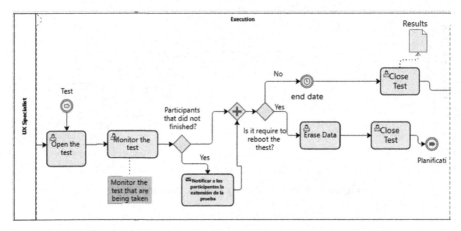

Fig. 5. Remote Tree Testing process. Test execution (UX Specialist).

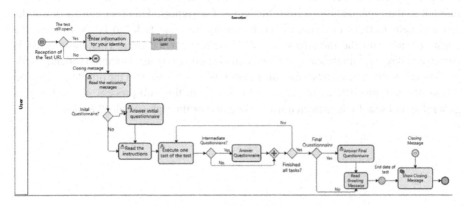

Fig. 6. Remote Tree Testing process. Test execution (User).

Finally, the fifth sub-process describes the Analysis, as we can see in Fig. 7. This diagram shows the interaction of the UX practitioner to perform the analysis of the information obtained during the execution of the test. With this information, UX Specialist is able to implement enhancements. All this with the purpose to improve three main indicators: execution time, user error rate and length of the path followed.

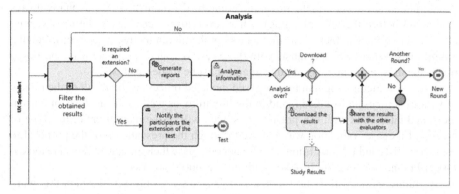

Fig. 7. Remote Tree Testing process. Analysis.

4.2 Validation

For the validation of the proposed process, interviews were conducted with UX practitioners and HCI experts. This validation resulted in the agreement of these experts, once the observations and suggestions provided by them in the aforementioned interviews were addressed and corrected.

It is worth noting that the experts highlighted the importance of carrying out this type of evaluation in the early stages of the projects. Given that, in accordance with what was found in the literature, the experts indicated that carrying out this type of evaluation is cheaper than other evaluations, and its corrections are less impactful in terms of cost and time.

5 Results and Future Works

Among the findings reported, it is important to mention that Tree Testing, as an Information Architecture technique, is very useful and practical in its remote application, and should be considered to be applied in the early stages of software projects; and a tool to support the whole process should be implemented.

Furthermore, a small number of papers on this subject were found in the SLR conducted. This has been contrasted in the interviews to UX practitioners conducted, and it is evident that the topic is new, the technique is not widely used and little disseminated, however, there is a growing interest in the subject.

In addition, it was observed, from the literature, that there was no standardized process to carry out remote tree testing. In the literature, several steps and activities were found that were decided to be applied due to the experience of the UX practitioners and due to the needs at the time of the studies in question. However, the systematic review serves as a source since many activities mentioned in these studies are common to all of them. Likewise, it was possible to determine and group several steps in three phases that, although not explicit in the literature, could be distinguished. A first phase always mentioned before the test (planning), where everything necessary is built. A second phase where users can then perform the tasks in the hierarchy tree (execution). Finally, a third phase where UX specialists with these results, can determinate if the proposed tree is the most appropriate or if adjustments must be made (analysis).

It is worth mentioning that the proposed modeled process is the result of the review of various sources and studies found in the literature, as well as the analysis of current tools, and interviews with UX practitioners, who will be the main users of this type of process. Likewise, validation was achieved through the presentation of the proposal to HCI specialists and UX practitioners, who not only gave their agreement but also looked forward to the next steps to be taken with this proposed process.

As future work, within the framework of the research project to which this work belongs, it is proposed to implement a tool that provides support to the whole process of remote execution of Tree Testing. However, this proposed process is an independent result of the tool. This means that other people who want to implement their tool or who wish to have a framework to apply Tree Testing remotely without necessarily using the tool that is expected to be implemented can also use the modeled process.

Acknowledgment. This work is part of the research project "Virtualización del proceso de eval-uación de experiencia de usuario de productos de software para escenarios de no presencialidad" (virtualization of the user experience evaluation process of software products for non-presential scenarios), developed by HCI-DUXAIT research group. HCI-DUXAIT is a research group that belongs to the PUCP (Pontificia Universidad Católica del Perú).

This work was funded by the Dirección de Fomento a la Investigación at the PUCP through grant 2021-C-0023.

References

1. Arslan, H., Yüksek, A.G., Elyakan, M.L., Canay, Ö.: Usability and quality test in software products to oriented user experience. Online J. Qual. High. Educ. **5**(3) (2018). http://www.tojdel.net/journals/tojqih/articles/v05i03/v05i03-11.pdf
2. Niranjanamurthy, M., Archikam, N., Himaja, G., Shetty, P.K.: Research study on importance of usability testing/User Experience (UX) Testing. Int. J. Comput. Sci. Mob. Comput. 78–85 (2014). https://www.semanticscholar.org/paper/Research-Study-on-Importance-of-Usability-Testing-%2F-Niranjanamurthy-Nagaraj/60dc55511afb1af8d78518ebdff5d1f746c41ee8
3. Mehic, A.: TreeTest: Online tree testing for information hierarchies. Master's thesis. Graz University of Technology (2019). https://ftp.isds.tugraz.at/pub/theses/amehic-2019-msc.pdf
4. Spencer, D.: Card-based classification evaluation. boxes and arrows (2003). https://boxesandarrows.com/card-based-classification-evaluation/

5. Türkyilmaz, A., Kantar, S., Bulak, M.E., Uysal, O.: User experience design: Aesthetics or functionality? Management, knowledge and learning. In: Joint International Conference 2015. Italy. ISBN: 978-961-6914-13-0. 27–29 May 2015 (2015). http://www.toknowpress. net/ISBN/978-961-6914-13-0/papers/ML15-111.pdf
6. Kitchenham, B., Charters, S.: Guidelines for performing systematic literature reviews in software engineering. Evidence based software engineering technical report. Keele University and Durham University Joint Report. Elsevier (2007). https://www.elsevier.com/__data/pro mis_misc/525444systematicreviewsguide.pdf
7. Petticrew, M., Roberts, H.: Systematic Reviews in the Social Sciences: A Practical Guide. Blackwell Publishing, Hoboken (2006).https://doi.org/10.1002/9780470754887
8. Association Computer Machinery: About the ACM Organization. ACM (2020). https://www. acm.org/about-acm/about-the-acm-organization
9. IEEE: IEEE - About IEEE. IEEE (2020). https://www.ieee.org/about/index.html
10. Elsevier: About Scopus - Abstract and citation database. Elsevier (2020). https://www.els evier.com/solutions/scopus?dgcid=RN_AGCM_Sourced_300005030
11. Ding, W., Lin, X., Zarro, M.: Information Architecture: The Design and Integration of Information Spaces (Synthesis Lectures on Information Concepts, Retrieval, and Services). Morgan & Claypool Publishers, San Rafael (2017).https://doi.org/10.2200/S00755ED2V01Y20 1701ICR056
12. Zhang, Q., Neitzel, A.J.: Methodological review: A systematic narrative review of screening tools for conducting systematic reviews in educational research. OSF preprints (2021).https:// doi.org/10.31219/osf.io/efs2n
13. OMG: Business Process Model and Notation (BPMN), Version 2.0. 538. OMG (2010). https:// www.omg.org/spec/BPMN/2.0/About-BPMN/
14. Hunt, V.D.: Process Mapping: How to Reengineer Your Business Processes. Wiley, New York. ISBN: 978-0-471-13281-3. February 1996 (1996)
15. ISO. ISO 9241-210:2019(en): Ergonomics of human-system interaction—Part 210: Human-centered design for interactive systems (2019). https://inacal.isolutions.iso.org/obp/ui#iso: std:iso:9241:-210:ed-2:v1:en
16. Morville, P.: User Experience Design. Semantic Studios (2004). http://semanticstudios.com/ publications/semantics/000029.php
17. Cardello, J.: Low: Findability and Discoverability: Four Testing Methods to Identify the Causes. Nielsen Norman Group (2014). https://www.nngroup.com/articles/navigation-ia-tests/
18. Nielsen, N. Usability 101: Introduction to Usability. Nielsen Norman Group, 2012. https:// www.nngroup.com/articles/usability-101-introduction-to-usability/
19. Wilson, D.: A is for Accessibility—12 top tips for designing an inclusive user experience. Medium (2019). https://uxdesign.cc/the-a-to-z-of-ux-a-is-for-accessibility-12-top-tips-for-designing-an-inclusive-user-experience-667eedaf5bca
20. Harley, A.: Trustworthiness in Web Design: 4 Credibility Factors. Nielsen Norman Group (2016). https://www.nngroup.com/articles/trustworthy-design/
21. Pillamarri, S.S., Huyett, L.M., Abdel-Malek, A.: Novel bluetooth-enabled tubeless insulin pump: A user experience design approach for a connected digital diabetes management platform. J. Diabetes Sci. Technol. **12**(6), 1132–1142 (2018). https://doi.org/10.1177/193229681 8804802
22. Mullins, C.: Responsive, mobile app, mobile first: Untangling the UX design web in practical experience. In: Proceedings of the 33rd Annual International Conference on the Design of Communication - SIGDOC 2015, pp. 1–6 (2015). https://doi.org/10.1145/2775441.2775478
23. Le, T., Chaudhuri, S., Chung, J., Thompson, H.J., Demiris, G.: Tree testing of hierarchical menu structures for health applications. J. Biomed. Inf. **49**, 198–205. Scopus (2014). https:// doi.org/10.1016/j.jbi.2014.02.011

24. Nurcahyanti, W.E., Suhardi: Information architecture assessment of BPS headquarters official website. In: 2014 International Conference on Information Technology Systems and Innovation (ICITSI), pp. 177–182 (2014). https://doi.org/10.1109/ICITSI.2014.7048260

25. White, B.J., Kapakos, W.A.: User Experience (UX) in the CIS Classroom: Better information architecture with interactive prototypes and UX testing. Issues in Information Systems, 2017, Vol. 18, Issue 2, pp. 59–70 (2017). https://doi.org/10.48009/2_iis_2017_59-70

26. Borisova, L.: How startups should evaluate their websites' UX? Comparison of UX evaluation methods through evaluation of UX of the prototype of a matching platform for the rental housing market in Finland – Sopia. Master's thesis, Aalto University School of Business. International Design Business Management (2019). https://aaltodoc.aalto.fi/handle/123456 789/42377?locale-attribute=en

27. Naview: Naview - Plans and Signup. Naview (2021). https://www.naviewapp.com/naview/ plans-and-signup

28. Raemy, J.: The International Image Interoperability Framework (IIIF): Raising awareness of the user benefits for scholarly editions. Thesis for Bachelor of Science in Information Science. University of Basel (2017). https://doi.org/10.13140/RG.2.2.34211.89125

29. Garrett Jesse James: The elements of user experience: user-centered design for the Web and beyond. Second edition. Berkeley, CA: New Riders. Voices that matter (2011). ISBN 978-0-321-68368-7

Developing Personas in UX Process: A Case Study for a Web-Documentary to Increase Empathy Among Social Groups

Elisângela Vilar[1,2]([✉]) [iD], Milena Monteiro[3], Sónia Rafael[2] [iD], Francisco Rebelo[1,2] [iD], and Paulo Noriega[1,2] [iD]

[1] CIAUD, Faculdade de Arquitetura, Universidade de Lisboa, Rua Sá Nogueira, 1349-063 Lisbon, Portugal
{ebpvilar,pnoriega}@edu.ulisboa.pt, frebelo@fa.ulisboa.pt
[2] ITI- LARSyS, Universidade de Lisboa, Rua Sá Nogueira, 1349-063 Lisbon, Portugal
srafael@campus.ul.pt
[3] Faculdade de Arquitetura, Universidade de Lisboa, Rua Sá Nogueira, 1349-063 Lisbon, Portugal

Abstract. This paper aims to present the process of personas development for a digital solution to increase empathy among social groups. It is a part of a research focusing on promoting empathy in university students related to external groups through a web-based platform, with the broader concern of contributing to the fight against prejudice and discrimination with immigrants in European countries. Research has demonstrated that empathy can have an important role in decreasing bias related to external groups. Also, developing personas is an important part of the UX process; however, its use is often misunderstood, and developers' interests bias its development. A reliable and well-prepared data collection comprising tools development – such as interviews and questionnaires- is crucial for personas creation. In this sense, this paper presents a case study of personas creation, from tools development and application to data analysis and personas definition. – As a result of data collection, three personas were developed based on 83 European university students' respondents.

Keywords: Interaction design · User experience · Personas · Ergodesign

1 Introduction

Europe is one of the major immigration destinations of both migration movements, from inside the European continent and intercontinental immigration. According to Eurostat [1], about 23 million non-EU citizens were living in an EU state at the end of 2019. Immigrants add their experiences, values, and biological and cultural diversity to the host countries. However, sometimes this diversity is not seen as good by locals, and frictions, from small prejudice demonstrations to significant hate crimes, among social groups may occur. Since 2011, the European Union has suffered the effects of a migratory crisis that arose with the Arab Spring and intensified in 2015–2016 [2].

M. M. Soares et al. (Eds.): HCII 2022, LNCS 13321, pp. 93–107, 2022.
https://doi.org/10.1007/978-3-031-05897-4_7

A considerable amount of legal and illegal immigrants arrived at member states from their birth countries. With this, discontent among the population became more usual, contributing to the increase of discriminatory acts, often hidden behind allegations of fear of loss of job opportunities, decreasing quality of life, canceling of local culture, and practicing non-European religions.

Authors identify and try to explain this behavior. Stephan & Finlay [3] define prejudice as negative attitudes towards different social groups. So, when there is a psychological distance between the prejudiced person (agent) and the person who is the target of the prejudice (focus), there is also little or no effort by the prejudice agent does in understand the other social group, increasing the difficulty of putting in the other shoes. In this sense, authors argue that diminishing this psychological distance between prejudice agent and prejudice focus through empathy could positively affect the relationships between social groups.

Considering this, a project to develop a digital solution to promote empathy among social groups based on the User Experience (UX) methodology was proposed, and it is under development. In this way, this chapter aims to present a pertinent concern during the UX methodology development: creating the personas.

The chapter is divided into five main sections, starting with the introduction followed by the theoretical background, where core concepts and principles are presented in the light of the focus of this paper, the development of the personas. The third section presents the methodology, followed by the fourth, with the main results and discussion, and the fifth section with the conclusions.

2   Theoretical Background

2.1   The Concept of Empathy

According to Crocetti and colleagues [4], barriers against immigrants are increasing in many countries, under the excuse of defending one's own nations against "foreigners". Favorable treatments for ingroup members compared to outgroup members, leading to discriminative behaviors, that is the core meaning behind prejudice definition [5, 6], is a reality that can be found worldwide. Despite this, research has shown that empathy can have a positive impact in decreasing this phenomenon. Stephan & Finlay [3] related empathy to prosocial behaviors and its absence is linked to the antisocial behavior. Also, the prejudice related to external groups are often associated to exaggerated perceptions about the differences between internal and external groups. In this way, empathy could be an important aspect to consider while developing positive solutions to act against prejudice among social groups.

According to Einsenberg and Fabes [7] empathy is described as an emotional response that has origin on the emotional state (or condition) from another person and that is in line with the emotional state (or condition) of this other person, considering a differentiation between the self and the other. This principle of "the other" recognition is also shared by Decety and Meyer [8].

Through empathy, we are able to connect with the other's feelings and thoughts, allowing us to understand the other intentions, predict their behavior, and experience ourselves an emotion that was triggered by the emotion of the other [9]. So, it is funda-mental for social skills and interactions, leading us to help people and preventing us to hurt them, making social interaction more efficient.

Authors point two different ways of empathy: the cognitive empathy and the emo-tional empathy. According to Stephan & Finlay [3], the cognitive empathy, also known as perspective taking, is a cognitive process related to the ability to put ourselves in each other's shoes, taking his/her perspective. It is related to the capacity of understand and evaluate how much pain a person is felling [10].

The emotional empathy, also known as sympathy, is defined as an emotional reaction based on the other's emotional state (or condition). It involves feelings of concern and sadness for the other person, instead of only reflecting the other's emotional state [11]. According to Stephan &Finlay [3], emotional empathy can be divided into:

- reactive empathy - that is a reaction to the emotional experiences of the other person. It is also subdivided into empathetic concern, that is emotions that are predominantly positive, related to compassion that arise from a feeling of concern with the suffering of the other. And personal distress, that is related to negative emotions, such as anxiety, threat and repulsion that arise from the feelings of anguish evoked by the feeling of the other.
- parallel empathy – that is related to emotional responses that are like those that the other person is experiencing (negative, if the other has negative experiences, and positive is the other is experiencing a positive emotion).

The empathetic attitudes are formed by a set of socially responsible empathic beliefs, where the people that identify themselves with these beliefs are more favorable to deal with problematic situations and to act accordingly.

Thus, being aware about our own feelings (self-awareness) and being able to regulate consciously regulate our own emotions (emotional regulation) may be what allow us to distinguish empathic response to others from our own personal distress. With only empathic responses leading to prosocial behavior [10].

Prosocial Behavior (Empathetic Attitudes). According to [12], the prosocial behav-ior comprises acts such as helping, sharing, comforting, donating or volunteering and cooperating, that aim to benefit other people, and it is shaped by cognitive and emotional process. Their motivations can be altruist (aiming to promote well-being of others), and selfish (aiming to promote one's own well-being). Empathetic attitudes are voluntary actions that give answer to the cognitive process, resulting from a conscious decision taking [13].

Decety & Meyer [8] point that in cognitive empathy -related tasks, when people imagine the other's feelings in certain situation versus what they imagine that are their own feelings in the same situation, different emotions arise. In the first case, people tend to feel sympathy or empathetic concern by the other, while the second case people can lead to personal distress. So, authors [10] argue that this could explain why empathy not necessarily leads to a prosocial behavior. In this way, any intend to develop solutions to promote empathy needs to rely on promoting empathetic concern, avoiding personal distress.

2.2   The User Experience (UX) Process

According to Xu [14], ergonomics and human-factors have been developing Human-centered approaches to deliver ergonomic products, namely the Human-Centered Design (HCD) methodology [15]. This approach is based on considering Human needs and expectations in the center of the developmental process, in order to promote interactive products (physical or digital) that meet Human requirements. ISO 9241-210:2019 [15] define experience as the perceptions and responses that users' have while using a system, product or service, including their emotions and beliefs.

As stated by Jetter and Gerken [16], nowadays people mediate their intention of having aa product not only because of their needs or product's superior technical and functional capabilities. Instead, they are interested in the whole experience products can provide, such us social integration, recognition, freedom, among others.

The empathic approach of UX process highlights the emotional nature of the experience, and the experiences that products elicit should be in line with user's needs, beliefs, motivations and expectations. For this, a rich and empathic understanding of the user's desired experiences is needed, with the objective of both, defining requirements truly reflects users and creating empathy in designers, inspiring them to feel like the users [17]. A useful tool in the UX design process are the Personas [18].

Personas. The concept was introduced by Cooper [18] and are very used when designing considering a Human-centered approach. According to the author, Personas are hypothetical archetypes of real users as they are developed based on empirical understanding of users' characteristics and behaviors. According to Goh and Romainoor [19], the advantage of using this technique is target group be seen in an empathetic way, encouraging communication about it among design and development team, supporting a holistic understanding of the user.

Personas' creations are supported by reliable data from qualitative and, sometimes quantitative, field research, in order to collect information from a broad range of real people, including extremes. Thus, this information is processed considering grouping users by their goals, motivations, beliefs, tasks, skills, and so on. According to Cooper [18], generally, despite of the dramatic variation among users, three groups with the same pattern will be detected. Personas are the representation of these groups of real people. Thus, developing focused and well-structured data collection tools, such interviews guides and questionnaires, are an important part of the personas' creation process. Most of the criticism about Personas are based on its biased development, that is when they are developed to justify and defend features proposed by the design and development team, based on the idea they have about the use, instead of to act as a tool to understand and to communicate the goals, motivations and desires of real users [20]. Authors [21] also argue that is a lack of validation in personas creation process.

Personas are goal directed fictional representations of real users, whose main characteristics are grouped considering pattern that arise from data analysis. They are described as vivid representations that are, in general, described in a text-basis, considering a name, basic demographic information, patterns of product usages, goals, behaviors, beliefs and attitudes. Usually, it is also attached to the textual information about the persona, a pictorial information [19].

In this context, this paper aims to present the personas creation process for the development of a digital solution to increase empathy among social groups. This is part of a larger project based on the development of a platform to host content related to the promotion of empathy between social groups.

3   Methodology

As already explained, Personas were developed for be used in a more complex project that aims to increase empathy among social groups (immigrants), namely among university students. Considering this, the focus of Personas creation were university students from Europe.

Qualitative data were collected through an online questionnaire directed to target group. Target group was comprised by European citizens, European residents, aged between 18 and 30 years old.

The methodology was developed in two main phases: questionnaire development and data collection.

3.1   Questionnaire Development

The questionnaire was developed mainly to understand the general characteristics of the target group, considering demographic data, their preferences, their personality, their level of empathy, their attitudes towards the other and their contact with immigrants. Questions were developed considering studies objective and were inspired by the Neris model, from the 16personalities website [22]. The questions were created in Portuguese and translated by a professional Portuguese-English speaker and retranslated by another professional to provide accuracy of translation process. Questionnaire was provided in both languages, Portuguese and English.

The questionnaire was comprised by eleven parts:

1st part: questionnaire explanation, objectives presentation and participation, data collection authorization.

2nd part: participants' selection according to their birthplace and country of residence.

3rd part: Understanding of participants preferences related to their personal choices that characterize their personality. With these data it would be possible to understand project requirements as well as more appropriated interactions to be used to allow the target group to reach the project's main objective.

4th part: Questions made with the objective to know if participants can separate their own feelings from those shared with others, as well as to know if they are able to control their emotions. With these data we could understand where the target group are considering the project's main objective and to contribute for decisions related to approaches directed to improve empathy with immigrants.

5th part: to understand participant's sociability level to develop the system based on their characteristics. For example, defining if participants would have a direct contact with immigrants through the system or if this option shouldn't be considered.

6th part: Understand how the relationship of the target with others is considering the possibility of conflict. With this, it is possible to define possible interactions without creating friction between social groups.

7th Part: Knowing the level of interests about the other. It can influence the way information is presented, the duration of the contact with the immigrant's narrative and its complexity.

8th Part: Knowing participant's (target-group) level of empathy, also perceiving if they are more framed into the emotional or cognitive empathy. It is necessary to avoid the personal distress caused by a high level of emotional empathy. Besides, understanding the empathy level allow us to have idea of the empathy level start point of the target group (university students) to plan what is needed to increase the empathy level with social group (immigrants).

9th part: Knowing the profile of the target group to perceive the type of interaction and content is part of their daily lives. With this, it would be possible to define, for example, the narrative type more suitable to catch and maintain target's attention as well as interaction's average duration.

10th part: knowing the level of proximity the target group (university students) has with immigrants to find out if they have contact with this social group. It would allow us to predict if using narratives about immigrants would represent a novelty for the university students, and how much of this contact would evoke the feeling of belonging to the group.

11th part: to make a demographic profile of the target group, also ensuring that respondents belong to this group (European university students from 18 to 30 years old).

The constructs list with the questions for each part of the questionnaire is presented on Table 1.

Application Protocol. Data were collected through an online questionnaire, distributed through Facebook groups and the Survey Cycle® for two weeks. Only European citizens were asked to participate. To ensure this, after presenting the study's objective and having authorization for data collection, the second part of the questionnaire directly asked participants if they born or live in Europe. If the answer was "yes", they could continue to fulfil the questionnaire, if they answered "No", they were directed to the end of the questionnaire.

Table 1. List of the parts of the questionnaire with their constructs, questions and answer's types

Part	Construct	Question	Answer's type
Part 1	Questionnaire Presentation	Q1 - Do you agree to participate in this questionnaire and share your answers as part of this study?	Multiple-choice (Yes/No)
Part 2	Participant's selection	Q2 - Were you born in Europe?	Multiple-choice (Yes/No)
		Q3 - Do you live in Europe?	Multiple-choice (Yes/No)

(continued)

Table 1. (*continued*)

Part	Construct	Question	Answer's type
Part 3	Personality - Priorities	Q4 - You get along better with:	Multiple-choice (Your family/Your friends)
		Q5 -You prefer:	Multiple-choice (Face to face conversations/Online conversations)
		Q6 - You prefer:	Multiple-choice (To listen/To talk)
		Q7 -You prefer:	Multiple-choice (To create/To contemplate)
Part 4	Personality – self-awareness and emotional regulation	Q8 -You react impulsively under pressure	Likert-type scale (always-never)
		Q9 - You envy other people	Likert-type scale (always-never)
		Q10 - You see yourself as an emotionally stable person	Likert-type scale (always-never)
		Q11 - You understand what you're feeling	Likert-type scale (always-never)
		Q12 -You let yourself be infected by the emotions of other people	Likert-type scale (always-never)
Part 5	Contact with others - Sociability	Q13 - You start conversations	Likert-type scale (always-never)
		Q14 - You like to be the center of attention	Likert-type scale (always-never)
		Q15 - A book or a video game is often better than a social event	Likert-type scale (always-never)
Part 6	Contact with others - Relationship	Q16 - You often feel superior to other people	Likert-type scale (always-never)
		Q17 - In an argument, speaking the truth is more important than how it affects people's feelings	Likert-type scale (always-never)
		Q18 - You care about how your actions affect other people's feelings	Likert-type scale (always-never)
Part 7	Contact with others - Interest in the other	Q19 - You are interested in knowing about other people's lives	Likert-type scale (always-never)

(*continued*)

Table 1. (*continued*)

Part	Construct	Question	Answer's type
		Q20 - When someone starts talking about himself/herself you get quickly distracted	Likert-type scale (always-never)
		Q21 - In a conversation, you usually find yourself talking more about yourself than listening to what the other person has to say about themselves	Likert-type scale (always-never)
Part 8	Empathy	Q22 - In a conversation, you pay attention on the person's reactions to what you are saying	Likert-type scale (always-never)
		Q23 - Even if the listener doesn't like it, you prefer to say what you think	Likert-type scale (always-never)
		Q24 - If a friend is sad, you try to find solutions to help instead of reproducing his emotions	Likert-type scale (always-never)
		Q25 - You feel happy when someone is ready to express their feelings and share them with you	Likert-type scale (always-never)
		Q26 - You can tell when people are upset about something	Likert-type scale (always-never)
		Q26 - If someone is sad get sad too	Likert-type scale (always-never)
		Q27 - Even if you don't agree with someone else's point of view, you can still appreciate the differences of opinion	Likert-type scale (always-never)
Part 9	Information Source	Q28 - On average, how much time a day do you spend on the internet? (not counting work, if applicable)	Multiple choice (less than 1 h/1 h–2 h/3 h–4 h/5 h–6 h/more than 6 h)

(*continued*)

Table 1. (*continued*)

Part	Construct	Question	Answer's type
		Q29 - You spend most of that time:	Multiple choices (Social networks/reading news/navigating in websites/Playing games/watching videos/shopping/other)
		Q30 - How often do you read?	Likert-type scale (always-never)
		Q31 - How often do you watch documentaries?	Likert-type scale (always-never)
		Q32 - How often do you watch videos in the first person? (f.e.: YouTube)	Likert-type scale (always-never)
		Q33 - How often do you listen to podcasts?	Likert-type scale (always-never)
		Q34 - How often do you visit museums?	Likert-type scale (always-never)
		Q35 - How often do you access Instagram or other photo sharing networks?	Likert-type scale (always-never)
Part 10	Contact with Immigrants	Q36 - Is anyone in your family an immigrant (came from another country)?	Multiple choice (I don't have immigrants' relatives or friends /Mother or father /Grandmother or grandfather /great-grandmother or great-grandfather /other)
		Q37 - Do you have any immigrant friends (who live in your country but were born in another)?	Multiple choice (I don't have immigrants' relatives/friends/I have a friend/ 2–3 friends/4–5 friends/More than 6 friends)
		Q38 - Do you interact with immigrants during your day?	Likert-type scale (always-never)
Part 11	Demographic data	Q39 - How old are you?	Multiple choice (18, 19, 20, 21, 22, 23, 24, 25, 26, 27, 28, 29, 30, other)
		Q40 - What is your gender?	Multiple choice (male/female/other)
		Q41 - What country were you born in?	Open answer

(*continued*)

Table 1. (*continued*)

Part	Construct	Question	Answer's type
		Q42 - What country do you live in?	Open answer
		Q42 - What is your level of education?	Multiple choice (completed high school/completed graduation/completed masters/completed doctorate)
		Q42 - What is your profession?	Open answer

4   Results and Discussion

At the end of two weeks period, 87 completed questionnaires were collected, and results were analyzed in order to group patterns of response.

From these 87 questionnaires, 63 reported as being students, consequently these are considered the valid ones. Demographic data was analyzed first, and three age groups were defined, as can be seen on Table 2.

Table 2. Results from demographic data

Age group	Female	Male	Total	N° of students	Country (born/live)
18–23	24	8	32	28 (87.5%) Graduation (68.8%)	Portugal (28.1%)/ Portugal (28.1%)
24–26	13	9	22	15 (68.1%) Graduation (59.1%)	Germany (27.3%)/Germany (27.3%)
27 - 30	14	19	33	20 (60.6%) Graduation (42.4%) Master (39.4%)	Germany/UK (51.5%)
Total	**51**	**36**	**87**	**63 (72.4%)**	

From demographic data three profiles were verified a female graduation student, from south of Europe, between 18 and 23 years old, a female graduation/master student, from a country of the western Europe, between 24 and 26 years old, and a male Master student and worker, from the north of Europe, between 27 and 30 years old.

Data from these three age groups were defined and their answers for each construct were analyzed. Likert-type answers were analyzed grouping points 1and 2 (never), 3 (medium point), 4 and 5 (always). Main results can be seen on Table 3.

Table 3. Main results for each construct grouped by age.

Age group	Priorities			
	You get along better with (n/%):	You prefer:	You prefer:	You prefer:
18-23	Family (20 – 62.5%)	Face-to-face (27 – 84.3%)	To listen (25 – 78%)	To contemplate (17- 53%
24 - 26	Family (11 – 50%) Friends (11 – 50%)	Face-to-face (18 – 82%)	To listen (15 – 68%)	To contemplate (11 – 50%)
27 - 30	Friends (18 – 54.4%)	Face-to-face (28 – 84.8%)	To listen (24 – 72.7%)	To create (19 - 57.5%)

Age group	Self-awareness and emotional regulation				
	You react impulsively under pressure (n):	You envy other people	You see yourself as an emotionally stable person.	You understand what you're feeling.	You let yourself be infected by the emotions of other people.
18-23	Never (11 - 34,4%) medium (10 – 31,2%) always (11 34,4%)	Never (18 – 56%)	Medium (14–43.7%) Always (13 -40.6%)	Always (20-62.5%)	To contemplate (17-53%
24 - 26	Never (11 – 50%)	Always (10 – 45.4%)	Never (9-40.9%) Always (9-40.9%)	Always (12-54.5%)	To contemplate (11 – 50%)
27 - 30	Never (11) medium (10) always (11)	Never 22 (66.6%)	Always (18-54.5%)	Always (23-69.6%)	To create (19 - 57.5%)

Age group	Contact with others - Sociability		
	You start conversations.	You like to be the center of attention.	A book or a video game is often better than a social event.
18-23	Medium (12–37.5%) Always (12-37.5%)	Never (22-68.7%)	Never (17-53.1%)
24 - 26	Medium (8-36.7%) Always (9-40.9%)	Never (13-59%)	Never (7-31.8%) Always (7 – 31.8%)
27 - 30	Always (20-60.6%)	Never (17-51.5%)	Never (17-51.5%)

Age group	Contact with others - Relationship		
	You often feel superior to other people	In an argument, speaking the truth is more important than how it affects people's feelings.	You care about how your actions affect other people's feelings.
18-23	Never (23-71.8%)	Always (26-81.2%)	Always (29-90.6%)
24 - 26	Never (10-45.4%)	Always (11-50%)	Always (17-77%)
27 - 30	Never (22-66.6%)	Never (12-36.4%) Always (14 – 42.4%)	Always (26-78.7%)

Age group	Contact with others - Interest in the other		
	You are interested in knowing about other people's lives.	When someone starts talking about himself/herself you get quickly distract-ed.	In a conversation, you usually find yourself talking more about yourself than listening to what the other person has to say about themselves.
18 - 23	Always (22-68.7%)	Never (25-78%)	Never (24-75%)
24 - 26	Always (18-82%)	Never (11-50%)	Never (10-45.4%)
27 - 30	Always (25-75.7%)	Never (19-57.5%)	Never (18-54.5%)

Age group	Information Source							
	On average, how much time a day do you spend on the internet? (not counting work, if applicable)	You spend most of that time:	How often do you read?	How often do you watch documentaries?	How often do you watch videos in the first person? (f.e.: YouTube)	How often do you listen to podcasts?	How often do you visit museums?	How often do you access Instagram or other photo sharing networks?
18 - 23	3-4h (11 – 34.4%)	Social Media (20-62.5%)	Never (12-37.5%) Always (11 – 34.8%)	Never (19-59.3%)	Never (17-51.5%)	Never (18-56%)	Never (26-81%)	Always (24-75%)
24 - 26	3-4h (11 – 50%)	Social Media (9-40.9%)	Always (12-54.5%)	Medium (10–45.4%)	Always (10-45.4%)	Never (10-45%)	Never (16-72.7%)	Always (12-54.5%)
27 - 30	3-4h (12 – 36.4%)	Social Media (10-30%)	Always (16-48.4%)	Always (16-48.4%)	Never (18-54.5%)	Never (17-51.5%)	Never (17-51.5%)	Always (16-48.4%)

Age group	Contact with Immigrants		
	Is anyone in your family an immi-grant (came from another coun-try)?	Do you have any immigrant friends (who live in your country but were born in another)?	Do you interact with immigrants during your day?
18 - 23	No (22-68.7%)	No friends (8-25%)	Never (13-40.6%)
24 - 26	No (16-72.7%)	1 friend (7-31.8%). 2-3 friends (7-31.8%)	Never (10-45.4%)
27 - 30	No (17 -51.5%)	More than 6 friends (12-36.4%)	Always (20-60.6%)

According to the data, the age group from 18 to 23 years old presented more family-oriented, being more contemplative than creative, a little shyer than the other two groups. People from this group sems interested in what others have to say and let themselves be infected by the others' emotions, being able to stop saying what they to not hurt the listener. This group had participants from eleven different countries but most of them are from Portugal.

The age group from 24 to 26 years old seems to be a middle term between the two other groups. They are both, family and friends-oriented, and they prefer to contemplate than to create. People from this group are shy. They like both, stay at home with family and to hang out with friends. They are very emotive, preferring to not saying what they think for not hurting another person. They are very worried in knowing how their actions affect the others, feeling sadness when the other is sad. Most of the participants from this group are from Germany, followed by Italy.

The oldest age group (27–30 years old) is very different from the youngest one (18–23 years old). This group is more friend-oriented and more creative than contemplative. A little impulsive and less shy than the other groups, they take the initiative in starting a conversation and don´t care in being the center of attentions, for example. However, this group shows less attention to the other emotions, showing less concerns about the effect of their acts in the others, preferring to say what they think. Most of participants from this group are from United Kingdom and Germany, followed by Portugal.

After data analysis, three personas were created according to Cooper and colleagues [23], a main persona, called Beatriz, and two secondaries that are Emma and Dave. Beatriz can be seen on Fig. 1. Emma and Dave can be seen on Fig. 2 and Fig. 3.

Fig. 1. A description of Beatriz, the main persona created from the questionnaire data.

Fig. 2. A description of Emma, a secondary persona created from the questionnaire data.

Fig. 3. A description of Dave, a secondary persona created from the questionnaire data.

5   Conclusion

The main objective of this paper was presenting the development of personas for a project to develop a digital system to increase empathy among social groups. The target group was the university students, mainly those from age group ranging from 18 to 30 years old.

For this a questionnaire based on constructs related to level of empathy, information source, contact with immigrants, among others, was developed and distributed online.

Attained results were analyzed and three main profiles were defined. From them, personas were created.

Despite the criticism around Personas, when used in a Human-Centered Design methodology approach, it has been considered a valuable contribute for the design process. Personas are a collection of human attributes specifically from the target users. This method allows us to promote project's decisions focused on the real users, avoiding that designers' personal beliefs may influence the design and development process. Besides, personas help the process as this tool promotes designer-user connection, promoting empathy. So, designer starts seen the user, not as data, requirements and features, but as a human being. It makes easy for the designers to put the focus on the necessities and expectations of real persons.

As literature explaining the process of personas creation is still difficult to find, data from this paper could be useful for those who want to implement this tool in UX design processes.

Acknowledgements. Research funded by CIAUD Project UID/EAT/4008/2020 and ITI - LARSyS-FCT Pluriannual funding's 2020–2023 (UIDB/50009/2020).

References

1. Eurostat - European Union: Migration and migrant population statistics - Statistics Explained: Retrieved February 8, 2022, from (n.d.) https://ec.europa.eu/eurostat/statistics-explained/index.php?title=Migration_and_migrant_population_statistics#Migrant_population:_23_million_non-EU_citizens_living_in_the_EU_on_1_January_2020
2. Karolewski, I.P., Benedikter, R.: Europe's refugee and migrant crisis. Politique Européenne **60**(2), 98–132 (2018). https://doi.org/10.3917/poeu.060.0098
3. Stephan, W.G., Finlay, K.: The role of empathy in improving intergroup relations. J. Soc. Issues **55**(4), 729–743 (1999). https://doi.org/10.1111/0022-4537.00144
4. Crocetti, E., Albarello, F., Prati, F., Rubini, M.: Development of prejudice against immigrants and ethnic minorities in adolescence: a systematic review with meta-analysis of longitudinal studies. Dev. Rev. **60**(100959), 100959 (2021). https://doi.org/10.1016/j.dr.2021.100959
5. Brown, R., Zagefka, H.: Ingroup affiliations and prejudice. In: Dovidio, J., Glick, P., Rudman, L. (Eds.), On the Nature of Prejudice: Fifty Years After Allport (2nd ed.). Blackwell, pp. 54-70 (2008)
6. Tajfel, H., Billig, M.G., Bundy, R.P., Flament, C.: Social categorization and intergroup behaviour. Eur. J. Soc. Psychol. **1**(2), 149–178 (1971). https://doi.org/10.1002/EJSP.2420010202
7. Eisenberg, N., Fabes, R.A.: (1990). Empathy: conceptualization, measurement, and relation to prosocial behavior. Motiv. Emot. **14**(2), 131-149 (1990) https://doi.org/10.1007/BF00991640
8. Decety, J., Meyer, M.: From emotion resonance to empathic understanding: a social developmental neuroscience account. Dev. Psychopathol. **20**(4), 1053–1080 (2008). https://doi.org/10.1017/S0954579408000503
9. Baron-Cohen, S., Wheelwright, S.: The empathy quotient: an investigation of adults with asperger syndrome or high functioning autism, and normal sex differences. J. Autism Dev. Disord. **34**(2), 163–175 (2004). https://doi.org/10.1023/B:JADD.0000022607.19833.00

10. Decety, J., Lamm, C.: Human empathy through the lens of social neuroscience. Rev. Article TheScientificWorldJOURNAL **6**, 1146–1163 (2006). https://doi.org/10.1100/tsw.2006.221

11. Eisenberg, N., et al.: The relations of emotionality and regulation to dispositional and situational empathy-related responding. J. Pers. Soc. Psychol. **66**(4), 776–797 (1994). https://doi.org/10.1037//0022-3514.66.4.776

12. Dovidio, J.F., Banfield, J.C.: Prosocial behavior and empathy. Int. Encycl. Soc. Behav. Sci. Second Edition, 216–220 (2015). https://doi.org/10.1016/B978-0-08-097086-8.24024-5

13. Gerdes, K.E., Lietz, C.A., Segal, E.A.: Measuring empathy in the 21st century: development of an empathy index rooted in social cognitive neuroscience and social justice. Social Work Res. **35**(2), 83–93 (2011). https://doi.org/10.1093/SWR/35.2.83

14. Xu, W.: Enhanced ergonomics approaches for product design: a user experience ecosystem perspective and case studies. Ergonomics **57**(1), 34–51 (2014). https://doi.org/10.1080/00140139.2013.861023

15. International Organization for Standardization: ISO 9241–210:2019 - Ergonomics of Human-System Interaction — Part 210: Human-Centred Design for Interactive Systems. International Organization for Standardization. p. 33, (2019). https://www.iso.org/standard/77520.html

16. Jetter, H.C., Gerken, J.: A Simplified Model of User Experience for Practical Application. In: NordiCHI 2006 Oslo: The 2nd COST294-MAUSE International Open Workshop "User EXperience :Towards a Unified View. pp. 106–111, (2007). http://nbn-resolving.de/urn:nbn:de:bsz:352-opus-31516

17. Battarbee, K., Koskinen, I.: Co-experience: user experience as interaction. CoDesign **1**(1), 5–18 (2010). https://doi.org/10.1080/15710880412331289917

18. Cooper, A.: The Inmates Are Running the Asylum: Why High Tech Products Drive Us Crazy and How to Restore the Sanity (2nd ed.). Sams. (2004) https://www.goodreads.com/book/show/44098.The_Inmates_Are_Running_the_Asylum

19. Goh, C.H., Romainoor, N.H.: User goals, behaviours and attitudes: developing web user personas of art and design students. Art and Design Rev. **7**(1), 1–9 (2018). https://doi.org/10.4236/ADR.2019.71001

20. Cooper, A.: Defending Personas. If you love a design tool, set it free | by Alan Cooper | Medium. Medium. (2021) https://mralancooper.medium.com/defending-personas-2657fe26dd0f

21. Chapman, C.N., Milham, R.P.: The personas' new clothes: methodological and practical arguments against a popular method. In: Proceedings of the Human Factors and Ergonomics Society Annual Meeting, 50(5), 634–636, (2006). https://doi.org/10.1177/154193120605000503

22. Neris Analytics: *16Personalities*. Retrieved February 14, 2022 (n.d.) https://www.16personalities.com/

23. Cooper, A., Reimann, R., Cronin, D., Noessel, C.: About Face: The Essentials of Interaction Design (4th ed.). Wiley (2014) https://www.wiley.com/en-us/About+Face%3A+The+Essentials+of+Interaction+Design%2C+4th+Edition-p-9781118766576

The Exploration of Tools and Methods for Designing Smart Products in User Experience

Yichen Wu[✉]

China Academy of Art, Hangzhou 310000, China
wuyc@caa.edu.cn

Abstract. The smart products or smart device, are updated from normal products by implanting electronic chips and system, connecting to the Internet or other devices, and users have to operate them through the physical the digital interface. Thanks to the popularity of smart products, the economy is increasing, the relevant market is expanding. Internet of Everything and everything became smart are seems to be the new trend for part of human civilization. Thereby, the design of these technology- related product becomes the mainstream for design education. Design as the force for innovation was given greater responsibility at this time. Thereby, this research attempted to produce specific design methodology for the smart product, included design process and methods. This design methodology could be novel or updated one for creating smart products with high quality of both product and experience. When the author took an in-depth interpretation of the research road for the smart products' design methodology, which is the leading research result of the design methodology. The research of classic or novel design approaches tries to define the factors from them, which could contribute to enhancing the quality of smart products. The final outcome of this research is a basic model of design methodology for smart products. This updated design methodology is concerning both the situation of rapid iteration and quality of user experience, which are the characteristics of consumer products in this age.

Keywords: Smart products · Design tools · Interaction design · User experience

1 The Future of Smart Products

With the development of information technology and the Internet of Things, the smart products are becoming the necessity to human's life. These smart products evolved from traditional, non-electrical products by implanting chips and digital system. They are penetrating our lives and changing our behaviors and habits. Thanks to the convenience, they are bringing new growth of the economy and changing the consuming habit of society. It is also becoming a hot field for design, and many design disciplines are involving to the smart products, e.g., industrial design, interaction design, user experience design, service design. However, the smart products have high failure rate actually, most of them failed at the concept phase. The failure comes from the low concept acceptability

© The Author(s), under exclusive license to Springer Nature Switzerland AG 2022
M. M. Soares et al. (Eds.): HCII 2022, LNCS 13321, pp. 108–119, 2022.
https://doi.org/10.1007/978-3-031-05897-4_8

on crowdfunding platforms, also from the user experience quality for the products that already released into the market. These failures lead to design waste. Although there are various reasons for the success of a product, design methodology as the approach to generate the solution from concept to product, it is playing an essential role for the smart products. Meanwhile, a design methodology is always the main content for design education, and it is also applied in the profession and industry. Therefore, a specific design approach for the design of smart products is required for both the design education and industry, to enhance the quality of the smart products, especially for the user experience quality.

2 The Design Methodologies of Smart Products

2.1 The Design Process and Methods

It is necessary to have a view of the process, methods and tools when to study the design methodology of smart products, which are the components of a design methodology. Design methodologies belong to the class of procedural approaches as they contain a procedural process model and methods [1]. With the context of this research, I selected standard methodologies of Industrial Design, Interaction Design and User Experience Design with the interpretation of the specific process, methods, to have a sound understanding of them and state of the art. With the definition of design methodology, the design process comprises phases in sequence, and each step usually combines with diverse methods and tools. Briefly, it is the flow for designers to manage the problem. Moreover, the design method in the process helps designers to understand the situation and problem, and then allows them to determine what the design solution needs to do [2]. Therefore, I conducted a study of the design process first.

By the process model which based on the problem-solution based methodology by JJ Foreman in 1967, the design process included four steps which from the problem to the solution. By the descriptive model of the design process by Nigel Cross, he sorted the phases from the perspective of designers in this model, and it concluded the main tasks of designers in each step. Another design process model proposed by Bruce Archer predicts the need for different approaches in different moments, systematic observation and inductive reasoning in the analytical phase, and subjective and deductive reasoning in the creative phase [3]. Michael French produced a more detailed model of the design process in 1985. It demonstrated the outputs and activities in each stage with feedback loops. On the other hand, when I studied the general process of the Industrial Design, it has there are three primary stages: planning, development, and production. These stages define the process beyond the activities of any specific discipline [4]. The development stage of this model includes research, conceptualization and refinement. Meanwhile, when I took IxD as a research object, the IxD design methodology, as Dan Saffer discussed. The most special features of this model are the second times' divergence and convergence from the begin to the end. It shows that in the middle point is the decision of structured findings, and structured findings are research data put into a form that can be easily understood. They can be stories, models, visualizations, personas-anything that makes the unfiltered data into something helpful and actionable [5]. It is the previous step with a specific proposal before the ideation phase. During a diverging phase, designers should try to open up as much as possible without limiting themselves, whereas a converging phase focuses on condensing and narrowing designers' findings or ideas.

J. Christopher Jones, in his book Design Methods, argued that design breaks down into three stages: Divergence, transformation and convergence. Briefly, divergence is the stage to define the objectives and the problem boundary; transformation is the stage to structure the problem into subproblems and to detail all the issues of the project, it is the stage when objectives, brief, and problem boundaries are fixed, when critical variables are identified, when constraints are recognized, when opportunities are taken and when judgements are made; convergence stage is to make decisions of the final design by designers.

In order to have a general view of the design process from the macro perspective, after the study of these representative design process in history, I compared all these process models by redrawing all these models in the horizontal view, and parted each step by tasks, activities and outcomes, all of them can ergonomics as with four steps. Whatsmore, I created a universal model which can be the theoretical design process to interpret the stages and the main purpose and activities of them (see Fig. 1).

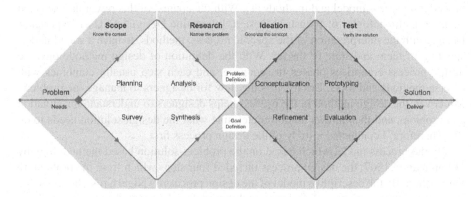

Fig. 1. The typical model of the design process

The model integrated the similar phases of the diverse models into four steps, which also follow the process of problem-establishing needs-satisfying needs-solution. Meanwhile, it applied the second divergence-convergence form for seeking more opportunities and possibilities of the solution. Specifically, in this model,

- The scoping stage is to plan the design project and to conduct the survey, and it includes the scheduling, understanding the competitors, it is the phase to collect the data for research;
- In the research stage, designers' task is to analyze the data, and to work out the explicit definitions of the problem and users' need;
- In the ideation stage, designers start to conceptualize the ideas and to refine them in time. The various concepts could include all the aspects of the product, such as the user interface, the functions, the interactive forms, and so on. Indeed, all of them should concern the experience of the user;

- Once the idea comes to visible by virtual model or sketches, they should be developed into perceptible prototypes or models in the stage of the test. Designers, users and other stakeholders have to evaluate as much as the factors of the products, such as aesthetics, ergonomics, perception, experience, and so on.

Besides the process, another component of the design methodology in the form is the method. By definition, a method is a procedure or technique for obtaining findings or knowledge. It is a philosophy and approach that lends clarity to and facilitates the designer's work. It helps designers understand the situation and problem, and then allows them to determine what the design solution needs to do [2]. According to the initial survey, there are over one hundred standard design methods for diverse design methodologies, although most of them are employed in the same design methodologies simultaneously. Certainly, it is still too much for me to research each of them. Thus, I selected and analyzed the methods and tools in the typical and emerging design methodologies those fits for the industrial design and interaction design, they included User-Cantered Design, Goal-Directed Design, typical Industrial Design, Agile, Lean UX and Design Sprint, these focused analyses were effective and efficient in this research context.

In this phase of research, I will discuss all the six standard and emerging design methodologies from the process to the methods. The study on each methodology will analyze the process, principle and features first, and then mention the methods of them. Because there are repeating methods among these approaches, the interpretations of them will discuss together with analyses. I intended to generate a new or updated design methodology for smart products to enhance the quality both of the product and experience by adopting the advantages from these conventional or new design approaches with concerning the quality factors of the smart product. By combining the previous research, the smart products are produced for enhancing the experience by making traditional products into smart ones or created for satisfying the new need of users, and the main characteristic of the smart product is the combination of the physical part and the digital part. Therefore, the new design has to fit the design of both the tangible and the virtual parts of the smart products.

2.2 The Methods and Tools of the Design Methodologies

Follow the study of both traditional and emerging design methodologies, and I realize the difference between the two kinds of approaches, especially in the new ones, there are some unique methods and tools. Therefore, after the process analysis, I intended to interpret the methods those adopted in the approaches I studied above, and to define the stages involves the specific methods. It is the preparation of the smart product design methodology research in next phase.

The methods and tools listed here are from the UCD, GDD, typical industrial design methodology, Lean UX and Design Sprint. The order of them followed the sequence of the approaches we discussed. Most of the methods are repeated in the design methodologies, especially in the standard design approaches (Table 1).

Table 1. The comparison of the methods' adoption

Method	Applied methodology	Applied stages			
		Scope	Research	Ideation	Test
Personas	UCD / GDD / Lean UX	/	●	●	/
Scenarios	UCD / GDD	/	●	●	/
Use case	UCD	/	●	/	/
Focus group	UCD	●	/	/	/
Usability testing	UCD / GDD	/	/	●	●
Card sorting	UCD	/	●	/	/
Co-design	UCD / GDD / Design Sprint	/	●	●	●
Interviews	UCD / GDD / Lean UX	/	●	●	●
Ethnography	GDD	/	●	/	/
Observations	UCD / GDD	/	●	/	/
Storyboards	GDD / Lean UX	/	/	●	/
Sketching	UCD / GDD / Design Sprint	/	/	●	/
Prototyping	UCD / GDD / Lean UX/ Design Sprint	/	/	●	●
Case study	UCD / GDD	/	●	/	/
Design brief	UCD / GDD / Lean UX/ Design Sprint	●	/	/	/
Brainstorming	UCD / GDD	/	/	●	/
Design charrette	Lean UX	/	●	/	/
Wireframes	UCD / GDD / Lean UX	/	/	●	●
Lightning talk	Design Sprint	●	/	/	/
Experience map	UCD / GDD / Design Sprint	/	●	/	/
Empathy	Design Sprint	/	●	/	/
User journey	UCD / GDD / Design Sprint	/	●	/	/
Success metrics & signals	Design Sprint	/	●	/	/
The golden path	Design Sprint	/	●	/	/
Future press release	Design Sprint	/	/	/	●
Crazy 8's	Design Sprint	/	/	●	/
Solution Sketch	Design Sprint	/	/	●	/

The result demonstrates the most adopted methods, which also the common ones in design activities, such as design brief, literature reviews, sketching, prototyping. It indicates there are the indispensable methods in the design process for a design approach. The methods those for user study are employed by many of the approach, which includes personas, scenarios, interviews, experience mapping. Furthermore, storyboards, case study, brainstorming are the usual methods for design activities. From the stages' point of view, several methods throughout the process and are used at least two stages, such as personas, scenarios, usability testing, participatory design, interviews, literature reviews, prototyping, 3D modelling, wireframes.

In contrast, most of the methods in emerging design approaches are used in only one stage by each of them, such as lighting talk, business model canvas, future press release, crazy 8's, they are specified and efficiency. Beside these targeted methods, there are some unique methods which only be employed by one approach and one stage, and they are including focus group, card sorting, ethnography, 3D modelling. To have detailed analyses of them, some of them used for specific object, for instance, 3D modelling is applied for physical product design; some of them need resource and time to carry out in the process, for example, ethnography need long term immersive, while focus group and card sorting require cooperation of users. Whatsmore, the emerging design methodologies adopt business-related methods to meet the current design trends and needs. In conclusion, as the result of comparing and combining the performance of applied methodology and stages, personas, scenarios, usability testing, interviews, observations, literature reviews, storyboards, sketching, prototyping, case study, design brief, brainstorming, brainstorming, 3D modelling, user journey, experience mapping and business-related methods can be referred to the design methodology of smart products.

2.3 The Flexibility of Design Methodology in Practice

The design methodology, as its definition I discussed at the beginning of this chapter. Briefly, it focused on the design process, to employ appropriate methods, and manage them for a sustainable solution for a problem. It is a translation to interpret designers' knowledge to a product by considering the diverse situation by practical design activities. The design methodology should contribute to the improvement of design practice, particularly by exploiting scientific methods [6].

Nevertheless, the conditions and context for each project are different from others, multiple constraints should be coordinated simultaneously, such as the environment, time, financial supports, the task for each participator in the team and so on, theses mass issues promote the designer to seek and set appropriate methodology for balancing all the constraints. Therefore, there are no restricted rules for the employment of the design methodology in designing a product. It is flexible and dynamic to organize the steps in the process and the specific methods.

A lot of effort has been invested in finding out that designers do not usually work to the guidelines of design methodology [7]. After all, the purpose of the design is to create a product bring benefit to all the stakeholders as much as possible, to satisfy users, clients, customers, and so on. To use a design methodology serves for finding an appropriate approach to promote innovation.

Furthermore, in most cases, the adoption of design methodologies and the strategies for using them are the tasks of individual designers or the design teams. It caused any of the personal and groups' factors will impact the application of the design methodology. As the characteristics and capabilities of the individual designers, the experience and knowledge of them influence thought and actions to choose the process and methods. With this feature, as a group of various practitioners, a design team should well organize each members' capabilities and knowledge to establish an available design approach.

In this case, as the component of the design methodology, the process is not fixed; it depends on the time and resource constraints. The designer has to plan and control the whole process by arranging the sub-process in a flexible way [8]. For instance, the design process of GDD takes a long term since it adopts ethnography and interviews which require a certain number of users to participate, designers then should spend time to observe and communicate with them. This kind of design approach not appropriate for the start-ups, which are short of the human, and financial resources, their designers have to allocate all the resources rationally and create market-competitive products within a particular time. Thus, for a start-up company, maybe to refer to the Agile related design approach for innovation is a more sensible choice. Designers can set the particular number of the stages and reorder the sequence of them in the process by the project and the realistic conditions.

On the other hand, the flexible adoption of methods in the process is also an issue for the designers. All the methods in the process should be adapted to the context by designers, their purpose is to support the design process, and they should not simply be undertaken as routine tasks [9]. Therefore, the designer must be able to choose appropriate methods in a particular situation, given a set of characteristics specific to the interaction between designer and the situation, to make the design methodology support designers appropriately [7]. Additionally, some of the methods still have a lack of professionalism and targeted dilemma, and they desire to be used flexibly from other methods, for instance, the design methods and tools for interaction design. There is not a clear and developed set of core tools that have been commonly accepted and given a well-defined purpose and place in the interaction design process, and interaction designers often draw upon many different existing design traditions and tools from fields as diverse as fine arts and graphic design to mechanical engineering [10]. From this point of view, designers have to employ the specific design methods with a clear understanding of the method, to define the advantage which fit for the design project.

In conclusion, the adoption of design process and methods by designers is dynamic. It is a coordination activity for the designer to consider the actual limitations and affordability of the design team to the project. Besides the knowledge of design methods, designers should have capabilities to choose appropriate methods for the design task, instead of employing them conventionally.

3   The Updated Design Process and Methods for Smart Products

By all the previous survey, analysis and discussion in this research, there is no specific design methodology for smart products, which includes hardware, software and service. The community requires an exploration of research a design methodology to enhance the quality of smart products, the quality focus on not only the product but also the user experience of the end-user. Meanwhile, from the results of the research on design methodology that had been completed, the specific design methodology of smart products was gradually formed. Additionally, combined with the character and quality factors of the smart product, the design approach of smart products shaped its features. The features distinguished the difference to other design methodologies and specified the unique design techniques for the interactive, technology products. Thereby, from the perspective of establishing a new design methodology or upgrading an existed design methodology, these features could be referred to as the basis at the same time. Based on the previous argument of the design methodologies and the survey of the design methodologies' adoption in Chinese industry, here I discuss the design methodology of smart products from the process to the methods.

3.1 The Design Process for Smart Products

As argued before, the design process as the framework for programing the methods to obtain the data and promote the project, it has to plan the main stages and their order clearly before the implementation. Therefore, the principles for developing the design process are the initial and critical task. Specifically, the principles include:

- It is a general model. First of all, it has to declare again that the design process is a general model in this research context as mentioned before, it constructs the main stages and the tasks in each of them, while the specific content in the process has to depend on the requirements of the specific project. From a macro perspective, therefore, it is the framework to divide the phases by following the procedure of problem-exploration-solution-testing. And the basic structure referred to the updated double diamond which worked out by the study of the diverse design process in the development history in the previous research section.
- There are two subprocesses. As argued in chapter two, the combination of physical and digital products is one of the main features of the smart products. In other words, the implementation of the design tasks in the entire process are the design of tangible objects and the software, in which they relate to Industrial Design and Interaction Design, and physical user interface and graphic user interface are the targets for the designers. Thereby, the design process of a smart product must include these two design parts as subprocesses, and they should be conducted paralleled in an ideal situation. Which means these two procedures begin simultaneously, both of them start from the scoping stage, then to through the stages of research, ideation and test. Indeed, the participators in these two subprocesses have to communicate continually, to ensure the conformity of the product and the software, for instance, the color and the form of the tangible product, even the interactive mode should be reflected in its application for the smartphone.
- It combines the process of both traditional and emerging design approaches. Since the design process relating to the design of the physical and digital product, it should adopt the Industrial Design, Interaction Design and User Experience Design, which are the traditional design methodologies I had analyzed and discussed before. Also, with considering state of the art of design approach's employment in the industry and

the competition of the market, Agile related design methodologies are the approaches to make the design of smart products satisfies the user need and adapts market requirements in time. Thus, on the one hand, the design process based on the traditional design process for creating a product in stable pace; on the other hand, the characteristic of emerging design methodologies provides the design process have the flexibility to adjust the steps, activities and the rhythm.

- The sprints in the process are frequently. By the complexity of the smart product, as a technology product to interact with the user, the experience of the user in the interaction is the primary measurement to determine the quality of the smart product to the user, which I had deduced in the previous chapter, it includes usability, reliability, communication and so on. Thereby, it requires designers to decide the most appropriate solution efficiently. By referring to the Agile design methodology, sprints are a beneficial approach to find the best solution. The design process should adopt the sprint strategy, either for the physical product or for the software, especially in the refinement and test phases. In order to find an appropriate solution for the user precisely, the prototypes or demonstrations must be tested by users or practitioner themselves several times. The sprint of ideation, test, refinement have to be conducted frequently, and they can be carried out not only for the design subprocess of tangible or digital products but also for the final solution with the integration of hardware and software.
- Setting the priority of design tasks, to use a main functional product occupy the market. Because of the fierce competition of the market and limited resources for the companies, especially for the start-ups, the timeliness of product entering the market is critical for these companies, the earlier, the better, to open up potential markets and brand awareness. However, it is impossible to create an ideal product for users. It is a step-by-step process to satisfy more need from users. Therefore, to create the product with main and essential functions is the primary requirement of a company from the business's point of view, then to optimize the product by constant iterations. Indeed, the product can be improved by the user's feedback from the usage of the initial generation product. Consequently, in the design process, the practitioners have to set the priority of the design tasks, to arrange the sequence of the importance of functions. It can guide the practitioners to focus on the creation of the first version product, and also consider and plan the design activities for future iterations.

About the setting of design methods, as the specific approaches in design activities, design methods help designers to collect the information and data, they are the tools for creativity. Based on the previous research, there are several methods from traditional and emerging design methodologies, they cover the typical approaches in Industrial Design, Interaction Design and User Experience design, although there are over one hundred design methods in the industry. In this design methodology for smart products, the adoption of methods refers to the popular ones in the previous research with principles.

- The flexible adoption. Through the previous discussion, we agree that the employment of the design methodology in practice is determined by the specific requirements of the stakeholders and the conditions of the practitioners. As a general model, like to the process, the methods in this design methodology for smart products are optional, they are the common ones to be referred. Designers could select the specific ones flexibly by considering the factors of the project.

- Focus on the time control and the efficient of the user study. Because of the fierce market competition and the rapid development of technology, the design of smart products requires to consider efficiency as the primary factor. Designers should seek the methods to create the product that satisfies the needs of users and has high quality in a short time. It means the methodology requires specific methods to control the cost of time in design and understand the users efficiently. From previous research, the design brief is the method for time control and schedule planning, and there are some sophisticated methods for enhancing the efficiency in user research, such as Participatory Design, Storyboards, Experience mapping, Crazy 8's and so on. On the contrary, the methods of consuming time and resources maybe not fit for short time development, such as the ethnography.

- To involve business-related methods. In the study of emerging design methodology, especially in the Design Sprint, it adopts the methods from business strategy, such as Business model canvas, Future press release. They are the typical approaches to make designers think about the feasibility of a potential solution from a commercial and operational perspective. After all, from the perspective of the value, the profitability of products is fundamental. On the other hand, the smart product as the tangible product to embody the service system; it is no longer the product that users use it unilaterally. It desires to adopt an appropriate business model to create commercial value while promotes users to use it continuedly.

- It encourages practitioners to employ crowdfunding platforms. With the research on the possibility of crowdfunding platform as the design methods, these on-line open platforms suitable for creative products. It is an integration of effective and efficient design tools for entrepreneurs to find potential users and communicate with them. It is a kind of user-oriented approach to meet the needs of users with the best solution. Moreover, it controls the design costs strictly, both the creators and backers involve in a project with minimal risk because of the all-or-nothing operating mechanism. Therefore, it is very worth trying to adopt the crowdfunding platform as an auxiliary design method from the stage of ideation in the process, to collect feedbacks of the concept and to refine it by sprints.

3.2 The Typical and Updated Design Methodology for Smart Products

From the design process, is based on the general model, which I developed from the integration of diverse design process in previous research. Since it has already been discussed before, I will not repeat this general process. The primary features of the updated process include the subprocess and the sprints. The physical product and the digital product are separated and developed at the same time in two lines, which means the design process of the hardware and the software of the products are carried out in parallel. The two subprocesses also apply the four stages with double diverges and converges, both of them require to communicate with each other in the procedure, to coordinate the time and deal with some design issues together. The frequent communications ensure the project to follow the schedule and in the same direction. Indeed, the principal purpose of communication is to promote the consistency of design, to unified the form, style, interaction for the enhancement of user experience. In the stages of ideation and test, the frequent sprints of evaluation and refinement are the main activity for the designers and developers. The efficiency is the core of both hardware design and software development in these two phases. Besides the sprints in each subprocess, the sprint of the final solution, which combined the physical and digital parts is the most critical activity. For instance, once the designers found value feedback or data from the test, to take a week to refine and verify it again is an efficient approach, as refer to the process of Design Sprint. The sprints in the controlled period drive the participators to improve the product into a better one to the users.

To base on the process framework, the specific contents in the methodology are demonstrated in Fig. 2.

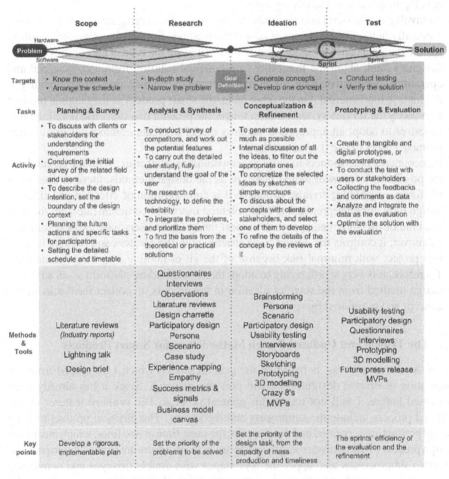

	Scope	Research	Ideation	Test
Targets	• Know the context • Arrange the schedule	• In-depth study • Narrow the problem	• Generate concepts • Develop one concept	• Conduct testing • Verify the solution
Tasks	Planning & Survey	Analysis & Synthesis	Conceptualization & Refinement	Prototyping & Evaluation
Activity	• To discuss with clients or stakeholders for understanding the requirements • Conducting the initial survey of the related field and users • To describe the design intention, set the boundary of the design context • Planning the future actions and specific tasks for participators • Setting the detailed schedule and timetable	• To conduct survey of competitors, and work out the potential features • To carry out the detailed user study, fully understand the goal of the user • The research of technology, to define the feasibility • To integrate the problems, and prioritize them • To find the basis from the theoretical or practical solutions	• To generate ideas as much as possible • Internal discussion of all the ideas, to filter out the appropriate ones • To concretize the selected ideas by sketches or simple mockups • To discuss about the concepts with clients or stakeholders, and select one of them to develop • To refine the details of the concept by the reviews of it	• Create the tangible and digital prototypes, or demonstrations • To conduct the test with users or stakeholders • Collecting the feedbacks and comments as data • Analyze and integrate the data as the evaluation • Optimize the solution with the evaluation
Methods & Tools	Literature reviews *(Industry reports)* Lightning talk Design brief	Questionnaires Interviews Observations Literature reviews Design charrette Participatory design Persona Scenario Case study Experience mapping Empathy Success metrics & signals Business model canvas	Brainstorming Persona Scenario Participatory design Usability testing Interviews Storyboards Sketching Prototyping 3D modelling Crazy 8's MVPs	Usability testing Participatory design Questionnaires Interviews Prototyping 3D modelling Future press release MVPs
Key points	Develop a rigorous, implementable plan	Set the priority of the problems to be solved	Set the priority of the design task, from the capacity of mass production and timeliness	The sprints' efficiency of the evaluation and the refinement

Fig. 2. The design methodology for smart products

To base on the process, the detailed contents of the methodology are demonstrated in Fig. 3. In this general framework, all the elements are for reference. There is not rules but pieces of advice and guidelines. The targets, tasks, activities and methods are suitable for the physical and digital product. Indeed, most of the participators in the project will involve both the hardware and software design. For instance, the interaction designers should take part in the design of the part of the tangible product with industrial designers and structural engineers, to take charge of the physical interface design. They also have to join the design of the application for smartphones with developers, to think the functionality, usability, accessibility of the software, and to design the user interface of it. Thereby, under this circumstance, the designers could play a role as coordinators in the communication between the two subprocesses.

The list of methods and tools in the framework is the result of integrated the previous research. It selected the methods in traditional and emerging design approaches by considering the actual limitations of time, funding, resource in the circumstance with the fierce market competition. All of the methods and tools are optional, and practitioners can choose any of them with the realistic situation of the project, to form their design approach for the design activity.

References

1. Gericke, K., Blessing, L.: Comparisons of design methodologies and process models across disciplines: a literature review. In: Proceedings of the 18th International Conference on Engineering Design. Design Society (2011)
2. Karjaluoto, E.: The design method: A philosophy and process for functional visual communication. New Riders (2013)
3. van der Linden, J.C.S., de Lacerda, A.P., de Aguiar, J.P.O.: The evolution of design methods. In: Conference: 9th International Conference of the European Academy of Design, Porto (2011)
4. Cuffaro, D., Zaksenberg, I.: The Industrial Design Reference & Specification Book: Everything Industrial Designers Need to Know Every Day. Rockport Publishers (2013)
5. Saffer, D.: Designing for Interaction: Creating Innovative Applications and Devices. New Riders (2010)
6. Kroes, P.: Design methodology and the nature of technical artefacts. Des. Stud. **23**(3), 287–302 (2002)
7. Badke-Schaub, P., Daalhuizen, J., Roozenburg, N.: Towards a designer-centred methodology: descriptive considerations and prescriptive reflections. In: Birkhofer, H. (ed.) The future of design methodology, pp. 181–197. Springer London, London (2011). https://doi.org/10.1007/978-0-85729-615-3_16
8. Birkhofer, H., Kloberdanz, H., Berger, B., Sauer, T.: Cleaning up design methods-describing methods completely and standardised. In: DS 30: Proceedings of DESIGN 2002, the 7th International Design Conference, Dubrovnik (2002)
9. Wallace, K.: Transferring design methods into practice. In: Birkhofer, H. (ed.) The future of design methodology, pp. 239–248. Springer London, London (2011). https://doi.org/10.1007/978-0-85729-615-3_21
10. Stolterman, E., Pierce, J.: Design tools in practice: studying the designer-tool relationship in interaction design. In: Proceedings of the Designing Interactive Systems Conference. ACM, pp. 25-28 (2012)

Building up Personas by Clustering Behavior Motivation from Extreme Users

Xin Xin[1], Yonghao Wang[2], Yiwen Zhang[1], Qianqian Wu[1], Wenmin Yang[1], Chenhong Yang[1], Rongrong Zhang[2], Michael T. Lai[2(✉)], and Wei Liu[1(✉)]

[1] Beijing Normal University, Beijing, China
Wei.liu@bnu.edu.cn
[2] X-Thinking Institute, Shanghai, China
Mike@tangux.com

Abstract. This paper introduces a new practical approach to developing a persona via the extreme user. The behavior of extreme users provides the distinguished dimension on grouping different persona. This research collects data from observation and deep-in interviews, with analyzed the interview data sentence by sentence, five dimensions are filtered by the principles that can provide guidance for the design and distinguish the user portrait. The scales on each dimension are used to describe the refine characters of the persona, to have the persona be stereo and vivid. Finally, five personas were set up in the theme of health in the middle class: "corporation slave sport by mind", "self-discipline middle in a dilemma", "sports talent overdo lead to injury", "home care keeper" and "ageless lady". Common trends are also understood thoroughly from interview data to support persona. This approach is trying to grab sensible information from typical users to build up a persona and to get precise user features for commercial use.

Keywords: Persona · Extreme user · Distinguished dimension

1 Introduction

1.1 Persona

Persona is a tool to describe the actual target user group with an abstract labeled virtual user representative model. Williams (2021) claims that persona has been widely used in various fields where systems, services, or products are being designed for human use. As a tool for describing target users, the significance of user profiling lies is in refining the target users and helping to explore their behavioral patterns and specific user needs (Huh et al 2016). On the other hand, it lies in further segmenting and fleshing out the users, providing the parts of the target users that form a differentiation from other user groups.

1.2 Manual Clustering Method of Persona Development

Concerning the persona development process, Brickey et al. (2012) summarized and suggested that "persona development teams often pursue various methods to developing

© The Author(s), under exclusive license to Springer Nature Switzerland AG 2022
M. M. Soares et al. (Eds.): HCII 2022, LNCS 13321, pp. 120–131, 2022.
https://doi.org/10.1007/978-3-031-05897-4_9

personas, including which type of data to use. Nonetheless, the different persona development methods are usually shared four steps": (1) Identify target users, (2) Collect user data, (3) Group users into personas, (4) Create and present persona details. Since users possess many attributes such as natural, social, and behavioral attributes, we need to identify which of the many attributes on users are responsible for the differences among users. As suggested by Mulder and Yaar (2012), grouping users into personas (step 3) is essential to the effectiveness of the final personas, capturing user needs, identifying key differences between users, and generating clusters.

The clustering of persona must be based on user data (step 2). Qualitative or quantitative data collection methods, such as user interviews, focus groups, and questionnaires can be used. Although, Jansen (2020) argues that conditions such as online social media (Khan et al. 2019), system analysis platforms (Berg et al. 2019) can help realize data-driven personas created by algorithms (An et al. 2018). In the persona development process, we cannot get the specific scenarios and psychological attributes of users from charts and figures of those quantitative data. As well as we can only portray the deep-seated attributes from reasons, demands, and motives behind users' behaviors. Therefore, most of the persona studies still use qualitative methods (Lee et al. 2021), although Cooper (1999) stated that designers should use qualitative data to create personas, and Goodwin (2002) strongly recommended it.

The method of collecting user data determines the technique of persona clustering. As Brickey (2010) argued persona recognition and clustering only rely on the same type of data, including manual operations to identify users and qualitative clustering techniques using semi-automated statistical software are the most commonly used techniques for clustering personas. Goodwin (2002) is one of the representative researchers who advocates the use of rich qualitative data from interviews or observations for manual clustering and summarizes the necessary steps to complete the creation of the final persona. Her manual clustering method as described in (Cooper et al. 2007) is to list the significant behaviors of users into several groups of behavioral variables (including several aspects of users' activities, attitudes, abilities, motivations, skills, etc.). Then the subjects of the interview and the behavioral variables correspond one by one, and the significant behavioral model combinations are identified and adjusted to form personas. This study is based on Goodwin's manual clustering method, which separates users with extreme attribute values at both ends of significant behavioral variables into a group after screening.

2   Method

This study develops a new approach to grouping persona, which is based on Goodwin's manual clustering method. This approach separates users with extreme attribute values by extremum significant behavioral variables. Meanwhile, common dimensional attributes should also be properly recruited according to the goal of the study (Fig. 1). The behavioral characteristics and needs of extreme users are often amplified and exaggerated from common users, and the descriptions of their ideas and behaviors will be clearer and more explicit than those of common users. Therefore, the research results on the demanding needs of extreme users can generally meet the needs of common users.

Meanwhile, it should be noted that all the personas cannot be separated from the data from interviews, we need to go back to the interviewee to see if there is a matching real persona archetype, and to ensure the personas are real and typical.

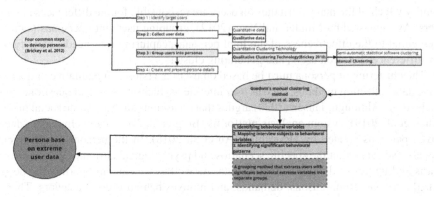

Fig. 1. Research flow chart

This study will present the whole process of grouping users into personas and dimensional segmentation filtering, explain specifically the proposed grouping method of extracting users with significant behavioral extremes into separate groups. The persona identified by this method could be flexibly fit the requirements and the true state of the project, and filtered by the distinct level.

3 Case Studies

3.1 Project Background

According to McKinsey's China Consumer Survey 2020, the number of middle-class shows a clear upward trend, is already exceeding 300 million and continuing to rise, and is expected to exceed 500 million by 2025. "National Health Insight Report" published by "Dingxiang Doctor" mentions that health consumption is increasing with the growth of health awareness. People believe that health is crucial in all their life, and the scale and number of people consuming health products online have been rising in recent years.

With the influence of pandemic from the new crown virus, the new health era has come, there is an apparent change in the middle class regarding their living status, consumption, and health concepts. The concepts of exercise and a healthy diet are receiving widespread attention. Their high consumption level and unique consumption style influence their attitude on healthy. The growth of the number, the urgent demand of middle-class people for health, and the change and improvement of their health concepts will inject new vitality and vigor into the development of the health industry.

As the backbone of Chinese society in the workplace and family, middle-class people are no longer just suffering from physical health problems caused by overtime work, insomnia, overwork, aging, and illnesses accumulated when they were young. There is also a sense of crisis and psychological anxiety brought about by work and family.

Accurately grasping this group can bring new opportunities for the health industry and usher in new market opportunities. User profiling is a labeled model abstracted from behavioral information, which can analyze potential users of products and market to specific groups for commercial purposes. Therefore, to grasp the new trend of the middle class in health consumption, building personals can help us clarify what their health concerns are, what their needs are, and what kind of life state they want to achieve. We can distinguish the main groups of the middle class and find new consumption scenarios, business models, and marketing channels.

3.2 Select Participants

The middle-class definition in this project is the annual personal income of 120,000 RMB per year or more in first-tier cities; 90,000 RMB per year or more in second-tier cities, with a stable living environment and stable economic income. In the preliminary desktop research, after the frequency analysis and clustering of crucial information in relevant information and industry reports. The project gets conclusion on: firstly, in terms of health consumption, 50% of the relevant information mentioned that the middle class is willing to pay for exercise, whether it is buying avant-garde fitness equipment or immersing themselves in the gym. Secondly, the middle class regards the label of homemade and natural foods as an important standard of healthy food (Devia et al. 2021), this indicates that the middle class is health-conscious and keen on their food choices. In addition, the middle class spends more attention on household health care and think a lot of features, formula, and branding. Finally, the health consciousness of the middle class is upgraded from problem-solving to prevention and management, physical to mental health, and mental health is gradually becoming a hot issue for the middle class. Thus, it can be shown that the four aspects: Sport, Diet, Health care, and Psychology are instructive for this study. Therefore, we set the selection criteria for the subjects from these four aspects (Table 1), and the subjects were shown with the corresponding characteristics. The percentage of these four criteria in the final recruited subjects are: 40% has significant behavior on diet, 30% has significant behavior on doing exercise, 16% has significant behavior on health care, and 14% has clear tendency to keep psychological health. These included subjects with extreme performance in one aspect, which could cover the relevant characteristics of the general subjects to a certain extent, and the behavioral characteristics were more significant.

Table 1. Participant selection criteria

Aspect	Meet the conditions
Diet	Regular meals a day with less sugar, salt, oil
	Drink no more than once a week
	Junk food no more than twice a week
Sport	Go to the gym or take a dance, yoga, or personal trainer class
	Jogging 5 km or swimming 2 km at least 3 times a week for more than 6 months

(*continued*)

Table 1. (*continued*)

Aspect	Meet the conditions
Psychology	Pay attention to mental health (paid classes, official accounts, etc.) more than 3 times a week
	Adhere to psychological therapy (meditation, mindfulness, group therapy, etc.) for at least one month
Health care	Take health care products every day or use a home therapy machine every week for more than six months
	Health therapy (massage, foot therapy, cupping, acupuncture, massage, etc.) more than once a month, and adhere to more than half a year

3.3 Research Procedure

After selecting the subjects, we conducted one-on-one in-depth interviews with subjects who met the specific health behaviors and clustered the information from the interview results. A total of 12 dimensions were acquired, namely age, family status, income, the primary source of information, disposable time, perception, urgency, motivation, behavior, diet, exercise, and health care. The process of producing user portraits is divided into two main stages. In the first stage, filter 12 dimensions, the advantageous dimensions should fully reflect the user's characteristics and the determine user's behavior. The filtered dimensions should be able to distinguish the crowd. The user's characteristics and the determination of user's behavior should be the standard of screening the dimension, after a large amount of discussion and iteration, we get the final critical dimensions: available time, the urgency of health, motivation of health, behavior of health and primary source of information (Fig. 2). In the second stage, scale the critical dimensions, the

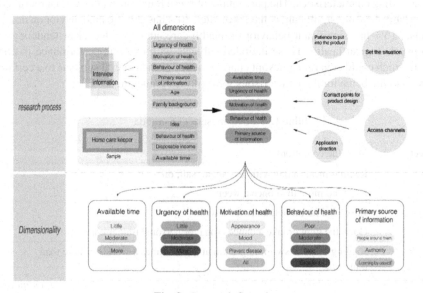

Fig. 2. Research flow chart

behavioral dimension characteristics are summarized to describe the person. The details of the interview text are mined to improve the characteristics of the profile and behavioral motivation (Fig. 2). With this rich information, the final personas and subsequent insights could be established.

Phase 1: Produce Dimensions
This phase aims to understand the subjects adequately and cluster as many dimensions as possible. In addition to the clustering, a behavioral dimension analysis of extreme users was used to find dimensions, that is to extract dimensions for the key characteristics of a user with significant behaviors. For example, one extreme subject was a full-time housewife, her husband's income can cover all the expenses of the whole family. She'd like to choose high-quality food and products. She learns a lot on health for the health of her husband and children by herself. Therefore, she is characterized by having a lot of disposable income and disposable time, having a scientific and comprehensive health concept and knowledge, and taking health activities regularly. Therefore, four dimensions of disposable income, disposable time, health perceptions, and health behaviors were extracted based on the characteristics of this extreme subject. In addition to this, other eight dimensions were also proposed in this way. Thus, the final output was 12 dimensions.

In dimension screening, the selection of dimensions is based on the principles that can provide guidance for the design and distinguish the user portrait (Fig. 3). Five dimensions emerged from the interview data.

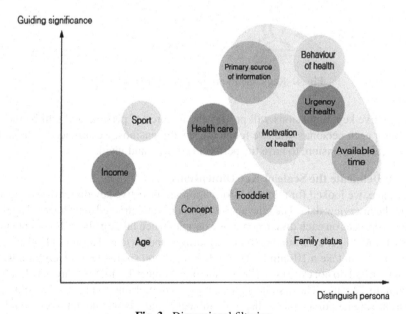

Fig. 3. Dimensional filtering

First, the source of information is the channel through which the user obtains information. The information source can clarify the scenarios and facilitate the identification of the touchpoints between the user and the product. It is possible to precisely deliver features and products to specific groups efficiently. Therefore, information sources are highly instructive and generally distinguishable to the portrait.

Second, motivation of health can help designers understand the psychology of users and find the internal need for features, operations, and design. Capturing users' psychological motivation can help better accomplish growth goals. Therefore, the differentiation of user motivation to the portrait is higher compared to information sources.

Third, the urgency of health can help designers target features properly. Urgency is how eagerly the users want to solve the pinpoint. The higher urgency of the pain points, the more likely the user want to use the product. The urgency has a high guiding meaning and a high degree to distinct the persona.

Fourth, available time, affects how much patience the user has to devote to health, it determines the user context and interaction. Therefore, the guiding meaning of disposable time and the differentiation of user portraits are both higher.

Fifth, the behavior of health, the behavior can restore the natural process when using a product. Therefore, the guiding meaning of behavioral performance and the differentiation of persona are both crucial. (Fig. 4).

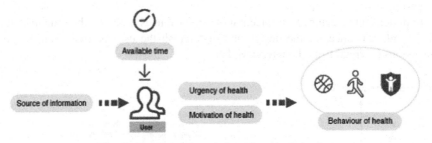

Fig. 4. Key dimensions influencing user behavior

These five key dimensions will portray the features of persona and will be the distinction for each persona. After we found the key dimensions, we still need to refine the scale on each dimension, to have the persona be stereo and vivid.

Phase 2: Delineate the Scale of Key Dimensions

In this stage, we looked for relevant information on these five key dimensions by going back to the interview data. The relevant information was extracted and clustered again to refine the degrees on each dimension. For example, when talking about disposable time, subject 1 said, "I get up around 6:10 in the morning and go to bed around 11:30 at night. Sometimes I can take a 10-min or 20-min break at noon so that I can sleep for a while, and sometimes I do not even take a break at noon." Subject 2 said, "My day may last from 6:30 a.m. to 12 p.m." These subjects were busy from morning to night, so we clustered them as having less time at their disposal. Subject 3 said, "Now I do not work, so it is all rest and no rest." In this case, we classify them as having more disposable time. Then we define the disposable time of users in between these two states as a medium. Similarly, we divided the other four dimensions into degrees at the same approach. Corresponding quantitative, as well as qualitative degree descriptions, are presented in Table 2.

Table 2. Dimensional scales

Dimensions	Degree			
Available time	Little Working seven days and having to work overtime every week	Moderate Working days from 9 am to 5 pm, two days off on weekends	More Freelance, more freedom	
Urgency of health	Little Relatively healthy and does not affect daily life	Moderate Indisposition and maintain consciously	More Need to take medical treatment	
Motivation of health	Appearance Manage the body and maintain skin beauty	Mood Keep healthy purely for fun and pleasure	Prevent disease Reduce disease and increase resistance	All No specific motivation
Behavior of health	Poor Not investing time and energy in managing health	Moderate Make healthy behaviors, at the same time, make unhealthy behaviors	Good Make efforts on healthy behavior, and get proper results	Excellent Comprehensive and systematic health management is very effective
The primary source of information	People around them (Friends, colleagues, family)	Authority (Doctor, coach)	Learning by oneself (Books, popular science, experience)	

In addition, while describing the dimensional scales, each subject was clustered on the corresponding dimension. Each category of users had the same scale on the same dimension, then the personals were named according to the most critical dimensional characteristics, the six personas were derived as Corporation slave sport by mind, Self-discipline middle in a dilemma, Sports talent overdo lead to injury, Homecare keeper, Ageless lady, and Scientific health rich woman.

4 Results

4.1 Personas and Insights

Among the six personas obtained in the second stage, the "rich woman in scientific health" and the "Home care keeper" have remarkable similarities in terms of available time (more), concept (scientific and comprehensive), and behavior (excellent), meanwhile, the representation of rich women are not strong, and the number of users is small compared with homemakers, so we merged them. Therefore, we have five personas left: Corporate slave sport by mind, Self-discipline middle in a dilemma, Sports talent overdo lead to injury, Homecare keeper, and Ageless lady. Table 3 shows the distinction of the five portraits on each critical dimension.

Table 3. Degree of user profiling dimensions

Personal	Available time	Urgency of health	Motivation of health	Behavior of health	The primary source of information
Corporation slave sport by the mind	Little	Moderate	Mood	Poor	People around them
Self-discipline middle in a dilemma	Moderate	More	Prevent disease	Moderate	Learning by oneself
Sports talent overdo lead to injury	Moderate	Little	Mood	Good	Authority
Home care keeper	More	Moderate	Prevent disease	Excellent	Learning by oneself
Ageless lady	Moderate	More	Appearance	Good	People around them

After building up the personas, we returned to the interview text again to dig behavior insight sentence by sentence for each persona. Only with the insight behind the behavior, we can find the common motivation to guide future functional design and product development.

Corporate Slave Sport by the Mind
Overtime work imprisoned more of their health freedom. They cannot squeeze in time to cook and do exercise, which is the biggest stumbling block on their health road. They are also aware of their poor health; they try to change, but the large amount of work limits their healthy behaviors. The office is where they spend most of the day and where they do their health behaviors. They want to do health activities without much effort anytime and anywhere.

Self-discipline Middle in a Dilemma
These people already understand the importance of health and have urgent needs for health care. However, they have to engage in unhealthy behaviors for various reasons, such as drinking or working overtime, but they often consider their work as their crucial task, and when the socializing activities and health behaviors conflict, they usually have to engage in the "unhealthy" behaviors. But they feel guilty and uneasy inside. They want to counteract those unhealthy behaviors by doing exercise or care products. They try their best to dedicate time to exercise every week as some compensatory relief and to remind themselves to maintain a healthy lifestyle. They want to live a healthy life and

keep the balance between life and work, but usually, they fall into self-contradiction. They need to break this situation in the strategy to achieve a "win-win" result.

Sports Talent Overdo Lead to Injury.
Playing sports with old friends is also a chance to promote communication, playing basketball is not only a sport but also a bridge to carry on the conversation with strangers. However, he has long been aware that his body is no longer the same as when he was young. Although the skills and experience are still slowly improving, there are times when they have to admit that they are no longer the rivals of the young generation. Even when they suffer injuries, they can still find their youthful mindset. They'd like to enjoy the moment of victory when they figure on the playground.

Home Care Keeper.
They are good at making delicious meals for the big family, they study nutrition and establish a set of health rules from a sensible diet. Their health concept influences the family. They know precisely what nutrition their children need most at different ages. As they work hard for their family's health, they reap the benefits of their family's health. Families rely more on them for their health.

Ageless Lady.
"Ageless lady": they usually pay attention to their body and skin; buying cosmetics and maintenance products has become their hobby. They constantly study the new skincare cosmetics that come out. The pursuit of beauty is a way for them to pursue a better life; not only constantly draw and learn new knowledge, but also enhance themselves to reap the joy of beauty. As they are getting older, the maintenance routine becomes more tedious and complicated. They are afraid of the traces of age being exposed, the more homework they do, the more they pay, the more beautiful they can come back from their youth, and they will do their best to stay young forever.

4.2 Common Trends

Distinctive features characterize the persona of typical users. However, the typical commonalities of the middle class cannot be ignored. Therefore, this study proposes four behavioral trends of the middle class based on the insights of all subjects.

Not Getting Sick Is the Bottom Line of a Healthy Life
Prevention is the essential thing that middle-aged people need to do for their health, but it is also the worst thing most of them do. It is not that they do not want to do it, but they do not know where to start. The most crucial thing is to develop a healthy lifestyle. The lack of health awareness among the middle-aged generation, coupled with the natural and fake science on the Internet and the mixed health care products in the market, has set up many obstacles for the middle-aged to live a healthy life. Therefore, some mechanisms and tools are needed to cultivate healthy living among middle-aged people. In addition to influence and authority, penetration is also a key point to note. This is why subtle

influence and other people's amenities will be the key to helping middle-aged people stay healthy.

Exercise Is the Breakthrough of Mid-life Crisis

People facing mid-life crises are trying to find a way to break through the situation, and sports is the weakest point in this circle that is easy to breakthrough. Nowadays, the main force of the middle class in the post-80s, most of them are only children, no siblings can share the responsibility of supporting their parents, and the competition for their children's education is becoming even more violent. To cope with their mid-life crisis, exercise is the lowest economic cost and can enhance their sense of self-efficacy, which is bound to get more and more attention from the middle class.

Health Communication Is a Responsibility

As the backbone of the family, the mainstay, especially the middle class who are married and have children. They need to worry about the whole family and pay particular attention to the health of family members. They have a greater sense of family responsibility and a greater sense of concern for the future. At the same time, middle-class people who are used to taking responsibility at home also play the role of the mainstay in society, and they are used to influencing more people with their health concepts. They have the responsibility to support their parents and the obligation to raise their children. They are not only suffering from stress from their families but also have a stronger sense of social responsibility. They hope to have a good and healthy atmosphere in their circle or even in society, and how to have them self-fulfillment is a potential opportunity point.

Mental Health Is Getting More Attention.

The key performance indicator, bills, medical reports are making their heartache, everything from childcare to mortgage repayments is driving them mad. The mainstay of the middle class should be able to carry the pressure of life and finish the negative emotions. Life goes on and on, and they do not have too much time to stay in their sad mood. A reasonably compliant and flexible outlet to vent to their heart's content may help them to release their spirits a little and cope better with tomorrow's life.

5   Discussion and Conclusion

The advantage of dividing dimensional output personas by extreme user attributes is that extreme users have significant behavioral characteristics in behavioral variables, which can meet ordinary users to a certain extent. Extreme users can help researchers develop significant behavioral dimensions efficiently. In addition, extreme users show more critical personal details, which can visualize and concretize personal, and make critical differences and attributes more apparent, which can play a more significant role in product design and decision making.

Extreme users are relatively niche and atypical compared to general users. Because it is emphasized on powerful features, it is slightly less comprehensive in terms of common features. Therefore, it does not apply to the customized services produced with a comprehensive combination of tags through extensive data analysis. The necessity of the existence of output portraits is also subject to trade-offs and variations according to specific project goals.

The project outputs five types of middle-class user personas, focusing on their state and behavior in health, and the health needs summarized based on the insight portraits provide new ideas for the health industry.

References

Williams, A.J., et al.: Fostering engagement with health and housing innovation: development of participant personas in a social housing cohort, JMIR Public Health Surveill. **7**(2), e25037 (2021)

Huh, J., et al.: Personas in online health communities. J. Biomed. Inform. **63**, 212–225 (2016)

Brickey, J., Walczak, S., Burgess, T.: Comparing semi-automated clustering methods for persona development. IEEE Trans. Software Eng. **38**(3), 537 (2012)

Redish, J.: The user is always right: a practical guide to creating and using personas for the web. Technical Commun. **55**(1), 74–76 (2008)

Jansen, B.J., Salminen, J.O., Jung, S.-G.: Data-driven personas for enhanced user understanding: combining empathy with rationality for better insights to analytics. Data Inf. Manage. **4**(1), 1–17 (2020)

An, J., et al.: Imaginary people representing real numbers. ACM Trans. Web **12**(4), 1–26 (2018)

Khan, F., Si, X., Khan, K.U.: Social media affordances and information sharing: an evidence from Chinese public organizations. Data Inf. Manage. **3**(3), 135–154 (2019)

Baig, M.I., Shuib, L., Yadegaridehkordi, E.: Big data adoption: State of the art and research challenges. Inf. Process. Manage. **56**(6), 102095 (2019)

Lee, J.H., et al.: A persona-based approach for identifying accessibility issues in elderly and disabled users. Interaction with Home Appliances. Applied Sci. **11**(368), 368 (2021)

Cooper, A.: The Inmates are Running the Asylum. SAMS, Indianapolis, IN (1999)

Goodwin, K.: Getting from research to personas: Harnessing the power of data. Cooper Newsletter, (2002) Retrieved August 6, 2009, from http://www.cooper.com/content/insights/newsletters/2002_11/getting_from_research_to_personas.asp

Brickey, J.: System for Persona Ensemble Clustering: A Cluster Ensemble Approach to Persona Development. the University of Colorado at Denver (2010)

Cooper, A., Reimann, R., Cronin, D.: About Face 3: The Essentials of Interaction Design. 3rd eds. Wiley, New York (2007)

Devia, G., et al.: References to home-made and natural foods on the labels of ultra-processed products increase healthfulness perception and purchase intention: Insights for policymaking. Food Qual. Prefer. **88**, 104110 (2021)

Effective Public Participation in Urban Open Space: Take Yangpu Waterfront Scenario Workshop as an Example

Peng Xu[✉]

Tongji University, No. 281 Fuxin Road, Shanghai, China
ben_xp223@tongji.edu.cn

Abstract. Effective public participation of urban open space can optimize the functional services of public spaces, enhance social interaction and the spirit of public cooperation. However, it mainly exists the problem of insufficient depth of participation, low willingness to participate and lack of participation mechanism, which often leads to the high-cost and low-efficiency during public participation. The Scenario Workshop as a participatory design approach, it is driven by shared visions, which have a positive impact on opening up equal communication and enhancing mutual understanding, fostering the public spirit and promoting potential opportunities for cooperation. Through the empirical research of Yangpu Waterfront Scenario Workshop, it is found that the capability of participation can be cultivated, the degree of participation can be deepened, the participation mechanism can be supplemented and the participation experience can be optimized. However, Scenario Workshop is restricted to the number of participants and tight time control so that it is hardly to involve every citizen. At last, strengthening information disclosure and providing policy support can make up for the shortcomings of the workshop to a certain extent.

Keywords: Scenario Workshop · Participatory design · Urban open space

1 Introduction

In recent years, the government of China has put forward the concept of "people's cities", which aims to enhance the quality of urban space, create human-centerd city and promote social cohesion by attracting a wide range of citizens to participate in the design of urban open space. Effective public participation of urban open space can optimize the functional services of public spaces, enhance social interaction and the spirit of public cooperation. At present, the mainstream public participation in Shanghai is to collect opinions and suggestions from the masses through online website submission and offline questionnaire and interview, etc. To a certain extent, these initiatives have expanded the scope of participation and the approach of participation, but there are still some problems of tokenism participation. In order to improve the effectiveness of public participation, this paper first analyzes the main problems in the public participation of urban open space, and then introduces the Scenario Workshop and takes Yangpu

M. M. Soares et al. (Eds.): HCII 2022, LNCS 13321, pp. 132–141, 2022.
https://doi.org/10.1007/978-3-031-05897-4_10

Waterfront Scenario Workshop as an example to carry out empirical research. Lastly, it discusses the advantages and disadvantages of the Scenario Workshop, and then propose suggestions to solve with current shortcomings.

2 Major Issues of Public Participation in Urban Open Spaces

Effective public participation means that citizens, in the process of participation, can propose effective problems or solutions based on the current situation. This means that the degree of participation should be deep and should not be superficial; the willingness to participate should be positive, and the participants should actively communicate and fully express their ideas and suggestions; the participation mechanism should be sound to ensure the orderly progress of participation. However, the public participation in the open space of the Shanghai city mainly exists the problem of insufficient depth of participation, low willingness to participate and lack of participation mechanism, it is difficult to express advantages of effective public participation, resulting in problem of high-cost and low-efficiency.

Firstly, the depth of public participation is relatively tokenism [1]. At this stage, the main ways of public participation in urban open space are publicity, symposiums, large-scale online questionnaires and face-to-face interviews. Although the scope of participation has been expanded to a certain extent, the depth of participation is limited. For example, Publicity is often based on the display of professional drawings, due to the lack of designers present to interpret, it is difficult for ordinary citizens without professional education to understand its connotation and professional terms. Symposiums are often presided over by experts and leaders, and one-way education is the mainstay, and the expression of citizens as listeners is limited. While the online questionnaire is convenient and conducive to dissemination and can collect large sample data, the public lacks a real understanding of the project overview information, cannot make effective recommendations, and finds it difficult to obtain immediate feedback. Although offline research interviews have established face-to-face communication, the number of single interviewees and stakeholders involved in the exchange are limited, and it is impossible to establish sufficient social dialogue.

Secondly, the enthusiasm for public participation is generally low. There are three main reasons, one is the lack of civic awareness, most citizens usually think that public space is the government's business, other people's business, and hold a negative and wait-and-see attitude towards public participation [2]. Second, some people believe that they do not have professional ability and cannot make effective suggestions. Third, some people think that the participation process is boring and unattractive.

Thirdly, participation mechanisms is not guaranteed. In contrast to residential space governance, residents are usually faced with more figurative problems in their daily lives, such as walking dogs without ropes, noise and smoke disturbing, informal constructions and so on. Such problems often have clear stakeholders, residents have a more consistent information background on the origin of the current situation. Through the establishment of appropriate guidance and orderly participation mechanism, many issues can be resolved in consultations within the residents. The participation mechanism is more complicated in the urban open space. First of all, different citizens have different professional and cultural backgrounds, and this difference is likely to make it difficult for both sides to establish a deep dialogue and smooth communication, resulting in high communication costs. Secondly, due to the lack of understanding of the actual project overview of urban open space, everyone asks questions from their own perspective, which makes it more difficult to collect and analyze information data. Moreover, since the participants do not directly contribute to the transformation of the public space, the citizens are in the role of rational people, of course, thinking that the higher the standard, the better, so that most ideas are unrealistic or too personal preferences, ignoring the trade-off between cost awareness and overall interests. Last but not least, there are few unique solutions in urban open space iterations. That is to say, whether the renewal of a field is a basketball court, a children's playground, a landscape garden or a temporary venue, it may have its own supporters, and there is almost no most correct and perfect solution. Therefore, when the design proposal is highly replaceable and triggers competition, the lack of appropriate communication and coordination mechanisms is easy to cause conflicts and it is difficult to ensure orderly participation [3].

In view of the plight of public participation in urban open space, in order to realize the promising goal of "people's city", it is urgent to supplement and introduce new ways of participation to improve the effectiveness of public participation.

3 Empirical Analysis Based on Yangpu Waterfront Scenario Workshop

Scenarios involve narrative descriptions of potential future problems that emphasize relationships between events and decision points. In addition, scenarios direct attention to causes, areas for development and the span of exigencies that may be met in a local community issue [4]. The workshop is the approach aspect of this method in which participants from a local community engage in discussion, produce some sort of action through deliberative discussion and act as decision-makers or create a communal plan of action.

The scenario workshop, a participatory design approach originally proposed by the Danish Science and Technology Commission, is a future-oriented, multi-participation and democratic consultation platform for communication. Scenario Workshops involve a group of citizens interacting with other participants to exchange knowledge, experience, develop common visions, debate, provide criticism and produce a plan of community action for potential future developments [5]. The aims of Scenario Workshop include raising awareness of future problems in a community, helping to develop a common definition of a desirable factor; facilitating discussions between different social groups within a society, cultivating steps and solutions for foreseen problems, and stimulating teamwork in coming up with a solutions or recommendations with the ideal result being consensus [6].

Scenario Workshop has the advantages of exploratory, open and inclusive, which is conducive to opening up equal communication and enhancing mutual understanding, fostering the public spirit and promoting potential opportunities for cooperation [7]. It was widely used in areas such as public policy [8], environmental governance [9], and urban and rural planning. Taking Yangpu Waterfront in Shanghai as an example, this paper explores the extent to which the Scenario Workshop can promote the effectiveness of public participation in urban open space.

3.1 Preparation

Discussion topics. In order to listen to the opinions and visions of different interest groups, there is no limit to the topic in advance. However, in order to avoid the discussion in the process of being aimless or getting into detail, the designer will gradually focus on a topic in the discussion from the open discussion under the guidance of the designer.

The recruitment of the participants. The consideration is taken as follows. The number of participants cannot be too large so that each participant is able to speak, and the mutual in-depth communication can be carried out. The participants are limited to 28 people being divided into four groups with seven people in each group. As the openness, inclusiveness and democracy of workshop is emphasized, and the discussion among heterogeneous groups is expected, the selection of participants are conducted mainly by two ways, namely "open recruitment from the Web" and "specific participants' invitation". The latter is to satisfy the diversity of participating groups. Seven people in each group contains representatives from three parties. One is from the residents. It is the main participating group, which consists of the people living or working nearby, citizens who frequently take the waterfront walk, families with children, university students and the elderly. Another community is the employees of the governments, who are from institutions like Yangpu District Planning and Resources Bureau, Market Superscenario Authority, Urban Management Integrated Law Enforcement Bureau etc. The third is the business representatives, who are the staff of the Yangpu Waterfront Development Co., Ltd. and the nearby merchants etc. Two designers are arranged in the group to organize and guide the discussions.

The toolkit design. To stimulate discussion and orderly workout, a toolkit for assisting thinking was designed (see Table 1). The toolkit consists of three sections, including "Personal Vision", "Shared Vision", and "Action Framework", each with several tool cards (see Fig. 1). The "personal vision" is from the individual perspective, encouraging participants to put forward more specific pain points; "shared vision" is a group perspective, through full dialogue and consultation, to establish a long-term shared vision; "Framework for Action" is based on panel discussion to explore diversified approaches to achieve the shared vision.

Table. 1. The Scenario Workshop toolkit.

Tpye	Toolkit	Description
Personal Vision	Emotion journey	Identify emotional reflections at important touchpoints in the user journey
	Persona	Identify problems with specific perspectives by given persona
	Public space evaluation index	Evaluate the current state of the public space experience
	Waterfront map	Recall the impressive moments

(continued)

Table. 1. (*continued*)

Tpye	Toolkit	Description
Shared Vision	City's vision cases	New York2050, London 2050, Seoul 2030
	High quality public space characteristics	Design features of high-quality public spaces
	Propose an open-ended question	"Where are the most impressive public spaces you've been to?"
	Propose an open-ended question	"If Yangpu Binjiang becomes…, I will prefer/often come/recommend to friends!"
Action Framework	Time clues	Visualize the fusion of different activities through the time dimension "day/week/month/quarter"
	Hybrid functions	Multiple types of activities and spaces to choose from
	Smart growth	Explore unused, loose spaces that can be used
	Stakeholders' map	Identify key people and co-create a win-win actor program

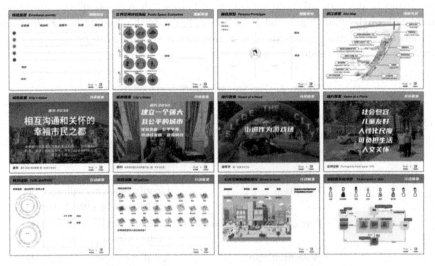

Fig. 1. The Scenario Workshop toolkit cards.

3.2 Implementation

The scenario workshop was held in September 2020 at Yangpu Waterfront Service Station for 6 h. The workshop process is divided into plenary meetings, pannel discussion and Freewheeling discussion (see Fig. 2). The discussion theme is divided into three stages, "Discover problem", "Build shared scenario" and "Action framework".

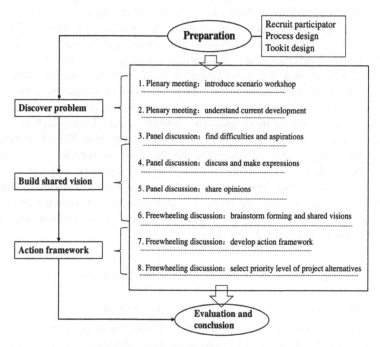

Fig. 2. Scenario Workshop process design.

In the plenary session, the organizers introduced the process, timing and use of the toolkit of the workshop, and the enterprise representatives from Yangpu Binjiang Investment and Development Co., Ltd. shared the planning and design, development overview and overall positioning of Yangpu Binjiang, which allowed participants to have a more macro and comprehensive understanding of the current situation of Binjiang and establish a consistent information background. In the pannel discussion, the designer's main task is to guide the discussion according to the task card of the toolkit, not only for each participant to speak, but also to control the individual speaking time to ensure that they all have the opportunity to express their personal ideas; the second is to promote effective and agreeable discussions, from divergent ideas to focus on the specific topic. In the freewheeling discussion, group representatives shared the process and results of the discussions within the group, on the basis of which a shared vision was established and a framework for action to achieve this goal vision was explored.

3.3 Presentation of Results

In Personal Vision phase, it can be summarized into six sub-topics: transportation facilities, sanitation facilities, visual facilities, commercial facilities, event organization and management mechanisms. Specifically, as many as 90% of people have raised the lack of transportation facilities, hoping to improve the accessibility of external transportation, increase parking spaces, and set up parking spots for shared bicycles. This was followed by visual tour facilities, where 70% of people advocated combining tour signage with digital technology to better deliver information, optimize experiences and improve services. Similarly, 70% of people believe that commercial hybrid functions should be enriched to meet diversified and personalized consumer needs. In addition, 60% of women have proposed that in terms of sanitation facilities, there should be more mother and baby rooms to facilitate the solution of physical problems for pregnant women and families with babies. A small number of 30% of people expect that in the organization of events, there will be more temporary activities in the future, such as markets, light shows, exhibitions, etc. Finally, basically everyone has about 90% of the initiative, and the management mechanism should be flexible, allowing for various spontaneous activities, such as dancing, kite flying, vendors, barbecues, skateboarding, etc.

In Shared Vision phase, four groups of delegates take turns speaking to share the scenario of goals reached within the group. Through collective open discussion, a shared vision of "People-centered, integrating historical humanities, eco-friendliness and digital technology" was finally formed (see Table 2).

Table 2. Shared vision based on panel discussion

	Panel discussion	Shared vision
A	Get rid of over-commercialization and mesh symbols and build an eco-friendly, dynamic, water-friendly environment	People-centered, integrating historical humanities, eco-friendliness and digital technology
B	Look forward to more interesting, more dynamic, more accessible, more readable	
C	To create a fusion of entertainment, leisure, business, residential, office and other diversified composite functions	
D	Inclusive coverage of all ages of civic activities, and truly reflect the "people's city" of the public platform	

In Action Framework phase, participants proposed a number of creative solutions. After voting screening, the widely welcomed and recognized programs are the digital twin waterfront platform, the light show combining historical buildings with new media art, the Pet Games Facility, the Story Crowdsourcing Museum and so on. Specifically, the workshop make the further discussion about digital twin technology, and think it combines many advantages. The first is to enhance the public's tour experience, and the platform is conducive to citizens' rapid and convenient access to information services by marking comprehensive information such as scenic spots, activities, exhibitions, shops, markers, and cycling routes. The second is to empower ordinary people to optimize program design. Through data collection and preference analysis such as human behavior trajectory, object usage frequency, and mobile phone remote sensing signals, the platform provides data support for designers and assists in design proposals. The third is to improve the refined governance ability of managers. Through sensors, cameras, the Internet of Things and information and communication technology, real-time monitoring and feedback of the real-time dynamics of Yangpu Waterfront, timely judgment of emergency situations, and improvement of responsiveness and refined governance. The fourth is to stimulate the vitality of public innovation. Grassroots makers can launch campaigns and "wishlists" on the platform to attract individuals with common interests to form a community and drive crowdfunding.

4 Conclusion

The future of the city depends on the vision of every citizen. Many international cities such as New York, Boston, London, etc. are devoted to develop citizens' vision and integrate it into the future development of the city. Scenario Workshop as a relatively simple, easy-to-operate and low-cost participatory negotiation method, in dealing with the future of uncertain issues, it provides a new way of thinking. The Scenario Workshop is problem-based, but not limited to problems and looks to the future. It identifies real problems and unmet potential needs, and at the same time, it fosters social dialogue and enhances the potential for mutual cooperation by bringing together multiple stakeholders to think, imagine and explore actions, forming a shared vision and framework for action for the future development of a region [10].

The innovation of this paper is to apply the Scenario Workshop to solve the problem of public participation failure in urban open space. In terms of the quality of questions, the atmosphere of the discussion, the output of the results, and the satisfaction of the participants, the Scenario Workshop, to a large extent, promotes an effective public participation in the following areas. First, the participation ability is first improved. The design kit provides non-professional individuals with traceable ideas to follow, providing a frame of reference for divergent ideas and stimulating imagination. At the same time, the idea is embedded in the design process from the proposal to how to implement it. In this way, a practical solution is no longer a self-interested or unrealistic proposal. Second, it increases the depth of participation. Through intensive dialogue among different stakeholders, the problem is gradually deepened, and empathy is established between groups, which is no longer a superficial superficial participation. As one participant put it, "In the past, public participation was to ask questions in a hurry, but this workshop is really sitting down, listening to each other, understanding each other and building a dialogue". Again, the participatory mechanism has been supplemented. In the process of participation, only participants who actively express suggestions and have the courage to take responsibility and obligation will win the final program. This will help to establish a participatory mechanism in which participants should have the right to propose and obtain benefits while also fulfilling their corresponding responsibilities and obligations.

Finally, the engagement experience was optimized. The Scenario Workshop was conducted in a fun, cheerful and entertaining manner, and was well received and actively engaged by the participants, many of whom expressed their willingness to participate continuously and gladly to be an volunteer for the next workshop.

Although the Scenario Workshop has many benefits, it still has some shortcomings due to its own characteristics. First, the number of participants is limited. In order to ensure the diversity of participants and the quality and effectiveness of the workshop, the size and capacity of the participants are limited, usually around 30 people, so that many citizens fail to participate. This requires that the diversity of social structures be guaranteed in the selection of participants and that long-term participation plans be developed. Second, easily to lose time-control. If the workshop lasts too long, participants will feel tired, but the time is too short to communicate in depth. At the same time, it often happens that a small detail is stuck in a small matter, or the theme is off course, making it difficult to form an effective discussion in a limited time. This requires designers to have a strong sense of rhythm, affinity and professionalism, and steadily promote the orderly development of the workshop. Nonetheless, Scenario workshop is a great way to cultivate citizen's capability, foster social dialogue, and facilitate civic engagement.

5   Discussion

5.1   Strengthen the Disclosure of Information

A full understanding of the current situation is the basis for public participation in raising effective questions, but these channels of information are often difficult for the general population to obtain.

For example, in the description of the current pain points of Yangpu Riverside, a considerable proportion believes that the accessibility of external traffic is not good, there are problems such as low recognition, easy to get lost, and inconvenient transportation, which seriously affect the tour experience. When the problem was stated, it was immediately explained and feedback from the project leader, "because the construction site and road near the riverside side are under construction, it has to be closed for safety reasons, resulting in the inability to improve riverside accessibility now. "However, in the future, a number of branch roads will be added in the planning map, and there will also be shuttle bus services, which will greatly improve the accessibility of the riverside." After several back-and-forth questions and answers, the negative emotions caused by information asymmetry were gradually resolved, and how to improve public services on the existing basis was discussed.

Therefore, the government should strengthen information disclosure, so that citizens can understand and grasp the relevant current situation in a timely, accurate and convenient manner, and reduce unnecessary loss of citizens' goodwill due to information asymmetry. Information disclosure is not only an important basis for the public to put forward effective opinions, but also an effective way to enhance the credibility of the government and promote political and social cooperation. Parallel to information disclosure, it is to improve the responsiveness to feedback, and the adoption of public opinions and the lack of rigid constraints on feedback are the key to affecting the continuity of public participation. The public wants their voices to be seen and valued, whether it is "fantasy" or "personal preference", and expects a certain degree of respect and response.

5.2 Policy Support

According to the proposals of current participants, many of them break the existing management rules, but breakthrough innovations are often discontinuous. Refined governance should not be "one size fits all", but should allow "mistakes" and explore innovative paths. In recent years, a new urban development model in Western countries, "temporary urbanism" refers to the temporary suspension of laws and regulations related to urban planning, and the community operation composed of a group of stakeholders within a certain space, through joint consultation, affects the development of the space in the future for a period of time []. The government is responsible for providing the necessary knowledge, skills, funding, talent, policies and other resources to support the community. This model has gradually been adopted by cities such as London in the United Kingdom, Berlin in Germany, and Amsterdam in the Netherlands, and has gradually become a new paradigm for flexible trial and error and iterative experimentation in the process of urban development. Yangpu Waterfront can also learn from it, the government provides relevant policy support for building a community platform, and drive the continuous innovation vitality of public open space.

References

1. Monno, V., Khakee, A.: Tokenism or political activism? Some reflections on participatory planning. Int. Plan. Stud. **17**(1), 85–101 (2012)
2. Mostert, E.: The challenge of public participation. Water Policy **5**(2), 179–197 (2003)
3. Rowe, G., Frewer, L.J.: A typology of public engagement mechanisms. Sci. Technol. Human Values **30**(2), 251–290 (2005)
4. Godet, M., Roubelat, F.: Creating the future: the use and misuse of scenarios. Long Range Plan. **29**(2), 164–171 (1996)
5. Scenario Workshop. https://participedia.net/method/529. Accessed 21 Dec 2021
6. Nilsson, A.E., Carson, M., Cost, D.S., et al.: Towards improved participatory scenario methodologies in the Arctic. Polar Geogr. **44**(2), 75–89 (2021)
7. Duranova, T., Bedwell, P., Beresford, N.A., et al.: CONFIDENCE dissemination meeting: summary on the scenario-based workshop. Radioprotection **55**(HS1), S17–S37 (2020)
8. Volkery, A., Ribeiro, T.: Scenario planning in public policy: understanding use, impacts and the role of institutional context factors. Technol. Forecast. Soc. Chang. **76**(9), 1198–1207 (2009)
9. Nygrén, N.A.: Scenario workshops as a tool for participatory planning in a case of lake management. Futures **107**, 29–44 (2019)
10. Van Vliet, M., Kok, K., Veldkamp, A., et al.: Structure in creativity: an exploratory study to analyse the effects of structuring tools on scenario workshop results. Futures **44**(8), 746–760 (2012)

Research on Product Design Process Based on the Integration of Perceptual Image and Brand Identity

Zhijuan Zhu, Ziyi Zhang[✉], Yan Qin, and Siyi Li

School of Mechanical Science and Engineering, Huazhong University of Science and Technology, Wuhan, People's Republic of China
1871309847@qq.com

Abstract. Perceptual image is an important theory often used in product design. However, under normal circumstances, product design does not rely on a single theory and method, but is the result of a combination of multiple considerations. This paper aims to integrate brand identity theory into the perceptual image design method and construct a comprehensive design process, in order to take into account the needs of function, perceptual and product identification. Taking a Chinese brand's smart home gateway product as an example, the cultural elements were obtained through enterprise-oriented desktop research and interview methods. Then, by establishing a sample library of similar products and performing hierarchical statistics, the mainstream design elements of gateway products were obtained as an auxiliary reference. Finally, the gateway products were perceptually measured and then quantitatively analyzed through the Semantic Difference Scale to establish the mapping relationship between image vocabulary and product appearance elements. The cultural elements, mainstream elements and perceptual image elements were summarized from the three dimensions of shape, color and material, and were used in the design practice of smart home gateway products. After inspection, it is determined that the design results meet the design objectives. This study provides a practical, comprehensive and systematic design process for product design based on perceptual image and brand identity.

Keywords: Perceptual image · Brand identity · Product design · Smart gateway

1 Introduction

1.1 Background and Motivation

Perceptual image has been widely used in product design as an important medium to understand users' emotional cognition of products. However, the practical application of perceptual images usually cannot meet the overall planning needs of an enterprise or brand, which means that a brand is easy to succeed in a single product, but it is difficult to leave a clear brand image to consumers. Therefore, brand identity characteristics are the elements that designers should fully consider when designing products for enterprises

© The Author(s), under exclusive license to Springer Nature Switzerland AG 2022
M. M. Soares et al. (Eds.): HCII 2022, LNCS 13321, pp. 142–154, 2022.
https://doi.org/10.1007/978-3-031-05897-4_11

[1]. This paper is committed to integrating the theory and method of brand identity into the process of perceptual image design, so that the designed series of products have similar brand intentions under the same brand, and enhance the correlation between product image and brand.

1.2 Literature Review

Perceptual Image. Products are the carrier that connects brands and users, so excellent design can effectively enhance product and brand recognition, as well as corporate image. Perceptual image is an important theory often used in product design, which integrates users' subjective feelings into product design. The research on product perceptual image is mainly based on the theory of Kansei Engineering, which has long been proposed in Asia, especially in Japan [2]. In 1970, the Research Department of Hiroshima University in Japan introduced sentiment analysis in the field of engineering. Subsequently, Professor Mitsuo Nagamachi of Hiroshima University [3] and Professor Harada Akira of Tsukuba University established a corresponding relationship between emotional needs and engineering projects. In Japan and South Korea, the "societies of Kansei engineering" has been established [4]. Perceptual image is the description, processing and association of people's visual perception of the space and size of things, reflecting people's psychological feelings and psychological changes. It is an important medium for understanding users' emotional cognition of products [5]. Perceptual image vocabulary is a word used by users to describe a product perceptually, and a subjective expression perceived by users through the appearance, characteristics, material, and structure of the product [6]. The formation process of the perceptual image is that the user's personal knowledge and experience are comprehensively processed by the brain to form the image description of the relevant product, such as the use of perceptual adjectives such as "technical" and "warm". There are five key aspects in the research of product perceptual image design [7]:

Extensive collection of product samples to determine representative samples;

1. Analyze product design elements;
2. Obtain the user's perceptual needs and locate the product design direction;
3. Establish the mapping relationship between user perceptual image and product design elements;
4. Product perceptual image based on intelligent algorithm.

At present, the design process related to perceptual image is mainly divided into three stages [8], which are acquisition of perceptual image, model establishment and design optimization, as shown in Fig. 1.

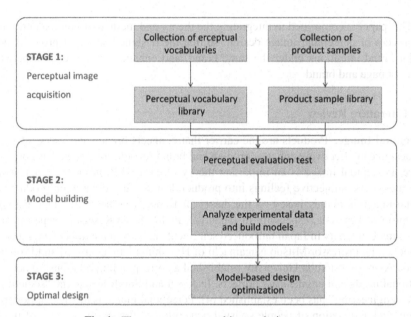

Fig. 1. The current perceptual image design process

Brand Identity. Brand Identity, or BI for short, is a relatively new concept compared to CI (Corporate Identity). On the concept of BI, different scholars have different expressions. Gardner et al. [9] pointed out that a brand image is a complex symbol that builds a series of associations over time to convey ideas, attributes, image, character and personality to consumers. David Aaker, an internationally renowned brand research expert, believes that brand identity is the association that brand strategists hope to create and maintain that can arouse people's good impression of the brand [10]. This definition emphasizes that brand recognition is an act of the owner of the brand, which plays the role of establishing a differentiating advantage through communication.

Under normal circumstances, the following two aspects can reflect the brand recognition of a product: first, the personality of the product. The distinctive personality helps to capture the consumer's consumption awareness, so that consumers can be deeply impressed by it in the shortest time. The second is continuity, which means that the re-creation of the original product is based on the brand image, so as to maintain the consistency of the appearance image of the product and the brand characteristics [11]. Brand identity is mainly composed of two parts. One is the identification through the five senses, such as graphics, colors, text, music, etc., which is a relatively simple and direct identification method. Another is cultural-based identification, such as corporate values. Brand characteristics can guide product design to achieve unity with brand tonality. At the same time, product design based on brand characteristics can strengthen brand image and positioning, as shown in Fig. 2.

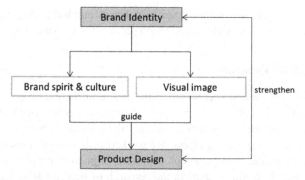

Fig. 2. The relationship between brand identity and product design

Based on the theories and methods of perceptual image and brand recognition, this paper proposes a comprehensive product design process in order to meet the needs of perceptual image and brand identity.

2 Method

2.1 Product Design Process Framework Based on Perceptual Imagery and Brand Identity

The design process framework proposed in this paper based on perceived image and brand identity is shown in Fig. 3. The research process is divided into two parts: the internal and external parts of the enterprise, covering the brand concept and characteristics, existing products, brand visual image, similar products in the market and the research of target consumers, so as to take into account the perceptual needs of users and the brand recognition needs of enterprises.

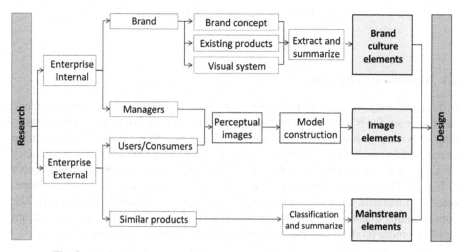

Fig. 3. Product design process based on perceptual image and brand identity

The research results are summarized into brand cultural elements, mainstream elements and perceptual image elements, which serve as the guidance for product design.

2.2 Brand Culture Elements

The first part of the research was aimed at the inside of the enterprise to explore the characteristics of brand culture, covering brand concept, existing products, and visual image. The source of the research were mainly the official website of the enterprise and interviews with enterprise managers. We worked with business managers to extract some keywords from the brand concept. Some of them were perceptual words, such as "technical", which would be used in the research of perceptual image. Some were figurative things, such as "fire", extracted from the culture of the brand in this case: "A single spark can start a prairie fire". Brand vision sets the tone of the brand and can provide color and abstract morphological features for product design, as shown in Fig. 4. In addition, if existing products had formed family characteristics, they could provide a basis for the design of subsequent products. Since the previous products of this enterprise did not form family characteristics in the design, this case did not include research on existing products.

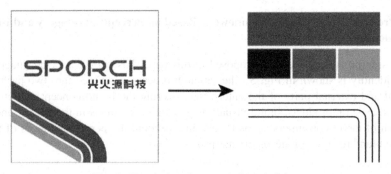

Fig. 4. Key design elements in brand vision

2.3 Mainstream Elements

In this part, firstly, we selected three gateway products including smart gateways, routers, and router-set-top box integrated devices as research objects. From offline stores, shopping websites and design websites, a total of 87 products were obtained as observation samples. After preliminary screening, some products with high appearance similarity were removed, and a total of 60 of them were retained to build a sample library (as shown in Fig. 5). Then the core elements of each product's design are split, including Shape, color, and material. Finally, all product design elements are coded and stratified. The corresponding quantity of each type of appearance element can reflect the mainstream trend of similar products and has reference value for subsequent design.

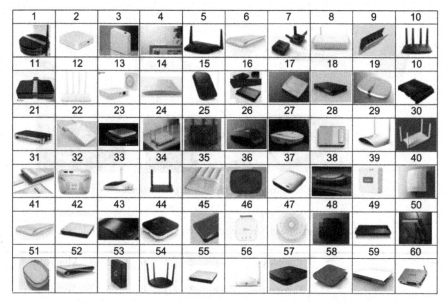

Fig. 5. A sample library containing 60 gateway products

2.4 Perceptual Image Elements

The third part of the research was the acquisition, measurement and mapping of perceptual image. The first was the acquisition of perceptual vocabulary, which came from three channels. One is enterprise managers, which is also the reflection of the brand's design needs at the perceptual level. The second is target users, which is also the core source of perceptual image collection. The third is External information, including the descriptive text of the company's website products, brand websites of similar products, books, literature, design websites, etc. Then, the perceptual words in the vocabulary database were classified and screened, and four target image words are finally determined, namely "technical", "elegant", "minimalist" and "professional". This result was negotiated by experts, enterprise managers, and target users.

Then, a perceptual evaluation experiment was performed. Based on the four perceptual words and the sample library mentioned above, 10 representative product samples with large differences (as shown in Fig. 6) were selected from the three dimensions of shape, color and material as the final experimental objects. This result were also negotiated by experts, enterprise managers, and target users. A seven-level semantic difference scale (as shown in Table 1) based on these 10 samples was used in the questionnaire, and the respondents were asked to rate each product sample based on their subjective feelings, ranging from −3 to 3, the higher the score, the higher the closer to the design goal. During the questionnaire survey, the gender and age distribution of the respondents were controlled to be roughly balanced.

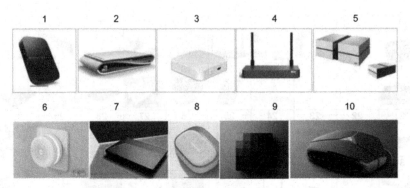

Fig. 6. Ten product samples for experimentation

Table 1. The semantic difference scale with sample 5 as an example

Sample 5	Complex	-3	-2	-1	0	1	2	3	Minimalist
	Conservative	-3	-2	-1	0	1	2	3	Technical
	Vulgar	-3	-2	-1	0	1	2	3	Elegant
	Dangerous	-3	-2	-1	0	1	2	3	Reliable

The final step was the establishment of the mapping relationship. Based on the above perceptual measurement questionnaire, the user's scores for each product image were averaged. If the result is greater than 0, it indicates that the appearance and feeling of the product are more in line with the image. Then, the shape, color, and material elements of these products were divided, as shown in Table 2, to establish the mapping relationship between each appearance element and the image.

Table 2. Product design elements including extraction of shapes, colors and materials

	Shape	Color（s）	Material（s）
	Tough regular shape	Black	Frosted plastic

3 Result

3.1 Brand Culture Elements

In the first part, the design elements extracted from the brand cultural characteristics can be divided into three categories, namely concrete things, abstract forms and colors. But failed to get element of material type. As shown in Fig. 3 (Table 3).

Table 3. Design elements provided by the brand

Shape (figurative)	Shape (abstract)	Colors
"Fire"		

3.2 Mainstream Elements

The mainstream element is an important result of research outside the enterprise. We summarize and code all kinds of the shapes, colors, and materials contained in the sample library as the basis for product classification. Then use the stratified method to count the usage of the shape, color and material elements of the existing products in the market (as shown in Table 4). The greater the corresponding quantity of each type of appearance element, the more representative the current gateway product popularity. Popularity is a double-edged sword, and these elements are repeatedly validated as "can't go wrong", but usually also mean mediocre and hard to stand out. Mainstream elements need to be considered together with other factors.

Table 4. Similar product design element statistics

Coding	Category		Quantity
A01	Shape	Tough regular shape	29
A02		Tounded regular shape	26
A03		Organic shape	5
B01	Color	Black/dark grey	11
B02		White	23
B03		Silver	1
B04		Black & white	7
B05		Black & silver	7

(*continued*)

Table 4. (*continued*)

Coding	Category		Quantity
B06		Black & colored	6
B07		White & silver	5
C01	Material	Frosted plastic	3
C02		Glossy plastic	8
C03		Frosted metal	9
C04		Frosted plastic & frosted metal	4
C05		Glossy plastic & frosted metal	5
C06		Glossy plastic with glossy metal	2

3.3 Perceptual Image Elements

In the third part of the study of perceptual image, a total of 67 questionnaires were recovered, of which 67 were valid questionnaires. The results of the questionnaires were averaged and summarized into Table 5. In addition, the shape, color and material characteristics of the ten samples are shown in Table 6. By comparing Figs. 5 and 6, the mapping relationship between image vocabulary and shape, color, and material can be established (as shown in Table 7). It can be concluded that the element codes satisfying the four image adjectives are A01, B01, B05, B06, C01, C03, c04 respectively.

Table 5. The mean of the semantic difference scale questionnaire

Sample number	Minimalist	Technical	Elegant	Reliable
1	2.433	1.881	0.970	1.731
2	−0.015	0.836	0.119	0.910
3	2.851	−2.701	−2.149	−1.687
4	1.886	2.672	0.940	2.030
5	1.149	2.701	1.881	1.746
6	−0.045	−0.015	0.896	0.731
7	−0.060	0.851	0.030	0.970
8	−0.104	2.075	0.731	1.776
9	−2.657	2.254	0.925	2.269
10	−2.224	2.248	0.104	1.761

Table 6. Shapes, colors, and materials of ten samples

Sample number	Shape	Color	Material
1	A01	B01	C02
2	A03	B05	C03
3	A01	B02	C01
4	A01	B01	C03
5	A01	B05	C04
6	A02	B02	C01
7	A01	B01	C01
8	A02	B07	C04
9	A01	B01	C02
10	A02	B01	C01

Table 7. The mapping relationship between perceptual image and shape, color and material

	Coding	Minimalist	Technical	Elegant	Reliable
Shape	A01	✓	✓	✓	✓
	A02	✓	✓		
	A03	✓			
Color	B01	✓	✓	✓	✓
	B02	✓		✓	
	B03				
	B04				
	B05	✓	✓	✓	✓
	B06	✓	✓	✓	✓
	B07		✓		✓
Material	C01	✓		✓	
	C02	✓	✓	✓	✓
	C03	✓	✓	✓	✓
	C04	✓	✓	✓	✓
	C05				
	C06				

3.4 Design and Verification

To sum up, through this process, brand culture and characteristic elements, mainstream elements and perceptual image elements are finally obtained to jointly guide the appearance design of the smart home gateway product, as shown in Fig. 7.

Fig. 7. Smart home gateway product appearance design scheme

As a verification, a seven-level semantic difference scale (as shown in Table 8) was established based on the design scheme and distributed in the form of a questionnaire. A total of 71 questionnaires were recovered, of which 71 were valid questionnaires. Input the questionnaire data into SPSS software, calculate the average score of each perceptual image vocabulary and summarize (as shown in Table 9). The scores of the four groups of perceptual images are all greater than 0, indicating that the appearance design of the smart home gateway product conforms to the perceptual images of "minimalist", "technical", "elegant" and "professional", and can stand out from similar products in appearance.

Table 8. The semantic difference scale for program evaluation

	Complex	-3	-2	-1	0	1	2	3	Minimalist
	Conservative	-3	-2	-1	0	1	2	3	Technical
	Vulgar	-3	-2	-1	0	1	2	3	Elegant
	Dangerous	-3	-2	-1	0	1	2	3	Reliable

Table 9. Design scores of smart home gateway

Perceptual image	Scores
Complex/Minimalist	1.68
Conservation/Technical	0.75
Vulgar/Elegant	0.96
Dangerous/Reliable	0.75

4 Conclusion

Most of the existing researches on perceptual image and brand identity are conducted in isolation, while product positioning, user perceptual needs and brand identity needs are usually important factors that must be considered in practical design projects.

The main innovation of this paper is to construct a comprehensive design process that focuses on perceptual image and integrates the theory of brand identity. This process systematically covers the research on brand culture and characteristics, popularity and perceptual image, so that product design is internally consistent with brand characteristics, and externally different from similar products. This study objectively enriches the image-based product design process.

The limitation of this paper is mainly reflected in the distribution of the perceptual evaluation questionnaire. In addition to individuals, real estate developers also account for a considerable proportion of consumers of this product. However, for real estate companies, it is difficult to collect enough data to directly study their perceptual preferences. Therefore, the research on perceptual image in this paper mainly considers the emotional preferences of individual consumers and the positioning of products and brands themselves.

Secondly, in the research of similar products, the method provided in this paper only counts the use of each design element in competing products more or less, which does not necessarily reflect user preferences. Enterprises should decide whether to choose conventional or unconventional appearance elements according to product and brand strategy.

In addition, this research focuses on the integration of the two theories and methods of perceptual image and brand identity in the design process. Due to the fact that this case is a real project, and the urgency of time, relatively simple approaches to both theories were chosen and used. Based on this research framework, the specific method can be modified and improved, which is also what we hope to do in the future.

Acknowledgments. This subject came from the entrusted design project of Wuhan SPORCH Technology Co., Ltd. We especially thank the enterprise and relevant staff for their trust, cooperation and necessary equipment support in the research process.

References

1. Li, X., Zou, S.: Research on product image design for brand recognition. Des. Res. **9**(03), 67–70+76 (2019)
2. Xiao, W., Cheng, J.: Perceptual design method for smart industrial robots based on virtual reality and synchronous quantitative physiological signals. Int. J. Distrib. Sens. Netw. **16**(5), 155014772091764 (2020). https://doi.org/10.1177/1550147720917646
3. Nagamachi, M.: Kansei engineering: a new ergonomic consumer-oriented technology for product development. Int. J. Ind. Ergon. **15**(1), 3–11 (1995). https://doi.org/10.1016/0169-8141(94)00052-5
4. Luo, S., Pan, Y.: Review of theory, key technologies and its application of perceptual image in product design. Chin J Mech Eng **43**, 8–12 (2007). https://doi.org/10.3901/JME.2007.03.008
5. Li, Y., Shieh, M.-D., Yang, C.-C.: A posterior preference articulation approach to Kansei engineering system for product form design. Res. Eng. Des. **30**(1), 3–19 (2018). https://doi.org/10.1007/s00163-018-0297-4
6. Hu, X., Wang, J., Xu, X.: Reader design for the blind person based on kansei engineering. J. Mach. Des. **33**(05), 121–212 (2016). https://doi.org/10.13841/j.cnki.jxsj.2016.05.025
7. Chen, L., Zhu, W.: Research on the modeling design of cultural creative products of "Leizhou Stone Dog." Int. J. New Dev. Eng. Soc. **4**(1), 226–235 (2020)
8. Ding, M., Cheng, Y., Huang, X., Zhao, L.: Status and progress of kansei engineering design method. J. Mach. Des. **37**(1), 121–127 (2020). https://doi.org/10.13841/j.cnki.jxsj.2020.01.022
9. Gardner, B., Levy, S.: The product and the brand. Harv. Bus. Rev. **33**(2), 33–39 (1955)
10. Dan, C.: Brands, consumers, symbols, and research: Sidney J Levy on marketing. J. Consum. Mark. (1984). https://doi.org/10.1108/jcm.2000.17.6.550.3
11. Aaker, D.: Building Strong Brands. Simon & Schuster, New York (1996). https://doi.org/10.1057/bm.1996.8

User Requirements, Preferences, and UX Influential Factors

IOHIVE: Design Requirements for a System that Supports Interactive Journaling for Beekeepers During Apiary Inspections

Theodora Chamaidi⬚, Katerina Malisova⬚, Vangelis Nomikos⬚,
Evangelos Vlachogiannis, Charalambos Alifieris, Chrysostomos Rigakis,
and Modestos Stavrakis$^{(\boxtimes)}$⬚

Department of Product and Systems Design Engineering, University of the Aegean,
84100 Syros, Greece
{theodora.chamaidi,katemalisova,v.nomikos,evlach,babis,
chr.rigakis,modestos}@aegean.gr

Abstract. In this paper, we present an ongoing project that focuses on designing interactive systems and their respective interfaces for monitoring and journaling of apiculture information acquired in the actual field during apiary inspections by the beekeepers. Initially, the paper provides a brief overview of the concepts and technologies found in the domain. Next, it examines the scenarios to be used for the design of interactions related to the actual beehive inspections and desktop use in the office. The paper mainly focuses on the design requirements based on user research. It provides a review of interaction techniques that can be implemented for journaling in the workplace of the apiary, briefly outlines the infrastructure and gives a system overview at its current state of development. Finally, the paper discusses future work including, guidelines towards the development of the various system components for journaling and a preliminary evaluation plan for the case studies that will follow.

Keywords: Journaling for beekeeping · Beehive inspection · Apiculture · IoT · Interaction design · Agriculture science · Bee management practices · Modern beekeeping

1 Introduction

In recent years there has been an increasing interest in the design of technologies for the agricultural and more specifically apiculture/beekeeping sectors. Graphical User Interfaces (GUIs) still dominate as the main user interface platform used in outdoor workplaces (field/farm), while non-traditional interfaces such as speech-based, gestural, haptics, multimodal, etc. are also incorporated more frequently in terms of human work interaction in pervasive and smart work environments [1, 2]. These interfaces create a natural link with the users' working environment and promote user performance in multitasking contexts where agricultural activities take place [3]. Researchers agree that there is a need to further investigate technology use in agriculture. Toward this goal, great attention is given to making it more efficient, easy to access and understand. Moving beyond the well-established GUI interaction [4], the new direction is to focus on the relation of the user, the technology, and the actual environment where most agricultural activities are taking place [5].

The general objectives of the project are the design and development of technological infrastructures and services for a) Remote hive monitoring of beekeeping data including bee biometrics, hive development in relation to local climatic conditions, honey production and other hive products, b) supporting beekeeping practices and management techniques that are aiming at the development and population expansion of the bees, c) supporting the utilisation of all products that are being produced by beekeeping. The quantitative and qualitative data that will be produced, will be gathered, processed, and presented in order to increase efficiency and improve the quality of the produced products [6]. In this paper, we focus on the design of the logging/journaling mechanisms that will be introduced to support inspection notetaking in an apiary. The paper also describes the methodology towards the general systems' design and architecture.

1.1 Precision Beekeeping/Apiculture

The field of agriculture that needs to follow this path is beekeeping. Beekeeping is a labour-intensive practice that focuses on preserving the health and productivity of bee colonies [6]. To monitor the progress of the hive, beekeepers inspect the frames of each hive almost daily, depending on the season and the goals that a beekeeper has. By journaling the practices and the data that were observed during the field visit, beekeepers can be drawn to conclusions regarding the state of the hive and be able to make predictions about the future of its state. It is also a way to verify that a practice is effective and aligned with beekeeping protocols, by monitoring its progress and results based on the journaling activity [6–8]. Journaling during the process of the beekeeping inspection can be distracting and difficult to follow because of the tools and processes involved. Beekeepers have been using empirical methods and tools such as paper journals, in order to take notes based on signs, symbols, and numbers [9], during or after the process of the inspection (Fig. 1).

Fig. 1. Empirical methods for note-taking in an apiary: journaling on paper, stones and other objects placed on the beehives to indicate an event of action (e.g. missing queen), markings on the frames (e.g. newly introduced frame since last inspection)

This type of method makes it extremely difficult to track the plurality and complexity of data that have been gathered during practices that took place over a beekeeping period.

A technological system could help to organise and keep track of the activities performed and evaluate their effectiveness. Remote monitoring, telemetry, and analysis of sensor data of a beehive isn't the only option to secure the colony strength and thus identify crucial factors for the productivity and the health of the bees. Often the observed hives might be in distant places, increasing the travelling costs and the time consumed [10]. Digital sensors installed on a beehive provide valuable data that can be stored and used in near real-time to assist in collecting data that can be later used to study the health and behaviour of individual honey bees and their hives [11–13]. This project supports the idea that this type of automated monitoring does exclude a large part of beekeeping, namely human observation, and intervention during beehive inspections. For this reason, the IOHIVE project focuses on designing a comprehensive system that affords both automated monitoring and logging of human empirical observation. Monitoring will be based on IoT sensor data, including commonly used in-hive sensors such as temperature, humidity, weight, sound etc., as well as environmental and weather data from weather stations either in the wider region or ones closely located to the apiaries that capture the microclimate of the area. The core idea of the project is to support beekeeper workers to log data while inspecting or intervening on a beehive. The purpose is to provide them with a usable interface/device that affords simple data entry interactions in the farm/field during actual work. This information can later become more valuable in terms of correlation with data sourced from sensors and other monitoring devices.

2   Related Work

There are several different systems and practices focusing on assisting beekeepers in the apiculture domain in journaling, keeping logs or diaries of their activities related to inspecting and intervening in a beehive.

2.1   Logging and Journaling Apiculture Practices

Hive inspection is one of the main tasks performed by beekeepers to manage their colonies. With this activity beekeepers try to turn a set of stimuli and scattered data into meaningful understanding about their colonies [14]. It is a practice that is usually taught by a more experienced beekeeper to beginners by collaborating over their inspections. To successfully manage a beehive, the amateur beekeeper needs to become more attentive, have the capacity to monitor certain information, and adapt their responses to situations that arise. There are certain lists and categories of information that one might look for in an inspection, although the more experienced a beekeeper becomes, the quicker it is to inspect a hive and to go further on what they observe during that time. Hive inspections can be taking place weekly, fortnightly, monthly, or even daily during harvesting season [15, 16]. Beekeepers usually assess the status of brood condition, the population size, they consider giving additional space to the hive during the flowering season or reducing it during winter, check for food reserve, queen's existence, or tendency to swarm [9, 15]. As it is a practice that is carried out regularly in every hive of an apiary, the amount of data produced in only one inspection can be overwhelming. To be able to manage this information, beekeepers keep records of hive inspections which can be helpful in order to follow colony progress and to plan for future work in the apiary [17]. This type of manual recording takes place in various ways, such as making notes on a hive, marking a hive with a rock, and keeping notes on paper [9, 17].

Beekeeping Diaries and Inspection Notebooks. Beekeepers started journaling those inspections, in order to manage this information and be able to make predictions about the well-being of the hive. Organizing this data makes it easier to verify that a practice is effective and aligned with beekeeping protocols, instead of having to memorize them. This task takes place during or after beehive inspections, preferably as soon as possible so that all qualitative and quantitative data can be recorded. They use paper journals or take notes based on signs, symbols, and numbers regarding usually the number of frames that have brood (eggs), the presence of the queen, and the number of frames that have food reserves (honey or pollen) [9]. Beekeepers are particularly interested in those data because they can indicate potential future problems. They also keep notes of abnormalities in hives or statuses that trouble them, in order to take further action about those hives in their next inspection. They keep comments on more abstract observations as well, given a reason exists, but this is not the usual case since there is a lack of time.

The main problems with keeping notes during hive inspections is that it is time-consuming, and the environment is not conducive to writing down observations. If the notes are written down after the inspections, the quality and quantity of the information that ends up in the journal is significantly lower than what was observed at the apiary. Traditionally, beekeepers solve this problem using empirical methods, marking hives with information that will be useful to them during their next inspection or at a later visit. This is only a short-term solution, as this type of recording is not stored somewhere and is often lost immediately after the next inspection to be updated with the new data. If the notes are written down during the inspections, the beekeeper must do so while wearing protective gear.

2.2 Related Systems and Software

Beehive Journaling. There is a wide range of systems, services and applications that focus on note-taking or journaling for inspections alongside monitoring from sensors [18]. These include research and commercially available systems and services, as well as mobile applications easily found on most mobile market stores. The two most well-known open-source systems that have attempted to address journaling more specifically include Beep App online webservice with its accompanying Beep Scale [19] and OSBee-hives application accompanied by the BuzzBox beehive monitoring system [20]. Both system services support beekeepers' diary functionality. The user can keep notes after creating each hive, about the current status, treatments, changes that have been made during the inspections etc. Moreover, monitoring from sensors is stored on databases and presented to the user through various visualisation techniques (graphs, charts, widgets etc.). Both services classify the information properly according to inspection lists, well known in the beehive community [21]. As both systems are under heavy development, their graphical user interfaces and core functionality are continuously updated, allowing users to navigate quickly through their mobile and desktop devices.

Beehive Monitoring. Manual journaling from the beekeeper is often accompanied by automation systems that monitor the current data of an apiary including the beehives and the microclimate of the area. Monitored data is captured and analysed by a number of systems and techniques including: audio / acoustics or sound analysis [22–25], motion/track analysis [26–29], population estimation and variability [30–34], behaviour analysis [35], vibration [36, 37], image analysis and computer vision for detecting diseases and parasites [38], energy consumption [39], environmental data [40] etc. A number of systems have also been developed to monitor combinations of the aforementioned data based on multi-sensor arrays that also fall within the domain of IOT. These usually monitor temperature, humidity, weight, audio, video, vibrations etc. Some recent examples are BeePi [41], Beemon [12], an IoT concept for precision beekeeping [42], and an IoT project of a low-power beekeeping safety and conditions monitoring system [43].

3 Methodology

One of the most important tasks of this project is to design interaction and interactive interfaces that afford the logging and journaling of specific beekeeping practices/tasks performed by the respective workers/beekeepers in the actual field/apiary. The methodology we follow in this project focuses to support several levels of design and development ranging from the design of the interactions based on user research to the analysis and outline of data architecture, to the development of the infrastructures, systems and services. We follow a user centered design approach for establishing the user requirements and establishing the interaction techniques to be used in the various interfaces [44, 45]. In terms of systems and services we follow a Service Oriented Architecture (SOA) for web service applications which defines an important stage towards the evolution of the actual application development and integration [46]. Therefore, the different layers of the project will be developed as independent sets of interacting services offering well-defined interfaces to their potential users. The technologies involved will be available in such a way to allow sub-component developers to browse collections of systems, technologies, and services, select those of interest, and combine them to create the required functionality in terms of user research and pre-established design requirements [47, 48]. The challenge here is to apply the SOA architecture for an IoT service-oriented architecture that takes into account a user centered design approach [49]. The IoT SOA architecture layers for this project include the following layers: Application Layer, Domain Services Layer, Common Services Layer, Infrastructure Layer. In combination with the user centered approach described earlier, the generic architecture of this focusing on: a) desktop research and stakeholder interviews for identifying the domain requirements, b) user (beekeepers and researchers) research for establishing requirements, c) design and development of infrastructure systems and services, d) design and development of common systems services, including the iterative design process of establishing working interactive prototypes and e) the evaluation of the various sub-systems and services in terms of a pilot case study. For the purposes of this paper, we will focus on the analysis of the user research, the interaction techniques and the architecture components implemented at the current state of the project.

3.1 User Research

Initially, the research focused on understanding beekeeping and its practices, the work environment that beekeepers experience in an apiary, the challenges they face during work, and the tools they use. The main part of beekeeping concerns hive inspections. It is craftsmanship where the beekeepers must understand the nature and the needs of the bee colonies, receive stimuli during their visit about the current status, and develop a plan of future actions [9, 10]. To better understand this process and identify the difficulties that arise due to the complexity of this work environment, the research and design team of the project conducted a set of field visits. We interviewed beekeepers and researcher by using semi-structured interviews. We also observed and recorded beehive inspections in the apiary on the basis of structured and semi-structured scenarios. The participants were asked a range of questions covering topics related to their activities. The purpose was to learn about the data they observe during the inspection, which of those they journal, what methods they use to record them, when they record them and how often they consult them. Some of the most important findings during the interviews were the following:

1. It is almost impossible to document all the practices each beekeeper follows, as they are often structured in terms of empirical knowledge,
2. due to the lack of appropriate tools, beekeepers only record a general review of their observations when and if they journal,
3. problematic situations are preferred to be solved on the spot, if not, beekeepers keep notes in order to remember to take further actions about those hives in their next inspection (e.g. disorder, missing queen etc.),
4. time and task completion are important factors and affect most of their decisions, as it is limited during their field visits,
5. journaling most of the times does not take place right after the individual beehive inspection,
6. depending on the season, their focus shifts, but during inspections they mainly observe the status of the brood, the food reserves, and the queen presence.
7. beekeepers manage how they are going to spend their time and what actions they are going to follow in their next inspection, before going to the field. They have a general overview of their hives and based on the season; they make plans about their actions. Even if they don't journal each hive's progress, they manage to filter the most important information and act on it. Each hive's status concerns them on a high level during the inspection, but after they are done with their actions, if it doesn't appear to have an abnormality, they keep a minimum amount of information about the hive.
8. Beekeepers are creative in inventing new ways to communicate this information, using signs, letters, objects to solve as fast and efficiently as possible. Although they manage to achieve their goal without the use of specifically designed tools for their work, these issues must be addressed.

Researchers of the field face similar issues; even though they have the time to observe and journal, there is not a user-friendly digital tool available to help them organize their observations. The data that they are recording must be accurate, consistent, and gathered in one place. It appears thorough user research in the available tools has yet to be done to take their needs and the field into account.

Finally, both beekeepers and researchers are using monitoring systems as a way to indicate important marks on their apiaries. Such systems do not seem to cover their needs as they can only monitor some parameters of a few hives that do not actually indicate what is happening in the hive. During the structured scenario, the beekeepers were questioned about the date, practices, and goals of the previous inspection, the goals, and practices during the present inspection and the tools they are going to use, as they approached the hive to follow certain steps to perform an inspection. Those steps were part of an inspection protocol, designed to understand how beekeepers would journal an observation, as well as their hand and body position, by giving the same instructions to multiple beekeepers. The tasks assigned to them included: 1) using the smoker and the hive tool during the inspection, 2) carrying out practices in the hive, 3) observing the frames, 4) moving around with and without the tools, 5) announcing what they observed in each frame regarding the hive population, brood status (egg and capped brood) and food reserve (honey, pollen) in percentages, as well as if there was a queen presence, while they were able to add any other comment (Fig. 2).

Fig. 2. Use of tools and hand interaction during beehive inspection

Through the structured scenario what was discovered was that although beekeepers could follow the instructions, they often preferred to follow a different workflow based on their way of working. Their attention was on the events that take place in the hive with the bees and not on their tools or the position of their hands. Although they were guided to leave their tools on the side while observing a frame, the hive tool seemed to be a part of their hand during the whole inspection. Both of their hands were busy most of the time, trying to perform quickly but steady what was requested.

They also mentioned that putting their tools far away or on the ground is an action they would avoid, so as to reduce their physical fatigue. According to the unstructured scenario, it was detected that the focus of the beekeepers was aimed inside the hives and not on the peripheral environment. They were mainly dedicated in observing, while acting almost instinctively. Their actions were fast but cautious and efficient, while using both hands and always holding the hive tool in one hand. Every tool and part of the hive was placed on a close range from the hive they were inspecting, in order to avoid large movements, bending over or lifting weights, as they wanted to minimize their physical effort per hive. Due to the weather conditions (cold, wind), beekeepers also reduced the information they were looking to keep for later and focused on minimizing the time they would keep the hive open.

Inspection Scenarios. Beehive inspection will possibly take place in two phases: a) by opening the beehive and identifying the current status, b) after finishing up the inspection. Before the next visit, the beekeepers review the data they have recorded so that they can properly prepare the inspection. To meet these requirements, the system must include all of the actions listed in these two stages. The data that the beekeeper will record per hive will include the number of frames, the population, the bees' behaviour, the quantity of brood and the stage it is in, the honey / pollen stocks, the presence of a queen, disorder identification, and food consumption. Thus, during a visit to inspect food consumption in their apiary, the beekeepers can approach a hive and check its condition using data collected by the sensors. They can then begin the inspection based on the protocol chosen and check the frames in relation to the food reserves. During the process, if they notice that there are fewer reserves of honey and pollen from the previous visit, they can proceed to feed them. They can journal the new hive's status in food consumption about food reserves (honey, pollen), and brood status before moving on to the next hive. After finishing the inspection, they return home and have an overall view about the apiary's food consumption during this month.

3.2   Interaction Requirements and Interaction Techniques

Beekeepers, like other agri-food workers, are often required to deal with painful everyday practices for the human body, like lifting and lowering brood and honey boxes that may harm their lower back in the long run [16]. Therefore, they need small and lightweight assistive technologies, as well as interactions that do not restrict their movement in the field. The interface's dialogue with the beekeeper via audiovisual notifications must be carried out carefully. Beekeepers feel it is necessary to use both their mind and their eyes to document the overall situation inside and outside the hive. Any distraction can result in incomplete journaling and, as a result, affect future beekeeping practices. Among the key insights provided by beekeepers during the field research were the inability to hold more tools or objects during beekeeping practices. As a result, it is not surprising that most of them suggested hands-free interactive tools during beekeeping inspections. Another vital requirement they highlighted is instant access to the history of all the beehive health data via GUIs, with an emphasis on previously critical data, particularly when inspecting beehives in a large-scale apiary. The information that was previously memorised or noted through the use of signs, must also be included in the digital journaling process, since a potential data loss or an incorrect interpretation of a past event may determine the future of a bee colony. Bare-hand interaction with touchscreens could not be considered a best practice, primarily because most beekeepers tend to avoid being stung and therefore wear uniforms and thick gloves that prohibit touch interaction, and secondarily because they will have traces of bee products on their bare hands that also makes difficult to interact with any touchscreen device. Furthermore, wearing thick or dirty gloves may make it difficult to perform subtle movements such as typing, tapping on options, or using a touchscreen or traditional keyboard in general. Consequently, multimodal user interfaces that combine tangible and voice interfaces might be an option when time is limited and adverse field conditions, such as low visibility, occur.

Web and mobile application interfaces are mainly used in order to keep beekeepers informed through charts and alert notifications about beehive health status and weather conditions either during apiary inspections or later on in the office [42–44]. Smartwatch interfaces for beekeeping, which are currently in a conceptual design phase, emphasize on displaying real-time changes in the beehive and alerts for the node's battery level [40]. On the other hand, no particular development has been observed in the use of smart emerging technologies, so that the beekeepers can maintain their own digital journal for the beehive inspection with Wearables and Augmented Reality technology. Nowadays, the design of interactive applications for this purpose is limited to the use of common user-platform interaction techniques, allowing beekeepers to type notes, create, input, edit, and delete information about their hives and apiaries, with the use of their keyboard from a desktop computer or a mobile device [45]. Portable devices, combined with the evolutionary capabilities of interaction like tangible interactions, speech recognition and gesture-based interactions are the proposed styles of interaction that can potentially evolve as the future interactions for beekeeping practices. A description of the existing types of interactions and their possible contribution to journaling during beekeeping inspection is mentioned below.

Wearable Interaction. Wearable Technology, wearable devices or wearables are small electronic gadgets with wireless communication capability, which are usually worn on the human body, or easily integrated into accessories and clothing [50, 51]. Physiological and kinematic parameters can be measured, so that users are able to enhance their perception about their performance, or even the conditions of their surroundings and the environment [52].

Ometov et al. (2021) presented a detailed classification of wearables based on the device technology, managing to name 27 different device types. Personal notification devices, Smart watches, Wearable cameras, Smart clothes, Smart contact lenses, Smart gloves, Smart rings, E-Textiles (smart fabrics) and AR devices, are some examples of the wearable technologies mentioned. Recognizing how many options are available and how many combinations could be used in beekeeping practices, we can get a taste of the innumerable ways we can provide the user to interact with both the environment and the interface.

Wearables can also be categorized into the following three types, based on how much energy they consume: low-power, medium-power, and high-power wearables. Devices with displays typically consume more power than those without a graphical output interface [53].

In terms of data collection, the following sensing techniques are already used in wearables: Participatory (active) sensing (gathering information through the user's action), Opportunistic (passive) sensing (gathering time-based or distance based data), and Opportunistic mobile social networks (point-to-point networks of devices that share information with one another) [50].

In this paper, wearables are considered as extremely useful for journaling during the inspection process. As previously stated, beekeepers frequently have their hands full and are usually unable to hold another item. Small smart devices are also easier to carry on the human body. Immediate access to charts of live data collected by sensors, combined with available technologies for manual data input, like speech-based [54] and gesture interaction, would increase presence and add significant value to user experience design.

Physical Object Manipulation and User Experience. Physical objects are characterized by shape, colors, ergonomy, metaphors, mobility, weight, texture, plasticity, functionality, indications, aesthetics and size. Using physical objects could activate innate spatial reasoning skills of the beekeepers, while simultaneously expanding the range of gestures with grasping behaviors [55]. Moreover, the manipulation of a physical object would enhance their user experience with the feeling of touch and response [56]. An interesting challenge when designing interactions is keeping users engaged with the feeling that they are actively participating in the process. Interacting with a physical object, would give beekeepers the feeling that the journaling process is still under their control.

Physical object interactions are based on the way users hold, move, touch an object and transform it. As mentioned above, subtle movements like typing may not be possible during beehive inspections whereas, moving, rotating and tapping on larger tangible interfaces can potentially provide more flexibility in data entry of simple values. Aside from important elements, such as form and functionality, user experience could also be improved with detailed design of other elements placed on the object, like colourful indicators, lighted surfaces, and symbols representing beekeepers' semiotics during beehive inspection.

Gesture-Based Interaction. Recent advances in real-time gesture recognition algorithms have resulted in the development of algorithms that are quite adaptable to different types of hands and have overall recognition accuracy rates greater than 94% [57]. A wider range of available gestures could lead to a more realistic and detailed journal about the behaviour of bees, the condition of each frame and the overall health of the beehive. Given the fact that difficult conditions may prevail during journaling, together with the inability of the beekeeper to grasp other things, wearables with eye-tracking interaction, can be potential alternatives for data input [50].

3.3 Basic Architecture and Infrastructure

This section aims at presenting a high-level overview of the IOHIVE architecture and its connection with the journaling sub-system. Starting from the user side, a user can interact with the IOHIVE platform both through a wearable/tangible device and a web application for visualising data in terms of mobile or desktop interfaces. Through the wearable/tangible interface, the user can record observed inspections. When the user moves away from the actual apiary, he/she can interact with the web application in order either to configure his/her hives for next inspection or to monitor them based on the installed IoT sensors and devices. Every hive has been associated with a list of devices including weather stations, temperature and humidity sensors in/outside the hive, scales, sound sensors etc.

The open and extensible architecture of the IOHIVE platform is designed to facilitate the integration of different end devices for remote beehive monitoring, acquisition of weather/environmental data as well as inspection data. Measurements such as a) the weight of a hive, b) the temperature inside/outside a hive, c) the humidity and d) the sound inside the hive provide valuable information about the status of bee colonies. Environmental or weather data provide a good valuable source of wide area climate and microclimate around the apiaries. In addition to the aforementioned, beehive inspection data, provided by the beekeepers, offer a valuable additional layer of information. This type of empirical data is based on observation or experience and is a subjective measurement of phenomena, as directly experienced by the beekeepers. This data is thus valuable and cannot be ignored. It can be further utilised in terms of correlation with sensed data from the instruments and sensors.

A brief description about the end devices that have been already integrated in the platform is presented on the following Fig. 3:

(a)   (b)   (c)   (d)

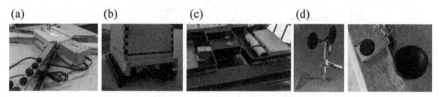

Fig. 3. IOHIVE end devices. a) BEEP base, b) SaveBees SMS scale, c) Kudzu scale based on Sprout, and d) MeteoHelix IoT Pro weather station MeteoWind IoT Pro wind sensor.

The focus of this project, according to the design requirements and research gathered at the early stages of its implementation, is to invest on IoT technologies that provide long-range wireless communications at a low bitrate among the connected objects, such as sensors that operate on a battery (Fig. 4).

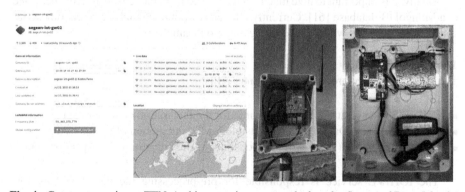

Fig. 4. Gateway overview at TTN. At this stage six gateways deployed at Syros and Paros Islands. These include custom made TTN Gateways based on RPi (3), Beaglebone (1) microcontrollers and LoRank (2).

Thus, the majority of devices used in this project operate over the LoRa low-power wide-area network modulation technique. A few node devices support 3G/4G connectivity for coverage in areas with limited network access or LoRa coverage and communicate through Simple Message Service (SMS) technology via an SMS gateway. In this way the absence of LoRa coverage at the area can be tackled. Therefore, the main goal is to have devices installed in the apiaries which are low power wide area (LPWAN) LoRa nodes that connect to the nearest LoRa gateway [58, 59]. The gateways forward the data to The Things Network (TTN) [60]. Using appropriate payload decoders and web hooks the payload is supplemented with a unique device ID and timestamp and is being pushed to the IOHIVE Service described in the following section (Fig. 5).

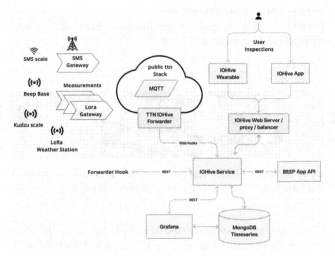

Fig. 5. High-level overview of the IOHIVE architecture

Finally, it is important to note that the data derived from the sensors is being persisted in a MongoDB database [61]. Currently, the latest Mongo 5 database offers timeseries collections combined with a powerful aggregation framework.

The IOHIVE Service
The IOHIVE service provides three distinct APIs:

- IOHIVE Sensor (Data) API - responsible for the integration of sensor data
- IOHIVE Weather (Data) API - responsible for the integration of weather data
- IOHIVE Inspection (Data) API - responsible for the integration of inspection data

The IOHIVE service is responsible for pre-processing the data (validate, format etc.) and store them into the database. The service has been implemented using NestJS/NodeJS technology. Apart from the push API, the service exposes endpoints to allow retrieval/aggregation of data by the IOHIVE App. Grafana has been used as the main framework for generating charts and embedding them into the IOHIVE App. The combination of MongoDB aggregation framework and Grafana offers a flexible framework for developing charts aiming at extracting useful insights about the data. So, data originating from continuous monitoring of a beehive and its surrounding environment can be correlated in time with data coming from inspections. For every cycle of an inspection (finished inspection → start new inspection) a data window can be extracted and analysed. Through appropriate visualization techniques the user has insights about what went wrong during the last inspection period and plans corrective actions (Fig. 6).

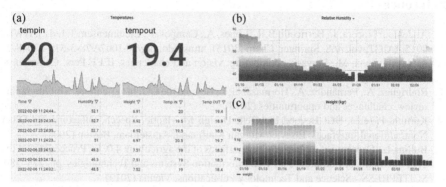

Fig. 6. Visualization of sensor data using charts and tables. Measurements from an SMS scale: a) temperature in/out, b) relative humidity, c) weight.

Furthermore, BEEP app and BEEP base have been integrated in our architecture [19]. Data from the different sensors are being forwarded to the BEEP app through the IOHIVE Service. In addition to them the IOHIVE wearable/tangible device will also feed with inspection data initially the IOHIVE API service and its forwarding services. Based on the user research described above, several inspection checklists will be developed. A data transformation layer, part of the IOHIVE Service, is responsible for transforming data from different sources to the suitable formats for an optimized consumption by the different interfaces. This allows for dynamic/configurable checklists based on the end user needs.

4   Future Work and Directions

Future work will focus on the design of the wearable/tangible system that will support journaling for beehive inspections. This will include the actual design of the physical product, the electronics and the interaction techniques. The design team will also focus on designing the web interfaces, the user roles and the visualisation mechanisms for providing charts and graphs to the end users. Moreover, further development is needed for the completion of the Sensor, Weather and Inspection APIs.

Another important task for the research and design team is to outline and organise the evaluation plan for the case studies that will follow the actual development of the prototypes.

Acknowledgements and Funding. This research has been co-financed by the European Union and Greek national funds through the Operational Program 'Research Innovation Strategies for Smart Specialisation in South Aegean ΟΠΣ 3437', under the call South Aegean Operational Plan 2014–2020 (project code: ΝΑΙΓ1-0043435). Parts of this work was done in collaboration with our project partners: the Institute of Mediterranean Forest Ecosystems and Forest Products Technology (Dr. Sofia Gounari) and Kudzu P.C [62].

References

1. Abdelnour Nocera, J., Barricelli, B.R., Lopes, A., Campos, P., Clemmensen, T. (eds.): HWID 2015. IAICT, vol. 468. Springer, Cham (2015). https://doi.org/10.1007/978-3-319-27048-7
2. Satyanarayanan, M.: Pervasive computing: vision and challenges. IEEE Pers. Commun. **8**, 10–17 (2001)
3. Rodríguez, A., Fernández, A., Hormazábal, J.: Beyond the GUI in agriculture: a bibliographic review, challenges and opportunities (2018)
4. Kortum, P. (ed.): HCI Beyond the GUI: Design for Haptic, Speech, Olfactory and Other Nontraditional Interfaces. Elsevier/Morgan Kaufmann, Amsterdam, Boston (2008)
5. Bollini, L., Caccamo, A., Martino, C.: Interfaces of the agriculture 4.0. In: Proceedings of the 15th International Conference on Web Information Systems and Technologies, pp. 273–280. SCITEPRESS - Science and Technology Publications, Vienna (2019)
6. Sperandio, G., et al.: Beekeeping and honey bee colony health: a review and conceptualization of beekeeping management practices implemented in Europe. Sci. Total Environ. **696**, 133795 (2019)
7. Durant, J.L., Ponisio, L.C.: A regional, honey bee-centered approach is needed to incentivize grower adoption of bee-friendly practices in the almond industry. Front. Sustain. Food Syst. **5**, 261 (2021)
8. Kulhanek, K., et al.: Survey-derived best management practices for backyard beekeepers improve colony health and reduce mortality. PLoS ONE **16**, e0245490 (2021)
9. Werner, G.: ΟΙ ΜΕΛΙΤΟΦΟΡΕΣ ΜΕΛΙΣΣΕΣ ΚΑΙ Η ΕΚΤΡΟΦΗ ΤΟΥΣ. ΒΑΣΔΕΚΗΣ (2009)
10. Zetterman, B.-E.A.: Beekeepers usage of IoT: Data collection, sharing and visualization in the domain of beekeeping (2018)
11. Fiedler, S., et al.: Implementation of the precision beekeeping system for bee colony monitoring in Indonesia and Ethiopia. In: 2020 21th International Carpathian Control Conference (ICCC), pp. 1–6 (2020)
12. Tashakkori, R., Hamza, A.S., Crawford, M.B.: Beemon: an IoT-based beehive monitoring system. Comput. Electron. Agric. **190**, 106427 (2021)
13. Zacepins, A., Brusbardis, V., Meitalovs, J., Stalidzans, E.: Challenges in the development of Precision Beekeeping. Biosyst. Eng. **130**, 60–71 (2015)
14. Adams, E.C.: How to become a beekeeper: learning and skill in managing honeybees. Cult. Geogr. **25**, 31–47 (2018)
15. Farinde, A.J., Soyebo, K.O., Oyedokun, M.O.: Improving farmers attitude towards natural resources management in a democratic and deregulated economy: honey production experience in Oyo state of Nigeria. J. Hum. Ecol. **18**, 31–37 (2005)
16. Fels, D.I., Blackler, A., Cook, D., Foth, M.: Ergonomics in apiculture: a case study based on inspecting movable frame hives for healthy bee activities. Heliyon. **5**, e01973 (2019)
17. Gentry, C.: Small Scale Beekeeping. Peace Corps Information Collection & Exchange (1982)
18. Hadjur, H., Ammar, D., Lefèvre, L.: Toward an intelligent and efficient beehive: a survey of precision beekeeping systems and services. Comput. Electron. Agric. **192**, 106604 (2022)

19. BEEP: digital tools for beekeepers. https://beep.nl
20. OSBeehives - BuzzBox Hive Health Monitor & Beekeeping App. https://www.osbeehives. com. Accessed 11 Feb 2022
21. beeXML.org – Collaboration platform for the standardization of the exchange of data about bees and beekeepers – BeeXML. https://beexml.org/beexml/. Accessed 30 Jan 2022
22. Hodzic, A., Hoang, D.: Detection of Deviations in Beehives Based on Sound Analysis and Machine Learning (2021)
23. Kulyukin, V., Mukherjee, S., Amlathe, P.: Toward audio beehive monitoring: deep learning vs. standard machine learning in classifying beehive audio samples. Appl. Sci. **8**, 1573 (2018)
24. Liao, Y., McGuirk, A., Biggs, B., Chaudhuri, A., Langlois, A., Deters, V.: Noninvasive beehive monitoring through acoustic data using SAS® event stream processing and SAS® Viya®. 24 (2020)
25. Terenzi, A., Cecchi, S., Spinsante, S.: On the importance of the sound emitted by honey bee hives. Vet. Sci. **7**, 168 (2020)
26. Kulyukin, V., Mukherjee, S.: On video analysis of omnidirectional bee traffic: counting bee motions with motion detection and image classification. Appl. Sci. **9**, 3743 (2019)
27. Magnier, B., Ekszterowicz, G., Laurent, J., Rival, M., Pfister, F.: Bee hive traffic monitoring by tracking bee flight paths. In: 13th International Joint Conference on Computer Vision, Imaging and Computer Graphics Theory and Applications, Funchal, Madeira, Portugal, 27–29 January 2018, pp. 563–571 (2018)
28. Spiesman, B.J., et al.: Assessing the potential for deep learning and computer vision to identify bumble bee species from images. Sci Rep. **11**, 7580 (2021)
29. Using artificial intelligence to decode dance patterns of bees. https://www.sas.com/en_us/cus tomers/beefutures.html. Accessed 30 Jan 2022
30. Campbell, J., Mummert, L., Sukthankar, R.: Video monitoring of honey bee colonies at the hive entrance. In: Workshop Visual Observation and Analysis of Vertebrate and Insect Behavior (VAIB) at International Conference on Pattern Recognition (ICPR), Tampa, FL, pp. 1–4 (2008)
31. Campbell, J.M., Dahn, D.C., Ryan, D.A.J.: Capacitance-based sensor for monitoring bees passing through a tunnel. Meas. Sci. Technol. **16**, 2503–2510 (2005)
32. Chen, C., Yang, E.-C., Jiang, J.-A., Lin, T.-T.: An imaging system for monitoring the in-and-out activity of honey bees. Comput. Electron. Agric. **89**, 100–109 (2012)
33. Ghadiri, A.: Implementation of an automated image processing system for observing the activities of honey bees, 100 (2013)
34. Mukherjee, S., Kulyukin, V.: Application of digital particle image velocimetry to insect motion: measurement of incoming, outgoing, and lateral honeybee traffic. Appl. Sci. **10**, 2042 (2020)
35. Tu, G.J., Hansen, M.K., Kryger, P., Ahrendt, P.: Automatic behaviour analysis system for honeybees using computer vision. Comput. Electron. Agric. **122**, 10–18 (2016)
36. Aumann, H.M., Aumann, M.K., Emanetoglu, N.W.: Janus: a combined radar and vibration sensor for beehive monitoring. IEEE Sens. Lett. **5**, 1–4 (2021)
37. Michelsen, A., Kirchner, W.H., Lindauer, M.: Sound and vibrational signals in the dance language of the honeybee, Apis mellifera. Behav. Ecol. Sociobiol. **18**, 207–212 (1986)
38. Schurischuster, S., Remeseiro, B., Radeva, P., Kampel, M.: A preliminary study of image analysis for parasite detection on honey bees. In: Campilho, A., Karray, F., ter Haar Romeny, B. (eds.) ICIAR 2018. LNCS, vol. 10882, pp. 465–473. Springer, Cham (2018). https://doi. org/10.1007/978-3-319-93000-8_52
39. Hadjur, H., Ammar, D., Lefèvre, L.: Analysis of energy consumption in a precision beekeeping system. In: Proceedings of the 10th International Conference on the Internet of Things, pp. 1–8. Association for Computing Machinery, New York (2020)

40. Rahman, A.B.M.S., Lee, M., Lim, J., Cho, Y., Shin, C.: Systematic analysis of environmental issues on ecological smart bee farm by linear regression model. IJHIT **14**, 61–68 (2021)
41. Kulyukin, V.: Audio, image, video, and weather datasets for continuous electronic beehive monitoring. Appl. Sci. **11**, 4632 (2021)
42. Zacepins, A., Kviesis, A., Pecka, A., Osadcuks, V.: Development of Internet of Things concept for Precision Beekeeping. In: 2017 18th International Carpathian Control Conference (ICCC), pp. 23–27 (2017)
43. Kontogiannis, S.: An Internet of Things-based low-power integrated beekeeping safety and conditions monitoring system. Inventions **4**, 52 (2019)
44. Sharp, H., Preece, J., Rogers, Y.: Interaction Design: Beyond Human-Computer Interaction. Wiley, Indianapolis (2019)
45. Benyon, D.: Designing User Experience: A Guide to HCI, UX and Interaction Design. Pearson, London (2019)
46. Brown, A., Johnston, S., Kelly, K.: Using service-oriented architecture and component- based development to build web service applications, 16 (2002)
47. Brown, A.W.: Large-Scale, Component-Based Development. Prentice Hall PTR, Upper Saddle River (2000)
48. Crnkovic, I.: Component-based software engineering — new challenges in software development. Softw. Focus **2**, 127–133 (2001)
49. Mishra, S.K., Sarkar, A.: Service-oriented architecture for Internet of Things: a semantic approach. J. King Saud Univ. – Comput. Inf. Sci. (2021, in press)
50. Ometov, A., et al.: A survey on wearable technology: history, state-of-the-art and current challenges. Comput. Netw. **193**, 108074 (2021)
51. Yoon, H., Park, S.-H.: A non-touchscreen tactile wearable interface as an alternative to touchscreen-based wearable devices. Sensors **20**, 1275 (2020)
52. Luczak, T., Burch, R., Lewis, E., Chander, H., Ball, J.: State-of-the-art review of athletic wearable technology: what 113 strength and conditioning coaches and athletic trainers from the USA said about technology in sports. Int. J. Sports Sci. Coach. **15**, 26–40 (2020)
53. Qaim, W.B., et al.: Towards energy efficiency in the internet of wearable things: a systematic review. IEEE Access **8**, 175412–175435 (2020)
54. Beenotes app
55. Fitzmaurice, G.W.: Graspable user interfaces. University of Toronto (1997)
56. Krestanova, A., Cerny, M., Augustynek, M.: Review: development and technical design of tangible user interfaces in wide-field areas of application. Sensors **21**, 4258 (2021)
57. Zhang, Q., Xiao, S., Yu, Z., Zheng, H., Wang, P.: Hand gesture recognition algorithm combining hand-type adaptive algorithm and effective-area ratio for efficient edge computing. J. Electron. Imag. **30**, 063026-1–063026-18 (2021)
58. Sinha, R.S., Wei, Y., Hwang, S.-H.: A survey on LPWA technology: LoRa and NB-IoT. ICT Express **3**, 14–21 (2017)
59. Bor, M., Vidler, J.E., Roedig, U.: LoRa for the Internet of Things. Presented at the EWSN 2016 Proceedings of the 2016 International Conference on Embedded Wireless Systems and Networks, AUT, 15 February (2016)
60. The Things Network. https://www.thethingsnetwork.org/. Accessed 11 Feb 2022
61. MongoDB: The Application Data Platform. https://www.mongodb.com. Accessed 11 Feb 2022
62. Kudzu, P.C.: https://kudzu.gr/. Accessed 11 Feb 2022

Combining Virtual Reality and Eye Tracking to Recognize Users' Aesthetic Preference for Product Modeling

Wanyu Chen and Haining Wang[(✉)]

School of Design, Hunan University, Changsha 410082, China
haining1872@qq.com

Abstract. As one of the unique cultural products and representative symbols of China, Yixing teapots have a unique aesthetic connotation. The cultural and creative products of Yixing teapot have played a positive role in the inheritance of intangible cultural heritage, however, they still face higher requirements in terms of design innovation and adaptation to users' aesthetic needs. Although several methods of evaluating and measuring user experience have been established, such as subjective reporting and questionnaire surveys, designers still need objective methods to evaluate users' perception and response for Yixing teapots modeling. This paper aims to combine virtual reality and eye tracking technology to recognize users' aesthetic preference for the 3D modeling of Yixing teapots. Eye tracking signals were recorded in a preference categorization task, and users' aesthetic preference was analyzed via eye tracking data and users' subjective evaluation. The results showed that the fixation count and time of first fixation in different AOIs had significant effects on users' subjective evaluation. The study provides an objective method in recognizing users' aesthetic preference, and can provide practical reference for the future modeling design of Yixing teapots.

Keywords: User's aesthetic preference · Product modeling · Virtual reality · Eye tracking · Yixing teapots

1 Introduction

The rapid development of global knowledge economy and experience economy has promoted the prosperity of cultural and creative industries. Teaware production and tea drinking have long history, Yixing teawares first appeared during the Sung dynasty (AD 960–1279) in the Yixing region. The use and production of Yixing ceramic teawares began to flourish in the late Ming dynasty (AD 1600s). For the following three centuries, scholars variously praised, made, inscribed and collected Yixing teawares, which made them renown throughout China and Europe [1]. Yixing teapots have a unique aesthetic connotation, being attractive mainly by elegant modeling and exquisite craftsmanship. Yixing ceramic cultural and creative products have contributed positively to the inheritance of intangible cultural heritage, but still face more challenges in terms of design

M. M. Soares et al. (Eds.): HCII 2022, LNCS 13321, pp. 173–181, 2022.
https://doi.org/10.1007/978-3-031-05897-4_13

innovation and adaptation to users' aesthetic needs. Further investigation of users' aesthetic preference for the modeling of Yixing teapots needs to be conducted to provide deeper insight into Yixing ceramic cultural and creative products design.

With regard to evaluating users' preferences for the modeling of cultural and creative products, researchers usually rely on traditional methods such as questionnaires or interviews to evaluate and measure user experience [2]. The existing findings revealed that traditional methods based on questionnaire surveys have limitations in evaluating user's perception and response. Data from traditional methods are easily affected by the respondent's surroundings, voluntary participation, difficulty of comparisons among product, false feeling of their inner state [3]. This drives a need to establish an integrated and objective method in evaluating user' aesthetic preference for product modeling to draw any conclusive or generalized guidelines for Yixing ceramic cultural and creative products design.

Noticeably, some physiological signals have been associated with the dynamic appreciation flow to distinguish aesthetics [4]. As one of physiological measurements, vision receives the largest amount of information about a product quickly [5]. A user's perceptions and responses to a product are mainly affected by the product's appearance [6]. In general, vision is the first channel to obtain information, and directly impact user's future behavior and intention to experience with the product [7]. Researchers also found that vision is the most important sense in the product-buying experience [8]. More and more researches have applied eye tracking method to product design and explain the meaning of eye movement [9].

The application of eye tracking to virtual reality environments combines the strengths of mobile and desktop-based eye tracking [10]. Virtual reality can provide more information and create a more realistic display experience than traditional two-dimensional media (such as photos) [11]. It provides simulated experiences that create the sensation of being in the real world. Virtual reality has been used in the new product development process for quite a while [12]. In the present, Virtual Reality represents a novel and powerful tool for behavioral research [13]. With the rapid development of VR technology, most scholars believe that combining VR technology with eye tracking will have a promising future, which can greatly promote the analytical research and application of cognitive behavior [14]. The combination of eye tracking and virtual reality has also been applied to study user behavior to provide shopper assistance [10]. The experimental design, technical application and data analysis of these studies laid an important foundation for future research. Whereas, to the best of our knowledge, it has not been utilized in recognizing users' preference for the modeling of cultural and creative products. Thus, a method combining virtual reality and eye tracking will provide a more accurate and objective reference for assessing users' aesthetic perception and experience of product modeling.

This study extends previous research by providing an objective evaluation of users' perception for product modeling. Specifically, we recorded the eye tracking signals of thirty participants in a preference task to investigate the correlation between eye tracking signals and users' subjective evaluation. The findings provide designers with an objective method in evaluating users' aesthetic preferences for product modeling, and provide a more accurate and objective reference basis for the future design of Yixing ceramic cultural and creative products.

2 Methods

2.1 Stimuli

Samples of Yixing teapots were widely collected through product catalogs, Yixing Zisha artistry museum website, related reports and shopping websites. After removing similar samples, a total of 75 preliminary pictures of Yixing teapots were selected according to the principle of clear morphology. Subsequently, thirty participants (15 females, mean age 25) were recruited to classify the 75 Yixing teapots by different features for similarity. Finally, five representative samples were selected using hierarchical cluster analysis (HCA) based on a user-defined similarity metric (see Fig. 1). 3d models of these representative samples were constructed to investigate users' aesthetic preference for the modeling of Yixing teapots in the formal experiment.

Fig. 1. Five representative Yixing teapot samples.

In a technical sense, the five Yixing teapot models were constructed in similar ways. The process consisted of modelling and rendering (see Fig. 2). Modelling was performed by using Rhinoceros v6.0 (www.rhino3d.com). The rendering was performed using the V-Ray 5 for 3ds Max (www.vray.com), operating with Autodesk 3ds Max v2019 (www.autodesk.es).

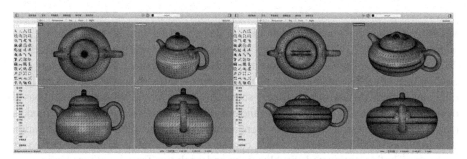

Fig. 2. 3D Yixng teapot models.

Excluding the interference of color and material, the study divided the Yixing teapot into six morphological components (see Fig. 3): the knob, the lid, the spout, the handle, the body, and the bottom, according to the criteria of the Yixing Zisha artistry museum website. These area divisions correspond to different area of interest (AOI), as shown in Table 1.

1. Pot knob

2.Pot lid

3. Pot spout

4.Pot handle

5.Pot body

6.Pot bottom

Fig. 3. Morphological components of Yixing teapot.

Table 1. Product AOI division.

AOI	Definition
AOI_1	Pot knob
AOI_2	Pot lid
AOI_3	Pot spout
AOI_4	Pot handle
AOI_5	Pot body
AOI_6	Pot bottom

VR Environment Set-up. A 3D simulation developed by means of the Unity game engine (Unity v2019.1.2f1; https://unity3d.com). The model was generated in SketchUp 2015 (http://www.sketchup.com), and the textures were extracted from the physical environment to achieve maximum realism. In order to realize the collection and analysis of eye-movement data, a simple display scene was set up for the VR environment based on the principle of being close to reality and not affecting the user's viewing of the models (see Fig. 4). The eye tracking signals were acquired using the Tobii Pro VR Integration based on the HTC Vive HMD, which can be used for a range of human behaviors analysis including automated visualizations and analytics for interaction, navigation, and eye tracking data.

Fig. 4. VR environment set-up.

2.2 Participants

Another thirty participants (15 females, mean age 22.17) were recruited from Hunan University. All participants had a normal or corrected-to-normal vision and were right-handed. They reported no history of neurological or psychiatric disorders. Before the experiment, they were fully informed of the experimental procedures and voluntarily signed written consent forms to participate.

2.3 Procedures

The experiment was conducted in Hunan University laboratory with noise prevented. The individuals were given a brief explanation of the experiment and signed their informed consent to participate. A total of 5 stimulus were used for the experiment, and each Yixing teapot sample rotated at a uniform speed and displayed in the VR environment.

At the beginning of the study, each participant sat down and relaxed for 10 min. Then they put on the Tobii Pro VR Integration based on the HTC Vive HMD (see Fig. 5), and watched a 1-min blank screen to create a common state of baseline calm. When the blank screen ended, a blank screen with a cross was presented in 2 s to draw participants' sight back. The stimulus was randomly presented with a duration of 30 s. After viewing the sample, the users were asking to orally evaluate the aesthetic preference of each Yixing teapot using a 7-point Likert scale embedded in the VR environment. The task paradigm of the experiment was shown in Fig. 6.

Fig. 5. Exemplary experimental set-up.

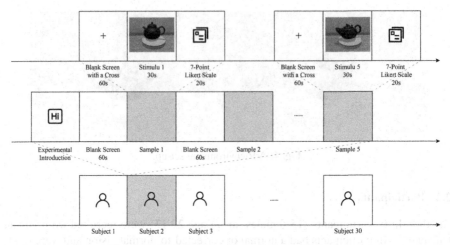

Fig. 6. Schematic illustration of an example trial.

2.4 Eye Tracking Data Recording

The eye tracking signals were acquired using the Tobii Pro VR Integration based on the HTC Vive HMD. Eye tracking signals were imported into Tobii Pro VR Analytics. Tobii Pro VR Analytics is an analysis software tool that integrates into new or existing Unity environments. The software enables collection and playback of eye tracking data in Unity environments. During the recording, the experimenter observed the participants' gaze cursor in real time on external screen. Participants were asked to avoid extensive or vigorous head movements when stimuli were presented. Metrics including fixation count, total fixation duration, average fixation duration, and time to first fixation were extracted.

2.5 Data Analyses

Homogeneity of variance test was conducted to test the user' subjective evaluation (liked-disliked) against the eye tacking indicator data in SPSS 26.0 (see Table 2). Eye tracking indexes included fixation count, total fixation duration, and average fixation duration. Results showed that all indicators passed the test with $p > 0.05$, allowing for the next step of one-way ANOVA.

Table 2. The result of Homogeneity of variance test.

Eye tracking index	Levene	df1	df1	Sig.
Fixation count	0.734	6	143	0.542
Total fixation duration	0.558	6	143	0.648
Average fixation duration	0.906	6	143	0.453

3 Results

One-way ANOVA was conducted to test whether eye tracking data influences users' perception for the modeling of Yixing teapots. Fixation count, total fixation duration, and average fixation duration were analyzed using users' subjective evaluation (dislikes-likes) as influencing factors (see Table 3). The ANOVA results indicated that fixation count had a significant effect on users' subjective evaluation (F = 3.358, p = 0.016), i.e., fixation count significantly reflected user' aesthetic preference.

Table 3. The correlation between users' subjective evaluation and eye tracking indexes.

Eye tracking index	F	Sig.
Fixation count	3.358	0.016
Total fixation duration	0.744	0.620
Average fixation duration	1.064	0.412

In order to study the relationship between fixation count and time to first fixation of different AOIs and users' aesthetic preference, fixation count and time to first fixation in different AOIs were analyzed using one-way ANOVA with users' subjective evaluation (liked-disliked) as the influencing factor, and the results are shown in Table 4 and Table 5.

Table 4. The correlation between users' subjective evaluation and fixation count in different AOIs.

AOI	F	Sig.
AOI_1	0.536	0.776
AOI_2	1.912	0.122
AOI_3	2.048	0.100
AOI_4	0.516	0.790
AOI_5	3.069	0.023
AOI_6	0.459	0.765

It can be seen from the tables that at the significance level of 0. 05, fixation count in AOI_5 had a significant effect on users' subjective evaluation, and time to first fixation in AOI_3, AOI_4 and AOI_5 had a significant effect on users' aesthetic preference. At the significance level of 0.1, fixation count in AOI_3 had a significant effect on users' subjective evaluation.

The results in Table 4 showed that fixation count was closely related to users' aesthetic. Specifically, fixation count in pot body and spout had a significant effect on users' subjective evaluation. Users will look more at important or interesting product design features than at unimportant or uninteresting ones [15]. This means that for the design of Yixing teapots, the design of the body and spout is crucial, which will influence the users' aesthetic preference.

Table 5. The correlation between users' subjective evaluation and time to first fixation in different AOIs.

AOI	F	Sig.
AOI_1	1.655	0.177
AOI_2	0.245	0.957
AOI_3	2.681	0.040
AOI_4	2.857	0.031
AOI_5	3.507	0.013
AOI_6	0.561	0.693

The results in Table 5 showed that time to first fixation in pot body, handle and spout had a significant effect on users' subjective evaluation. Time to first Fixation is the time from the start of a task until a particular AOI is fixated for the first time. It can provide information about how certain aspects of a visual scene are prioritized. Thus, the design of the body, handle and spout should be prioritized by the designer to attract users' attention.

4   Conclusion

Enhancing users' overall aesthetic experience of Yixing ceramic cultural and creative products is essential for designers. However, existing methods in evaluating users' aesthetic preference for product modeling cannot provide designers with integrated and objective guidelines. This work provided an objective evaluation of users' preference via combining virtual reality and eye tracking. Five representative Yixing teapot samples were selected to a preference task. Participants' eye tracking signals were recorded when they observed and judged their preferences for the product modeling.

The results showed that two indicators, fixation count and time of first fixation in different AOIs, had significant effects on users' subjective evaluation. Specifically, fixation count in pot body and spout significantly influenced the user' subjective evaluation, and time to first fixation in pot body, handle and spout also had a significant effect on user preference. This means that for Yixing teapot design, the design of these features should be more visual salient to attract user's visual attention.

The evaluation method via eye tracking could enable designers to objectively evaluate users' aesthetic experience and perception for the modeling of Yixing teapots when the designers establish prototypes. It will help improve the situation that previous scholars predominantly rely on questionnaires or interviews when evaluating users' preferences. This study can guide the cultural and creative product design of designers, and enhance user' overall aesthetic experience and perception of Yixing teapots. The cultural and creative products of Yixing teapots will be more in line with the users' aesthetic needs in the future.

Although considerable efforts have been devoted to optimizing the research scheme, limitations still exist in this study. Only eye tracking metrics involved in visual information access were employed. More physiological signals that might be involved in evaluating user' preference, such as electrocardiogram (ECG), electrodermal activity (EDA), electroencephalography (EEG), should be investigated. In the future work, more attention would be paid to enrich product categories.

References

1. Chow, S.-K., Chan, K.-L.: Reconstruction of photorealistic 3D model of ceramic artefacts for interactive virtual exhibition. J. Cult. Herlt. **10**(2), 161–173 (2009)
2. Zhu, S.S., Dong, Y.N.: Evaluation of liangzhu cultural artifacts based on perceptual image. Appl. Mech. Mater. 2187 (2013). https://doi.org/10.4028/www.scientific.net/AMM.268-270.1986
3. Ariely, D., Berns, G.S.: Science and society neuromarketing: the hope and hype of neuroimaging in business. Nat. Rev. Neurosci. **11**(4), 284–292 (2010)
4. Guo, F., et al.: Evaluating users' preference for the appearance of humanoid robots via event-related potentials and spectral perturbations. Behav. Inform. Technol. 1–17 (2021)
5. Schifferstein, H.N.J., Desmet, P.M.A.: The effects of sensory impairments on product experience and personal well-being. Ergonomics **50**(12), 2026–2048 (2007)
6. Ho, C.H., Lu, Y.N.: Can pupil size be measured to assess design products? Int. J. Ind. Ergonm. **44**(3), 436–441 (2014)
7. Moshagen, M., Thielsch, M.T.: Facets of visual aesthetics. Int. J. Hum Comput Stud. **68**(10), 689–709 (2010)
8. Fenko, A., Schifferstein, H., Hekkert, P.: Looking hot or feeling hot: What determines the product experience of warmth? Mater. Des. **31**(3), 1325–1331 (2010)
9. Guo, F., et al.: Can eye-tracking data be measured to assess product design? Visual attention mechanism should be considered. Int. J. Ind. Ergonm. **53**, 229–235 (2016)
10. Meissner, M., et al.: Combining virtual reality and mobile eye tracking to provide a naturalistic experimental environment for shopper research. J. Bus. Res. **100**, 445–458 (2019)
11. Luo, S., et al.: Sit down and rest: use of virtual reality to evaluate preferences and mental restoration in urban park pavilions. Landsc. Urban Plan. **220**, 104336 (2022)
12. Purschke, F., Schulze M., Zimmermann P.: Virtual reality-new methods for improving and accelerating the development process in vehicle styling and design, pp. 789–797. IEEE Hannover, Germany (1998)
13. Chicchi Giglioli, I.A., et al.: A novel integrating virtual reality approach for the assessment of the attachment behavioral system. Front. Psychol. **8**, 959 (2017)
14. Jacob, R.J.K., et al.: Eye tracking in human-computer iteraction and usability research: ready to deliver the promises. In: The Mind's Eye, pp. 573–605 (2013)
15. Henderson, J.M.: Eye movements and scene perception (2012)

A Study of the Affordance of Haptic Stimuli in a Simulated Haunted House

Gina Clepper[1] , Aravind Gopinath[1] , Juan S. Martinez[1] ,
Ahmed Farooq[1,2] , and Hong Z. Tan[1](✉)

[1] Haptic Interface Research Lab, Purdue University, West Lafayette, IN, USA
gclepper@alumni.purdue.edu, {gopinath,mart1304,hongtan}@purdue.edu
[2] Tampere Unit for Computer-Human Interaction (TAUCHI), Tampere University,
Tampere, Finland
ahmed.farooq@tuni.fi

Abstract. The present study investigates the affordance of vibrotactile
signals in a simulated haunted house. Participants experienced a virtual
séance using a head-mounted display, sound, and haptic stimuli on the
palm and thighs. In one condition, six unique, handcrafted haptic signals (*cicadas, frog, thunder, earthquake, heartbeat, knock*) were presented
alongside appropriate events in the narrative. In another condition, a single multiplexed stimulus was presented for every event; this signal was a
composite of the six distinct signals. Adjective ratings were collected for
both conditions for each participant. Results showed that the extent to
which a haptic signal enhanced the sense of immersion depended on the
match between the signal and the natural phenomenon it represented.
The unique, handcrafted signals generally were rated as more immersive
than the multiplexed signal. However, the signal *cicadas* had a distinct
spectral signature that stood out in the multiplexed signal. Participants
rated the distinct *cicadas* signal and the multiplexed signal as similarly
immersive. Our results demonstrate that carefully handcrafted vibrotactile signals can enhance the sense of immersion in virtual reality. Furthermore, participants may rate a haptic signal as more immersive if it
contains features congruent with the natural event it represents, regardless of extraneous, incongruent features.

Keywords: Haptic affordance · Haptic design · Distinctiveness of
haptic signals

1 Introduction

As our ability to create rich and novel haptic sensations grows, so too does the
interest in the potential of haptics to enhance immersion in remote and virtual
environments. *Immersion* here refers to the degree to which a simulated environment envelopes or surrounds a user, a key factor in how engaged the user
feels in the simulation [10]. Many studies have examined the role that haptics

© The Author(s), under exclusive license to Springer Nature Switzerland AG 2022
M. M. Soares et al. (Eds.): HCII 2022, LNCS 13321, pp. 182–197, 2022.
https://doi.org/10.1007/978-3-031-05897-4_14

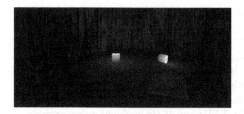 

Fig. 1. Left: A scene simulating a séance in the virtual haunted house, with a representation of a hand on the *palmScape*. Right: A participant wearing the VR headset with one hand resting on the *palmScape* display.

Fig. 2. The two vibrotactile displays employed in this study. Left: the *palmScape*. Right: a chair with tactors concealed, with an inset showing the two tactors on each side of the seat cushion.

plays in enhancing users' experience from various perspectives such as affective communication [4,5,12,18]. The present study explores the affordance of vibrotactile stimuli in a simulated haunted house VR with accompanying visual and audio events (Fig. 1).

When properly synchronized with high congruency, multimodal stimuli can enhance the user's experience in a virtual scenario by leveraging sensory experiences we are familiar with from our daily lives. While most VR environments may be dominated with sight and sound, including haptic feedback can contribute to the extensiveness (the range of sensory modalities presented) and vividness (quality) of a simulation [6]. But how distinctive and realistic those signals need to be to immerse the user is still an open question. While conventional wisdom may prefer high-fidelity systems for better immersion, research that employs stimuli of different levels of realism points to similar levels of effectiveness [11,19]. For example, a number of relatively high-fidelity wearable haptics that simulate grasping or touching virtual objects have been shown to be effective in enhancing the user's sense of realism in VR [9]. Passive haptics—objects in the real world (often static and low-fidelity) that represent virtual objects—have also shown to be effective at enhancing presence [6]. In one study, participants wearing VR headsets experienced significantly higher changes in heart rate and skin conductance when a 20-foot pit in the virtual world was simulated by a drop in the floor of the physical world—even though the real drop was only several inches deep [6].

Table 1. Haptic signals employed in the present study

	Signal name	Location	Description
1	Cicadas	*palm*	Rough, rhythmic: 120-Hz background noise with 32-Hz amplitude modulation and four 60-Hz bursts with 32-Hz modulation
2	Frog	*palm*	Rough, rhythmic: 50 Hz and 120 Hz superimposed with 1.7 Hz and 16 Hz modulation, respectively
3	Thunder	*palm*	Impact then decay: initial 135 Hz and 150 Hz at high amplitude, then attenuation following Gaussian envelope
4	Earthquake	*palm*	Build-up then decay: 30 Hz modulated with Gaussian envelope
5	Heartbeat	*palm*	Smooth beating: 20–30 Hz pulses
6	Knock	*palm*	Short pulses: 30 Hz and 300 Hz superimposed
7	Multiplex	*palm*	Complex: derived from signals 1–6
8	Rattling chair	*seat cushion*	Rumble: 170 Hz pulses below each leg

The present study explores how haptic stimulation can enhance one's sense of immersion, novelty, and creepiness in a haunted house. Two types of haptic stimuli were used: distinct signals that were hand-curated to match the sight and sound of a specific event, and a single multiplexed signal that was employed for all events. Participants experienced séance-themed visual and sound effects. At key points in the narrative, such as the arrival of a croaking frog or booming thunder, vibrotactile stimuli were presented to the user's palm (Fig. 2, left). Concealed actuators embedded in the seat cushion also rattled the user's chair (Fig. 2, right). After the five minute presentation, participants completed a questionnaire on their experience. By assigning the participants randomly to the condition of distinct stimuli followed by the multiplex condition or vice versa, we hoped to determine the degree to which the distinctiveness of the haptic stimuli affected their affordance in the haunted house experience.

2   Related Work

This study utilizes the vibrotactile signals on a *palmScape* haptic display developed by Shim and Tan [14]. The *palmScape* signals were designed to imitate calm and pleasant (low arousal, high valence) natural phenomena using features like intensity, frequency, and rhythm. The present study uses a subset of these signals, shown in Table 1.

Prior to the present study, a pilot study was conducted, in which the *palmScape* signals were incorporated into a haunted house narrative [2]. Twenty-two participants volunteered to sit in a dark booth and feel haptic, visual, and audio effects as part of a fictitious séance. A questionnaire was used to determine whether the haptic effects affected the participants' sense of immersion, novelty, and creepiness. The results indicate that the *rattling chair*, *heartbeat*, *frog*, and *thunder* signals were most effective in eliciting positive perceptions and a sense of creepiness. Moreover, stimulus-label compatibility seemed to be an important factor in those perceptions; for the three most positively received *palmScape* signals, "expected," "familiar," and "life-like" were the most common neutral or positive adjectives chosen, and "confusing" was the most common negative adjective chosen overall.

The findings of the pilot study suggest that life-like haptic effects may increase perceived immersion and enjoyment of a haunted house. However, it is not clear to what degree the distinctiveness of the haptic stimuli determined this enjoyment, as opposed to the context in which the stimuli were presented in the narrative. It is possible that less distinctive, less unique, and even less realistic stimuli might be sufficient to achieve the same emotional effect. The present study was designed to test the affordances of distinct and scenario-specific haptic signals vs. a complex but general vibrotactile signal.

3   Methods

3.1   Participants

Thirty-one participants (10 females) aged 21 to 32 years (25 ± 3 years) took part and were compensated $10.00 for their participation. All participants signed an IRB-approved informed consent form.

3.2   Apparatus

The *palmScape* display employed in the present study is comprised of a 2-by-2 array of 30-mm diameter, wide-band audio exciters (Tectonic Elements, Model TEAX13C02-8/RH) embedded within a silicon disk, shown in Fig. 2 (left). To feel the signals, the user rests a hand on the plastic housing, with the palm covering the four tactors. For further details about the *palmScape* signals and apparatus, see [14].

Besides the *palmScape* display, an additional four actuators (Tectonic Elements, Model TEAX25C10-8/HS) were hidden in the participant's seat cushion, two under each thigh, as shown in Fig. 2 (right). The actuators were freely suspended using a plastic attachment within the chair cushion to ensure that they could be excited up to 1.5 mm under the weight of the leg. Black cloth was used to conceal the chair tactors, and participants were not informed in advance that haptic feedback would occur from that location. Audio and visual stimuli were presented using an Oculus Quest 2 headset (https://www.oculus.com/), as shown in Fig. 1 (right).

3.3   Stimuli

In trial A, the participant experienced multiple, distinct, nature-inspired haptic stimuli at key points in the narrative (see Signals 1 to 6 in Table 1). In trial B, the participant experienced a single multiplexed stimulus repeated at each of those key points in the narrative (see Signal 7 in Table 1). This composite stimulus was derived from six of the distinct stimuli used in trial A and modulated according to both frequency and amplitude to ensure that the perceptual output of key individual characteristics of each of the original six signals could be felt by the user. Amplitude, frequency, and time variations were counterbalanced such that the multiplexed signal had a similar perceived intensity as the six distinct signals [8].

3.4 Experimental Conditions

Each participant completed two trials, A and B, varying only in the haptic stimuli presented to the palm. The order of the two trials was randomly assigned to each participant. The *rattling chair* setup remained identical for both trial A and trial B and therefore was expected to garner similar responses in each trial.

3.5 Procedure

For each trial, participants were asked to sit down in the chair with the concealed actuators, lay their right hand gently on the *palmScape*, and watch a five-minute 3D video via the VR headset. In virtual reality, participants were led by a narrator through a fictitious séance, a form of ghostly entertainment popular in the 19th century in which participants sit in the dark, join hands, and attempt to commune with spirits [15]. Scenes of a haunted marsh and wooden cabin were rendered using Unity (https://unity.com/). Participants could lean, twist, and turn their heads to explore their surroundings. Synchronous sounds, visuals, and haptics were integrated into the narrative. For instance, the narration "come quickly now; there is a storm approaching" was accompanied by the *thunder* vibration delivered by the *palmScape*, visuals of lightning striking a nearby virtual tree, and the sound effect of thunder. At the end of the séance, the actuators in the chair vibrated to signify a spirit's arrival.

Afterward, participants sat with an experimenter and answered a questionnaire. First, they were asked a series of open-ended questions:

> *How did it go?*
> *Have you been to a haunted house before?*
> *Have you been to a séance before?*
> *What did you expect (to feel, sense, or see)?*
> *What surprised or was novel to you?*
> *Tell me about an experience that stands out to you.*
> *Did the haptic sensations make you feel more/less immersed?*

Next, participants chose an adjective to describe each of the haptic stimuli in the order of their first appearance in the narrative. A word bank of suggested adjectives, shown in Table 2, was provided, and participants were given the choice to select from these suggestions or to choose another word entirely. These adjectives were sourced from the Microsoft Desirability Toolkit, with the

Table 2. Adjectives provided in random order to participants as suggestions during the questionnaire.

Immersive	Neutral	Not immersive
Exciting	Calm	Boring
Clear	Complex	Confusing
Effective	Expected	Ineffective
Satisfying	Unpredictable	Undesirable
Consistent	Familiar	Inconsistent
Comfortable	Unconventional	Overwhelming
Engaging	Slow	Distracting
Creepy	Fast	Simplistic
Scary		

exception of "creepy" and "scary," which were haunted house context-specific additions [1]. The numbers of words with positive, negative, and neutral connotations were balanced in the word bank, based on the recommendations of the Toolkit designers. The order of the words in the bank was randomized for each participant. Unbeknownst to the participants, these adjectives were categorized by experimenters as "immersive," "neutral," and "not immersive," as shown in Table 2. *Creepy* and *scary* were categorized as "immersive" given the haunted house context. If participants generated an adjective from outside the word bank, e.g. "realistic," clarification was sought by the experimenter. The word would then be categorized accordingly and kept consistent across all participants. Likewise, if participants selected a "neutral" adjective with ambiguous valence (e.g. "expected"), clarification was sought, and the response was categorized as "immersive" or "not immersive" if possible. This was done in order to gather as much information as possible related to immersion. Participants also chose a modifier for their adjective on a 5-point Likert scale ranging from "Not _____" to "Very _____."

During the questionnaire, participants were provided a *palmScape* to feel the stimuli again if desired. For trial A, these stimuli were the distinct, nature-inspired haptic signals. For trial B, the single multiplexed stimulus was presented every time, just like during the narrative experience. Experimenters did not comment on the fact that the same stimulus was being repeatedly presented in trial B, or the fact that the stimuli differed at all between the two trials.

After completion of the questionnaire, the VR experience and adjective rating exercise were repeated for the second trial.

3.6 Results

Overall Impressions Were Positive for Both Trials. From the open-ended questions, it was learnt that most participants (24 out of 31) had previously

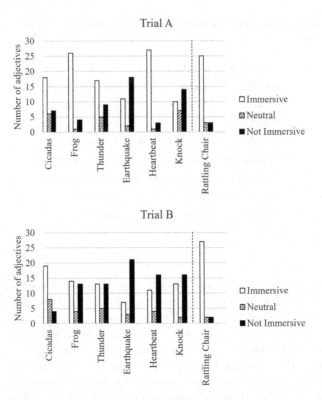

Fig. 3. Adjective responses for distinct *palmScape* signals in trial A (top) and repeated multiplexed signal in trial B (bottom). The number of "immersive" (white), "neutral" (striped), and "not immersive" (black) adjective responses aggregated across all 31 participants are shown for each of the 6 haptic stimuli presented to the palm in order of first appearance. The *rattling chair* stimulus (right of the dotted line) was the same for trials A and B.

been to a haunted house, though none had experienced a séance. Overall, all but one participant responded positively to the question, "how did it go?" after experiencing the first trial. Twenty-three participants explicitly stated that the haptic effects made them feel "more" immersed after experiencing the first trial; on this question, little difference was observed between those who experienced trial A first (of whom 11 reported "more" immersed) and those who experienced trial B first (12 reported "more" immersed). Like in the pilot study, the *rattling chair* was cited most often as surprising, novel, or stand-out; twenty participants mentioned it in their freely recalled answers. Feelings of creepiness were definitely achieved; the words "creepy" or "scary" were mentioned 49 times across the 31 questionnaires, with the *rattling chair*, *knock*, and *thunder* signals receiving the most accolades.

Responses to the Distinct, Nature-Inspired Signals Varied. Figure 3 summarizes the adjective responses. The upper plot shows responses from trial A, in which participants felt distinct, nature-inspired *palmScape* signals. These signals are listed along the x-axis. The adjectives that participants chose to describe these signals were categorized as "immersive," "neutral," or "not immersive." The total number of adjectives in each category for each signal were aggregated across all participants and plotted as columns. The higher the "immersive" column (in white), the more participants chose words like "effective" and "realistic" to describe that signal. The higher the "not immersive" column (in black), the more participants chose words like "confusing" and "distracting."

As might be expected for the diverse signals presented in trial A, the adjectives chosen by participants varied from signal to signal. For the *heartbeat*, *frog*, and *rattling chair*, participants largely responded positively and overwhelmingly selected "immersive" adjectives. Likewise for *cicadas* and *thunder*, the majority of responses were "immersive." However, for *earthquake* and *knock*, more participants responded with "not immersive" adjectives than with "immersive" ones. Participants' answers to the open-ended questions offer some insight into this variation, as will be discussed in the following section.

Responses to the Multiplexed Signal Were Not Uniform. The lower plot of Fig. 3 shows responses from trial B, in which the same multiplexed signal was repeated each time a haptic stimulus was presented to the palm. Even though only a single repeated signal was presented to the palm in trial B, the responses to that multiplexed signal were not uniform across the narrated events. Adjective responses were more positive when the signal was labelled as *cicadas* (19 positive responses) than when labelled as *earthquake* (7 positive responses), for example. This may reflect the different ways that the multiplexed signal used in trial B resembled the sensations felt with the six distinct signals used in trial A, as will be discussed in the next section.

Distinct Signals Were Perceived as "More Immersive" than the Multiplexed Signal in Most Cases. Comparing the two trials in Fig. 3, participants generally selected more "immersive" adjectives and fewer "not immersive" adjectives when describing the handcrafted *palmScape* signals used in trial A than when describing the repeated multiplexed stimulus used in trial B. This was true when responses were aggregated across all signals and participants. It was also true for four of the six signals presented to the palm (*frog*, *thunder*, *earthquake*, *heartbeat*); for each of these signals, participants chose more "immersive" adjectives and fewer "not immersive" adjectives in trial A than B. One of the two exceptional cases was *cicadas*, for which the multiplexed stimulus garnered responses very similar to the signal specifically designed to imitate a cicada. The other exception was *knock*, which was described more neutrally in trial A than in B but with otherwise similar responses between the two trials.

Notably, the magnitude of the difference between trials A and B was the greatest for the two signals that garnered the most "immersive" adjective responses in trial A, *frog* and *heartbeat*. For all other signals, the difference in the number of "immersive" adjective responses in the two trials was small (no more than 4 adjectives difference).

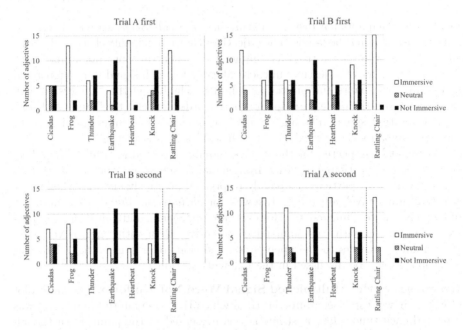

Fig. 4. Adjective responses for distinct *palmScape* signals in trial A (top) and repeated multiplexed signal in trial B (bottom), for two groups of participants: those who experienced trial A then trial B (left, $n = 15$), and those who experienced trial B then trial A (right, $n = 16$). The number of "immersive" (white), "neutral" (striped), and "not immersive" (black) adjective responses aggregated across all n participants are shown for each of the 6 haptic stimuli presented to the palm in order of first appearance. The *rattling chair* stimulus (right of the dotted line) was identical for trials A and B.

The difference in response between the two trials is also apparent when we divide the participants into two groups based on trial order. The left hand side of Fig. 4 shows the responses for the 15 participants who experienced the handcrafted signals in trial A first (above) and the multiplexed signal in trial B second (below). These participants gave many more "not immersive" responses in trial B (49) than they had in trial A (36). For each individual signal presented to the palm, they selected at least as many "not immersive" adjectives to describe trial B than they had selected for trial A, with one exception (*cicadas*).

Likewise, the right hand side of Fig. 4 shows responses for the 16 participants who experienced trial B (above) then A (below). These participants gave more "immersive" responses to describe trial A (51) than they had in trial B (42). For each *palmScape* signal, they selected more "immersive" adjectives in trial A than they had in B, with the exception of *knock*. On the whole, these results suggest participants responded positively to most of the handcrafted signals after previously experiencing the multiplexed signal—and responded mostly negatively to the multiplexed signal after having previously experienced the handcrafted signals.

Likert Scores Offer Some Support of Preference for Distinct Signals.
Due to a programming error, the instructions for the Likert score portion of the
questionnaire were inconsistent. Fifteen of the participants were asked, "how
[insert adjective] was the signal?" while the remaining sixteen participants were
asked specifically "how lifelike was the signal?" For the first question, responses
tended to be stronger for the distinct trial A signals than the multiplexed trial B
signal, save for *knock* and *cicadas*, though no statistically significant difference
was found between the trials ($p = 0.10$). For the second question, the distinct
trial A signals were by far perceived as more lifelike than the multiplexed signal
($p << 0.001$).

**Most Participants—But Not All—Were Aware that the Haptic Sig-
nals Changed Between the Two Trials.** When asked "how did it go?" over
half of the participants (18 of 31) mentioned unprompted that the haptic signals
in the second trial felt different than those in the first. Most of those participants
(10 of 18) expressed a preference for the distinct *palmScape* signals in trial A;
one expressed preference for the multiplexed signal in trial B, and the remainder
(7 of 18) noted the difference but didn't mention any preference. Those who preferred the handcrafted *palmScape* signals described them as "completely different," "much better," and "more realistic" compared to the "not as clear," "more
nois[y]" multiplexed signal. Some described differences in perceived magnitude
(i.e. signals in trial A were "stronger," "closer," "more aggressive," "powerful")
or synchronicity (more "in sync," "flows better") that led them to prefer the
handcrafted signals.

Interestingly, other participants were less certain that a change had occurred.
In fact, some (3 of 31) thought there was clearly no difference between the haptic signals in trials A and B. When asked "how did it go?" after experiencing
trial B then trial A, one participant attributed the increased "fun" of the second trial to "now knowing what to expect," supposing that he "could focus
more on calibration between audiovisual and [haptics] on the hand" after experiencing two trials. Another hypothesized that any perceived differences were
attributable to experiencing the signals "separate" from context (while completing the questionnaire) versus the "immersion" of feeling the signals "together."
A third participant confirmed in debriefing that he had no idea that trials A
and B featured different signals, or that trial B featured repetitions of the same
signal. The remaining participants (10 of 31) fell somewhere between on the
spectrum between full awareness and total lack of awareness. Many noticed the
multiplexed signal was being repeated only midway through the questionnaire,
after being allowed to replay the signal multiple times.

3.7   Discussion

Touch is a particularly promising channel for enhancing immersion. First, touch
is well-suited for presenting information unobtrusively in the ambience rather
than at the center of attention [7]. Second, touch is inherently affective. We are
socialized to convey intimate emotions through touch, so even haptic feedback

generated mechanically can be laden with emotional implication [17]. Third, touch requires proximity. By encroaching on the user's personal space, touch has the unique potential to invoke uncomfortable, unsettling, or even creepy feelings [3,13].

In our everyday lives, we are constantly experiencing haptic sensations that accompany visual and auditory stimuli. Yet except for a few cases where we focus on the haptic sensations alone (such as a heartbeat), most haptic sensations do not convey specific meanings when they are presented alone in the absence of visual or auditory counterparts. One of the authors vividly remembers how, in the absence of any auditory stimuli, moving the end effector of a force-feedback display back and forth gave rise to friction and viscosity perception but not the mental image of a cello bow. During the development of the *palmScape* display [14], each handcrafted vibrotactile signal was explicitly designed for a target scenario, such as *cicadas* and *thunder*. One may argue that such an approach invariably *biased* or *tainted* the users' perception of the *palmScape* signals. If that were the case, then we would expect the signals in trial A to lead to more positive and neutral adjective responses than that in trial B. A second possibility is that users may exhibit a haptic form of "confirmation bias," in that participants can selectively focus on characteristics of a haptic signal that are relevant to the current context. As long as the haptic signals in either trial A or trial B contain sufficient features that may lend themselves to the context, similar adjective responses are expected in trials A and B. The third possibility is that the adjective responses to the multiplexed signal in trial B would be more positive than those to the individual haptic signals in trial A. This seems unlikely given the effort in designing the trial A signals to fit the context they were mapped to. The results of the present study yield evidence towards the first two possible outcomes.

In Some Cases Distinct, Handcrafted Signals May be Preferable to a Multiplexed Signal. For certain events in the present study (*heartbeat, frog, thunder,* and *earthquake*), the handcrafted signals had a more immersive effect than the multiplexed signal when placed in the same narrative context. In the most extreme case (*heartbeat*), perceptions of the signal totally reversed between the two trials; when presented the handcrafted signal, the majority of participants chose "immersive" adjectives (e.g. "expected" or "familiar" in a positive way), whereas for the multiplexed signal, the majority chose "not immersive" adjectives ("confusing" or "inconsistent").

It Is Possible to Induce Selective Focus on Specific Characteristics of a Multiplexed Signal Relevant to the Current Context. For *cicadas*, results were similar when the handcrafted and multiplexed signals were presented, with the majority of participants selecting "immersive" adjectives in both cases. If anything, participants may have favored the multiplexed signal slightly. Likewise for *knock*, results were similar between the two trials, though the multiplexed signal was the more polarizing of the two options, garnering fewer "neutral" adjective responses.

What could account for this variation? Why were only certain handcrafted signals preferred to the multiplexed signal, whereas in other cases, the multiplexed signal was sufficient to garner a similar response? And what role do other modalities play in inducing focus on selective characteristics of multiplexed signal? We offer several conceivable possibilities to address these questions:

Suitability of Signals: One explanation is that some handcrafted signals were more successful than others in fitting their labels. For example, of all the handcrafted signals, *knock* garnered the fewest positive or "immersive" responses. In fact, the most commonly adjectives chosen to describe it were "simplistic" (4 participants) and "boring" (3 participants). Even among the group of participants who experienced the multiplexed signal before the handcrafted signals—and who otherwise expressed preference for the handcrafted signals across the board (see Fig. 4, right)—*knock* was the one signal that was received more negatively in the second trial than the first. It is therefore possible that neither the handcrafted haptic *knock* nor the multiplexed signal resemble the sensation of a real knock. It is reasonable that the bias toward handcrafted, artificial haptic signals would only extend to signals that bear resemblance to the real phenomena they are intended to imitate.

The inability to disentangle participants' perceptions of realism and immersion is perhaps a limitation of the present study. Given the open-ended nature of the adjective selection process, participants were not questioned explicitly about the appropriateness of the signals. Future studies on this topic could employ a multidimensional rating system that polls participants about realism and immersion separately, to better understand this potential link. It could also be revealing to ask participants what they expect each phenomenon to feel like, particularly phenomena that are not usually experienced haptically. For instance, most participants had likely heard or seen cicadas but not held a cicada in their hands. Exploring what it means for a haptic representation of a typically aural or visual experience to be "realistic" is a subject ripe for exploration, though beyond the scope of this study.

Myriad Multiplexings: The particular multiplexed signal employed here could also be a factor in why participants exhibited bias toward certain handcrafted signals but not others. The composite signal used in trial B was created from the six handcrafted signals using amplitude and frequency modulation [8]. Although care was taken to balance the perceived intensity of the multiplexed signal against the other *palmScape signals*, and to conserve the characteristics of the individual signals, this was a design process done by hand. The resulting signal may have borne more resemblance to some *palmScape* signals than others. Therefore, it could be that counter balancing modulated amplitude and frequency parameters to achieve a combination of considerably different hand crafted signals, which may have originally had various degrees of perceptual arousal, stripped them of their unique tactile signatures.

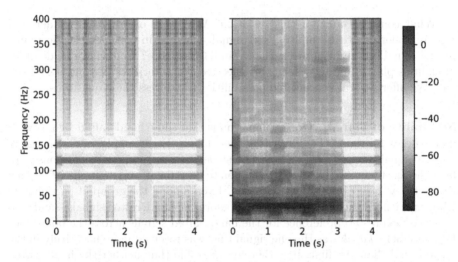

Fig. 5. Spectrograms of the signal on tactor #1 of the *palmScape* device for the *cicadas* (left) and the multiplexed (right) haptic effects. The color scale ranges between 10 dB (red) and −90 dB (blue) for the energy of the signals. (Color figure online)

To understand how the original and multiplexed signals were rendered on the *palmScape* device itself, we utilized spectrograms to compare both outputs. The purpose of doing so was to ensure limitations in the output efficiency (resonance frequency, acceleration, displacement etc.) of the actuation components utilized within the *palmScape* device did not affect the results. For that reason, we focused on energy distribution for both the handcrafted and multiplexed signals. The spectrograms from Fig. 5 compare the energy distribution of the signals from the *palmScape cicadas* (left) and the multiplexed (right) haptic effects. The spectrograms were estimated using a multitaper approach with 4 Discrete Prolate Spheroidal Sequences (or DPSS tapers) and 400 ms-long segments (for more information about spectrum estimation using DPSS see [16]). Three distinct frequencies at approximately 90, 120 and 150 Hz are constantly present with high energy in both plots. They are some of the most salient features of the multiplexed signal. This similarity may explain the similar responses garnered by the *palmScape cicadas* and multiplexed signals when both signals were labeled as "cicadas."

Certain haptic features may be more critical than others for characterizing a signal, and the fact that this relative importance should be taken into consideration when multiplexing various tactile primitives is one of the main outcomes of this research. We could hypothesize that for some phenomena, frequency and rhythm variations might be the key and that amplitude variations play a lesser role. A muffled heartbeat still feels like a heartbeat; even at a lower amplitude, a heartbeat still maintains the frequency characteristics that makes it so distinctive. Conversely, amplitude variations are key to conveying the impact and rumbling decay of a thunderbolt. In fact, in their open-ended responses, fourteen participants mentioned being underwhelmed by the amplitude of the thunder or earthquake signals, a comment rarely made of the other four *palmScape* signals.

There are a whole host of features that could prove essential to defining haptic phenomena. Perhaps some signals can't be selectively picked out of a multiplexed signal at all; the broadband nature of the multiplexed signal might be fitting for a buzzy cicada but unusual for a crisp, discrete knock on wood. Perhaps some phenomena are so deeply familiar that they must be rendered exactly to be effective (like the feel of one's own heartbeat), while others are abstract enough to leave room for interpretation (like the arrival of a ghostly spirit). Familiarity, rhythm, liveliness—these factors and more were not expressly considered in this study but ought to be explored. One could imagine designing a variety of multiplexed signals, each with different features of the constituent signals emphasized, and comparing their effectiveness in mimicking the original signals. Using this approach, it would be possible to develop an algorithm to dynamically assign weights to core parameters of the varied signals, to be multiplexed and achieve a more consistent outcome. However, as yet this work opens up more questions than answers.

Inability to Identify Changes Within Tactile Output Parameters: Perhaps the most unexpected result was participants' awareness or lack thereof regarding the multiplexed stimulus. Some participants experienced a haptic analogue to the visual phenomenon of *change blindness*. To varying degrees, these participants did not notice that the haptic signals were different in the two trials or that the multiplexed signal was being repeated. This outcome seems to support the idea that participants can selectively focus on relevant components of the multiplexed stimulus. In fact, more than one of these participants mistook their positive perceptions of the *palmScape* signals for merely improved focus, remarking on their newfound ability to notice the differences among the signals better than they had before. Yet participants who exhibited this effect still followed the overall pattern of responding more positively to the distinct trial A signals than to the trial B signal—even if they justified these changes as the result of improved clarity. A larger sample size would be useful to determine the significance of this intriguing trend.

4   Conclusion

This study provides evidence for the utility of vibrotactile stimuli for enhancing immersion, novelty, and creepiness in a simulated haunted house. Most participants in the study reported that the haptic signals helped them feel immersed in the virtual environment. Unique signals that were handcrafted to imitate natural phenomena were more effective at eliciting this sense of immersion than a repeated multiplexed signal—with two exceptions. First, the handcrafted *knock* signal failed to resemble a real knock, and participants did not prefer it to the multiplexed signal. This result suggests a bias toward signals that are both distinctive and evocative of their labels. In another exception, the handcrafted *cicadas* signal and multiplexed signal had similar characteristics in the spectral domain, and participants gave very similar responses to both signals. In doing so, participants demonstrated an ability to selectively focus on the relevant features of the multiplexed signal.

The present study opens up future questions, especially regarding the potential of multiplexed stimuli. Some participants did not notice the changes in haptic stimuli between the two trials or failed to note the repetition of the multiplexed stimulus, which warrants further investigation. New multiplexing algorithms that give relative weight to specific parameters of the modulated signal could also yield results more capable of mimicking a wider range of signals. Additional research may also be required to gauge how the efficiency of actuation components (*palmScape*) being used to create the feedback play a role in delivering the multiplexed signals to the skin contact. We hope this research and its subsequent findings encourage the design and development of even more evocative vibrotactile stimuli and novel multiplexing methods.

Acknowledgements. The authors thank Alyse M. Allred, Kevin A. McDonald, Ian J. Carr, and Austin L. Toombs at the Department of Computer Graphics Technology at Purdue University for their design contributions. Thanks also to Jaehong Jung, Husein A. Khambata, Yixuan Bian, and Matthew L. Winger for their contributions and to Sang-Won Shim for the use of the *palmScape* device.

References

1. Benedek, J., Miner, T.: Measuring desirability: new methods for evaluating desirability in a usability lab setting. Proc. Usabil. Prof. Assoc. **2003**(8–12), 57 (2002)
2. Clepper, G., et al.: Feeling creepy: a haptic haunted house. In: IEEE Haptics Symposium 2020. IEEE (2020)
3. Culbertson, H., Nunez, C.M., Israr, A., Lau, F., Abnousi, F., Okamura, A.M.: A social haptic device to create continuous lateral motion using sequential normal indentation. In: 2018 IEEE Haptics Symposium (HAPTICS), pp. 32–39. IEEE (2018)
4. van Erp, J.B.F., Toet, A.: Social touch in human-computer interaction. Front. Digit. Hum. **2**(2) (2015). 14 pp
5. Huisman, G., Frederiks, A.D., van Erp, J.B.F., Heylen, D.K.J.: Simulating affective touch: using a vibrotactile array to generate pleasant stroking sensations. In: Bello, F., Kajimoto, H., Visell, Y. (eds.) EuroHaptics 2016. LNCS, vol. 9775, pp. 240–250. Springer, Cham (2016). https://doi.org/10.1007/978-3-319-42324-1_24
6. Jerald, J.: The VR Book: Human-Centered Design for Virtual Reality. Morgan & Claypool (2015)
7. MacLean, K.E.: Putting haptics into the ambience. IEEE Trans. Haptics **2**(3), 123–135 (2009)
8. Morley, J.W., Rowe, M.J.: Perceived pitch of vibrotactile stimuli: effects of vibration amplitude, and implications for vibration frequency coding. J. Physiol. **431**(1), 403–416 (1990)
9. Pacchierotti, C., Sinclair, S., Solazzi, M., Frisoli, A., Hayward, V., Prattichizzo, D.: Wearable haptic systems for the fingertip and the hand: Taxonomy, review, and perspectives. IEEE Trans. Haptics **10**(4), 580–600 (2017)

10. Proctor, R.W., Van Zandt, T.: Human Factors in Simple and Complex Systems, 3rd edn. CRC Press, Boca Raton (2018)
11. Rakkolainen, I., et al.: Technologies for multimodal interaction in extended reality- a scoping review. Multimodal Technol. Interaction **5**(12), 81 (2021)
12. Seifi, H., MacLean, K.E.: A first look at individuals' affective ratings of vibrations. IEEE World Haptics Conference, pp. 605–610 (2013)
13. Severgnini, F.M., Martinez, J.S., Tan, H.Z., Reed, C.M.: Snake effect: a novel haptic illusion. IEEE Transactions on Haptics (2021)
14. Shim, S.-W., Tan, H.Z.: palmScape: calm and pleasant vibrotactile signals. In: Marcus, A., Rosenzweig, E. (eds.) HCII 2020. LNCS, vol. 12200, pp. 532–548. Springer, Cham (2020). https://doi.org/10.1007/978-3-030-49713-2_37
15. The Editors of Encyclopaedia Britannica: Séance (2018)
16. Thomson, D.: Spectrum estimation and harmonic analysis. Proc. IEEE **70**(9), 1055–1096 (1982)
17. Van Erp, J.B., Toet, A.: Social touch in human-computer interaction. Front. Digit. Hum. **2**, 2 (2015)
18. Y. Yoo, T.Y., Kong, J., Choi, S.: Emotional responses of tactile icons: Effects of amplitude, frequency, duration, and envelope. In: IEEE World Haptics Conference, pp. 235–240 (2015)
19. Yang, T.H., Kim, J.R., Jin, H., Gil, H., Koo, J.H., Kim, H.J.: Recent advances and opportunities of active materials for haptic technologies in virtual and augmented reality. Adv. Func. Mater. **31**(39), 2008831 (2021)

Research on the Influencing Factors of Shopping Mall Experiential Marketing on Consumer Attitudes: A Case of Guangzhou Sunac Mall

Yiwen Cui[✉], Dan Wu, Lulu Ge, and Xiaomin Xu

Management School, Guangzhou City University of Technology, Guangzhou 510800,
People's Republic of China
cuiyiwencj@qq.com

Abstract. The consumption of Chinese residents has entered a new stage, changing from focusing on the material enjoyment brought by the product itself to focusing on the satisfaction of material and affective needs, and also paying more attention to the process experience. This article conducted a field survey of consumers in Guangzhou Sunac Mall, based on the 10 major influencing factors of shopping environment experience, service experience, activity experience, preferential promotion experience, parking service experience, and 5-dimensional format combination experience. Use SPSS tools to perform confirmatory factor, correlation and regression analysis on the data, and perform statistical tests on the factors affecting shopping mall consumer attitudes and their relationships. From its impact on the three dimensions of attitudes, cognitive, affective and behavioral, construct a model of the influence of shopping mall consumer attitudes. It is expected to provide a reference for the improvement and upgrading of shopping malls in terms of core IP, business combination, service system, shopping environment, and physical facilities.

Keywords: Consumer attitudes · Experiential marketing · Shopping mall · Guang-zhou Sunac Mall

1 Introduction

The emergence of shopping mall marked a leap forward in the global retail industry in the 20th century. The convenience, multiple options and entertainment features of shopping malls have had a significant impact on the world economy and residents' lives and have played an increasingly important role in urban industrial upgrading, business environment improvement, and social and economic development.

Entering the 21st century, the supply of large-scale shopping malls in China is continuing to increase, and the scope of residents' consumption choices is expanding, therefore, the development environment of shopping malls becomes more and more severe. The continuous integration of new media and new technologies as well as the emergence of new retail formats also pose more severe challenges to traditional shopping malls. At the same time, the consumption of Chinese residents has reached a new level, changing

© The Author(s), under exclusive license to Springer Nature Switzerland AG 2022
M. M. Soares et al. (Eds.): HCII 2022, LNCS 13321, pp. 198–219, 2022.
https://doi.org/10.1007/978-3-031-05897-4_15

from focusing on the material enjoyment brought by the product itself to focusing on the satisfaction of material and emotional needs, and also paying more attention to the process experience. During the consumption process, the experience brought about by the relevant environment, services, and business formats that customers are exposed to has an increasing influence on the improvement of consumer attitudes.

Therefore, this article study from the perspective of the influencing factors of experiential marketing on consumer attitudes, conducted a field survey of consumers in Guangzhou Sunac Mall, based on 10 major influencing factors which include 5-dimensional format combination experience. Then use SPSS tools to perform confirmatory factor, correlation and regression analysis on the data, and perform statistical tests on the factors affecting shopping mall consumer attitudes and their relationships. From its impact on the three dimensions of attitudes, cognitive, affective and behavioral tendencies, construct a model of the influence of shopping mall consumer attitudes. It is expected to provide a reference for the improvement and upgrading of large shopping malls in terms of core IP, business combination, service system, shopping environment, and physical facilities.

2 Literature Review

2.1 Experiential Marketing

Since 1982, two American scholars Holbrook and Hirschman [1] introduced the concept of "experience" into consumer and marketing research in their pioneering classic paper, this concept has gradually become a core concept of understanding consumer behavior [2]. " Experience arise when consumers search for products, shop and receive services, as well as consumer products or brands [3].

The existing research mainly involves product experience, shopping and service experience, consumer experience and brand experience. (1) Product experience: arising from the interaction between consumers and products, such as consumer search, inspection and evaluation of products. When consumers have physical contact with the product the product experience is direct but when the product is virtually presented or present in advertising the product experience is indirect. (Hamilton et al. 2007) (2) Shopping and service experience: When consumers interact with store's physical environment, service staff, policies, and management practices, a shopping and service experience is created (Arnould et al. 2005). (3) Consumer experience: When consumers consume or use the products, consumption experience will be produced. Most explanatory studies on consumption experience have analyzed the consumption processes of visiting museums, rafting, enjoying basketball games, skating and their hedonistic goals. (4) Brand experience: Brand experience refers to a subjective internal (sensory, emotional, cognitive) response and behavioral response caused by the brand-related stimuli of consumers. Related stimuli include brand design, brand identification, packaging, communication, and the environment [4].

Brakus et al. (2009) follow the rigorous scale development procedures to construct a brand experience scale that accord with the psychometric standards start from marketing, philosophy, cognitive science, management practice. They divide the brand experience into four dimensions: sensory, affective, behavioral, and intellectual [5].

2.2 Consumer Attitude Theory

The term "attitude" was first proposed as a psychological concept, which refers to the stable and continuous psychological tendency of an individual to a certain object. It was later introduced into the field of consumer psychology as the core concept of consumer psychology research. Different scholars have different definitions of attitudes, as shown in Fig. 1:

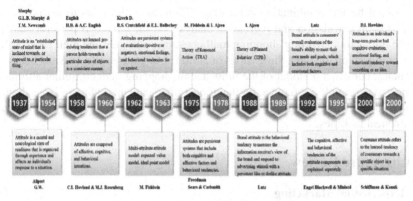

Fig. 1. Definition of attitude by scholar

The two widely recognized models in attitude research are the ABC model and the multi-attribute model of Fishbein, both of which establish connections between attitude and purchase intention (Guo Guoqing 2003) [6].

The ABC model believes that attitude includes three elements: affective, behavioral and cognitive. The model assumes that the consumer is a reasonable person to systematically process or utilize the relevant information as much as possible. So the model argue that "the consumer thinks fully about later action". There are different levels of effectiveness between the three elements of attitude, as follows: the high level of participation (effective order is cognitive, affective, behavioral), the low level of participation (effective order is cognitive, behavioral, affective), and the experience level (effective order is affective, behavioral, and cognitive).

Fishbein's multi-attribute model is a compensation model for brand attributes, in which consumers can compensate for its defects in another with the advantage of one brand on one attribute, and the consumer determines its attitude towards the brand by the sum of all attributes. Fishbein's ABC attitude model deem the attitude is composed of cognitive, affective and behavioral tendency. Between the three is not a single influence on attitude output, but emphasizes the influence through the mutual relationship between the three. All three factors are important factors. The model can be applied to study the influence of consumer attitude in multiple scenarios.

2.3   Research on the Influence Factors of the Consumer Attitudes or Purchase Intentions in Shopping Centers

For shopping center, the affective, cognition and purchase intention, is the most important dimension of the enterprise. Research the factors and make consumer has a better feeling to improve its purchase intention, that is, have a good attitude to commercial real estate, can help commercial real estate to improve its profit level and customer loyalty. Many experts and scholars have studied and analyzed the influencing factors of consumption attitude and purchase, as summarized in Table 1.

Table 1. Impact consumer attitudes or purchase intentions in shopping mall

Scholar	Object of study	Influence factor
Schmitt (1999) [7]	Mall	Sociocultural environment, use and consumption scenarios, product experience, and brand experience
Wen Tao (2007) [8]	Department store	Customer, situation, and traffic factors
Mi Xue (2008) [9]	Department store	The diversity of the store formats, the quality of the products, the store convenience felt by the consumers, the store name, trademarks and signs, the service level of the store staff, and the experience of the internal environment
Ge Xiangxi (2009) [10]	General merchandise enterprise	The complexity of the product, the services provided by the mall, and its internal environment
Wang Xianqing (2010) [11]	Shopping mall	Attraction of main stores, merchant combination factors, non-business form combination factors, commodity cost performance combination factors, environmental factors, personnel and service factors, site selection factors, overall and lasting customer gathering force

(*continued*)

Table 1. (*continued*)

Scholar	Object of study	Influence factor
Zhao Jing (2014) [12]	Large retailers	Impact consumer engagement: online factors are community involvement, website attraction, convenience, entertainment and customer satisfaction; offline factors are reputation, scale perception, conversion cost, offline trust
Zhang Hui (2015) [13]	Shopping mall	Environmental factors, employee factors, convenience factors, leisure and entertainment factors, and commodity factors

In summary, the existing research on shopping mall focuses on the power of customer's gathering, consumer behavior, preference. Except the factors to macro environmental factors, such as policy, economy, history, the main influence factors are the commercial real estate stores, business combination, shopping environment, products, services, brand effect, etc. Traditional retail pays more attention to brand, price, transportation, environment and other factors, while modern retail adds service, personnel interaction, leisure and other content.

This paper takes Guangzhou Sunac Mall and its consumer customers as the research object, takes the ABC attitude model as the theoretical basis, and constructs the influence model of Sunac Mall's consumer attitude from the three attitude dimensions of cognitive, affective and behavioral. Based on the research results of other scholars and the practical research indicators of the commercial real estate consulting company Winshang.com, the 10 influencing factors of shopping mall experience marketing have been determined, including shopping environment experience, service experience, activity experience, preferential promotion experience, parking service experience, and 5 dimensions of business combination experience. Use SPSS tool to carry out confirmatory factor, correlation and regression analysis on the data, and carry out statistical test on the influencing factors of shopping mall consumer attitude and their relationship. This paper fills the gap of existing research to a certain extent, and also has some reference significance for the research of other shopping malls.

3   Study Design and Descriptive Statistical Analysis

3.1   Research Objects and Data Sources

The shopping mall studied in this paper—Guangzhou Sunac Mall, its developer is Sunac China Holdings Co., Ltd. Sunac China, which was established in 2003. Through high-quality products, services + high-end residence, cultural tourism, commercial supporting resources, etc., it provides Chinese families with a perfect solution for a better life, which is highly recognized by customers.

Guangzhou Sunac Mall is located in the Guangzhou Airport Economic Circle, on the central axis of the CBD of Huadu District, with a total area of about 346,000 square meters, of which the commercial operation part is about 107,000 square meters. As a stage for one-stop experience of eating, drinking and playing in Sunac Cultural Tourism City CIMC, Sunac Mall's main body has 4 floors and over 160 brands. In addition, Sunac Mall is adjacent to Sunac Water World, Snow World and Sports Paradise, giving consumers a new large-scale experience commercial place integrating tourism, entertainment, eating and drinking, which stands out in traditional commercial real estate.

This paper conducts a questionnaire survey on consumers of Guangzhou Sunac Mall. A total of 203 questionnaires were recovered in this survey, 14 invalid samples were excluded, and 189 valid questionnaires were obtained. Among the 189 valid questionnaires returned, men accounted for 33.3% and women accounted for 66.7%, which is in line with the market situation that there are slightly more female customers than male customers in shopping malls. In terms of family status, the largest proportions are "single living alone/sharing with friends, colleagues and classmates" and "living with parents or other relatives", accounting for 38.6% and 32.3% respectively, followed by "couples/third generations together, existing children (under 18 years old)" and "living with men/girlfriends" accounted for 12.7% and 7.9%. Its monthly disposable income range is dominated by 1,000 to 5,000, followed by 5,000 to 7,000. It can be seen from the above data that the recovered samples of this questionnaire survey basically cover the main customer groups of Sunac Mall in terms of gender, family status and monthly disposable income.

3.2 Research Hypothesis and Model Construction

This paper conducts a questionnaire survey based on the ABC attitude model, and constructs a consumer attitude influence model from the three attitude dimensions of Cognitive, Affective and Behavioral.

Based on the research results of other scholars and the practical research indicators of the commercial real estate consulting company Winshang.com, the 10 influencing factors of shopping mall experience marketing have been determined, including shopping environment experience, service level experience, activity experience, preferential promotion experience, parking service experience, and 5 dimensions of business combination experience. Use SPSS tool to carry out confirmatory factor, correlation and regression analysis on the data, and carry out statistical test on the influencing factors of shopping mall consumer attitude and their relationship. The influence model is constructed from the influence of experiential marketing on the three attitude dimensions of cognition, affection and purchase behavior. The influencing variables and measurement items are shown in Table 2.

Table 2. The variable measurement items of experiential marketing's impact on consumption attitudes

Module	Variable	Secondary indicators	Measurement item
Experiential marketing	Shopping environment experience	–	Comfortable interior decoration environment (spacious, sanitary, bright, etc.) Distinctive architectural style Internet celebrity check-in place/shop Rich and complete supporting facilities (mother and baby room, rest seats, drinking water, etc.) Shopping environment and public facilities are not crowded High quality of customers
	Service experience	–	Clear guidelines for shopping mall ancillary facilities, such as WiFi/clear guidelines Service staff have the enthusiasm to help customers solve problems Service staff can respond to customer requests in a timely manner The service staff always treat customers politely and make customers feel comfortable Service staff understand customer needs and preferences Attractive membership system
	Activity experience	–	Rich shopping mall theme activities Attractive shopping mall theme activities (excluding discounts and preferential promotions)
	Preferential promotion experience	–	Frequent preferential promotions and discounts in shopping malls Great preferential promotions in shopping malls

(*continued*)

Table 2. (*continued*)

Module	Variable	Secondary indicators	Measurement item
	Parking service experience	–	There are plenty of free parking spaces in the mall Parking fees in shopping malls are within an acceptable range The mall has plenty of different parking facilities
	Business combination experience	Retail experience	There are more comprehensive fashion clothing collection stores and characteristic brands. There are favorite clothing/shoes/bags/skincare cosmetics brands; fashionable clothing styles and many cosmetic brands; supermarket goods are complete and attractive
		Food and beverage experience	There are many types of meals, many options for dinner, and a wide range of snacks. There are exotic restaurants with special flavors, restaurants suitable for leisure/afternoon tea, and themed casual dining bars/bars. There are favorite catering brands, Internet celebrity catering brands, bakery desserts, tea and other food brands
		Entertainment experience	The entertainment industry is rich, and there are new and interesting leisure and entertainment. There are high-quality cinemas and KTVs, Internet cafes and video games, gyms, ball sports venues, and leisure places, such as bookstores, tea houses, etc.

(*continued*)

Table 2. (*continued*)

Module	Variable	Secondary indicators	Measurement item
		Life service experience	The shopping center has a wide variety of beauty, health, beauty and body services (beauty, hairdressing, manicure, etc.). There are brands of photo studios and photography services. There are related brands that provide convenience services, such as laundry care, housekeeping intermediaries, etc. Stores with travel service types, such as travel agencies, ticket sales points, etc.
		Parent-child experience	The shopping center has a wealth of children's retail brands, children's amusement brands, children's education brands, and high-quality children's education brands. There are types of maternal and child services such as confinement centers, baby swimming pools, etc.
Attitude variables	Cognitive	–	I think Sunac Mall is the largest and most complete commercial complex in Huadu District I think Sunac Mall can meet my shopping needs I think Sunac Mall can meet my entertainment needs I think Sunac Mall can meet my food needs I think Sunac Mall's facilities, services and goods are very good
	Affective	–	I prefer Sunac Mall I trust Sunac Mall more I am more interested in Sunac Mall

(*continued*)

Table 2. (*continued*)

Module	Variable	Secondary indicators	Measurement item
	Behavioral	–	When I need to shop, I prefer to go to Sunac Mall When I need entertainment, I prefer to go to Sunac Mall When I need food, I prefer to go to Sunac Mall Sunac Mall has become an indispensable part of my life I would like to recommend Sunac Mall to others

This paper will propose hypotheses H1, H2, H3 based on the mutual influence within the ABC attitude model. The independent variables are 10 major influencing factors (including 5 secondary subdivision variables of business combination), and the dependent variables are cognitive, affective, behavioral. Hypotheses H4–H33 are proposed to form a hypothetical model. The hypothetical model is shown in Fig. 2.

Consumer attitudes internal influence relationship hypothesis:

- H1: The higher the consumer's cognitive attitude towards Sunac Mall, the higher the purchasing behavior of Sunac Mall's products.
- H2: The higher the consumer's cognitive attitude towards Sunac Mall, the higher their affective attitude towards Sunac Mall's products
- H3: Consumers' cognitive attitude towards Sunac Mall affects their affective attitude, which in turn affects their purchasing behavior tendency to Sunac Mall's products

The influence of shopping environment experience on consumer attitudes:

- H4: The better the shopping environment of Sunac Mall, the better the consumers' cognitive attitude towards Sunac Mall
- H5: The better the shopping environment of Sunac Mall, the better the affective attitude of consumers towards Sunac Mall
- H6: The better the shopping environment of Sunac Mall, the higher the attitude of consumers towards the purchase behavior of Sunac Mall's products
- The effect of service experience on consumer attitudes:
- H7: The better the service level provided by the service personnel of Sunac Mall, the better the consumers' cognitive attitude towards Sunac Mall
- H8: The better the level of service provided by the service personnel of Sunac Mall, the better the affective attitude of consumers towards Sunac Mall
- H9: The better the level of service provided by the service personnel of Sunac Mall, the higher the attitude of consumers towards the purchase of Sunac Mall's products

The influence of activity experience on consumer attitudes:

- H10: The higher the consumer's evaluation of the experience of the activities held by Sunac Mall, the better the consumer's cognitive attitude towards Sunac Mall.
- H11: The higher the consumer's evaluation of the experience of the activities held by Sunac Mall, the better the consumer's affective attitude towards Sunac Mall
- H12: The higher the consumer's evaluation of the experience of the activities held by Sunac Mall, the higher the attitude of consumers towards the purchase of Sunac Mall's products.

The influence of preferential promotion experience on consumer attitudes:

- H13: The higher the degree of preferential promotion of Sunac Mall's products, the better the consumers' cognitive attitude towards Sunac Mall.
- H14: The higher the degree of preferential promotion of Sunac Mall's products, the better the consumers' affective attitude towards Sunac Mall.
- H15: The higher the degree of preferential promotion of Sunac Mall's products, the higher the attitude of consumers towards the purchase of Sunac Mall's products.

The influence of parking service experience on consumer attitudes:

- H16: The better the parking service provided by Sunac Mall, the better the consumers' cognitive attitude towards Sunac Mall
- H17: The better the parking service provided by Sunac Mall, the better the affective attitude of consumers towards Sunac Mall
- H18: The better the parking service provided by Sunac Mall, the higher the attitude of consumers towards the purchase of Sunac Mall's products

The influence of business combination experience on consumer attitudes:

- H19-H23: The types of retail, catering, entertainment, life services, and parent-child business within Sunac Mall, the higher the degree to which they can meet the needs of consumers, the better the consumers' cognitive attitude towards Sunac Mall.
- H24-28: The types of retail, catering, entertainment, life services, and parent-child business within Sunac Mall, the higher the degree to which they can meet the needs of consumers, the better the affective attitude of consumers towards Sunac Mall.
- H29-33: The types of retail, catering, entertainment, life services, and parent-child business within Sunac Mall, the higher the degree to which they can meet the needs of consumers, the higher the attitude of consumers towards the purchase of Sunac Mall's products.

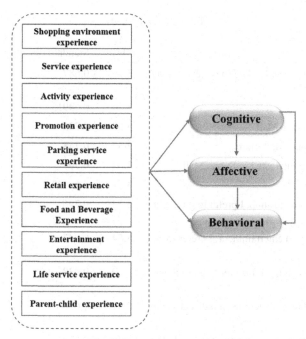

Fig. 2. Hypothetical model

3.3 Descriptive Statistical Analysis

Statistical Analysis of Consumer Attitude Dimension. In this survey, the overall evaluation of the consumer groups on Guangzhou Sunac Mall is divided into three points: cognitive, affective and behavioral attitude. Each aspect is set up with more than three measurement items. The average score statistics are shown in Table 3.

Table 3. Descriptive statistics of consumer attitudes (N = 189)

Measurement item	Mean	Standard deviation	Variance
RZ Cognitive	3.82	0.5127	0.263
RZ-1 I think Sunac Mall is the largest and most complete commercial complex in Huadu District	4.01	0.688	0.473
RZ-2 I think Sunac Mall can meet my shopping needs	3.70	0.790	0.625
RZ-3 I think Sunac Mall can meet my entertainment needs	3.80	0.701	0.491
RZ-4 I think Sunac Mall can meet my food needs	3.83	0.790	0.624

(*continued*)

Table 3. (*continued*)

Measurement item	Mean	Standard deviation	Variance
RZ-5 I think Sunac Mall's facilities, services and goods are very good	3.76	0.687	0.472
QG Affective	3.60	0.64913	0.421
QG-1 I prefer Sunac Mall	3.67	0.735	0.541
QG-2 I trust Sunac Mall more	3.52	0.748	0.559
QG-3 I am more interested in Sunac Mall	3.60	0.797	0.635
GM Behavioral	3.41	0.68142	0.464
GM-1 When I need to shop, I prefer to go to Sunac Mall	3.53	0.796	0.633
GM-2 When I need entertainment, I prefer to go to Sunac Mall	3.54	0.847	0.718
GM-3 When I need food, I prefer to go to Sunac Mall	3.60	0.938	0.879
GM-4 Sunac Mall has become an indispensable part of my life	2.91	1.056	1.114
GM-5 I would like to recommend Sunac Mall to others	3.48	0.879	0.772
Total	3.61	0.77	0.61

It can be seen from Table 3 that in the 5-point evaluation scale, the overall score of consumers' attitude towards Sunac Mall is 3.61 points, indicating that consumers generally have a high evaluation of Guangzhou Sunac Mall. Among the three attitude dimensions, cognitive attitude has the highest score, reaching 3.82 points, affective attitude is the second, and behavioral attitude is lower.

In the detailed measurement items, in terms of cognitive attitude, it is considered that "Sunac Mall is the largest and most complete commercial complex in Huadu District" and "Sunac Mall can meet the needs of food and entertainment" has high scores. In terms of affective attitude, consumers have higher scores for "more like Sunac Mall" and "more interested in Sunac Mall". It shows that consumers have a high evaluation of Sunac Mall's cognition and affective attitude, which is basically consistent with Sunac Mall's positioning. In the behavioral attitude, "I prefer to go to Sunac Mall when I need catering and entertainment", which indicates that Sunac Mall can better meet the needs of consumers in terms of entertainment and catering. The relatively low scores in shopping, life and recommending to others indicate that Sunac Mall has not been able to well match the needs of consumers in these aspects and needs to be further improved.

Descriptive Statistical Analysis of Influencing Factors of Consumption Attitude. It can be seen from Table 4 that consumers' satisfaction evaluation score for Sunac Mall's experiential marketing is 3.60 points, which is very close to the total evaluation score of consumers' attitude towards Sunac Mall, which is 3.61 points. The overall evaluation of Sunac Mall by consumers is good. Among them, the satisfaction of shopping environment, catering format and parking service is relatively high and can be maintained continuously; the score of life service format is the lowest and needs to be optimized and improved; the score of preferential promotion, parent-child format and service level is the second lowest and needs to be further adjusted according to the needs of consumers.

Table 4. Average score of experiential marketing consumer satisfaction (N = 189)

Influencing factors	Satisfaction score
Shopping environment experience	3.76
Food and Beverage Experience	3.71
Parking service experience	3.64
Activity experience	3.63
Retail experience	3.62
Entertainment experience	3.59
Service experience	3.56
Parent-child experience	3.56
Preferential promotion experience	3.52
Life service experience	3.36
Total	3.60

4 Empirical Research

4.1 Reliability and Validity Test

Using SPSS25 to conduct reliability analysis, it can be seen from Table 5 that the Cronbach'α coefficient of the overall scale is higher than 0.7, and all higher than the coefficients of 13 variables, and the scale has excellent reliability. The standard load coefficients of the corresponding analysis items in the 13 dimensions are all greater than 0.5, and the p-values are significant, indicating that each analysis item is highly representative; at the same time, the CR values are all greater than 0.6, the AVE is higher than 0.36, and the square root of the AVE of the variable is both It is not significantly lower than the correlation coefficient, and the validity of the comprehensive scale is good.

Table 5. Reliability and validity analysis

Variable dimension	Cronbach'α	Analysis item	Standard load factor	Sig.	CR	AVE
Cognitive	0.739	RZ1	0.53	–	0.73	0.36
		RZ2	0.57	.000		
		RZ3	0.57	.000		
		RZ4	0.57	.000		
		RZ5	0.75	.000		
Affective	0.814	QG1	0.85	–	0.82	0.61
		QG2	0.71	.000		
		QG3	0.77	.000		
Behavioral	0.807	GM1	0.80	–	0.81	0.47
		GM2	0.60	.000		
		GM3	0.65	.000		
		GM4	0.72	.000		
		GM5	0.62	.000		
Shopping environment experience	0.813	HJ1	0.65	–	0.81	0.42
		HJ2	0.66	.000		
		HJ3	0.65	.000		
		HJ4	0.68	.000		
		HJ5	0.55	.000		
		HJ6	0.71	.000		
Service experience	0.868	FW1	0.69	–	0.87	0.53
		FW2	0.75	.000		
		FW3	0.76	.000		
		FW4	0.74	.000		
		FW5	0.77	.000		
		FW6	0.64	.000		
Activity experience	0.704	HD1	0.69	–	0.70	0.54
		HD2	0.71	.000		
Preferential promotion experience	0.817	YH1	0.87	.000	0.82	0.70
		YH2	0.77	.000		
Parking service experience	0.521	TC1	1.00	–	1.00	0.99
		TC2	0.99	.000		
		TC3	0.99	.000		
Retail experience	0.891	LS1	0.75	–	0.89	0.58

(*continued*)

Table 5. (*continued*)

Variable dimension	Cronbach'α	Analysis item	Standard load factor	Sig.	CR	AVE
		LS2	0.77	.000		
		LS3	0.80	.000		
		LS4	0.79	.000		
		LS5	0.74	.000		
		LS6	0.72	.000		
Food and beverage experience	0.886	CY1	0.71	–	0.89	0.47
		CY2	0.61	.000		
		CY3	0.68	.000		
		CY4	0.68	.000		
		CY5	0.73	.000		
		CY6	0.65	.000		
		CY7	0.72	.000		
		CY8	0.67	.000		
		CY9	0.72	.000		
Entertainment experience	0.864	YL1	0.61	–	0.88	0.52
		YL2	0.61	.000		
		YL3	0.44	.000		
		YL4	0.79	.000		
		YL5	0.83	.000		
		YL6	0.79	.000		
		YL7	0.75	.000		
Life service experience	0.857	SH1	0.67	–	0.87	0.62
		SH2	0.88	.000		
		SH3	0.80	.000		
		SH4	0.77	.000		
Parent-child experience	0.604	ET1	1.00	–	1.00	0.99
		ET2	1.00	.000		
		ET3	1.00	.000		
		ET4	1.00	.000		
		ET5	0.98	.000		
Overall scale	0.923	–	–	–	–	–

4.2 Correlation Analysis and Regression Analysis

Correlation analysis was carried out on the 13 variables in this study, and it was concluded that there was a positive correlation between the variables, which was used as the basis of regression analysis.

Consumer Attitudes Internally Influence Relationships. Based on the theoretical basis of ABC attitude, the step-by-step regression test method is used. From Table 6, the regression model 1 is established for cognitive attitudes and purchasing behavior attitudes. There is a significant positive correlation, Hypothesis 1 was established. A regression model 2 was established for cognitive attitudes and affective attitudes. The results showed that the R-square value was 0.436, which was an increase of 0.185 compared with model 1, and the p value was 0.000, which had a significant positive correlation. Hypothesis 2 was established.

Model 3 takes cognitive and affective attitudes as independent variables, and purchase behavioral attitudes as dependent variables for analysis. The results show that the p value between cognitive and purchase behavior is 0.830, which is not significant, and the p value between affective and purchase behavior is 0.000, which is very significant. Therefore, the complete mediating effect of affective attitude is established. Cognitive attitude affects consumers' purchasing behavioral attitude by affecting affective attitude. Hypothesis 3 is established.

Table 6. Analysis of the mediating effect of cognitive, affective and behavioral attitude

	Behavioral (Model 1)			Affective (Model 2)			Behavioral (Model 3)		
	B	t	p	B	t	p	B	t	p
Constant	0.868**	2.680	0.008	0.407	1.520	0.13	0.553*	2.203	0.029
Cognitive	0.666**	7.921	0.000	0.836**	12.016	0.000	0.019	0.215	0.830
Affective							0.775**	11.384	0.000
R^2	0.251			0.436			0.559		
Adjust R^2	0.247			0.433			0.554		
F value	$F_{(1,187)} = 62.739$, p = 0.000			$F_{(1,187)} = 144.392$, p = 0.000			$F_{(2,186)} = 117.743$, p = 0.000		

The Influence of Predictors on Consumer Attitudes. Analyze the relationship between the 10 influencing factors of consumer attitudes and cognitive, affective, and behavioral, and build regression models I, II, and III respectively., as shown in Table7. The three models have $R^2 > 0.4$, $F > 11$, the significance is less than 0.05, indicating that the models have a good degree of fitting. The DW value is close to 2, the tolerance is greater than 0.1, and the VIF is less than 10, indicating that the model basically has no autocorrelation and multicollinearity problems.

The regression results of model I show that the Beta values of service level, life service experience, and preferential promotion are 0.309, 0.363, and 0.283, respectively, and the significance is less than 0.05, that is, the service level, life service format, and preferential promotion has a positive and significant impact on consumers' cognitive attitudes, Hypotheses 7, 13, 22 are supported.

The regression results of Model II show that the Beta values of children's parent-child business formats are 0.455 and 0.003 respectively, which means that it has a positive and significant impact on consumers' affective attitudes. Hypothesis 28 is supported. The Beta values of the shopping environment are 0.320 and the significance is 0.031, that is, the shopping environment has a positive and significant impact on consumers' affective attitudes, and Hypothesis 5 is supported.

The regression results of Model III show that the Beta value of the parking service is 0.611, and the significance is 0.000, that is, it has a positive and significant impact on the attitude of consumers' purchasing behavior. Hypothesis 18 is supported; the Beta value of the shopping environment is 0.470, and the significance is 0.001., that is, it has a positive and significant impact on consumer purchasing behavior attitude, Hypothesis 6 is supported.

Table 7. Regression analysis of influencing factors and attitudes

Model	Influencing factors	Standardized coefficient	Sig.	Collinearity Statistics		R^2	F	p	DW
		Beta		Tolerance	VIF				
Model I Cognitive	Service experience	0.309	0.049	0.583	1.716	0.576	14.491	.000	1.988
	Life service experience	0.363	0.017	0.640	1.561				
	Preferential promotion experience	0.283	0.033	0.820	1.219				
Model II Affective	Parent-child experience	0.455	0.003	0.884	1.131	0.408	11.379	.000	2.015
	Shopping environment experience	0.320	0.031	0.884	1.131				
Model III Behavioral	Parking service experience	0.611	0.000	0.669	1.495	0.408	11.379	.000	2.015
	Shopping environment experience	0.470	0.001	0.783	1.277				

4.3   A Revised Model of the Influence of Consumer Attitudes

Based on the mutual influence within the ABC attitude model, this paper proposes three research hypotheses. According to the regression analysis results, all three hypotheses are supported. The 30 research hypotheses proposed in this paper on the influencing factors of experiential marketing on consumer attitudes, through empirical research, the following 7 hypotheses are supported.

- H1: The higher the consumer's cognitive attitude towards Sunac Mall, the higher the purchasing behavior of Sunac Mall's products.
- H2: The higher the consumer's cognitive attitude towards Sunac Mall, the higher their affective attitude towards Sunac Mall's products
- H3: Consumers' cognitive attitude towards Sunac Mall affects their affective attitude, which in turn affects their purchasing behavior tendency to Sunac Mall's products
- H5: The better the shopping environment of Sunac Mall, the better the affective attitude of consumers towards Sunac Mall
- H6: The better the shopping environment of Sunac Mall, the higher the attitude of consumers towards the purchase behavior of Sunac Mall's products
- H7: The better the service level provided by the service personnel of Sunac Mall, the better the consumers' cognitive attitude towards Sunac Mall
- H13: The higher the degree of preferential promotion of Sunac Mall's products, the better the consumers' cognitive attitude towards Sunac Mall
- H18: The better the parking service provided by Sunac Mall, the higher the attitude of consumers towards the purchase of Sunac Mall's products
- H22: The life service experience has a significant positive impact on consumers' cognitive attitude. The more the business type of Sunac Mall's life service can meet the needs of consumers, the better the consumer's cognition of Sunac Mall.
- H28: Parent-child business experience has a significant positive impact on affective attitudes. The higher the degree to which the parent-child business types of Sunac Mall can meet the needs of consumers, the better the consumers' affective experience with Sunac Mall.

The modified impact model is shown in Fig. 3.

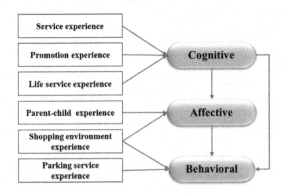

Fig. 3. Influence relationship correction model

5 Conclusion and Suggestion

The results of this research show that (1) shopping environment experience has significant positive impact on consumer affective and behavioral attitude; (2) service experience, preferential promotion and life service experience has significant positive impact on cognitive attitude; (3) parent-child experience has significant positive impact on affective attitude; (4) parking service has significant positive effect on behavioral attitude; (5) cognitive attitude has significant positive correlation with affective attitude and behavioral attitude. The cognitive attitude influence behavioral attitude by influencing affective attitude.

Based on the above research conclusions and the descriptive statistical analysis results of consumers on Guangzhou Sunac Mall, this paper puts forward six improvement suggestions, in order to form executable and valuable suggestions for the development and operation of Guangzhou Sunac Mall and other large shopping mall.

5.1 Suggestions Based on the Parent-Child Business Experience

- Optimize the current children's parent-child brand, replace the original brand with poor customer effect. Introduce more quality-oriented, well-known child parent-child brands and children's quality to expand education brands. At the same time, try to launch children or parent-child projects and surrounding areas with Sunac Snow World, Water World and Sports Park.
- On parent-child entertainment, create children's exclusive services, and hold children parent-child activities by reconciling intelligent software, robot, etc., with entertainment, catering and education. For example, increase VR experience hall or organize special activities, such as the animal world, galaxy phantom, ocean world and other diversified theme scene to open a special parent-child interaction. This can improve the mall of parent-child interaction experience.

5.2 Suggestions for Improvement Based on Life Service Business Experience

- Make appropriate adjustment and supplement to the existing store life service brands. Introduce quality brands in pet service, health care, hairdressing and beauty categories.
- Innovative life services are forming a trend. We can introduce innovative service brands, such as Haima photo studio, KOKOWAN, etc., or combined with the diversified characteristics of internal skiing and park, to carry out characteristic activities such as "one-stop diversified experience of Sunac" and "one stop to enjoy the style of the four seasons".

5.3 Suggestions for Improvement Based on the Service Experience

- In the operation of the WeChat official account platform, you can push the brand preferential promotion, preferential promotion activities, life small encyclopedia and other customer preference content. Secondly, promote user activity and stickiness through integral offset and gift exchange. Finally, realize the intellectualization and automation of member points, simplify the parking preferential exchange process, and improve the parking exchange experience of the car members.

- Provide convenient services, such as renting umbrellas, free hot water, charging port / charging facilities, clean trash cans and clear identification, etc.
- Improve the attitude and effectiveness of service personnel reception, and set up online public account or offline reception guidance.

5.4 Suggestions for Improvements Based on Parking Services Experience

- For entering the parking lot, the outside parking guidance's main goal is beautiful and clarity. After parking, the walking route and logo can be optimized and improved.
- For departure payment link, it can strengthen the personnel diversion of traffic flow during peak hours, and reduce the parking charging standard and fast charging appropriately. Members can redeem free parking vouchers for three hours four times a month.

5.5 Suggestions for Improvement Based on Preferential Promotions Experience

- Strengthen the management of the online public account platform, and timely update the information of preferential promotions in shopping malls.
- Create a variety of preferential promotions. Such as the new store can hold preferential promotional activities, and the members can enjoy preferential benefits if they consume for many times.
- Promote activities by combining with festival theme, such as interactive activities such as brand runway shows, music festivals and creative fairs.

5.6 Suggestions for Improvement Based on the Shopping Environment Experience

- In public environment designing, the external wall advertising of shopping malls can add creative and beautiful theme elements, such as specific festivals or seasonal elements, hot topic elements, etc., and can strengthen the ornamental nature of green plants.
- In IP operation, integrate the original IP image into the shopping mall's art exhibition, staff clothing, publicity and preferential promotion operation, to make the shopping mall more personalized charm and emotional temperature. You can also set up characteristic clock points, launch IP peripheral products, joint ride products. At the same time, in conduct propaganda, IP can be integrated into the public account tweets and the art exhibitions to unify the IP image. It will be easier to form a memory point and to spread by creating scenes.
- In scenic spot operation, realize the function from single to multiple. We will improve the functions of leisure, parent-child, entertainment, art, food, tourism, and social networking, etc. In the scenic shopping centers, increase the personal experience activity, especially the parent-child business and life service business.

References

1. Holbrook, M., Hirschman, E.: The experiential aspects of consumption: consumer fantasies, feeling and fun. J. Consum. Res. **9**(2), 132–140 (1982)
2. Addis, M., Holbrook, M.: On the conceptual link between mass customization and experiential consumption: an explosion of subjectivity. J. Consum. Res. **1**(1), 50–66 (2001)
3. Brakus, J.J., Schmitt, B.H., Zarantonell, L.: Brand experience: what is it? How is it measured? Does it affect loyalty? J. Mark. **73**(3), 52–68 (2009)
4. He, H., Liu, Y., Zhou, Z.: Mark. Res. Front. Rev. Foreign Econ. Manag. **32**(08), 42–50 + 65 (2010)
5. Rousseau, D.M.: Idiosyncratic deals: flexibility versus fairness? Organ. Dyn. **29**(4), 260–271 (2001)
6. Schmitt, B.: Experiential marketing. J. Mark. Manag. (15), 53–67 (1999)
7. Wen, T.: Mechanism of customer experience on service brand rights and interests —based on empirical research in department stores. Manag. Rev. (11), 24–29+63 (2007)
8. Mi, X.: Department store consumer experience on store loyalty impact research. Renmin Univ. China (09), 19–29 (2008)
9. Ge, X.: Analysis of the own brand influence factors of department stores in China-Based on the consumer's willingness to buy. Contemp. Econ. (21), 80–83 (2009)
10. Wang, X., Wang, X.: Research in large shopping centers based on AHP analysis. Bus. Res. (04), 165–170 (2010)
11. Zhao, J.: Study on consumer viscosity of large traditional retailers. Zhejiang Univ. Finan. Econo. (05), 29–41 (2015)
12. Zhang, H., Lin, M., Xu, Y., Yuan, Q.: Empirical study on influactors of customer experience in shopping center. Soc. Sci. Guizhou Province (07), 143–147 (2015)
13. Hou, X., Wu, S., Fan, J.: Research on the scenic spot management mode of large shopping centers and the evaluation index system construction. Bus. Econ. Res. (23), 111–114 (2019)

Different Sample Sources, Different Results?
A Comparison of Online Panel and Mail Survey Respondents

Aki Koivula[ID] and Jukka Sivonen[✉][ID]

Department of Social Research, University of Turku, Turku, Finland
{aki.j.koivula,jukka.e.sivonen}@utu.fi

Abstract. This paper compares data and results from two different survey modes: a probability sampled postal survey and a nonprobability sampled online panel. Our main research objective was to explore if there are differences between the sample methods in terms of nonresponse, item response bias, and selectivity. Both the postal survey and online panel data consist of Finns aged 18–74. Altogether, 2470 respondents were included in the probability sample gathered randomly from the population register of Finland (sample size was 8000 with a response rate of 30.9%), and 1254 respondents were from an online panel organized by a market company. We collected the data in late 2017. The findings confirmed that an online panel can improve the representativeness by including more respondents from groups that are underrepresented within the traditional probability sample. However, we found that panel respondents were more likely to leave unanswered questions perceived as sensitive, which may be a sign of a measurement bias related to intrusiveness. Moreover, the results indicated selection differences between samples related to respondents' media interests.

Keywords: Online panel data · Survey research · Representativeness · Measurement error · Selectivity

1   Background

1.1   Introduction

The traditional probability sampling method in survey research has recently met growing difficulties linked to rising data collection costs and decreasing response rates [1]. At the same time, using online panels (e.g., Qualtrics, Dynata, Ipsos Mori) in research and as a source of different kinds of polls has become increasingly common. They offer a relatively cost-effective and fast way to access large and diverse populations and enable or facilitate the usage of new types of survey research techniques [2]. Moreover, the combination of two or more collection methods, ie. mixed-response modes, as become more popular in recent years [3, 4]. In addition to the mixed-response modes, the mixed-survey modes has become more popular [5, 6].

© The Author(s), under exclusive license to Springer Nature Switzerland AG 2022
M. M. Soares et al. (Eds.): HCII 2022, LNCS 13321, pp. 220–233, 2022.
https://doi.org/10.1007/978-3-031-05897-4_16

The data from online panels and mixed modes are constantly taken as reliable, without further elaborating on the problems that might be related to the quality of online collected data based on nonprobability sampling, especially regarding representation and generalization. Accordingly, it is possible that online panel data do not represent various population groups as there is high *nonresponse error*. A potential error may also be due to the *measurement error* and the overlapping bias related to sensitive questions; that is, panel respondents may identify the social norms associated with questions differently than traditional survey respondents. Finally, the online panel data can also be made up of *self-selected* respondents differing from the general population, especially regarding different attitudinal and ideological questions.

This study aims to fulfill the information gap regarding the errors mentioned above. The paper compares the results gathered with a probability sample from the population register and a nonprobability sample from the online panel. The surveys were conducted with similar questionnaires at the same time, enabling a precise comparison of the two distinct data-gathering procedures. Our research questions are as follows:

1. How do the (nonprobability sampled) online panel and the (probability sampled) postal survey respondents represent the population demographically?
2. How do online panel and mail survey respondents differ by item nonresponse?
3. How do online panel and mail survey respondents differ in selectivity when examining interest toward news?

Before going into the empirical analysis, we conceptualize our research questions according to recent literature on survey methodology. Then, we introduce our data and methodology. Finally, we demonstrate our results and discuss what conclusions can be made based on this study.

1.2 Background

Nonresponse Error

One of the main problems in implementing valid surveys is nonresponse error. Even though surveys are still the most popular method to collect research data and the budgets to conduct them have increased, the survey response rates have fallen over the past four decades. The decrease in the response rate is not directly related to the nonresponse bias in the research results. With regard to the representation and generalization of survey results, the problems are concretized after the response is no longer random between different population groups [7].

A well-established problem with regard to online surveys is that not everyone has access to the internet; hence, many people from specific groups cannot be reached online, and internet panels do not represent the overall population [8]. However, in many Western countries, the penetration rates of the internet, computers, and mobile devices are so high that online panels have real potential to cover various populations. Previous studies have also indicated that online panel respondents do not necessarily differ from benchmark data collected using postal or face-to-face modes and probability samples [9, 10].

At their best, online panels can provide more opportunities to reach various populations compared to traditional surveys. It is well known that younger people in particular are underrepresented when surveys are implemented through traditional survey methods using probability samples [11–15]. Invitations to online panels can be sent, for example, on social media, through which young respondents can be recruited more effectively [16–18].

Moreover, previous studies have indicated that it is possible to gather an online panel that is demographically representative, but important improvement would be to include offline households in the online panel [19]. It is possible that including offline households in the panel would improve its representativeness regarding qualitative questions such as interestedness in politics.

Measurement Errors

The main goal of the survey is to get a truthful picture of the respondents in the sample, which makes it possible to generalize the sample to the population. However, various measurement errors are common in survey research. For example, respondents may lie to or skip response questions that are perceived to be very sensitive [20]. Item nonresponse addresses questions that respondents missed, even if they had taken part in the survey. Previous research has suggested that item nonresponses can be the result of the survey design, the placement of the question, the characteristics of the participant, and the mode of data collection [21, 22].

For example, it has been put forth that online surveys might be understood by participants in a different way than other methods used in conducting surveys [3] Moreover, surveying some issues, such as income level, religiosity, or sexual behaviors, may be considered culturally too delicate or even taboo. Respondents may also feel offended if their privacy is challenged by intrusive questions [for a review, see 23].

It has also been observed that pen-and-paper and web-based surveys do not yield identical results, particularly when examining sensitive questionnaire items [e.g. 24]. Kays et al. [25] for example, found that respondents tend to be more likely to answer sensitive questions on the internet compared to a pen-and-paper option. Web participants' feelings of anonymity likely play a role here [26].

However, it has been noted that online respondents more readily answer "I do not know" and elicit more nondifferentiation on rating scales [27, 28]. Another concern is related to the "professional" respondents in online panels, whose answers are supposed to differ from the rest of the population. However, this worry does not seem to be as serious as often presumed [29].

Selectivity Bias

Nonresponse and item response biases are insufficient measurements to evaluate the total quality and representativeness of surveys. In addition to sociodemographic factors, the survey topic is an important factor with regard to response rates [30]. For instance, people who feel they are in a better position in the dating world are more likely than others to respond to a dating survey [31]. For example, it has been proposed that an environmental survey may receive more responses from environmentalists than others [4]. One study revealed there are multiple reasons to join online panels; for example, two-thirds of an online panel's participants mentioned that they joined a panel to have fun [32]. It might be that there are numerous motives to join online panels or answer mail surveys, and this might at least partially explain the differences in answering certain questions.

Several studies addressing different phenomena across various countries have highlighted differences between online panelists and respondents from traditional survey modes. Grönlund and Strandberg [9] and Sivonen et al. [33] found that the interest in politics differed significantly across respondents from postal surveys and online panels in Finland. Lee et al. [34] found that online panelists in South Korea were more likely to have substance-abuse and mental health problems when compared to randomly collected respondents of a telephone survey. Hemsworth et al. [35] indicated there were multiple differences between the online panel sample and a random-digit telephone survey when comparing respondents' attitudes and behavior toward the red meat industry in Australia. On the other hand, a meta-analysis regarding applied psychology found that results from online panel data do not differ significantly from data collected though more traditional sampling techniques [36]. On the other hand, it is worth noting that when it comes to data and data collection quality, there are also differences between online panel providers [37].

However, prior research has not studied how respondents from different survey modes vary in their interest in media consumption. Media interest creates an interesting phenomenon that is also central when considering the flow of information in the current multidimensional media environment. For example, during the COVID-19 outbreak, media consumption has become a particularly important factor that separates citizens' propensity to adapt to an uncertain situation across countries [38–40].

2 Method

2.1 Participants

This study is based on the comparison of mail and online panel surveys. Both studies were executed in December 2017. The mail survey was sent to 8000 18- to 74-year-old Finnish speakers selected with a simple random sampling technique from the population register.[1] The respondents had two options to answer the survey: either by mail or by filling out a similar form on the internet. One reminder was sent to the survey respondents by post. 2011 respondents answered by post and 459 through the internet. Altogether, 2470 Finns (30.9%) answered the survey.

In addition to the mail survey, we collected a sample of 1254 respondents aged 18–74 from an online panel of volunteer respondents administered by a market research company, namely Taloustutkimus Inc. We recruited the members of the online panel in question both on- and offline. The panel could be classified as a so-called general population panel: it has a large group of people and aims to represent the different subpopulations [41]. Panel data were gathered on December 5–12, 2017, including one reminder. The final data consist in total of 3724 respondents, of which 66.3% were gathered by mail survey and 33.7% by online panel survey.

---

[1] Due to the very small amount of Finnish speakers, the Åland-area was excluded from the study.

2.2 Measures

Our independent variable is survey mode, which distinguishes 1) "mail survey" respondents who participated in the survey based on probability sampling from 2) "online survey" respondents who participated in the survey via an internet panel.

In the first stage of analysis, we analyzed potential nonresponse bias by comparing the demographic representativeness of survey modes. To determine the age of the respondents, we asked them to disclose their birth year. We requested respondents' household income as follows: "After adding all household income (including social, retirement, and other benefits), what is your household's total income after taxes per month? If you do not remember exact amounts, make the closest possible estimation." In terms of residential information, we requested the respondents' postal code. Based on the postal code, we classified respondents according to the NUTS 2 statistical regions of Finland: Helsinki-Uusimaa, South Finland, West Finland, and North & East Finland.

Respondents' gender was considered as binary variable: 1 "Male", 2 "Female". Education was coded as a three-class variable: 1 "Primary level education" (original options 1 and 2), 2. "Secondary level education" (original options 3 and 4), and 3. "Higher level education" (original options 5–7). Moreover, the questionnaire included the question "What is your main activity?": 1 = "Salary work/on leave", 2 = "Entrepreneur", 3 = "Unemployed/seeking employment", 4 = "Retired", 5 = "Student", and 6 = "Other, what". We combined the categories "Salary work/on leave" and "Entrepreneur" to the category "Working". We also considered these demographic variables as control variables in additional multivariate models.

The second part of the empirical analysis involved searching for differences between survey modes in item-response bias. We assessed the extent to which respondents have answered an income question often considered as a sensitive variable [20]. We categorized respondents according to whether they had answered the question. Respondents who answered the question received a score of 1, and those who refused to answer received a score of 0.

Finally, to analyze selectivity differences in survey modes, we examined respondents' media interest. We analyzed questions that initially asked the following: "How interested are you in the following forms of news?" (1 = "Not interested at all", 5 = "Very interested"): "Entertainment news", "Arts and cultural news", "Political news", and "Science news".

The descriptive statistics of independent variables are shown in Table 1.

Table 1. Descriptive statistics of study variables

Variable(s)	Obs	Mean	Std. Dev.	Min	Max
Age	3,704	4.18	1.61	1	6
Gender	3,706	1.50	.50	1	2
Education	3,632	2.22	.649	1	3
Main activity	3,724	2.08	1.12	1	4

(*continued*)

Table 1. (*continued*)

Variable(s)	Obs	Mean	Std. Dev.	Min	Max
NUTS2 Region	3,698	2.45	1.11	1	4
Income (non-missing)	3,724	.94	.24	0	1
Media interests					
Entertainment	3,681	2.60	1.02	1	5
Art	3,667	2.75	1.10	1	5
Politics	3,686	3.29	1.08	1	5
Science	3,686	3.31	1.14	1	5

2.3 Analysis Techniques

We began the analysis by comparing the relative representativeness of online and mail respondents compared to population figures. When estimating the shares of various groups, we considered the margins of error at the 95% confidence level.

In the following steps, we used multivariate models to assess the extent to which the response mode is related to nonresponse and various interest variables. We performed a logistic regression analysis for a binary variable and an ordinal regression analysis for Likert-scale variables. We estimated the confounding effect of the background variables using the KHB method, which provided us the direct and total effects of the response mode, as well as the indirect effect according to the different background variables. The KHB method has been widely used in recent years to analyze the effect of various mediating and confounding factors when comparing nested nonlinear models [42].

3 Results

3.1 Nonresponse Bias

Tables 2 and 3 point out the demographic representativeness of online panel and mail survey respondents. As shown, men among the age groups 18–24, 25–34, and 35–44 are underrepresented, whereas the 55–64 and older age groups are overrepresented. Regarding the group of 65- to 74-year-old men, the online panel evens out in terms of the respondents' overrepresentation in the data but does not fix the overrepresentation in the total data. Women are especially overrepresented among the age groups 65 − 74 and 55–64. Particularly in the case of a group of 65- to 74-year-old women, the online panel caused the respondents' overrepresentation to level out somewhat. The differences in the representation of the oldest group (65–74 years) between the postal survey and online panel were statistically significant.

When moving to a residential area (Table 3), the online data corresponded relatively well with the population proportions. In total, the data proportion of the Helsinki-Uusimaa Region was slightly underrepresented, and South Finland was underrepresented, but the online panel evened out a little for both distortions. West Finland seemed to be slightly overrepresented in all data sources compared to the share of the population. The North & East Finland area matched precisely with the proportion of the population in the region.

Table 3 shows that when it comes to the more highly educated participants, both data sources are overrepresented. In particular, the online panel data included a high share of highly educated participants in relation to the population. The share of those with secondary education is relatively well represented within the data, whereas the proportion of those with primary education is underrepresented, especially in the case of the online panel data. In this respect, the online panel did not correct the traditional nonresponse error but addressed the overrepresentation of highly educated citizens.

The proportion of employed citizens is underrepresented in all data sources (Table 3). Instead, pensioners are overrepresented, particularly in the mail survey data. The students are relatively well represented in both data sources. The unemployed are underrepresented, but here the online panel balanced out the bias to some extent.

Table 2. Distribution of respondents of mail survey and online panel and population by age groups and gender. The population information is from 2017 [43]. 95% confidence intervals are in parentheses

	Mail survey		Online panel		Population (18–74 years)	
	Male	Female	Male	Female	Male	Female
Age group	%	%	%	%	%	%
18–24	5.9	9.7	4.2	8.2	11.6	11.1
	(4.6–7.4)	(8.2–11.4)	(2.9–5.9)	(6.2–10.9)		
25–34	10.9	12.2	14.0	20.2	18.4	17.4
	(9.2–12.9)	(10.5–14.1)	(11.7–16.8)	(17.0–23.8)		
35–44	11.0	10.8	15.6	11.4	17.8	16.9
	(9.3–13.0)	(9.2–12.6)	(13.1–18.4)	(9.0–14.3)		
45–54	15.2	14.6	21.3	17.2	17.8	17.6
	(13.2–17.4)	(12.8–16.7)	(18.4–24.4)	(14.2–20.6)		
55–64	25.7	24.1	23.6	20.7	18.2	18.9
	(23.2–28.4)	(21.9–26.5)	(20.7–26.9)	(17.5–24.2)		
65–74	31.4	28.6	21.3	22.2	16.2	18.1
	(28.7–34.2)	(26.2–31.1)	(18.4–24.4)	(18.9–26.0)		
Total	**100**	**100**	**100**	**100**	**100**	**100**

Table 3. Distribution of respondents of mail survey and online panel and population by NUTS 2 statistical regions of Finland, education, and main activity. The population information is from 2017 [43]. 95% confidence intervals are in parentheses

NUTS 2 statistical regions of Finland	Mail survey		Online panel		Population
	%	95%CI	%	95%CI	%
Helsinki-Uusimaa	25.7	(24.0–27.5)	29.1	(26.6–31.6)	30.9
South Finland	24.8	(23.1–26.5)	22.1	(19.9–24.5)	21.1
West Finland	26.5	(24.8–28.3)	26.2	(23.9–28.8)	24.8
North & East Finland	23.0	(21.4–24.7)	22.6	(20.4–25.0)	23.1
Education					
Primary level	15.12	(13.7–16.6)	7.64	(6.28–9.3)	19.9
Secondary level	53.77	(51.8–55.8)	52.01	(49.2–54.8)	56.0
Higher level	31.11	(29.3–33.0)	40.35	(37.7–43.1)	24.0
Main activity					
Working	48.3	(46.3–50.3)	50.84	(48.1–53.6)	58.0
Unemployed	5.2	(4.4–6.2)	8.61	(7.2–10.3)	9.1
Students	6.7	(5.7–7.7)	7.64	(6.3–9.3)	6.0
Pensioner	36.9	(3.5–3.9)	31.05	(28.5–33.7)	22.7
Other	2.9	(2.3–3.7)	1.85	(1.2–2.8)	4.3
Total	100		100		100

3.2 Item Response Bias

The second stage of analysis focused on item response bias related to the question of household income. Table 4 reveals that online panelists had a lower likelihood of responding to the question of income ($B = -0.56$; $p < 0.001$). Moreover, we found that controlling for underlying factors did not weaken the difference between the panel and survey but conversely widened the difference. This confirmed that respondents recruited from the online panel are significantly more unwilling to answer the sensitive questions.

The analysis also indicated that education had a statistically significant confounding effect. However, controlling for education did not weaken the difference between the survey and panel; instead, it had the opposite effect. This means that, in the direct comparison, the correlation between the online panel and the non-item response is lower due to the variation in the level of education; that is, the online panel involves more highly educated respondents who are generally more likely to answer the income question. The actual impact of an online panel is therefore higher if we consider the suppression effect of education.

- Total effect refers to unadjusted effect of the online panel
- Direct effect refers to demographic-adjusted effect of the online panel
- Indirect effect refers to confounding effect of demographic factors

3.3 Selectivity Bias

Finally, we examined the extent to which different kinds of participants are selected as online and mail survey respondents in terms of news interest. According to the analysis presented in Table 5, the respondent groups clearly differed regarding how interested they were in a different kind of news source. Those who responded through the postal survey were less interested in politics, science, and art when compared to those who responded through the online panel. Instead, postal survey respondents were more interested in entertainment news.

Table 4. Predicting the probability of responding to the income question according to the survey mode. Direct and demographic-adjusted effects of the online panel (ref = mail survey) with indirect effects of demographic variables.

	B	SE	z	p-value	[95% confidence interval]	
Total effect	**−0.56**	**0.16**	**−3.55**	**0.00**	**−0.86**	**−0.25**
Direct effect	**−0.68**	**0.16**	**−4.2**	**0.00**	**−1.00**	**−0.36**
Indirect effect	**0.13**	**0.03**	**3.95**	**0.00**	**0.06**	**0.19**
via						
Age	0.00	0.01	−0.59	0.55	−0.02	0.01
Gender	0.03	0.02	1.56	0.12	−0.01	0.06
Education	0.08	0.02	3.34	0.00	0.03	0.13
Main activity	0.01	0.01	−0.89	0.37	−0.02	0.01
Residential area	0.01	0.01	1.04	0.30	−0.01	0.02

We also analyzed the confounding effects of demographic variables. First, the results confirmed that the differences between survey formats were not only related to differences in demographic factors. This confirms our assumption that respondents with different interests are selected for online panels and mail surveys.

However, the results suggested that controlling for gender and education had a significant effect on the differences between respondents of mail and online panel surveys in each news category. Age was also related to the differences between survey modes when examining politics, entertainment, and art and culture.

- Total effect refers to unadjusted effect of the online panel
- Direct effect refers to demographic-adjusted effect of the online panel
- Indirect effect refers to confounding effect of demographic factors

Table 5. Predicting interest in entertainment, art and culture, politics, and science according to the survey mode. Unadjusted and demographic-adjusted effects of the online panel (ref = mail survey) with confounding effects of demographic variables

	B	SE	z	p	[95% Conf Interval]	
Entertainment						
Total effect	**−0.32**	**0.07**	**−4.49**	**0.00**	**0.18**	**0.46**
Direct effect	**−0.26**	**0.07**	**−3.55**	**0.00**	**0.12**	**0.40**
Indirect effect	**0.06**	**0.02**	**−2.52**	**0.01**	**0.01**	**0.11**
Via *Age*	*0.02*	*0.01*	*1.95*	*0.05*	*0.00*	*0.03*
Gender	*0.08*	*0.02*	*−5.19*	*0.00*	*−0.11*	*−0.05*
Education	*−0.03*	*0.01*	*−2.25*	*0.03*	*−0.05*	*0.00*
Main activity	*−0.01*	*0.01*	*−1.38*	*0.17*	*−0.02*	*0.00*
Residential area	*0.00*	*0.00*	*0.56*	*0.57*	*−0.01*	*0.01*
Art and culture						
Total effect	**0.19**	**0.07**	**2.75**	**0.01**	**−0.33**	**−0.06**
Direct effect	**0.19**	**0.07**	**2.62**	**0.01**	**−0.33**	**−0.05**
Indirect effect	**0.00**	**0.03**	**−0.15**	**0.88**	**−0.06**	**0.05**
Via *Age*	*−0.01*	*0.01*	*−1.78*	*0.08*	*−0.03*	*0.00*
Gender	*−0.09*	*0.02*	*−5.34*	*0.00*	*−0.13*	*−0.06*
Education	*0.09*	*0.02*	*5.47*	*0.00*	*0.06*	*0.12*
Main activity	*0.00*	*0.01*	*0.34*	*0.74*	*−0.01*	*0.02*
Residential area	*0.01*	*0.01*	*1.25*	*0.21*	*−0.01*	*0.03*
Politics						
Total effect	**0.50**	**0.07**	**6.79**	**0.00**	**−0.64**	**−0.36**
Direct effect	**0.39**	**0.08**	**5.15**	**0.00**	**−0.53**	**−0.24**
Indirect effect	**0.11**	**0.03**	**4.19**	**0.00**	**−0.17**	**−0.06**
via *Age*	*−0.02*	*0.01*	*−1.90*	*0.06*	*−0.04*	*0.00*
Gender	*0.06*	*0.01*	*4.67*	*0.00*	*0.03*	*0.08*
Education	*0.09*	*0.02*	*5.07*	*0.00*	*0.05*	*0.12*
Main activity	*0.00*	*0.01*	*0.45*	*0.65*	*−0.02*	*0.03*
Residential area	*0.01*	*0.01*	*1.33*	*0.18*	*−0.01*	*0.03*
Science						
Total effect	**0.95**	**0.07**	**13.39**	**0.00**	**−1.09**	**−0.81**
Direct effect	**0.70**	**0.07**	**9.89**	**0.00**	**−0.84**	**−0.56**

(*continued*)

Table 5. (*continued*)

	B	SE	z	p	[95% Conf Interval]	
Entertainment						
Indirect effect	**0.24**	**0.03**	**8.05**	**0.00**	**−0.30**	**−0.18**
via *Age*	0.01	0.00	1.51	0.13	0.00	0.02
Gender	0.09	0.02	5.31	0.00	0.06	0.12
Education	0.12	0.02	6.00	0.00	0.08	0.16
Main activity	0.00	0.01	0.18	0.85	−0.01	0.02
Residential area	0.01	0.01	1.18	0.24	−0.01	0.02

4 Discussion

This study provided an opportunity to compare two survey modes regarding demographic representation, item nonresponse, and selectivity differences. In summary, the demographic representativity was significantly different across the survey modes. The online panel had a positive balancing effect on the bias in distributions of age, gender, and residential area, although its effects for the generalizability of the data were uncertain. Moreover, the results provide an indication of the qualitative difference between the respondents of survey modes and that panel respondents are more susceptible to decline when responding to sensitive questions.

Our first research question considered the demographic representativeness of online panel data in relation to the whole population. The findings indicate that the online panel improves the demographic representativeness by including more respondents from groups that are underrepresented within the traditional survey data. For instance, people living in the Helsinki-Uusimaa Region (capital region) and working in the private sector are better represented in the online panel. However, the online panel did not properly cover some groups; for example, older people and people with primary education are clearly underrepresented, whereas people with higher education are overrepresented within the panel data.

Our second question concerned measurement bias, which we measured using answers to the question considering respondents' monthly household income. When compared to the postal survey respondents, online panel respondents were more likely to miss the income question. This could be the sign of a measurement bias: panel respondents may easily skip over questions that handle more sensitive topics. Controlling for education and other underlying factors even strengthened the difference. One possible explanation for this could be that respondents do not trust the companies that admin the online panel as much as the universities that implement the population survey.

The final research question handled selectivity bias among the online panel. The results point out that this is a serious problem regarding the quality of online panel data; the panel respondents were distinctly more interested in science and political news than the survey respondents. Taking demographic factors into account moderated the results, but the differences remained statistically significant. Can we, however, conclude that online panel data are badly biased? It is difficult to provide an exact answer to the question as it is possible that the panel included respondents who do not typically respond to postal surveys. Still, the results of this and earlier studies [9] suggest that researchers should elaborate on how credible the results received from online panels actually are.

Selectivity creates a bias that cannot be corrected with weighting techniques [8]. It has recently been debated that estimates of vaccine hesitancy and willingness based on large-scale online surveys, for example, do not correspond to actual statistics [44]. In this respect, the representativeness of the non-probability survey has potentially remarkable implications for policymaking. However, previous studies have suggested that nonprobability and online-based samples can be useful when conducting experimental studies and the effect of treatment in experiment is known to be homogeneous from one subpopulation to another [45].

As this study included data from only one online panel, future studies could collect data from several different online panel companies to gain more comprehensive research results. Since news media and many others frequently use data from online panels, it would be fruitful to compare how well their results match with each other, as well as with the postal surveys (and, when possible, with population-level data). Finally, it should be noted that responsive activity (30.9%) in mail survey could be considered as a study limitation because a higher response rate would offer more reliable results. However, such a response rate is quite typical these days, and in the context of this study, the results offered us a good change to compare the data of relatively typical postal surveys with online panel data and population information.

References

1. Stoop, I., Billiet, J., Koch, A., Fitzgerald, R.: Improving Survey Response: Lessons Learned from the European Social Survey (2010)
2. Hays, R.D., Liu, H., Kapteyn, A.: Use of Internet panels to conduct surveys. Behav. Res. Methods **47**, 685–690 (2015)
3. Hox, J.J., De Leeuw, E.D., Zijlmans, E.A.O.: Measurement equivalence in mixed mode surveys. Front Psychol.**6**, 87 (2015)https://doi.org/10.3389/fpsyg.2015.00087
4. Dillman, D.A., Smyth, J.D., Christian, L.M.: Internet, Phone, Mail, and Mixed-Mode Surveys: The Tailored Design Method, 4th edn. Wiley, New Jersey (2014)
5. Dillman, D.A., Hao, F., Millar, M.M.: The SAGE handbook of online research methods. In: Fielding, N.G., Lee, R.M., Blank, G. (eds.) The SAGE Handbook of Online Research Methods. SAGE, Los Angeles, pp. 220–240 (2017)
6. Atkeson, L.R., Adams, A.N.: Mixing survey modes and its implications. In: Atkeson, L.R., Alvarez, R.M. (eds.) The Oxford Handbook of Polling and Survey Methods, pp. 53–75. Oxford University Press, Oxford (2018)
7. Pohjanoksa-Mäntylä, M., Turunen, J.: Kyselytutkimus. In: Hämeen-Anttila, K., Katajavuori, N. (eds.) Yhteiskunnallinen lääketutkimus – ideasta näyttöön, 2nd edn., pp. 80–96. University of Helsinki, Helsinki (2021)
8. Rich, R.C., Brians, C.L., Manheim, J.B., Willnat, L.: Empirical Political Analysis: Quantitative and Qualitative Research Methods, 9th edn. Routledge, New York (2018)

9. Grönlund, K., Strandberg, K.: Online panel research : representativeness and attrition in the finnish eopinion panel. In: Callegaro, M., Baker, R.P., Bethlehem, J., et al. (eds.) Online Panel Research : A Data Quality Perspective, pp. 86–103. John Wiley & Sons, Chichester (2014)

10. Lehdonvirta, V., Oksanen, A., Räsänen, P., Blank, G.: Social media, web, and panel surveys: using non-probability samples in social and policy research. Policy Internet **13**, 134–155 (2021). https://doi.org/10.1002/POI3.238

11. Koivula, A., Sirppiniemi, R., Koiranen, I., Oksanen, J.: Workingpapers in Economic Sociology: Arkielämä ja osallistuminen -kyselyn tutkimusseloste. University of Turku, Department of Social Research, Turku (2017)

12. Van Loon, A.J.M., Tijhuis, M., Picavet, H.S.J., et al.: Survey non-response in the Netherlands: effects on prevalence estimates and associations. Ann. Epidemiol. **13**, 105–110 (2003). https://doi.org/10.1016/S1047-2797(02)00257-0

13. Antholz, B.: Cover letter reduces response rate. Bull Me´thodologie Sociol **137**(1), 140–156 (2018)

14. Saari, H., Koivula, A., Sivonen, J., Räsänen, P.: Working papers in Economic Sociology : Suomi 2019 – kulutus ja elämäntapa. Tutkimusseloste ja koodikirja (2019). https://www.utu pub.fi/handle/10024/148680

15. Rosentiel, T., Witt, E., Best, J.: How Different Are People Who Don't Respond to Pollsters? l Pew Research Center. In: Pew Res. Cent. (2008). https://www.pewresearch.org/2008/04/21/how-different-are-people-who-dont-respond-to-pollsters/. Accessed 4 Feb 2022

16. Ramo, D.E., Prochaska, J.J.: Broad reach and targeted recruitment using facebook for an online survey of young adult substance use. J. Med. Internet Res. **14**, e1878(2012). https://doi.org/10.2196/JMIR.1878

17. Retention of College Students with Type 1 Diabetes via Social Media: An Implementation Case Study. J. Diabetes Sci. Technol. **13**, 445–456. https://doi.org/10.1177/1932296819839503

18. Survey Research: Using Facebook and Instagram Advertisements and In-Person Intercept in LGBT Bars and Nightclubs to Recruit LGBT Young Adults. J. Med. Internet Res. **20**(6), e197 (2018). https://www.jmir.org/2018/6/e197. https://doi.org/10.2196/JMIR.9461

19. Blom, A.G., Gathmann, C., Krieger, U.: Setting up an online panel representative of the general population: the German internet panel. Field Methods **27**, 391–408 (2015)

20. Tourangeau, R., Yan, T.: Sensitive questions in surveys. Psychol. Bull **133**, 859–883 (2007). https://doi.org/10.1037/0033-2909.133.5.859

21. Ziegenfuss, J.Y., Easterday, C.A., Dinh, J.M., et al.: Impact of demographic survey questions on response rate and measurement: a randomized experiment. Surv. Pract. **14**(1), 26126 (2021)

22. Pollien, A., Herzing, J.M.E., Antal, E.: Preparation of survey data : FORS Guide No. 13, Version 1.0. Swiss Centre of Expertise in the Social Sciences (FORS) (2020)

23. Gnambs, T., Kaspar, K.: Disclosure of sensitive behaviors across self-administered survey modes: a meta-analysis. Behav. Res. Methods **47**, 1237–1259 (2015). https://doi.org/10.3758/S13428-014-0533-4/FIGURES/3

24. Naus, M.J., Philipp, L.M., Samsi, M.: From paper to pixels: a comparison of paper and computer formats in psychological assessment. Comput. Human Behav. **25**, 1–7 (2009). https://doi.org/10.1016/J.CHB.2008.05.012

25. Kays, K., Gathercoal, K., Buhrow, W.: Does survey format influence self-disclosure on sensitive question items? Comput. Human Behav. **28**, 251–256 (2012). https://doi.org/10.1016/J.CHB.2011.09.007

26. Huang, H.M.: Do print and Web surveys provide the same results? Comput. Human Behav. **22**, 334–350 (2006). https://doi.org/10.1016/J.CHB.2004.09.012

27. Heerwegh, D., Loosveldt, G.: Face-to-face versus web surveying in a high-internet-coverage population differences in response quality. Public Opin. Q **72**, 836–846 (2008). https://doi.org/10.1093/POQ/NFN045

28. de Leeuw, E.D., Hox, J.J., Boeve, A.: Handling do-not-know answers: exploring new approaches in online and mixed-mode surveys. Soc. Sci. Comput. Rev. **32**, 116–132 (2016)
29. Matthijsse, S.M., De Leeuw, E.D., Hox, J.J.: Internet panels, professional respondents, and data quality. Methodology **11**, 81–88 (2015). https://doi.org/10.1027/1614-2241/a000094
30. Goyder, J.: The Silent Minority: Non-respondents in Sample Surveys. Routledge, New York (2019)
31. Zillmann, D., Schmitz, A., Skopek, J., Blossfeld, H.-P.: Survey topic and unit nonresponse: evidence from an online survey on mating. Qual. Quant. **48**, 2069–2088 (2014)
32. Keusch, F., Batinic, B., Mayerhofer, W.: Motives for joining nonprobability online panels and their association with survey participation behavior. In: Online Panel Research. John Wiley & Sons, Ltd., Chichester, UK, pp. 171–191 (2014)
33. Sivonen, J., Koivula, A., Saarinen, A., Keipi, T.: Working Papers in Economic Sociology : Research Report on the Finland in the Digital Age -Survey. University of Turku, Department of Social Research, Turku (2018)
34. Lee, C.K., Back, K.J., Williams, R.J., Ahn, S.S.: Comparison of telephone RDD and online panel survey modes on CPGI scores and co-morbidities. Int. Gambl. Stud. **15**, 435–449 (2015). https://doi.org/10.1080/14459795.2015.1068353
35. Hemsworth, L.M., Rice, M., Hemsworth, P.H., Coleman, G.J.: Telephone survey versus panel survey samples assessing knowledge, attitudes and behavior regarding animal welfare in the red meat industry in Australia. Front Psychol. **12**, 1024 (2021). https://doi.org/10.3389/FPSYG.2021.581928/BIBTEX
36. Walter, S.L., Seibert, S.E., Goering, D., O'Boyle, E.H.: A tale of two sample sources: do results from online panel data and conventional data converge? J. Bus Psychol. **34**, 425–452 (2019). https://doi.org/10.1007/S10869-018-9552-Y/TABLES/6
37. Eyal, P., David, R., Andrew, G., et al.: Data quality of platforms and panels for online behavioral research. Behav. Res. Methods (2021)
38. Bendau, A., Petzold, M.B., Pyrkosch, L., et al.: Associations between COVID-19 related media consumption and symptoms of anxiety, depression and COVID-19 related fear in the general population in Germany. Eur. Arch. Psychiatry Clin. Neurosci. **271**, 283–291 (2021). https://doi.org/10.1007/S00406-020-01171-6
39. Nekliudov, N.A., Blyuss, O., Cheung, K.Y., et al.: Excessive media consumption about COVID-19 is associated with increased state anxiety: outcomes of a large online survey in Russia. J. Med. Internet Res. **22**, e20955 (2020). https://doi.org/10.2196/20955
40. Nabi, R.L., Wolfers, L.N., Nathan, W., Qi, L.: Coping with COVID-19 stress: the role of media consumption in emotion- and problem-focused coping. Psychol. Pop Media (2022)
41. Callegaro, M., Baker, R.P., Bethlehem, J., et al.: Online panel research: history, concepts, applications and a look at the future. In: Callegaro, M., Baker, R.P., Bethlehem, J., et al. (eds.) Online Panel Research : A Data Quality Perspective, pp. 1–54. John Wiley & Sons, Chichester (2014)
42. Karlson, K.B., Holm, A., Breen, R.: Comparing regression coefficients between same-sample nested models using logit and probit a new method. Sociol. Methodol. **42**, 286–313 (2012)
43. Statistics Finland. Statistics Finland's PX-Web databases: Statfin (2018). http://pxnet2.stat.fi/PXWeb/pxweb/en/StatFin/?rxid=99142dcd-2c78-437d-8172-6a68fbadccfa. Accessed 15 May 2018
44. Bradley, V.C., Kuriwaki, S., Isakov, M., et al.: Unrepresentative big surveys significantly overestimated US vaccine uptake. Nat **6007890**(600), 695–700 (2021). https://doi.org/10.1038/s41586-021-04198-4
45. Coppock, A., Leeper, T.J., Mullinix, K.J.: Generalizability of heterogeneous treatment effect estimates across samples. Proc. Natl. Acad. Sci. **115**, 12441–12446 (2018). https://doi.org/10.1073/PNAS.1808083115

The Effect of Music Type Association on Design Product Styling

Chi-Meng Liao[✉], Chih-Wei Lin, Lan-Ling Huang, and Li-fen Ke

School of Design, Fujian University of Technology, No.3 Xueyuan Road, University Town, Minhou County, Fuzhou, Fujian, China

jameslgm88@sina.com.cn, copy1.copy2@msa.hinet.net

Abstract. This study explores how music types impact the product styles and characteristics presented in design concept sketches. This empirical study asked the subjects to draw sketches of lamp designs while listening to New Age music and opera music, fill out a design styling association table, retrace their design process through retrospective reports. The experimental results show that the subjects prefer using natural objects as design materials and geometric, simple, monolithic, and handmade design styles in the case of New Age music, while they prefer using artifacts objects as design materials and bionic, curved, ornate, and bright design styles in the case of opera music. It is assumed that the context-dependent memories phenomenon caused by listening to music during the design process may have prompted the subjects to associate music-related auditory experiences and translate their characteristics into product design styles.

Keywords: Music · Association · Product styling

1 Introduction

The musical activities depicted in cave paintings from ancient times suggest that people have been engaged in similar musical activities for thousands of years [1]. There have been many studies on the effects of listening to music, which mostly used word tests or brainstorming experiments [2, 3], while few have explored the effects of music on design creativity when sketching designs. As technological advances make product styling less restricted by manufacturing and production, there is more room for the development of product styling than in the past. This, coupled with the fact that the demands of modern consumers for products depends on both the function and price of the product, whether the product styling can meet the expectation of consumers will be one of the considerations to purchase products.

Design is an act of discovery, a way of bringing people's dreams to life through observation, imagination, knowledge, and experience. In addition to applying existing knowledge and experience in the stage of designing concepts, designers often utilize external stimuli, such as collecting information and pictures, deconstructing samples, or posting collected pictures on walls, to create a design-friendly environment that triggers memories, association, and creative ideas [4]. Previous studies have shown that designers often listen to music during the design process [5], and ubiquitous music is like a part of the design activity, thus, the effect of music on idea creation is worthy of further exploration.

2 Literature Review

2.1 The Effect and Association of Music

Music has been closely correlated with human life since ancient times and has generated different applications and effects over time. In the past, Areni and Kim probed into the effects of classical music and popular songs on consumer behavior in a downtown hotel in the United States, and the results showed that playing classical music causes consumers to spend more money [6]. The effect of music on people's cognitive abilities has also been explored, such as the use of background music to stimulate the emotional responses of the subjects. One study also suggested that the performance of female students during language tests improved significantly when music was played in a major key, while male students performed better on spatial tasks [7]. Recent studies have investigated the effects of music on design creativity, including the effect of music on brainstorming, and the results showed that music stimulates emotions that could influence creative ideas, with both positive and negative emotions increasing the number of ideas in low-stimulation situations, and conversely, neutral emotions help to increase the number of ideas in high-stimulation situations [3]. The effect of music on creativity has also been explored using the Remote Associates Test, with findings showing that listening to music has a positive effect on the subjects' creative cognition, semantic retrieval, and mood [2]. However, these recent studies do not easily capture the effects of listening to music on the actual design task, thus, this study explored the effects of music on design ideas by performing design tasks.

Listeners often have mental changes when listening to music, meaning they associate matters related to the music. People will generate different imaginations based on their experience of listening to similar music; for example, Yeoh and North showed that rock music evokes more objects related to rock characteristics, such as electric guitars, tattoos, and men with long hair; similarly, classical music recalls more classical objects, including cigars, champagne, and pens, and such findings reflect the influence of the characteristics of music types on associations [8]. It has also been shown that music with distinctive local features will help to associate local objects and cultural characteristics in the imagination, and the characteristics of such mental images can be applied to design objects that express local features [9].

2.2 Design Idea and Association

Association is the basis of perception, concept, memory, and imagination. In the creative process, designers often use association to connect existing perceptions and knowledge, and then, gradually expand new ideas to generate a large number of concepts. To stimulate more creative ideas, designers utilize association to link internal long-term memory with external information and stimuli to inspire different design ideas during the idea development stage [10]. The case in point is to collect relevant information and shape the environment that helps to generate design creativity. The environment provides different information from smells, sounds, colors, and indoor arrangements, to the view from the window, which may shape our perceptions [11]. McCoy and Evans found that environmental factors seem to have a strong influence on design creativity [12]. Goldschmidt and Smolkov experimentally revealed that different visual environments affect the performance of designers in feasibility, originality, and creativity. Moreover, designers' creative thinking is very sensitive to the environment, which can provide potential clues to help solve design problems [13]. Music has a unique role in shaping the ambiance in environmental information; just like a movie soundtrack, we feel differently about what is going on around us as it changes. Therefore, this study aims to explore whether the ambiance created by music affects the designers' creative thinking and how the designers apply the characteristics of music to their design concepts.

2.3 The Style of Product Styling

A product is composed of its external styling and internal functions, meaning the combination of shape, color, material, and function. The style of a product's shape and imagery are important mediums of communication between designers and consumers. In addition to its actual function, the shape style enables consumers to experience the symbolic meaning of a product, meaning when designers determine the stylistic attributes of the product, its shape style is also created. How can designers make their abstract design concepts materialize features prominently in the design process. In the early stage of conceptual development, designers often make abstract design concepts concrete through hand-drawn sketches to facilitate communication with customers and meet their needs [14]. Thus, designers have the important responsibility of designing products with appropriate stylistic imagery that is in line with the design theme and requirements.

Style consists of multiple differentiated units, and these different basic units enable people to identify the differences in products and perceive the messages conveyed by the products to distinguish the style characteristics [15]. Style characteristics change with social background, conventions, customs, knowledge, mental images, and personal preferences [16]. Style is reflected in the external physical characteristics of the designed product, and this prominent stylistic feature depends on how it is perceived by the observer. Chang and Van studied design trends and the redesign of product styles, and determined that the elements of product styles include four profiles, styling, color, material, and detail processing [17]. When probing into the language of shape and style, Chen and Owen decomposed the style profile into 6 categories, form elements, component relationships, detail treatments, materials, color treatments, and textures. Each profile corresponds to specific adjectives with polarized style to express the product style, which means basic product profiles and style features are matched in detail, in order to facilitate communication between designers [18]. A study that explored the formal representation of simple design styles found that the appearance characteristics of products were decomposed into seven profiles, shape, color, decoration, components, materials, technology, and function, to elaborate the product style [19]. However, the technological and functionality of profiles require in-depth understanding, it's difficult to judge products from the appearance of images. Therefore, this study investigates what specific elements or characteristics designers use to describe their design style according to form, color, material, decoration, and construction profiles.

3 Research Method

People's perceptions of music are related to their listening experience and imagination, meaning when listening to the same piece of music, different listeners will have different feelings, thus, there will inevitably be individual differences in the design abilities of designers recruited to participate in this experiment. Consequently, this study adopted the experimental method of within-group design, in which each participant listened to two different styles of music, New Age and opera music, and drew a sketch to show their design concept, which was intended to minimize the impact on the experimental result by reducing the variation of errors caused by individual differences in the participants' design abilities. In the post-experimental stage, the subjects were asked to orally retrace their design process and fill out a music perception table, in order to obtain a correlation between the subjects' design thinking and music characteristics.

3.1 The Method and Design Assignments of the Experiment

Sixteen designers were invited as subjects, 8 male and 8 female, with 2–8 years of design experience, an average of 3.8 years. The subjects were divided into two groups, A and B. Group A performed the experimental task in the first experiment with opera music; after a week, the experimental task was counted with New Age music. In group B, the experimental task was performed for the first time while listening to New Age music; one week later, the experimental task was counted for the second time while listening to opera music. The three experimental tasks in this study are, as follows:

1. Design task: The subjects were asked to design a lamp, where the client wants "a lamp that is designed to express the style of music played in the restaurant (New Age music/opera music)", meaning the hand-drawn conception sketch was required to fit the music characteristics. In order to ensure the consistency of difficulty between the two tasks, the designers were asked to design lamps. However, to reduce the carry over effect caused by performing the design task twice, the subjects were asked to design floor or ceiling lamps separately while listening to the two types of music.
2. Verbal retrospect: Although the styling features presented in the design sketches can be interpreted, the verbal retrospect of the subject's thoughts and opinions at the time of sketching can be used to understand the design thinking of the subjects [20].
3. Music perception table: The subjects were asked to write about their design styles, and how their associations were triggered by the music they heard.

3.2 Procedure of the Experiment

The experiment was conducted based on research ethics, meaning the subjects were informed that the experiment was intended for academic research only, did not involve commercial behavior, and the experimental operation did not involve invading the body. Nevertheless, if the subjects preferred, they could leave the experiment at any time. The experiment was conducted with the consent of the subjects, and the procedures were, as follows:

1. Experimental task description: The researcher stated the purpose of the experiment, explained how the experiment would be conducted, and provided the estimated time required for the experiment.
2. Warm-up before the experiment: The subjects were given 5 minutes to warm up before the experiment, where they could sit for rest or doodle at will to relax.
3. Perform the experimental design task: The researcher played music and asked the subjects to draw their lamp conception sketches by hand, and the subjects were given 40 min to complete the task.
4. Break time: Rest for 10 min。
5. Conduct the verbal retrospect: The subject looked at their design sketches and retrospectively explained the correlation between the conception features and the music.
6. Fill in the music perception table: After the experimental task, the subjects completed their basic information and the "music-induced design style association table".

3.3 Profile of the Design Sketches

In order to deconstruct the appearance characteristics of the design concept sketches, this study referred to the product style profile proposed by Chen and Owen, as well as Lin's seven profiles [18, 19], explored the appearance characteristics of the products in this study, meaning the formal representations of design styles, and considered the characteristics of this study. The deconstruction in this study covers five profiles, product profile styling, surface color, composed materials, decorative elements, and component relationships.

3.4 Music-Induced Association Design Style Measureme

This study adopted the semantic differential method to explore the design style association caused by music. The music-induced association style table was created based on five bipolar adjective pairs of stylistic styles, including angular-rounded, geometric-biomorphic, single-multiple, hard-soft, and matte-glossy, in order to extract style adjectives regarding the form profiles of the products, as deconstructed by Chen and Owen [18], and explore the form language and style description. Moreover, the table was also based on five adjectives pairs, plain-luxurious, coarse-delicate, straight-curvature, and hand-made-hi-tech, which were selected from the stylistic adjectives used to study cell phone styles by Chuang et al. [21]. In addition, the normal-particular style adjectives were transformed into regular-random. This study applied a total of 10 semantically opposed style adjectives to create the design style table for this experiment, which includes seven grades, as shown in Table 1.

Table 1. The examples of music-induced design style association measurement.

Measurement items		Measurement scale
		-3 -2 -1 0 1 2 3
The music-induce your design style tended to	Plain	☐ ☐ ☐ ☐ ☐ ☐ ☐ Luxurious
The music-induce your design style tended to	Single	☐ ☐ ☐ ☐ ☐ ☐ ☐ Multiple
The music-induce your design style tended to	Coarse	☐ ☐ ☐ ☐ ☐ ☐ ☐ Delicate

3.5 Tool and Music of Experiment

This experiment was carried out in a school classroom with no hanging objects except for a whiteboard on the wall, and conducted in the same place and at the same time to minimize environmental interference. Drawing tools included blank A4 paper, pencil, atomic pen, or marker pen. The conception sketches were hand-drawn by pencil or pen, which the subjects were free to choose according to their usual drawing habits. This study chose four pieces of New Age music and four pieces of opera music with high view rates on YouTube as the stimuli for the experiment, and the music tracks are shown in Table 2. In order to explore the influence of New Age music on product design style, four pieces of New Age music were played in turn; the same procedure was applied to explore the influence of opera music on design style. In terms of the music playing devices, the subjects could choose either a laptop computer with an external speaker or headphones to perform the design task.

Table 2. List of the experimental music

New Age music		Opera music	
Performer	Music	Performer	Music
Kevin Kern	Through the Arbor	Sofia Philharmonic Orchestra	Nessun Dorma
Bandari	Moonlight	New York Philharmonic	The Marriage of Figaro
Omar Akram	Take My Hand	New York Philharmonic	La donna è mobile
Ron Korb	Tokaido Eastern Sea Route	New York Philharmonic	Bizet_ Carmen-Toreador

4   Results and Analysis of the Experiment

4.1   Music Type and Conceptual Sketch Features

The sketches of the lamp concept were drawn by the subjects while listening to the New Age music, as shown in Fig. 1. The subjects tended to employ bionic objects, such as trees, bamboo, and tiles, to present the profile styling of their sketch and simplify a lamp shape with geometric or large curvature; or they would choose the musical instruments from the music, such as drums, to simplify the appearance of the instruments and present a lamp with a gentle curve; according to notes about their sketches and the verbal retrospect of the subjects, the materials for making lamps were mainly bamboo, wood, and cloth; the surface colors were mostly the color of the applied raw materials, including the color of wood, green grass, and bamboo colors; the lamp sketches showed less decorative elements; in terms of the lamp component relationship, the styling characteristics of the sketches are shown in units. In general, in the case of the New Age music, the subjects tended to apply handmade methods and used natural materials and simple design styles.

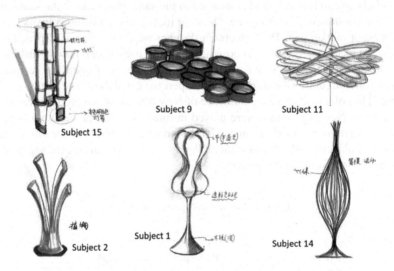

Fig. 1. Sketches of some subjects under New Age music condition.

When the subjects listened to opera music, the sketches of the lamp concept as shown in Fig. 2. The profile styling of these lamps utilized bionic objects, such as gorgeous crystals, in order to display angular surfaces and small curvature arcs; or they would use items common to opera stages, such as cloth curtains, performer's costumes, etc. Regarding the lamp materials, artificial materials were widely used, including metal, crystals, and cloth. In terms of surface colors, the notes about the sketches and the verbal retrospect descriptions show that bright colors were mostly used, such as red, the combination of yellow and black, or brilliant crystals; in terms of the decorative elements, more decorative elements were used, such as tassels, crystals, and scroll grass on the lampshade; in terms of the component relationship, while the conceptual sketches were relatively diversified, similar units were repeatedly superimposed to show the characteristics of the lamp, as shown in Fig. 2.

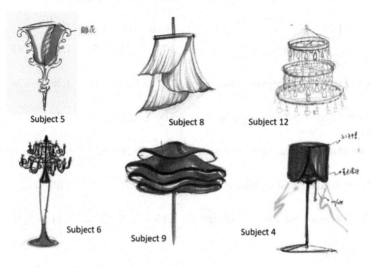

Fig. 2. Sketches of some subjects under Opera music condition.

4.2 Music and Design Style Association

The music-induced design style association measurements, as completed by the subjects, conducted Paired Sample T-testing to examine the design style associations applied by the subjects when performing the design tasks while listening to New Age and opera music, and the test results are shown in Table 3.

Table 3. Paired Sample T-test of music-induced design style association

Test items	New Age music		Opera music		t	p
	Mean	SD	Mean	SD		
The music-induced of "hard-soft" design style	5.62	0.96	4.31	1.30	4.67	0.00*
The music-induced of "angular–rounded" design style	5.38	0.89	4.52	1.11	2.93	0.01*
The music-induced of "hand-made-hi-tech" design style	2.32	0.72	4.57	0.93	−7.23	0.00*
The music-induced of "plain-luxurious" design style	2.63	0.89	6.13	0.50	−15.65	0.00*

(continued)

Table 3. (*continued*)

Test items	New Age music		Opera music		t	p
	Mean	SD	Mean	SD		
The music-induced of "single-multiple" design style	2.73	1.18	5.56	1.11	−7.12	0.00*
The music-induced of "regular-random" design style	2.31	0.87	3.16	1.26	−1.74	0.11
The music-induced of "straight-curvature" design style	5.06	1.39	5.51	0.73	−1.45	0.17
The music-induced of "matte-glossy" design style	3.31	1.30	6.25	0.58	−8.18	0.00*
The music-induced of "coarse-delicate" design style	5.31	0.71	5.25	1.06	0.19	0.89
The music-induced of "geometric-biomorphic" design style	3.13	1.06	5.37	0.81	−9.32	0.00*

$\alpha = 0.05$, *$p < 0.05$

Among the 10 bipolar design style adjective pairs, regular- random ($t = -1.74$, $p = 0.11$), straight-curved ($t = -1.45$, $p = 0.17$), and coarse -delicate ($t = 0.19$, $p = 0.89$), have p values over 0.05, which reach significant difference. This result indicates no significant difference in the style association when the subjects listened to these two types of music. However, regarding the design style association of the straight-curved, the average p values are greater than 5 in both New Age music ($M = 5.06$) and opera music ($M = 5.51$), which suggests that the subjects were strongly inclined to feel the style association of the curve in the cases of New Age and opera music. Similarly, regarding coarse -delicate, the average p values are greater than 5 in both New Age music ($M = 5.31$) and opera music ($M = 5.25$), which shows that the subjects tended to feel delicate style association from these two music, as shown in the trend chart of design style association in Fig. 3.

Among the bipolar design style adjective pairs, hard-soft ($t = 4.67$, $p = 0.00$), angular-rounded ($t = 2.93$, $p = 0.01$), hand-made-hi-tech ($t = -7.23$, $p = 0.00$), plain-luxurious ($t = -15.65$, $p = 0.00$), single-multiple ($t = -7.12$, $p = 0.00$), matte-bright ($t = -8.18$, $p = 0.00$), and geometric-biomorphic ($t = -9.32$, $p = 0.00$) have p values less than 0.05, which reach significant difference, and indicates that there are significant differences in subjects' style associations when listening to New Age and opera music. When listening to New Age music, compared with opera music, the subjects obviously associated with soft, rounded, hand-made, plain, single, matte, and geometric design styles; when listening to opera music, compared with New Age music, the subjects obviously associated with hard, angular, hi-tech, luxurious, multiple, glossy, and biomorphic design styles, as shown in the trend chart of design style association in Fig. 3.

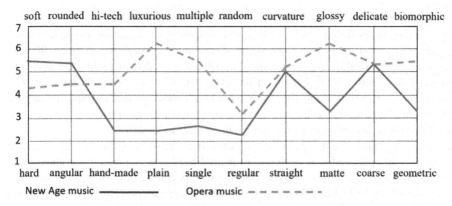

Fig. 3. Music-induce design style association tendency.

5 Discussion and Conclusion

5.1 Discussion

According to the concept sketch and music style association measurement drawn by the subjects, New Age and opera music can trigger specific design style associations. In both of these two music types, the subjects mainly chose biomorphic objects for product shape and composed materials, but different imitation objects. In the case of New Age music, the subjects preferred to use natural objects as design materials, such as trees, bamboo, and textile. In the case of opera music, they preferred imitation artificial objects as the design materials, such as items common to opera stages, including cloth curtains and performer's clothing. Regarding the style characteristics of the surface color of lamps, natural materials and matte colors were mainly used when the subjects listened to New Age music; while those listening to opera music preferred to apply bright colors and those with strong contrast. There are some differences in the style of lamp decoration according to the contexts of New Age music and opera music. In the case of New Age music, fewer decorative elements were applied, the relationship between lamp components was relatively simple, and the styling characteristics were mostly presented in units. However, in the case of opera music, more decorative elements were widely used, such as tassels and crystals on the lampshade, and the component relationships were more diversified.

These phenomena of the above lamp design sketches, according to the verbal retracing of the subjects, "listening to New Age music leads to a natural and simple feeling. Therefore, when designing the outline, and composing the materials and surface color of lamps, imitating natural materials or the original color of materials is preferred and fewer decorative elements are used. The component relationship is expressed in a simple form, which can reflect the natural and simple style feeling brought by listening to music." As a result, in this music context, the styling of lamps and lanterns is presented through geometric, plain, monomeric, and man-made design methods. These design style features are consistent with the test results of the music association measurement. Please refer to Fig. 3. The lamp styles designed on the opera music are based on the above phenomena.

After listening to opera music, the subjects said that "the opera music triggers a gorgeous style feeling. When designing the outline, and composing the materials and surface color of the lamps, we strongly associated with the curtain tassels of the opera stage, the gorgeous costumes of the performers, and the brilliant crystal lighting in the scene, and regarded them as the styling characteristics of the lamps". Therefore, the characteristics of the lamp sketches were mostly expressed in biomorphic, curved, multiple, luxurious, and bright design forms. These design style characteristics are consistent with the test results of music association feeling table. Please refer to Table 2.

This study takes the design sketches, music-induce association measurements, and the oral recall of the subjects as the experimental results, which lead to the abovementioned phenomena, and may be related to the way people retrieve memories and their cognition of music features. When external stimuli appear (playing music), it arouses people's attention, which stimulates the long-term memory area to search for memories matching the current stimulus [22], just like people recall the past when listening to music and generate associations from the music. Listening to music while designing is like adding a stimulus connection, meaning it helps to inspire the brain's memory network to connect to specific memory blocks, thus, generating the imagination required for design creativity [23]. Studies have shown that people's response to music is based on the listener's expectation of the music, meaning music leads people to associate with things that have moved them [24], and the listener's familiarity with music patterns enables the ear to find relevant connections, like automatic navigation [25]. In other words, in this experiment, cognition was generated by listening to music to create an associated atmosphere, and the subjects could generate context-dependent memories from listening to similar music in the past. The extraction of elements related to music and applying them to lamp design [23], echo the findings that music evokes the listener's autobiographical memory, which allows them to enter the situation of hearing similar music in the past [26].

5.2 Conclusion

This study empirically explored the influence of music type on design style, and the results show that both New Age and opera music can trigger specific design style associations. In the case of New Age music, the subjects preferred natural and simple design styles. In the case of opera music, most of the subjects expressed their design styles in multiple and gorgeous ways. Music stimulated the subjects' context-dependent memories, which prompted them to recall memories of listening to similar music in the past, and select the available materials to express the design style.

The effect of music is extensive, the impact of music on people's behavior is complex, and the design behavior involves a wide range of levels. This study did not intend to explain the complex design behavior stimulated by the phenomenon of listening to music to present the development of design concepts, but only put forward the idea of making good use of the characteristics of music to help stimulate creative ideas to enable designers to enhance and improve their design ideas.

References

1. Ziegler, R.: Music, the Definitive Visual History. Dorling Kindersley, London, UK (2013)
2. Eskine, K.E., Anderson, A.E., Sullivan, M., GolobFirst, E.J.: Effects of music listening on creative cognition and semantic memory retrieval. Psychol. Music **48**(4), 513–528 (2020)
3. Gültepe, B., Coskun, H.: Music and cognitive stimulation influence idea generation. Psychol. Music **44**(1), 3–14 (2016)
4. Eckert, C., Stacey, M.: Source of inspiration: a language of design. Des. Stud. **21**(5), 523–538 (2000)
5. Liao, C.M., Chang, W.C.: A survey on effects of music on design association. Bull. Japanese Soc. Sci. Des. **61**(5), 47–56 (2015)
6. Areni, C.S., Kim, D.: The influence of background music on shopping behavior: classical versus top-forty music in a wine store. Adv. Consum. Res. **20**, 336–340 (1993)
7. Sutton, C.J.C., Lowis, M.J.: The effect of musical mode on verbal and spatial task performance. Creat. Res. J. **20**(4), 420–426 (2008)
8. Yeoh, J.P.S., North, A.C.: The effect of musical fit on consumers' memory. Psychol. Music **38**(3), 368–378 (2010)
9. Liao, C.M., Chang, W.C.: Effects of listening to related music on idea generation in design project. Bull. Japanese Soc. Sci. Des. **62**(5), 11–20 (2016)
10. Lai, I.C., Chang, T.W.: A distributed linking system for supporting idea association during the conceptual design stage. Des. Stud. **27**(6), 685–710 (2006)
11. Seelig, T.: InGenius : A Crash Course on Creativity. HarperOne, New York (2012)
12. McCoy, J.M., Evans, G.W.: The potential role of the physical environment in fostering creativity. Creat. Res. J. **14**(3 & 4), 409–426 (2002)
13. Goldschmidt, G., Smolkov, M.: Variances in the impact of visual stimuli on design problem solving performance. Des. Stud. **27**(5), 549–569 (2006)
14. Purcell, A.T., Gero, J.S.: Drawings and the design process: a review of protocol studies in design and other disciplines and related research in cognitive psychology. Des. Stud. **19**(4), 389–430 (1998)
15. Wang, K.: Research on product formal design based on style description. In: 2009 IEEE 10th International Conference on Computer-Aided Industrial Design & Conceptual Design, pp. 213–215. IEEE, Wenzhou (2010)
16. Chan, C.S.: Can style be measured. Des. Stud. **21**(3), 277–291 (2000)
17. Chang, W., Van, Y.: Researching design trends for the redesign of product form. Des. Stud. **24**(2), 173–180 (2003)
18. Chen, K., Owen, C.L.: Form language and style description. Des. Stud. **18**(3), 249–274 (1997)
19. Lin, M.H.: The characters and tendencies of minimalism in design. J. Des. **17**(1), 79–99 (2012)
20. Dorst, K.: Analysing design activity: new directions in protocol analysis. Des. Stud. **16**(2), 139–142 (1995)
21. Chuang, M.C., Chang, C.C., Hsu, S.H.: Perceptual factors underlying user preferences toward product form of mobile phones. Int. J. Ind. Ergon. **27**, 247–258 (2001)
22. Best, J.B.: Cognitive Psychology. 5th edn. Wadsworth, Belmont, CA (1999)
23. Santrock, J.W.: Psychology: Essentials. 2nd edn. McGraw-Hill, New York (2004)
24. Winner, E.: Invented Worlds: The Psychology of the Arts. Harvard University Press, Cambridge, Massachusetts (1982)
25. Maconie, R.: The Concept of Music. Oxford University Press, New York (1993)
26. Janata, P., Tomic, S.T., Rakowski, S.K.: Characterisation of music-evoked autobiographical memories. Memory **15**(8), 845–860 (2007)

The Effect of Camera Viewing Angle on Product Digital Presentation Perception

Rafał Michalski[✉] [iD] and Jerzy Grobelny[iD]

Faculty of Management, Wrocław University of Science and Technology, 27 Wybrzeże Wyspiańskiego st., 50-370 Wrocław, Poland
{rafal.michalski,jerzy.grobelny}@pwr.edu.pl

Abstract. The digital presentation of a product is ubiquitous today. It appears in both online stores and outdoors in various types of displays. Thus, it is important to know as much as possible how such product demonstration should be designed. This study presents an experimental investigation of the impact of product packaging viewing perspective on the purchasing intentions of people. Unlike previous studies, the issue is examined in a systematic way. It involved six viewing angles ($\pm 15°$, $\pm 30°$, and $\pm 45°$) that varied in two dimensions: vertical and horizontal. In general, 12 variants were assessed. The article confirms previous studies indicating that the presentation of people or objects from different angles may affect the perception of observers. Our findings showed that the willingness to buy is greatest when packages are viewed from a top angle. This is in contrast to the results presented previously on picturing individuals or advertising products. Unexpectedly, there were no differences in demonstrating packages on the left- or right-hand side. The bigger camera angles used to picture packages produced lower and lower values of preferences. The findings expand our knowledge of human visual behavior in a specific context and provide useful suggestions on display design usability. The results are of potential interest to computer graphics designers in various areas.

Keywords: Visual information usability · Display design · Subjective preferences · Viewing angle · Marketing

1 Introduction

Knowledge about the usability of visual content demonstration is essential in various fields, especially in a modern highly digitized world. The graphical presentation of digital versions of classic banners or packages influences perception and affects user preferences and, as a result, their decisions. This impact depends on a number of factors.

In recent years, Grobelny and Michalski [5] examined user preferences in this regard. They revealed, among other things, that the location of product brand name closer to the right edge of the package is preferred to the left side. Another finding regarded larger preferences for a larger and more concentrated text than the smaller and spreader one. The study also involved background color preferences. Although women liked and men

© The Author(s), under exclusive license to Springer Nature Switzerland AG 2022
M. M. Soares et al. (Eds.): HCII 2022, LNCS 13321, pp. 246–258, 2022.
https://doi.org/10.1007/978-3-031-05897-4_18

dislike pink versions, the color factor was considerably more significant for men than for women. The color feature in conjunction with the dimensionality was subject to investigation in [21]. They found that people favored in this context, rather blue-colored background than the red and green ones. The results also showed the superiority of three-dimensional looking packages over two-dimensional ones and the advantage of rounded edges as compared with sharp variants. The roundedness effect was further explored using the eye tracking methodology in [20]. The effects of various three-dimensional shapes on preferences were systematically examined in [19]. Curved, tapered, and tilted packages appeared to be markedly less liked than a classic cuboid option.

Another factor that could possibly influence people's decisions is the angle at which the product is pictured. In real situations, consumers search for products and look at them from various distances, so the viewing angle of a specific article changes. Naturally, there are large interpersonal differences in this regard related, for example, to consumers' body heights. In a digital world, the angle at which the product is presented seems to be even more important, however, there is surprisingly little research dealing with this issue.

Among the few investigations in this regard, work [24] reports that there exist specific viewing angles for everyday objects that speed up their perception. They called them canonical views. These results were further confirmed and extended in [12]. They additionally demonstrated that these canonical perspectives are considered to be more aesthetically pleasing than less canonical ones. Gardner [4], in turn, indirectly considered the effect of viewing angle by analyzing depth perception with respect to digital spheres placed within a rectangular, three-dimensionally bounded artificial space. The space resembled a room with different positions of horizon height.

Another study by Sammartino & Palmer [29] involved various angles of digitally presented real objects. They examined, inter alia, preferences for a bowl and a light fixture placed within a frame displayed in five different perspectives 0° (pure side view), 18°, 36°, 54°, and 90° (direct view above the bowl and below the light fixture). For items presented in the center of the frame, the highest preferences for both types of object were observed for 90° while in the second place there were pictures with items rotated by the smallest angle from the profile view (0°). Under other conditions, the differences were not so distinctive. In a follow-up experiment, the same authors explored flying eagle and swimming stingray images from four different perspectives (above 90°, side above 45°, side below –45°, and below -90°) and, similarly as in the previous experiment, situated within a frame in five different locations. When the animals were located in the center of the frame, the highest preferences were obtained for versions above (90°) and below (–90°). In general, these investigations revealed a significant impact of the effect of viewing angle on people's preferences. The results also showed strong interactions between types of objects, their positions in the frame, and the applied perspective.

The camera angle effect was subject to interest for photographers and filmmakers. For example, Tiemens [30] found that placing the camera below the communicator increased his credibility, while Mandell and Shaw [17] showed that a person shot slightly from the bottom was considered more active or potent. Kraft [15] generally confirmed these findings and extended them to boxes. Their findings additionally indicate that significant effects of camera angle are more probable if consumers are low or moderately motivated to process the advertisement presented.

In a marketing context, the effects of the camera angle were examined in [18]. In this study, individuals perceived the bicycles examined as stronger or more potent when they were presented from a below eye-height level and weaker and more inferior when demonstrated from a downward-looking angle.

Although there is some research indicating that the viewing angle could be an important effect shaping people's preferences, comprehensive, experimentally based studies are still very scarce in this respect. Therefore, in this investigation, a variety of viewing angles have been applied to a typical box-shaped product package to assess its impact on the subjects' preferences. As far as we are aware, this effect has not been systematically investigated in the context of product visual presentation design.

2   Method

2.1   Participants

There were 99 students who took part in the study – 61 women and 38 men. Their age ranged from 19 to 29 years with an average of 20.7 and standard mean error of 0.17. They all reported normal or corrected to normal visual acuity. The participants were briefly reported on the procedure and the possibility of resigning from the study at any time without the need to state any reason. They also gave their informed consent to participate in the experiment. Data collected were related to the subjects' opinions on the product package and were not directly linked with a specific participant.

2.2   Stimuli

This study investigates the willingness of participants to buy a fictitious smartphone device after presenting its digital image placed on a virtual packaging. We use the unreal brand name presented in black font. The product was presented in the picture as turned off and was also mainly black with a silver outline. The mockup packages were prepared in 3D Studio Max software and resembled a three-dimensional gray box. Its dimensions followed the golden proportion.

The stimuli were differentiated by the way the camera was placed. Three factors were examined: (1) *Camera horizontal location* (Left, Right), (2) *Camera vertical location* (Bottom, Top), and (3) *Camera angle* (15, 30, 45) degrees. A mixture of these three factors produces 12 different experimental conditions as demonstrated in Fig. 1.

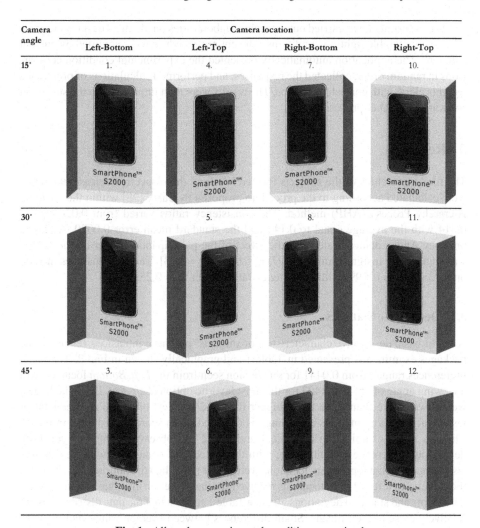

Fig. 1. All twelve experimental conditions examined.

2.3 Experimental Design and Procedure

A full factorial within-subjects design was applied, which means that each participant evaluated all 12 experimental conditions: 2 (*Camera horizontal locations*) × 2 (*Camera vertical locations*) × 3 (*Camera angles*). Subjects were presented with two versions of the packaging at the same time. They were asked to express their opinion about which of them incline them to purchase the product more and to what extent. Subjects specified the degree of their preference on a five-point ordered linguistic scale.

A given pair was demonstrated once, and we did not compare the same variants. Since there were 12 different packaging variants, the number of pairwise comparisons amounted to $\frac{(12^2-12)}{2} = 66$.

The experiment was carried out in teaching laboratories on identical desktop computers and comparable lighting conditions. The entire procedure was supported by custom software. The application automatically presented the experimental condition comparisons in random order, collected the responses, and performed calculations of preference weights along with consistency ratios. The results were then imported into the statistical software for further processing.

3   Results

The final hierarchies of the subjects' preferences and the respective consistency ratios were calculated according to the procedure proposed by Saaty [28] within the Analytic Hierarchy Process (AHP) method. The consistency ratios varied from 0.0264 up to 0.414 with the average equal to 0.143 and the standard mean error 0.0070. A classic one-way Anova demonstrated that the effect of the participants' gender on mean CRs was statistically insignificant [$F(1, 97) = 0.0074, p = 0.93$]. The next analyzes include only 93 subjects (of 99) with consistency ratios lower than 0.25.

3.1 Descriptive Statistics

A list of basic descriptive characteristics of subjects' purchase intensions related to the packages examined is presented in Table 1 and graphically shown in Fig. 2. The mean preferences ranged from 0.0441 for the version seen from the *Left-Bottom* location with a viewing angle of 45° to 0.1403 for the most favorite option (*Left-Top*, 15°). The largest weight was more than three times bigger than and smallest one. The arrangement of tested package presentations according to computed mean scores is provided in Fig. 3. Through initial examination of Table 1 and Fig. 2 one observes a trend of generally decreasing preference weights along with the increase of camera view angles. It may also be noticed that top camera locations were better rated than the bottom ones, whereas the cameras in left and right locations received similar scores on average. The mean standard errors and standard deviations given in Table 1 suggest that the data distributions are relatively close to their means. Small differences between average values and medians indicate that variable distributions do not deviate markedly from a symmetrical shape. Post-hoc pairwise comparisons computed according to Fischer's LSD procedure, presented in Table 2, revealed statistically significant differences on various levels between the mean weights of almost all conditions. No meaningful differences were observed for pairs of conditions that differ in the *Left-Right* camera locations e.g. *Left-Bottom_15°* vs. *Right-Bottom_15°*, *Left-Bottom_30°* vs. *Right-Bottom_30°* etc. This analysis confirms the initial notion that discrepancies between package presentations from cameras located on the left- or right-hand side are probably negligible. A very clear pattern that is emerging from Fig. 2 and Table 1 is further explored by means of Anova in the next section.

Table 1. Basic descriptive statistics for all experimental conditions ($n = 93$) with $CR < 0.25$.

Experimental condition			Basic descriptive statistics					
No	Camera location	Camera angle	Mean	SME[*]	Median	Min	Max	SD[**]
1	Left-Bottom	15°	0.0848	0.0035	0.0796	0.0278	0.1786	0.0334
2	Left-Bottom	30°	0.0617	0.0025	0.0569	0.0218	0.1651	0.0243
3	Left-Bottom	45°	0.0441	0.0025	0.0373	0.0204	0.1620	0.0242
4	Left-Top	15°	0.1403	0.0046	0.1416	0.0421	0.2398	0.0448
5	Left-Top	30°	0.1067	0.0037	0.1045	0.0331	0.2380	0.0354
6	Left-Top	45°	0.0700	0.0031	0.0627	0.0235	0.1690	0.0301
7	Right-Bottom	15°	0.0834	0.0037	0.0795	0.0292	0.1793	0.0353
8	Right-Bottom	30°	0.0570	0.0022	0.0544	0.0198	0.1328	0.0214
9	Right-Bottom	45°	0.0457	0.0028	0.0377	0.0157	0.1651	0.0266
10	Right-Top	15°	0.1393	0.0042	0.1374	0.0453	0.2522	0.0402
11	Right-Top	30°	0.1024	0.0032	0.0998	0.0469	0.1918	0.0308
12	Right-Top	45°	0.0644	0.0030	0.0583	0.0223	0.1806	0.0291

[*] SME– Standard Mean Error,
[**] SD– Standard Deviation.

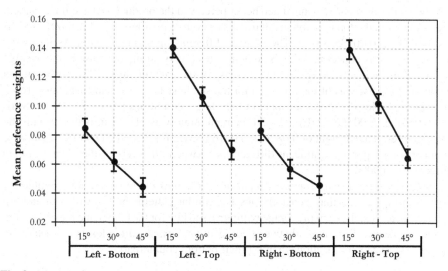

Fig. 2. Mean preference weights for all experimental conditions. Whiskers denote 0.95 confidence intervals.

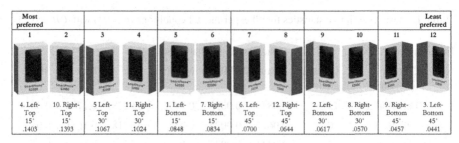

Most preferred											Least preferred
1	2	3	4	5	6	7	8	9	10	11	12
4. Left-Top 15° .1403	10. Right-Top 15° .1393	5 Left-Top 30° .1067	11. Right-Top 30° .1024	1. Left-Bottom 15° .0848	7. Right-Bottom 15° .0834	6. Left-Top 45° .0700	12. Right-Top 45° .0644	2. Left-Bottom 30° .0617	8. Right-Bottom 30° .0570	9. Right-Bottom 45° .0457	3. Left-Bottom 45° .0441

Fig. 3. Final preference hierarchy.

3.2 Analysis of Variance

A three-way Anova was used to check if the mean participant scores were significantly influenced by the following three factors: *Camera horizontal location*, *Camera vertical location*, and *Camera angle*. The results obtained presented in Table 3 revealed a statistically significant influence of *Camera vertical location*, [$F(1, 1104) = 460, p < 0.0001, \eta^2 = 0.29$], *Camera angle* [$F(2, 1104) = 285, p < 0.0001, \eta^2 = 0.34$] and the interaction between them (*Camera vertical location* × *Camera angle*) [$F(2, 1104) = 27, p < 0.0001, \eta^2 = 0.046$]. Taking into account the Cohen's [2] rule of thumb, the effect sizes of *Camera vertical location* and *Camera angle* can be regarded as large while their significant interaction as medium. The *Camera horizontal location* effect was meaningless [$F(1, 1104) = 1.7, p = 0.19$]. The three-way interaction along with all other two-way interactions did not affect the mean intentions of the subjects to buy either.

Mean purchase intents for statistically important effects are illustrated in Figs. 4, 5, 6. As shown in Fig. 4 participants much better perceived the product package if the camera was situated in the top location in contrast to its bottom position (0.104 ± 0.00135 SME vs. 0.0628 ± 0.00135 SME). The relative difference amounts to 65%. As far as the *Camera angle* is concerned, Fig. 5 demonstrates a very strong decrease in the average scores of the subjects along with the increase of the camera angles. The highest mean intent to purchase was of the observed for the smallest 15° angle and was almost twice as high as the lowest scores attributed to 45° angle conditions (0.112 ± 0.00166 SME vs. 0.0561 ± 0.00166 SME). The 30° camera angle was placed in between with the average preference weight of 0.0820 ± 0.00166 SME. Fischer's LSD post-hoc pairwise comparisons reported significant differences between all levels of the *Camera angle* effect ($\alpha = 0.00001$).

Analyzing the *Camera vertical location* × *Camera angle* interaction, graphically shown in Fig. 6, one may generally observe similar patterns both for bottom and top camera locations: the drop in average willingness to buy for the bigger and bigger camera angles. However, differences between consecutive *Camera angle* levels are decidedly larger for top camera locations than for their bottom counterparts.

Table 2. Fischer's LSD post-hoc pairwise comparisons for all conditions (n = 93 with CR < 0.25; * $\alpha < 0.1$; ** $\alpha < 0.05$; *** $\alpha < 0.001$

			Left Bottom			Left Top			Right Bottom			Right Top		
			15°	30°	45°	15°	30°	45°	15°	30°	45°	15°	30°	45°
Left	Bottom	15°	×	< 0.0001***	< 0.0001***	< 0.0001***	< 0.0001***	0.0016**	0.77	< 0.0001***	< 0.0001***	< 0.0001***	0.0002***	< 0.0001***
		30°		×	0.0002***	< 0.0001***	< 0.0001***	0.077*	< 0.0001***	0.32	0.0007***	< 0.0001***	< 0.0001***	0.56
		45°			×	< 0.0001***	< 0.0001***	< 0.0001***	< 0.0001***	0.0059**	0.73	< 0.0001***	< 0.0001***	< 0.0001***
	Top	15°				×	< 0.0001***	< 0.0001***	< 0.0001***	< 0.0001***	< 0.0001***	0.85	< 0.0001***	< 0.0001***
		30°					×	< 0.0001***	< 0.0001***	< 0.0001***	< 0.0001***	< 0.0001***	0.36	< 0.0001***
		45°						×	0.0042**	0.0059**	< 0.0001***	< 0.0001***	< 0.0001***	0.24
Right	Bottom	15°							×	< 0.0001***	< 0.0001***	< 0.0001***	< 0.0001***	0.0001***
		30°								×	0.016**	< 0.0001***	< 0.0001***	0.12
		45°									×	< 0.0001***	< 0.0001***	0.0001***
	Top	15°										×	< 0.0001***	< 0.0001***
		30°											×	< 0.0001***
		45°												×

Table 3. Three-way analysis of variance results. The influence of *Camera horizontal location*, *Camera vertical location*, and *Camera angle* on mean preference weights.

Effect	Sum of squares	Degrees of freedom	Mean sum of squares	F	p	η^2
Camera horizontal location (CHL)	0.0018	1	0.0018	10.7	0.19	0.0016
Camera vertical location (CVL)	0.47	1	0.47	460	<0.0001*	0.29
Camera angle (CA)	0.58	2	0.29	285	<0.0001*	0.34
CHL × CVL	0.00031	1	0.00031	0.31	0.58	0.00028
CHL × CA	0.00056	2	0.00028	0.27	0.76	0.00050
CVL × CA	0.054	2	0.027	27	<0.0001*	0.046
CHL × CVL × CA	0.00090	2	0.00045	0.44	0.64	0.00080
Error	10.1	1104	0.0010			

* $\alpha < 0.0001$

The results obtained revealed a very clear pattern of increasing the buying intents along with decreasing the viewing angle. A similarly strong effect of *Camera vertical location* was observed: subjects markedly preferred top over bottom views. The *Horizontal camera location* factor, in turn, did not meaningfully differentiate the purchase intentions.

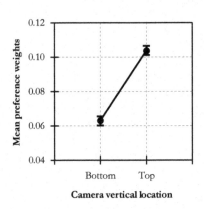

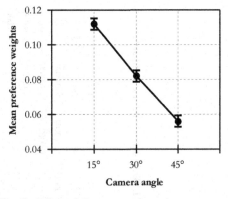

Fig. 4. Effect of *Camera vertical location* on the mean preference weights. [$F(1, 1004) = 460, p < 0.0001, \eta^2 = 0.29$]. Whiskers denote 0.95 confidence intervals

Fig. 5. Effect of *Camera angle* on the mean preference weights. [$F(2, 1004) = 285, p < 0.0001, \eta^2 = 0.34$]. Whiskers denote 0.95 confidence intervals

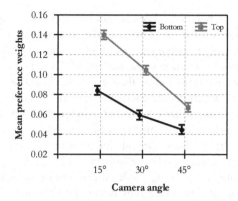

Fig. 6. Effect of *Camera vertical location* × *Camera angle* interaction on mean preference weights [$F(2, 1104) = 27, p < 0.0001, \eta^2 = 0.046$]. Whiskers denote 0.95 confidence intervals

4 Discussion

The experiment focused on presenting the product package from various perspectives. The obtained results revealed a very clear-cut pattern of increasing the purchase willingness along with decreasing the viewing angle. A similarly strong effect of *Camera vertical location* was observed: subjects markedly preferred top over bottom views. The *Camera horizontal location* factor did not meaningfully differentiate purchase willingness.

The effect of *Camera angle* could possibly be explained by the reluctance of subjects to positively rate objects with skewed lines versus horizontal or perpendicular ones. This phenomenon called "the oblique effect" was reported by Jastrow already in 1892 [9]. A review of this type of study is provided by Appelle [1]. This behavior may be related to the way people process simple lines in the primary visual cortex, where particular groups of neurons are specialized in detecting specific angles of processed lines. The mechanism was first discovered in cats by Nobel Prize winners Hubel and Wiesel in 1959 [8]. Further physiologically based developments in this regard were presented by, e.g., Furmanski & Engel [3], Li et al. [16], or Wurtz [33]. It seems that the less is the number of skewed lines, the less processing needs to take place, which may increase the preference towards a specific object shape. As a result, the best scored forms were those presented at the smallest angle because most of the package edges were very close to horizontal or vertical lines.

The obtained finding may also be related to experiments showing that people tend to identify horizontal or vertical axes of symmetry faster than skewed symmetries. A support for this hypothesis for two-dimensional abstract shapes was presented in [10, 22, 23, 27, 31, 32], and for three-dimensional objects, e.g., by Koning & Wagemans [14]. Thus, for packages presented in the current study, at smaller angles the symmetry was noticed more quickly and, according to [26], this may lead to higher preferences.

The finding of vertical and horizontal camera locations is interesting and to some extent surprising. In the context of brain lateralization research outcomes (e.g., [6, 7]), it could be assumed that the *Left–Right* camera location somehow influences the subjects' perception of the product, but the analysis did not no support this supposition. However, participants strongly favored the top views over the bottom ones, which is in contrast to the results obtained in [18]. Possible reasons for obtaining this result can be connected with the typical purchasing situation in the real world. Usually, customers see products on shelves or shopping windows below their eyesight. A similar explanation relating to a typical situation in which people encounter specific objects was provided in [29] where, generally, higher preferences of placing a digital bowl image in the upper parts of the displayed frame were accompanied by better perceptions of a light fixture located near the bottom of the frame. These typical situations may, in turn, develop the "*best*" perspective view of a package called by Palmer et al. [24] as the canonical one.

Furthermore, the natural viewing angle, the so-called normal line of sight, lies approximately between 25 and 35 degrees below the horizontal line of sight if both the head and eyes are relaxed [25, p. 461]. Thus, the biological cost of looking at products from the bottom is greater than that for objects visible from the top. Users might subconsciously consider these real-life experiences while expressing their willingness to purchase towards digital product demonstrations.

Although the research was conducted thoroughly, there are some limitations that must be considered when interpreting the results. The study involved participants with similar demographic, cultural, and social characteristics. Although it can be seen as an advantage in some circumstances, the subjects are not representative of the whole population of target product buyers. Another issue relates to the fact that we examined purchase intentions by computing relative preferences. These data could not fully reflect actual buying behavior in real-life. Furthermore, our findings can be specific to small electronic products, which should be verified in further research.

5   Conclusions

This research investigated the impact of product packaging viewing perspective on people purchase intentions. Unlike previous studies, we examined the issue in a considerably more systematic way by involving a number of specific viewing angles that varied in two dimensions: vertical and horizontal.

This article confirms prior studies indicating that the presentation of peoples or objects from different angles may affect the perception of observers. Our findings showed that purchase willingness is the greatest when packages are pictured from a top viewing angle. This is in contrast to the outcomes presented in previous studies on picturing and filming of persons or advertising products. Unexpectedly, there were no differences in the presentation of packages on the left or right side, which could have been the case in light of brain lateralization research. The larger camera angles used to picture packages produced lower and lower values of purchase willingness, which was not reported earlier to the best knowledge of the authors.

The findings of this study expand the corpus of knowledge on human visual processing behavior of various three-dimensional shapes in a specific context. They provide useful practical implications regarding the usability of product digital presentations, which are of potential interest for computer graphics designers in various areas.

Acknowledgments. The research was partially financially supported by Polish National Science Centre Grant No. 2017/27/B/HS4/01876.

References

1. Appelle, S.: Perception and discrimination as a function of stimulus orientation: the "oblique effect" in man and animals. Psychol. Bull. **78**(4), 266–278 (1972). https://doi.org/10.1037/h0033117

2. Cohen, J.: Statistical Power Analysis for the Behavioral Sciences, 2nd edn. Erlbaum, Hillsdale, NJ (1988)

3. Furmanski, C.S., Engel, S.A.: An oblique effect in human primary visual cortex. Nat. Neurosci. **3**(6), 535–536 (2000). https://doi.org/10.1038/75702

4. Gardner, J.S., Austerweil, J.L., Palmer, S.E.: Vertical position as a cue to pictorial depth: height in the picture plane versus distance to the horizon. Atten. Percept. Psychophys. **72**(2), 445–453 (2010). https://doi.org/10.3758/APP.72.2.445

5. Grobelny, J., Michalski, R.: The role of background color, interletter spacing, and font size on preferences in the digital presentation of a product. Comput. Hum. Behav. **43**, 85–100 (2015). https://doi.org/10.1016/j.chb.2014.10.036

6. Hellige, J.B.: ERIC/ECTJ annual review paper: cerebral hemisphere asymmetry: methods, issues, and implications. Educ. Commun. Technol. **28**(2), 83–98 (1980)

7. Hellige, J.B.: Hemispheric asymmetry. Annu. Rev. Psychol. **41**(1), 55–80 (1990). https://doi.org/10.1146/annurev.ps.41.020190.000415

8. Hubel, D.H., Wiesel, T.N.: Receptive fields of single neurones in the cat's striate cortex. J. Physiol. **148**(3), 574–591 (1959)

9. Jastrow, J.: Studies from the University of Wisconsin: on the judgment of angles and positions of lines. Am. J. Psychol. **5**(2), 214–248 (1892). https://doi.org/10.2307/1410867

10. Kayaert, G., Wagemans, J.: Delayed shape matching benefits from simplicity and symmetry. Vis. Res. **49**(7), 708–717 (2009). https://doi.org/10.1016/j.visres.2009.01.002

11. Kayaert, G., Wagemans, J.: Infants and toddlers show enlarged visual sensitivity to nonaccidental compared with metric shape changes. i-Perception, **1**(3), 149–158 (2010). https://doi.org/10.1068/i0397

12. Khalil, S., McBeath, M.: Canonical representaion: an examination of preferences for viewing and depicting 3-dimensional objects. J. Vis. **6**(6), 267 (2010). https://doi.org/10.1167/6.6.267

13. Koczkodaj, W.W.: Testing the accuracy enhancement of pairwise comparisons by a Monte Carlo experiment. J. Stat. Plan. Inference **69**(1), 21–31 (1998). https://doi.org/10.1016/S0378-3758(97)00131-6

14. Koning, A., Wagemans, J.: Detection of symmetry and repetition in one and two objects. Exp. Psychol. **56**(1), 5–17 (2008). https://doi.org/10.1027/1618-3169.56.1.5

15. Kraft, R.N.: The influence of camera angle on comprehension and retention of pictorial events. Mem. Cognit. **15**(4), 291–307 (1987). https://doi.org/10.3758/BF03197032

16. Li, B., Peterson, M.R., Freeman, R.D.: Oblique effect: a neural basis in the visual cortex. J. Neurophysiol. **90**(1), 204–217 (2003). https://doi.org/10.1152/jn.00954.2002

17. Mandell, L.M., Shaw, D.L.: Judging people in the news — unconsciously: effect of camera angle and bodily activity. J. Broadcast. **17**(3), 353–362 (1973). https://doi.org/10.1080/08838157309363698

18. Meyers-Levy, J., Peracchio, L.A.: Getting an angle in advertising: the effect of camera angle on product evaluations. J. Mark. Res. **29**(4), 454–461 (1992). https://doi.org/10.2307/3172711

19. Michalski, R.: The role of virtual package shapes in digital product presentation. In: Rebelo, F., Soares, M. (eds.) AHFE 2020. AISC, vol. 1203, pp. 24–30. Springer, Cham (2020). https://doi.org/10.1007/978-3-030-51038-1_4

20. Michalski, R., Grobelny, J.: An eye tracking based examination of visual attention during pairwise comparisons of a digital product's package. In: Antona, M., Stephanidis, C. (eds.) UAHCI 2016. LNCS, vol. 9737, pp. 430–441. Springer, Cham (2016). https://doi.org/10.1007/978-3-319-40250-5_41

21. Michalski, R., Grobelny, J.: The effects of background color, shape and dimensionality on purchase intentions in a digital product presentation. In: Antona, M., Stephanidis, C. (eds.) UAHCI 2016. LNCS, vol. 9739, pp. 468–479. Springer, Cham (2016). https://doi.org/10.1007/978-3-319-40238-3_45

22. Palmer, S.E.: Goodness, gestalt, groups, and garner: local symmetry subgroups as a theory of figural goodness. In: Lockhead, G.R., Pomerantz, J.R. (Eds.), The Perception of Structure: Essays in Honor of Wendell R. Garner, pp. 23–39. Washington, DC, US: American Psychological Association (1991). https://doi.org/10.1037/10101-001

23. Palmer, S.E., Hemenway, K.: Orientation and symmetry: effects of multiple, rotational, and near symmetries. J. Exp. Psychol. Hum. Percept. Perform. 4(4), 691–702 (1978). https://doi.org/10.1037/0096-1523.4.4.691

24. Palmer, S.E., Rosch, E., Chase, P.: Canonical perspective and the perception of objects. In: Long, J., Baddeley, A. (eds.) Attention and Performance IX. Hillsdale, NJ: Erlbaum (1981)

25. Proctor, R.W., Zandt, T.V.: Human Factors in Simple and Complex Systems, Second Edition. CRC Press, Boca Raton (2008)

26. Reber, R., Schwarz, N., Winkielman, P.: Processing fluency and aesthetic pleasure: is beauty in the perceiver's processing experience? Pers. Soc. Psychol. Rev. 8(4), 364–382 (2004). https://doi.org/10.1207/s15327957pspr0804_3

27. Royer, F.L.: Detection of symmetry. J. Exp. Psychol. Hum. Percept. Perform. 7(6), 1186–1210 (1981). https://doi.org/10.1037/0096-1523.7.6.1186

28. Saaty, T.L.: A scaling method for priorities in hierarchical structures. J. Math. Psychol. 15(3), 234–281 (1977). https://doi.org/10.1016/0022-2496(77)90033-5

29. Sammartino, J., Palmer, S.E.: Aesthetic issues in spatial composition: representational fit and the role of semantic context. Perception 41(12), 1434–1457 (2012). https://doi.org/10.1068/p7233

30. Tiemens, R.K.: Some relationships of camera angle to communicator credibility. J. Broadcast. 14(4), 483–490 (1970). https://doi.org/10.1080/08838157009363614

31. Wagemans, J.: Skewed symmetry: a nonaccidental property used to perceive visual forms. J. Exp. Psychol. Hum. Percept. Perform. 19(2), 364–380 (1993). https://doi.org/10.1037/0096-1523.19.2.364

32. Wagemans, J., Gool, L.V., d'Ydewalle, G.: Orientational effects and component processes in symmetry detection. Quarterly J. Exp. Psychol. Section A 44(3), 475–508 (1992). https://doi.org/10.1080/14640749208401295

33. Wurtz, R.H.: Recounting the impact of Hubel and Wiesel. J. Physiol. 587(12), 2817–2823 (2009). https://doi.org/10.1113/jphysiol.2009.170209

Demographic Census: Searching for the Best User Experience

Patricia Zamprogno Tavares[1]([⊠]), Luiz Agner[2], and Simone Bacellar Leal Ferreira[3]

[1] Instituto Brasileiro de Geografia e Estatística (IBGE), Universidade Federal do Estado do Rio de Janeiro (UniRio), Rio de Janeiro, RJ, Brazil
`pztavares@gmail.com`
[2] Instituto Brasileiro de Geografia e Estatística (IBGE), Faculdades Integradas Helio Alonso, Rio de Janeiro, RJ, Brazil
[3] Universidade Federal do Estado do Rio de Janeiro (UniRio), Rio de Janeiro, RJ, Brazil
`simone@uniriotec.br`

Abstract. Brazil is conducting tests to offer questionnaires on the Web as an option for collecting data for the demographic census. This research aims to contribute to the census's success in approaching human-computer interaction and user experience (UX) design. Our goal is to focus on the respondent, analyze problems of online data collection, and propose strategies to enhance UX design. Citizens responding to the census online is a substantial innovation in obtaining data. This condition is a considerable challenge, as there is an immense diversity of respondents: they will have to interpret the questions and interact independently with the questionnaire. This article sought to comprehend some critical aspects of the interaction and maximize the usability of the online survey. Communication between the questionnaire and citizens must be clear and intuitive to accomplish a satisfactory user experience. This study examined 365 recommendations from census takers – grouped by themes. It developed a set of fourteen proto heuristics for self-administered online questionnaires.

Keywords: Computer-Assisted Web Interviewing · Heuristics · UX

1 Introduction

With systematic data collection, demographic censuses are one of the primary reference sources for producing information on people's profile and living conditions. It monitors changes and socioeconomic characteristics of a population, which is vital for understanding the economy and society [1].

The most considerable difficulties of demographic censuses are related to the cost and complexity, which represent challenges for any country. The traditional method of data collection, characterized by face-to-face visits to households carried out by census takers, has been increasingly questioned.

M. M. Soares et al. (Eds.): HCII 2022, LNCS 13321, pp. 259–274, 2022.
https://doi.org/10.1007/978-3-031-05897-4_19

The data collection phase could cost up to 75% of the census operation budget. Another unfavorable fact is the population's decreasing willingness to participate in surveys. Ultimately, the Covid-19 crisis reinforced the need to rethink face-to-face data collection [2].

These difficulties have led several countries to consider other forms of data collection without the direct support of census takers [3]. One of the alternatives is the adoption of online forms. National statistics offices have encouraged people to respond to questionnaires on the Web – an innovation regarding the traditional way of obtaining data. However, citizens will need to independently interpret and effectively interact with the questionnaire without the support of a census taker. This issue can impact data quality.

Difficulties and limitations in using the Web are essential concerns: technological problems can lead to an abandonment of questionnaires. In addition, communication between citizens and the electronic questionnaire must be clear and intuitive, ensuring an adequate user experience. Usability and UX strategies are recommended in self-administered interviews to increase citizens' satisfaction and improve their experience when filling out the questionnaires (Kaczmirek 2008) [4].

1.1 The Brazilian Demographic Census

The Brazilian Institute of Geography and Statistics (IBGE) is responsible for the Brazilian census. IBGE's census is budgeted at around US\$615 million[1] for an estimated population of 212.2 million people [1]. This operation may involve more than 250 thousand census takers[2] visiting 70 million addresses in 5,570 geographically dispersed cities in a territory with continental characteristics.

Brazil has been carrying out regular tests for the demographic census, which will apply a mixed-mode data collection, using traditional techniques (face-to-face and telephone interviews) and internet data collection. The Institute practitioners developed a testing website [5], where census takers tested the questionnaire and collaboratively shared their experiences. In total, census takers produced 365 comments describing opinions, ideas, criticisms, and recommendations, emphasizing the crucial aspects of online data collection. This study analyzed all these comments, grouping them by theme and identifying fourteen critical areas. The goal was to comprehend the recurrent data collection problems and lower their effects in designing the online questionnaire.

We aim to support scientific understanding on constructing an online questionnaire with acceptable usability and help offer the population a friendly, understandable, and efficient solution. Focusing on the respondent and analyzing the problems of online data collection, this research aims to contribute to the census's success by approaching human-computer interaction and user experience (UX) design issues.

---

[1] R\$ 3.4 billion (Brazilian Reais). Exchange rate in 01/17/2022: US\$ 1 = R\$ 5.5350. (Source: Bloomberg).

[2] Brazil has teams spread across the country to carry out in-person and telephone interviews, made up of two types of professionals: census takers, who collect data from respondents, and the supervisors, who manage teams of census takers. This article preferred to call these professionals census takers to simplify the comprehension.

2   Data Collection Methods in Demographic Censuses

The typical instrument for data collection in demographic censuses is a questionnaire. Questions can be answered through face-to-face or telephone interviews, mediated by census takers, or answered by the citizen through the post office or the internet. This article will focus on the data collection method supported by questionnaires on the Web.

In the CAWI (Computer-Assisted Web Interviewing) method, data collection does not require the intervention of the census taker: the citizen himself reads and answers the questions on the screen.

The problem, in this case, is that the rate of online responses varies among countries, and not all countries have reasonable rates in this kind of experience [3]. It is not possible to predict the acceptance of the population. Particular characteristics are essential, such as the proportion of access to the internet and how society behaves towards technologies. The online approach runs the risk of excluding specific groups (such as the elderly or poor people) and determining the predominance of particular audiences, such as younger people or those residing in urban areas [6].

3   The Importance of Usability and UX

Usability is a software quality requirement that aims to make the communication between the user and the systems transparent and intuitive. It defines guidelines that determine whether the handling of a product is easily and quickly learned, hardly forgotten, does not cause operational errors, offers a high degree of satisfaction, and efficiently solves tasks for which it was designed (Leal Ferreira and Nunes 2008) [7]. In addition to usability, there are complementary criteria that we can add to the user experience proposal, such as emotion, credibility, aesthetics, performance, and security. The user experience (UX) approach can encourage users to use the product (or service) not only because they find it easy to achieve their goals but also because they transmit positive emotions (Agner 2018) [8].

The application of usability principles must be a priority when migrating from paper questionnaires to online medium: the process requires much more than simply converting the paper instrument into a web format, said Kaczmirek (2008) [4]. The development of the questionnaire must be centered on users' needs – in this case, citizens – since questions and answer options can be dependent on the interface design. We must carefully conceive the interface design, from visual presentation of questions and answers, to support and help functions (Tavares 2011) [9].

Kaczmirek (2008) [4] pointed out that census takers receive training to operate and interpret the questionnaire, but there is no training in the case of questionnaires completed by citizens. Therefore, usability studies are even more recommended for self-administered questionnaires.

It is essential to create a user interface with simple navigation. Clear text and usable help instructions – easy to use and independent of prior knowledge – can minimize data entry errors, emphasized Kaczmirek (2008) [4]. Reducing the probability of generating mistakes, inaccurate interpretations, and avoiding interaction problems increases the quality of a census and contributes to user satisfaction.

4   Research Method: Affinity Diagram

Using a testing questionnaire on the Internet, hundreds of skilled census takers spread throughout the country shared their suggestions to improve it. Three hundred and fifty-six reports included opinions, ideas, evaluations, or recommendations, emphasizing the critical aspects of online data collection. This study analyzed these suggestions, which were full of essential advice and diverse points of view. The systematic reading of contributions supported the construction of specific practical guidelines to evaluate the UX design.

4.1   Classifying the Suggestions: A Bottom-Up Analysis

An affinity diagram is a tool for managing voluminous and qualitative data to organize ideas and create groups according to similarity. Courage and Baxter (2005) [10] proposed that an affinity diagram could contribute to structuring a diversity of opinions. This study performed a bottom-up analysis to organize the suggestions. The objective was to explore unique ideas, look for relationships between them, and group them into categories with the same topic.

The suggestions were grouped into topics with similar concepts. Researchers should avoid determining categories in advance, as the ideas need to flow according to intuition and creativity. After analyzing all recommendations, this research placed them on stacks that contained common issues. Some suggestions had more than one idea, so they were duplicated to be represented in different stacks. Other suggestions raised doubts and went to a separated group for future classification. This process was repeated until all notes had a suitable group (Courage and Baxter 2005) [10]. In the end, fourteen categories emerged to classify all suggestions. Results stimulated us to search for complementary issues.

5   Proto Heuristics for On-Line Self-administered Questionnaires

Hermawati and Lawson (2016) [11] suggested that heuristics developed exclusively for specific domains may identify usability problems more precisely than generic heuristics. Ignacio (2022) [12] shared this hypothesis: he bet on creating heuristics contextualized to the business models of specific companies where they will be applied.

Beyond Nielsen's heuristics (2020) [13], Couper (1994) [14] offered specific heuristics to evaluate the interaction between the interviewer and the collection instrument, and Kaczmirek (2008) [4] proposed a specific framework to analyze the respondents' cognitive capacities and processes during the task of answering an electronic questionnaire. Despite proposals by renowned authors, this research noted a gap in heuristics for the specific context of online data collection through questionnaires answered directly by the respondent (in the Brazilian context).

According to Wilson (2020) [15], we can learn a lot from the interviewers about problems associated with face-to-face data collection. Therefore, based on census takers' observations, we developed an initial proposition of a set of specific heuristics for evaluating the usability of online self-administered census questionnaires. They are called 'proto heuristics' (the prefix *proto* expresses the notion of 'first' or 'previous') since the effectiveness of these heuristics has not yet been validated through experiments (Hermawati and Lawson 2016) [11]. The fourteen proto heuristics and the percentage of suggestions associated with them appear in Table 1:

Table 1. Proto heuristics for online questionnaires and the percentage of suggestions associated with them (Source: the authors).

Proto heuristics	Percentage
Help and documentation	**21,10%**
Make help available on all screens	
Explain the research concepts	
Offer extra help on items that traditionally cause doubt	
Enable personalized help	
Clarity of texts and information	**20,27%**
Make questions and answer choices self-explanatory	
Keep the questionnaire communicable	
Show useful supplementary data	
User interface (UI) design	**17,81%**
Provide efficiency to the UI design	
Employ adequate elements to highlight important information	
Validation rules and questionnaire flow	**15,89%**
Reduce the respondent's cognitive effort	**5,48%**
Simplify data input	
Perform automatic calculations and procedures	
Communication with the respondent	**4,93%**
Take care of the starting approach	
Explain the importance of research	
Establish a two-way dialogue between the research and the respondent	
Consistency and standardization of the questionnaire	**3,29%**
Visual standardization	
Organization and navigation	
Corrections and text revisions	**2,74%**
Remove instructions for the census taker	
Remove technical terms	
Respondent's mental model	**2,74%**
Household composition	
Use real-world language	

(continued)

Table 1. (*continued*)

Proto heuristics	Percentage
Respondent control and freedom	2,74%
Ensure survey accessibility	1,64%
Independence from technology	0,55%
Security and authentication	0,55%
Data privacy	0,27%
Total	100%

Next, we present the descriptions and subdivisions of the set of proto heuristics. This research pursued conceptual foundations in the literature to explain each one and provided quotes from the census takers' suggestions.

5.1 Help and Documentation

One of the main characteristics of the questionnaire on the Web is that it is self-administered by the citizen. There is no census taker to explain the concepts or interpret the question for the respondent. Therefore, it is up to the system to support the respondent directly. The topic Help was the most cited by census takers (21% of the suggestions), who examined efficient ways to assist the respondent. Help and documentation has four subdivisions:

Make Help Available on All Screens. The questionnaire should have a help area oriented to the context of each question or task that the respondent is completing. Help should be useful, simple, well-written, and straightforward. It must always be visible, highlighted, and easily accessible whenever necessary. The following are some quotes from the census takers:

> *"This question does not have a 'Help' button: there is no alternative to clarify doubts."*

> *"The 'Help' menu is not available throughout the whole questionnaire."*

Explain the Research Concepts. Most suggestions pointed out concerns about the concepts used in the questionnaire. Citizens must understand the principles to answer the questionnaire correctly. Descriptions must clearly and concisely explain the concepts to citizens uninitiated on the matter. Some quotes from census takers are:

> *"What is the difference between 'occupation' and 'activity'? People will have doubts here."*

> *"It's better to explain what a 'collective household' is."*

> *"Answering the number of rooms presupposes that the citizen knows some concepts behind the number."*

Offer Extra Help on Items that Traditionally Cause Doubt. There are sensitive questions that may need detailed instructions, either because they contain complex texts, take longer to answer, or because they deal with topics that typically generate controversy. It is essential to add extra help to avoid interruptions, abandonment, or incorrect responses in these cases. Some quotes from census takers are:

> *"Brazil has a remarkable diversity of religions. This characteristic can generate confusion."*

> *"All questions about fertility should have a help icon next to it."*

> *"The 'Occupation and activity' questions frequently challenge the respondent's comprehension."*

Enable Personalized Help. Even with traditional help, the citizen may not answer specific questions correctly and may need personalized help. In this case, automated answering tools such as chatbots and virtual assistants can be good options. The respondent can ask the question in natural language and better understand the matter. Some quotes from census takers are:

> *"A help box on the concepts of autism is essential."*

> *"Can a Ph.D. degree be considered as a paid work/internship?"*

> *"For a person who does the cleaning on their own, this question might be somewhat confusing."*

5.2 Clarity of Texts and Information

In the absence of a census taker for direct support, communication between the questionnaire and the respondent becomes crucial for online data collection. Communication should help the respondent to correctly fill in the answers and guide their navigation in the questionnaire. Vague, ambiguous texts that cause doubts or insecurity in the respondent must be avoided. Poorly written questions can negatively impact the experience (Agner 2018) [8]. The clarity of the texts, cited by about 20% of the suggestions, can be improved in three situations:

Make Questions and Answer Choices Self-explanatory. The texts must be clear and detailed, with no grammar mistakes. The technical language, codes, and acronyms must be converted into a natural language to make it closer to a personal interview (Wilson 2018) [16]. Understanding the question is essential not to cause discomfort to the respondent. In addition, a poorly understood answer can lead to inconsistencies in later questions. Some quotes from census takers are:

> *"Questions about the municipality can state the name of the city instead of 'this municipality' to avoid confusion."*

> *"What was the highest course you have attended previously? The word 'previously' is confusing."*

Keep the Questionnaire Communicable. The alert messages and the help area intend to provide security and guide the respondent. Mismatched information can generate uncertainty and augment the respondent's chances of dropping out of the questionnaire.

"The question asks the citizen to answer in months, but the help guides to answer in years."

"This question asks for the value, but it does not have an option to mark the value."

Show Useful Supplementary Data. Some additional data already stored by the system can be helpful and provide a significant differentiator for the task flow.

"In the area about the household, it would be interesting if the age of each resident appeared next to the name."

"The household resident's name appears without a surname. It's not good: there may be residents with the same name and different surnames..."

5.3   User Interface (UI) Design

The questionnaire's user interface design influences the respondent's engagement in the survey as taught by Bosnjak and Tuten (2001) [17] and Couper (2008) [18]. As 18% of the messages indicated, complex interfaces or poor graphic design can trigger problematic behaviors, such as interruptions, omission of data, or increased time completion. The user interface (UI) should drive the citizen to better understand the information and facilitate his task (Tavares, 2011) [9]. This recommendation includes two aspects:

Provide Efficiency to the UI Design. Each visual element of the user interface (UI) must emphasize questions and answer options. Questions with mutually exclusive answer choices may solicit drop-down menus. Instead, radio buttons involve less effort to complete, as they require only a single click, stated Bosnjak and Tuten (2001) [17]. UI designers must avoid excessive scrolling and grids with many items. Those items are complex and negatively impact response rate (especially on mobile), as argued by Couper (2008) [18]. Poorly designed screens and improper visual elements may confuse citizens, causing data entry errors.

"The 'Previous' and 'Next' buttons overlap the response options."

"In the registration screen, the 'Save and End List' and 'Save and Register New' buttons are extremely close to each other and may cause errors."

"The 'Agree' button is on the left side and the 'Disagree' button on the right. I think it should be the other way around."

Employ Adequate Elements to Highlight Important Information. Adding suitable design elements (highlights, bold or highlighted text boxes) improves the user experience. The purpose is to increase attention to some critical areas to better understand the information and efficiently complete the task. Each informative element, if properly designed, contributes to providing support in the questionnaire navigation (Agner 2018) [8].

"Even though I am an expert, I hardly noticed the 'Help' menu."

"The field for income information must gain prominence (a box, for example), or most people will not realize it exists."

"Some questions are related to 'Up to the reference date'; others are on the 'reference date'. The graphic interface should alert users about the distinction."

"Bad visualization of the minimum age to provide information. Insert visible information: the respondent must be at least ten years old."

5.4 Validation Rules and Questionnaire Flow

One of the advantages of electronic questionnaires is the automatic inspection of the responses. Consistency checks and validation rules can be performed for data verification, avoiding errors during typing. The questionnaire flow follows an algorithm that guarantees correct automatic skips (Couper 2008) [18]. Since the census taker is not there to inquire about incoherent answers, these procedures guarantee a reduction of the errors made by the respondent. Among the suggestions, 16% drew attention to the importance of validation rules for the questionnaire.

"You can answer 99 bathrooms without a warning message? There should be an automatic inspection."

"It is possible to have a 5-month-old mother!"

"You may have an 18-year-old resident who can have ten, twenty, or thirty children?"

"Does your father live in your household? There are no men in the household... So, I believe there should be a skip here."

5.5 Reduce the Respondent's Cognitive Effort

The characteristics of the respondent vary, from their capability to answer questions to their motivation. Therefore, the need to resort to memory, such as performing calculations, translating codes, or recalling previous answers, requires a high cognitive load from the respondent. This issue may discourage citizens from answering the questionnaire (Tavares 2011) [9]. For this topic, covered by 5% of the census takers' suggestions, the following points emerged:

Simplify Data Input. Using computer resources to minimize typing effort is critical to avoid the respondent abandoning the task.

"State, city, and country could open on the same screen to speed up..."

"The page about knowing how to read and write could show all residents at the same time to speed up...."

"Questions about work open a screen for each resident... It is tedious!"

Perform Automatic Calculations and Procedures. Date and value calculations, field autocompletion, and recurring task automation capabilities are good approaches to reduce the time required to complete the task and minimize the respondent's memory overhead.

"If the resident does not know the day of birth but knows the month and year, the system should estimate his or her age."

"The answers should be automatically saved."

"The questionnaire can cause fatigue, depending on the number of residents. Consequently, the citizen may evaluate it as a bad user experience."

5.6 Communication With the Respondent

Census takers represent the institution during face-to-face interviews. However, questionnaires become the only communication channel between the research institute and the respondent during online surveys. This criterion, commented on by 5% of the suggestions, can be subdivided into the following items:

Take Care of the Starting Approach. Census takers master respondents' approach creating a bond of trust and putting them at comfort so that the interview flows easily. They are friendly and elegant, as it is mainly at the beginning of the interview that refusals occur. As there is no census taker online, the system should play its role, offering a "welcome" to the respondent. The interface must be engaging and easy to understand, increasing reciprocity and motivation (Agner 2018) [8].

"If the citizen forgets his/her password, a severe warning appears... This message can lead citizens to give up."

"It is intimidating to ask for the Individual Taxpayer Identification Number in the opening questions."

Explain the Importance of Research. The respondents are curious about the research goals (Tavares 2011) [9]. A simplified explanation about how the government uses the data and how each question will contribute to society would be constructive. Knowing the relevance of the census, the respondent may feel stimulated to fill out the questionnaire, increasing its response rate.

"The question includes no explanation about the significance of examining color or ethnicity in the census."

"It would be helpful if there was a short exposition of the goals of each question."

Establish a Two-Way Dialogue Between the Research and the Respondent. The survey builds credibility and confidence and engages the respondent when demonstrating professionalism. The official communication channels of the research institute must be highlighted so that the respondent can maintain direct contact in case of doubts, as suggested by Couper (2008) [18].

"The bottom bar shows the call center number but no opening hours."

"The message 'a census taker can visit you to confirm the information' should appear in large letters."

5.7 Consistency and Standardization of the Questionnaire

As the citizens do not have previous training to respond to the census, it is vital to maintain a design standard throughout the filling process. By creating consistency, the respondent learns more quickly and feels confident to use his knowledge in the following questions.

Visual Standardization. Standardization helps the respondent's mental effort to understand the questions and the accuracy of the answers. In addition to the respondent's cognitive effort to complete the task alone, the visual complexity can be prejudicial. A clear and organized layout of the information, colors, fonts, and other visual or textual elements must maintain a standard from the beginning to the end of the questionnaire. Standardization may extend to other surveys within the same institution (Tavares 2011) [9].

> *"Keep all income questions consistent."*
>
> *"This question seems less formal than the other questions."*
>
> *"These two options should be standardized for the next six questions."*

Organization and Navigation. The organization of questions and answers and the number of pages of the questionnaire may vary as it must consider the characteristics of the survey (complexity and size). The entire survey can be presented on a single page (scrolling survey design) or one question per page (paging survey design), remarked Couper (2008) [18]. It is also possible to organize according to the residents. The questionnaire may be presented in its entirety for each resident or by questions. In this case, each question requests all residents to respond. Regardless of how they are organized, it is essential to choose a pattern and respect the navigation structure (Tavares 2011) [9].

> *"In some parts, the questionnaire asks questions to all the residents at once. In other parts, it follows a flow for a specific resident. I did not find consistency."*
>
> *"Concerning 'occupation and activity, it would be better to show a list of options, as in other surveys...."*

5.8 Corrections and Text Revisions

When migrating from questionnaires administered by census takers to self-completion modes, it is essential to review texts, answer options, buttons, error messages, and help. In this matter, one can list the following developments:

Remove Instructions for the Census Taker. All instructions to the census taker should be deleted and rewritten, focusing on the respondent. Avoid forgetting instructions that are only useful in a face-to-face interview.

> *"Help is aimed at the census taker, not the citizen. It does not clarify the topic."*
>
> *"Help text is very similar to the census manual, although it has a different target audience."*
>
> *"Here is an explanation that seems to make sense only to the interviewer in a face-to-face interview...."*

Remove Technical Terms. The target audience of the online questionnaire is diverse, and there is no training to answer the questionnaire. Census takers are trained in the terms used by the research institute, but the general public may not be familiar with the jargon.

"In the help menu, the explanation is extremely technical."

"The definitions of 'domicile' and 'resident' were taken from the census taker's manual. The explanations must adapt to the respondent."

5.9 Respondent's Mental Model

We must understand how the respondent thinks and conceptualizes a topic to build the questions and questionnaire flow. The respondent bases himself on his reality to understand the questions. Therefore, he builds his answers according to the mental models[3] of his daily life.

Household Composition. The registration of basic demographic information about each family member is the foundation of the questionnaire. The questions will appear later following residents' data. Understanding how the respondent visualizes the family hierarchy is essential to design this interface. Residents must be registered and classified with their correct relationship with the householder. All functionalities and navigation must be based on this list.

"Understanding the idea of 'resident' will help start the questionnaire correctly."

"The resident chart should be better organized. There is no logical hierarchy in the residents' chart."

Use Real-World Language. Understanding the concepts already established in citizens' daily lives is necessary to maintain easy-to-understand communication and help them answer the questionnaire efficiently.

"Time format as we are used (HH:MM) would make things easier."

"Requesting the first name in one field and the last name in another field can be difficult. Usually, the forms request the first and last name in the same field."

5.10 Respondent Control and Freedom

A good experience in using the questionnaire allows the respondent to feel that he or she has control of filling out the data. Suppose he or she forgot to include a resident in the household or needs to go back to correct the answer to a previous question. The questionnaire should provide signaled mechanisms to correct the mistakes without prejudice to the data.

---

[3] The notion of a mental model has already been defined by Nielsen as follows: "A mental model is based on belief, not facts: that is, it is a model of what users know (or think they know) about a system." (Nielsen, J.: Mental Models. (2010). https://www.nngroup.com/ articles/mental-models, accessed 13 Oct 2020). In an online census, one must consider the citizen's expectations about how information should be structured and how its flow should be.

"Field for comments, criticisms or suggestions is limited to a few characters."

"The system does not allow access after the end of the questionnaire. It should allow access to correct data."

"If the respondent does not have the taxpayer identification number, he or she should have the possibility to inform it later."

"Regarding religion, one cannot manually fill in the answer."

5.11 Ensure Survey Accessibility

Besides technological diversity, it is necessary to address human diversity. The audience of a census is extensive, and the proportion of the population utilizing the Internet is still variable, mainly characterized by young people with higher education living in urban areas [19]. The census should not favor a particular audience or exclude other groups – such as people with limitations, the visually impaired, the elderly, less educated individuals, low-income populations, and citizens living in rural areas. The online census should be an opportunity to increase the reach, so accessibility is essential to encourage everyone to participate [6].

"The font size and graphic presentation make it difficult to read the questions."

"It is important to highlight the sign language options icon."

"Insert an option to increase the font size of the questionnaire."

5.12 Independence from Technology

Designers must ensure that the questionnaire works on old computers or with slow connections and can offer the possibility of being read by assistive technologies. One should think of a minimalist design that does not rely on specific technologies. According to Wilson (2018) [16], designers must develop within the mobile-first concept to create the interface first for mobile devices and then perform adaptations for other platforms. By focusing on limited screen space, the designer optimizes the layout and displays only what is necessary to convey the concepts of the survey.

"On the laptop, the user has to move the scroll bars many times... It is not pleasant..."

"In rural areas, the captcha is quite slow and may discourage filling out the questionnaire."

5.13 Security and Authentication

Online data collection brings information security a significant challenge. Besides maintaining the availability of the questionnaire during the census period and protecting the confidentiality of the data, a secure technological infrastructure must prevent malicious damage. The login must have two attributes: (a) be simple to prevent the respondent from giving up before starting, and (b) be reliable, providing security controls to ensure individual access so that respondents trust their personal information is protected.

"The access is blocked after entering an incorrect password three times. The system should allow more attempts..."

"It is worth noting that the login and password can lead the user to failure. The sequences of numbers, letters, and symbols are often confusing. Some citizens confuse the letter O with the digit zero."

5.14 Data Privacy

Online surveys bring the opportunity to link respondents' answers to paradata (Couper 2008) [18], (Tavares, Agner and Leal Ferreira 2021) [20]. Paradata are additional data tracked during the completion of the questionnaire, such as geographic location, time, IP address, among others. Data privacy regulations say that the respondent must be warned about such tracking and express his or her agreement. The survey should be transparent about the collection, use, and data storage, and keep with good practices in statistical production [21], statistical confidentiality [22], and personal data protection as described in legislation [23].

"To ease access to the respondent and obtain authorization regarding the use of personal data, I suggest inserting a link to LGPD [Brazilian personal data protection law] information."

6 Conclusion and Notes for Discussion

The Internet brought opportunities for research institutes to offer online questionnaires to be filled out by citizens. Online censuses request an easy-to-use, accessible, and elegant design that matches user experience (UX) requirements. The respondents will largely depend on the interface design, as they will not have the census taker to support and interpret the questions and the answer options.

This study aimed to deeply comprehend the recurring problems in online data collection. Its goal was to learn from census takers, who collect data by approaching respondents in their households. This work sought to understand the critical points and minimize their impact on the online survey. By offering an excellent user experience to the respondent, he or she can be motivated to conclude the questionnaire. Therefore, the response rates – indicators of statistical quality – can grow.

This research analyzed 365 suggestions from census takers containing observations, evaluations, and recommendations about the online questionnaire – plenty of suggestions to improve the user experience.

Aspects such as help, clarity, revision, and screen design, were broadly commented on by census takers to ensure independence, efficacy, ease of use, accessibility, security, and guidance. Good communicability plays a vital role in inviting the citizen to answer the questions – a role analogous to a census taker approaching a household for the first time.

The importance of preventing errors highlighted the necessary input data checks, skips among questions, and overall flow, which are methods that may guarantee integrity and data quality.

Some recommendations proposed standardization to reduce citizens' cognitive effort. Other suggestions brought the need to apprehend the mental model of the respondents, their constraints, abilities, and expectations for the understanding of the questionnaire (questions, answers, messages, and instructions).

The suggestions also emphasized the diversity of respondents and technologies. Before the Web, the questionnaires were restricted to census takers holding equipment supplied by the research institutes. After the Web, they reached a broader audience and included various devices, browsers, and network connections. Web accessibility standards request suitable data collection instruments that seek to avoid excluding specific groups due to intellectual, physical, or technological limitations.

The percentages presented in Table 1 show the census takers' points of view. They are not necessarily the issues that may occur during the actual access of citizens. Despite the significant differences observed in the percentages, all the problems deserve attention to improve usability and user experience (UX).

This work is part of doctoral research; it proposes identifying possible UX inconsistencies and contributing to a suitable online data collection from the point of view of human-computer interaction. Further development can involve detailing case studies and undertaking remote usability testing with prototypes to validate the effectiveness of the proto heuristics built in this study.

Note
The content of this article is the sole responsibility of the authors, and does not reflect the opinion of the Brazilian Institute of Geography and Statistics (IBGE).

References

1. IBGE, Instituto Brasileiro de Geografia e Estatística: Números mostram o valor do Censo para o avanço de políticas públicas no país. Agência IBGE. Revista Retratos, 17 Jan 2019. https://censos.ibge.gov.br/2012-agencia-de-noticias/noticias/23594-numeros-mos tram-o-valor-do-censo-para-o-avanco-de-politicas-publicas-no-pais.html. Accessed 05 Nov 2020
2. UNSD, United Nations Statistics Division: Statistics - COVID-19 response. Department of Economic and Social Affairs (2021), https://covid-19-response.unstatshub.org. Accessed 26 July 2021
3. INE. Instituto Nacional de Estatística: Estudo de viabilidade para os Censos 2021. Avaliação dos modelos censitários utilizados noutros países e a sua adequabilidade a Portugal. 30 de junho de 2014. Lisboa, Portugal (2014), https://Censos.ine.pt/xurl/doc/265781490. Accessed 31 Mar 2020
4. Kaczmirek, L.: Human-Survey Interaction Usability and Nonresponse in Online Surveys (2008), https://madoc.bib.uni-mannheim.de/2150/1/kaczmirek2008.pdf. Accessed 03 June 2021
5. IBGE, Instituto Brasileiro de Geografia e Estatística: Bem-vindo ao Censo 2022 (2022), https://questionario2022.ibge.gov.br. Accessed 21 Jan 2022
6. UNECE, United Nations Economic Commission for Europe: Conference of European Statisticians Recommendations for the 2020 Censuses of Population and Housing – prepared in cooperation with the Statistical Office of the European Communities (EUROSTAT). United Nations Publications, Geneva, Swiss (2015), https://www.unece.org/fileadmin/DAM/stats/publications/2015/ECECES41_EN.pdf. Accessed 28 Apr 2020

7. Leal Ferreira, S.B., Nunes, R.: e-Usabilidade. LTC, Rio de Janeiro (2008)
8. Agner, L.: Ergodesign e Arquitetura de Informação: Trabalhando com o Usuário. Rio de Janeiro: Editora Senac Rio, 2018. 240 p. 4ª edição (2018)
9. Tavares, P.Z.: Estudo de usabilidade para PDAs utilizados em coleta de dados nas entrevistas pessoais para pesquisas domiciliares. Dissertação (Mestrado em Informática). Universidade Federal do Estado do Rio de Janeiro, Rio de Janeiro (2011), http:// www.repositorio-bc.uni rio.br:8080/xmlui/handle/unirio/12742. Accessed 25 May 2021
10. Courage, C., Baxter, K.: Understanding your Users: A Practical Guide to User Requirements Methods, Tools, and Techniques. ISBN: 1–55860–935–0. Morgan Kaufmann Publishers (2005)
11. Hermawati, S., Lawson, G.: Establishing usability heuristics for heuristics evaluation in a specific domain: is there a consensus? Appl. Ergon. **56**, 34–51 (2016), ISSN 0003–6870, https://doi.org/10.1016/j.apergo.2015.11.016. Accessed 21 Oct 2021
12. Ignacio, Elizete. Ainda vale a pena fazer análise heurística? (2022), https://www.design2022. com.br/artigos/ainda-vale-a-pena-fazer-analise-heuristica. Accessed 12 Jan 2022
13. Nielsen, J.: 10 Usability Heuristics for User Interface Design (2020), https://www.nngroup. com/articles/ten-usability-heuristics. Accessed 21 Oct 2021
14. Couper, M.: Discussion: What Can CAI Learn from HCI?. In: Proceedings of the Seminar on New Directions in Statistical Methodology, pp. 363–377 Washington: Statistical Policy Office, Office of Management and Budget (1994), https://nces.ed.gov/FCSM/policy.asp. Accessed 15 May 2020
15. Wilson, L.: User-centred design approach to surveys. Government Statistical Service. Office for National Statistics (ONS), 4 November 2020, https://gss.civilservice.gov.uk/policy-store/ a-user-centred-design-approach-to-surveys. Accessed 02 Feb 2022
16. Wilson, L.: Using respondent centric design to transform Social Surveys at ONS. Office for National Statistics (ONS). Survey Methodology Bulletin No.78, January 2018, https://www.ons.gov.uk/methodology/methodologicalpublications/generalmetho dology/surveymethodologybulletin. Accessed 15 Oct 2021
17. Bosnjak, M., Tuten, T.L.: Classifying response behaviors in web-based surveys. J. Comput. Mediated Commun. **6**(3), JCMC636 (2001). https://doi.org/10.1111/j.1083-6101.2001.tb0 0124.x, Accessed 14 Feb 2021
18. Couper, M.: Designing Effective Web Surveys. Cambridge University Press, p. 416 (2008)
19. PASC, Public Administration Select Committee: Options for the future of the census. UK Parliament, 25 February 2014. United Kingdom, https://publications.parliament.uk/pa/cm2 01314/cmselect/cmpubadm/1090/109005.htm#a2. Accessed 02 Apr 2020
20. Tavares, P.Z., Agner, L., Leal Ferreira, S.B.: Censo Demográfico e Paradados: Em Busca da Melhor Experiência para o Usuário. Revista Estudos em Design (online), Rio de Janeiro, RJ, Brasil, vol. 29, no. 3, pp. 87–101 (2021), ISSN Eletrônico: 1983–196X, https:/estudos emdesign.emnuvens.com.br/design/article/view/1275. Accessed 22 Dec 2021
21. IBGE, Instituto Brasileiro de Geografia e Estatística: Código de boas práticas das estatísticas do IBGE. 2a edição. Rio de Janeiro (2021), https://biblioteca.ibge.gov.br/visualizacao/livros/ liv101744.pdf. Accessed 21 Dec 2021
22. Brasil: Obrigatoriedade de prestação de informações estatísticas. Lei N° 5.534, de 14 de novembro de 1968 (1968), http://www.planalto.gov.br/ccivil_03/leis/l5534.htm. Accessed 13 May 2021
23. Brasil: Lei Geral de Proteção de Dados Pessoais (LGPD). Lei N° 13.709, de 14 de agosto de 2018 (2018), http://www.planalto.gov.br/ccivil_03/_ato2015-2018/2018/lei/L13709.htm. Accessed 13 May 2021

Usability in Automated Teller Machines Interfaces: A Systematic Literature Review

Rosangela Valenzuela$^{(\boxtimes)}$ ⓘ, Arturo Moquillaza ⓘ, and Freddy Paz ⓘ

Pontificia Universidad Católica del Perú, Lima 32, San Miguel, Peru
rosangela.valenzuelah@pucp.edu.pe, {amoquillaza,fpaz}@pucp.pe

Abstract. Due to technological progress, financial institutions have included ATMs as one of their main channels as a way to decentralize their services. However, there is a gap between user expectations and their perceptions regarding what ATM interfaces offer. As a result, several users feel dissatisfied after using ATMs and many times this dissatisfaction is related to the difficulty of use, design flaws and the fact of committing many errors when interfaces have a low degree of usability. In this sense, in this study we present a Systematic Literature Review (SLR) about usability on ATM interfaces. With this study, we want to understand the current situation of the problems mentioned before, so we seek to know the problems and challenges that have been presented lately for these electronic media, as well as the solutions that have addressed these problems, and the techniques and methods used to carry out these designs or redesigns. For this, the protocol proposed by Kitchenham was followed. Scopus, ACM Digital Library, Alicia and IEEE Digital Library were searched, and finally 51 papers were selected as relevant. With this information it was possible to identify and analyze challenges, usability issues, usability evaluations, and techniques and methods used to carry out designs or redesigns, as well as case studies of designs or redesigns in the ATM domain. We found that this topic is being developed in recent years, that there are common challenges encountered, and that designs, redesigns and usability evaluations have been carried out in this domain under different methods, techniques and frameworks. However, several of these usability issues persist today.

Keywords: Human-computer interaction · Automatic teller machine · Usability · Systematic literature review · Banking system

1 Introduction

ATMs are electronic media that allows users to carry out transactions without the need to interact with a representative of a bank [1]. Currently, ATMs have become an important channel for both financial institutions and their customers due to the benefits that these offers; such as the fact that banks can provide their services 24 h a day through ATMs and those customers do not need to go to banks to take advantage of these services [2]. Therefore, it can be said that practically no bank operates without ATMs [3] as well as that anyone has a credit or debit card [1] and some even use cardless technology, which consists of carrying out transactions without the use of a physical card [4].

© The Author(s), under exclusive license to Springer Nature Switzerland AG 2022
M. M. Soares et al. (Eds.): HCII 2022, LNCS 13321, pp. 275–294, 2022.
https://doi.org/10.1007/978-3-031-05897-4_20

However, according to Aguirre, the lack of consideration for users in the design of ATM interfaces has caused usability issues [5]. Also, in a study carried out in Peru [2], it is mentioned that a gap exists between user expectations and their perceptions regarding what ATM interfaces offer. As a result, several users feel dissatisfied after using ATMs and ask questions such as why ATMs do not remember the accounts they use [6]. It is also mentioned in another study [7] that user dissatisfaction with ATMs is due to their difficulty in use, their design and the many mistakes they made.

In this paper, a Systematic Literature Review (SLR) was carried out to identify case studies, methodologies, problems, challenges and good practices related to the design and redesign of interfaces in ATMs, in order to know how the relationship between usability and ATMs has developed.

This paper has the following structure: Sect. 2 presents the most relevant concepts and how they are used in this research. Section 3 details the planning and execution of the SLR, and Sect. 4 details the results obtained. Finally, Sect. 5 presents the main conclusions and future work.

2 Theoretical Background

In this section, we present the most important concepts related to this research.

2.1 ATM

ATMs (Automatic Teller Machines), are computerized electronic telecommunication devices that are established as a method of direct communication between clients of financial institutions and their respective bank accounts [8]. It is also mentioned that ATMs are self-service banking terminals that have, among their functionalities, making deposits and withdrawals, as well as other banking transactions such as balance inquiries.

Usually, its operation begins with the entry of a bank card and the Personal Identification Number (PIN), and then follow the flow of the process of some functionality.

In 1967, the first ATM was opened in London and since then no bank has operated without these devices [5], thus they form an important part of the smart transformation of bank branches [1].

2.2 Interface

This term refers to user interfaces. According to ISO 9241–210, user interfaces are all the components of an interactive system that provide information and control to the user in such a way that they can achieve specific tasks with the interactive system described above [9]. For example, in an interface, users can select and move objects on the screen, in each of these cases, users must initialize the interaction with an action and the interface must communicate with a change in its state by showing a response to the user [10].

2.3 Usability

According to ISO 9241–210 [9], usability is the extent to which a system, product or service can be used by specific users in such a way that they achieve the objectives of effectiveness, efficiency and satisfaction in a specific context of use. Nielsen [11] proposes that usability has multiple components and that in a traditional way an association is made with the following 5 components:

- Learning ability, which means that the system must be easy to learn so that users can quickly start working with it.
- Efficiency, which refers to the fact that a high level of productivity will be reached when the system has been learned to use.
- Memory capacity, which means that the system must be easy to remember, so users will not have to struggle to relearn the system when they want to use it after a while.
- Errors, this component refers to the fact that there should be a low rate of errors per users and that, if an error occurs, users will be able to recover from them.
- Satisfaction, this component means that the system must be pleasant to use in such a way that users feel satisfied.

2.4 User Centered Design

According to ISO 9241–210 [9], User Centered Design (UCD) is an approach for the design and development of systems whose objective is to make such systems more usable in terms of their use through the utilization of knowledge, techniques of human factors and usability. A similar concept is found in another study [12] where it is mentioned that UCD incorporates the point of view of users in the software development process with the aim of obtaining a system with a high degree of usability.

3 Planning and Executing a SLR

In this section, we describe the research process that allowed obtaining relevant studies that address usability in the ATM domain. This exploration of the literature aimed to identify case studies, methodologies, problems, challenges, and good practices related to the design of ATM interfaces. This (SLR) was carried out using the protocol proposed by Kitchenham [13].

3.1 Objectives of the SLR

The main objectives of this SLR are detailed as follows:

- Determine the challenges that have emerged in the user interaction with ATM interfaces and their relationship with the user needs.
- Identify usability issues that have been reported in relation to ATM interfaces and how these issues have affected the User Experience.
- Collect frameworks, methodologies, and good practices in case studies in which a design or redesign of ATM interfaces has been carried out and how these projects have been performed.

3.2 Research Questions

To achieve the review objectives, the following research questions were formulated:

- **RQ1:** What challenges have been identified in the use of ATMs, and how do they relate to the users' needs?
- **RQ2:** What usability issues have been perceived in ATM interfaces, and how do they affect the user experience?

  - **RQ2.1:** What usability evaluations have been reported in the development of ATM interfaces, and how do the results affect the degree of usability perceived by users?
  - **RQ2.2:** What techniques have been reported in the literature for the design and redesign of ATM interfaces according to the UCD phases, and in what way have they been used?

- **RQ3:** What case studies on the design and redesign of ATM interfaces have been reported in the literature, and how were they carried out?

For the SLR, the PICOC criteria [14] are used, which are the following: (1) Population, referring to the object of study, (2) Intervention, related to those aspects that will be studied from the population and how the research will be carried out, (3) Comparison, referring to comparisons between several interventions, (4) Outcomes, which is related to what is expected to be obtained from the systematic review, and (5) Context, which establishes under what scenario or circumstances the case studies to be identified were carried out. These criteria are presented in Table 1, and are recommended to guide the search for studies based on the concepts described in the research questions. In this research, the comparison criterion was not considered since the objective of this review does not seek to compare designs and redesigns of ATM interfaces but rather to study them to obtain information about the aspects described in Table 1.

Table 1. Definition of the general concepts using PICOC

Criterion	Description
Population	Automated Teller Machines
Intervention	Interface design and redesign
Comparison	(N.A.)
Outcomes	Case studies, methodologies, challenges, good practices
Context	Academic and industrial

3.3 Search Strategy

Following the Kitchenham protocol, to perform the search for primary studies, key concepts were defined from the criteria presented in Table 1. Then, synonyms or related words of the extracted concepts were defined. As a result, Table 2 was obtained, which was used to establish search strings. The process of obtaining these strings is detailed in Sect. 3.5.

Table 2. Terms associated with the PICOC criteria

Keyword	Synonyms	Criterion
Automated bank teller	Automated teller machine, automatic teller machine, cash-machine, cash machine	Population
Interface design	HCI, redesign, screen, sketch, UI design, usability, UX	Intervention
Best practices	Guideline, recommendation	Outcomes
Case study	Application, experience	Outcomes
Challenge	Difficulty, problem	Outcomes
Methodology	Approach, framework, method, procedure, process, technique	Outcomes

3.4 Search Engines

For the search of primary studies, recognized databases in the field of Software Engineering have been considered [15]. In addition, with the aim of having a search engine that includes thesis works, the Alicia database has been considered, which brings together research works from various public and private entities, including recognized universities in Peru. The search engines selected for the present systematic review are the following:

- Scopus (http://www.scopus.com)
- ACM Digital Library (http://portal.acm.org)
- Alicia (https://alicia.concytec.gob.pe/vufind/)
- IEEE Digital Library (http://ieeexplore.ieee.org)

3.5 Search Strings

According to the search strategy proposed for the systematic review, the search strings were formulated according to the terms defined in Table 2 in such a way that those that belong to the same criteria and are established as synonyms were joined with the operator "OR". In addition, the asterisk symbol was added at the end of those terms in which a search for derived words was required. As a result, the following strings were formed:

```
C2: ("interface design" OR "HCI" OR "redesign*" OR
"screen*" OR "sketch" OR "UI design" OR "usability" OR
"UX")
C3: ("best practices" OR "guideline*" OR "recommenda-
tion*")
C4: ("case study" OR "application*" OR "experience*")
C5: ("challenge*" OR "difficult*" OR "problem*")
C6: ("methodolog*" OR "approach" OR "framework*" OR
"method*" OR "procedure*" OR "process*" OR "technique*")
```

Based on the strings described above, those that belong to the same criterion were joined with the "OR" operator. On the contrary, those that belong to different criteria were joined with the "AND" operator. In this way, the string (C1 AND C2 AND (C3 OR C4 OR C5 OR C6)) was obtained. This string has been customized for each database since each one has its own search query syntax. The resulting chains are detailed in Table 3.

3.6 Inclusion and Exclusion Criteria

For the selection of scientific papers, inclusion criteria have been established, which allow identifying the primary studies that are relevant and that provide meaningful information to answer the research questions. The inclusion criteria are the following:

- **CI1:** The paper describes the application of the (UCD) framework for the design of ATM interfaces.
- **CI2:** The paper describes the user experience or usability of ATM interfaces.
- **CI3:** The paper describes case studies on the design or redesign of ATM interfaces.
- **CI4:** The paper is related to the functionalities of ATMs over time.
- **CI5:** The paper reports methodologies for the design of interfaces in ATMs.

With the aim of discarding studies that do not provide relevant information in relation to the research questions, exclusion criteria have been established. The CE1 criterion is defined for articles that have no relationship with ATMs. In the same way, the CE2 criterion is established for articles dealing with ATMs, but from an approach not relevant to the research questions such as information technology, communication networks, security, mobile banking, virtual reality, games, ATM tracking ATMs, advertisements, hardware, design algorithms, and software that control the internal workings of ATMs. Also, for studies that have been published before 2010, the CE3 exclusion criterion has been established because the purpose was to obtain a balance between case studies, methodologies, challenges, and good practices. Finally, for studies that use a language other than English or Spanish, the exclusion criterion CE4 is applied. In this sense, the exclusion criteria defined are the following:

- **CE1:** The paper is not related to the topic of ATMs.
- **CE2:** The paper is about ATMs, but it departs from the focus of the study.

Table 3. Search string used in the selected databases

Search Engine	Resulting Search String
SCOPUS	TITLE-ABS-KEY(("automated bank teller" OR "automated teller machine" OR "automatic teller machine" OR "cash-machine" OR "cash machine") AND ("interface design" OR "HCI" OR "redesign*" OR "screen*" OR "sketch" OR "UI design" OR "usability" OR "UX") AND ("best practices" OR "guideline*" OR "recommendation*" OR "case study" OR "application*" OR "experience*" OR "challenge*" OR "difficult*" OR "problem*" OR "methodolog*" OR "approach" OR "framework*" OR "method*" OR "procedure*" OR "process*" OR "technique*"))
ACM Digital Library	("automated bank teller" OR "automated teller machine" OR "automatic teller machine" OR "cash-machine" OR "cash machine") AND ("interface design" OR "HCI" OR "redesign*" OR "screen*" OR "sketch" OR "UI design" OR "usability" OR "UX") AND ("best practices" OR "guideline*" OR "recommendation*" OR "case study" OR "application*" OR "experience*" OR "challenge*" OR "difficult*" OR "problem*" OR "methodolog*" OR "approach" OR "framework*" OR "method*" OR "procedure*" OR "process*" OR "technique*")
Alicia	(cajero automático OR automated teller machine OR cash machine OR automatic teller machine OR automated bank teller OR cash-machine) AND (diseño de interfaces OR interface design OR rediseño OR redesign OR HCI OR human center design OR pantalla OR screen OR usabilidad OR usability OR experiencia de usuario OR UX OR sketch OR bosquejo) AND (best practices OR buenas prácticas OR caso de estudio OR case study OR marco de trabajo OR framework OR metodología OR methodology OR problem OR problema OR process OR proceso OR procedure OR procedimiento OR method OR método OR technique OR técnica OR challenge OR desafío OR application OR aplicación OR guideline OR guía OR recommendation OR recomendación)
IEEE Digital Library	("automated bank teller" OR "automated teller machine" OR "automatic teller machine" OR "cash-machine" OR "cash machine" OR "ATM") AND ("interface design" OR "HCI" OR "redesign*" OR "screen*" OR "sketch" OR "UI design" OR "usability" OR "UX") AND ("best practices" OR "guideline*" OR "recommendation*" OR "case study" OR "application*" OR "experience*" OR "challenge*" OR "difficult*" OR "problem*" OR "methodolog*" OR "approach" OR "framework*" OR "method*" OR "procedure*" OR "process*" OR "technique*")

- **CE3:** The paper has been published before 2010.
- **CE4:** The paper is written in a language other than English or Spanish.

3.7 Documents Found

The search was carried out on March 15, 2021. After entering the previously established search strings in their corresponding search engines, a total of 488 results were obtained, which are distributed in Table 4. From this total, 51 papers were accepted in accordance with the inclusion criteria stated before. The details of the search results are shown in Table 4 and Table 5.

Table 4. Search results by search engines

Search engines	Results	Duplicates	Relevant
Scopus	144	0	39
ACM digital library	231	25	5
Alicia	10	4	1
IEEE digital library	103	16	6
Total	**488**	**45**	**51**

Table 5. Selected papers

Paper	Title
1 [6]	Analysis and Optimization of Cash Withdrawal Process Through ATM in India from HCI and Customization. Smart Innovation, Systems and Technologies
2 [4]	Applying a UCD Framework for ATM Interfaces on the Design of QR Withdrawal: A Case Study
3 [1]	Applying a UCD approach to redesign functionality on ATM: A case study in the context of university and business collaboration
4 [2]	Security guidelines for the design of atm interfaces
5 [3]	A Systematic Literature Review About Quantitative Metrics to Evaluate Usability and Security of ATM Interfaces
6 [16]	A Systematic Review of Usability Evaluation Methods and Tools for ATM Interfaces
7 [1]	Usability Testing of Bank of China Automatic Teller Machine
8 [17]	A contextual usability exploration of cash and ticket machines
9 [3]	A User-Centered Framework for the Design of Usable ATM Interfaces
10 [5]	Methodologies for the Design of ATM Interfaces: A Systematic Review. Advances in Intelligent Systems and Computing

(*continued*)

Table 5. (*continued*)

Paper	Title
11 [18]	Redesigning a Main Menu ATM Interface Using a User-Centered Design Approach Aligned to Design Thinking: A Case Study
12 [19]	Development and Validation of Usability Heuristics for Evaluation of Interfaces in ATMs
13 [20]	The Effect of ATM Service Quality on Customer Satisfaction and Customer Loyalty: An Empirical Analysis. Global Business Review
14 [21]	Developing QR Authentication and Fingerprint Record in an ATM Interface Using User-Centered Design Techniques
15 [22]	The design guideline for dyslexics-friendly Chinese ATM interface
16 [23]	PocketATM: Understanding and improving ATM accessibility in India
17 [24]	The interplay between usability, sustainability and green aspects: A design case study from a developing country
18 [25]	A Graphical PIN Entry System with Shoulder Surfing Resistance
19 [26]	Interactive Systems in the Student-Bank Relationship: A Research on the Views of the University of Bucharest Students on the Utility and Adaptability of HCI Technologies
20 [27]	Design of graphical user interfaces to implement new features in an ATM system of a financial bank
21 [28]	Availability Test of Automated Teller Machine Based on Eye-Tracking Data
22 [29]	Adaptive & dynamic interfaces for automated teller machines using clusters
23 [30]	Designing talking ATM system for people with visual impairments
24 [31]	Token access: Improving accessibility of automatic teller machines (ATMs) by transferring the interface and interaction to personal accessible devices
25 [32]	Designing technologies for Africa: Does culture matter?
26 [33]	Revolving Flywheel PIN Entry Method to Prevent Shoulder Surfing Attacks
27 [34]	Developing an ATM interface using user-centered design techniques
28 [35]	Applying a user-centered design methodology to develop usable interfaces for an automated teller machine
29 [7]	Public system usability analysis for the valuation of cognitive burden and interface standardization: A case study of cross-ATM design
30 [36]	A Usability Study of an Assistive Touch Voice Interface Based Automated Teller Machine (ATM)
31 [37]	Generic menu optimization for multi-profile customer systems
32 [38]	SafetyPIN: Secure PIN entry through eye tracking
33 [39]	Enhanced security for ATM machine with OTP and facial recognition features
34 [40]	SEPIA: Secure-PIN-Authentication-as-a-Service for ATM Using Mobile and Wearable Devices
35 [41]	Developing convenience store ATMs as social infrastructure

(*continued*)

Table 5. (*continued*)

Paper	Title
36 [42]	Security Notions and Advanced Method for Human Shoulder-Surfing Resistant PIN-Entry
37 [8]	A survey on human computer interaction technology for ATM
38 [43]	Money on the Move Workload, Usability and Technology Acceptance of Second-Screen
39 [44]	Usability study of fingerprint and palmvein biometric technologies at the ATM
40 [8]	A survey on human-computer interaction technology for financial terminals
41 [45]	Don't Queue up! User Attitudes towards Mobile Interactions with Public Terminals
42 [46]	How accessible are the voice-guided automatic teller machines for the visually impaired?
43 [47]	Enhancing accessibility: Mobile to ATM case study
44 [48]	Personalized ATMs: Improve ATMs usability. Communications in Computer and Information Science
45 [49]	User-centered design approach for interactive kiosks: Evaluation and redesign of an automatic teller machine
46 [50]	Usability in ATMs
47 [51]	Usability Comparisons of Seven Main Functions for Automated Teller Machine (ATM) Banking Service of Five Banks in Thailand
48 [52]	A New Design of ATM Interface for Banking Services in Thailand
49 [53]	Towards Understanding ATM Security: A Field Study of Real World ATM Use
50 [54]	ColorPIN: Securing PIN Entry through Indirect Input
51 [55]	Elaboración y validación de un marco de trabajo para el diseño de interfaces para cajeros automáticos

4   Results of the Systematic Review

In this section, we present the answers to the research questions in Sect. 3.2. Additionally, in Fig. 1, we show the distribution of studies accepted by country. Interest in this topic can be observed in several countries.

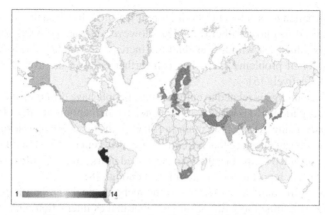

Fig. 1. Distribution of studies accepted by country.

4.1 Challenges in the Use of ATMs

Regarding the first question: "What challenges have been identified in the use of ATMs, and how do they relate to the users' needs?", The challenges that were found in the primary studies are listed in Table 6.

Table 6. Challenges in the use of ATMs

Category	Papers	Total
Security	2, 4, 18, 26, 32, 33, 34, 37, 38. 39, 40, 41, 49, 50, 51	15
Accessibility	6, 8, 15, 16, 23, 24, 29, 30, 38, 42, 43, 44, 47	13
Functionality	1, 2, 3, 5, 7, 10, 14, 22, 38, 39, 40, 41	12
Culture	6, 9, 14, 21, 25, 31, 35, 36, 37, 44, 47	11
Technology gap	25, 36	2

The first challenge found is related to security, since ATMs are subject to scams and fraud [39], which have increased drastically mainly due to the PIN usage [54]. This problem is frustrating for users, because for them the perception of security is important [2]. Additionally, it was mentioned on an interview with 8 people that safety is the main concern when using an ATM [8].

The second challenge is about accessibility, since many of the ATMs have not considered users with disabilities in the design of their interfaces. For example, in India [23], only 18% of 107 ATMs tested in a study are accessible, which is not very encouraging for a country where 12 million blind people live out of the 36 million that exist in the world. In China [22], people with dyslexia have difficulties interpreting the instructions presented on the ATM screens. In the case of older adults [17], their capacities related to motor activity, sight and memory are not the same as that of young people; therefore, they need more time to use ATMs.

The third challenge is related to both current and new functionalities. ATMs were initially only used to make withdrawals [3]. However, nowadays ATMs can perform more operations than just withdrawals and the increase in functionalities can turn out to be a generator of problems since they can further confuse the user if they are not implemented effectively [5].

The fourth challenge is related to culture, since people have different attitudes, experiences and occupations [51], which can influence the perception of difficulty of ATMs and performance using ATMs. The main problem with this challenge lies in the complexity of providing an interface that accommodates different user profiles. This problem can be seen represented by the fact that inexperienced users have difficulties using ATMs while frequent users report that they are not fast enough [8].

Finally, the fifth challenge is related to the technological gap on the part of users due to the lack of interaction with technology that makes interaction with ATMs more difficult, as in Africa where there is technological illiteracy [32]. In addition, there is also the resistance of some users to changes in the interface, especially those who are not used to technology [42].

4.2 Usability Issues

In order to answer the question "What usability issues have been perceived in ATM interfaces, and how do they affect the user experience?" we present Table 7, where we show the usability issues that have been found.

Table 7. Usability issues

Issue	Papers	Total
Menu structure or hierarchy is not understood	3, 10, 11, 17, 20, 22, 25, 31, 37, 40, 44, 45, 48, 51	14
Uninformative or confusing instructions	2, 7, 11, 12, 14, 15, 19, 21, 51	9
Unintuitive interfaces	3, 7, 16, 20, 21, 40, 46	7
Too many elements (buttons, texts)	3, 7, 10, 11, 12, 15, 21, 25	8
Important information not displayed or not found	17, 21, 25, 30, 40, 51	6
Complexity of operations	3, 11, 21, 44, 46	5
Confusing buttons	1, 3, 16, 51	4
Sensitive information is displayed	3, 4, 49, 50	4
It does not prevent the user from errors	3, 29, 40, 45	4
Confusing icons	3, 15, 25	3
There is no reminder to withdraw the card after performing an operation	7, 16, 37	3
The font size is not correct	12, 14, 15	3

(continued)

Table 7. (*continued*)

Issue	Papers	Total
Colors or backgrounds are not pleasant	15, 17, 46	3
The user cannot recover from errors or if he can, it is not done quickly	40, 45	2
It is necessary to standardize elements (buttons, texts, etc.)	12, 15	2
The design feels old	7	1
Fear is perceived when interacting with the interface	21	1

One of the main issues found is related to the main menu structure. It has been mentioned in studies that the design of the menu structure is very difficult to access [1], confusing [18], overloaded with options [5], not user-friendly [32], causes queues to be generated [37], among others.

Another problem is related to uninformative or confusing instructions. For example, in a case study where a QR code was used [4], users commented that instructions on how to scan the QR code should be included. Also, in another case study [1], two users were concerned about pressing the wrong buttons because the text on the buttons was not clear.

Usability Evaluations. To answer the question "What usability evaluations have been reported for the development of ATM interfaces, and how do the results impact the degree of usability perceived by users?" usability evaluations are listed in Table 8. These evaluations are mostly part of the analysis of an existing interface to identify usability issues or obtain the validation of a prototype to which improvements have been incorporated. Within these evaluations, heuristic evaluations and user tests have been identified.

Table 8. Usability evaluations

Type of intervention	Studies	Total
Interface redesigned	2, 3, 11, 12, 14, 20, 22, 27, 30, 35, 38, 40, 43, 48, 50, 51	16
Interface no modified	3, 7, 12, 15, 17, 21, 40, 42, 45, 47	10

An example of an evaluation on existing ATM interfaces happened in Nigeria [24], where ATMs were randomly visited and 500 participants were taken for a usability evaluation. As a result, it was obtained that most of the participants were not satisfied with the designs of the interfaces that the ATMs had and some required assistance to be able to complete the transactions they wanted to carry out.

Another case was that of a heuristic evaluation [1] was carried out at Banco Continental (BBVA) of Peru, as part of the evaluation phase of UCD. The prototypes evaluated were a proposal of the credit card payment functionality, consequently, 3 usability problems were obtained regarding metaphors, visibility of sensitive information and error prevention.

Techniques for Design and Redesign of ATM Interfaces. According to the question "What techniques have been reported in the literature for the design and redesign of ATM interfaces according to the User-Centered Design phases, and in what way have they been used?" The techniques used for the design and redesign of ATM interfaces are listed in Table 9, in which the User Centered Design (UCD) was used as a division, because several studies carry out this classification [1, 3, 4]. It should be noted that UCD is divided into four steps: Context, Requirements, Design and Evaluation.

Table 9. Techniques for design and redesign ATM interfaces

Phases	Techniques	Studies	Total
Context	Identify Stakeholders, Interviews, Preliminary User Questionnaire, Study Field, User Groups, Face-to-face Meeting	2, 7, 9, 11, 48, 51	6
Requirement	Competitor Analysis, Focus Group, Interviews, User profile, Scenario of Use, Polls, Persona, User Requirements Interview, UX Story, Card Sorting, Tag cloud, Empathy Map	2, 3, 7, 9, 11, 14, 20, 51	8
Design	Brainstorming, Prototyping, Storyboarding, Parallel Design, Video Prototyping, Visual Thinking	2, 3, 6, 9, 11, 14, 27, 28, 50, 51	10
Evaluation	Expert Evaluation, User Evaluation, Heuristic Evaluation, Satisfaction Questionnaire, Controlled User Testing, Interviews, Polls, Free Exploration, Face-to-face Meeting, Tasks, Cognitive Inspection, Thinking Aloud	1, 2, 3, 6, 7, 9, 11, 12, 14, 15, 17, 20, 21, 27, 35, 37, 38, 40, 42, 45, 46, 47, 48, 50, 51	25

In the context phase, in a study [4] the following techniques were used: User Groups, to hold meetings between the team; Identify Stakeholders, to list the people involved as developers or business Users; and Study Field, to observe users interact with ATM interfaces, especially using the withdrawal functionality.

In the requirements phase, in a case study [21] an interview of 10 questions was conducted with users so that relevant information can be obtained such as name, age, gender, their experience using ATMs and reasons for using them. From this, through the Person technique, two profiles were obtained: users with experience in technology and users without experience with which it is possible to work on a prototype.

In the design phase, the prototyping technique [4] was used to design interfaces that improve the process of cardless withdrawals. In another study [18], the Card Sorting and Brainstorming techniques were used with the purpose of identifying a simpler taxonomy for the main menu of an ATM interface that gives priority to the most used operations.

In the evaluation phase, techniques such as Free Exploration [1] were used, which was useful for users to carry out tasks that they normally do in an ATM. Also, in the same study, the System Usability Scale (SUS) questionnaire was used after each task to find out the degree of user satisfaction, as well as the users' feelings and the level of perceived ease of use.

4.3   ATM Interface Design and Redesign Case Studies

In order to answer the question "What case studies on the design and redesign of ATM interfaces have been reported in the literature, and how were they carried out?", different banks have been identified in the world that have carried them out, among which the BBVA Peru stands out. This bank has carried out redesigns or designs of the following functionalities: obtaining a new credit card as a new user, obtaining a duplicate of a credit card as a customer of the bank using QR authentication, withdrawals without a card using QR codes, redesign of the main menu among others [1, 4, 18, 21, 27, 34, 55].

BBVA Peru has followed frameworks such as User-Centered Design or Design Thinking for the design of the functionalities mentioned before. For example, for the cardless withdrawals functionality [4] UCD was used and the following was done: in the context phase, stakeholders were identified in order to understand the problem from their point of view, a field study or observation was also carried out where only 33% of users had made withdrawals without a card. Then, in the requirements phase, an analysis of the BBVA bank's competitors was carried out, where Interbank and BCP were identified as the main competition at the national level and a bank in Hong Kong, which had a solution similar to the withdrawal functionality without card, in the international level. In this phase the requirements were also listed. In the design phase, brainstorming was done on how to optimize cardless withdrawal and then make proposals in the form of prototypes and evaluate them. Finally, in the evaluation phase, a test was carried out with users that had positive results. However, some observations were also identified that were corrected and thus a new prototype was obtained, which was validated.

In Nigeria [24] a more sustainable and usable ATM interface redesign was performed using environmental heuristics. In Thailand [52] an interface design based on the 7 most used transactions in ATMs has been proposed, which seeks to improve the effectiveness, efficiency and user satisfaction and finally, a design of an adaptive interface [29] that changes according to the information of user transactions has been proposed, this is personalized.

5   Conclusions and Future Works

After conducting the SLR, we found that there are several studies that deal with the issue of usability in ATMs, which makes this a quite developed topic in recent years. In these studies, we identified that remained relevant even in the most recent papers, such as accessibility, security and usability issues that affect the User Experience. These problems have been addressed through several techniques and methods, and even some studies have made use of a framework for the design of ATM interfaces based on User Centered Design. However, in general, ATM interfaces still present usability issues related to: ease of use, learning capacity, error rates, user satisfaction, etc. [1, 7, 26, 27]. This is due to the insufficient analysis of use scenarios taking into account to stakeholders, the insufficient consideration of the needs of the users, and the reduced use of metrics and techniques that allow determining the degree of usability. These problems impact on the perception of the users about the usability of the interfaces [8, 16, 32].

Finally, as future work, it is proposed to carry out a design from scratch, following a user-centered framework, since it has been identified that most of the case studies of the review had a previous basis on which the design was carried out. Furthermore, most studies have not used methodologies or frameworks focused on the user in such a way that the interface design is oriented towards obtaining a high degree of usability, which generates a gap between the expectations of the user and their perceptions regarding what the ATM interfaces offer [2].

Acknowledgement. We want to thank to the "HCI, Design, User Experience, Accessibility & Innovation Technologies (HCI DUXAIT)" a research group from the Pontificia Universidad Católica del Perú (PUCP) for its support along the whole research.

References

1. Kitchenham, B., Charters, S.: Guidelines for Performing Systematic Literature Reviews in Software Engineering. Keele University and Durham University (2007)
2. Petticrew, M., Roberts, H.: Systematic Reviews in the Social Sciences: A Practical Guide. Blackwell Publishing, USA (2005)
3. Brereton, P., Kitchenham, B.A., Budgen, D., Turner, M., Khalil, M.: Lessons from applying the systematic literature review process within the software engineering domain. J. Syst. Softw. **80**(4), 571–583 (2007). https://doi.org/10.1016/j.jss.2006.07.009
4. Weng, Y., Xia, S., Liang, S., Soares, M.M.: Usability testing of bank of China automatic teller machine. In: Marcus, A., Rosenzweig, E. (eds.) HCII 2020. LNCS, vol. 12202, pp. 189–199. Springer, Cham (2020). https://doi.org/10.1007/978-3-030-49757-6_13
5. Quiroz, M.A., Coz, H.J.C.: "Percepción de La Calidad del Servicio de Cajeros Automáticos en Universidades Particulares del distrito de San Isidro." Universidad Peruana de Ciencias Aplicadas (UPC) (2018). https://doi.org/10.19083/tesis/624770
6. Aguirre, J., Moquillaza, A., Paz, F.: A user-centered framework for the design of usable ATM interfaces. In: Marcus, A., Wang, W. (eds.) HCII 2019. LNCS, vol. 11583, pp. 163–178. Springer, Cham (2019). https://doi.org/10.1007/978-3-030-23570-3_13
7. Aguirre, J., Benazar, S., Moquillaza, A.: Applying a UCD framework for ATM interfaces on the design of QR withdrawal: a case study. In: Marcus, A., Rosenzweig, E. (eds.) HCII 2020. LNCS, vol. 12202, pp. 3–19. Springer, Cham (2020). https://doi.org/10.1007/978-3-030-497 57-6_1
8. Aguirre, J., Moquillaza, A., Paz, F.: Methodologies for the design of ATM interfaces: a systematic review. In: Ahram, T., Karwowski, W., Taiar, R. (eds.) IHSED 2018. AISC, vol. 876, pp. 256–262. Springer, Cham (2019). https://doi.org/10.1007/978-3-030-02053-8_39

9. Jain, A., Subhedar, S., KumarGupta, N.: Analysis and optimization of cash withdrawal process through ATM in India from HCI and customization. In: Senjyu, T., Mahalle, P.N., Perumal, T., Joshi, A. (eds.) ICTIS 2020. SIST, vol. 196, pp. 203–211. Springer, Singapore (2021). https://doi.org/10.1007/978-981-15-7062-9_20

10. Shafiq, M., Ahmad, M., Choi, J.-G.: Public system usability analysis for the valuation of cognitive burden and interface standardization: a case study of cross-ATM design. J. Organ. Comput. Electron. Commer. **27**(2), 162–196 (2017). https://doi.org/10.1080/10919392.2017.1297654

11. Zhang, M., Wang, F., Deng, H., Yin, J.: A survey on human computer interaction technology for ATM. Int. J. Intell. Eng. Syst. **6**(1), 20–29 (2013). https://doi.org/10.22266/ijies2013.0331.03

12. International Organization for Standardization: "Ergonomics of human-system interaction — Part 210: Human-centred design for interactive systems (ISO Standard No. 9241–210:2019)," (2019). https://www.iso.org/standard/77520.html

13. Dillon, A.: "User Interface Design," in Encyclopedia of Cognitive Science, American Cancer Society (2006)

14. Nielsen, J.: Usability Engineering. Morgan Kaufmann, San Diego (1993)

15. Maguire, M.: Methods to support human-centred design. Int. J. Hum. Comput. Stud. **55**(4), 587–634 (2001). https://doi.org/10.1006/ijhc.2001.0503

16. Silva, D., Falconi, F., Aguirre, J., Moquillaza, A., Paz, F.: "Applying a UCD approach to redesign functionality on ATM: a case study in the context of university and business collaboration". In: CEUR Workshop Proceedings, 2020, vol. 2747, pp. 15–24, [Online]. https://www.scopus.com/inward/record.uri?eid=2-s2.0-85096917289&partnerID=40&md5=56d0a1114f0d39913390b2b1e54c70b0

17. Falconi, F., Zapata, C., Moquillaza, A., Paz, F.: Security guidelines for the design of ATM interfaces. In: Ahram, T., Falcão, C. (eds.) AHFE 2020. AISC, vol. 1217, pp. 265–271. Springer, Cham (2020). https://doi.org/10.1007/978-3-030-51828-8_35

18. Falconi, F., Zapata, C., Moquillaza, A., Paz, F.: A systematic literature review about quantitative metrics to evaluate usability and security of ATM interfaces. In: Marcus, A., Rosenzweig, E. (eds.) HCII 2020. LNCS, vol. 12202, pp. 100–113. Springer, Cham (2020). https://doi.org/10.1007/978-3-030-49757-6_7

19. Sahua, J., Moquillaza, A.: A systematic review of usability evaluation methods and tools for ATM interfaces. In: Marcus, A., Rosenzweig, E. (eds.) HCII 2020. LNCS, vol. 12202, pp. 130–141. Springer, Cham (2020). https://doi.org/10.1007/978-3-030-49757-6_9

20. Uggla, K., Eriksson, Y.: A contextual usability exploration of cash and ticket machines. In: Gao, Q., Zhou, J. (eds.) HCII 2020. LNCS, vol. 12207, pp. 245–255. Springer, Cham (2020). https://doi.org/10.1007/978-3-030-50252-2_19

21. Moquillaza, A., Falconi, F., Paz, F.: Redesigning a main menu ATM interface using a user-centered design approach aligned to design thinking: a case study. In: Marcus, A., Wang, W. (eds.) HCII 2019. LNCS, vol. 11586, pp. 522–532. Springer, Cham (2019). https://doi.org/10.1007/978-3-030-23535-2_38

22. Chanco, C., Moquillaza, A., Paz, F.: Development and validation of usability heuristics for evaluation of interfaces in ATMs. In: Marcus, A., Wang, W. (eds.) HCII 2019. LNCS, vol. 11586, pp. 3–18. Springer, Cham (2019). https://doi.org/10.1007/978-3-030-23535-2_1

23. Aslam, W., Tariq, A., Arif, I.: The effect of ATM service quality on customer satisfaction and customer loyalty: an empirical analysis. Glob. Bus. Rev. **20**(5), 1155–1178 (2019). https://doi.org/10.1177/0972150919846965

24. Chumpitaz, D., et al.: Developing QR authentication and fingerprint record in an ATM interface using user-centered design techniques. In: Marcus, A., Wang, W. (eds.) HCII 2019. LNCS, vol. 11586, pp. 420–430. Springer, Cham (2019). https://doi.org/10.1007/978-3-030-23535-2_31

25. Shih, M.-S., Chang, J.-H., Cheng, T.-Y.: "The design guideline for dyslexics-friendly Chinese ATM interface. In: ACM International Conference Proceeding Series, pp. 416–420 (2019). https://doi.org/10.1145/3306500.3306519

26. Singanamalla, S., Potluri, V., Scott, C., Medhi-Thies, I.: "PocketATM: Understanding and improving ATM accessibility in India," (2019). https://doi.org/10.1145/3287098.3287106

27. Oyedeji, S., Adisa, M.O., Naqvi, B., Abdulkareem, M., Penzenstadler, B., Seffah, A.: "The interplay between usability, sustainability and green aspects: a design case study from a developing country". In: CEUR Workshop Proceedings, vol. 2382 (2019). https://www.scopus.com/inward/record.uri?eid=2-s2.0-85067805013&partnerID=40&md5=69fe1832145cbb225680342211bde9ab

28. Salman, M., Li, Y., Wang, J.: A graphical PIN entry system with shoulder surfing resistance. In: 2019 IEEE 4th International Conference on Signal and Image Processing (ICSIP), pp. 203–207 (2019). https://doi.org/10.1109/SIPROCESS.2019.8868388

29. Leoveanu, V.M., Sandu, M.C., Coman, A.: Interactive systems in the student-bank relationship: a research on the views of the university of bucharest students on the utility and adaptability of HCI technologies. In: Nah, F.-H., Siau, K. (eds.) HCII 2019. LNCS, vol. 11588, pp. 159–173. Springer, Cham (2019). https://doi.org/10.1007/978-3-030-22335-9_11

30. Meléndez, R., Paz, F.: Design of graphical user interfaces to implement new features in an ATM system of a financial bank. In: Marcus, A., Wang, W. (eds.) DUXU 2018. LNCS, vol. 10919, pp. 247–257. Springer, Cham (2018). https://doi.org/10.1007/978-3-319-91803-7_18

31. Xu, J., Wang, Y., Lv, F.: "Availability test of automated teller machine based on eye-tracking data. In: Proceedings - 2018 11th International Symposium on Computational Intelligence and Design, ISCID 2018, vol. 1, pp. 161–164 (2018). https://doi.org/10.1109/ISCID.2018.00044

32. Imran, M., Hussaan, A.M.: "Adaptive & dynamic interfaces for automated teller machines using clusters". In: 2018 International Conference on Computing, Mathematics and Engineering Technologies: Invent, Innovate and Integrate for Socioeconomic Development, iCoMET 2018 - Proceedings, vol. 2018-January, pp. 1–6 (2018). https://doi.org/10.1109/ICOMET.2018.8346346

33. Magdum, D., Patil, T., Suman, M., Patil, T.B.M.: "Designing talking ATM system for people with visual impairments," Int. J. Eng. Technol. 7, 657–660 (2018). https://www.scopus.com/inward/record.uri?eid=2-s2.0-85082350551&partnerID=40&md5=4c051fa9d7a8a74857e8c5c3397d110f

34. Zaim, E., Miesenberger, K.: TokenAccess: improving accessibility of automatic teller machines (ATMs) by transferring the interface and interaction to personal accessible devices. In: Miesenberger, K., Kouroupetroglou, G. (eds.) ICCHP 2018. LNCS, vol. 10896, pp. 335–342. Springer, Cham (2018). https://doi.org/10.1007/978-3-319-94277-3_53

35. Sikhuphela, A., Gawuza, N., Maka, S., Jere, N.R.: "Designing technologies for Africa: Does culture matter?". In: ACM International Conference Proceeding Series, pp. 275–276 (2018). https://doi.org/10.1145/3283458.3283504

36. Kasat, O.K., Bhadade, U.S.: "Revolving flywheel PIN entry method to prevent shoulder surfing attacks". In: 2018 3rd International Conference for Convergence in Technology (I2CT), 2018, pp. 1–5, doi: https://doi.org/10.1109/I2CT.2018.8529758

37. Moquillaza, A., et al.: Developing an ATM interface using user-centered design techniques. In: Marcus, A., Wang, W. (eds.) DUXU 2017. LNCS, vol. 10290, pp. 690–701. Springer, Cham (2017). https://doi.org/10.1007/978-3-319-58640-3_49

38. Moquillaza, A., Paz, F.: Applying a user-centered design methodology to develop usable interfaces for an automated teller machine. In: ACM International Conference Proceeding Series, vol. Part F131194 (2017). https://doi.org/10.1145/3123818.3123833

39. Muneeb, S., Naseem, M., Shahid, S.: A usability study of an assistive touch voice interface based automated teller machine (ATM). In: Proceedings of the 2015 Annual Symposium on Computing for Development, pp. 114–115 (2015). https://doi.org/10.1145/2830629.2830635
40. Karimov, J., Ozbayoglu, M., Tavli, B., Dogdu, E.: Generic menu optimization for multi-profile customer systems. In: 2015 IEEE International Symposium on Systems Engineering (ISSE), pp. 163–169 (2019). https://doi.org/10.1109/SysEng.2015.7302750
41. Seetharama, M., Paelke, V., Röcker, C.: SafetyPIN: secure PIN entry through eye tracking. In: Tryfonas, T., Askoxylakis, I. (eds.) HAS 2015. LNCS, vol. 9190, pp. 426–435. Springer, Cham (2015). https://doi.org/10.1007/978-3-319-20376-8_38
42. Karovaliya, M., Karedia, S., Oza, S., Kalbande, D.R.: Enhanced security for ATM machine with OTP and facial recognition features. In: Procedia Computer Science, 2015, vol. 45, no. C, pp. 390–396 (2015). https://doi.org/10.1016/j.procs.2015.03.166
43. Khan, R., Hasan, R., Xu, J.: SEPIA: secure-PIN-authentication-as-a-service for ATM using mobile and wearable devices. In: 2015 3rd IEEE International Conference on Mobile Cloud Computing, Services, and Engineering, pp. 41–50 (2015). https://doi.org/10.1109/Mobile Cloud.2015.16
44. Ohta, T., Matsuda, T., Murata, N., Hinago, N., Fujita, S.: Developing convenience store ATMs as social infrastructure. NEC Tech. J. 8(3), 60–63 (2014). https://www.scopus.com/inward/record.uri?eid=2-s2.0-84907004808&partnerID=40&md5=a045c12832415cb618ca515cfc1c1622
45. Lee, M.: Security notions and advanced method for human shoulder-surfing resistant PIN-entry. IEEE Trans. Inf. Forensics Secur. 9(4), 695–708 (2014). https://doi.org/10.1109/TIFS.2014.2307671
46. Regal, G., Busch, M., Deutsch, S., Hochleitner, C., Lugmayr, M., Tscheligi, M.: Money on the move workload, usability and technology acceptance of second-screen atm-interactions. In: Proceedings of the 15th International Conference on Human-Computer Interaction with Mobile Devices and Services, pp. 281–284 (2013). https://doi.org/10.1145/2493190.2493211
47. Peevers, G., Williams, R., Douglas, G., Jack, M.A.: Usability study of fingerprint and palmvein biometric technologies at the ATM. Int. J. Technol. Hum. Interact. 9(1), 78–95 (2013). https://doi.org/10.4018/jthi.2013010106
48. Seifert, J., De Luca, A., Rukzio, E.: Don't Queue up! User Attitudes towards Mobile Interactions with Public Terminals (2012). https://doi.org/10.1145/2406367.2406422
49. Oswal, S.K.: How accessible are the voice-guided automatic teller machines for the visually impaired? In: SIGDOC 2012 - Proceedings of the 30th ACM International Conference on Design of Communication, pp. 65–70. https://doi.org/10.1145/2379057.2379071
50. Pous, M., Serra-Vallmitjana, C., Giménez, R., Torrent-Moreno, M., Boix, D.: Enhancing accessibility: mobile to ATM case study. In: 2012 IEEE Consumer Communications and Networking Conference (CCNC), pp. 404–408 (2012). https://doi.org/10.1109/CCNC.2012.6181024
51. Kamfiroozie, A., Ahmadzadeh, M.: Personalized ATMs: improve ATMs usability. Communications in Computer and Information Science. CCIS, no. PART 1, vol. 173, pp. 161–166 (2011).https://doi.org/10.1007/978-3-642-22098-2_33
52. Camilli, M., Dibitonto, M., Vona, A., Medaglia, C.M., Di Nocera, F.: User-centered design approach for interactive kiosks: evaluation and redesign of an automatic teller machine. In: ACM International Conference Proceeding Series, pp. 85–91 (2011). https://doi.org/10.1145/2037296.2037319
53. de Moraes, R.P., Pereira, E.C., de Freitas, J.C.J., da Cunha, I.T.: Usability in ATMs. In: 2011 IEEE Systems and Information Engineering Design Symposium, pp. 71–75 (2011). https://doi.org/10.1109/SIEDS.2011.5876847

54. Taohai, K., Phimoltares, S., Cooharojananone, N.: Usability comparisons of seven main functions for automated teller machine (ATM) banking service of five banks in Thailand. In: 2010 International Conference on Computational Science and Its Applications, pp. 176–182 (2010). https://doi.org/10.1109/ICCSA.2010.50

55. Cooharojananone, N., Taohai, K., Phimoltares, S.: A new design of ATM interface for banking services in Thailand. In: 2010 10th IEEE/IPSJ International Symposium on Applications and the Internet, pp. 312–315 (2010). https://doi.org/10.1109/SAINT.2010.49

56. De Luca, A., Langheinrich, M., Hussmann, H.: Towards understanding ATM security: a field study of real world ATM use (2010). https://doi.org/10.1145/1837110.1837131

57. De Luca, A., Hertzschuch, K., Hussmann, H.: ColorPIN: Securing PIN entry through indirect input. In: Proceedings of the SIGCHI Conference on Human Factors in Computing Systems, pp. 1103–1106 (2010). https://doi.org/10.1145/1753326.1753490

58. Aguirre, J.: Elaboración y validación de un marco de trabajo para el diseño de interfaces para cajeros automáticos. Pontificia Universidad Católica del Perú (2019). http://hdl.handle.net/20.500.12404/16055

User Experience Research in China: A 15-Year Bibliometric Analysis

Wenfeng Xia[1] and Zhen Liu[2(✉)]

[1] Management School, Guangzhou City University of Technology, Guangzhou 510800, People's Republic of China
[2] School of Design, South China University of Technology, Guangzhou 510006, People's Republic of China
liuzjames@scut.edu.cn

Abstract. With the continuous development of China's economy, the proportion of added value of service industry in gross domestic product in China has exceeded 50%, and reached 54.5% in 2020. User experience is an important link in the economy of the service industry, analyzing the development trend of academic research in the area of user experience in China, focusing on the hot issues of user experience research in China, and understanding the current needs of user experience research in the Chinese market will serve as a guide for future research directions for research scholars in the area of user experience. However, at present time, little has been done in user experience of China from the very beginning to 2021 through knowledge mapping analysis. This paper uses a scientific bibliometric method to make a comprehensive analysis with literature visualization by using CiteSpace and SATI selecting the core journal articles indexed by Chinese National Knowledge Infrastructure (CNKI) from 2006 which is the beginning year of Chinese user experience research to November 2021. User experience as a research keyword is started in 2006 in China, which has involved in a wide distribution of subject areas, mainly focused on computer software, graphics, industrial technology, press media, and internet technology. There is a need of collaboration of schools in discipline research in the area of user experience research in China. The research hotspots in the field of user experience in China in recent years mainly focus on the perspective of user sensory experience, interactive experience, and internet application experience. In the future, the research trend of user experience in China may focus on the impact of user sensory factors and situational factors on user experience, the interdisciplinary research of China's aging population and intelligent devices, and the user experience research of virtual reality interaction in Experience Metaverse.

Keywords: User experience · Knowledge map · Bibliometric analysis · Experience metaverse

1 Introduction

With the development of China's economy, the scale of experience economy in the current Chinese market shows a large growth trend. The American futurist Alvin Toffler, first introduced the term "experience" in 1970 and proposed that economic development would go through three stages in turn, from "manufacturing economy" to "service economy" to "experience economy" [1]. In 1992, the Central Committee of the Communist Party of China and the Chinese State Council made the decision on "Accelerating the Development of the Tertiary Industry", which decide to propose vigorous promotion of tertiary industry and development of service economy [2].

Experience economy is the extension of service economy and the fourth type of economy after agricultural economy, industrial economy and service economy. In the report of the 19th national congress in China, President Xi pointed out that China's economy has changed from a high-speed growth stage to a high-quality development stage, and pointed out that the connotation of high-quality development is to meet the people's needs for a better life [3]. Therefore, user experience which is the most important link in the experience economy has become the focus of research and attention in all walks of life.

The research based on user experience has a long history, Alvin Toffler (1970) believes that experience is the psychological product of tangible goods and intangible services [1]. Pine II and Gilmore (1998) proposed four dimensions of negative experience, attraction experience, positive experience and immersion experience from the process of customer psychological change [4]. This classification is limited to the process of user psychological change. Schmitt (1999) proposed the customer holistic experience, which consists of five aspects, namely sensory experience (awareness), emotional experience (feeling), cognitive experience (thinking), physical experience (action), social identity experience (Association) [5].

User experience is an important link in experiential Economics. Combined with the needs of China's high-quality economic development, the essence of improving user experience in the experience economy is to meet the people's needs for a better life. Therefore, the study of the development process of user experience in China and the overall understanding of the current research situation in the academic field of user experience can lay a foundation for the continuous and innovative research in this field.

2 Methods

2.1 Data Sources

This paper takes the CNKI (Chinese National Knowledge Infrastructure) academic journal database as the data source, and carries out literature retrieval with the Theme = "User Experience", Keyword = "User Experience", time span for all years. SCI, EI, Peking University core journals, CSSCI and CSCD are selected for source selection. The retrieval time is November 11, 221. A total of 1069 documents were obtained by searching. As the main research object of this paper is "User Experience", the unrelated documents such as meeting information and review report were manually excluded from the search results, and 510 valid documents were finally obtained as research samples.

2.2 Research Method

CiteSpace and SATI (Statistical Analysis Toolkit for Informetrics) are two commonly used tools for literature analysis. Citespace a JAVA platform-based document visualization analysis tool developed by Dr. Chen Chaomei. It can achieve a diversified, dynamic and time-sharing visual analysis of document samples, which helps us to find the historical research path and future development trend of academic research points from a large number of sample documents [6]. Since its development, CiteSpace has been widely used in many disciplines. It is the most characteristic and influential knowledge map analysis tool in the literature analysis tools in recent years. SATI (Statistical Analysis Toolkit for Informetrics) is a general statistical analysis tool for bibliographic information, which can analyze document information in endnote format in a multidimensional way.

This paper uses CiteSpace 5.8 R3C to analyze keyword co-occurrence, keyword cluster and burst words. At the same time, it is combined with SATI online analysis tool to analyze the trend of journal publication, literature publication and institutional cooperation. This paper combines two analysis tools to do multidimensional comparison analysis on the sample of literature analysis, draws the knowledge map of "User Experience" research, and grasps the research hot spots and trends in the academic research field of "User Experience" from a macro perspective, which provides reference for the further research in this field.

3 Results and Analysis

3.1 Bibliometric Analysis

Analysis of Document Quantity Distribution Based on Time Axis. The number and time of papers in academic field is one of the criteria to judge the research heat in this field. This paper gives a rough view of the year distribution of 1069 journals retrieved from CNKI journals with the Theme = "User Experience", Keyword = "User Experience", finds that 1 article was published in 2004 and 2005 respectively in China, which has increased gradually from 2006 to 2008 and reached its peak in 2018. Research in this field continues to be hot, as shown in Fig. 1.

This paper manually filters 1069 documents, eliminates conference information and reports that are not related to the "User Experience" study, and finally selects 510 sample documents. The statistical analysis tool of sati was used to produce information sheets on the year of publication and quantity of literatures shows as in Fig. 2. It can be seen from the publishing trend that the academic research in the field of "User Experience" in China started in 2006, increased significantly from 2010 to the first research peak in 2012, with an annual publication volume of 31 articles, and then entered the hot research stage, reaching the first research peak in 2015, with an annual publication volume of 48 articles. In 2016, the number of publications declined slightly, but in 2017, it increased explosively, reaching the second peak period with 62 articles. Overall, the research trend of "User Experience" research is increasing year by year.

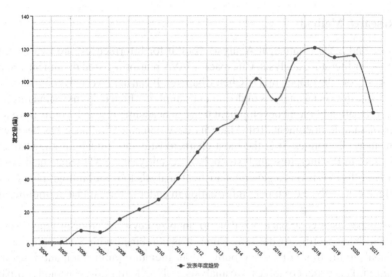

Fig. 1. Number of papers published in the "User Experience" area in China (2004–2021.11) in China.

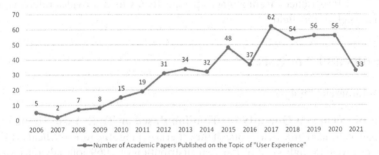

Fig. 2. Number of core academic papers published on the topic of "User Experience" from 2006 to 2021 in China.

Distribution and Research Topics of Documentation Discipline Analysis in China.
The distribution of research subjects across disciplines can be found by analyzing the distribution of research subject areas in the literature. Because the CNKI database can only analyze raw literature data, this paper gives a rough outlook on 1069 retrieved journals, and through charting analysis finds that the distribution of discipline categories in this subject design of "User Experience" is wide, and the distribution of their main literature categories as shown in Fig. 3 below. It can be found that the largest number of academic papers published area is "Computer Software and Computer Applications", accounting for 19.05%, followed by "Library and Information Science and Digital Library", accounting for 14.37%. The third is "Industrial General Technology and Equipment", accounting for 13.95%, the fourth is "News and Media", accounting for 7.77%, and the fifth is "Internet Technology", accounting for 7.02%.

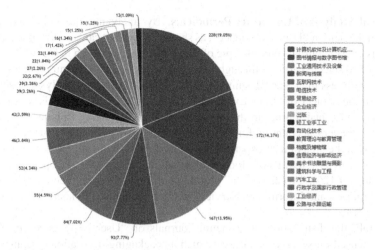

Fig. 3. Distribution of subject areas of "User Experience" research in China.

Through the cross-analysis of 1069 search results of CNKI (Chinese National Knowledge Infrastructure) as shown in Fig. 4. This paper finds that the main cross-research fields of "User Experience" topic are user-based user experience research, user experience-based research, design-based user experience research, user experience research based on APP and user experience research based on experience perspective. At the same time, the research on user experience in mobile library, Digital Library and empirical research fields also has a close cross-section.

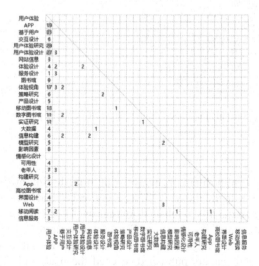

Fig. 4. Cross-research analysis map of "User Experience" theme in China.

Statistical Analysis of Literature Periodicals. By analyzing the published journal papers in the field of "User Experience", as shown in Fig. 5, it can provide an insight into the focus of core journals on this topic of user experience research in China. This paper analyzed 510 selected articles through SATI online platform and manually merged publications with less than 5 articles into "Other". A graphical visual analysis of academic papers on the subject of "User Experience" from 2006 to 2021 reveals that the most frequently published journal in this research area is "Packaging Engineering", with a total of 132 papers, accounting for up to 25.9% which shows that this journal has a very high focus in the area of user experience. The next most frequently published journal in this research area is "Journal of Modern Information", with a total of 21 papers, accounting for up to 4.12%. "Art & Design" journal published 19 papers, accounting for up to 3.72%. "Library and Information Service" journal published 17 papers, accounting for up to 3.33%.

Overall, the distribution of academic journals on "User Experience" research is mainly focused on several major areas, such as packaging decoration, graphics, computers, telecommunications, and media, which has a consistent with the distribution of disciplines analysis, as shown in Fig. 5.

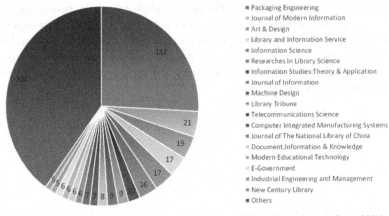

Fig. 5. Distribution of journals published on the theme of "User Experience" from 2006 to 2021 in China.

Through the SATI online literature analysis platform, the time analysis of the journals that 510 core articles with the theme = "User Experience" had been published is shown in Fig. 6. The most frequently published journal in "User Experience" research area is "Packaging Engineering", as shown in Fig. 6, which started to rise a focus on user experience since 2010, gradually to the stage of high-frequency published articles starting in 2015, the number of papers published reached the peak with 22 papers in 2019. Other journals do not fluctuate significantly in the number of articles published in "User Experience", with annual articles published in 5 or less.

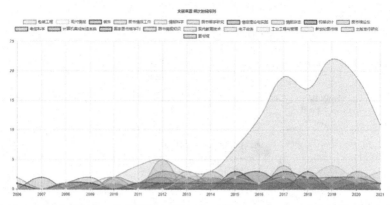

Fig. 6. Trend chart of the number of "User Experience" theme papers published by journals from 2006 to 2021 in China.

3.2   Core Authors and Institutional Analysis

Core Author Visualization Map. By analyzing 510 published articles on SATI online platform, it is found that the top 10 authors of "User Experience" topics from 2006 to November 2021, as shown in Fig. 7, are Yongfeng Li, Qinghua Zhu and Shengli Deng, who have published 7 academic articles respectively, Liping Zhu and Yanzhang Xu have published 6 articles respectively, Jinjun Xia and Xiaopu Jin have published 5 articles respectively, and Yi Ding, Shiyang Yu, Keren He publish four articles respectively.

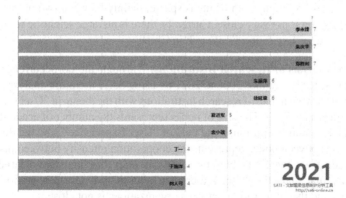

Fig. 7. Ranking chart of the number of core authors published on the theme of "User Experience" from 2006 to 2021 in China.

The co-citation analysis via CiteSpace software is mapped in Fig. 8, which calculated 253 nodes with generating 105 lines in which the size of the node is proportional to the amount of publication, the lines between the nodes represent the cooperation between the authors, and the thickness of the line segment represents the closeness of its cooperation.

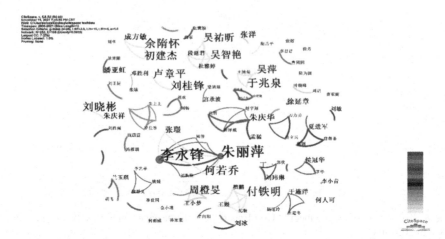

Fig. 8. Collaboration map of core authors of "User Experience" research in China.

By analyzing the graph, it can be seen that the most of the researchers of "User Experience" in China are scattered. YongFeng Li and Liping Zhu, who have published a large number of research papers in the field of "User Experience", have formed a seven-person collaborative team, and their main research field is the research in the field of "User Experience" for the elderly. Qinghua Zhu has formed a 5-person cooperative team whose main research area is Human-Computer Interaction user experience in the field of library and information science. Other authors in the top 10 volumes did not form an obvious group of over 5 people. Overall, the cooperation between most researchers in the field of "User Experience" in China is sparse, mainly between two or three people, and the cooperation is not very close. Currently, there is no large scientific research team in the field of "User Experience" research in China.

Visual Map Analysis of Research Institutions. Through the co-occurrence analysis of 510 papers since November 2006 to 2021 by using SATI literature analysis software, it is found that the visual map of research institutions with the theme in "User Experience" in China is shown in Fig. 9. The size of nodes represents the number of academic papers issued by the research institution in the field of "User Experience", and the thickness of the connection between nodes represents the cooperation intensity between institutions. It can be seen from the SATI literature analysis map that there are a large number of institutions that study the "User Experience", but there is less cooperation between organizations and the cooperation between organizations is not close.

Through the analysis of the institution cooperation network, it is found that the number of documents issued by the School of Information Management of Wuhan University, Jiangnan University, the School of Information Management of Nanjing University, and Hunan University are high. The most notable collaboration networks were formed between the School of Information Management of Nanjing University and the School of Engineering Management of Nanjing University, School of Economics and Management of Nantong University, School of Economic Management of Nanjing University of

Technology, Nanjing University Library, and Institute of Scientific and Technical Information of Chinese Academy of Tropical Agricultural Sciences, and brought together the Library of Xijiao Liverpool University, School of social science, Soochow University, the Wenzheng College of Soochow University forms a triangular cooperation network. Secondly, the School of Information Management of Wuhan University, the information resources research center of Wuhan University, the Information Management Department of the School of Public Management of Huazhong Agricultural University, the School of Management of Tianjin Normal University, the library of Tianjin Normal University and the Public Security Bureau of Lvliang City, Shanxi Province have formed a chain cooperation. Hunan University and Shanghai Huawei Technology Co., Ltd. have formed a bilateral cooperation network. Jiangnan University, National Information Center informatics research Jiangsu Normal University has a significant volume of academic research publications, but all are independent research status.

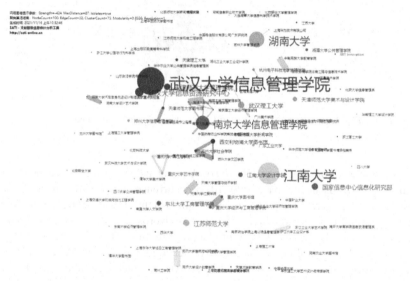

Fig. 9. Map of "User Experience" research cooperation among institutions in China.

4 Research Hot Spots and Frontier Analysis

4.1 Analysis of Research Hotspots

Keywords Analysis

Keyword Co-occurrence Map Analysis. The analysis of keyword co-occurrence map by CiteSpace is shown in Fig. 10. There are 375 nodes, 655 connections, and the overall network density is 0.0074. The larger the number of nodes, the higher the frequency of keyword co-occurrence [6]. Therefore, key words such as user experience, product design, usability, design, experience, interactive design, experience design, service design, library, influencing factors, government website, the elderly, search engine appear more frequently. Most of the keywords are presented in network and few isolated nodes, which indicates that the correlation between keywords is strong. At the same time, the node of user experience, interaction design, older people, product design, influencing factors, service design in the graph is larger, which indicates that the research of Chinese "User Experience" is hot in these several cross-over areas.

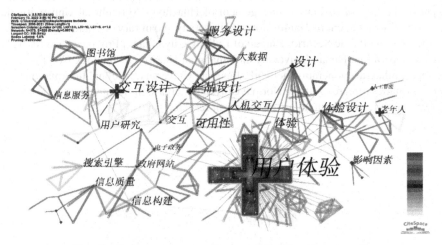

Fig. 10. Cooccurrence map of keywords in "User Experience".

Keywords Frequency and Centrality Analysis. Sorting and analyzing the frequency and centrality of keywords in CiteSpace keyword co-occurrence map provides further insight into the developmental research hotspots and frontiers of the "User Experience" in China. As shown in Table 1, the top ten high-frequency keywords are user experience, interactive design, the elderly, service design, product design, innovative design, and optimal design. Keyword as Usability, Interactive Experience juxtaposed eighth. Keywords as Design, Influence Factor, Five Senses Experience, AR (Augmented Reality), QFD (Quality Function Deployment), Children's Cognition, Kano juxtaposed ninth. Keyword as Experience Design, Physical Resources juxtaposed tenth.

Table 1. Statistics of high frequency keywords, word frequency and centrality of "User Experience" research in China

Keyword frequency			Keyword centrality		
No.	Frequency	Keyword	No.	Centrality	Keyword
1	594	User experience	1	1.28	User experience
2	52	Interaction design	2	0.96	Usability
3	38	Elderly group	3	0.92	Government website
4	30	Service design	4	0.91	Interface

(continued)

Table 1. (*continued*)

Keyword frequency			Keyword centrality		
No.	Frequency	Keyword	No.	Centrality	Keyword
5	25	Product design	5	0.91	Satisfaction
6	20	Innovative design	6	0.9	E-Government
7	19	Optimal design	7	0.72	Product design
8	17	Usability, interactive experience	8	0.44	Experience design
9	16	Design, influence factor, five senses experience, AR, QFD, children's cognition, Kano	9	0.39	Experience
10	15	Experience design, physical resources	10	0.27	Service design

Analysis of Hot Research Topics. The keyword co-occurrence network can be obtained by using the keyword co-occurrence analysis of CiteSpace. This paper selects the top 10 clusters for analysis, as shown in Fig. 11. Among them, Modularity Q = 0.8036, generally Q > 0.3 means the cluster structure is significant [7]. Silhouette S = 0.9827, generally S > 0.5 cluster classes are considered reasonable, S > 0.7 means cluster is convincing. These clusters can reflect that the top 10 studies in the field of "User Experience" research in China from 2006 to November 221 focused on environmental psychology, usability, service design, interactive design, design, user research, information construction, government websites, experience design, and libraries.

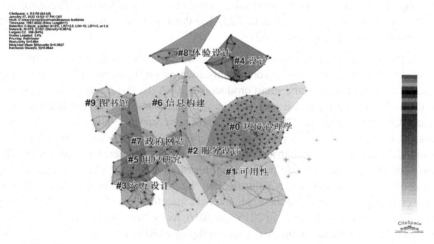

Fig. 11. Keyword clustering map of "User Experience" research via CiteSpace.

Keyword Burstness Analysis. Keywords burstness are hot research keywords that have surged in a certain period. CiteSpace burstness can find keywords that occur frequently over a period of time, and the intensity and time of keyword emergence can be used to analyze research hot spots and trends over a period of time. In order to get a better analysis result, Minimum Duration is set to 1 year. $\gamma = 0.8$, a visual analysis can produce a keyword highlight map, as shown in Fig. 12.

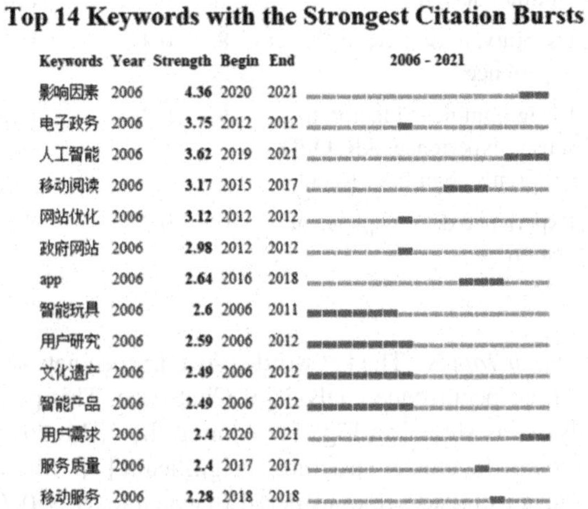

Top 14 Keywords with the Strongest Citation Bursts

Keywords	Year	Strength	Begin	End	2006 - 2021
影响因素	2006	4.36	2020	2021	
电子政务	2006	3.75	2012	2012	
人工智能	2006	3.62	2019	2021	
移动阅读	2006	3.17	2015	2017	
网站优化	2006	3.12	2012	2012	
政府网站	2006	2.98	2012	2012	
app	2006	2.64	2016	2018	
智能玩具	2006	2.6	2006	2011	
用户研究	2006	2.59	2006	2012	
文化遗产	2006	2.49	2006	2012	
智能产品	2006	2.49	2006	2012	
用户需求	2006	2.4	2020	2021	
服务质量	2006	2.4	2017	2017	
移动服务	2006	2.28	2018	2018	

Fig. 12. Keywords burstness analysis map of "User Experience" research via CiteSpace.

There are 14 burstness keywords in the research area of "User Experience". Studies of impact factors related to "User Experience" that began to burst in 2020 have a maximum intensity of 4.36. The second highest ranking is the emergence of keyword E-government in 2012 with a burst intensity of up to 3.75. The third is artificial intelligence that burst in 2019 with the intensity up to 3.62.

From the year of the overall burstness keywords, studies based on the area of "User Experience" from 2006 to 2012 were mainly focused on the areas of smart toys, user research, cultural heritage, and smart products. In 2012, the "User Experience" research on E-government and website optimization in China burst with a high intensity very clearly. Combined with the "2012 UN E-Government Survey", China has made steady progress in the overall development of e-government. China E-Government Development Index (0.5359) ranked 78th in 2012. The Chinese Government has made remarkable achievements in promoting the publicity of information and has improved the quality of the official portal website. It indicates that the government paid more attention to E-government at that time and the academic field therefore had a higher research focus. With the rise of mobile Internet in 2015 and 2016, research on mobile reading and user experience of app is heating up. Artificial Intelligence (AI) has received much attention in 2019 and has become a research hotspot till today. "User Experience" research based on user needs and influencing factors has also become a hot trend since 2020.

Time Zone Map Analysis of Keyword Clustering. The change of research keywords over time can show the change and development trend of research hotspots. Through cluster analysis, CiteSpace can arrange the hotspots in the same year in chronological order and gather them in the same area. Therefore, the cluster timezone view generated by CiteSpace is shown in Fig. 13.

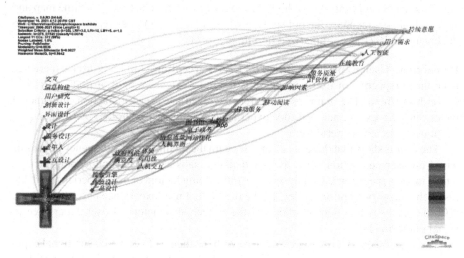

Fig. 13. Keyword clustering Timezone map of "User Experience" research via CiteSpace.

From the evolution of keywords in the overall Timezone diagram, it can be seen that the research in the field of user experience in China is roughly divided into five stages. The first stage is the research stage of "design" based on user experience. The research in this stage is mainly concentrated from 2006 to 2009. As shown in the gray line in Fig. 13, the research keywords are embodied in experience design, product design, service design, and interface design. The second stage is the user experience research stage of informatization and digitization. The research period of this stage is from 2009 to 2013, as shown in the dark blue line in Fig. 13. The research keywords are mainly e-government, library, big data, man–machine interface, and app. The third stage is the user experience research stage in the mobile Internet era. The research period is from 2014 to 2015, as shown by the light blue line in the Fig. 13. The research keywords are mainly mobile services and mobile reading. The fourth stage is the research based on the influencing factors and evaluation methods of user experience. The research period of this stage is from 2016 to 2018, as shown in the green line in the Fig. 13. The research keywords are mainly influencing factors, service quality, and evaluation system. The fifth stage is the user experience research based on the user perspective. From 2018 to 2021, as shown by the red line in the Fig. 13, the research keywords are mainly user needs, and continuous willingness.

5 Discussion

5.1 Hotspots of User Experience Research in China

This paper combs the academic research papers on the theme and keywords of Chinese user experience. At the same time, combined with the analysis of keyword co-occurrence map, frequency and centrality of high-frequency keywords, clustering timeline map and keyword emergence map, the hot spots of Chinese user experience research from 2006 to November 2021 are summarized into three aspects.

Research on User Experience Based on User Perception. Studying user experience from the perspective of user perception is the most extensive field of user experience research in China. The main research areas involved are user satisfaction, influencing factors of user experience, sensory experience, cognitive psychology, willingness to continue, and scene experience.

The results show that there are 27 articles with the theme of high-frequency keywords based on user perception, such as user demand, satisfaction and influencing factors, which involve the empirical analysis of the influencing factors of user experience [8], the research of user perception model [9], the research of user experience based on website [10], the analysis and demonstration of the influencing factors of user experience of social platform [11].

There are 66 articles on user experience with the theme of keywords emotional experience, sensory experience, cognitive psychology, sustained willingness and psychological model, which involve the research on user experience of psychological stratification theory [12], sustained willingness of reading experience to the elderly group [13], and visual search experience [14]. At the same time, there are continuous user experience research for the elderly user group. There are 38 articles on the user experience research involving the elderly group, mainly related to the optimization of APP use experience of the elderly group [15], and the evaluation of user experience of electronic products for the elderly group [16].

Based on the keyword cluster timezone view, the keyword "user research" is mainly focused on user experience interface design of digital memory resource recommendation system [17], user research and user experience design [18], website classification system [19], and automobile after-sale service scene [20].

Research on User Experience Based on Interactive Design. The results indicate that there are 45 academic papers on user experience research with the theme of user experience research keywords based on interaction design, such as human-computer interaction, human-computer interface, information interaction, and interaction and interactive experience. The content mainly involves cultural heritage AR (Augmented Reality) interaction design [21], comparative research on human-computer interaction interface of digital reading platform from the perspective of user experience [22], service design of handheld mobile devices [23], context based user experience design in mobile phone interface [24], user experience design research of internet shopping website [25], emotional voice interaction design [26], and touch interaction interface design of numerical control press [27].

Based on the keyword cluster timezone view, there are 52 articles related to the keyword "interactive design", which are mainly involved in the language learning APP design research of user experience [28], the interactive design research of children's smart toys guided by touch experience [29], the relationship between interaction and user experience in interactive web advertising [30], the interactive design of children's smart toys [31], the design of interactive visual experience under the environment of autonomous communication [32], the emotional research of interactive products [33], and the interactive design of food consumption websites [34]. At the same time, with the development of Metaverse virtual reality interaction research, user experience research based on Metaverse field has also become a research focus in China [35].

Research on User Experience Based on Internet Application. There are 39 articles on user experience research based on artificial intelligence, big data, search engine, e-government, and information construction. The content involves the impact of the anthropomorphic characteristics of artificial intelligence on user experience [36], the innovative design of unmanned stores based on the full link user experience path [37], the impact of the matching degree between artificial intelligence and product types on user experience [38], the effectiveness evaluation of search engines based on user experience [39], the classification and update strategy of large website pages for user experience [40], and the optimization of government websites [41].

Based on the keyword cluster Timezone view, there are 7 articles related to the keyword "government website", which include the performance evaluation of government website based on user experience [42], the research on user satisfaction of government website based on user experience [43], and the optimization of government website based on user experience [44] with dynamic adjustment of columns, careful design of service interface and accurately identified user needs.

The above research in the field has conducted in-depth research in their respective fields, enriched the research and development theory of user experience in China, and laid a foundation for the optimization of user experience in various fields.

5.2 Research Trend of User Experience in China

The research in the field of user experience in China has obvious interdisciplinary, policy-oriented and market-oriented characteristics in the last 15 years from 2006 to 2021. The research attention has been increasing year by year, and the amount of publications has been growing steadily in recent years. The future research on user experience in China may focus on the following areas.

Research on User-Oriented Experience. China's economy has gradually upgraded from service economy to experience economy. The analysis of influencing factors of user experience based on user perspective has been transformed from traditional satisfaction to multi-dimensional research, such as sensory factors, psychological factors, and situational factors. The specific theoretical model of user experience factors has a preliminary research foundation. With the deepening of cross research in various fields and disciplines, the improvement of services and experience to meet the growing material needs of the people will be the focus of research in various fields in the future.

Research on Market-Oriented User Experience. With the emergence of new technology in the market, such as artificial intelligence, robots, big data, and Metaverse, and the changing structure of users in the Chinese market, such as the aging trend of China's social population, new research hotspots appear to the field of user experience. With the impact of COVID-19 on China's society since 2019, the theme of user experience will change with the change of China's market structure. The interactive user experience research of Metaverse virtual reality integration, the aging social product experience research of artificial intelligence associated with home-based elderly care mode, and the experience research of internet user behavior with big data analysis are all in line with the development trend of China's future market demand. The efforts to improve the user experience of emerging market products could be the focus of future research.

Multidisciplinary and Interdisciplinary Research. In recent years, the research theme of user experience has appeared in the interdisciplinary field. The results indicate that there are few empirical research on the improvement of user experience in cross fields. It is more common to do theoretical and model based research, product design research, and satisfaction research. The empirical research on the influencing factors will also be a new development trend in this field. In addition, the research of Metaverse user experience is a new hot spot of interdisciplinary research. The research of user experience based on Metaverse virtual real interaction may also become a new trend of user experience research in China.

6 Conclusion

This paper uses CiteSpace 5.8 R3C and SATI bibliometric analysis software to analyze the literature on "User Experience" as the theme and keyword via CNKI (Chinese National Knowledge Infrastructure) database, selecting the more representative SCI, EI, Peking University core, CSSCI and CSCD literature for multi-level analysis and visual knowledge map analysis.

In terms of the number and time of articles published, the research on the theme of "User Experience" began to appear in five relevant academic literatures in 2006, and then gradually developed. In terms of the growth rate of the number of articles published, it has entered a period of rapid development since 2010. In 2010, 15 relevant subject research literatures were retrieved, and then increased year by year. Since 2012, more than 30 articles have been published each year. Since 2015, an average of nearly 40 articles have been published annually, of which 37 were published in 2016, but 62 were published in 2017. Considering the delay in publication time due to the periodical review cycle, it still reflects the increasing research heat year by year. From 2017 to 2020, the average annual number of papers published increased to more than 50. Overall, research on user experience is on the rise and will continue to grow in the future.

From the perspective of research fields and published journals, journals with the theme of "User Experience" have obvious interdisciplinary characteristics, involving many disciplinary fields, such as computer, graphics and information, industrial technology, news media, Internet, telecommunications, trade, construction, automobile, and administrative management. Among them, the research fields of computer, graphics and information, and industrial technology account for the top three. In the field of user experience in China are also scattered due to the interdisciplinary nature of their disciplines. Since 2015, the core journal in the design field is Packaging Engineering that has significantly increased the volume of publications on the subject of user experience, while the volume of other journals does not fluctuate significantly. This also indicates that the research on user experience in design field in China is starting to deepen gradually, which conforms to the people-oriented policy direction advocated by the state.

From the distribution of core authors and institutions, most researchers of user experience research in China are independent researchers, and only a few have formed research teams. Most of the research institutions are universities, few independent scientific research institutions, and the cooperation network between them is sparse. From the perspective of geographical location, there are few cross regional and cross unit cooperation networks, and the distribution of scientific research is decentralized as a whole.

From the perspective of research hotspots, the research based on user experience mainly focuses on the research based on user sensory perspective, interactive perspective, and internet application perspective. In recent years, with the emergence of artificial intelligence devices and the in-depth study of Metaverse virtual real interaction, China has gradually entered the stage of population aging and the popularization of mobile internet applications. The user experience of virtual real interaction of Metaverse, the user experience of intelligent devices of aging people and the related user experience based on mobile internet applications may become the research focus and future trend.

Acknowledgements. This research is supported by project "Research on two-way decision-making and low-carbon policy impact of e-commerce packaging in green closed-loop supply chain, 57-CQ190029", and project "T. I.T college students' innovation and entrepreneurship practice base construction, JY191401", Guangzhou City University of Technology.

References

1. Toffler, A.: Future Shock, Reissue. Bantam, New York (1985)
2. Zhang, J.: Reflections on accelerating the development of tertiary industry in China. J. Cent. Univ. Financ. Econ. **08**, 1–2 (1994)
3. Xi, J.: The Governance of China, 2nd edn. Foreign Language Press, Beijing (2020)
4. Pine, I.I., Gilmore, J.H.: Welcome to the experience economy. Harv. Bus. Rev. **76**(7–8), 97–105 (1998)
5. Schmitt, B.H.: Experiential marketing. J. Mark. Manag. **15**(1–3), 53–67 (1999)
6. Chen, C., Chen, Y., Hou, J.: CiteSpace II: identification and visualization of new trends and trends in scientific literature. J. China Soc. Sci. Tech. Inf. **28**(3), 401–421 (2009)
7. Chen, C.: Predictive effects of structural variation on citation counts. J. Am. Soc. Inform. Sci. Technol. **63**(3), 431–449 (2012)
8. Peng, X., Cheng, N., Pei, X., Fang, H., Ma, Y., Qian, S.: Analysis of factors affecting user experience of mobile video platform. Packag. Eng. **42**(12), 9 (2021). https://doi.org/10.19554/j.cnki.1001-3563.2021.12.022
9. Zhang, L., Li, Z., Wang, J.: User perception model of e-business ecosystem. Inf. Sci. **38**(8), 145 (2020). https://doi.org/10.13833/j.issn.1007-7634.2020.08.022

10. Xu, Z., Shang, S., Shi, Y.: Research on key influencing factors of user experience of electronic health website based on DEMATEL. Library **11**, 33 (2020)
11. Chen, J., Zhong, Y., Deng, S.: An empirical study and analysis of influencing factors of the user experience of mobile social networking platform. Inf. Stud.: Theory Appl. **39**(1), 95 (2016). https://doi.org/10.16353/j.cnki.1000-7490.2016.01.016
12. Li, X.: Web user experience model based on general psychological stratification theory. Inf. Doc. Serv. **01**, 62–65 (2010). https://doi.org/10.3969/j.issn.1002-0314.2010.01.014
13. Hou, G., Li, Y.: Effects of reading experience for the elder adults on continuous willingness of information behavior: an empirical study. J. Natl. Libr. China **30**(02), 54–66 (2021). https://doi.org/10.13666/j.cnki.jnlc.2021.0205
14. Zhu, M., Zhu, Q.: Study on the scale development of the influencing factors of mobile visual search user experience. J. Mod. Inf. **41**(02), 65–77 (2021). https://doi.org/10.3969/j.issn.1008-0821.2021.02.007
15. Li, Y., Liu, H., Zhu, L.: Optimization design approach for user experience of the elderly APP based on Kano model and conjoint analysis. Packag. Eng. **42**(02), 77–85 (2021). https://doi.org/10.19554/j.cnki.1001-3563.2021.02.012
16. Li, Y., Zhou, J., Zhu, L.: Research of user experience evaluation of electronic product for the elderly based on Taguchi-quality-thinking. J. Mach. Des. **37**(02), 131–137 (2020). https://doi.org/10.13841/j.cnki.jxsj.2020.02.019
17. Zhang, Y., Luo, T., Nunes, M.B.: Interface design of digital memory resource recommender system based on user experience. Libr. Dev. **9**(06), 1–13 (2021)
18. Tan, H., You, Z., Peng, S.: Big data-driven user experience design. Packag. Eng. **41**(02), 7–12 (2020). https://doi.org/10.19554/j.cnki.1001-3563.2020.02.002
19. Qian, M., Gan, L.: Experimental study of users' experience of website classification system. Inf. Stud.: Theory Appl. **35**(09), 103–108 (2012). https://doi.org/10.16353/j.cnki.1000-7490.2012.09.027
20. Liu, Y.: User experience design of automotive after-sales service scenarios. Packag. Eng. **40**(02), 31–38 (2019). https://doi.org/10.19554/j.cnki.1001-3563.2019.02.005
21. Tan, P., Wang, M., Fu, T., Ji, Y.: Interaction design of cultural heritage type augment reality application based on experiential learning theory. Packag. Eng. **42**(4), 1–7 (2021)
22. Zheng, F., Zhao, Y., Zhu, Q.: Comparative studies on the human-computer interaction and digital reading platform: from the perspective of user experience. Libr. J. **34**(07), 50–58 (2015). https://doi.org/10.13663/j.cnki.lj.2015.07.009
23. Zhou, Y., Luo, S., Zhu, S.: User-centered service design in handheld mobile devices. Comput. Integr. Manuf. Syst. **18**(02), 243–253 (2012). https://doi.org/10.13196/j.cims.2012.02.21.zho uyx.019
24. Luo, S., Zhu, S., Ying, F., Zhang, J.: Scenario-based user experience design in mobile phone interface. Comput. Integr. Manuf. Syst. **16**(02), 239–248 (2010). https://doi.org/10.13196/j.cims.2010.02.17.luoshj.009
25. Wu, J., Huang, C., Cai, J.: Research on user experience design of internet shopping website. Packag. Eng. **33**(08), 68–71 (2012). https://doi.org/10.19554/j.cnki.1001-3563.2012.08.019
26. Liao, Q., Wang, M., Feng, Z.: Voice interaction design of smart home products based on emotional interaction. Packag. Eng. **40**(16), 37–42+66 (2019). https://doi.org/10.19554/j.cnki.1001-3563.2019.16.006
27. Yuan, H., Lao, C., Zhang, Q., Liang, B., Zang, C.: Design of industrial servo press touch-type interactive interface based on user experience. Packag. Eng. **40**(12), 229–235 (2019). https://doi.org/10.19554/j.cnki.1001-3563.2019.12.040
28. Liu, Y., Wang, F.: Design of language learning APP to optimize user experience. Packag. Eng. **42**(04), 103–108 (2021). https://doi.org/10.19554/j.cnki.1001-3563.2021.04.013
29. Wu, Z., Wu, Y., Du, Y., Duan, Y.: Interactive design of children's intelligent toys guided by tactile experience. Packag. Eng. **7**(28), 1–9 (2021)

30. Li, W.: On the relationship between the interactive online advertisement and the client experience. Art Des. (05), 96–97 (2008). https://doi.org/10.16272/j.cnki.cn11-1392/j.2008.05.035

31. Wang, Y., Wang, X., Niu, J., Liu, J.: Research on the interaction design of smart dolls based on children's sensory interaction experience. Design **34**(19), 4–5 (2021)

32. Shen, T., Hao, Y.: Interactive visual experience design in autonomous communication environment. Packag. Eng. **39**(24), 70–75 (2018). https://doi.org/10.19554/j.cnki.1001-3563.2018.24.013

33. Lan, Y., Liu, P.: Emotionalization of interactive products based on user experience. Packag. Eng. **40**(12), 23–28 (2019). https://doi.org/10.19554/j.cnki.1001-3563.2019.12.005

34. Chen, H., Zhou, B.: User experience research of catering consumption website interaction design. J. Donghua Univ. (Nat. Sci.) **41**(04), 546–550 (2015)

35. Wu, J., Cao, Z., Chen, P., He, C., Ke, D.: Users' information behavior from the perspective of metaverse: framework and prospect. J. Inf. Resour. Manag. **12**(12), 1–17 (2021)

36. Mou, Y., Din, G., Zhang, H.: The influence of anthropomorphic characteristics of artificial intelligence on user experience. Econ. Manag. **33**(04), 51–57 (2019). https://doi.org/10.3969/j.issn.1003-3890.2019.04.008

37. Zhang, J., Chen, S.: Innovative design of all link user experience driven unmanned store. Packag. Eng. **40**(04), 9–10 (2019). https://doi.org/10.19554/j.cnki.1001-3563.2019.04.004

38. Wang, X., Lei, S., Guo, Y.: Research on the impact of artificial intelligence and product type matching on user experience -- from the perspective of quasi social interaction. J. Commer. Econ. (10), 67–69 (2020). https://doi.org/10.19554/j.cnki.1001-3563.2019.04.004

39. Xu, Y., Chen, S.: Evaluation of search engine effectiveness based on user experience. Chin. J. Ergon. (03), 9–12 (2008). https://doi.org/10.13837/j.issn.1006-8309.2008.03.014

40. Ouyang, L., Yi, X., Li, X., Yang, Z.: Classified webpage refresh strategy for user's experience-oriented large-scale websites. J. Huazhong Univ. Sci. Technol. (Nat. Sci. Ed.) **38**(09), 18–21 (2010). https://doi.org/10.13245/j.hust.2010.09.027

41. Yu, S., Yang, D.: Government website optimization based on user experience: general idea. E-Government (08), 6–7 (2012). https://doi.org/10.16582/j.cnki.dzzw.2012.08.003

42. Wang, J., Yang, D.: Performance evaluation of government websites based on user experience: exploration and practice. E-Government (05), 35–41 (2014). CNKI: SUN: DZZW.0.2014-05-007

43. Cao, Q.: Research on satisfaction of government web-site based on user experience. Inf. Sci. **27**(10), 1470–1474 (2009). CNKI: SUN: QBKX.0.2009-10-007

44. Wang, J, Yu, S.: government website optimization based on user experience: carefully designed service interface. E-Government (08), 35–44 (2012). CNKI: SUN: DZZW.0.2012-08-008

Why Some "User-Centred" Medical Devices do not Provide Satisfactory User Experiences? An Investigation on User Information Factors in New Device Development Processes

Fan Yang, Liuzhuang Wang[(✉)], and Xiong Ding

Guangzhou Academy of Fine Arts, 168 Waihuan Xilu, Higher Education Mega Center, Panyu District, Guangzhou, China
fanyang@gzarts.edu.cn

Abstract. Many medical devices on the market are labelled "user-centred"; however, a large percentage of them are not designed to adequately reflect the needs and features of the end-users. Design issues have led to accidents in which poor experiences impair product functionality and even threatens users' safety. This study explored the user information factors that hindered the success of new medical devices that were effective, safe and easy to use, and also the correlations between these factors. A case study methodology was utilised to gain improved understanding of the factors that substantially influence the user performance of new products. In specific, the project processes of sixteen medical devices produced by two carefully selected manufacturers were analysed, through analysing the project archives of the devices, interviewing team members playing key roles in the development processes, and validation workshops. The results also revealed that the design of most of the devices in the study was based on insufficient user insights. This owed to the issues embedded in both the ways of obtaining user information and using the information. These are as follows: 1) unreliable information sources; 2) linear and unidirectional data delivery manner; 3) inconsistent ways of translating and presenting data; and 4) lack of central governance of project information.

Keywords: Creativity · User information factors · Medical device · Product design

1 Introduction

Improving the design of medical devices plays an important role in minimising the risk of an incident occurring during use, given that the usability of many devices are ill considered in the design processes, affecting the end-users' psychological state and/or their abilities to engage with the devices [1, 2]. Historically, the healthcare delivery system has been criticised for its "culture of blame" in which culpability for failure has been attributed to the human elements of the system: people make errors, therefore

© The Author(s), under exclusive license to Springer Nature Switzerland AG 2022
M. M. Soares et al. (Eds.): HCII 2022, LNCS 13321, pp. 314–324, 2022.
https://doi.org/10.1007/978-3-031-05897-4_22

people must change their behaviour to reduce errors [3]. Recent studies have revealed that human errors are more generally associated with latent causes hidden within systems and processes [4]. In England, for example, The National Health Services England received over forty-thousand reports of patient safety incidents involving medical devices in 2013 [5]. Chris Smyth, Health Correspondent of The Times, even pointed out that thousands of patients were killed or seriously injured because of mistakes caused by the poor design of drugs packets and confusing medical equipment [6].

The analysis of the design of failed medical devices by authoritative bodies like the Medicines and Healthcare Products Regulatory Agency (MHRA) and the National Patient Safety Agency (NPSA) further identified a lack of systematic considerations of human factors, rather than flawed technology, as a major contributor to patient-related incidents [e.g., 7]. For example, manual override is positioned such that it is difficult to access during surgery; diathermy hook is not compatible with lead; and a female size catheter length is used on a male patient due to the difficulty in discriminating the equipment [8].

Furthermore, merely addressing the clinical needs of the users and the safety needs of the systems will not guarantee the success or prevent dissatisfaction or ad hoc modification of the devices. Additional user factors like their working and living patterns must be considered during design to ensure a good fit with user requirements - ideally users should not have to modify either the device or their working pattern or lifestyle in order for it to be used. The system where devices will be used in conjunction with other equipment by different users for the treatment of numerous conditions and in a variety of settings [9].

Despite beginning to understand the value of "good" design in developing new medical devices, the manufactures are typically pressed by resources to engage with formal user research and design methods [10]. As a result, the approaches utilised in developing new devices need to evolve, to ensure that the end devices reflect both the latest progress in medical science and technology, and also the continuously rising demands in terms of human factors i.e., safety, ease of use, and the users' subjective wellbeing. This would in turn require effective, accurate, credible and up-to-date information being applied in the process of designing MDs.

Addressing the above concerns, this study explored the user information factors that hindered the success of new medical devices that were effective, safe and easy to use, and also the correlations between these factors.

2   Method

According to Flyvbjerg [11], case studies are necessary to understand a phenomenon to any degree of thoroughness, while statistical studies are necessary to understand the prevalence of a phenomenon. Following this understanding, case studies were engaged with two carefully selected medical device manufacturers that had shown a successful record in the design, implementation, and delivery of innovative medical and healthcare solutions, to acquire improved understanding of the factors that substantially influence the user performance of medical devices on the market. The two manufacturers are hereafter referred to as M1 and M2, for reasons of confidentiality agreements.

Sixteen devices produced by M1 and M2 (eight from each) between 2011 and 2021 were selected as case examples for investigation, including two hearing aids, four blood glucose meters, three wheelchairs, two chair absence sensors, and three forced airway devices, and two electrocardiogram monitors. In terms of functionality, the devices could be categorised into three types, namely assistive technologies, respiratory equipment, respiratory equipment. In terms of intended users, they incorporated both hospital-based devices intended for use by surgeons, and household devices intended for use by residents and carers.

Information about the practices that lead to the development of the devices was obtained from (i) analysing the project archives, (ii) interviewing with the company staff playing key roles in developing the devices, and (iii) validation workshops. The three different methods were combined to validate our data by triangulation.

Given the author's limited knowledge about the two manufacturers prior to the stud, the Snowball Sampling method [12] was adopted in selecting the interviewees. The author initially contacted M1's chief technology officer and M2's innovation director. With the two contact persons' input and help, the other company staff that played key roles in developing the twenty example devices were identified and reached. The first author contacted twenty company staff in total, and twelve participated in this study (5 from M1, 7 from M2), including one innovation director, one chief technology officer, three project managers, two innovation researchers/designers, one service manager, two installation engineers and one marketing director. They represented critical functions including board level management, project management, product design, manufacturing preparation, quality control, marketing, and after-sale services.

A total of twenty-five interviews were carried out, each lasted from 30 to 80 min (total duration ≈24 h). Ten of the informants were interviewed twice, and the other one three times, because the latter had additional information about the example devices that was not covered in earlier interviews. The interviewer was made aware of this through other interviews. The interviews were conducted either face to face or via virtual conference platforms. The interview format was qualitative and semi-structured [13, 14] to reflect the exploratory nature of the study. Table 1 summarises the types of devices investigated in the study, the individuals consulted, and the research activities (See Table 1).

The interview questions were structured to capture three types of data: (i) the role the user is perceived to play within the development processes of the example devices; (ii) what human factors engineering methods they applied (if any) within the development process; and (iii) what they saw as the barriers and benefits to effectively involving users within the development processes. Before beginning, a preliminary interview guide was prepared, which evolved as individual interviews progressed, allowing the interviewees to provide greater depth on matters that the author found important [15, 16]. The author also explained the purpose and format of the interview to the interviewee, and informed consent to participate, and for the audio recording of the interview, was obtained. All interviews were audio-recorded and later transcribed, and the author also took notes during the interviews. In addition, the archives of the sample devices incorporating design/product specifications, reports, and meeting records were reviewed to gain contextual knowledge, and also to consolidate the interviews.

Table 1 The samples devices and the interviewees within the manufacturers

Devices (sum = 16)	Manufacturers	Individuals consulted (n = 12)	Interviews (sum = 23, total duration ≈24 h)	
			Face-to-face interviews (sum = 12)	Interviews via virtual conference platforms (sum = 13)
Two hearing aids, Four blood glucose meters, Two electrocardiogram monitors	M1	Two project managers	n = 2	n = 2
		Innovation director	n = 1	n = 1
		Marketing director	n = 1	n = 1
		One researcher/designer	n = 1	n = 1
Three forced airway devices, Two chair absence sensors, Three wheelchairs	M2	Two project managers	n = 2	n = 2
		Chief technology officer	n = 1	n = 1
		One researcher/designer	n = 1	n = 2
		One service manager	n = 1	n = 1
		Two installation engineers	n = 2	n = 2

After gathering the case information, two validation workshops were held to give both the author and the interviewees the opportunities to comment and elaborate on the case facts and findings as well as the constructed time line of actions and events.

2.1 Data Analysis

All the interviews were transcribed successively, and the transcriptions were read several times and coded manually [16]. With reference to the case study undertaken by [17], the data analysis in this study was conducted in three steps with some iteration. The first step was an open coding where discrete incidents were given a label that represented a phenomenon, e.g., no internal design team, little experience (in user research), and low priority. During this process, questions were asked, such as "What is this?" And different incidents were compared and categorised. In the second step, an axial coding was performed, where the author focused on the conditions that gave rise to the phenomenon associated with the application of human factors research and engineering methods, the context in which the phenomenon was embedded, the strategies by which it was handled, and the effect produced on the example devices.

As a check on the analysis, thirty percent of the transcripts were analysed by both the first author and the second author. After this the two researchers discussed their readings of the interviews and came to an agreement on the theme categories before analysis proceeded onto the subsequent transcripts. The first author then analysed the rest of the data. Descriptive statistics were reported for the quantitative data collected in this study.

3   Results

3.1   Source of User Data

The results from this study showed that the user insights utilised in the development of the sixteen example medical devices were established from the four sources: clients, in-house front-end user research, after-sale services practices, and team members' intuition and experience.

Intuition and experience influenced team members' user insights that were utilised within the development of all of the sample devices; and was the sole source of user knowledge for 31.25% (n = 5) of the devices. In addition to intuition and experience, user information for 31.25% (n = 5) of the devices came solely from clients; 25% (n = 4) came solely from after-sale service practices; 6.25% (n = 1) came from a combination of clients and in-house user research, and 12.5% (n = 2) came from a combination of in-house user research, and service and installation practices. It needs to be noted that for none of the devices user information came from all of the four sources. Overall, the clients contributed to 37.5% (n = 6) of the devices with user information; after-sale service practices to 37.5% (n = 6) of the devices; and in-house front-end user research to only 18.75% (n = 3) of the devices.

When interviewed, 83% (n = 10) of the informants regarded after-sale service practices as an economical and efficient in-house source of user information. The most common reason given by the informants was that the service engineers accessed the end-users more frequently compared with other company staff, e.g., to solve technical problems, install new products and replace components. A more practical reason pointed out by the informants from both M1 and M2 was:

"front-end user research was rarely carried out in the design innovations".

The R&D researcher from M1 held a different view because:

"the user data provided from this source is sometimes inaccurate and unreliable"; and the installation engineer from M2 stated:

"he was not trained to do this job probably", and

"there was not a formal structure to encourage to withdraw user data from the service practices".

Although M1 and M2 have their own R&D teams, the interviewed researcher and the innovation director indicated that both of the two R&D teams rarely engaged font-end user research activities in daily product development practices. Even for the three (18.75%) devices that in-house front-end user research occurred, the research of one device was performed by the service engineers.

3.2   Application of User Data

3.2.1   Information Transmission

The interviews and the analysis of the project archives showed that critical project data produced and/or applied in developing the example devices was transferred among team members a linear fashion comprising multiple layers. In M1, for example, the common way of delivering a piece of user information or any "blue-sky thinking ideas" was like this: a staff member obtained the information that he/she considered valuable; he/she then reported it to the department leader; the latter gathered such information from the whole department then passed those he/she selected through the business hierarchy via group meetings held every four-six weeks. In other words, user information obtained by a service engineer needed to go through the installation manager, the quality management department, the R&D department and the product management department, in order to reach design engineers that applied the information in designing new devices (See Fig. 1).

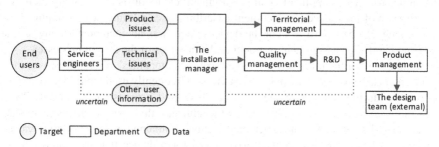

Fig. 1 The process of exploring and communicating market and client information, in M1

On the other hand, the company master data (including the principal NPD process and quality policies) did not determine when and how the many different transmitters should act in data delivery, nor was there consistent understanding among the transmitters to ensure that the data reach the recipients in time. As per the interviewed service engineer:

> *"Even when I have fed back to the company an improvement idea from the user, I often do not know what has happened to it. It is like a black hole..."*

Information Translation. In the course of delivery, original data was processed by different transmitters. For example, in M1, user information received by the designer had already been selected, interpreted and synthesised by transmitters from Installation, Quality Management, R&D and Product Management (See Fig. 1). Finding from a combination of the interviews and the analysis of the project documents showed that the transmitters deployed diverse formats for recording, presenting and communicating data. For example, a long written description of design assignment could be over fifty pages, while a short statement was only half an A4 page. Even for central documents like design specifications, they were found in the project archives to be communicated between team members via an interactive presentation, a template, an email or even a verbal agreement.

In such instances, information receivers had difficulties in decoding the sender's information, because the information was received in relatively unfamiliar formats [18]. As per one of the M1's project manager,

> *"over 50% of time in a project was consumed by transferring the format of documents across platforms".*

Besides, the innovation director at M2 and the design engineer at M1, as data consumers, pointed out that there was no opportunity to trace back to the data source, to either validate the credibility or to discover further details as needed for designing.

Data Storage. The interviewees from both M1 and M2 confirmed the companies' policies required project information to be kept in the corresponding folder saved on the central drive (on-line data safe). While the interviews showed that all of the twelve projects in this study had their own respective project folders. As a result, valuable information was found by the author to be missing, incomplete, duplicated or inaccurate, and was kept in heterogeneous application silos with insufficient consistency among them. For 75% (n = 9) of the devices, a document describing user-relevant design requirements was missing. For 58.3% (n = 7) of the devices, there was no document, in any format, depicting the design assignment or tracking the progress of the design processes.

Although all of the interviewees agreed that the companies' central drive was more secure and also easy to access, only 33.3% (n = 4) frequently used the folder to manage information during a project cycle; 25% (n = 3) used it occasionally; and 41.7% (n = 5) rarely used it. Most (66.7%, n = 8) established their own archives to manage project related documents. These personal archives contained information that was not available in the companies' central drive. Even for a device that was launched two months prior to this study, the project manager could not recall the exact details of initial design requirements when being interviewed. Nor was he able to recover any document accommodating user information.

4   Discussion

The above results revealed that effective and valid user information was absent in the design processes of the majority (88%, n = 23) of the example medical devices. This situation was attributed to the issues in two design innovation management areas: (1) the sources of user information, and (2) the application of user information.

4.1   Issues Concerning the Sources of User Information

Firstly, for both M1 and M2, there was lack of systematic front-end user research to produce reliable, accurate, in-depth and complete information regarding the end-user and the market, within the processes of developing new medical devices. This issue led to critical and valuable information being omitted, with unreliable and inaccurate insights being taken on-board during project formulation and product designing. User insights utilised in formulating project strategies were established solely from team members' intuition and experience, for 31.25% (n = 5) of the devices (See Sect. 3.1). Exploiting intuition in decision-making at the front end of NPD increases new product creativity [19], whereas making intuitive judgments alone may lead to inaccurate or erroneous decisions [20]. Although there was unanimity among the interviewed company staff that intuition was strongly related to "the right experience and knowledge", intuition needs to be used in addition to generally accepted rational approaches, in fuzzy front-end decision-making [e.g., 21, 22, 23]. Even for a combination of cognitive and intuitive judgment, its effectiveness can be associated with other factors, for example, the level of stress under which team members were working [19].

Secondly, the manufacturers investigated tended to depend on "second-hand user information" which quality cannot be promised. As elaborated in Sect. 3.1, the clients contributed to 37.5% (n = 6) of the example devices with user information, that was more than any other user information sources determined. For 31.25% (n = 5) of the devices, user input even came from clients solely. In the medical device sector, user information acquired from the clients can be beneficial, given that some clients like hospitals and non-hospital healthcare facilities, and local authorities and housing associations have expertise in the medical and healthcare area, and also frequently engage the device users. However, the accuracy, completeness, broadness and credibility of the information provided by these sources cannot be promised, not to mention meeting the particular needs from the design perspective. This is because that in these cases the user information was produced by external organisations, at different locations, using unknown methods, and with purposes that might not be in line with the strategy and/or requirements of a specific new device design project.

4.2 Issues Concerning the Application of User Information

Information Transmission. While original user information might not be reliable with regard to the information sources, its quality was further eroded throughout the delivery process. This issue was attributed to both the inefficient data delivery manner and the unclear roles and responsibilities of the transmitters.

Section 3.2 reveals that at both of the two manufactures user information was transmitted in a linear manner wherein multiple communication layers existed between the information producers and consumers. An excessive amount of time was consumed during data transmission, while success in medical device development requires designers and other key stakeholders to solve product issues in a timely fashion [24]. More importantly, the consistency and quality of information was easily eroded when being handed over from one transmitter to another, without a data quality monitoring framework. This issue became more prominent with the unidirectional nature of the information delivery manner, particularly between the sources of user information and its consumers. Besides, the designers were only passive recipients, although the bi-directional relation between data discovery and usage and within iterative feedback loops between different divisions has been broadly recognised by researchers and practitioners to be essential in successful product innovations [e.g., 25, 26–28]. These factors explained why the informatics system at both M1 and M2 failed to keep project data "alive".

To further exacerbate the inefficiency in the delivery of user information, there was a lack of consistent definitions on the roles and responsibilities of both the data transmitters and the providers. This not only diluted the efficiency and quality, but also strangled the data generator's motivation in producing data and the transmitter's motivation in ensuring the data reach the right recipients in time. As described in Sect. 3.2.1, some in-house information producers lacked sufficient sense of contribution that was supportive to a feeling of being responsible, in charge, proud, and involved with work output (Mongiat and Snook 2007).

Information Translation. Data transmission in design innovations commonly starts with a broad perspective and then reaches specific implications for solutions in an iterative way. At M1 and M2, this process involved multiple transmitters who had various knowledge background, used different "language", and were motivated by diverse concerns. As a result, richness, validity and accuracy of data was easily corrupted; valuable data fragments were frequently lost; and too much time was consumed. This highlights the necessity for applying a company level guideline determining how data should be processed, with the purpose of ensuring accuracy, credibility and traceability.

Moreover, the informatics system at the company needs to be changed, to enable both present and future data consumers access raw data, allowing them to repeat the translation process according to different purposes. This is because original data should be translatable in different perspectives, at various levels and in diverse departmental terminologies, to produce effective insight as needed for different applications within the development processes. In user testing, for example, marketers tend to prefer actionable input; whereas designers want to know who the users are, how they interact with the product, and what their comments are in detail.

Information Storage. At both M1 and M2, the corresponding folder established on the companies' central drive was rarely used. These folders were barely visited after the projects were completed, albeit knowledge and insights gained from individual projects can serve as reference data that is supportive to other/future projects [29]. One critical cause was that there was no effective data governance to ensure that all team members apply a format that is distributable across platforms, to enable consistent understanding of master data entities and their relationships. Besides, the project folders stored in the central drive were poorly maintained, as no company staff was dedicated to this job. As a result, finding useful data across projects and/or tracing back to the data source became increasingly difficult, with the day-to-day growth of data volumes. This reduced team members' willingness to use the central drive, which in turn affects the efficiency in data usage.

This issue concerning data storage can also create difficulties for device maintenance, support services and future device upgrades. For example, if a product suddenly starts to "fail" a few years after it was first produced, comparing current data with the original would be essential to unfold the causes – whether it is because the design process in the first place was flawed; there are fundamental changes in customer expectations; or service engineers do not do their job properly.

5 Contribution, Limitation and the Next Step

Actual or potential applications of this study include the facilitation of the appropriate application of human factors methods in developing new medical devices. It also provides a reference for revising industrial standards and guidelines in the sector.

The main concern is related to the possibility of generalising the conclusions to other entities. This means that the findings may not be considered conclusive, and would benefit from investigating a broader spectrum.

Acknowledgements. This study was supported by the Department of Education of Guangdong Province (Grant 2020GXJK135 and Grant 2020KZDZX1136). The funding sources had no role in the design of the study and collection, analysis, and interpretation of data and in writing the manuscript.

References

1. Blache, L., Robbins, P., Brown, S., Jones, P., Liu, T., LeFever, J.: Risk Management and its Application to Medical Device Management, 1st edn. Institute of Physics and Engineering in Medicine, York (2007)
2. Renda, G., Jackson, S., Kuys, B., Whitfield, T.A.: The cutlery effect: do designed products for people with disabilities stigmatise them? Disabil. Rehabil. Assist. Technol. **11**(8), 661–667 (2016)
3. American College of Clinical Engineering: Enhancing Patient Safety - The Role of Clinical Engineering (2001). http://accenet.org/downloads/ACCEPatientSafetyWhitePaper.pdf. Accessed 20 Dec 2017
4. Perrow, C.: Normal Accidents: Living with High Risk Technologies. Princeton University Press, New York (2011)
5. NHS England: Preventing medical device incidents (2016). https://www.england.nhs.uk/patientsafety/medical-device-incidents/. Accessed 1 Aug 2017
6. Smyth, C.: Thousands of patients killed by drug and equipment errors (2014). https://www.thetimes.co.uk/article/thousands-of-patients-killed-by-drug-and-equipment-errors-k7m7c5zjpcx. Accessed 2 Oct 2017
7. Rinkus, S., et al.: Human-centered design of a distributed knowledge management system. J. Biomed. Inform. **38**(1), 4–17 (2005). https://doi.org/10.1016/j.jbi.2004.11.014
8. National Patient Safety Agency: Design for patient safety: user testing in the development of medical devices (2010). http://www.nrls.npsa.nhs.uk/resources/?EntryId45=74946. Accessed 7 Dec 2017
9. Sharples, S., Martin, J., Lang, A., Craven, M., O'Neill, S., Barnett, J.: Medical device design in context: a model of user–device interaction and consequences. Displays **33**(4), 221–232 (2012)
10. Yang, F., Renda, G.: The design briefing process matters: a case study on telehealthcare device providers in the UK. Disabil. Rehabil.: Assist. Technol. **14**(1), 91–98 (2019)
11. Flyvbjerg, B.: Case study. In: Denzin, N.K., Lincoln, Y.S. (eds.) The Sage Handbook of Qualitative Research, pp. 301–316. Sage, Thousand Oaks (2011)
12. Bryman, A.: Social Research Methods. Oxford University Press, Oxford (2001)
13. Smith, J.A.: Semi-structured interviewing and qualitative analysis. In: Smith, J.A., Harre, R., Van Langenhovc, L. (eds.) Rethinking Methods in Psychology. Sage, London (1995)

14. Kvale, S.: Interviews: An Introduction to Qualitative Research Interviewing. Sage Publications, Thousand Oaks (1996)
15. Kvale, S., Brinkmann, S.: InterViews: Learning the Craft of Qualitative Research Interviewing. Sage, Los Angeles (2009)
16. Gish, L., Hansen, C.T.: A socio-technical analysis of work with ideas in NPD: an industrial case study. Res. Eng. Des. **24**(4), 411–427 (2013)
17. Yang, F., Al Mahmud, A., Wang, T.: User knowledge factors that hinder the design of new home healthcare devices: investigating thirty-eight devices and their manufacturers. BMC Med. Inform. Decis. Mak. **21**(1), 166 (2021). https://doi.org/10.1186/s12911-021-01464-3
18. Maltz, E., Kohli, A.K.: Market intelligence dissemination across functional boundaries. J. Mark. Res. **33**, 47–61 (1996)
19. Dayan, M., Di Benedetto, C.A.: Team intuition as a continuum construct and new product creativity: the role of environmental turbulence, team experience, and stress. Res. Policy **40**(2), 276–286 (2011)
20. Fredrickson, J.W.: Effects of decision motive and organizational performance level on strategic decision processes. Acad. Manag. J. **28**(4), 821–843 (1985)
21. Armstrong, S.J., Hird, A.: Cognitive style and entrepreneurial drive of new and mature business owner-managers. J. Bus. Psychol. **24**(4), 419 (2009)
22. De Brentani, U., Reid, S.E.: The fuzzy front-end of discontinuous innovation: insights for research and management. J. Prod. Innov. Manag. **29**(1), 70–87 (2012)
23. Eling, K., Griffin, A., Langerak, F.: Using intuition in fuzzy front-end decision-making: a conceptual framework. J. Prod. Innov. Manag. **31**(5), 956–972 (2014). https://doi.org/10.1111/jpim.12136
24. Xue, L., Yen, C.C., Boucharenc, C., Choolani, M.: The design evolution of medical devices: moving from object to user. J. Des. Res. **7**(4), 411–438 (2008)
25. Phillips, P.L.: Creating the Perfect Design Brief: How to Manage Design for Strategic Advantage, 2nd edn. Allworth Press, New York (2012)
26. Keller, R.T.: Cross-functional project groups in research and new product development: diversity, communications, job stress, and outcomes. Acad. Manag. J. **44**(3), 547–555 (2001)
27. Gilley, A., Dixon, P., Gilley, J.W.: Characteristics of leadership effectiveness: implementing change and driving innovation in organizations. Hum. Resour. Dev. Q. **19**(2), 153–169 (2008)
28. Hoegl, M., Gemuenden, H.G.: Teamwork quality and the success of innovative projects: a theoretical concept and empirical evidence. Organ. Sci. **12**(4), 435–449 (2001)
29. Haug, A., Stentoft Arlbjørn, J.: Barriers to master data quality. J. Enterp. Inf. Manag. **24**(3), 288–303 (2011)

Comparison of Usability and Immersion Between Touch-Based and Mouse-Based Interaction: A Study of Online Exhibitions

Qijuan Yu[✉], Xinmiao Nie[✉], Haining Wang, and Zilong Li

Hunan University, Changsha 414000, China
cooyqi@foxmail.com, imnxm@foxmail.com

Abstract. Equipment in the next few years. As large-screen personal devices to view virtual exhibitions, tablet computer and computers have two interactive modes of touch and mouse. This study aims to investigate whether mouse and touch affect users' usability and immersion experience. During the process, the typical interactive actions of viewing online exhibitions under the two methods of tablet pc touch and computer mouse were extracted, and 2 typical tasks were set up. The operation count and operation time were recorded, and then the usability and immersion scores were obtained by subjective scale. Finally, a brief experience interview was conducted to investigate the experience differences of viewing virtual exhibitions under different interactive modes. The results showed that the usability score and immersion score of using tablet pc touch were better than using computer mouse, and the operation time was more for the table pc than for computer mouse. The results of this research can be used as a reference for the interactive design of the online virtual exhibition on tablet pc and computer.

Keywords: Online exhibition · Immersion · Usability · Interaction mode

1 Introduction

1.1 Background

With the development of 3D reconstruction technology, the real scene is reconstructed in the digital world, and online exhibition brings people innovative experience. Because of the epidemic, online exhibitions have become a way for the public to communicate with museums since 85,000 museums closed around the world in 2020. For viewing virtual exhibitions, VR display equipment is undoubtedly the best display carrier at present. However, due to the limitation of application scenarios and high price, VR equipment is not widely owned by people. In the next few years, the experience of such scenes will still be dominated by computers, mobile phones and tablet pcs for most users. Therefore, optimizing the experience of online exhibitions on such devices is still a matter of concern.

Tablet pcs and computers, as large-screen personal devices, have two typical interaction methods of touch and mouse, which have an important impact on users' experience of viewing online exhibitions. Previous studies have been conducted to compare different types of scenes and confirmed the difference of usability between mouse and touch [1]. [2] found that the touch screen performed as equally well as the mouse when tested with a web map. [3] found evidence that touch-based input was better than mouse-based input in a tablet pc interaction context and in terms of throughput and movement time [3]. However, in contrast, [1] showed that the mouse-based interaction was faster, caused fewer errors and was preferred by the participants, they had two abstract type tasks and one contextualized task [1]. Also, [4] proposed that users' perception of digital content may differ based on the device they use. For example, using a touch interface results in higher engagement with games and education content [4]. These studies demonstrate that different interactions lead to different user experience of online content [5]. However, little research has examined how the touch devices differ from mouse devices on the sense of immersion when viewing online exhibition. Therefore, this study aims to investigate the experience differences of viewing online exhibitions using the two interaction methods.

1.2 User Behavior in Online Exhibition

Panoramic online exhibition provides users with the best sense of scene restoration. Its advantage is that it can restore the real scene, nonetheless, it has the shortcomings of single content and difficult to focus on the viewpoint [6, 7]. The audience need to actively explore in the online exhibition. Referring to the research of [8], the audience's viewing behavior of viewing exhibitions can be divided into dynamic and static categories according to the length of stay. In the panoramic online exhibition, users can stand and click to view the details of the three-dimensional model of the exhibits, and can walk and browse freely in the exhibition (Table 1). Under the two interaction modes, mouse and touch correspond to the same operation purpose in different interactive methods [9, 10]. In mouse mode, click the left mouse button to move, drag the right mouse button to switch the 2D viewing angle, drag the left mouse button to switch the 3D viewing angle, and use the mouse wheel to zoom the screen. In touch mode, tap with one finger to move, drag with two fingers to convert the 2D perspective, drag with one finger to convert the 3D perspective, and pinch with two fingers to zoom the screen. [9, 10] (Table 2).

Table 1. User behaviors in exhibition

User Behaviors in Exhibition	Example
ᴜᴨ Dynamic behavior	Look around Go straight Turn
◉ Static behavior	Look at an exhibit

Table 2. Interactive actions in online exhibition

Heading level	Mouse	Touch	Interactive action
Move Position or switch interface			Click
Transform 3D perspective			Drag
Transform 2D perspective			Drag
Zoom the model or screen			Zoom

1.3 Immersion of Online Exhibition

Online exhibition restores the real scene, which is like online 3D games. It has multiple interactive user interfaces and allows users to move freely in virtual scenes. Therefore, like the experience in the game scene, usability [7] and immersion [11] are important for users viewing virtual exhibitions. The immersion measurement of online exhibition refers to game scene and virtual space [11, 12], which includes four dimensions: spatial immersion (The correlation between users and virtual scenes), [12] focused attention (the degree of ignoring the external world) [4], scene realism (the similarity between the virtual scene and the real scene), and continuing intention (being attracted by the exhibition and hoping to continue to experience such content) [13, 14]. In this study, users ' immersion in the exhibition is defined as feeling that they exist in virtual space, that attention is fully attracted, that experience is consistent with the real scene, and want to continue experiencing the exhibition.

2 Research Purpose

To explore the user experience of online exhibitions in different interactive modes, this study will measure the differences in usability and immersion between the two interactive modes. The study first extracts the typical interactive actions of subjects viewing virtual exhibitions: click, drag, and zoom, and designs experimental tasks based on static and dynamic behaviors. Since the user' s subjective experience is often associated with its operation level [1], the operation data of the participants are also recorded. The operation time is the time for the participants to complete the task. The operation count on the computer side is the number of mouse clicks and rollers. The operation count on the tablet pc side is the number of single finger and double finger operations. In this study, different devices are used for touch screen display and mouse display as independent variables, the operation count and operation time are set as objective dependent variables, and the usability score and immersion score are set as subjective dependent variables.

Based on previous studies, The hypothesis and expectations are as follows:

Hypothesis 1: The usability of using tablet pc touch is better than that of using computer mouse.

Hypothesis 2: The immersion of using tablet pc touch is better than that of using computer mouse.

3   Method

3.1   Participants

18 college students were recruited from Hunan University in China. The participants included 9 males and 9 females (Mean age = 24.11 years). All participants were right-hand dominant and had no hand disease, pain, or touch impairment. They had at least four years of experience of using a computer or tablet pc, and they have experience in using mobile phones to view online exhibitions. Among them, the data of 2 participants were excluded, and 16 valid data were retained.

3.2   Experiment Design

In this study, touch and mouse were used as independent variables, the operation count and duration of operations were used as objective dependent variables, usability score and immersion score were used as subjective dependent variables. Participants were asked to complete two experimental tasks using two devices. Task 1: Go forward to see the exhibition (participants need to go straight along the designated route, and scan one exhibits on the left, and click to check one of the exhibits carefully); Task 2: Turn around to view the exhibition (participants need to turn around in the scene and view the exhibits on the right). Finally, participants were asked to fill out usability and immersion questionnaires and make a brief subjective statement.

3.3   Materials

This experiment used "Nepal 3D Statue Art Exhibition" [15] (Fig. 1) as the experimental scene. The exhibition was launched in 2021. It is a typical panoramic 3D online exhibition, which can be adapted to both computer and mobile terminals. In order to reduce the difference caused by the display screen quality, the mouse-based device used in the experiment is a 13.3-in. MacBook pro, and the touch-based device is an 11-inch iPad pro.

Fig. 1. The experiment scene: Nepal 3D statue art exhibition [15].

3.4 Questionnaire

After the participants entered the laboratory, the experimenter asked them to read and sign the informed consent form and verbally reminded them about their rights. Firstly, the participant needs to be familiar with the online exhibition under the two interaction modes then inform the experimenter that they are ready to start up. The experiment consisted of two tasks which users had to complete with both the mouse and the touch screen. To reduce bias users were split into two groups. Group A completed tasks first with the mouse, then with the touch screen whilst group B completed tasks with the touch screen first then the mouse. The participants need to score system usability and immersion subjectively for each task (Tables 3 and 4), and after that they need to fill in personal information and preference for exhibition interest on the mobile phone. Finally, the experimenter conducted a brief experience interview with them. The experiment took about 25 min.

Table 3. Usability components and scale items.

Usability component	Measure items
Effectiveness	This system's capabilities meet my requirements
Satisfaction	Using this system is a frustrating experience
Overall	This system is easy to use
Efficiency	I have to spend too much time correcting things with this system

Table 4. Immersion components and scale items.

immersion component	Measure items
Spatial immersion	1. I feel like this is in a virtual space, not pictures 2. I feel I ' m roaming inside the exhibition, rather than operating it outside 3. I feel like I 'm in virtual space
Focused attention	1. When I was roaming the virtual world I 'm very concerned about what was happening around me 2. I still noticed the real environment 3. I was totally attracted to the virtual exhibition
Scene realism	1. It is same as the real exhibition 2. The experience in the virtual exhibition is consistent with that in the real environment for me

(continued)

Table 4. (*continued*)

immersion component	Measure items
Continuance intention	1. When interrupted, I feel disappointed that the experience was over 2. If I could, I would like to continue experience this kind of exhibition

Notes: All items on 7-point "strongly disagree/strongly agree" scale were measured

Fig. 2. Experiment process.

3.5 Procedure

After the participants entered the laboratory, the experimenter asked them to read and sign the informed consent form and verbally reminded them about their rights. Firstly, the participant needs to be familiar with the online exhibition under the two interaction modes then inform the experimenter that they are ready to start up. The experiment consisted of two tasks which users had to complete with both the mouse and the touch screen. To reduce bias users were split into two groups. Group A completed tasks first with the mouse, then with the touch screen whilst group B completed tasks with the touch screen first then the mouse. The participants need to score system usability and immersion subjectively for each task, and after that they need to fill in personal information and preference for exhibition interest on the mobile phone. Finally, the experimenter conducted a brief experience interview with them. The experiment took about 25 min (Fig. 2).

4   Results

4.1   Usability Score

Table 5 lists the mean (M) and standard deviation (SD) of usability scores for the two interaction methods. Two-factor repeated-measure ANOVAs were conducted on these

Table 5. Usability scores for the computer mouse and tablet pc.

Variable	Method	Task 1			Task 2		
		M	SD	p	M	SD	p
Usability	Computer	4.88	0.74	0.00**	4.19	1.42	0.01**
	Tablet pc	5.97	0.76		5.48	1.10	

**. Correlation is significant at the 0.01 level.
*. Correlation is significant at the 0.05 level.

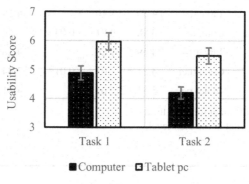

Fig. 3. Usability scores

usability scores. The main effect of the interaction method variable is statistically significant in two tasks (all p < 0.01). In task 1, The usability score is significantly higher for the tablet pc (M = 5.97, SD = 0 .76) than for the computer mouse (M = 4.88, SD = 0 .74). In task 2, the usability score is significantly higher for the tablet pc (M = 5.48, SD = 1.01) than for the computer mouse (M = 4.19, SD = 1.42) (see Fig. 3).

4.2 Immersion Score

Table 6 lists the M and standard SD of immersion scores for the two interaction methods, including the four dimensions of spatial immersion, focused attention, scene realism, continuance intention and total immersion. Two-factor repeated-measure ANOVAs were conducted on these immersion scores. The results show that the main effect of the interaction method variable is statistically significant only on the dimensions of continuance intention and total immersion in task 1(all p < 0 .05). In task 1, the continuance intention score is significantly higher for the tablet pc (M = 4.69, SD = 1.26) than for the computer mouse (M = 3.88, SD = 0.81), the total immersion score is significantly higher for the tablet pc (M = 5.31, SD = 1.01) than for the computer mouse (M = 4.31, SD = 1.01) (see Fig. 4).

Table 6. Immersion scores for the computer mouse and tablet pc.

Variable	Method	Task 1			Task 2		
		M	SD	p	M	SD	p
Spatial immersion	Computer	4.06	1.19	0.08	3.63	1.14	0.06
	Tablet pc	4.83	1.24		4.46	1.26	
Focused attention	Computer	4.08	1.12	0.30	3.98	1.08	0.11
	Tablet pc	4.54	1.33		4.65	1.18	
Scene realism	Computer	3.81	1.14	0.09	3.69	1.21	0.30
	Tablet pc	4.50	1.10		4.19	1.47	
Continuance intention	Computer	3.88	0.81	0.04*	3.63	1.02	0.10
	Tablet pc	4.69	1.26		4.28	1.15	
Total immersion	Computer	4.31	1.01	0.01**	3.94	1.53	0.08
	Tablet pc	5.31	1.01		4.81	1.22	

**. Correlation is significant at the 0.01 level.
*. Correlation is significant at the 0.05 level.

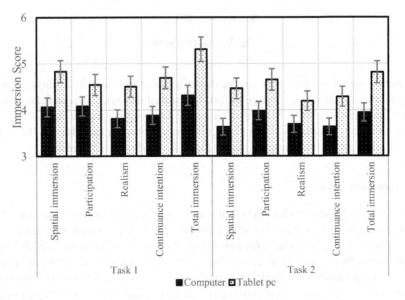

Fig. 4. Immersion scores

4.3 Gender Difference

Usability Difference

Table 7. Usability scores for the computer mouse and tablet pc for male and female

Variable	Gender	Method	Task 1			Task 2		
			M	*SD*	*p*	*M*	*SD*	*p*
Usability	Male	Computer	4.60	0.76	0.02*	4.31	1.89	0.13
		Tablet pc	5.75	0.92		5.63	1.37	
	Female	Computer	5.15	0.66	0.00**	4.06	0.86	0.01**
		Tablet pc	6.19	0.79		5.34	0.82	

**. Correlation is significant at the 0.01 level.
*. Correlation is significant at the 0.05 level.

Table 7 lists the M and SD of usability scores for male and female in the two interaction methods. Two-factor repeated-measure ANOVAs were conducted on these usability scores separately. In task 1, the main effect in the interaction method variable are statistically significant for usability score in male and female (all $p < 0.05$), the male usability score is significantly higher for the tablet pc (M = 5.75, SD = 0.92) than for the computer mouse (M = 4.60, SD = 0.76) and the female usability score of is significantly higher for the tablet pc (M = 6.19, SD = 0.79) than for the computer mouse (M = 5.15, SD = 0.66). In task 2, the main effect in the interaction method variable isn't statistically significant for male usability score ($p = 0.13$), but it's statistically significant for female usability score ($p < 0.01$), the female usability score is significantly higher for the tablet pc (M = 5.34, SD = 0.82) than for the computer mouse (M = 4.06, SD = 0.86).

Immersion Difference

Table 8. Immersion scores for the computer mouse and tablet pc for male and female.

Variable	Gender	Method	Task 1			Task 2		
			M	SD	p	M	SD	p
Spatial immersion	Male	Computer	3.67	1.30	0.40	3.29	1.35	0.36
		Tablet pc	4.25	1.41		3.92	1.33	
	Female	Computer	4.46	0.99	0.04*	3.96	0.84	0.04*
		Tablet pc	5.42	0.71		5.00	0.99	

(continued)

Table 8. (*continued*)

Variable	Gender	Method	Task 1			Task 2		
			M	SD	p	M	SD	p
Focused attention	Male	Computer	3.83	0.94	0.57	3.83	1.23	0.78
		Tablet pc	4.21	1.53		4.00	1.13	
	Female	Computer	4.33	1.28	0.38	4.13	0.96	0.02*
		Tablet pc	4.88	1.10		5.29	0.86	
Scene realism	Male	Computer	3.44	1.43	0.44	3.31	1.58	0.94
		Tablet pc	3.94	1.05		3.38	1.69	
	Female	Computer	4.19	0.65	0.04*	4.06	0.56	0.00**
		Tablet pc	5.06	0.86		5.00	0.53	
Continuance intention	Male	Computer	3.56	0.86	0.24	3.50	1.20	0.37
		Tablet pc	4.38	1.66		4.06	1.24	
	Female	Computer	4.19	0.65	0.03*	3.75	0.89	0.16
		Tablet pc	5.00	0.65		4.50	1.10	
Total immersion	Male	Computer	3.87	1.25	0.13	3.62	2.07	0.42
		Tablet pc	4.88	1.25		4.38	1.51	
	Female	Computer	4.75	0.46	0.00**	4.25	0.71	0.01**
		Tablet pc	5.75	0.46		5.25	0.71	

**. Correlation is significant at the 0.01 level.
*. Correlation is significant at the 0.05 level.

Table 8 lists the M and SD of immersion scores for male and female in the two interaction methods, including the four dimensions of spatial immersion, focused attention, scene realism, continuance intention and total immersion. In both task 1 and task 2, the main effect in the interaction methods variable isn't statistically significant for male immersion score (all $p > 0.05$). In task 1, the main effect in the interaction method variable is statistically significant on the dimensions of spatial immersion, scene realism, continuance intention and total immersion in female (all $p < 0.05$). In task 2, the main effect in the interaction method variable is statistically significant on the dimensions of spatial immersion, focused attention, scene realism and total immersion in female (all $p < 0.05$).

4.4 Operation Behavior

Table 9 lists the M and SD of operation count and operation time for the computer mouse and tablet pc. Two-factor repeated-measure ANOVAs were conducted on the operation count and operation time.

Table 9. Operation count and time for the computer mouse and tablet pc.

Variable	Method	Task 1			Task 2		
		M	SD	p	M	SD	p
Operation Count	Computer	35.12	13.83	0.32	17.06	6.13	0.13
	Tablet pc	40.25	15.04		21.62	10.00	
operation Time	Computer	57.75	25.23	0.50	26.53	12.15	0.01**
	Tablet pc	52.38	18.46		40.25	15.04	

**. Correlation is significant at the 0.01 level.
*. Correlation is significant at the 0.05 level.

Operation Count

In task 1, the operation count for the tablet pc (M = 40.25, SD = 15.04) is more than for the computer mouse (M = 35.12, SD = 13.83) (see Fig. 5). In task 2, the operation count for the tablet pc (M = 21.62, SD = 10.00) is more than for the computer mouse (M = 17.06, SD = 6.13). However, the main effect of the interaction method variable isn't statistically significant for operation count in both task 1 and task 2(all p > 0.05).

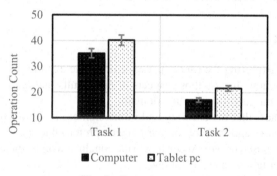

Fig. 5. Operation count

Operation Time

In task 1, the main effect of the interaction method variable isn't statistically significant for operation time (p = 0.50). In task 2, the main effect of the interaction method variable is statistically significant for operation time (p < 0.01). The operation time for the tablet pc (M = 40.25, SD = 15.04) is more than for the computer mouse (M = 26.53, SD = 12.15) (see Fig. 6).

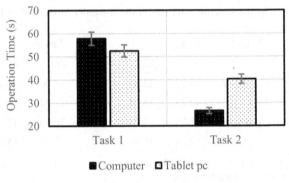

Fig. 6. Operation time

4.5 Subjective Preference

In addition to the measured values, we asked for participants' preferences. Of the 16 participants, 15 preferred tablet pc and only 1 preferred computer mouse. In addition, five participants said they were more accustomed to computer mouse; two participants thought that using mouse click and drag on the computer to switch the spatial perspective was not used to and would increase their fatigue.

5   Discussion

With our goal of exploring the user experience of online exhibitions in different interactive modes, we now discuss those aspects of our results that are most surprising/or most relevant for our target application domain.

The results show that the usability and immersion are better for the tablet pc than for computer mouse, and 94% of the participants prefer tablet pc. This validates two hypotheses we proposed before. According to the conclusion of the interview, the reasons participants prefer tablet pc are as follows:

1. The tablet pc is similar to the mobile phone in operation, so they are more familiar with the interaction method of touch;
2. Touch has a stronger sense of control than the mouse in dragging, and it is more natural and fluent;
3. The movement of eyes and hands during the viewing of the exhibition is more consistent, which makes the user's attention more concentrated;
4. When the tablet touch operation, the physical distance between people and the exhibition is closer, and a clearer viewing experience can be obtained.

These are consistent with the research findings of [2]. However, this conclusion is contrary to the research of [1]. The reasons for this may be improvements in touchscreen technology (the new iPad pro uses a higher-resolution retina screen, unlike previous capacitive screens), and the placement of the screen has a comfortable slope, while the touchscreen in Charlotte's research for vertical placement.

It is worth mentioning that 5 participants said that although they are more accustomed to computer operation, they rated the usability of computer mouse operation lower than tablet. Because they often play computer games and modeling, they are more accustomed to the operation of the mouse and keyboard. They noted that "on the computer side it requires manual clicking and dragging to change the perspective, while in the game I can change the perspective and position by simply moving the cursor."

In task 1, the immersion score was significantly higher for tablet pc than for computer mouse. In task 2, the main effect of interaction variable was not statistically significant for immersion score. This shows that the degree of immersion difference is related to the task setting, and the immersion difference of the task that requires careful viewing of exhibits is greater. One of the reasons is that all the participants have experience in computer modeling and are very familiar with the operation of viewing 3D models. When they associate the exhibits on the computer with the previous product models, the realism of the exhibits will be weaker.

6 Conclusion

This study explores the differences in usability and immersion between computer mouse and tablet pc for users viewing virtual exhibitions. Experiments had confirmed that the usability and immersion of using tablet pc to view virtual exhibition is better than computer mouse. Moreover, there were gender differences in the degree of immersion difference between the two interaction methods. In addition, we found the operation time was less for the tablet pc than for the computer mouse, and the immersion of viewing virtual exhibitions has scene differences and was affected by its own operating habits. The findings broaden the study of both touch and mouse interactions. In addition, the differences in spatial immersion experience of interactive methods in virtual three-dimensional space are explored, which has certain design guiding significance for the interactive design of online panoramic exhibitions on tablet pc and computer.

For design suggestions, the usability is worse for the tablet pc than for the computer mouse when clicking, and tablet touch usability is better when dragging. The space switching operation of two interaction methods needs to be optimized.

In the selection of participants, the participants in this study were all experienced users of 3D modeling software. We did not investigate the differences in the experience of viewing exhibitions for users without 3D manipulation and modeling experience. In the selection of influencing factors, this paper focused on comparing the differences in the experience of viewing exhibitions between the two interactive methods. The impact of task type and device size on immersion can be further studied.

References

1. Travis, C., Murano, P.: A comparative study of the usability of touch-based and mouse-based interaction. Int. J. Pervasive Comput. Commun. **10**, 115–134 (2014)
2. Wu, F.G., Lin, H., You, M.: Direct-touch vs. mouse input for navigation modes of the web map. Displays **32**(5), 261–267 (2011)

3. Sasangohar, F., MacKenzie, I.S., Scott, S.D.: Evaluation of mouse and touch input for a tabletop display using Fitts' reciprocal tapping task. In: Proceedings of the Human Factors and Ergonomics Society Annual Meeting, vol. 53, no. 12, pp. 839–843. Sage, Los Angeles (2009)
4. Chung, S., Kramer, T., Wong, E.M.: Do touch interface users feel more engaged? the impact of input device type on online shoppers' engagement, affect, and purchase decisions. Psychol. Mark. **35**(11), 795–806 (2018)
5. Jihua, Z., Xiaojian, C., Ming, T.: Click or slide ? research on the effect of page-turning actions on users' online immersion intensity. Fore. Econ. Manag. **42**(02), 59–70 (2020)
6. Widjono, R.A.: Analysis of user experience in virtual art exhibition during pandemic. In: International Conference of Innovation in Media and Visual Design (IMDES 2020), pp. 93–99. Atlantis Press (2020)
7. Tan, P., Ji, Y.: Research on interaction design of mobile panoramic virtual museum based on knowledge visualization. Pack. Eng. **2022**, 1–9 (2022)
8. Hu, Y., Li, P., Wang, Z.: Research on spectatorship of exhibition space based on three-dimensional cumulative visualization. South Arch. **2020**(01), 60–66 (2020)
9. Wu, J.: Usability Research of 2D and 3D Interactive Gestures. Zhejiang Sci-Tech University, Hangzhou (2016)
10. Chen, P.: Research and Practice of Human-Computer Interaction in Mouse. Hunan University, Changsha (2013)
11. Jennett, C., Cox, A.L., Cairns, P., et al.: Measuring and defining the experience of immersion in games. Int. J. Hum Comput Stud. **66**(9), 641–661 (2008)
12. Ryan, M.-L.: Narrative as Virtual Reality 2: Revisiting Immersion and Interactivity in Literature and Electronic Media. John Hopkins University Press, Baltimore (2015)
13. Chang, C.C.: Examining users' intention to continue using social network games: a flow experience perspective. Telematics Inform. **30**(4), 311–321 (2013)
14. Witmer, B.G., Singer, M.J.: Measuring presence in virtual environments: a presence questionnaire. Presence **7**(3), 225–240 (1998)
15. Nepal 3D Statue Art Exhibition. https://tinyurl.com/y9w5yf4k/2022, Accessed 11 Feb 2022

Identifying Key Factors Influencing Mobile Music App User Experience in China Using a Fuzzy DEMATEL Method

Meiyu Zhou[✉], Hanwen Du, Zhengyu Wang, Li Wang, Yibing Wu, Jinyao Zhang, Yajing Xu, and Lu Zhong

East China University of Science and Technology, Shanghai, China
398172541@qq.com

Abstract. The main purpose of this paper is to construct the evaluation index of the system and study the degree of influence of the main factors affecting the design of mobile music app from the perspective of user experience. By means of literature research and questionnaire survey, the index system of influencing factors of user experience was established, and the fuzzy DEMATEL model was established. This paper constructs an index system of influencing factors of mobile phone music app user experience, which includes five dimensions (reliability, usability, ease of use, interaction, security) and 19 influencing factors. The 10 key factors affecting the mobile music App user experience were identified, namely, music richness, personalized service, listening function, copyright information protection, interpersonal interaction, system performance, personal information protection, audio quality, interface design and payment protection. Finally, the index system of influencing factors of mobile music App user experience is constructed, and the importance of influencing factors of mobile music App user experience is analyzed.

Keywords: Fuzzy DEMATEL model · Mobile music app · User experience

1 Introduction

As we enter the second decade of the 21st century, smartphones are developing rapidly. With the help of smart apps, the primary way to listen to music is to switch from downloading to listening online. This shift has made it easier to access and distribute music, and mobile music listening is not limited by time or space. In the age of fragmented entertainment, online music is beloved and has entered everyone's daily life. As of February 2021, China had 657 million mobile network music subscribers, accounting for 66.6 percent of all mobile phone users [1]. In October 2020, our mobile network music active user week averaged 105.8 min, second only to gaming and web-video apps in mobile entertainment applications [2]. Access to online music services via various mobile music apps has become an important form of entertainment in people's daily lives. Since 2010, China's mobile music industry has entered a mature and stable period. As the largest digital music market in the world, there are now hundreds of mobile music

© The Author(s), under exclusive license to Springer Nature Switzerland AG 2022
M. M. Soares et al. (Eds.): HCII 2022, LNCS 13321, pp. 339–350, 2022.
https://doi.org/10.1007/978-3-031-05897-4_24

apps on every platform in China, and the online music service industry is becoming saturated. The number of monthly active users of mobile music app is stable against a backdrop of peaking overall internet traffic. In recent years, with the strong investment of capital and competition from many commercial forces, the pattern of music copyright has stabilized [3]. Therefore, as copyright and market size gradually stabilize, it is very important to improve the user experience, not only to improve user stickiness, but also to improve the quality of mobile music services, and to promote the healthy and sustainable development of mobile music app. The user experience has surpassed traditional factors such as resource rights, platforms and user groups as one of the key factors that distinguish mobile music app from fierce competition [4].

At present, the commercial development of mobile music app is quite mature. Most of the existing research on Music App has focused on the development of features such as song catalogs [5] and playback pages [6] in music player interface design, which in some ways measures the availability of mobile music Apps. Online music platforms have been systematically evaluated by scholars [7], However, there are few theoretical researches on user experience, and there is no systematic analysis of the key influencing factors of mobile phone music app user experience, mainly for single system such as music retrieval [8] and music recommendation [9].

Most related studies collect data by means of questionnaires and semi-structured interviews [10], which is subjective and may lack some important relevant factors, which leads to the one-sidedness of the evaluation system, which can not fully assess the importance of the factors. Based on the 5E model proposed by Quesenberry [11] and the cellular model proposed by Morville [12], this paper constructs an index system of influencing factors for mobile phone music App user experience, including five dimensions: reliability, availability, ease of use, interaction, security, and 22 influencing factors. Then we corrected the influencing factors to 19 through a questionnaire. Using the Decision-Making Trial and Evaluation Laboratory (DEMATEL) method, we introduced triangulated fuzzy numbers, built fuzzy-DEMATL models, and extended the single values of the comparison matrix to a fuzzy interval, giving decision makers an appropriate judgment space to identify key factors affecting the mobile music app user experience.

2 Construction of the Index System of Influencing Factors of Mobile Music App User Experience

In this study, the index system of influencing factors of mobile phone music app is constructed from 5 dimensions by summarizing and analyzing the related research of product user experience, referring to the 5E model proposed by Quesenberry and user experience honeycomb model proposed by Morville (Figs. 1 and 2).

Fig. 1. 5E model proposed by Whitney Quesenberry

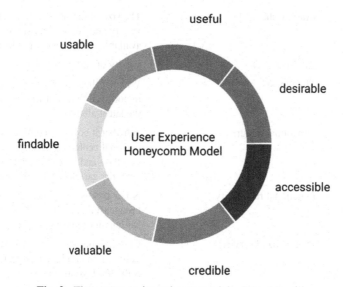

Fig. 2. The user experience honeycomb by Peter Morville

By means of literature analysis and questionnaire survey, an index system of influencing factors of mobile phone music App user experience is constructed. First, the study used literature analysis to search and summarize a literature review of the CNKI (China

National Knowledge Infrastructure) from 2000 to 2020. The 22 influential factors affecting the mobile music App user experience were selected using the terms Mobile Music, Mobile Music, Mobile App, User Experience, User Satisfaction, User Perception, User Willingness, Influencers, and User Evaluation.

Then, the 22 influencing factors were revised by means of a questionnaire. A total of 100 effective questionnaires were issued, of which 91, or 91%, of the respondents were between the ages of 15 and 50, with students and young and middle-aged workers (Table 1).

Table 1. Index system of influencing factors of mobile music app user experience.

Dimension	Influencing factors	Instructions
Reliability	Stability	Software has fewer flashes and a low error rate Vulnerability can be fixed in a timely manner and software crash rate is low
	Fluency	When using the software, it responds quickly, with no time lag
	System performance	Software compatibility is high Small software package with low memory usage
Usability	Music richness	The size of the software library, the variety and genre of music resources available, and the length of time covered
	Audio quality	Clarity of audio provided
	Timeliness	Whether the singer's new album is included in time and whether there is the latest album
	Functional integrity	Whether it covers recommendation, personal center, community, music purchase and other complete services to meet the various needs of users
	Functional rationality	No or less useless functions such as live broadcast and mall Rationality of charging price
Ease of use	Personalized service	Classify and push content based on your search and listening preferences Software layouts and wallpaper can be customised Personal centers have personalization, etc

(continued)

Table 1. (*continued*)

Dimension	Influencing factors	Instructions
	Convenience	Users can easily and quickly retrieve information, search for music they have heard before, easily view music information, collect and download music
	Song listening function	Software provides features such as setting up song lists, sound effects, loop modes, lyrics or MV displays to improve the listening experience
	advertisement	No malicious ads, no bundles and fewer ads in the software to reduce interference during listening
	Usage mode	Software offers different modes of use such as driving mode, night mode, small window mode
Interaction	Interface design	The beauty and comfort of software interface design, including icon and font design, content layout, and color scheme
	Interpersonal interaction	Software should support comments, likes and retweets of songs Support for user-to-user viewing and chat to create opportunities for like-minded users to meet and interact Have a user community and can retweet and comment on content within the community
	Feedback system	There should be sound and effective communication between users and customer service personnel, regular consultation with clients, timely processing of feedback from users
Security	Personal information protection	Individual registration information, listening records, song lists created, comments, purchase information, etc., are protected
	Payment protection	Payment security, diversity of payment channels, availability of after-sales service, etc
	Music copyright protection	Protection of original music by software. Protection of the intellectual property rights of resident musicians and users to upload original audio

3   Research Method

3.1   Fuzzy-DEMATEL Model

DEMATEL is a systematic analysis method that uses graph theory and matrix tools to screen for influencing factors in complex systems [13, 14]. It has evolved into a well-established methodological system, but its application still has limitations. It uses expert knowledge to determine the degree of impact between the two factors, typically using the Richter scale to get clear values, but in most cases, uncertainty in expert judgment makes it difficult to directly express accurate numbers due to the ambiguity of the technical terms. So, to get more accurate results, introducing fuzzy math to quantify terms goes some way to solving the uncertainty in language terms [15–20]. In view of the advantages of the fuzzy DEMATEL method, this study uses this method to determine the importance of influencing factors in the user experience evaluation system.

3.2   Establishment of the Model

Establishing Judgement Matrix. The influencing factors were $a_1, a_2, ..., a_n$. Based on the degree of influence between each of the two factors given by the experts, a judgment matrix A is established in which the element a_{ij} indicates the degree of influence of factor a_i on factor a_j. The degree of influence from weak to strong is divided into five levels: no influence, weak influence, certain influence, strong influence and strong influence, corresponding to 0, 1, 2, 3 and 4.

Establishing the Initial Direct Relationship Matrix. The initial direct relation matrix B is obtained by triangulating fuzzy number to deal with judgment matrix A. According to the relationship between expert semantic code and triangular fuzzy number, the element a_{ij} in judgment matrix A is transformed into (l_{ij}, m_{ij}, u_{ij}), as shown in Table 2. l_{ij} means the least likely value of factor a_i's effect on factor a_j, m_{ij} means the most likely value of factor a_i's effect on factor a_j, and u_{ij} means the most likely value of factor a_i's effect on factor a_j.

Table 2. Relationship between expert semantic code and triangulated fuzzy numbers.

Expert semantic code	Triangulated fuzzy numbers
No impact	(0, 0, 0.25)
Weak impact	(0, 0.25, 0.5)
Certain impact	(0.25, 0.5, 0.75)
Strong impact	(0.5, 0.75, 1)
Extremely influential	(0.75, 1, 1)

Constructing Direct Relation Matrix. Triangle fuzzy number obtained from expert semantic evaluation cannot be directly used for data analysis and processing, so it is necessary to defuzzy the triangulation fuzzy number to obtain accurate value. In this study, the CFCS method was used to clarify matrix B, and the direct relation matrix Z was obtained. Assuming that a total of K experts are involved in the assessment of the degree of impact between each factor, the triangular fuzzy number corresponding to the degree of impact of factor a_i on factor a_j assessed by expert P is shown below

$$z_{ij}^P = \left(l_{ij}^P, m_{ij}^P, u_{ij}^P\right), (P = 1, 2, \ldots, K) \tag{1}$$

Specification triangle fuzzy number:

$$xl_{ij}^P = \frac{l_{ij}^P - minl_{ij}^P}{maxu_{ij}^P - minl_{ij}^P}$$

$$xm_{ij}^P = \frac{m_{ij}^P - minm_{ij}^P}{maxu_{ij}^P - minl_{ij}^P} \tag{2}$$

$$xu_{ij}^P = \frac{u_{ij}^P - minu_{ij}^P}{maxu_{ij}^P - minl_{ij}^P}$$

Standardizing the left and right values of triangular blurs:

$$xll_{ij}^P = \frac{xm_{ij}^P}{1 + xm_{ij}^P - xl_{ij}^P} \tag{3}$$

$$xul_{ij}^P = \frac{xu_{ij}^P}{1 + xu_{ij}^P - xm_{ij}^P} \tag{4}$$

Calculate the clear value of each expert evaluation after the fuzzy value is deblurred:

$$z_{ij}^P = minl_{ij}^K + [\frac{xll_{ij}^P\left(1 - xll_{ij}^P\right) + \left(xul_{ij}^P\right)^2}{1 - xll_{ij}^P + xul_{ij}^P}](maxu_{ij}^P - minl_{ij}^P) \tag{5}$$

Calculate the average and get the direct relation matrix Z:

$$z_{ij} = \frac{1}{K}(z_{ij}^1 + z_{ij}^2 + \cdots + z_{ij}^K) \tag{6}$$

$$Z = (z_{ij})_{n*n} = \begin{bmatrix} 0 & z_{12} & \ldots & z_{1n} \\ z_{21} & 0 & \ldots & z_{2n} \\ \vdots & \vdots & \ddots & \vdots \\ z_{n1} & z_{n2} & \ldots & 0 \end{bmatrix} \tag{7}$$

Establishing Normalized Direct Relation Matrix. The normalized direct relation-ship matrix D is obtained by using the matrix Z as a molecule and the maximum sum of rows and columns as denominator.

$$D' = max \sum_{j=1}^{n} z_{ij}, (1 \leq i \leq n)$$
$$D'' = max \sum_{i=1}^{n} z_{ij}, (1 \leq j \leq n) \tag{8}$$
$$D = \frac{Z}{max(D',D'')}$$

Establishing Total Relation Matrix. The normalized direct relation matrix is a binary relation matrix, which can only describe the direct influence between factors. In complex systems, the multivariate influence occurs simultaneously, so the total relation matrix T needs to be calculated.

$$T = D^1 + D^2 + D^3 + \cdots + D^n \tag{9}$$

when n nears infinity,

$$T = D(I - D^{-1}) \tag{10}$$

I is the unit matrix

Calculating the Influence Degree and Affected Degree of Each Factor. Based on the Total Relationship Matrix T, the influence degree R_i and affected degree C_i were calculated. R_i being the sum of the i row n elements of matrix T and C_i being the sum of the i row n elements of matrix T.

$$R_i = \sum_{j=1}^{n} t_{ij}$$

$$C_i = \sum_{i=1}^{n} t_{ij} \tag{11}$$

Calculating the Centrality and Cause Degree of Each Factor. The center degree E_i and cause degree F_i were calculated as:

$$E_i = R_i + C_i$$

$$F_i = R_i - C_i \tag{12}$$

The larger the center degree E_i value, the more important the factor is in the system, which is a cause factor if the cause degree F_i is > 0, and a result factor if the cause degree F_i is < 0.

Constructing the Causal Diagram. The causal diagram is constructed by using the center degree of each factor as horizontal coordinate and the cause degree of each factor as vertical coordinate. From the vertical coordinates, the point greater than 0 is the cause factor, and the point smaller than 0 is the result factor. From the horizontal coordinates, from left to right, the influencing factor becomes more and more important in the system. Identify the key elements of the system according to their degree of centrality.

4   Results and Discussion

Ten professional music reviewers and senior Music App users were invited to rate the impact of each factor on a scale of five (0, 1, 2, 3, 4). Matlab was used to calculate the degree of center and cause of each factor, with the results shown in Table 3.

Table 3 .

Serial number	Influencing factors	中心度	原因度
1	Stability	2.79084	0.24363
2	Fluency	2.79502	0.04963
3	System performance	2.87865	0.82849
4	Music richness	3.12715	1.33597
5	Audio quality	2.84583	−0.92001
6	Timeliness	2.77321	−1.47024
7	Functional integrity	2.78690	−0.34502
8	Functional rationality	2.77483	0.07901
9	Personalized service	3.06725	1.20635
10	Convenience	2.77672	0.51136
11	Song listening function	3.01145	−0.71602
12	Advertisement	2.76869	−0.14741
13	Usage mode	2.76685	−0.13839
14	Interface design	2.82347	0.21093
15	Interpersonal interaction	2.93732	−0.64981
16	Feedback system	2.76754	−0.37965
17	Personal information protection	2.85691	−0.42235
18	Payment protection	2.80139	−0.22156
19	Music copyright protection	2.98434	1.08732

Based on the data in Table 3, map the causal factors, as shown in Fig. 3.

From Fig. 3, 19 factors are ranked from large to small by center degree: music richness, personalized service, song listening function, music copyright protection, interpersonal interaction, system performance, personal information protection, audio quality, interface design, payment protection, fluency, stability, functional integrity, convenience, timeliness, functional rationality, advertising, feedback system, usage mode.

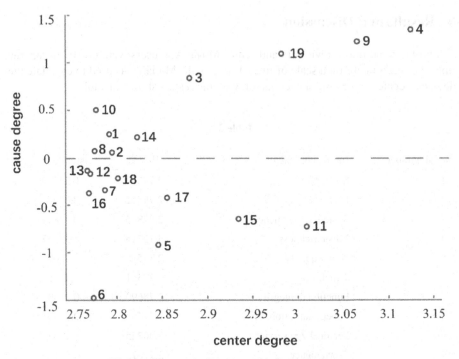

Fig. 3. Cause-and-effect map of influencing factors

Of the 19 influencing factors, 9 were cause factors (cause > 0), 10 were result factors (cause < 0), the top 5 cause factors were no. 4 (music richness), no. 9 (personalized services), no, 19 (music copyrighted information), no. 3 (system performance), no. 10 (convenience); the lowest 5 were no. 6 (timeliness), no. 5 (audio quality), no. 11 (song listening function), no. 15 (interpersonal interaction), no. 17 (personal information protection).

Centrality was the basis for determining the importance of the influencing factors, with the top 10 influencing factors being no. 4 (music richness), no. 9 (personalized services), no. 11 (song listening function), no. 19 (music copyright protection), no. 15 (interpersonal interaction), no. 3 (system performance), no. 17 (personal information protection), no. 5 (audio quality), no. 14 (interface design), and no. 18 (payment protection), suggesting that these factors were more important than others.

Based on the above findings, this paper makes three recommendations:

Increase Professionalism and Quality of Music. Music richness and audio quality are among the most important key factors. Music platforms need to improve their professionalism, expand their repertoire and improve audio quality, as well as do a good job of system-optimizing App.

Provide Personalized Services With a Focus on Interpersonal Communication.
To highlight their own design style, optimize the interface UI, focus on listening to
the design of common functions, to provide personalized services to customers. In addition, we should pay attention to the construction of the music community, which will
effectively improve user stickiness and improve user retention.

Protection of User Privacy With Emphasis On Information Security. As an online
service platform, paying attention to protecting user privacy is an important guarantee
to build user trust. As well as focusing on the performance of the system, we should
also ensure the security of users' personal information. When analyzing user behavior,
be moderate and make sure you don't "cross the line" to build bridges of trust between
users and platforms.

5   Conclusion

From the perspective of user experience, this paper constructs the index system of influencing factors of mobile phone music APP user experience by means of literature analysis
and questionnaire survey. On this basis, by introducing triangle fuzzy number and establishing fuzzy DEMATEL model, we can effectively solve the defect of expert subjective
judgment bias in traditional DEMATEL method, which is difficult to express directly
by exact number, and extend the application range of DEMATEL model.

Based on the results of the fuzzy-DEMATEL model, the analysis concludes with the
identification of 10 key factors affecting the mobile phone music App user experience—
music richness, personalized service, song listening function, music copyright protection, interpersonal interaction, system performance, personal information protection,
audio quality, interface design, and payment protection.

This study enriches the theory and practice of mobile music field to a certain extent,
provides a new research angle for mobile music field, and puts forward suggestions to
improve mobile music App user experience, and provides reference for mobile music
App developers.

This study was not able to analyze the actual case. In future research, we can select
QQ Music, NetEase Cloud Music, Cool Me Music, Cool Dog Music and other mobile
music APPs to analyze and compare to better improve the mobile music APP user
experience.

References

1. China Internet Network Information Center: The 47th Statistical Report on Internet Development in China. China Internet Network Information Center, Beijing (2021)
2. Fastdata: 2020 China Online Music Industry Report. Fastdata, Tianjin (2020)
3. iiMedia Research: iiMedia Report l 2019 Chinese Music Mobile Application Market Research
   Report. iiMedia Research, Hongkong (2019)
4. Zhao, Y., Xue, X.: Conceptualizing perceived affordances in user experience design for mobile
   music applications: a content analysis of version data. Libr. Tribune **39**(5), 67–78 (2019)

5. Xue, X., Zhao, Y.: Exploring user mental models of online music classification system: case study of college students. Data Anal. Knowl. Disc. **3**(2), 1–12 (2019)

6. Tan, J., Huang, F.: Exploring user mental models of online music classification system: case study of college students. Comput. Eng. Softw. **11**, 42–44 (2014)

7. Urbano, J., Schedl, M., Serra, X.: Evaluation in music information retrieval. J. Intell. Inf. Syst. **41**(3), 345–369 (2013). https://doi.org/10.1007/s10844-013-0249-4

8. Hu, X.: Evaluating mobile music services in china: an exploration in user experience. J. Inf. Sci. **45**, 16–28 (2018)

9. Cremonesi, P., Garzotto, F., Negro, S., Papadopoulos, A.V., Turrin, R.: Looking for "Good" recommendations: a comparative evaluation of recommender systems. In: Campos, P., Graham, N., Jorge, J., Nunes, N., Palanque, P., Winckler, M. (eds.) INTERACT 2011. LNCS, vol. 6948, pp. 152–168. Springer, Heidelberg (2011). https://doi.org/10.1007/978-3-642-23765-2_11

10. Xue, X., Zhao, Y.: Research on user experience evaluation of mobile music app based on the theory of perceived affordances. Doc. Inf. Knowl. **4**(6), 88–100+156(2020)

11. Quesenbery, W.: Balancing the 5Es: usability. Cutter IT J. **17**, 4–11 (2004)

12. User experience design. http://semanticstudios.com/user_experience_design/, Accessed 20 July 2021

13. Bavafa, A., Mahdiyar, A., Marsono, A.K.: Identifying and assessing the critical factors for effective implementation of safety programs in construction projects. Saf. Sci. **106**, 47–56 (2018)

14. Mahdiyar, A., Tabatabaee, S., Abdullah, A., Marto, A.: Identifying and assessing the critical criteria affecting decision-making for green roof type selection. Sustain. Cities Soc. **39**, 772–783 (2018)

15. Zhou, Q., Huang, W., Zhang, Y.: Identifying critical success factors in emergency management using a fuzzy DEMATEL method. Saf. Sci. **49**(2), 243–252 (2011)

16. Wu, W.W., Lee, Y.T.: Developing global managers' competencies using the fuzzy DEMATEL method. Expert Syst. Appl. **32**(2), 499–507 (2007)

17. Li, Y., Hu, Y., Zhang, X., Deng, Y., Mahadevan, M.: An evidential DEMATEL method to identify critical success factors in emergency management. Appl. Soft Comput. **22**, 504–510 (2014)

18. Sangaiah, A., Subramaniam, P., Zheng, X.: A combined Fuzzy DEMATEL and fuzzy TOPSIS approach for evaluating GSD project outcome factors. Neural Comput. Appl. **26**(2), 1025–1040 (2015)

19. Jafari, H., Malinowski, M.T., Ebadi, M.J.: Fuzzy stochastic differential equations driven by fractional Brownian motion. Adv. Diff. Equ. **2021**(1), 1–17 (2021). https://doi.org/10.1186/s13662-020-03181-z

20. Soner, O.: Application of fuzzy DEMATEL method for analysing of accidents in enclosed spaces onboard ships. Ocean Eng. **220**, 108507 (2021)

Usability, Acceptance, and User Experience Assessment

Augmented Reality Books: A User Experience Evaluation

Joana Casteleiro-Pitrez[(⊠)] [ID]

Universidade da Beira Interior, LabCom-Comunicação e Artes, Covilhã, Portugal
`joana.casteleiro.ferreira@ubi.pt`

Abstract. The rise of information society and the profound mediatization phenomenon led to a book use decrease. On the other hand, the attempt to promote book use and widen the capacities of the traditional book led to the application of computational resources, one of these resources is Augmented Reality (AR).

This study is about AR published Books and their User Experience (UX). We want to know if publishing AR books shows sufficient UX. We chose three AR books published in Portugal and applied a quantitative empirical study to evaluate their UX and answer this research question. Sixty users read the AR books and then answered the User Experience Questionnaire (UEQ) used as the research instrument of this study. We also compare the results with a benchmark. The results show a positive evaluation in almost all the means of the scales of the three AR books. Only in one book do we find a neutral evaluation in the scales of Stimulation and Novelty. Regarding the benchmark, the scales Attractiveness, Novelty and Stimulation achieved Excellent/Good category levels. On the other hand, the pragmatic quality aspects like Perspicuity, Dependably, and Efficiency revels a below "Good category" level, emphasizing the urgent need to improve the UX of AR books.

Keywords: Augmented reality books · User experience · User experience questionnaire

1 Introduction

The publishing market has been facing a sector crisis for some years now. Faced with the emergence of more attractive forms of leisure and learning arising from technological media coverage, the use of books decreased. This trend is particularly noticeable in younger generations. According to the results of the project "What our children read" [1], reading appears as the fifth leisure time activity with 26% of references. Multimedia uses got fourth place with 64%. Trying to remedy the situation, several formats of digital works, such as e-books, app-books, and AR books, have been created and exploited. All these products use computational resources to promote reading for the alpha generation.

The publishing sector has also encouraged these new editorial experiences by instituting prizes for digital books, such as the Bologna Ragazzi Digital Award promoted by the Bologna Children's Book Fair or the UKLA Digital Book Award, among others. Given this scenario, AR brings new possibilities to the publishing market, allowing, on

M. M. Soares et al. (Eds.): HCII 2022, LNCS 13321, pp. 353–368, 2022.
https://doi.org/10.1007/978-3-031-05897-4_25

the one hand, to maintain the traditional book format and, on the other hand, enabling the superposition of digital interactive layers over the book. Nevertheless, is this enough to increase book use? Do the users have a good experience using this product? The objective of this study is precisely to understand the UX in AR books.

The UX in AR books is often neglected due to the lack of integration between the editorial team and the AR content team (frequently contracted in an outsourcing mode). Also, the ease of developing an application using AR technology, especially by non-professional developers/designers, results in inadequate/low UX applications, which affects the overall quality of the developed applications [2]. Additionally, different practitioners have also pointed out that the research community lacks an understanding of how well AR applications have been accepted by the end-users, what kind of UX they evoke, and what the users perceive as the strengths and weaknesses of AR applications overall [3]. Thus, it is no longer sufficient to offer products focused only on novelty or functionality. Instead, users expect to learn how to use the system without much effort, solve their tasks fast and efficiently, and control the system at each point. In addition to these pragmatic, goal-oriented interaction qualities, it is also relevant that the product catches the user's attention and interest and that using the product is exciting. Consequently, hedonic, not directly goal-oriented interaction qualities have to be considered to create a successful product, system, or service [4, 5].

In the face of the situations described above, it is essential to ask, do publishing AR books shows sufficient UX? This is the research question that supports this study. To answer this question and achieve the purposed objective: a) we carried out a literature review in the domains of AR books and UX; b) we applied a quantitative methodology. We chose three of the sixteen AR books published in Portugal and evaluated their UX for the empirical work. The research instrument used was the Portuguese Version of the UEQ [6] because the main goal of the UEQ is to allow a fast and immediate measurement of UX. The UEQ also considers aspects of pragmatic and hedonic quality and results from a careful construction process [4]. To interpret scale results from the UEQ we used the UEQ Analysis Data Tool to analyze each scale item and compare it with a benchmark. Thus, the question of whether an AR book UX is sufficient can be answered by comparing its results to a larger sample of other used products, a benchmark data set. If the AR book scores high compared to the products in the benchmark, this can indicate that users will generally find this book UX satisfactory [7]. We used a sample of 60 users (20 for each book) to provide a stable measurement [8].

2 Literature Review

The vast majority of research in the fields of the augmented book is technological [9–13] or educational [14–18]. The study of UX in AR focuses on systematic literature reviews. [19–21], on mobile AR systems [22], in proposing frameworks [23] and models [24] to improve the end-user experience, and proposals for the improvement of the theoretical foundations [25]. The specific UX study in AR books focuses on understanding users' feedback [26, 28] and revealing issues that can improve AR books [20, 27, 29, 31].

Regarding the technological aspect, several studies present prototypes of AR books. One of the first studies related to the AR book is the study of Rekimoto [9], which in

1998 focuses on developing 2D matrix markers, the superposition of virtual contents, and their application on various products, one of which is a book. Although Rekimoto already had the underlying idea that augmented reality could be applied to editorial products, Billinghurst, Kato, and Poupyrev [10] present the first prototype of an AR book – the Magic Book.

Even today, the prototyping of augmented books motivates researchers to propose new approaches, such as creating multiple levels of interaction and the possibility of individual or shared reading [11], integration of different types of content such as videos, animations, sounds, and various interfaces, such as gesture-based interfaces [12] or the exploration of other kinds of reading like the syntopical reading experience [13].

Concerning the educational nature, the vast majority of studies aim to assess the learning impact of an AR book or AR textbook [14–17]. For example, a work [18] about students" beliefs of AR books in teaching reinforced that motivation is a possible advantage over traditional books.

Regarding UX studies, the presented systematic reviews focus on AR applications, not specifically AR books. The work of Swan and Gabbard [19] represents one of the first systematic reviews related to usability/user experience in AR applications in general. The results indicated that three lines caught researcher's interest:

1. Those that study low-level tasks to understand how human perception and cognition operate in AR contexts.
2. Those that examine user task performance within specific AR applications to understand how AR technology could impact underlying tasks.
3. Those that examine user interaction and communication between collaborating users.

Another systematic review [20] concludes that until 2014 there was an increase in the number of usability studies performed in AR research and a shift towards more studies on handheld displays. However, most of these studies are formal user studies, with little field testing and almost no heuristic evaluations. The most popular experimental task involves filling out questionnaires, which lead to subjective ratings being the most widely used dependent measure. This study suggests increased research opportunities in collaboration, field studies, and a more comprehensive range of evaluation methods. The study of Law and Heinz [21] on usability and UX in AR applications concludes that:

1. There is insufficient grounding in usability/UX.
2. Lack of innovative AR-specific usability/UX evaluation methods and the continuing reliance on questionnaires may hamper the advances of AR educational applications.

Many studies try to understand UX with mobile AR services [22]. For example, Olsson, Lagerstam, Ka¨rkka¨inen, and Vainio-Mattila's [22] study concluded that UX of mobile AR services is expected to be multifaceted and affected by various components of the underlying technology. The participants directed a set of expectations towards such services, ranging from proactivity, relevance, and the context sensitivity to social, surprising, immersive, and inspiring elements. Some works [23] proposed frameworks to enhance the UX of mobile AR, others [24] recommended a UX model that can be implemented to provide an engaging and seamless mobile AR experience for end-users. Another study [25] advocated for theoretical foundations of the UX in Augmented and Mixed Reality and proposed several directions for more scientific research in this regard. These directions involve:

1. A revisiting generic UX theory.
2. Revisiting the theoretical foundations for AR.
3. Structuring design knowledge for the UX of content, devices, interactions, applications, and contexts of use for AR/MR.
4. Practical user studies and controlled experiments for applying UX design knowledge to AR/MR and evaluating users' experience beyond aspects of usability or acceptability of AR/MR technology.
5. Connecting to the XR Access initiative for making VR, AR, and MR more accessible.

In the specific domain of AR books and UX, the first works are limited to collecting the user's opinions, through interviews or observations. Only user feedback is measured in the Grasset, Dünser, and Billinghurst study [26]. The conclusion is that people like to discover the system and interact with the various features. They were particularly amazed by the visual effects and the animations. The Dünser and Hornecker [27] work on AR books supporting reading and working through predefined storybooks reveals that the choice of stories and integrated interactive sequences is essential. Navigation turned out to be an essential issue when combining paper and on-screen elements, in particular if these are not integrated into one visual area and deploy tangible and desktop-based input devices. Gázcon and Castro [28] introduced the AR Book System, an interactive and collaborative application for traditional books augmentation. To validate the proposed system, they designed and conducted an experimental study and obtained very positive feedback from participants confirming the usefulness of the ARBS. Cao and Hou [29] studied AR picture books for children aged 5 to 8. They designed a usability test for their prototype. The results indicated the feasibility of AR books and figured out some issues in the interaction processes. These issues are the weak guidance in the interactive operation, the incomplete essential information in the interface, and children's preference for visible interaction and touch operations. Children are also more sensitive to large objects. Polyzou, Botsoglou, Zygouris, and Stamoulis [30] presented an empirical study of AR-published books for preschool children. The conclusion indicated that AR books are not intuitive for preschool children. These children's motor skills are not yet ready to use the fine touch screen movements needed to handle an AR object, and AR books turned out to be a fun and exciting way to capture preschool children's attention. Children perceived AR books as an excellent way to have fun. Even though the AR book appeared to have a better chance of keeping children's attention for longer, this was not practicable due to the highly delicate screen manipulation limitations imposed. Another study [31] reported a user test with 136 children examining the impact of content length and presentation in a digitally-augmented comic book. The results reveal that authors and designers need to balance physical and digital mediums while designing digital augmentation for comic books. In order to achieve the holistic experience and equal engagement with both mediums, the experience needs to be carefully designed by:

1. Avoiding or reducing duplication, especially when duplication means the reader gets no real benefit from engaging with both mediums.
2. Integrating augmented content only if it has high relevance to a particular frame in the comic book.
3. Using appropriate frequency and length of the augmented content to maintain the interest in both digital and physical medium.
4. Selecting the technology carefully as it still presents an interaction barrier (e.g., the access method).

Our brief literature review shows that the first studies related to AR books and UX focused on hedonic qualities and captured the users' feedback. This feedback is usually positive where the motivation and the capacity of the AR book to capture attention are highlighted. More recent studies focused mostly on pragmatic qualities and some guidelines to improve AR books result from the findings. Still, there is a need for studies that join hedonic and pragmatic qualities.

3 Materials and Methods

3.1 Quantitative Experimental Design

The objective of our study is to research whether three AR-published books have enough UX. Therefore, the research question driving this study is: RQ. Do publish AR books have sufficient UX? Furthermore, have a positive evaluation on Attractiveness, Perspicuity, Efficiency, Dependability, Stimulation, and Novelty? Moreover, fit in the category of good compared to the benchmark values?

We elaborated an experiment with three groups of users that read and tested the three selected books to answer the research question. The three groups responded to the UEQ.

3.2 Procedure

We assigned each one of the three books to a group of users. Then, between 8 to 11 November 2021, we ask users to go to a university laboratory where they read and experiment with the AR book assigned to them and, after the experience, respond to the online UEQ questionnaire. The UEQ was accessed easily with a link placed in University Beira Interior Moodle, and Google forms support it.

3.3 Participants

We recruited sixty participants (N = 60) voluntarily. The participants were undergraduate students of the 1st Cycle Degree in Multimedia Design, Art Department, University Beira Interior, Portugal. The 60 participants were randomly assigned to a group of 20 users. According to the UEQ handbook, there should be at least 20–30 respondents to get reliable results [8].

3.4 Data Collection

Data were collected through the Portuguese version of the UEQ questionnaire [6]. The UEQ enables the analysis of the entire UX beyond mere usability. The questionnaire considers the respondents' feelings, impressions, and attitudes and creates a format that supports the direct expression of these elements. The scales collect usability aspects (Efficiency, Perspicuity, and Dependability) and UX aspects (Stimulation, Novelty) and thus offer a comprehensive impression of the UX of product/system touchpoints [7]. The UEQ consists of 26 items distributed among six scales. The scales are the following: Attractiveness, Perspicuity, Efficiency, Dependability, Stimulation, and Novelty. The UEQ uses a 7-point Likert-type scale. The UEQ's items form a semantic differential; two contradictory terms represent every item. Terms are randomly ordered per item; half of the scale items begin with the positive term, and the other half begin with the negative one. UEQ uses a seven-stage scale to decrease the central tendency bias for the types of items. The items are scaled from -3 to $+3$. Accordingly, -3 denotes the most negative answer, 0 a neutral answer, and $+3$ the most positive answer [7]. The reliability and validity of the UEQ was investigated in several studies [4, 8].

3.5 Materials

1) Independent variables

The independent variables of this study were the three AR-published books. The chosen books are "Star Wars Galaxy Explorer Guide" (see Fig. 1) from Leya/D. Quixote, published in 2019. "Frozen II the Ice Kingdom: An Enchanted Adventure" (see Fig. 2) from Leya/D. Quixote, published in 2019 and "Toy Story 4 Woody the Adventure of Augmented Reality" (see Fig. 3) from Leya/D. Quixote, published in 2019.

Fig. 1. Star Wars Galaxy Explorer Guide, AR book.

The book Star Wars Galaxy Explorer Guide has a hybrid interface. The digital contents are 3D and 2D animations, sounds, videos, and text. The access mode is through an app, and the book is classified as juvenile literature.

Frozen II the Ice Kingdom: An Enchanted Adventure is a juvenile literature book with a hybrid interface. The digital contents are 3D animations and sounds, and an app accesses these contents.

Fig. 2. Frozen II the Ice Kingdom: an enchanted adventure, AR book.

Fig. 3. Toy story 4 woody the adventure of augmented reality, AR book.

Toy Story 4, Woody, the Adventure of Augmented Reality has a hybrid interface. The digital contents are 3D animations and sounds. The access mode is through an app and is classified as children's fiction book.

2) Dependent variables

The dependent variables used in this study were the six scales that consist of the UEQ:

a) Attractiveness reflects the overall impression of the product and shows whether users like the product.
b) Efficiency shows whether users can solve their tasks without unnecessary effort.
c) Perspicuity indicates whether it is easy to become familiar with the product or learn how to use it.
d) Dependability shows whether users can feel control over the interaction.
e) Stimulation shows whether it is exciting and motivating to use the product.
f) Novelty indicates whether the product is innovative and creative and whether the product catches the user's interest.

Attractiveness is a pure liability dimension. Efficiency, Perspicuity, and Dependability are aspects of pragmatic quality, while Stimulation and Novelty are aspects of hedonic quality [4].

3.6 Data Analysis

The quantitative data are obtained from a UEQ. The data was then processed to investigate the UX level of the chosen AR Books. The system's UX is measured in six scales: Attractiveness, Perspicuity, Efficiency, Dependability, Stimulation, and Novelty. First, we Calculate the level of UX for each scale by processing statistical data using UEQ Analysis Data Tool. Values for the single items between −0.8 and 0.8 represent a neutral evaluation of the corresponding scale, values > 0,8 represent a positive evaluation, and values <−0,8 represent a negative evaluation (see Table 1). After obtaining the score for each scale, the data is analyzed using a benchmark graph to know the quality of AR Books compared with other products contained in the data set UEQ Analysis Data Tool. The data set contains 21175 persons from 468 studies concerning different products (business software, web pages, webshops, social networks). Next, we consider the benchmark intervals (see Table 2) for the UEQ presented in Schrepp, Hinderks and Thomaschewski [7]. The feedback is limited to five categories:

- Excellent: The evaluated product is among the best 10% of results.
- Good: 10% of the results in the benchmark are better than the evaluated product, 75% of the results are worse than the evaluated product.
- Above Average: 25% of the results in the benchmark are better than the evaluated product 50% of the results are worse.
- Below Average: 50% of the results in the benchmark are better than the evaluated product 25% of the results are worse.
- Bad: The evaluated product is among the worst 25% of results.

To test the viability of the questionnaire scales, we also used Cronbach's Alpha. A Cronbach's Alpha between 1–0.90 indicates an excellent internal consistency, between 0.70–0.90 a good internal consistency, between 0.60–0.70 an acceptable consistency, between 0.50–0.60 a poor consistency, and less than 0.50 an unacceptable consistency.

Table 1. Interpretations of the UEQ scales means

Positive evaluation	>0,8
Neutral evaluation	−0.8 and 0.8
Negative evaluation	<−0,8

Table 2. Benchmark intervals for the UEQ scales (Schrepp, Hinderks & Thomaschewski; 2017b)

	Attractiveness	Efficiency	Prespicuity	Dependability	Stimulation	Novelty
Excellent	≥1.75	≥1.78	≥1.9	≥1.65	≥1.55	≥1.4
Good	≥1.52 <1.75	≥1.47 <1.78	≥1.56 <1.9	≥1.48 <1.65	≥1.31 <1.55	≥1.05 <1.4

(continued)

Table 2. (*continued*)

	Attractiveness	Efficiency	Prespicuity	Dependability	Stimulation	Novelty
Above average	≥1.17 <1.52	≥0.98 <1.47	≥1.08 <1.56	≥1.14 <1.48	≥0.99 <1.31	≥0.71 <1.05
Below average	≥0.7 <1.17	≥0.54 <0.98	≥0.64 <1.08	≥0.78 <1.14	≥0.5 <0.99	≥0.3 <0.71
Bad	<0.7	<0.54	<0.64	<0.78	<0.5	<0.3

4 Results

Considering the completion of the UEQ carried out by 60 participants, we can see that the average age of our sample is 21 years old, with 22 (36.7%) male respondents and 38 (63.3%) female respondents.

4.1 The Star Wars Galaxy Explorer Guide, AR Book

The reliability analysis of the scales Attractiveness ($\alpha = .96$), Perspicuity ($\alpha = .93$), Efficiency ($\alpha = .93$) Stimulation ($\alpha = .97$) indicated an excellent internal consistency, the analysis of the scales Novelty ($\alpha = .88$) and Dependability ($\alpha = .74$) indicated a good internal consistency. The experience with The Star Wars Galaxy Explorer Guide book produced two types of results. First, we can observe the value of each UEQ item (see Fig. 4), where the average reveals a positive evaluation of the UX for each scale. The value of the Attractiveness scale is 1,865; Perspicuity 1,393; Efficiency 1.238; Dependability 1,012; Stimulation 1,536; and Novelty 1,667.

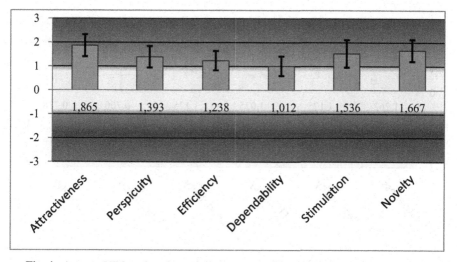

Fig. 4. Average UEQ scale values of the Star Wars Galaxy Explorer Guide, AR Book.

We obtained the other results about the UEQ benchmark (see Fig. 5). We analyze the UX of the AR book Star Wars Galaxy Explorer Guide compared to other products. The diagram shows that the scale value of Attractiveness and Novelty are in the Excellent category. This AR book corresponds to the 10% best results in these scales. The scale Stimulation is in the Good category, in the 25% best results. The scale Perspicuity and Efficiency is in the Above Average category, which means that 25% of the benchmark products are better than this AR book. Finally, the scale Dependability is Below the Average, which means that 50% of the benchmark products are better than this AR book.

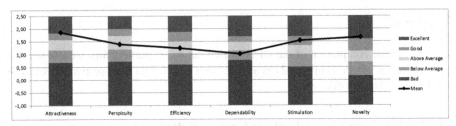

Fig. 5. UEQ benchmark diagram on the Star Wars Galaxy Explorer Guide, AR book

4.2 Frozen II the Ice Kingdom: An Enchanted Adventure, AR Book

The reliability analysis of the scales Attractiveness ($\alpha = .91$), Perspicuity ($\alpha = .90$), Stimulation ($\alpha = .94$) and Novelty ($\alpha = .91$), indicated an excellent internal consistency, the analysis of the scales Efficiency ($\alpha = .89$) and Dependability ($\alpha = .71$), indicated a

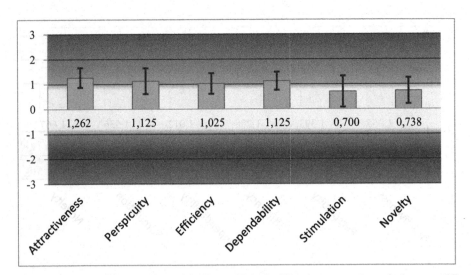

Fig. 6. Average UEQ scale values of the Frozen II the Ice Kingdom: an enchanted adventure, AR book.

good internal consistency. With the AR book Frozen II experience, we can observe the value of each UEQ item (see Fig. 6). The analysis of the average reveals a positive evaluation of the UX for the scales of Attractiveness (1,262), Perspicuity (1,125), Efficiency (1.025), and Dependability (1,125). It also reveals a neutral evaluation for the scales of Stimulation (0,700) and Novelty (0,738).

The results of the UEQ benchmark (see Fig. 7) for this AR book show that the scale value of Attractiveness and Novelty are in the Above Average category, which means that 25% of the benchmark products are better than this AR book. On the other hand, the scale Perspicuity, Efficiency, Dependability and Stimulation are in the Below.

Average category, which means that 50% of the benchmark products are better than this.

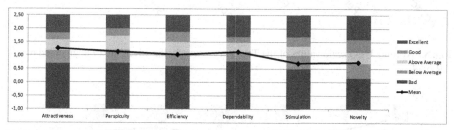

Fig. 7. UEQ benchmark diagram on the Frozen II the Ice Kingdom: an enchanted adventure, AR book.

4.3 Toy Story 4 Woody the Adventure of Augmented Reality, AR Book

The reliability analysis of the scales Attractiveness ($\alpha = .95$) and Stimulation ($\alpha = .94$) indicated an excellent internal consistency, the analysis of the scales Perspicuity ($\alpha = .86$), Efficiency ($\alpha = .79$), Dependability ($\alpha = .76$) and Novelty ($\alpha = .87$) indicated a good internal consistency. The experience with the AR book Toy Story 4 Woody, the Adventure of Augmented Reality, also produced two types of results. First, we can observe the value of each UEQ item (see Fig. 8), where the average reveals a positive evaluation of the UX for each scale. The value of the Attractiveness scale is 2,000; Perspicuity 1,475; Efficiency 1.475; Dependability 1,325; Stimulation 1,613; and Novelty 1,438.

We obtained the other results about the UEQ benchmark (see Fig. 9). The diagram shows that the scale value of Attractiveness is in the excellent category. This AR book corresponds to the range of 10% best results in this scale. The scale Stimulation and Novelty are in the Good category, meaning this book is in the 25% best results compared to the other benchmark products. Finally, the scale Perspicuity, Efficiency, and Dependability are in the Above Average category, which means that 25% of the benchmark products are better than this AR book in these scales.

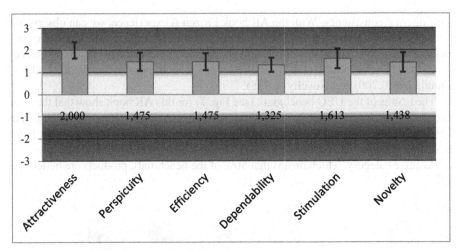

Fig. 8. Average UEQ scale values of the Toy Story 4 woody the adventure of augmented reality, AR book

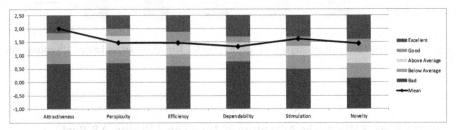

Fig. 9. UEQ benchmark diagram on the Toy Story 4 woody the adventure of augmented reality, AR book.

5   Discussion

The hypothesis: do AR published books show sufficient UX by having a positive evaluation in the scales of Attractiveness, Perspicuity, Efficiency, Dependability, Stimulation, and Novelty and fit in the Good/Excellent category in the benchmark analysis guided this fieldwork study. However, the fieldwork produced empirical evidence that does not entirely support this hypothesis. The same publisher publishes the three AR books in the same year. They have the same interface, and an app makes access to the contents. The essential differences are the themes of the books. Also, the book Star Wars Galaxy Explorer Guide has more content (text and 2D Animations). The book's classification also represents a difference. Toy Story 4, Woody the Adventure of Augmented Reality, is a children's fiction book, and the other two are juvenile literature.

Through the UEQ, the AR book Star Wars Galaxy Explorer Guide, and the AR book Toy Story 4, Woody the Adventure of Augmented Reality evaluated all the scales positively. The scale with the higher mean in the three books is Attractiveness, which means users liked the product. On the other hand, AR book Frozen II the Ice Kingdom: An Enchanted Adventure obtained a positive evaluation only in Attractiveness, Perspicuity,

Efficiency, Dependability, and a neutral evaluation in the scales of Stimulation and Novelty. These results show that the Frozen II AR book is a little exciting and motivating product, and that the product is less innovative and creative and catches less of the user's interest.

The benchmark analysis reveals curious results. In the Star Wars Galaxy Explorer Guide AR book, Attractiveness and Novelty are in the Excellent category. This result means that this book is in the range of 10% best results in the benchmark, meaning users like it and think it is more innovative and creative than 90% of the products. In the Good category is the Stimulation scale. Meaning this book is in the best 25% of the products in terms of the excitement and motivation it is to use it. Above Average are the Perspicuity and Efficiency scales, which means 25% of the products in the benchmark perform better in solving tasks without unnecessary effort and learning to work with the product efficiently. The scale Dependability is in the Below Average category. It is to say that 50% of the products in the benchmark are better in making users feel control over the interaction.

In Frozen II the Ice Kingdom: An Enchanted Adventure AR Book, 25% of the products in the benchmark perform better in the Attractiveness and Novelty scales. These two scales are in the Above Average category. However, users' response after experimenting with this book indicates that 50% of the products in the benchmark perform even better in the scales of Perspicuity, Efficiency, Dependability, and Stimulation. These scales are in the Below Average category.

In Toy Story 4 Woody the Adventure of Augmented Reality, Attractiveness is in the Excellent category. The scales Novelty and Stimulation are in the Good category. The Perspicuity, Efficiency, and Dependability scales are in the Above-average category.

Has said by Schrepp, Hinderks, & Thomaschewski [7, p43] "the general UX expectations have grown over time. Since the benchmark also contains data from established products, a new product should reach at least the Good category on all scales".

As we showed before, the three AR books do not reach the Good category in all the scales compared to the benchmark. The scales that in all the books are in the categories below the Good category are Perspicuity, Efficiency, and Dependability (the goal-oriented categories also named pragmatic quality aspects). It is to say that, despite our groups of users thought AR books are exciting, motivating to use, innovative, creative, could catch user's interest, and liked the overall product, our users also thought AR books could be improved. This improvement concerns solving tasks without unnecessary effort, making learning how to use the product more accessible, becoming familiar with it, and making users feel control over the interaction.

This study contributes towards the emergent body of quantitative studies whose aim is to evaluate the UX/usability of AR books [27, 29, 31] the UX of AR systems [22–24, 32] with both hedonic and pragmatic qualities [33] and comparing it with other products [30, 32]. This study can assess that our users liked the presented AR books, considered them an innovative product, and felt motivated to use them. In this concern, the results we obtained from our study are consistent with the results of other studies [18, 26, 28]. However, we cannot just depend on the hedonic qualities of AR books. As users feel more familiar with this type of product, these qualities tend to have less impact on users' opinions. Also, hedonic qualities are not sufficient to make a good UX of a product, meaning that users will use it for the first time because they think it is exciting to use it but will not use it continuously if the pragmatic qualities of the product are not ensured. In this sense, it is necessary to improve pragmatic aspects to achieve a better UX. The resulting guidelines of other studies [27, 29–31] and the results we obtained in this experience prove that AR books need improvements.

Future studies should also include long-term UX evaluations of AR books. Also, it would be interesting to create from scratch the measuring instruments specifically for AR products bringing novelty and usefulness for the Human-computer interaction study area. As in any study, there were limitations to the present study. We recognize we use a UEQ for this evaluation on AR books. This study could be completed by an ergonomic inspection or a usability test. Despite our users reading the AR books as we observed, we did not use that information in this study.

6   Conclusion

This research is the first study to evaluate the UX of AR published books that includes pragmatic and hedonic qualities to the best of our knowledge. Thus, this study is a first step towards improving AR published books through a holistic UX approach. Although books obtained positive evaluation from users in almost all the scales, the comparison with the benchmark showed that the pragmatic qualities need improvement. The analyzed books failed to meet the UX goals requirements, in what respects to Efficiency, Perspicuity, and Dependability.

As we know, AR can widen the capacities of the traditional book, and it offers the opportunity to create new layers of information, including visual contents. If, in the beginning, AR was treated more like a gimmick than an essential part of the book, today's readers expect more integration and equilibrium between real and virtual contents and a better UX. So, we cannot rely anymore only upon the freshness aspect of this product. Our findings indicate that users liked the overall product, though it was innovative and creative, caught users' interest, and thought it was exciting and motivating to use it. However, the obtained results indicate that not all UX dimensions have a good enough level. The pragmatic dimensions need improvement so AR books can be used as an editorial product capable of facing the demands and expectations of the new generations.

References

1. Gomes, A,. Esteves, M., Duarte, S.: Hábitos de leitura de livros. Relatório. MC'Donald's - PNL2027 – Expresso (2019)
2. Arifin, Y., Sastria, T., Barlian, E.: User Experience metric for augmented reality application: a review. Procedia Comput. Sci. **135**, 648–656 (2018). https://doi.org/10.1016/j.procs.2018.08.221
3. Irshad, S., Awang, D.: A UX oriented evaluation approach for mobile augmented reality applications. In: Proceedings of the 16th International Conference on Advances in Mobile Computing and Multimedia (MoMM 2018), pp. 108–112. Association for Computing Machinery, New York (2018) DOI:https://doi.org/10.1145/3282353.3282357

4. Laugwitz, B., Held, T., Schrepp, M.: Construction and evaluation of a user experience questionnaire. In: Holzinger, A. (ed.) USAB 2008. LNCS, vol. 5298, pp. 63–76. Springer, Heidelberg (2008). https://doi.org/10.1007/978-3-540-89350-9_6

5. Schrepp, M., Hinderks, A., Thomaschewski, J.: Design and evaluation of a short version of the user experience questionnaire (UEQ-S). IJIMAI 4(6), 103–108 (2017)

6. Cota, M., Thomaschewski, J., Schrepp, M., Goncalves, R.: Efficient measurement of the user experience: a portuguese version. Procedia Comput. Sci. 27, 491–498 (2014). https://doi.org/10.1016/j.procs.2014.02.053

7. Schrepp, M., Hinderks, A., Thomaschewski, J.: Construction of a benchmark for the user experience questionnaire (UEQ). Int. J. Interact. Multimedia Artif. Intell. 4(4), 40–44 (2017)

8. Schrepp, M., Hinderks, A., Thomaschewski, J.: Applying the user experience questionnaire (UEQ) in different evaluation scenarios. In: Marcus, A. (ed.) DUXU 2014. LNCS, vol. 8517, pp. 383–392. Springer, Cham (2014). https://doi.org/10.1007/978-3-319-07668-3_37

9. Rekimoto, J.: Matrix: a real time object identification and registration method for augmented reality. In: 3rd Asia Pacific Computer Human Interaction, Shonan, 17 July 1998, pp. 63–68 (1998)

10. Billinghurst, M., Kato, H., Poupyrev, I.: The magicbook-moving seamlessly between reality and virtuality. IEEE Comput. Graph. Appl. 21(3), 6–8 (2001)

11. Vanderschantz, N., Hinze, A., AL-Hashami, A.: Multi-level engagement in augmented reality children's picture books. In: Lamas, D., Loizides, F., Nacke, L., Petrie, H., Winckler, M., Zaphiris, P. (eds.) INTERACT 2019. LNCS, vol. 11749, pp. 558–562. Springer, Cham (2019). https://doi.org/10.1007/978-3-030-29390-1_37

12. Hita, Z., Lee, Y.: Interactive spatial augmented reality book on cultural heritage of Myanmar. J. Inf. Commun. Conv. Eng. 18(2), 69–74 (2020). https://doi.org/10.6109/JICCE.2020.18.2.69

13. Shinhyo, K., Jihyun, P., Jusub, K.: E-mmersive Book: the AR book that assists the syntopical reading. In: Proceedings of the 9th Augmented Human International Conference (AH 2018), Article 37, pp. 1–2. Association for Computing Machinery, New York (2018). https://doi.org/10.1145/3174910.3174942

14. Garcia-Sanchez, J.C.: Augmenting reality in books: a tool for enhancing reading skills in Mexico. Publ. Res. Q. 33(1), 19–27 (2017). https://doi.org/10.1007/s12109-017-9499-2

15. Cheng, K.: Reading an augmented reality book: an exploration of learners' cognitive load, motivation, and attitudes. Austr. J. Educ. Technol. 33(4), 53–69 (2017). https://doi.org/10.14742/ajet.2820

16. Bakri, F., Oktaviani M., Muliyati, D.: Textbooks equipped with augmented reality technology for physics topic in high-school. Jurnal Penelitian Pengembangan Pendidikan Fisika 5(2), 113–122 (2019). https://doi.org/10.21009/1.05206

17. Weng, C., Otanga, S., Christianto, S., Chu, R.: Enhancing students' biology learning by using augmented reality as a learning supplement. J. Educ. Comput. Res. 58(4), 747–770 (2020). https://doi.org/10.1177/0735633119884213

18. Swan, J., Gabbard, J.: Survey of user-based experimentation in augmented reality. In: Proceedings of 1st International Conference on Virtual Reality, vol. 22, pp. 1–9 (2005)

19. Koutromanos, G., Mavromatidou, E.: Augmented reality books: what student teachers believe about their use in teaching. In: Tsiatsos, T., Demetriadis, S., Mikropoulos, A., Dagdilelis, V. (eds.) Research on E-Learning and ICT in Education, pp. 75–91. Springer, Cham (2021). https://doi.org/10.1007/978-3-030-64363-8_5

20. Billinghurst, M., Lindeman, R., Swan, J.: A systematic review of usability studies in augmented reality between 2005 and 2014. In: 2016 IEEE International Symposium on Mixed and Augmented Reality (ISMAR-Adjunct), pp. 49–50 (2016). https://doi.org/10.1109/ISMAR-Adjunct.2016.0036

21. Law, E., Heintz, M.: Augmented reality applications for K-12 education: a systematic review from the usability and user experience perspective. Int. J. Child-Comput. Interact. **30**, 100321 (2021)

22. Olsson, O., Lagerstam, E., Kärkkäinen, T., Väänänen-Vainio-Mattila, K.: Expected user experience of mobile augmented reality services: a user study in the context of shopping centres. Pers. Ubiq. Comput. **17**(2), 287–304 (2013). https://doi.org/10.1007/s00779-011-0494-x

23. Irshad, S., Rambli, D.: Multi-layered mobile augmented reality framework for positive user experience. In: Proceedings of the 2nd International Conference in HCI and UX Indonesia 2016 (CHIuXiD 2016), pp. 21–26. Association for Computing Machinery, New York (2016). https://doi.org/10.1145/2898459.2898462

24. Irshad, S., Rambli, D., Sulaiman, S.: Design and implementation of user experience model for augmented reality systems. In: Proceedings of the 18th International Conference on Advances in Mobile Computing & Multimedia (MoMM 2020), pp. 48–57. Association for Computing Machinery, New York (2020). https://doi.org/10.1145/3428690.3429169

25. Pamparău, C, Vatavu, R.: A research agenda is needed for designing for the user experience of augmented and mixed reality: a position paper. In: 19th International Conference on Mobile and Ubiquitous Multimedia (MUM 2020), pp. 323–325. Association for Computing Machinery, New York (2020) DOI:https://doi.org/10.1145/3428361.3432088

26. Grasset, R., Dünser, A., Billinghurst, M.: Edutainment with a mixed reality book: a visually augmented illustrative childrens' book. In: Proceedings of the 2008 International Conference on Advances in Computer Entertainment Technology (ACE 2008), pp. 292–295. Association for Computing Machinery, New York (2008). https://doi.org/10.1145/1501750.1501819

27. Dünser, A., Hornecker, E.: Lessons from an AR book study. In: Proceedings of the 1st International Conference on Tangible and embedded interaction (TEI 2007), pp. 179–182. Association for Computing Machinery, New York (2007). https://doi.org/10.1145/1226969.122 7006

28. Gazcón, N., Castro, S.: ARBS: an interactive and collaborative system for augmented reality books. In: De Paolis, L.T., Mongelli, A. (eds.) AVR 2015. LNCS, vol. 9254, pp. 89–108. Springer, Cham (2015). https://doi.org/10.1007/978-3-319-22888-4_8

29. Cao, R., Hou, W.: Research on the interaction design of AR picture books via usability test. In: Tang, Y., Zu, Q., Rodríguez García, J.G. (eds.) HCC 2018. LNCS, vol. 11354, pp. 524–534. Springer, Cham (2019). https://doi.org/10.1007/978-3-030-15127-0_53

30. Polyzou, S., Botsoglou, K., Zygouris, N., Stamoulis, G.: Interactive books for preschool children: from traditional interactive paper books to augmented reality books: listening to children's voices through mosaic approach. Education, 3–13 (2022). https://doi.org/10.1080/03004279.2021.2025131

31. Kljun, M., et al.: Augmentation not duplication: considerations for the design of digitally-augmented comic books. In: Proceedings of the 2019 CHI Conference on Human Factors in Computing Systems (CHI 2019), Paper 103, pp. 1–12. Association for Computing Machinery, New York (2019). https://doi.org/10.1145/3290605.3300333

32. Stumpp, S., Knopf, T., Michelis, D.: User experience design with augmented reality (AR). In: Proceedings of the ECIE 2019 14th European Conference on Innovation and Entrepreneurship, pp 1032–1040 (2019)

33. Alenljung, Z., Lindblom, J.: User experience in augmented reality: a holistic evaluation of a prototype for assembly instructions. In: Soares, M.M., Rosenzweig, E., Marcus, A. (eds.) HCII 2021. LNCS, vol. 12781, pp. 139–157. Springer, Cham (2021). https://doi.org/10.1007/978-3-030-78227-6_11

G4NHE Second Edition: Refining a Generic Gamification Technique to Engage HCI Evaluators in Consolidation Tasks

José Cezar de Souza Filho[1]([✉]), Andréia Libório Sampaio[2],
Ingrid Teixeira Monteiro[2], and Paulyne Matthews Jucá[2]

[1] Institute of Computing, Federal University of Amazonas, Manaus, Brazil
`cezar@icomp.ufam.edu.br`
[2] Graduate Program in Computing, Federal University of Ceará, Quixadá, Brazil
`andreia.ufc@gmail.com`, {`ingrid,paulyne`}`@ufc.br`

Abstract. Heuristic Evaluation is an inspection method widely used to evaluate the usability of interactive systems. Some studies investigated collaboration to reduce the boredom and frustration evaluators tend to have in this evaluation process. One such proposal is G4NHE (Game for aNy Heuristic Evaluation), a generic gamification technique that can be instantiated to any usability heuristics set. This paper presents the G4NHE evaluation through two exploratory studies. The first one aims to evaluate the specialization guide, while the second one aims to evaluate the new rules' acceptance. From the participants' perception, G4NHE allows a rich and effective discussion about the problems found in a Heuristic Evaluation, increasing the evaluators' motivation. However, it was also apparent the difficulty in understanding and performing the specialization guide activities and the lack of information in the new rules, which caused doubts during the gamification rounds. Finally, we considered the improvement suggestions obtained in the studies to generate a refined version of the G4NHE and its specialization guide.

Keywords: Heuristic evaluation · Usability heuristics · Gamification · Card game · G4NHE

1 Introduction

Heuristic Evaluation [15], proposed by Nielsen and Molich in the 1990s, is a widely used inspection method to identify usability issues in user interfaces. In this method, Human-Computer Interaction (HCI) evaluators perform individual inspection tasks at the interface through a set of general usability principles (the usability heuristics, e.g., Nielsen's heuristics [11]) and assign a severity grade to each issue found [12,13] in order to prioritize fixing efforts. This process also includes a consolidation step [19], in which evaluators perform tasks collectively - they meet to discuss the usability issues found individually to reach a consensus on the heuristics violated by each issue and their severity grade.

However, previous research reports several challenges on the Heuristic Evaluation (cf. [5]). For instance, this evaluation process tends to be boring and frustrating for the evaluators, which can affect the final evaluation quality [16]. In this context, some initiatives have been proposed to promote collaboration among evaluators and support the evaluation process, such as Game for Heuristic Evaluation (G4H) [8], a gamification technique presented as a card game to improve motivation and engagement of different evaluators during Heuristic Evaluation-based consolidation tasks.

The authors of the G4H's original version [8] developed the technique considering only Nielsen's usability heuristics [11], not allowing its application with other sets of heuristics (cf. [1,6]). Thus, G4H evolved into a custom, generic gamification technique named Game for aNy Heuristic Evaluation (G4NHE) [22]. G4NHE has generic heuristic cards with templates to allow adaptation to different sets of usability heuristics. Also, G4NHE presents two activity cycle rules and a specialization guide to support its instantiation.

Although G4NHE was developed based on evidence from the literature [22], there is a lack of empirical evidence regarding its use by HCI evaluators, the target audience of this technique, in order to contribute to its validation. Therefore, in this paper, we aim to empirically investigate the use of G4NHE from the perceptions of HCI evaluators in an academic setting.

Our investigation was divided into two exploratory studies. The first one was conducted to investigate the use of the G4NHE specialization guide, while the second one was conducted to investigate the acceptance of the new activity cycle rules, to be chosen when the severity classification step will not be applied. In the first study, we conducted two rounds intertwining qualitative data collection and analysis with improvements to the G4NHE specialization guide. The second study involved novice HCI evaluators who used the new activity cycle rules in four gamification rounds, one demonstration and three effective rounds.

In both studies we conducted observations of use [19] while the participants applied the technique. At the end of each observation, we collected qualitative data through individual semi-structured interviews [4] in the first study and focus group [10] in the second one, in order to obtain the participants' perceptions, including strengths, weaknesses, difficulties, and improvement suggestions. We analyzed the qualitative data applying Discourse Analysis procedures [7].

The findings from both studies indicated that participants perceived benefits through G4NHE, such as related to motivation and better discussion of usability issues found in a Heuristic Evaluation. However, in the first study, participants had difficulties in understanding and performing the activities of heuristic cards development and activity cycle selection from the G4NHE specialization guide, while the participants in the second study revealed that the new rules were not entirely clear. From the empirical evidence obtained in the studies, we performed refinements in the technique and presented the G4NHE second edition.

2   Related Work

Gamification is "the use of game design elements in non-game contexts" [2]. In the HCI field, gamification is applied for enhancing the engagement in user experience [23]. Our research explored gamification through a different lens: to improve evaluator experience when applying HCI evaluation methods instead of addressing user experience.

Also, we highlight related works that present games about HCI evalua- tion methods and concepts. UsabiliCity [3] and UsabilityGame [20] are Web games that can be used to support the teaching of Heuristic Evaluation. Still, UsabiliCity focuses on Nielsen's usability heuristics [11] and UsabilityGame also includes requirements analysis and prototyping, other activities based on May- hew's Usability Engineering Life Cycle [9]. MACteaching [17] is an Android game developed to support the teaching of Communicability Evaluation Method (Método de Avaliação de Comunicabilidade - MAC, in Portuguese), a Semiotic Engineering method for evaluating software communicability [21].

G4NHE also was proposed for Heuristic Evaluation, similar to UsabiliCity and UsabilityGame but different from MACteaching. However, this gamification technique was developed as a card game rather than a digital game. Their main goal is improving the conduction of Heuristic Evaluation, focusing on consoli- dation tasks instead of teaching this method. G4NHE itself is not new, but we present its application by HCI evaluators in this paper. The main novelty of this paper is our findings that contribute towards G4NHE's validation.

3   Game for aNy Heuristic Evaluation (G4NHE)

Game for Heuristic Evaluation (G4H) [8] is a card-based gamification technique whose main goal is to engage and motivate evaluators in the execution of the Heuristic Evaluation, specifically in consolidating the results. Game for aNy Heuristic Evaluation (G4NHE) is a generic gamification technique developed to apply G4H gamification with any set of usability heuristics. G4NHE provides generic items and a specialization guide, allowing its users to specialize this generic gamification for any set of usability heuristics. G4NHE is limited to usability heuristics, so there may be limitations to applying it with established heuristics for other attributes, such as playability and accessibility [22].

G4NHE was developed using a structured literature survey, which identified common and different characteristics related to the specification of different sets of usability heuristics [22]. For instance, heuristics are commonly specified with ID, name, and definition; however, some sets classify heuristics in categories. It was also observed that, usually, the traditional method of Heuristic Evaluation [15] is applied to validate the proposed heuristics. However, some authors modify this method to exclude the severity classification step of the problems found.

In this way, G4NHE provides generic templates for the cards representing the heuristics, offering an option that only presents the heuristic ID, name, and definition, and another option that includes the heuristic category. Also, this model presents an adaptation of the original G4H rules [8] to allow apply the gamification in cases where the severity classification of the violations does not occur [22]. Finally, a specialization guide was also provided, whose goal is to guide the G4NHE user in creating gamification from G4NHE considering any set of usability heuristics. G4NHE guide has three activities [22]:

1. Develop the heuristic cards: the user should create a heuristic card for each usability heuristics proposed by the chosen set of heuristics. To do so, it can follow one of the generic heuristic card templates provided by G4NHE;
2. Develop the heuristics guide: the user should write a simple document with the brief or complete specification of the heuristics chosen to create the gamification from G4NHE. This guide is important so that players can remember, if necessary, the heuristics' definition during the gamification rounds;
3. Activity cycle selection: finally, the user needs to select which activity cycle (or set of rules) will be used in the gamification. If the heuristics use the traditional Heuristic Evaluation [15], he/she should choose the original G4H rules [8]. However, if the heuristics used in G4NHE does not use severity classification, he/she should choose the G4NHE rules adapted for that.

Details about the G4NHE generic items and its specialization guide can be found in its initial proposal [22].

4   G4NHE Evaluation

This section presents two exploratory studies to evaluate the G4NHE proposal and its specialization guide. To provide a base for comparison, the researcher also performed an specialization that serves as a baseline. Both researcher and participants performed their tasks using the activities established in the G4NHE specialization guide as defined in [22] and using the Ubiquitous Heuristics [18] (also called HUbis). This set of 15 usability heuristics faces the challenge of evaluating the quality-in-use of ubiquitous systems, which have specific characteristics compared to traditional systems (e.g., desktop and web), such as context-awareness, transparency, attention, calm, and mobility. Each heuristic was specified with ID, name, definition, and quality characteristics [18].

To evaluate the gamification, observation tests were performed [19] in a laboratory environment, with potential users of the G4NHE, which may be students, researchers, and HCI practitioners. This exploratory evaluation was divided into two studies. The first one is related to the G4NHE specialization guide. The second one is regarding the new rules adopted by G4NHE, used when the heuristic set does not use severity classification. The results referring to each validation step are presented in the next sections.

5   Evaluating the G4NHE Specialization Guide

The objective of the first study is to evaluate the G4NHE specialization guide to verify if it contains enough information to guide an specialization of the G4NHE from any set of usability heuristics.

5.1   Participants' Profile

Students and HCI experts participated in this study. Participants would need to know the Heuristic Evaluation method to understand the terms and concepts covered in the study. This information can be verified from the participants' responses to the applied profile questionnaire. Participants P1 and P4 are experts in HCI, while participants P2 and P3 are students in the field. Both P2 and P3 participants took the HCI and HCI Evaluation courses. Participant P1 had been a monitor for HCI course during her master's course, and participant P4 had already taught courses related to HCI in undergraduate courses. Considering a scale from 0 to 10 to assess the participant's level of experience with the Heuristic Evaluation, the experts said they knew a lot about the method, selecting high values (P1 - 9 and P4 - 8). Both student participants (P2 and P3) rated their experience with grade 7. The scale from 0 to 10 was also used to assess participants' level of experience with gamification. Participant P1 assigned a grade of 7 for her experience. However, it is interesting to note that she had declared that the current study would be her first contact with gamification. Participant P4 evaluated her experience as 1, considering that she knew little or nothing about gamification. Student participants rated their experience with similar grades (P2 - 7 and P3 - 8).

Finally, it is important to consider in this analysis the fact that most participants (P2, P3, and P4) already knew and participated in G4H rounds, which is the main basis of the G4NHE proposal evaluated in this study. This can indicate that it was easier for these participants to perform the study tasks than participant P1, who had no previous experience with the G4H.

5.2   Procedure

Individual tests were applied to observe the use of the G4NHE specialization guide by its potential users. Participants were asked to use the specialization guide to generate a G4NHE instance from Ubiquitous Heuristics. The tasks requested from each participant, following the format (ID: Task), are the same three activities in the G4NHE specialization guide – T1: Develop the heuristics cards; T2: Develop the heuristics guide; T3: Select the activity cycle (the rules of the gamification).

The following script guided the conduction of each individual test. Initially, the researcher proposing this work read the consent form with the participant. Then, the participant was asked to answer a profile questionnaire about their experience with the Heuristic Evaluation method and the gamification technique. All were made available to participants through an electronic form created with Google Forms. After that, the researcher explained the Heuristic Evaluation method when necessary. Then the test scenario was presented, which consisted of using the specialization guide from the Ubiquitous Heuristics. Soon, the G4NHE specialization guide was delivered to the participant. In addition, the participant also received the two activity cycles to select one of them; the Microsoft PowerPoint file where the heuristics cards were created; the complete specification of the Ubiquitous Heuristics set; and finally, a file that describes how to report the issues found using the Ubiquitous Heuristics, where the participant could verify whether the severity classification should be performed or not to help to decide which activity cycle to use. The complete Ubiquitous Heuristics specification and the problem report file were extracted directly from Rocha et al. [18] so participants used the source of this set of heuristics, avoiding bias.

The test was performed after the items were delivered to the participant. During tests, the activities were audio-recorded with the permission of the participant. Finally, a semi-structured post-test interview was carried out to collect the opinion of each participant about the G4NHE proposal, the use of its specialization guide, including positive points and improvement suggestions.

5.3   Initial Test

The initial test was applied with the participation of expert P1. First, the researcher proposing this work presented the proposal and the terms of the G4NHE to the participant so that she did not need to read this introductory content, starting her reading from the explanation of the activities in the specialization guide. However, the goal is that users can perform the activities of the specialization guide alone, not needing someone to explain the terms of the proposal.

Task T1 - Develop the Heuristics Cards. In task T1, the participant created three (3) heuristics cards. She didn't need to create cards for all 15 heuristics proposed in the Ubiquitous Heuristics set since the objective of this activity is for the participant to have experience in creating the cards so that she can give her opinion on this and that difficulties are revealed. The participant did not notice the space destined for the heuristic ID in the heuristics cards, as she inserted this information next to the heuristic name, separating the two pieces of information with a hyphen (Fig. 1).

Upon completing the test, the participant was asked if she had noticed the heuristic ID space on the heuristics cards. She claimed not to have identified this space and pointed out that the ID of a heuristic will not always be just a number to fit in the small area of a circle, as is the case with Ubiquitous Heuristics. So she suggested that this circle could have the same letter "H" that identifies the heuristic card, and the ID could be inserted next to the name of the heuristic, as she had done.

The participant had understood that the category present in the heuristics cards would refer to a usability problem to be evaluated in the gamification, as shown in her speech: "If it is uncategorized, what will they play? Will the problem be fixed or not?". However, the category refers to heuristics. For instance, a set of heuristics could be categorized into usability heuristics, accessibility heuristics, or for children heuristics. The participant felt worried about the act of summarizing the definition of the heuristic, as shown in her speech: "This worries me. Summarize, got it? Based on what, right? I do not know. I think not

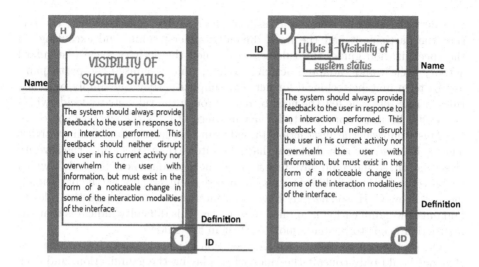

Fig. 1. Cards created by the researcher and participant P1.

to summarize, but put the text as it is there, and about three dots at the end in parentheses, understand? To know that there is a sequel". This was because she understood that summarizing would have the meaning of rewriting, and this could affect the validity of the heuristic. Then, it was explained to the participant that she could delete some lines of the definition without rewriting the text. She understood and continued recommending the three dots to represent a continuation and that the player could consult the rest of the definition in the heuristics guide. The objective is that the player can consult the complete specification in the heuristics guide; however, using three dots makes the card meaningless. The ideal would be to delete the text that did not fit in the letter, ending its content with a complete sentence.

Task T2 - Develop the Heuristics Guide. During task T2, the participant prepared the heuristics guide for Ubiquitous Heuristics. She entered the specification of all 15 heuristics specified in this set and not just the heuristics (Ubiquitous Heuristics 1, 2 and 3) for which she had created the heuristics cards in task T1. The participant did not think it necessary to include the quality characteristics present in the Ubiquitous Heuristics in the heuristics guide. She participated in creating these heuristics and informed that the quality characteristics were used only as part of the methodology to establish the Ubiquitous Heuristics. Thus, these characteristics are not considered by the evaluators during the Heuristic Evaluation using Ubiquitous Heuristics.

Task T3 - Activity Cycle Selection. In task T3, participant P1 selected the appropriate activity cycle, which contains the rules initially proposed by G4H, since the execution of the Heuristic Evaluation using Ubiquitous Heuristics [18] considers the stage of severity classification. However, this task was the one that the participant had the most difficulty understanding and executing. In the specialization guide, the rule sets are called the activity cycle ("standard activity cycle", and "adapted activity cycle"), which confused the participant, as this term may be technical for her. For simplicity, they can simply be called rules or rule sets. She felt the need to read through the rule sets to decide which one would be most appropriate for her instance of G4NHE, whereas she could have just followed the instruction provided in the description of this activity. That is because she already knew that Ubiquitous Heuristics apply the severity classification, so she could have just selected the "standard activity cycle", which contains the G4H rules. This fact may also have occurred because the participant did not know G4H, so she may have been interested in consulting the rules to find out how gamification is applied in practice. This difficulty indicates that the instruction needs to be made more explicit in the guide.

The participant recommended the inclusion of instruction to inform the user that he should only consult the rules when playing the gamification, and even that the existing instruction could indicate to the user that he should use a set of rules and not choose, as is currently written in the guide because it might lead the user to want to compare the two sets to decide which one is better. However, the appropriate word is "choose", as the user needs to choose between the two existing sets of rules. To do so, he must follow the guide's instruction that guides this choice rather than comparing the two sets of rules. Also, the word "use" can mean that the user needs to use the chosen ruleset when the gamification is being created, but this should only happen when he decides to play the gamification.

The participant suggested mentioning, in the guide prepared for the test, the name of the file that contains the activity cycles to be selected. This is because the description of this activity in the guide presents only the following instruction: "The two existing cycles can be consulted in the files made available to you", not indicating the name of the file, which made understanding difficult. The participant was also confused because the renegotiation card is only used in the "adapted activity cycle", which contains the rules adapted by the G4NHE to allow the application of gamification when the severity classification is not performed. Thus, the participant suggested that this card could be used in both activity cycles.

Post-Test Interview. Regarding the G4NHE, participant P1 showed a lot of interest: "I really liked the idea. It is a nice idea. Congratulations, congratulations on the idea. And... I think there are, in general, these little things just to adjust". The participant's adjustments are the recommendations given by her during the test. She considered the specialization guide to be simple: "The guide itself is simple. What does it really need? There are only three simple things you need: create the heuristics cards, because the severity ones already exist, the others already exist, make it clear that they already exist, and the guy [G4NHE user] won't need to work with it; [...] this guide that he will be able to put there on the side to be able to deliver to each player; and the choice of cycle".

Regarding the potential for using the G4NHE, participant P1 stated: "I think the potential is good. It's simple, it's a game, it's competitive. So, it's not a boring business, as you... oh, what a pain! I'll have to consolidate the heuristics and the severities now. No, let's play! It's cool. It's a good proposal". After finalizing her suggestions, the participant still showed enthusiasm in playing the proposed gamification. She said, "I'm looking forward to playing this game. Call me to play it there." The results of this initial test indicate that the G4NHE specialization guide was still not simple to understand, and also the occurrence of some unwanted behaviors during the execution of the activities of this guide (e.g., the participant read both sets of rules, which did not was the purpose of the test). Therefore, it was considered that the guide would need to be improved before being used by the other participants (P2, P3 and P4). In this way, the G4NHE specialization guide was improved from the application of the test with participant P1, and its new version was tested with the other participants (P2, P3, and P4).

G4NHE Specialization Guide Modifications. Based on the recommendations made by participant P1, some modifications were made to the specialization guide to improve its understanding, generating a new version. The following changes have been applied:

- All occurrences in the text referring to activity cycles have been replaced by rules. The "Standard Activities Cycle" was named "Rules for Heuristics with Severity Classification" and the "Adapted Activities Cycle" was replaced by "Rules Heuristics without Severity Classification";
- The flowchart that presents the cycle of activities in the specialization guide has been improved to better understand. For example, the input artifacts necessary for the execution of each activity/step were better positioned, and a diamond was also included to represent that the conditional structures of the first and third activities are an alternative (i.e., the user must choose one option or another);
- The name of each activity in the guide has been changed. The first activity was renamed "Prepare the heuristics cards"; the second activity was named "Prepare the heuristics guide"; and finally, the name of the third activity was changed to "Selection of the set of rules to be used";
- In the first activity (prepare the heuristics cards), an example of creating the heuristics cards for the first Nielsen heuristics (Visibility of the system state) was inserted;
- In the first activity, it was also said that the use of category cards is optional and that G4NHE provides these generic card templates only to allow greater flexibility and adaptability to the needs of those who create the gamification;
- Still, in the first activity, it was better explained that the text of the definition of a heuristic can be cut so that it is readable in the heuristic card, but it should not be rewritten with the user's words;

- In the second activity (prepare the heuristics guide), the purpose of the heuristics guide was better explained so that users understand that it is a support material on heuristics to be provided to gamification players;
- In the third activity (selection of the set of rules to be used), an instruction was inserted to clarify to the user that he does not need to know the details about the sets of rules when creating the gamification since they are provided as a set ready that should not be modified, and only when playing the gamification should the chosen set of rules be consulted;
- In the third activity of the guide prepared for the test, the names of the files containing the sets of rules to be chosen were inserted;
- Finally, in the file containing the "Rules for Heuristics with Severity Classification", the citations to G4H were removed.

5.4   Final Test

After obtaining a new version of the specialization guide, the final test was performed with the other participants (P2, P3, and P4). Contrary to what happened in the initial test, the participants read the document from the explanation of the proposal and the terms of the G4NHE, since it is important to verify if they can understand the activities of the specialization guide alone, not needing someone to explain related terms. The doubts that arose during the test with each participant were resolved by the researcher proposing this work. The results for each task established for the test are presented in the next sub-sections.

Task T1 - Develop the Heuristics Cards. Again, participants did not create heuristics cards for all 15 heuristics established in the Ubiquitous Heuristics set. They were instructed to create as many cards as they wished in order to prevent the work from becoming repetitive and also due to the test's time limitation. The number of cards created by participants P2, P3, and P4 were, respectively, 3, 4, and 9. Thus, participant P4 was the one who made more cards in the test.

Participants P2 and P4 noticed the space destined for the heuristic ID in the heuristics cards, while participant P3 did not identify this space (Fig. 2). Participant P2 did not use only a numerical value for the ID, as was done by the researcher, and did not consider the original ID of the Ubiquitous Heuristics [18], which follows the format (HUbis + numerical value). He believed that the ID starting with "HUbis" has the context of the dissertation that proposes this set of heuristics, so he preferred to create his ID, which follows the format (H + numeric value), as he finds it simpler. This is not a problem, as the user can use the heuristic ID as they prefer.

Participant P4, on the other hand, used the original ID of the Ubiquitous Heuristics, which may be the ideal approach since it is interesting to maintain the identity of the Ubiquitous Heuristics in the gamification that is being created. Initially, she was unsure whether to enter only the numeric value or the full ID of the heuristic, as much as she preferred to enter the full ID. That's because she noticed that the space destined for this information in the heuristics cards would

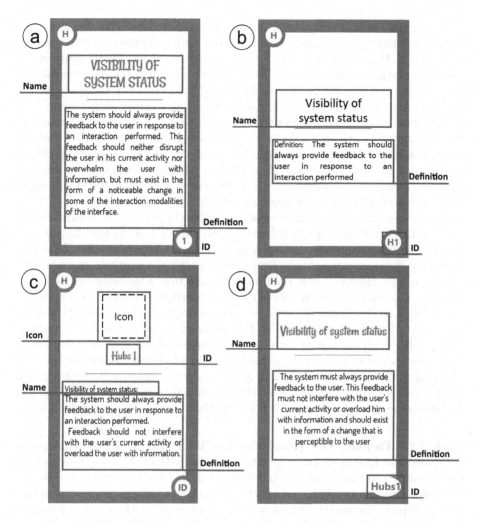

Fig. 2. Cards created by the researcher and participants P2, P3, and P4.

not support the Ubiquitous Heuristics ID and could misconfigure the layout of the cards. The participant was insecure about making changes to the template. Participant P3 also made suggestions for changes to the proposed layout, such as changing the position of the upper left "H" with the lower right "ID" of the card. P2 and P3 suggested changing the background color of the circle to attract attention. Modifying the template does not represent a problem since G4NHE does not require that the cards follow a defined template, and the template provided is only a support for the elaboration of the necessary cards.

Regarding the representation icon, all participants chose to create the heuristics cards without this element, which could be optionally inserted if the participant wanted. However, participant P4 was the only one who used the appropriate generic template for heuristics cards, which contains only textual elements. In contrast, participants P2 and P3 used the model that includes the space for the representation icon, making adaptations. Regarding the heuristic category, initially, participant P2 had doubts whether the quality characteristics present in the Ubiquitous Heuristics could be the card categories. Subsequently, the participant declared that he could clear his doubt through the example provided in the guide that the Ubiquitous Heuristics set has no categories. He considered that the category is an optional element of the card, so when in doubt, the cards would not need to include the heuristic category.

Regarding summarizing the heuristic definition to place in the heuristic card, it was noticed that participants P2 and P4 only cut parts of the text. In contrast, participant P3 rewrote the definition in his own words, as he said: "I rewrote looking at it [specification of the heuristics], I didn't put anything more or anything less no". However, it is important to note that a usability heuristic is a usability guideline or golden rule [11]; thus, rewriting its definition can affect the validity of the heuristic. Still, in relation to this, participant P4 showed insecurity: "I summarize, right, but I don't know to what extent I'm summarizing well, you know? Since I am not the person who created the heuristic." The researcher explained to the participant that she could summarize the definition of the heuristic as she wished, as long as it was not rewritten in her own words. This difficulty indicates that the instruction in the guide regarding how to summarize the definition of the heuristic also needs to be more enlightening.

Task T2 - Develop the Heuristics Guide. During task T2, participants developed the heuristics guide for the Ubiquitous Heuristics set. Contrary to participant P1 in the initial test, participants in this test included in the heuristics guide only the heuristics for which the heuristics cards were created in task T1. Both participants P2 and P4 were in doubt whether there was a template for creating the heuristics guide. Participant P4 stated that she expected the existence of this template. The researcher informed that this document could be freely written to allow it to be better adapted to each set of heuristics.

Participant P4 was the one who had the most doubts when performing this task: "I just think that the guide is going to be complicated, right? Make a guide? I do not know". The researcher asked if she understood the purpose of this guide, in which she said: "The heuristics guide is explaining better what heuristics are, like... how can I better explain heuristics if I didn't create it? the heuristics?". Thus, the participant was instructed to read the meaning of the heuristics guide again. After that, she understood that this guide only presents the specification of the heuristics that are being gamified. This indicates that the name of the artifact generated in this activity (heuristics guide) may not be ideal, as participant P1 of the initial test had already suggested.

Task T3 - Activity Cycle Selection. In task T3, the participants selected the set of rules with severity classification, which contains the appropriate rules for instantiating the G4NHE using the Ubiquitous Heuristics, since these heuristics uses severity classification [18]. Again, this task was the one that the participants had the most difficulty in understanding and executing.

Participant P4 did not understand the instruction of the guide when it explained how to choose the set of rules, since she questioned whether she would be free to choose either of the two sets. She was confused because the traditional Heuristic Evaluation considers severity classification, and she did not know heuristics without severity classification. Then, the participant was explained why G4NHE provides two sets of rules. She recalled that the Ubiquitous Heuristics followed the traditional Heuristic Evaluation, so she selected the set of rules with severity classification. Like participant P2, participant P4 also did not notice the file that describes how Ubiquitous Heuristics are used in the Heuristic Evaluation, informing that the severity classification is performed.

Both participants P2 and P4 indicated the fact that a user who knows the set of heuristics and wants to use it in gamification will quickly know how to choose the correct set of rules. To try to solve this difficulty, participant P4 suggested explaining that Heuristic Evaluation usually perform the severity classification of the problems found. Still, some people adapt the method to perform only the classification of violated heuristics. It also recommended the inclusion of the following statement: "Then check that your heuristics follow this method".

Participant P3 was the one who had more difficulty performing the task compared to the others. After some questions and problems, participant P3 chose the set of rules severity classification. As a correction suggestion, the participant recommended that the condition for selecting the ruleset to be highlighted in the specialization guide.

Post-Test Interview. Regarding the G4NHE proposal, all participants showed interest in gamification to promote dialogue and fun. On the understanding of the proposal, participant P2 said that he understood the terms of the G4NHE better after reading the specialization guide, where he was able to understand what would need to be done in the test. All participants read the guide completely before starting any task. About this, participant P2 considered that it is normal for no person to understand the guide with just one reading and said that he read this slowly, step-by-step, and twice. Thus, he concluded that the user would be able to better understand the specialization guide while reading it more often, requiring time. However, participant P4 reported that, initially, she did not understand which tasks would need to be performed: "I don't know, like... you gave me this [specialization guide] here. Then I decided to read everything, and I could have something like this: read and do it, read and do it. It was not very clear that I can read and do at the same time, you know". For P4, the guide could include the following instruction: "To use G4NHE in your heuristic sets, follow this [guide activities]". Participant P3 also did not understand which tasks needed to be performed when reading the guide only once.

5.5   Consolidation of Results

With the results found in the final test, it can be seen that the expert participant P4 made more suggestions for improvement compared to the participants who are students (P2 and P3). However, the difficulty in understanding the G4NHE specialization guide and performing its activities was the same, with the exception of only participant P3, who had an unexpected performance, which was justified by the fact that this participant was tired and, visibly, sleepy during the test application.

To facilitate the understanding and refinement of the G4NHE and its specialization guide, the modifications to be carried out were summarized. In this set of changes, the suggestions made by participant P1 of the initial test that have not yet been applied were also included. The modifications are:

- Modify the layout of heuristics cards to allow an ID of more than two characters to be legibly entered into these cards;
- Increase the size of the blue line that separates the name and definition of the heuristic on the heuristic card so that it can occupy the entire length of the white part of the card;
- Remove the separator line from scoring and renegotiation cards;
- Insert the less than ("¡") and greater than ("¿") symbol between the labels that define the space where the heuristics information will be inserted in the heuristics cards;
- Insert an instruction informing the user that to use G4NHE in his heuristic sets; he must follow the activities in the specialization guide;
- Insert a textual scenario usage describing a complete G4NHE round;
- In the first activity (prepare the heuristics cards), clarify that the use of these icons is optional;
- In the first activity, when summarizing the definition of a heuristic inform that it should be readable in a heuristic card;
- In the second activity (prepare the heuristics guide), a more precise name must be presented for the artifact that is generated;
- In the second activity, inform that there is no template for the creation of the heuristics guide;
- In the second activity, insert one more example of how the heuristics guide can be written for another set of heuristics that are specified with other information;
- In the second activity, inform that the user creates the heuristics guide based on how the heuristics selected by him were documented;
- In the third activity (selection of the set of rules to be used), as some people adapt the method to perform only the classification of violated heuristics, instruct that the user needs to check whether the heuristics chosen by him follow the traditional method (with severity) or not;
- In the third activity, emphasize that the condition that defines which set of rules should be chosen;
- In the third activity, instruct that the severity, score, and renegotiation cards already exist and only need to be printed;

- In step 2 of the rule sets, mention the use of the card that represents "not a violation";
- In step 4 of the set of rules with severity classification, replace "heuristic violations" with "violated heuristics";
- In step 5 of the set of rules with severity classification, it is possible to indicate in which step of the gamification the initial choice of severity will be used;
- In step 2 of the set of rules without severity classification, it is possible to indicate in which step of the gamification the initial selection of violated heuristics will be used;
- In step 8 of the ruleset with severity classification and in step 10 of the ruleset with severity classification, explain that when a round ends, the player on the left will be the next owner of the round.

6 Evaluating G4NHE New Rules

The objective of the second study is to evaluate the acceptance of the new rules proposed by G4NHE, which are an adaptation of the original rules of the G4H to allow the gamification to be applied without the severity classification step. This evaluation was also applied to verify that the balance of the rules is adequate.

6.1 Participants' Profile

The participants of this test were students of undergraduate courses related to the area of information technology. In order to participate, they would need to know the Heuristic Evaluation method so that they would be able to understand the terms covered in the test. Regarding the training of participants in relation to the HCI, players J1 and J4 took the HCI Evaluation course in 2018.1, while players J2 and J3 in 2016.2. Regarding the Heuristic Evaluation, players J1, J2, and J4 applied this method in other situations outside the courses. Player J3 reported that he vaguely remembered what was given in the classroom.

Considering a scale from 0 to 10 to evaluate the experience level of players with the Heuristic Evaluation, player J3 was the one who evaluated his experience with the lowest score (3). The score given by the other players (J1, J2, and J4) ranged between 7 and 8.5. This indicates that player J3 may have more difficulty performing test activities compared to other players.

6.2 Procedure

A group test was applied, which consisted of observing players' behavior during some rounds of the G4NHE, in which the set of rules with no severity classification was used. Players were asked to carry out an individual inspection of a web system[1], which allows them to compare product prices and sell them. Then, they consolidated the problems found using the G4NHE. Considering that the

---

[1] http://mercadolivre.com.br.

objective of this study is only to test the new rules of G4NHE, any set of heuristics could be used by the players, noting that they only performed an association of the problems found with the violated heuristics and not the execution of the Heuristic Evaluation method itself. Players applied Nielsen's usability heuristics [11], as they have previous experience with the use of these heuristics. It is important to consider that the results of this evaluation depend a lot on the evaluators' experience with the heuristics; thus, it would not be feasible to ask the players to use heuristics that they did not know [14]. Thus, the cards used in the test were the originals of the G4H, which were already created with Nielsen's heuristics in mind, as well as the renegotiation cards proposed by the G4NHE. All cards were delivered to players in prototype versions.

Conducting the group test was guided by the following script. Initially, the researcher proposing this work read the consent form with the participants. Then, the participants were asked to answer a profile questionnaire about their experience with the Heuristic Evaluation. In this study, the consent form and the profile questionnaire were provided to the participants in printed form. After that, the researcher revised the Heuristic Evaluation method quickly. Then, the test was explained to the participants, describing that they would need to carry out the individual inspection of a pre-established web system and, later, consolidate the identified problems using the G4NHE. Therefore, the materials to be used in the test were delivered to the participants electronically. They are the set of rules to be used in the gamification rounds so that players can consult them in case of doubts; the usage scenario for the individual inspection; the Nielsen's heuristics guide, which contains the specification of these heuristics; a worksheet so that players can record problems identified in the individual inspection; and finally, the heuristics and severity cards. Subsequently, each player performed an individual inspection. They were then asked to consolidate the identified issues using the G4NHE, in which a demonstration round and three effective rounds took place.

One of the participants, player J4, had to arrive later in the test room. However, the test started without his participation since he could not have been present. So he started performing the tasks well after the other participants. This may indicate that this participant identified the lowest number (2) of usability problems in the individual inspection. Player J2 identified the highest number of issues individually (7) and was also the one who scored the most in the rounds of the G4NHE, earning three (3) points.

The G4NHE rounds lasted quite a while, hitting the player's availability timeout. Thus, the planned focus group was carried out only on the following day. In the current study, this technique was applied with the objective of collecting players' opinions on the G4NHE proposal and identifying positive points and suggestions for improvement. In the application of the focus group, player J4 could not be present. Thus, only players J1, J2, and J3 participated in this part of the study.

6.3   Focus Group

In general, players enjoyed using a gamified approach to perform the Heuristic Evaluation. Player J1 stated that gamification makes the consolidation of results more effective: "I think it helped because there is something more certain there, more serious, that you chose such a heuristic. It's a card that you're showing, right, so others can already visualize it, different from just arguing. And you can even better develop the arguments to discuss. Ah... I don't agree with that card, I don't agree with that one". Player J2 highlighted the improvement in learning: "It generates learning, right, because everyone learns from everyone else according to the cards that are thrown, and in a not very bureaucratic way since it is a gamified way of doing the evaluation".

Players demonstrated increased motivation and stimulation to perform the evaluation using the G4NHE. The player J2 highlighted that the discussion about the problems becomes richer: "I think that with the game it motivates people to want to defend their point of view, to debate on that issue, you formulate a much broader thought to be able to win the point". Player J1 pointed out the fact that players can broaden their understanding of problems: "I think it also encourages people to look not only for a problem, a card, a heuristic. People are looking for more and more. Keep looking, keep looking, looking, and looking again. Something that maybe if it were without the cards, the person would look at one: there, I found it, it's here, it's good, and it's over". Player J2 confirmed her point of view: "And then knowledge about that would be limited, right, because people wouldn't go into much depth". In addition, player J3 showed the difference between carrying out the evaluation using the G4NHE and without it, as traditionally happens in HCI courses: "And then it stimulates more discussion, because, for example, a work to assess how it is done in the course... there was not as much discussion as there was in the experiment".

6.4   Consolidation of Results

To facilitate the understanding and refinement of the G4NHE rules, the discovered changes that need to be made are summarized below:

- Change the points distribution rule (step 5) in the ruleset with no severity classification to handle the case in which the final selection of violated heuristics does not correspond to the initial selection of any player;
- Change the points distribution rules (step 5) without severity classification ruleset to distribute more points per round and make the score an element of reward;
- Include the renegotiation card in the rules with severity classification, which were originally proposed by the G4H.

The refinements applied to the G4NHE technique can be find at a supplementary document[2].

---

[2] http://www.repositorio.ufc.br/handle/riufc/39472.

7   Conclusion

Game for aNy Heuristic Evaluation (G4NHE) is a generic gamification technique to allow the application of G4H with any set of usability heuristics. G4H aim to increase the engagement and motivation of different evaluators during the HCI evaluation process based on Heuristic Evaluation, in which only Nielsen's usability heuristics were considered. Thus, G4NHE emerges as an approach to allow G4H to be used with any set of usability heuristics. The main users of this proposal are HCI students, researchers, and practitioners, who often apply Heuristic Evaluation to evaluate the usability of interactive systems. G4NHE is not recommended to measure the performance or skills of an HCI evaluator or even to promote bonuses or additional remuneration in companies, as this can change the dynamics of gamification.

This paper presents the G4H evaluation with HCI evaluators. To do this, two exploratory studies were carried out. The first one aimed to evaluate the specialization guide in order to verify if it contains enough information to guide the creation of gamification based on G4NHE. The results of this step indicate that users were interested in the proposal and considered that it has good potential, highlighting the positive factors that are provided by G4NHE: motivation, competitiveness, and better debate on the problems found in a Heuristic Evaluation. However, they had difficulty understanding and executing the activities of the specialization guide, especially the preparation of heuristics cards and the choice of the set of rules to be used in gamification. In this last activity, the participants had some doubts related to whether the set of heuristics chosen for the gamification considered the severity classification or not.

The second study aimed to evaluate the acceptance of the new rules proposed by G4NHE, which are an adaptation of the original G4H rules, to allow the gamification to be applied without the severity classification step. The findings show that the use of G4NHE allowed users to consolidate the results of an evaluation, which was based only on the categorization of violated heuristics, with greater motivation and effectiveness, highlighting that this gamification allows for a richer discussion of usability problems identified. However, the established rules were not entirely clear. For instance, the points distribution rule did not balance the appropriate number of points to be distributed in each round and also did not handle the case where the final selection of violated heuristics does not match the initial selection of any player. Also, it was observed that players were not interested in buying a renegotiation, which may have occurred because they were more consensus-oriented. However, this factor may be related to the cultural aspects of the players, such as the fact that they are students and do not have a high level of technical expertise, which may have made them insecure to contest the assessment of other players/evaluators. Thus, these results may be different if the same test is applied to users with different cultural habits.

Finally, the improvement suggestions, which were obtained through the studies, were applied in the gamification proposal. Thus, generating a refined version of the G4NHE and its specialization guide. The main refinements carried out were: similar cards were unified and excerpts from the activity cycle rules were improved to facilitate understanding; a textual usage scenario was added to exemplify the technique execution; finally, activities' names and descriptions in the G4NHE specialization guide have been rewritten to make it easier to understand and execute.

As a future perspective, we aim to investigate the acceptance of the new activity cycle rules from the perspective of HCI evaluators with different cultural styles. We also intend to expand the G4NHE proposal by exploring their use with playability and accessibility heuristics.

References

1. Desurvire, H., Wiberg, C.: Game usability heuristics (PLAY) for evaluating and designing better games: the next iteration. In: Ozok, A.A., Zaphiris, P. (eds.) OCSC 2009. LNCS, vol. 5621, pp. 557–566. Springer, Heidelberg (2009). https://doi.org/ 10.1007/978-3-642-02774-1_60
2. Deterding, S., Dixon, D., Khaled, R., Nacke, L.: From game design elements to gamefulness: defining "gamification". In: Proceedings of the 15th International Academic MindTrek Conference: Envisioning Future Media Environments, pp. 9–15. ACM, New York (2011)
3. Ferreira, B., Rivero, L., Lopes, A., Marques, A.B., Conte, T.: Apoiando o ensino de qualidade de software: Um serious game para o ensino de usabilidade. In: VII Fórum de Educação em Engenharia de Software, pp. 12–21. SBC, Porto Alegre (2014) (in Portuguese)
4. Fontana, A., Frey, J.: Interviewing: the art of science. In: Denzin, N., Lincoln, Y. (eds.) The Handbook of Qualitative Research, pp. 361–376. Sage Publications, Thousand Oaks (1994)
5. Herr, S., Baumgartner, N., Gross, T.: Evaluating severity rating scales for heuristic evaluation. In: Proceedings of the 2016 CHI Conference Extended Abstracts on Human Factors in Computing Systems, pp. 3069–3075. ACM, New York (2016)
6. Inostroza, R., Rusu, C., Roncagliolo, S., Rusu, V., Collazos, C.A.: Developing SMASH: a set of smartphone's usability heuristics. Comput. Stand. Interfaces **43**, 40–52 (2016)
7. Johnstone, B.: Discourse Analysis, 3rd edn. Wiley, Hoboken (2018)
8. Jucá, P.M., Teixeira Monteiro, I., de Souza Filho, J.C.: Game for heuristic evaluation (G4H): a serious game for collaborative evaluation of systems. In: Kurosu, M. (ed.) HCI 2017. LNCS, vol. 10271, pp. 341–352. Springer, Cham (2017). https:// doi.org/10.1007/978-3-319-58071-5_26
9. Mayhew, D.J.: The Usability Engineering Lifecycle: A Practitioner's Handbook for User Interface Design, 1st edn. Morgan Kaufmann, San Francisco (1999)
10. Morgan, D., Spanish, M.: Focus groups: a new tool for qualitative research. Qual. Sociol. **7**, 253–270 (1984)
11. Nielsen, J.: 10 usability heuristics for user interface design. http://www.nngroup. com/articles/ten-usability-heuristics/. Accessed 3 Feb 2022
12. Nielsen, J.: Severity ratings for usability problems. http://www.nngroup.com/ articles/how-to-rate-the-severity-of-usability-problems/. Accessed 3 Feb 2022
13. Nielsen, J.: Finding usability problems through heuristic evaluation. In: Proceedings of the SIGCHI Conference on Human Factors in Computing Systems, pp. 373–380. ACM, New York (1992)

14. Nielsen, J.: Enhancing the explanatory power of usability heuristics. In: Proceedings of the SIGCHI Conference on Human Factors in Computing Systems, pp. 152–158. ACM, New York (1994)
15. Nielsen, J., Molich, R.: Heuristic evaluation of user interfaces. In: Proceedings of the SIGCHI Conference on Human Factors in Computing Systems, pp. 249–256. ACM, New York (1990)
16. Petrie, H., Buykx, L.: Collaborative heuristic evaluation: improving the effectiveness of heuristic evaluation. In: Proceedings of the UPA 2010 International Conference, Munich (2010)
17. Queiroz, W., Beltrão, R., Fernandes, M., Bonifácio, B., Fernandes, P.: MACteaching: Um jogo para o ensino do método de avaliação de comunicabilidade. In: Companion Proceedings of the 14th Brazilian Symposium on Human Factors in Computing Systems, pp. 70–71. SBC, Porto Alegre (2015). (in Portuguese)
18. Rocha, L.C.: HUbis: heurísticas de usabilidade para avaliar sistemas ubíquos. M.sc. thesis, Universidade Federal do Ceará (UFC), Fortaleza, Brazil (2017). (in Portuguese)
19. Sharp, H., Preece, J., Rogers, Y.: Interaction Design: Beyond Human-Computer Interaction, 5th edn. Wiley, Indianapolis (2019)
20. Sommariva, L., Benitti, F.B.V., Dalcin, F.S.: UsabilityGame: jogo simulador para apoio ao ensino de usabilidade. In: Proceedings of the 10th Brazilian Symposium on Human Factors in Computing Systems and the 5th Latin American Conference on Human-Computer Interaction, pp. 61–65. SBC, Porto Alegre (2011) (in Portuguese)
21. de Souza, C.S.: The Semiotic Engineering of Human-Computer Interaction, 1st edn. MIT Press, Cambridge (2005)
22. de Souza Filho, J.C., Monteiro, I.T., Jucá, P.M.: Game for aNy heuristic evaluation (G4NHE): a generalization of the G4H gamification considering different sets of usability heuristics. Univ. Access Inf. Soc. 18(3), 489–505 (2019). https://doi.org/10.1007/s10209-019-00674-x
23. Tondello, G.F.: An introduction to gamification in human-computer interaction. XRDS 23(1), 15–17 (2016)

Towards More Clean Results in Data Visualization: A Weka Usability Experiment

Jaime Díaz[1], Roberto Espinosa[2(✉)], and Jorge Hochstetter[1]

[1] Depto. Cs. de la Computación e Informática, Universidad de La Frontera, Temuco, Chile
[2] Dpto. de Ingeniería en Computación e Informática, Universidad de Tarapacá, Arica, Chile
respinosa@academicos.uta.cl

Abstract. The development of Information Technologies has contributed to the increase and complexity of data, implying a greater diversity of mechanisms for knowledge extraction. This high data availability has made citizens increase their interest in analyzing data and making more informed decisions. Data mining is an intrinsically complex process that expert users generally use. The non-expert users are overwhelmed because they lack relevant techniques for analyzing and understanding these results. This proposal presents a usability experiment to evaluate the level of understanding of the results when applying classification techniques. The users worked with decision trees, one of the "friendliest" of existing patterns. We need to start focusing on new patterns for non-expert users from the results exposed.

Keywords: Data mining · Pattern analysis · Human computer interaction · User interfaces · Data visualization

1 Introduction

The exponential growth of data in recent years has led to an increase in the use of knowledge extraction mechanisms that allow data to be exploited more intelligently, intending to make better-informed decisions. This availability of data makes it possible for citizens to increase their interest in analyzing them to make informed decisions [1].

Data mining techniques, given their complexity, are generally used by expert users, leaving the majority of users in the background. The massification of data mining techniques for all types of users has brought some problems, among those originated in interaction with the resulting patterns. Although the number of options for applying data mining techniques has increased, in general, they are not yet ready to be consumed by non-expert users. There is a gap between the need for analysis by population and the possibility of understanding the results obtained.

The usability of the resulting patterns is a problem that has been mentioned before [2], although it is still unsolved. Paradoxically, this problem has been increasing, considering the increase in the complexity of the data and the patterns obtained, for example, in Big Data.

M. M. Soares et al. (Eds.): HCII 2022, LNCS 13321, pp. 389–400, 2022.
https://doi.org/10.1007/978-3-031-05897-4_27

Some techniques serve to evaluate the usability of software systems [3], but they can be extrapolated to different areas of computer science. These techniques are known as cognitive accompaniment that evaluate time, goal accomplishment, and conclusions drawn from observations of experiments [4].

In the context of presenting the results obtained after applying data mining techniques, it would be desirable that they are easily understandable and avoid the need for an expert user for their interpretation.

This work aims to analyze how users perceive the resulting visualizations after applying data mining algorithms. The aim is to recreate a common knowledge scenario where a particular situation is experienced. Considering many mining techniques and algorithms, we will focus on studying the level of understanding of expert and non-expert users after interpreting the results of classification techniques. Specifically, decision trees will be analyzed in this case since they are among the most widely used supervised learning algorithms.

2 Related Concepts

2.1 Usability

Usability is a crucial concept in Human-Computer Interaction (HCI). According to ISO 9241-210 [5], it is defined as: "The extent to which specific users can use a product to achieve specific objectives with efficiency, effectiveness, and satisfaction in a specific context of use". In a complementary way, ISO 20282 [5] indicates that all interactive products must have a user interface and that the quality of this interface can significantly affect the fulfillment of the objectives. In our case, usability is an essential quality parameter for understanding data extraction and interpretation processes.

2.2 Knowledge Discovery in Databases

The "Knowledge discovery in databases" (KDD) was defined by Fayyad et al. in 1996 as "the non-trivial process of identifying valid, novel, potentially useful, and ultimately understandable patterns in data" [6]. This process can be grouped into three major stages: integrating and preprocessing the data into a single repository, selecting attributes and algorithms for data mining, and ending with the analysis and interpretation of the resulting patterns.

On the other hand, data mining is understood as a set of techniques and algorithms that allow obtaining patterns not perceptible to the naked eye in data sources. This phase is considered the core of the KDD process. Its objective is to produce new knowledge that users from the analyzed data can use.

2.3 Classification Techniques

Classification techniques are one of the most widely used techniques in data mining [7, 8]. These techniques analyze a set of input data and from them construct corresponding classes based on the characteristics of the data [9]. The idea is to establish a rule where the analyst can classify each new observation into an existing class.

3 Related Works

There is an increasing need for mechanisms that allow non-expert users to analyze their data quickly. The big challenge is to make the application of data mining techniques user-friendly.

Some approaches focus on the realization of interactive data mining systems by considering an adaptive and efficient communication between human users and computer systems [10–12]. The main drawback of these proposals is that knowledge about the KDD process is required. Therefore, users without prior knowledge of data mining cannot take advantage of these approaches.

Additionally, some proposals aim to assist non-expert users in applying data mining focused basically on a specific application domain. For example, Camiolo and Porceddu [13] propose an alternative to generating genomic sequences. Bodt et al. presents a specific user-friendly tool for data mining and integration in biology [14]. Salcines et al. introduces at the educational field a collaborative recommender system using distributed data mining for the continuous improvement of e-learning courses [15]. Espinosa et al. presents an alternative for the application of data mining techniques by non-expert users [16]. However the issue of visualization of the patterns obtained is still under development.

Kriegel et al. address the issue of "increasing usability", but from the perspective that the complexity and alternatives of mining algorithms will increase and the number of variables to be considered [2].

In order to find proposals related to our topic, we performed a preliminary search through the "ScienceDirect" engine, restricting the results to the last five years. This time restriction was mainly based on changes in technology and visualization trends.

First Approach. "Data Mining + User Experience". There are very few relevant results that manage to mix both needs. The initial search resulted in the proposal by Rojas et al. [17], where they comment on new techniques using augmented reality for improved perception of results. While it is true that user experience cannot be minimized to interface concepts, it is a second edge to the search spectrum.

Second Approach. A combination of concepts: "visualization for data-mining models"/"data visualization"/"visual data mining". Integrating this approach, known as "visual data mining", allows us to combine human exploration ability with the analytical processing capability of computers for problem-solving.

Graphical visualizations often aid data mining to facilitate a better understanding of the data and results [18]. This is especially true for visual and very detailed data, too complex to be easily understood with hard data alone.

Interactive data visualization allows us to leverage human visual and cognitive perception to improve the accuracy and efficiency of data analysis [19, 20]. When integrated with data mining algorithms, data visualization systems combine human strengths with the computational power of machines to solve problems that neither approach can solve in isolation [21].

In summary, proposals are found that try to support the application of data mining techniques in some specific domains, but solutions that support non-expert users are still needed [22].

4 Methods and Materials

This section describes the methodology applied to conclude the users' understanding of the resulting patterns obtained after applying data mining techniques.

In this case, we analyzed how the results were obtained after applying the J48 algorithm of classification techniques. This algorithm was selected because it is one of the most user-friendly patterns obtained from classification techniques since it presents its results in a tree form. The individual results and training were obtained with the Data Mining and Machine Learning software Weka [23].

A set of tasks were carried out to identify the usability of the resulting patterns (decision trees). The designed experiments were applied considering two groups of users: (i) experts and (ii) non-experts in data mining techniques.

We take as a reference whether or not they had taken any subject related to data mining or pattern recognition. They were between 20 and 40 years old, with similar experience in using technologies, students, or university professionals. 70% of the participants were men, and 30% were women. All the experiments were conducted in person, either in a classroom or a work office. The selection of the surveyed users was randomized.

For the experimentation, it was considered to present three graphic patterns to the users. After applying the same data mining algorithm on three data sources with different characteristics, these patterns were obtained but related to the same application domain. It is intended to increase the complexity of the patterns shown to analyze user reactions in each case.

Initially, users are introduced to the study, indicating the objectives of applying data mining techniques to the different data sources analyzed. Then it is explained to them what type of question they should answer when analyzing the patterns presented. In general, the aim is to store information on three criteria:

- Whether or not they get the correct answer to the question asked.
- How long it takes to obtain a solution.
- What observations are identified while performing the exercise.

4.1 Experimentation Details

The three data sources used contain information obtained from the interaction of university students in different courses available in virtual learning platforms. The objective of the applied algorithm is to predict whether or not a student passes or fails the course he is taking, based on the information gathered from his interaction with the activities available on the virtual platform during the course. In this opportunity, we seek that the user evaluator, given the actual data of a student, manages to determine from each resulting graph whether he/she will pass or fail the course. In other words, to evaluate the degree of visualization interpretation of the classification model obtained as its complexity increases.

Three alternative patterns obtained by applying the same algorithm to each data source will be presented. Table 1 describes the number of attributes, instances, and classes that were used in the exercise for each dataset.

The number of "attributes" are the characteristics to measure from the data source. The "instances" refer to the number of observations, and the "classes of the target attribute", refer to the number of possible values that the attribute to predict has, for example: For data source (1), the target attribute is "complete rating", where its possible values are two: {fail, pass}.

Table 2 shows the parameters and their respective values of the student who is asked to determine whether or not he will be able to pass the course in one of the exercises applied to the surveyed users.

Table 1. Description of some general characteristics of the data sources.

Datasource	Number of attributes	Number of instances	Number of classes of the objective attribute
(1)	12	65	2
(2)	14	64	2
(3)	27	193	5

Table 2. Attributes and values of the used instance of dataset 2.

Attribute	Value	Attribute	Value
tiempo_total	5133	tiempo_total_abril_assignements	101.383
num_sesione	117	clicks_febrero_contenidos	12
media_tiempo_semana	342	clicks_febrero_foro	92
media_sesiones	7	clicks_mayo_assignements	26
tiempo_total_contenidos	1135.316	mensajes_leidos_foro	137
num_sesiones_abril_assessment	1	mensajes_escritos_foro	20
tiempo_total_marzo_foro	627.266		

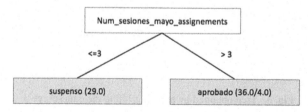

Fig. 1. Tree obtained by applying J48 to the data source 1.

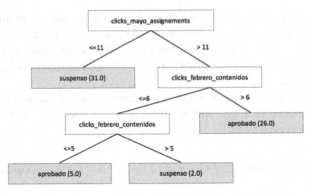

Fig. 2. Tree obtained by applying J48 to the data source 2.

Regarding the experimentation activities: (i) Each student was given interaction values of the evaluated activities (parameters). From the evaluation of these values, it should be determined whether they will finally pass or fail the course. The latter is the question to be solved.

The resulting trees (see Fig. 1 and 2) increase the complexity from 1 to 3 evaluated parameters. However, Fig. 3 shows that the number of attributes to be evaluated is higher, adding complexity to the results. Please note that the data expressed in the graph are not relevant, but the important thing is to show the complexity acquired as attributes are added to the scenario.

When an expert analyzes the third tree (see Fig. 3), he identifies overfitting from the degree of branching of the tree presented. To solve this, some pre-processing techniques are applied to the data source to simplify the resulting visualizations. However, as non-expert users should also use this, the graphical representations should still be as "usable and friendly" as possible.

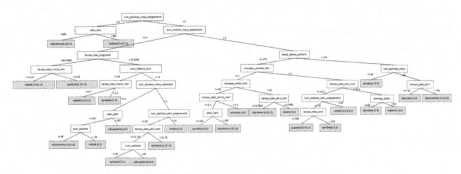

Fig. 3. Tree obtained by applying J48 to the data source 3.

Table 3. Results from datasource (1) non-experts users.

	Correct results	Incorrect results	Does not know/Does not answer
#	26	6	2
%	76.5%	17.6%	5.9%

Table 4. Results from datasource (2) non-experts users.

	Correct results	Incorrect results	Does not know/Does not answer
#	32	1	1
%	94.1%	2.9%	2.9%

5 Results

5.1 Non-expert Users

Regarding the experimentation on non-expert users (without previous experience in data mining). Of the 34 participants, all responded without significant problems.

Case (1) - Using Data Source (1). Average resolution time 88.57 s (see Table 3). With a standard deviation of 84.46 s. Although there were users who managed to solve it within the expected time (between 90 and 120 s, considering the time to read instructions), others took twice as long.

It should be remembered that the first experiment has a low level of complexity, taking into account that only one parameter is analyzed ("num_sesiones_mayo_assignements"), out of a maximum difficulty of eight (Fig. 3).

Table 5. Results from datasource (3) non-experts users.

	Correct results	Incorrect results	Does not know/Does not answer
#	25	7	2
%	73.5%	20.6%	5.9%

There was a hypothesis of correct answers higher than 90%. However, only 76.5% of the participants performed the test correctly. This is an exciting figure to analyze; 23.5% of the users in this stage made some error when asked for a specific answer.

Table 6. Results from datasource (1) experts users.

	Correct results	Incorrect results	Does not know/Does not answer
#	12	0	0
%	100%	0%	0%

Case (2) - Using Data Source (2). Average resolution time 87.83 s (see Table 4). With a standard deviation of 71.47 s. As in the previous scenario, there were users within the expected time averages (between 80 and 90 s), but the standard deviation indicates that some took almost twice as long to solve the same problem. However, this time, users began to understand the essential workings, taking about the same amount of time but with 94.1% correct results. Only 5.8% of the total had errors or failed to reach the result.

Case (3) - Using Data Source (3). Average resolution time 171.17 s. With a standard deviation of 98.61 s (see Table 5). The last scenario had the highest resolution difficulty (with a maximum of 8 parameters to be evaluated). Although the evaluation times exceeded what was expected (120–150 s), the deviation was not twice as high as in the previous cases. However, they were considerably lower than in the previous case and equal to the error levels of the first case. Only 73.5% of the users managed to get the correct answer to the exercise. Where 20.6% did not manage to arrive correctly (ended up in the wrong branch within the decision tree) and 5.9% did not manage to solve it.

5.2 Expert Users

The results achieved by the expert users are presented below. Of the 12 participants, it can be observed.

Table 7. Results from datasource (2) experts users.

	Correct results	Incorrect results	Does not know/Does not answer
#	12	0	0
%	100%	0%	0%

Case (1) - Using Data Source (1). Average resolution time 49.83 s (see Table 6). With a standard deviation of 37.17 s. 100% of the users answer correctly, within the expected time (less than 60 s).

Case (2) - Using Data Source (2). Average resolution time 26.17 s (see Table 7). With a standard deviation of 10.47 s. Like the previous case, 100% of the users complete the task without significant inconveniences.

Table 8. Results from datasource (3) experts users.

	Correct results	Incorrect results	Does not know/Does not answer
#	11	1	0
%	91.7%	8.3%	0%

Case (3) - Using Data Source (3). Average resolution time 92.5 s. With a standard deviation of 51.85 s (see Table 8). 91.7% of the evaluated users were able to solve the problem. Although only one of them indeed made an error (due to the size of the sample), this proves the hypothesis that the error can also be present in advanced or expert users.

These were separated by scenario based on the comments and observations perceived during the experimentation.

- First case: 75% dealt with the performance of the trees and the appropriate attribute association. The perception of the exercise and functioning of the decision trees was not immediate. After verifying the initial operation, the remaining 25% referred to how instinctive it was.
- Second case: 60% of the perceived observations dealt with the case's complexity. It was noted that the more attributes, the greater the complexity of the visualization. The rest of the comments ranged from (i) "not much work" and (ii) "solved after further review."
- The third case: 57% found the solution very complex. 29% that, although the participants marked the correct answer by indicating that they had "passed" the evaluated student. They came to a hasty conclusion (they did not follow the correct path). The rest of the comments referred to not having adequate knowledge to assimilate the attributes (once) or not "to find the graph to be evaluated" (once). Note: No comments were perceived at this stage.

5.3 Preliminary Approach

The results obtained show that the patterns used are not entirely user-friendly, and their presentation is not understandable for non-expert users, which is our target audience.

The following is a first approximation of a solution to this problem (see Fig. 4). After applying the decision tree algorithm, the visualization of the results was designed following two initiatives: (i) The final result is the relevant one. It is desired to know if the student passes or fails the subject in question, so it is the first thing that should be made known. (ii) If the end-user wishes to detail the classification given and extend the logistics of solving the algorithm, he can perform a retrospective visualization to analyze the reason for the answer. This provides the space to analyze the constraints and possible solutions, ensuring that the first option shows the predicted classification.

In this iteration, we only cover a gap of a complete KDD process. A good alternative would be to use the proposal presented in previous work [16]. The general objective is to assist the end-user by automatically selecting and applying the algorithm to obtain the best result according to the information extracted from the data the user wants to analyze. Subsequently, add our visualization proposal to achieve an acceptance and understanding of the results by the end-users after their data is processed using decision trees.

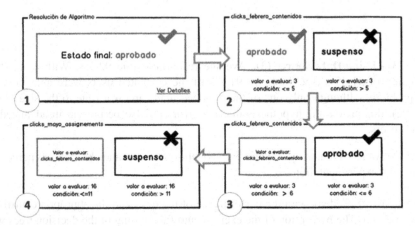

Fig. 4. Proposal to visualize the tree obtained from data source 2.

6 Discussion

The development of Information Technologies has contributed to the increase and complexity of the data currently generated [24]. This high availability of data has increased citizens' interest in analyzing them to make more informed decisions.

The results obtained in the proposal reaffirm that we are facing an open problem, where the scientific community should focus its efforts due to the growing current need. We conclude our analysis by addressing the following questions:

- What would happen then if the results were presented abruptly and early to non-expert users? We would likely encounter a percentage of users with errors, and it is worth noting that a graphical form of representation is being used. In contrast, usually, results are presented by plain text files.
- Is the description of parameters or language relevant when presented to non-expert users? Curiously, a few errors are due to attributes in different languages or without any context for the end-users. This type of representation should be more careful when displaying results.

As future work, it is interesting to highlight two initiatives (i) "Thick Data," a concept coined in 2009 by Tricia Wang [25], which uses qualitative and ethnographic research methods that capture the emotions, stories, and mental models of target users. The author indicates that "what is measurable is not necessarily valuable" and gives us an example of the wrong predictions that occurred during the United States elections [25].

The initiative calls for an integrative research approach, where the results of Big Data can be contextualized and told through stories, adding the human dimension. This integrated approach produces different types of insights at different scales and depths.

Secondly, (ii) search for and design new techniques for data visualization. Although we were indeed able to verify that there is a significant shortcoming in the interpretation of results, it is intended in the next iteration to compare data presentation techniques that aim to arrive at the correct solution obtained after applying data mining techniques. This allows us to meet the objectives of "digital literacy 2.0", where not only "Data Science" specialists will be able to use these large amounts of data to obtain/generate knowledge, as an expert in the field could do. Finally, the possibility of applying these recommendations to improve specific visualization software should be highlighted.

Acknowledgment. This work was partially funded by the Project UTA Mayor No 8729-20 of the Universidad de Tarapacá, Arica, Chile.

References

1. Boyd, D., Crawford, K.: Six provocations for big data. in internet time: Symposium on the dynamics of …. (2011)
2. Kriegel, H.-P., Borgwardt, K.M., Kroger, P., Pryakhin, A., Schubert, M., Zimek, A.: Future trends in data mining. Data Min. Knowl. Discov. **15**, 87–97 (2007)
3. Nielsen, J.: Usability inspection methods. In: Conference Companion on Human Factors in Computing Systems, pp. 413–414. ACM, New York (1994)
4. Nielsen, J.: Designing Web Usability: The Practice of Simplicity. New Riders Publishing, Thousand Oaks (1999)
5. Iso 9241-210: ISO 9241-210:2010 - Ergonomics of human-system interaction - Part 210: Human-centred design for interactive systems
6. Fayyad, U.M., Piatetsky-Shapiro, G., Smyth, P., et al.: Knowledge discovery and data mining: towards a unifying framework. In: KDD, pp. 82–88 (1996)
7. Osipovs, P.: Classification tree applying for automated CV filtering in transport company. Procedia Comput. Sci. **149**, 406–414 (2019)
8. K. Goswami, P., Sharma, A.: Realtime analysis and visualization of data for instant decisions: a futuristic requirement of the digital world. Materials Today: Proceedings (2021). https://doi.org/10.1016/j.matpr.2021.02.193
9. Breiman, L., Friedman, J., Stone, C.J., Olshen, R.A.: Classification and regression trees (1984)
10. Zhao, Y.: On interactive data mining. Encyclopedia of Data Warehousing and Mining (2009)
11. Li, T., et al.: FIU-Miner (a fast, integrated, and user-friendly system for data mining) and its applications. Knowl. Inf. Syst. **52**(2), 411–443 (2016). https://doi.org/10.1007/s10115-016-1014-0
12. Dimitropoulos, H., et al.: AITION: a scalable platform for interactive data mining. In: Ailamaki, A., Bowers, S. (eds.) SSDBM 2012. LNCS, vol. 7338, pp. 646–651. Springer, Heidelberg (2012). https://doi.org/10.1007/978-3-642-31235-9_51
13. Camiolo, S., Porceddu, A.: gff2sequence, a new user friendly tool for the generation of genomic sequences. BioData Min (2013)
14. Bodt, S.D., Carvajal, D., Hollunder, J.: CORNET: a user-friendly tool for data mining and integration. Plant (2010)
15. Salcines, E.G., Romero, C., Ventura, S.: Sistema recomendador colaborativo usando minería de datos distribuida para la mejora continua de cursos e-learning. IEEE-RITA (2008)

16. Espinosa, R., García-Saiz, D., Zorrilla, M., Zubcoff, J.J., Mazón, J.-N.: S3Mining: a model-driven engineering approach for supporting novice data miners in selecting suitable classifiers. Comput. Stand. Interfaces. **65**, 143–158 (2019)

17. Rojas, W.C., Quispe, F.M., Villegas, C.M.: Augmented visualization for data-mining models. Procedia Comput. Sci. **55**, 650–659 (2015)

18. Schuh, M.A., Banda, J.M., Wylie, T., McInerney, P., Pillai, K.G., Angryk, R.A.: On visualization techniques for solar data mining. Astronomy Comput. **10**, 32–42 (2015)

19. Steed, C.A.: Chapter 7 – interactive data visualization. In: Data Analytics for Intelligent Transportation Systems, pp. 165–190 (2017)

20. Laher, R.R.: Thoth: software for data visualization & statistics. Astronomy Comput. **17**, 177–185 (2016)

21. Ltifi, H., Benmohamed, E., Kolski, C., Ben Ayed, M.: Enhanced visual data mining process for dynamic decision-making. Knowl.-Based Syst. **112**, 166–181 (2016)

22. Mazón, J.-N., Zubcoff, J.J., Garrigós, I., Espinosa, R., Rodríguez, R.: Open Business Intelligence: on the importance of data quality awareness in user-friendly data mining

23. Weka 3 - Data Mining with Open Source Machine Learning Software in Java. https://www.cs.waikato.ac.nz/ml/weka/. Accessed 14 Jan 2022

24. Pavez, R., Diaz, J., Arango-Lopez, J., Ahumada, D., Mendez-Sandoval, C., Moreira, F.: Emo-mirror: a proposal to support emotion recognition in children with autism spectrum disorders. Neural Comput. Appl., 1–12 (2021)

25. Wang, T.: Why Big Data Needs Thick Data – Ethnography Matters – Medium. https://medium.com/ethnography-matters/why-big-data-needs-thick-data-b4b3e75e3d7

Usability Assessment and Improvement Plan for Treadmills in Campus Gym

Mingxia Gao[1], Sihui Peng[1], Zhengxian He[1], Huaming Peng[1(✉)], and Marcelo M. Soares[2]

[1] School of Design, South China University of Technology, Guangzhou 510006, People's Republic of China
huamingpengedu@163.com
[2] School of Design, Hunan University, Changsha 410000, Hunan, People's Republic of China

Abstract. In recent years, more and more Chinese colleges and universities have set up gyms on campus in order to enhance students' physical fitness. As an important part of the sports fitness industry, campus gyms have huge development space, and due to the particularity of the user groups, there are certain differences from ordinary gyms. Treadmills are the most common and basic fitness equipment in campus gyms. At present, there is no treadmill specially designed for campus gyms. Therefore, there is still a lot of room for improvement in user experience of campus treadmills. This study takes the gym of Guangzhou International Campus of South China University of Technology as an example. In terms of hardware, the OWAS scale is used to evaluate the user's running posture, and the treadmill is improved for problems such as heart rate measurement; in terms of interface, QUIS is used to evaluate the treadmill interface. And according to the evaluation results, the interface layout of the treadmill is optimized.

Keywords: Usability assessment · Campus treadmill · OWAS · QUIS · Redesign

1 Introduction

In recent years, China's fitness industry has begun to rise rapidly, and college students have become the main force in physical fitness. More and more colleges and universities have set up gyms on campus in order to enhance students' physical fitness. As an important part of the sports fitness industry, campus gyms have huge development space, and due to the particularity of user groups and use scenarios, there are certain differences from ordinary gyms. Most of the campus gyms are open to students for free or at a lower price, not for profit, and are not large in scale and have many users. Treadmills are the fitness equipment most commonly used by students in campus gyms, and there is still room for improvement in user experience. In order to improve the usability of campus treadmills, this study took the gymnasium of Guangzhou International Campus of South China University of Technology as an example, and used several analysis methods to evaluate and optimize the hardware and interface of campus treadmills.

M. M. Soares et al. (Eds.): HCII 2022, LNCS 13321, pp. 401–413, 2022.
https://doi.org/10.1007/978-3-031-05897-4_28

2   Research Method and Process

This study employed several methods to evaluate the usability of campus treadmill hardware and its interface. We first conducted a field survey, and in order to obtain more data, we designed a preliminary questionnaire in terms of functions, interface interaction, and user queuing experience. For the product, OWAS was used to assess the user's posture while using the treadmill. For the interface, the Questionnaire for User Interface Satisfaction (QUIS) was used to assess users' subjective satisfaction with specific aspects of the treadmill interface.

2.1   Field Observation

From 8:30 pm to 9:30 pm on December 23, we observed the whole process of 6 men and 3 women using the treadmill in the campus gym, recorded their using behaviors, and conducted user interviews with them after they finished running.

In order to obtain more information about the use of treadmill, we designed and distributed a questionnaire, which contained the basic information of users, their habits when using the treadmill, common functions and troubles encountered in using it. Through a combination of online and offline methods, we obtained 128 questionnaires, 91 of which were valid. We used this as the basis to draw a user journey map (Fig. 1).

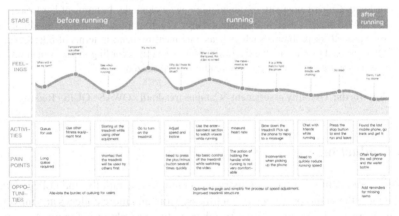

Fig. 1. User journey map.

2.2   Treadmill Hardware Evaluation Method

For treadmill hardware evaluation, we used OWAS (Ovako Working Posture Analysis Sustem), developed by Ovako Steel in Finland in 1973. This method is used to define the position of the user's body while using the treadmill and to classify the degree of injury that may result.

The investigator followed the user without interfering with the subject's normal running, and ensured the integrity of the user's whole body in the filmed images. The investigators recorded the whole process of users using the treadmill from 15:00–15:30 in the afternoon and from 19:00–19:30 in the evening. A total of 9 videos were sampled during the 1-h observation period. Investigators then measured the frequency of various combinations of postures in the exercise category and identified poor working postures. Then, we coded each bad working posture using the OWAS posture coding map, and the codes were counted to determine the action class (AC, ActionCategories) of the user's posture, and then the corresponding treatment plan was selected.

The action categories are divided into four levels, including AC1, AC2, AC3 and AC4, and the classification of each level is based on: AC1 = normal posture, no need to deal with; AC2 = posture with minor hazards, need to take improvement measures in the near future; AC3 = posture with obvious hazards, need to take improvement measures as soon as possible; AC4 = posture with serious hazards, need to take improvement measures immediately [1] (Fig. 2).

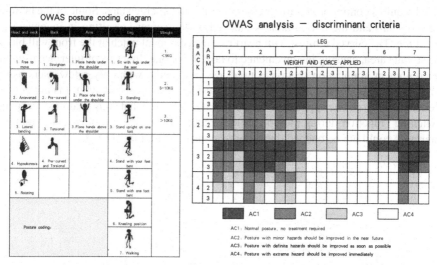

Fig. 2. OWAS posture coding diagram and discriminant criteria.

2.3 Treadmill Interface Evaluation Method

For treadmill interface evaluation, we used Questionnaire for User Interface Satisfaction (QUIS). The QUIS was designed to assess user's subjective satisfaction with specific aspects of the HMI.

The QUIS contains a demographic questionnaire, a measure of overall system satisfaction along six scales, and hierarchically organized measures of four specific interface factors (screen factors, terminology and system feedback, learning factors, and system capabilities) [2].

Each area measures the overall satisfaction with that facet of the interface, as well as the factors that make up that facet, on a 9-point scale [3]. A total of 20 users (meeting the minimum number of samples) accepted our survey. These samples were screened and used the treadmill 1–2 times a month. In earlier studies, it is found that men and women do not differ in their level of positive affectivity (Watson, 2000). Therefore, responses were not categorized according to the gender.

We used a simplified version of the QUIS scale for four aspects: screen factors, terminology and system feedback, learning factors, and system capabilities.

3   Results

3.1   Result of Field Observation

Field Observations and User Interviews. In the process of field survey and user interview, it was found that almost all users experienced queuing, and users might give up using the treadmill in the process of long queuing. In terms of product usage, users prefer buttons when turning on and adjusting speed in the middle. However, adjusting the speed requires continuous button presses or continuous screen taps. Some of the buttons are too small and the button area is blocked by the screen, resulting in inconvenient operation. The curved armrest with heart rate measurement patch at the front will block the storage area, causing inconvenience to take the phone. In terms of interface use, the entertainment application section is used less frequently, with only a few users using Street View and only one user using video. Besides, users feedback that it is not convenient to jump from one application to another. It is observed that there is almost no "page switching" function during the operation. Except for Street View, other entertainment interfaces could not be opened during basic control operations (Fig. 3).

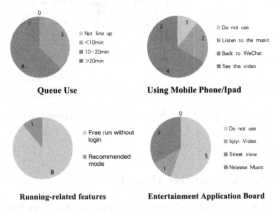

Fig. 3. Field research information.

Questionnaire. With 91 valid questionnaires, we can conclude that most users think the queue is too long and requires too many clicks when adjusting the speed. Most users use the buttons more often than the screen, and more users tend to put the "heart rate widget" in front than on either side. This is consistent with the results of our field observations and user research (Fig. 4).

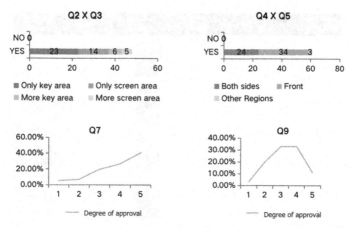

Fig. 4. Questionnaire information.

3.2 Result of Treadmill Hardware Evaluation

Through OWAS evaluation (Fig. 5), it can be concluded that among the user's posture of using the treadmill, the posture of "using buttons" and "using cell phone" is AC1, which means that this posture is the normal posture of the user and does not need to be dealt with.

The user's posture of "holding the cell phone", "using the handrail" and "clicking the screen" during the running process is AC2, which means that the posture is slightly harmful and needs to be taken recently. Improvement measures are needed in the near future. In the process of observation, we found that the "home" and "back" keys, which are used more frequently, are set in the upper left corner of the screen, so the posture appears more frequently and lasts longer. The user is more affected by the posture of clicking the upper left corner.

The user's posture of "measuring heart rate with the handle" while running belongs to AC3, which is obviously harmful and needs to be improved as soon as possible. Hand-held heart rate monitoring is at present the most widely used heart rate monitoring method on the treadmill, must hold the heart rate card in both hands at the same time in order to measure the heart rate, this way is more accurate and convenient to test, but the posture of measuring heart rate while running often makes the user feel uncomfortable, and the posture of measuring heart rate with the handle generally needs to be maintained for 10–20 s.

There is no obvious harm to the user's other postures, so the relevant hardware is not considered for improvement.

3.3 Result of Treadmill Interface Evaluation

Reliability analysis was used to measure the reliability of the sample response results, and after SPSS analysis, the Cronbach alpha coefficient value of this questionnaire was 0.955, so the questionnaire results were reliable.

Serial numbe	Action	Frequency	Average duration of	The worst position	Code	Analysis results
1	Use the heart rate handle	11	23s		42141	AC3
2	Take the phone	6	2.5s		24171	AC2
3	Use the buttons	18	10s		21121	AC1
4	Use the armrest	4	7s		22171	AC2
5	The use of mobile phones	6	49s		21171	AC1
6	(Running at high speed) Click on the bottom right corner of the screen	8	3s		22171	AC2
7	(Running at high speed) Click in the lower left corner of the screen	3	3s		24171	AC2
8	(Running at high speed) Click in the upper left corner of the screen	11	5s		24271	AC2
9	(Unexpected) Click in the middle of the screen	15	2s		52171	AC2

Fig. 5. OWAS assessment results.

In this questionnaire, screen factors include Q4, Q6, Q7, Q8, Q20, Q26 (Fig. 6), terminology and system feedback include Q3, Q10, Q11, Q12, Q14, Q21 (Fig. 7), learning factors include Q13, 15, 17, 19, 24, 28 (Fig. 8), the system functions include Q9, Q16, Q22, Q23, Q27 (Fig. 9).

The evaluation results show that: In terms of Screen design & layout, the page skipping steps are cumbersome, and the buttons highlighted on the screen fail to guide effectively; In terms of Terms & system information, system error messages (such as login failure) frustrate users; In terms of Learning, the process of exploring features is complicated, which makes the system less interesting; In terms of System capabilities, the system itself is not perfect and the function level is not clear enough, which makes it difficult for users to find featured functions (such as starting).

In addition, the back button and home button, which are frequently used, are located in the top left corner of the screen, and Chinese users are right-handed, which makes them inconvenient to click. The existing interface lacks a navigation bar, so users cannot

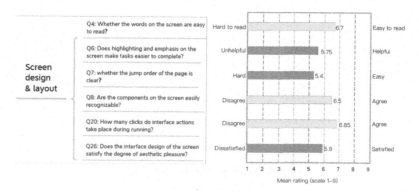

Fig. 6. Result of screen factors.

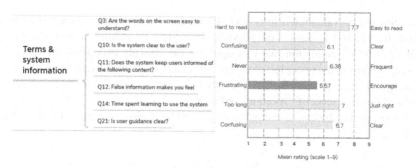

Fig. 7. Result of terminology and system feedback.

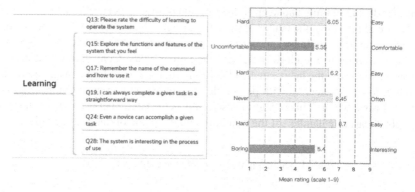

Fig. 8. Result of learning factors.

switch applications easily. The user bar is not frequently clicked and is not suitable for easy to click area. The area for adjusting speed only has plus and minus buttons, which makes users click too many times when adjusting speed.

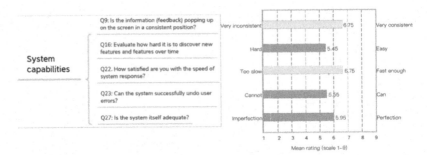

Fig. 9. Result of system capabilities.

4 Improvement Plan

According to the evaluation results of QUIS, we decided to optimize the interface design mainly for "partial buttons" and "navigation mode". In addition, combined with the results of OWAS evaluation, we will optimize the clicking experience of "back" and "Home" buttons in the upper left corner of the screen. On the hardware, we will optimize the design of "heart rate controller". Based on the results of "field observation", we will optimize the click level of "speed up and down";

In the whole process of using treadmill, we will also introduce the "reservation queue" function.

4.1 Improvement Program of Treadmill Hardware

The main function of the "heart rate controller" is that the user squeezes his hand on the controller during running and keeps it for a period of time to get accurate heart rate data.

The height between the center of the left and right "heart rate handle" and the plane of the running belt should be appropriate to the user's body height, and the height when standing can refer to the elbow height of the human body. Considering that users are accustomed to using the heart rate handle during running. in order to ensure convenient operation for most users, the 5th percentile of female standing posture elbow height – 899 mm (as shown in Table 1 below) is selected as the height between the center of left and right "heart rate handle" of the treadmill and the plane of the running belt [4].

Table 1. Standing body size of Chinese female adults.

Age group	18–55 years old						
Percentile	1	5	10	50	90	95	99
Height of eye	1337	1371	1388	1454	1522	1541	1579
Height of shoulder	1166	1195	1211	1271	1333	1350	1385

(continued)

Table 1. (*continued*)

Age group	18–55 years old						
Percentile	1	5	10	50	90	95	99
Elbow height	873	899	913	960	1009	1023	1050
Functional hand height	630	650	662	704	746	757	778
The perineum high	648	673	686	732	779	792	819
Ti-floor	363	377	384	410	437	444	459

The design of heart rate handle should adapt to the biological characteristics of human hand. First, keep the wrist in a straight state in the process of use; Second, to avoid pressure on the palmar tissue; Third, avoid repeated finger movements. So in the design of the handle shape can use arc shape to adapt to grasp.

By placing electrodes on the left and right handles of the electric treadmill, the ecg signals of the human body can be obtained, and the heart rate information of the trainer can be obtained by measuring the time interval of two adjacent R waves in the ecg signals. Therefore, the holding time of the heart rate handle is difficult to shorten. In order to reduce the impact of the heart rate detection process on running posture, we designed the "heart rate handle" to be removable.

According to the evaluation results of OWAS and the man-machine dimension analysis of the product and the measurement principle of human ecg signal proposed in this section, we optimized the "heart rate handle" and obtained the following design scheme (Fig. 10).

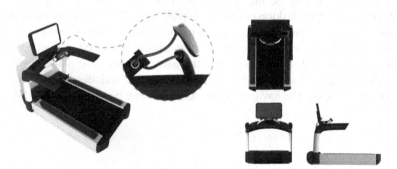

Fig. 10. Scheme rendering.

The optimized design is coordinated with the overall style, and the heart rate measurement handle can be pulled out and held in the hand, without affecting the user's running posture. In addition, we adjusted the shape, size and placement Angle of the handle to better adapt to the biological characteristics of the human hand. At the same time, the adjustment of the handle size reduces the cover of the handle over the basket, so that it does not interfere with the user's access to the phone.

4.2 Improvement Program of Treadmill Interface

Through experiments, according to the measurement of task completion time, error book, supervisor comfort and other indicators, Ye Hanyao analyzed and concluded that the interface area with the highest operation efficiency and the most comfortable feeling for users on the new treadmill interface (Fig. 11).

A3: Place parts with high click through rate/use frequency and strong demand.

A2: Place parts with average click through rate/use frequency and normal demand.

A1: Place components with low utilization rate/frequency and weak demand [5].

The circular area is the area where the user's line of sight is concentrated during running. It is suitable for placing parts that do not require user click operation but display necessary information, such as sports status display/prompt [6].

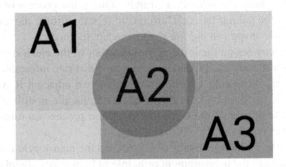

Fig. 11. Interface area.

Therefore, we redesigned the existing interface of the treadmill (Fig. 12), mainly including five sections: desktop (1), status display area (2), user bar (3), navigation bar (4), and basic control area (5). Among them, the desktop mainly displays the user's motion status information, and when the user adjusts the speed, a floating window of "current speed" will be displayed for the user to adjust. The status display area mainly includes device status and settings. The user bar includes login button/avatar and application menu. The navigation bar includes Home button and application icons,

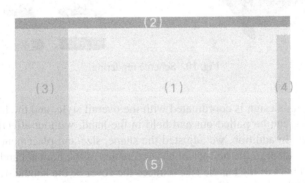

Fig. 12. Redesigned interface partition.

which can return to desktop or switch to other applications with one click. The basic control bar includes the start button, pause button and end button of the treadmill, and the speed and incline control buttons.

Click "speed" to pop up the floating window of digital panel, which is convenient for users to quickly adjust their favorite speed. When the user adjusts the speed, a floating window will pop up to display the current speed, which is convenient for the user to better control the speed. The user can adjust the speed by "_" / "+".

When the user pauses the run, there are two options: continue/end, where the user can choose to take a short break or just end the run and the next student takes their turn on the treadmill (Fig. 13).

Fig. 13. Redesigned low-fidelity interface.

The interface of the treadmill has been redesigned with clearer functions of the buttons, moving the user bar to the left side and adding a more frequently used navigation bar on the right side to facilitate user operation (Fig. 14).

Fig. 14. Redesigned homepage.

Move the frequently used "Back" and "Home" keys from the top left corner to the right navigation bar, so that when the user has used an application, the most recently used application will appear in the navigation bar, and the user can return to the home page with one click or switch to other applications with one click (Fig. 15).

In order to solve the problems of users not knowing whether there is a free treadmill before they arrive at the gym and the long queue for the treadmill, users can make a reservation in the APP to queue up and enter the reservation password to turn on the treadmill after arriving at the number. If the user does not come to open the treadmill after the countdown, the reservation will be cancelled (Fig. 16).

Fig. 15. Redesigned street view interface.

Fig. 16. Redesigned street view interface.

5 Summary and Discussion

This paper discusses the availability of shared treadmills in public gyms on the International Campus of South China University of Technology. The specific work is as follows:

Firstly, this paper conducted a field survey of 9 users (including ordinary users and experienced users) during the whole process of using treadmills, and made a preliminary analysis of users' experience of using treadmills on campus.

Secondly, OWAS and QUIS were used to evaluate hardware usage and user interface satisfaction of campus treadmills, and questionnaires were designed specifically.

Thirdly, according to the evaluation results, the problems of heart rate measurement module design, user interface design and user experience of "Good Family" indoor treadmill in the use of campus were found, and the optimization scheme was put forward.

The study proposed detailed improvements, including changing the interactive (pull-out), size and grip Angle of the handle to reduce physical injury caused by the use of existing heart rate modules. Rearrange the 5 functional plates of the existing interface according to the frequency of use, add digital panel for fast speed regulation, change the shape of buttons, add navigation bar and so on. The improvement plan adds the reservation queuing function to optimize the user experience.

Due to the limited research time and limited capability of project team members, there are still many deficiencies to be added in this paper:

Firstly, due to the limited time of the project, the study did not recruit enough participants, especially the questionnaire survey.

Secondly, due to the limited capacity of the members, the field observation method used in the experiment is insufficient.

In the end, we proposed detailed improvements based on the evaluation results, but due to time and funding issues, the usability of these options has not yet been experimentally evaluated.

References

1. Zuo, H., Yi, C., Li, K.: An analysis of the musculoskeletal disorders of the workers in manual demolition based on OWAS. Chin. J. Ergon. **27**(3), 23–26 (2021)
2. Sitting, D.F., Kuperman, G.J., Fiskio, J.: Evaluating physician satisfaction regarding user interactions with an electronic medical record system. In: Proceedings/AMIA Annual Symposium, vol. 6(1), pp. 400–404 (1999)
3. Chin, J.P., Diehl, V.A., Norman, K.L.: Development of an Instrument Measuring User Satisfaction of the human-computer interface. In: Proceedings of the SIGCHI conference on Human Factors in Computing Systems, pp. 213–218 (1988)
4. Sun, Y.: Design of Household Treadmill Based on Fuzzy Kano Model. Xi'an University of Technology, Xi'an City (2020)
5. Ye, H.: Research on interactive interface design of new treadmill based on micro interaction. Southern University of Science and Technology, Shenzhen City (2019)
6. Zhu, Y.: Research on human-computer interaction interface of treadmill. Zhejiang University of Technology, Hangzhou City (2015)

Examining the Usability of a Short-Video App Interface Through an Eye-Tracking Experiment

Wu Jia[✉], Rui Zhou, Nan Chen, and Yujie Shi

Baidu Mobile Ecosystem User Experience Design Center, Beijing, China
jiawu@baidu.com

Abstract. This study explored the visual strategies and operational implications of users scrolling through short videos provided by a short-video app. A within-subjects design with 2 (title position: title above video/title below video) × 2 (interaction area position: lower left interaction area/lower right interaction area) conditions was adopted. The eye-tracking experiment and questionnaire survey were combined to understand participants' preferences for different conditions. A total of 30 participants were recruited for the experiment. Both the eye-tracking experiment and questionnaire survey data showed that the participants preferred the design with the title above the video and the lower right interaction area. A plausible explanation is that the title above video arrangement facilitated information filtering and was congruent with the participants' existing browsing habits. Meanwhile, the lower right interaction area was easy to operate and more accommodating.

Keywords: Eye-tracking · Short-video · Interface design · Usability

1 Introduction

The widespread popularity of short-video apps has substantially changed the way individuals obtain information. Moreover, many are spending increasing amounts of time using these apps. As of February 2021, there were 873 million short-video users in China, accounting for 88.3% of the country's total Internet users [1]. Experts and scholars have defined short-video apps as applications that feature videos ranging from several seconds to a few minutes in length, including those generated by users and professionals. Compared with traditional text-based and image-based social media applications, they are more capable of meeting user demands for information and social interaction [2]. Due to fierce competition in the Chinese short-video market, players in the industry often have difficulty differentiating their products. The market is currently dominated by the top two players, Douyin and Kuaishou, thus leaving little space for similar products that do not contain distinct features. In this context, rivals must quickly understand how to meet the needs of short-video users, increase their product usage, and successfully retain customers [2, 3].

Gross argued that thoughtful product design is the key to exceeding user expectations, thus enhancing user adherence and satisfaction by giving the product a competitive edge through differentiation [4]. Regarding the UI system design for short-video apps, Zhang et al. recommended that the ICONS and visual placements in the interface design of short video APPs should match to users' usage behaviors, which may improve the app's usability [5]. As for short videos on popular science, Zhang suggested that strict logic in content presentation and well-organized screen layouts and compositions could effectively improve user browsing experiences, increase their access to knowledge, and encourage interactions such as sharing and reposting [6]. Tian analyzed the design of Douyin, thus identifying several characteristics of a good design, including a straightforward UI system and features, a user-friendly screen layout, and intuitive operation [7]. As can be seen, thoughtful user interface (UI) designs can simultaneously be aesthetically pleasing while adequately guiding or facilitating user interactions, as both qualities increase the usability of app pages [8]. But, among users, which design is the most popular? Questionnaires, user interviews, and other methods are commonly used in conventional research to uncover experience concerns and understand consumers' subjective preferences and selection criteria [9, 10]. It's also challenging to find the right words to explain some little behaviors that are difficult for consumers to notice [9]. Eye tracking technology can capture the user's eye movement data while browsing page, and the data can objectively reflect real user interaction behavior by identifying different behavior characteristics and significance, which can assist product designers in deciding whether to improve, adapt, or change the design to meet the users' potential demand [9, 10].

In sum, the usability of short video apps is influenced by interface design and layout. Users' surfing experience can be improved by good interface design and layout, which encourage interactions and increase user engagement and adherence. This study focused on the Haokan Video App offered by Baidu, Inc., which relies on Baidu technology to provide high-quality short videos for 110 million daily active users. Specifically, we manipulated the UI designs of the app to conduct an eye-tracking experiment aimed at understanding how different layout conditions affected users. We also obtained subjective data from participants via questionnaire survey. The main goal was to identify the most preferred design option, thus informing the design of other short-video apps.

2 Research Methods

2.1 Experiment Objective

Using the UI design of the Haokan Video App and its different layouts, we aimed to understand user preferences in relation to four conditions that were created by combining two possible locations of the title and interaction area. Considering possible operations while browsing through short videos, we also examined whether the layouts affected their operational efficiency as it pertained to the interaction area.

2.2 Experiment Design

A 2 × 2 within-subjects design was adopted for the experiment; Independent Variable 1 was the position of the title, which may appear above or below the video area (referred to as "title above video" and "title below video," respectively), while Independent Variable

2 was related to the position of the interaction area, which may appear below the left corner or right corner of the video area (referred to as "lower left interaction area" and "lower right interaction area," respectively). The following conditions were examined: title above video and lower left interaction area (Condition A1), title below video and lower left interaction area (Condition A2), title above video and lower right interaction area (Condition A3), and title below video and lower right interaction area (Condition A4). Figure 1 illustrates each condition.

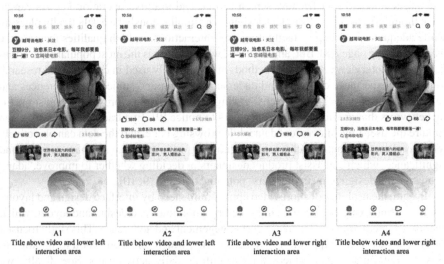

A1	A2	A3	A4
Title above video and lower left interaction area	Title below video and lower left interaction area	Title above video and lower right interaction area	Title below video and lower right interaction area

Fig. 1. Experimental scheme

2.3 Experiment Materials

As scrolling through short videos is often a continuous, dynamic, and immersive experience, it was vital to replicate the real user experience during the experiment, thus ensuring data validity. For this experiment, we developed the SDK version of Haokan Video (as shown in Fig. 2), which contains the same features that are available in the official version of the app, with four conditions for the test. The experimenter could switch between different conditions during the experiment by selecting from the eye-tracking UI types on the Haokan Video App's settings page.

2.4 Experimental Environment and Equipment

The experiment was conducted in a laboratory setting to ensure a consistent operating environment for each participant. We used the Tobii Pro Glasses 2 eye-tracking device, which features wireless real-time observation capabilities and is ultra-lightweight, thus allowing us to obtain the most natural visual behavior data. The device's sampling frequency was 60 Hz, which provides the pupil with images of optimal contrast for

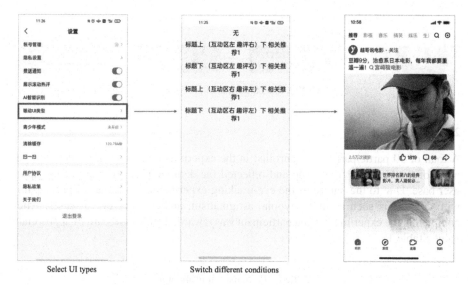

Select UI types   Switch different conditions

Fig. 2. SDK prototype

most indoor environments. The device captures the wearer's eye movement trajectory and analyzes their gaze (e.g., changes in gaze duration and frequency). To control for additional effects induced by the cell phone screen and brightness, each participant used the same brand and model (Huawei P30, resolution of 2340×1080), thus ensuring consistent conditions during the experiment.

2.5 Experimental Process

Prior to the experiment, all participants were given time to familiarize themselves with the phones and their operation, thus reducing the impact of differences between the experiment phones and their personal phones. The experimenter then provided the participants with explanations of the experimental process and relevant instructions. Following this, the participants were required to complete a calibration process to ensure data accuracy. The experiment formally began upon successful calibration. During the experiment, the participants freely used the Haokan Video App under different conditions, with eye-tracking data recorded during this time. To control for the learning effects, the conditions were presented in the order determined by a Latin square. We also observed the natural behaviors of participants during the experiment. If they did not click on the interactive area, they were guided to finish the clicking task after browsing to end the eye-tracking test. After they completed the experiment, we asked the participants to rate each design option and explain their ratings (Fig. 3).

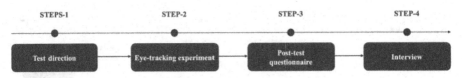

Fig. 3. Experimental process

2.6 Participants

A total of 30 participants were enrolled in the experiment. All were considered target users of the Haokan Video App and reflected the demographic structure of the app's user base. Due to the nature of the eye-tracking experiment, we excluded participants with conditions such as high myopia, astigmatism, and/or other eye diseases. After completing the experiment, each participant was rewarded with a gift card of appropriate value (Table 1).

Table 1. Participant information

Variables	Categories	Number	Percentage
Gender	Male	16	55.0%
	Female	14	45.0%
Age (years)	18–24	5	16.0%
	25–30	7	24.0%
	31–35	6	19.0%
	36–40	5	16.0%
	41–45	3	11.0%
	Above 46 (inclusive)	5	15.0%

3   Data Analysis

3.1   Areas of Interest

Areas of interest (AOI) refers to gaze areas on the UI. These were examined as basic units in the eye-tracking analysis. AOI may be responsive areas of the touch screen and target areas in the experiment [11]. In this study, the Haokan Video UI was divided into several different AOI for the purpose of recording and analyzing experimental data; specific AOI included the title and interaction area (Fig. 4).

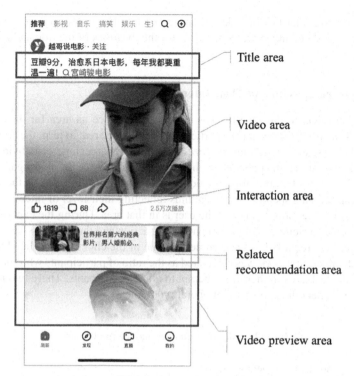

Fig. 4. Areas of interest

3.2 Evaluation Dimensions

In this study, we evaluated the six following dimensions: salience, level of interest, ease of operation, comfort design, aesthetic design, and preferred option. Saliency is related to the human visual perception and reflects the visual attractiveness of UI elements [12]. We assessed saliency to understand which locations of the title and interaction area were most conspicuous to participants. In relation to an image, visual experience entails that the eye is drawn to different levels of interest in different areas. Researchers are thus able to determine which areas of products are most interesting to users [13]. We assessed the level of interest to understand which locations of the title and interaction area were most effective for arousing user interest to gaze or tap. Intuitively, ease of operation refers to the degree of ease users experience when engaging with responsive areas (e.g., the interaction area). Visual comfort is typically evaluated based on data obtained through surveys and post-experiment interviews with users; specifically, this reflects the visual information and psychological perceptions that users acquire while using an app [14]. The visual aesthetics of a product interface affect how it is experienced and influence its usability; these qualities are most often subjectively evaluated by designers or researchers, thus providing insights into the aesthetic feelings users develop when engaging with products and aiding investigators in judging and obtaining aesthetic expressions that match the psychological feelings of users [15]. Finally, we evaluated preferred option to clarify which design options users subjectively preferred, with a particular focus on their subjective preferences for the locations of the title and interaction area.

3.3 Eye-Tracking Data and Their Interpretations

First fixation refers to the time it takes a participant to see an area for the first time. The shorter the time, the earlier the participant notices the area; in turn, the area is more salient. Visible scale, or the ratio of gaze, refers to the percentage of individuals who see an area. The higher the percentage, the more individuals see the area; again, the area is more salient [16]. Fixation time is calculated for a given AOI based on the browsing time that participants spend in that area, thus reflecting their level of interest [17]. The longer the time, the more interested the user is in that area. During the experiment, the time between a participant's obvious hand lifting action and their successful clicking of the task area was recorded as the completion time of the clicking task. In addition, the success rate of the first click was calculated as the ratio of participants who successfully tapped on the task area in their first attempt to all 30 participants. These two indicators were used to reflect the app's ease of operation (Table 2).

Table 2. Indicator meanings and interpretations

Eye-tracking indicators	Definitions	Explanations
First fixation	The time it takes for a participant to see an AOI for the first time after loading a page	The shorter the time, the earlier the participant notices the AOI
Visible scale	The percentage of all 30 participants who see an AOI	The higher the percentage, the greater number of participants who see the AOI
Fixation time	Cumulative time spent looking at an AOI	The longer the time, the more interested the user is in the AOI
Completion time of the clicking task	The user (spontaneously or prompted) produces a visible action of the lifting of the hand and clicking on the task area. It is the time between the two movements	The shorter the time, the easier the operation
The success rate of the first click	The user (spontaneously or prompted) clicks on the task area The rate is the percentage of all 30 participants who were successful in their first attempts	The higher the rate, the easier the operation

4   Results

4.1   Eye-Tracking Data Analysis

Eye movement data and subjective data are separated from the experimental data. The eye tracker automatically collects eye movement data, and when the data is generated, all values are averaged, and the final data preserves one decimal place. After the eye movement test, the subjective data was collected by filling out a questionnaire.

Title Position
By comparing the eye-tracking data for different title positions, we found that each position was associated with different participant behaviors (see Table 3). For example, the first fixation for the title above video condition was 421.8 ms (A1) and 540.7 ms (A2) which was shorter than that for the title below video condition, which took 586.7 ms (A3) and 709.9 ms (A4). Simultaneously, the visible scale for the title above video condition was 80.0% (A1) and 86.7% (A2), which is significantly larger than the visible scale for the title below video condition. This suggests that the title above video condition is more salient and easier for users to find. Moreover, the fixation time for the title above video condition was 198.0 ms (A1) and 286.3 ms (A2), which is longer than that for the tile below video condition. This indicates that the former condition produced higher user interest and increased the willingness to view the title.

Table 3. Data on title position

Eye-tracking indicators	Title above video		Title below video	
	A1	A3	A2	A4
First fixation/ms	421.8	540.7	586.7	709.9
Visible scale	80.0%	86.7%	56.7%	50.0%
Fixation time/ms	198.0	286.3	136.3	192.0

The typical user track map shows that users will quickly check up on the title for the title above video condition, but for the title below video condition, users will explore the video more times, be more distracted by other components in the interface, and later browse the title (Fig. 5).

Position of Interaction Area
The first fixation for the lower right interaction area was 755.3 ms (A3) and 728.7 ms (A4) which was shorter than that for the lower left interaction area, which took 1164.0 ms (A1) and 1036.0 ms (A2). The visible scale for the lower right interaction area was 43.3% (A3) and 56.6% (A4), which is significantly higher than the visible scale for the lower left interaction area (Table 4). This indicates that the lower right interaction area was both more salient and more attractive to users. Further, the fixation time for the lower right interaction area was 456.4 ms (A3) and 340.6 ms (A4), which is longer than that for the lower left interaction area, thus suggesting that it more effectively aroused user

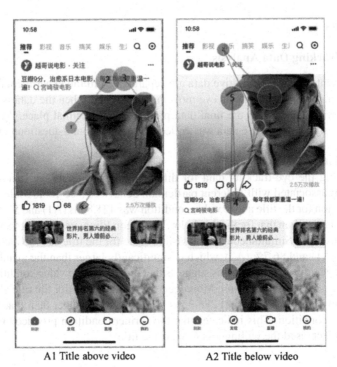

A1 Title above video   A2 Title below video

Fig. 5. Track map

interest. Regarding the ease of operation, the clicking task took less time to complete for the lower right interaction area when compared to that for the lower left interaction area, although the success rate for the first click was roughly identical. Still, this suggests that the lower right interaction area was easier to operate than the lower left interaction area.

Table 4. Data on interaction area position

Eye-tracking indicators	Lower left interaction area		Lower right interaction area	
	A1	A2	A3	A4
First fixation/ms	1164.0	1036.0	755.3	728.7
Visible scale	43.3%	36.6%	43.3%	56.6%
Fixation time/ms	335.0	226.3	456.3	346.0
Completion time of the click task/ms	442.6	392.4	382.3	360.6
The success rate of the first click	86.7%	93.3%	90.0%	86.7%

Based on the number of fixations, we superimposed the data from all 30 participants to obtain a heat map reflecting their browsing and fixation behaviors (Fig. 6). The redder the area, the stronger the user attraction; as shown, the title above video and lower right interaction area were most attractive.

Fig. 6. Heat map

In sum, the eye-tracking data revealed that the title above video was associated with better salience and higher interest than the title below video. For salience, level of interest, and ease of operation, the lower right interaction area was more favorable than the lower left interaction area. Overall, a significant advantage is produced when the title above video and lower right interaction area are combined.

4.2 Subjective Rating Results

As shown in Table 5, Condition A3 (title above video and lower right interaction area) had the highest subjective ratings, at 4.17 for comfort design and 4.23 for aesthetics. To test whether for differences between user scores for different design conditions in terms of aesthetics and comfort, we conducted a repeated measures ANOVA on the

Table 5. Aesthetic and comfort ratings for different design conditions

Experimental scheme	Aesthetic design		Comfort design	
	M	SD	M	SD
A1 title above video and lower left interaction area	3.60	0.89	3.37	0.85
A3 title above video and lower right interaction area	4.23	0.82	4.17	0.87
A2 title below video and lower left interaction area	3.30	1.15	2.97	1.19
A4 title below video and lower right interaction area	3.83	0.99	3.83	1.17

questionnaire data. The results showed that the main effects of design aesthetics differed significantly for design conditions with different interaction area positions ($F = 14.77$, $p < 0.05$), while neither the main effects of the title position ($F = 2.36$, $p > 0.05$) nor the interaction between the positions of the title and interaction area were significant. The main effects of comfort design differed significantly for design conditions with different interaction area positions ($F = 33.26$, $p < 0.05$), while neither the main effects of the title position ($F = 2.17$, $p > 0.05$) nor the interaction between the positions of the title and interaction area were significant. In regard to aesthetics and comfort design, these results indicate that the lower right interaction area was a better option than the lower left interaction area.

We also conducted a questionnaire survey to assess subjective preferences for the positions of the title and interaction area. As shown in Fig. 7, 63% of participants preferred the title above video, while 27% preferred the opposite. As shown in Fig. 8, 73% of users preferred the lower right interaction area, while 17% preferred the opposite.

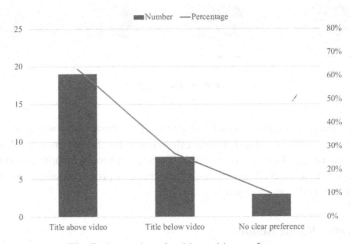

Fig. 7. Proportions for title position preference

As shown in Fig. 9, 60% of participants preferred Condition A3. In other words, most participants preferred the combination of title above video and lower right interaction area.

To conclude, both the objective eye-tracking data and subjective questionnaire data showed that users preferred the UI design with the title above video and lower right interaction area; that is, Condition A3 was the most preferred.

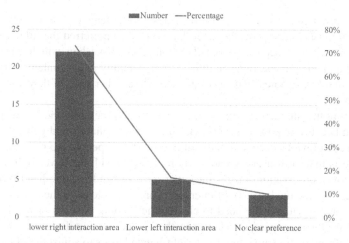

Fig. 8. Proportions for specific interaction area position preference

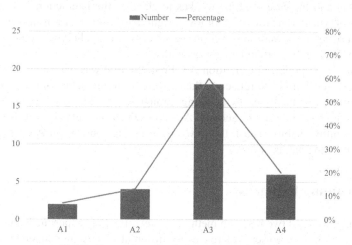

Fig. 9. Proportions for design scheme preference

5 Discussion

This study explored both usability and user preference for four design conditions for the Haokan Video App. The results suggested that Condition A3 (title above video and lower right interaction area) was the most preferred. Our qualitative analysis indicated that this preference could be explained by the fact that title above video was more salient; therein, it is easier for users to decide whether to watch the recommended video based on the contents of the title. Moreover, the Haokan Video App lists videos that are comparatively medium to long in duration, with no title presented on the preview image. As users need additional information to make quick judgments about video contents, the title above video arrangement is more user-friendly for those types of videos. By contrast, the title below video arrangement makes it more difficult for users to distinguish between the title and recommendation area. Additional design elements on the lower part of the screen create visual crowding. We posit that users who preferred the title below video arrangement may have been accustomed to Douyin and Kuaishou, which list videos that are shorter and contain less relevant titles. Users generally judge contents very quickly, during the first few seconds, and can easily scroll to another video if they do not like the one presented.

Regarding the interaction area position, most users preferred the lower right interaction area because it was congruent with their existing habits and generated a better experience. A previous survey found that about 90% of people are right-handed [18]. This suggests that most users would be more satisfied with the lower right interaction area. Moreover, observations during the experiment showed that one-handed operations were easier because the lower right interaction area was closer to the right thumb, thus facilitating usage without the need to change the holding position or hand. For these same reasons, the users perceived better aesthetics and comfort design. To the contrary, the lower left interaction area may force right-handed users to adjust their holding position or switch to their other hand to click on items. These additional actions may both be annoying and increase the time it takes to click on the interaction area. However, regardless of whether the lower left or lower right interaction area was implemented, no significant differences were observed in the success rate of clicking on the interaction area when the thumb operation area was nearby.

Overall, users preferred Condition A3. First, the title was placed above the video, making is easier to find and reflecting the existing browsing habits of users. Moreover, visual comfort was increased by avoiding arrangements with crowded and redundant middle sections of the screen. Second, A3 represented a regular layout that reflected existing cognitive habits. Third, the lower right interaction area in A3 catered to the existing operating habits of users.

6 Concluding Remarks

In this study, we used two research methods (an eye-tracking experiment and questionnaire survey) to explore user preferences for different UI designs implemented via the Haokan Video App. The experiment helped us understand the attention distributions of users when using the app in a natural setting based on objective recordings of their behaviors. During this time, we achieved additional benefits by observing users and inquiring about their usage. As such, any problems with lag, mistaken touches, click unresponsiveness, and/or interactional operations could be more easily recorded and effectively detected. While recorded footage was better than textual descriptions in this context, we omit extensive discussions for brevity.

Following the eye-tracking experiment, we conducted a questionnaire survey to analyze subjective user preferences for different design conditions. Compared with either research method alone, the combined approach adopted in this study supplemented objective information with subjective judgment, this enabling us to draw more reasonable and effective conclusions. Moreover, the Haokan Video App designers launched a version tailored to Condition A3 based on our findings. Excellent performance based on subsequently obtained online data verified these results. However, we only considered the design and layout of the title position and interaction area position. In other words, we did not assess other design elements of the Haokan Video App, including the video area and related recommendation area, nor did we examine how the title contents or video types affected users. In the future, comprehensive studies should explore the effects of these elements on browsing behaviors and operations.

References

1. The 47th "Statistical report on the development of Internet in China" is released. China (2021). www.cac.gov.cn
2. Li, S., Ji, Z.: A review of research on the continuous use of mobile short video application users. In: Conference on Big Data Economy and Information Management (BDEIM). IEEE, pp. 192–201 (2020)
3. Zhang, X., Wu, Y., Liu, S.: Analysis of factors affecting browsing and creation behavior of users in mobile short video. Library Inf. Serv. 63(6), 103–115 (2019)
4. Gross, A.M.: Unexpected Events and User Experience: Surprise as a Design Strategy for Interactive Products. Technische Universitaet Berlin (2016)
5. Zhang, B., Zhang, D., Hu, G.: Research on short video APP design based on heart flow theory. Design. 33(7), 144–146 (2020)
6. Zhang, G., Ma, X.: Research on the visual design of popular science short videos based on compositional interpretation. Art Design. 2(12), 49–51 (2020)
7. Tian, Xi, Zhao, W.: Music and video APP interaction design based on flow experience. Packaging Eng. 41(10), 181–185 (2020)
8. Poole, A., Ball, L.J.: Eye tracking in HCI and usability research. Encyclopedia of human computer interaction. IGI global, pp. 211–219 (2006)
9. Guo, F., Ding, Y., Liu, W.: Can eye-tracking data be measured to assess product design? visual attention mechanism should be considered. Int. J. Ind. Ergon. 53, 229–235 (2016)
10. Qu, QX., Zhang, L., Chao, W.Y., et al.: User experience design based on eye-tracking technology: a case study on smartphone APPs. In: Duffy, V. (eds.) Advances in Applied Digital Human Modeling and Simulation. AISC, vol. 481, pp. 303–315. Springer, Cham (2017). https://doi.org/10.1007/978-3-319-41627-4_27
11. Blascheck, T., Kurzhals, K., Raschke, M., et al.: Visualization of eye tracking data: a taxonomy and survey. Comput. Graph. Forum. 36(8), 260–284 (2017)
12. Leiva L A, Xue Y, Bansal A, et al.: Understanding visual saliency in mobile user interfaces. In: Conference on Human-Computer Interaction with Mobile Devices and Services, pp.1–12(2020)
13. Punchoojit, L., Hongwarittorrn, N.: Usability studies on mobile user interface design patterns: a systematic literature review. Advances in Human-Computer Interaction (2017)
14. Huan, T.: Research on Visual Comfort of Color Design in Digital Interface. Southwest University of Science and Technology China (2019)
15. Khalighy, S., Green, G., Scheepers, C., et al.: Quantifying the qualities of aesthetics in product design using eye-tracking technology. Int. J. Ind. Ergon. 49, 31–43 (2015)
16. Krafka K, Khosla A, Kellnhofer P, et al.: Eye tracking for everyone. Conference on Computer vision and pattern recognition, pp. 2176–2184 (2016)
17. Wang, J., Antonenko, P., Celepkolu, M., et al.: Exploring relationships between eye tracking and traditional usability testing data. Int. J. Hum.-Comput. Interact. 35(6), 483–494 (2019)
18. De Kovel, C.G.F., Carrión-Castillo, A., Francks, C.: A large-scale population study of early life factors influencing left-handedness. Sci. Rep. 9(1), 1–11 (2019)

Usability Evaluation and Redesign of an Integrated Chair

Lin Liu[1], Sijia Cheng[1], Haoran Li[1], Marcelo M. Soares[2], and Meng Li[1(✉)]

[1] South China University of Technology, Guangzhou, China
mengli@scut.edu.cn
[2] Hunan University, Changsha, People's Republic of China

Abstract. The integrated chair we choose is already a well-designed product, but we're still trying to find design flaws that are harder to spot through usability evaluation. This paper evaluates the usability of the product from the perspectives of ease of learning, ease of use, task match, user satisfaction, and ergonomics. In order to complete the usability evaluation, the experiment was designed accordingly. In this process, methods such as field observation, questionnaire survey, and user interview were used to find out the deep pain points and improve the design of more mature products.

Keywords: Usability evaluation · Ergonomics · Redesign · Integrated chair

1 Product Introduction

Learn2 seating (see Fig. 1) is an all-in-one desk and chair, but its usage scenarios are different from traditional all-in-one desks and chairs. This product is mainly to facilitate students to communicate and discuss in the process of learning and stimulate creativity, so it has the advantages of high adjustability and flexible movement.

However, in the process of using, we found that most users have difficulties in using and other problems. Therefore, a usability evaluation was carried out for the design of Learn2 seating. First, the user journey map was sorted out, and task analysis was carried out around the use of Learn2. Second, according to the characteristics of the target users and the use environment of Learn2, reasonable evaluation methods and evaluation models are screened. Last, combined with the evaluation results, we can screen the pain points, so as to carry out targeted redesign.

2 User Journey Map

In order to directly and clearly describe the user's human-computer interaction experience from the user's point of view, the method of creating a user journey map is adopted to visualize a series of tasks of using Learn2 (see Fig. 2).

M. M. Soares et al. (Eds.): HCII 2022, LNCS 13321, pp. 428–446, 2022.
https://doi.org/10.1007/978-3-031-05897-4_30

Fig. 1. Learn2 seating

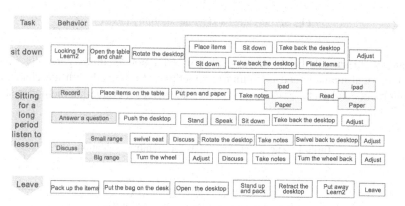

Fig. 2. User journey map of Learn2 seating

3   Usability Evaluation

3.1   Models and Methods of Usability Evaluation

Models of Usability Evaluation. Usability is user-centered design, which is used to measure the effectiveness, efficiency, satisfaction, etc. of a specific user in the process of using a product in a specific scenario.

Leventhal and Barnes Usability Model not only involves user characteristics, product interface design, but also evaluates various tasks in the process of using the product. Combined with the characteristics of the product's target users and use environment, the model is more suitable for the usability evaluation of learn2.

The principles of this model are shown in Fig. 3. Based on the characteristics of this product, four principles are selected for usability evaluation.

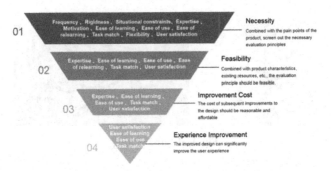

Fig. 3. Leventhal and barnes usability model.

Methods for Usability Evaluation. Usability evaluation methods generally include both empirical methods and non-empirical methods. Combined with the characteristics of product and usability evaluation model, the selected evaluation method is shown in the Table 1.

Table 1. The selected methods for usability evaluation.

Methods		Reason for choice
Empirical methods	Controlled experiments	Experiments are usually carried out under strictly controlled conditions, so it is possible to objectively and truly record be different problems that different users have in the process of using the product.
	Field observation	It is possible to observe the user's use of the product in a natural state, and obtain more realistic data. But avoid looking directly at the subject and minimise the impact on the subject, which may change the way they normally use the product.
	Questionnaires	It can quickly obtain the usage of the product by a large number of users, and it is easier to obtain general data.
	Interviews	By directly interviewing respondents, you can gain a deep understanding of user needs and uncover real pain points. It makes up for the lack of data depth of the questionnaire survey.
Non-Empirical methods	Task analyses	Predict what difficulties users will encounter when completing specific tasks without user involvement.
	Cognitive walkthroughs	The process of using the product can be decomposed into a series of tasks, and then the tasks can be further decomposed into a series of activities, so that it is easier to gain insight into the pain points in the process of using the product

3.2 Usability Evaluation Based on Leventhal and Barnes Usability Model

Ease of Use and Ease of Learning. To evaluate the Ease of use and Ease of learning, we designed an experiment and observed it in the field. And recorded video, detailed analysis of the use of different users.

Design Experiment.   The experiment focus on the common actions of Learn2. After task analysis, three tasks (6 actions) are designed, as shown in the Fig. 5 for details. In the experiment, 5 subjects were recruited. Combined with the recorded video, the subjects' use of Learn2 was repeatedly observed. After analysis and thinking, we choose three indicators to evaluate the Ease of use and Ease of learning of Learn2: time, mistakes and task completion. The detailed design of the experiment is shown in the Table 2.

Table 2. The detailed design of the experiment.

Task	Behavior	Principle			
		Ease of use	Ease of learning	Task match	User satisfaction
Task 1: Sit down	1. Choose a desk and chair, place your bag,stationery, etc.	☆☆☆☆	☆☆	☆☆☆☆	☆☆☆
	2. Sit down in your comfortable position, and prepare for class.	☆☆☆☆	☆	☆	☆☆
Task 2: Sedentary	1. Imagine that you are listening to the teacher for at least one hour.	☆☆☆	☆	☆	☆☆☆☆☆
	2. Imagine you need to take notes and record the specified sentence.	☆☆	☆	☆	☆☆☆☆
	3. Imagine you want to hand a pen to a classmate who is 2 meters away from you, behind the left.	☆☆☆	☆	☆	☆☆☆
	4. You need to transform your desktop from the current orientation to the other side	☆☆☆☆	☆☆☆☆☆	☆☆☆	☆☆☆☆
Task 3: Leave	1.Pack up your bags, stationery, etc. and get up.	☆	☆	☆	☆☆
	2.Return the tables and chairs to their original appearance, place them in the designated positions, and leave the classroom.	☆☆☆	☆☆☆☆	☆☆☆	☆☆☆☆
NOTICE	① The staff timed each task separately and recorded data such as error rate and accuracy rate. ② A video will be recorded when subjects participate in the experiment, but only for observation and analysis by the experimenter, and no personal information will be disclosed.				

Observations of the Experiment. The dynamic movement *and* static sitting position of 5 subjects were observed respectively (see Fig. 4).

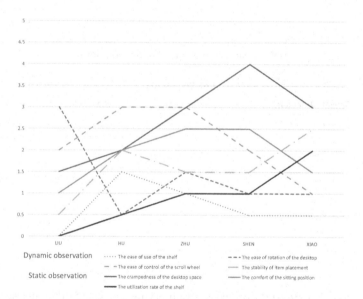

Fig. 4. Dynamic and Static sitting observation

The usage and duration of different subjects were recorded, as shown in the Table 3 for details. The errors and task completion of all subjects were comprehensively recorded, as shown in the Table 4 for details.

Table 3. Observation record of the experiment.

subject	Product usage				Duration			Task Completion
	Storage	Desktop	Chair	Joint Rotation	sit down	Rotate the desktop	Leave	
LIU	• Unused shelves, schoolbags, water glasses, etc. are placed on the ground.	• Item on table on desktop. • Desktop in the middle. • Strip and circular grooves not used.	• No use other than sedentary	• Rotate the tabletop slightly while sitting. • Use the scroll wheel when borrowing pen and paper.	41s	/	33s	Rotate desktop task: Not performed
HU	• Unused under chair shelf.	• Computer, water cup, pen and paper are all placed on the table. • Strip and circular grooves not used	• Shoulder bag on chair	• Rotate the tabletop slightly while sitting. • Use the scroll wheel when borrowing pen and paper.	60s	91s	41s	Rotate desktop task: more difficult
ZHU	• Unused under chair shelf.	• Computer, water cup, pen and paper are all placed on the table. • Desktop left • Strip and circular grooves not used	• Shoulder bag on chair	• Rotate the tabletop slightly while sitting. • Use the scroll wheel when borrowing pen and paper. • Uncontrollable small rotation of the seat.	38s	10s	25s	Rotate desktop task: relatively smooth
SHEN	• Shelving not used earlier. • When writing, remove the water glass and place it in the round hole of the shelf.	• Computer, water cup, pen and paper are all placed on the table. • Desktop right • Strip and circular grooves not used	• Shoulder bag on chair	• Rotate the tabletop slightly while sitting. • Use the scroll wheel when borrowing pen and paper. • Small uncontrollable rotation of seat surface and wheels when seated.	19s	28s	38s	Rotate desktop task: Basically smooth
XIAO	• The backpack is placed on the right shelf, but it often falls off. • The water cup is placed in the round hole of the left shelf.	• Desktop left • Computer on desktop • Strip and circular grooves not used	• No use other than sedentary	• When sitting, tentatively rotate the table top and adjust the posture on the horizontal axis. • Use the scroll wheel when borrowing pen and paper.	61s	30s	67s	Rotate desktop task: A little difficult

Table 4. Observation record of the experiment.

Task Completion		
Efficient (Duration)	**Effect (%)**	**Rotate desktop task error condition**
Enter to sit down 24s (control group) 43.8s (average)		When the subjects completed the task, it took many attempts to find the right way.
Rotate the desktop 39.75s (average)	100%	Main mistakes: ①The rotatable angle of the crossbar is not clear. ②Desktop rotatability is not clear
Pack up and leave 17s (control group) 40.8s (average)		③The front and back of the desktop can be pushed and pulled is not clear.

Analysis of the Experiment. By repeatedly observing the usage 5 different users, recording the indicators of the time, mistakes, task completion, the following conclusions are obtained:

(1) Learn2 basically cannot meet the needs of users to place items. Most users will not use the shelf located at the bottom of Learn2 or will have a poor experience while using it.

(2) Compared with traditional integrated desks and chairs, users can achieve 100% task completion when using Learn2, but it takes longer to learn.

(3) Learn2 is highly flexible and therefore highly adjustable. However, in the two task of rotating the table and changing the left and right positions of the table, subjects need to make several attempts to complete the specified action, and the error rate is high in this process.

Usability Evaluation. In terms of ease of use, it is evaluated from two dimensions: task completion efficiency and task completion effect:

(1) Efficient: According to the comparison between the subjects' average time to complete the task and the time of the control group (common matching desks and chairs), the task completion time of the smart desks and chairs is relatively long, and the task completion efficiency is low.

(2) Effect: All subjects completed the three designated tasks, but the functions of Learn2 were not fully used in the process. The amount of tasks completed reached the standard, but it was observed that the quality of task completion was not high. In terms of ease of learning. When completing the designated task of rotating the desktop, most subjects need to make multiple attempts to successfully complete the task, and even some subjects are close to giving up the task, and the learning error rate is high, indicating that the product is not easy to learn.

Conclusion. After the experiment, a series of pain points are summarized, as shown in Table 5.

Table 5. Pain points.

Items	Pain points	Evaluation			
		Ease of use	Ease of learning	Task match	User satisfaction
Storage	①The inclination of the rack is too large, the capacity is small, and the structure is unreasonable.	☆	☆☆☆☆	☆	☆
	②The water cup slot utilization rate is not high and the location is unreasonable.	☆	☆☆☆☆	☆☆	☆
Desktop	①Round hole grooves and long grooves are basically not noticed and used, and there are problems of unclear semantics.	☆☆	☆☆☆	☆	☆☆☆
	②The desktop space is small, and the water cup is easy to fall.	☆	☆☆☆	☆	☆
Chair	①Sitting for long periods of time can lead to back pain	☆	☆☆☆☆	☆☆☆☆	☆
Joint Rotation	①The joints are too flexible, making it inconvenient to control when sitting or moving tables and chairs.	☆☆	☆	☆☆☆	☆☆☆
	②The rotation angle and direction of each rotary joint are unclear, and multiple attempts are required.	☆	☆☆	☆☆☆	☆
	③There are many joint adjustment parts, and the body is prone to twisting and incorrect sitting posture when sitting still.	☆	☆	☆	☆

Task Match. To evaluate the Task match of Learn2, we conducted a questionnaire.

Design of Questionnaire. In order to design the specific question of the questionnaire, the user journey map is firstly analyzed, and some major pain points are screened peliminarily. After thinking and analysis, we found that the problems of Task match were mainly concentrated in two aspects: unclear signification design and too much flexibility between table and chair structures.

The former leads to users not understanding the partial functions of the *product*[1], while the latter leads to know how to use the product. Therefore, aiming at the two aspects: signification design, flexibility between structures, the questionnaire was designed, and 56 valid questionnaires were collected in total.

Usability Evaluation. In order to evaluate the Task match of Learn2 Seating, the analysis is mainly carried out from two aspects: signification design, flexibility between structures. In terms of signification design: It mainly focuses on the desktop and shelf. The questionnaire data, result analysis and evaluation are shown in the Table 6.

In terms of flexibility between structures: The adjustable structure of Learn2 seating mainly includes four parts. The questionnaire data, result analysis and evaluation are shown in the Table 7.

User Satisfaction. To evaluate the User satisfaction of Learn2 seating, we conducted a questionnaire and user interview.

Questionnaire. In order to evaluate the user satisfaction of Learn2, the design of specific questions in the questionnaire mainly focuses on ease of use, practicality, aesthetics, comfort and overall satisfaction. The subjects were asked to rate them on a scale of 1 to 5. And 56 valid questionnaires were collected in total. The questionnaire data, result analysis and evaluation are shown below.

In terms of ease of use, practicality, aesthetics: Nearly 80% of users' scores for ease of use and practicality are concentrated in 3 and 4, and nearly 70% of users' scores for aesthetics are concentrated in 3 and 4—which means the most users' scores are concentrated in 3 and 4 points (see Fig. 5).

So most users are satisfied with the ease of use, practicality and aesthetics of the product.

In terms of comfort: About 41% of users gave 3 points, about 33% of users gave it a score of less than 3, and about 25% of users gave it a score of higher than 3—which means the score for comfort is relatively neutral, but the overall score is low, so most users are less satisfied with comfort (see Fig. 6).

So most users are not satisfied with the comfort of the product.

In terms of overall satisfaction: About 53% of users gave 3 points, about 9% of users were lower than 3 points, and about 37% of users were higher than 3 points—which means the overall satisfaction score is relatively neutral, but the overall score is high, so most users have a good overall satisfaction with the product (see Fig. 6). However, nearly 18% of users still expressed their unwillingness to use the product again, which

---

[1] 1. Donald A. Norman. Design Psychology [M]. Beijing: CITIC Press, 2015.

Table 6. The evaluation of the signification design.

Item	Questionnaire	Data Analysis	Usability Analysis	Evaluation
Desktop bar groove	What do you think is the role of the strip grooves on the desktop?	About 67% of users think it is to put a pen, about 30% of users think it is to prevent items from falling, and the remaining 37% of users are unclear.	By contacting the manufacturer, the author learned that the desktop bar-shaped groove is equivalent to a card slot. The main function is to prevent the desktop items from falling, but most users mistake it for a pen.	Unreasonable
Desktop circular groove	What do you think the circular grooves on the desktop do?	About 55% of users said they did not know, about 35% of users thought it was the focus of adjusting the desktop, and 8% of users thought it was to place the eraser.	By contacting the manufacturer, the author learned that the circular groove on the desktop is the focal point for adjusting the desktop, but the vast majority of users said they did not know its function.	Unreasonable
Shelve	Q1:Based on your experience, what kind of items do you usually use this shelf for? Q2:Based on your experience, do you think this shelf meets your storage needs?	About 94% of users will use this shelf, and the usage rate is extremely high. However, about 75% of users believe that the design of the shelf does not meet their needs for placing items, and there are problems such as unreasonable structure and small space.	The vast majority of users know its storage function, and the usage rate is high, so the symbol design is clear. However, the vast majority of users believe that the design of the rack is unreasonable and does not meet their needs for placing items.	Unreasonable
Round hole in the shelf	According to your experience, what kind of items do you usually put in this hole on the shelf?	About 84% of users will use the holes on this shelf for placing water glasses, drinks, umbrellas, etc. Only 16% of users would not use it.	The usage rate is high, so the signification design is clear.	Reasonable

to a certain extent indicates that there are major defects in some designs of the product (see Fig. 7).

So most users are satisfied with the product as a whole, but there are major defects in some designs of the product.

User Interviews. The questionnaire survey is only a preliminary understanding of the user's usage, but in order to understand the user's inner needs and eliminate false needs, it is necessary to conduct more in-depth user interviews.

Table 7. The evaluation of the flexibility between structures.

Item	Questionnaire	Data Analysis	Usability Analysis	Evaluation
Back and forth movement of the desktop	Based on your experience, do you think the desktop can be pushed back and forth?	About 92% of users know that the desktop can be moved back and forth, and only 8% of users do not know.	The vast majority of users know that the desktop can be moved back and forth, so the signification design is clear.	Reasonable
Desktop Rotation	Based on your experience, do you think the desktop can be rotated?	About 90% of users know that the desktop can be rotated, and only 10% of users do not know that the desktop can be rotated, or think that the desktop cannot be rotated.	The vast majority of users know that the desktop can be rotated, so the signification design is clear.	Reasonable
Stool surface rotation	According to your experience, do you think the stool surface can be rotated?	About 57% of users know that the stool surface can be rotated, and about 43% of users do not know that the stool surface can be rotated, or think that the stool surface cannot be rotated.	Most users know that the stool surface can be rotated, but there are still a large proportion of users who do not know that the stool surface can be rotated, or think that the stool surface cannot be rotated, so the signification design is not clear.	Unreasonable
Crossbar rotation (crossbar: between table top and stool surface)	Based on your experience, do you think the crossbar between the table top and the stool surface can be rotated?	About 70% of users know that the bar can be rotated, and about 30% of users do not know that the bar can be rotated.	The vast majority of users know that the bar can be rotated to control the position of the desktop, so the signification design is clear.	Reasonable

In order to mine the core demands of users, the author conducted user interviews with 5 users. Through face-to-face communication, a more in-depth, focused and quality communication was conducted. Accordingly, more in-depth pain points have been excavated.

The user interview content is shown in the Table 8. After sorting out and analyzing the content of user interviews, it is found that most users' problems mainly focus on goods storage, difficulty in rotating the desktop and uncomfortable sitting.

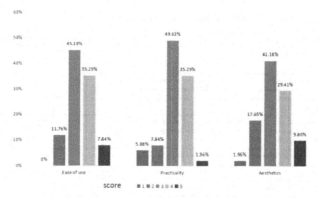

Fig. 5. The data of ease of use, practicality and aesthetics

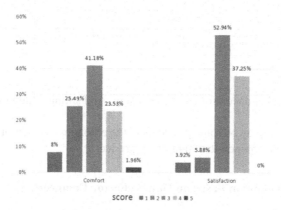

Fig. 6. The data of comfort

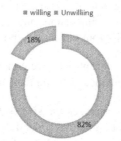

Fig. 7. The data of satisfaction

Most users think that the structural design of the purchase frame is unreasonable, the space is too small, and does not meet the demand of goods receiving. Although the signifier design between structures is reasonable, it is still difficult to use, and the ease of use is poor. And learning is also more difficult, need to go through a certain attempt, so easy to learn poor. In addition, a considerable number of users said that the product

Table 8. Recording of user interviews.

subjects	content	Evaluation			
		Ease of use	Ease of learning	Task match	User satisfaction
User 1	The user said that the structural design of the shelf was unreasonable, and he was unwilling to place the schoolbag there. And thinks that the hole on the shelf is for garbage, and is not willing to put the water cup on the shelf. All items can only be placed on the table, resulting in too many items on the table, insufficient space and very crowded.	☆	☆☆☆☆	☆☆☆	☆
User 2	The user believes that the comfort of this set of tables and chairs is poor, and the sitting posture is relatively restrained due to the cramped space. Compared with traditional desks and chairs, after sitting for a long time, it is easier to feel lower back pain.	☆	☆☆☆	☆☆☆	☆
User 3	The user said that it is more expensive to learn to move the desktop from the left to the right, and that the desktop on the left or right side of the body has no effect on him.	☆	☆	☆☆	☆
	In addition, the user said that the design of the shelf is unreasonable, and has not willing to put the schoolbag on the shelf, but because there is no other place to put it, he can only put it there.	☆	☆☆☆	☆☆☆	☆
User 4	The user said that he did not know that the holes on the shelf were used to put water cups, and he was still reluctant to put the water cups on the shelf even after he knew that the water cups could be placed. Users think that the shelf is made of steel, which may bump the water cup and cause psychological discomfort.	☆☆☆	☆☆☆	☆	☆☆
User 5	The user felt that there were too many places to rotate between the structures and too much flexibility. A certain task can only be completed after a reasonable combination, but it increases the user's learning burden.	☆	☆	☆☆☆	☆
	In addition, the user believes that there is a big problem with placing the item. I don't want to put things on the shelf, but everything is on the table, which makes the table space very cramped.	☆	☆☆☆	☆☆☆	☆

space is cramped, feel uncomfortable when using. And sitting a little longer, there will be back pain.

Therefore, there may be some problems in the ergonomic design of the product, so we then analyze the ergonomic design of the product.

3.3 Usability Evaluation Based on Human Factor Engineering

Some users said that the comfort of this set of desks and chairs is poor, and the sitting posture is more restrained due to the cramped space. Compared with traditional desks and chairs, after sitting for a long time, it is easier to feel lower back pain.

Therefore, measure the relevant dimensions, and analyze whether the size design of the tables and chairs is reasonable from the perspective of human factors engineering.

Measurement. In order to get relevant data, we conducted data measurement on the smart table and chair. The relevant measurement data are shown in Table 9.

Size Analysis. This part mainly analyzes the size of the stool surface and the table-top. According to the principle of ergonomics, the determination of product functional size is divided into five steps: determine the type of product, select the percentage of human body, determine the functional correction amount, determine the psychological correction amount, and set the product functional size[2].

---

[2] Ding Yulan. Ergonomics [M]. Beijing: Beijing Institute of Technology Press, 2011.4.

Table 9. Dimensional drawing of the product.

Item	measurement
A=Desk Length	54cm
B=Desk Width	33cm
C=Desk Height	75.5cm
a=Seat Depth	39cm
b=Seat Width	47cm
c=Seat Height	43cm
d=Seat Back Width	44cm
e=Seat Back Height	83.5cm

Stool Surface. First, select the appropriate percentile of the human body in combination with the product type. Second, select the corresponding percentile from the table, and consider the functional correction amount and the psychological correction amount, and set the size of the seat width, seat depth and seat height respectively. The calculation results are as follows:

(1) Seat width: the left and right distance of the single seat surface. It must meet the required width between the elbows in the natural position in the sitting position. Considering that most operators are to be accommodated, the hip width of the adult female P95 is selected. Considering the thickness and allowance of the clothes, leave 13 mm on the left and right sides.

$$\text{Seat width} = 382 + 13 \times 2 = 408 \text{ mm.} \tag{1}$$

(2) Seat depth: the distance in front of and behind the seat. Select the sitting depth size of adult female P5, and consider the functional modification items: clothing and hip-knee distance to ensure that the hips can be fully supported.

$$\text{Seat depth} = 401 + 13 + 5 = 419 \text{ mm.} \tag{2}$$

(3) Seat height: the vertical distance from the stool surface to the ground. Choose adult women's P5 calf to increase the foot height, and consider the heel height at the same time to ensure that the foot can be placed on the ground naturally.

$$\text{Seat height} = 342 + 38 = 380 \text{ mm.} \tag{3}$$

Tabletop. According to the relevant theories of ergonomics and biomechanics, four indicators, such as neck bending angle, trunk angle, elbow height, and visual distance, are selected to evaluate the health status of sitting posture under different desktop heights[3], The four indicators and their weights are shown in the Table 10.

---

[3] Yi Xiqiong, Chen Haomiao, Shen Liming.Research on the height optimization of desk table top based on ergonomics[J].Packaging Engineering,2011,32(04):44–46?+?73.

Table 10. The weights of the four indicators.

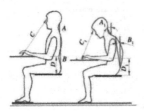

	Torso angle	Neck curvature	Sight distance	Elbow height	weighted Q_i	Compre-hensive weighting Q
Torso angle	1	1	4	4	0.414	0.424
Neck curvature	1	1	3	3	0.358	0.348
Sight distance	1/4	1/3	1	2	0.134	0.130
Elbow height	1/4	1/3	1/2	1	0.094	0.098

λ max=4.117,C I =0.024, R I =0.9.CR=0.027<0.1

According to relevant papers, when the height of the desktop is 790 mm, the value of the trunk angle is the smallest (the smaller the trunk angle, the closer the curvature of the spine is to the natural standing state), and the mean value of the curvature of the neck is also the smallest at this time, which is more conducive to the health of the cervical spine; When the table top height is 710 mm, the elbows are placed most reasonably and the eyes are the most comfortable.

Combined with the weight of each index, as the Table 11 shows, the optimal height of the desktop is calculated to be 770 mm.

Table 11. The weight of each index.

Index	Single optimal value (H_i)/mm	weighted Q_i	Comprehensive optimal value(H)
Torso angle	790	0.424	
Neck curvature	790	0.348	$H=\Sigma H_i \times Q_i=$
Sight distance	710	0.130	770 mm
Elbow height	710	0.098	

Note: The subjects are college students, and the average height is selected: male 17.7cm, female 160.7cm

Improved Size. In summary, according to the relevant theories of ergonomics and biomechanics, the more reasonable table height, seat width, seat depth, seat height, and the evaluation results are shown in the Fig. 8.

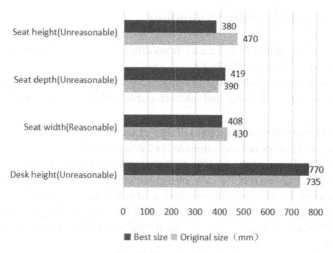

Fig. 8. Improved size

Human Hand Grasp Analysis. The human hand has great flexibility. From the point of view of grasping action, it can be divided into force grasping and precise grasping[4]. The use of this product only involves the force grip, namely the hole above the seat back and the circular force point on the table top (see Fig. 9).

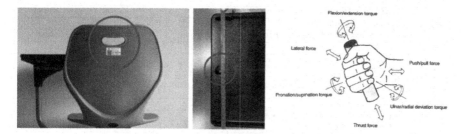

Fig. 9. Learn2's hand grasp design

When grasping forcefully, the grasping axis is almost perpendicular to the forearm, the slightly bent fingers form a grip with the palm, and the thumb exerts force, as shown in Fig. 9. And during use, keep your wrist in a straight state all the time. It can be seen that the two partial designs of the product are unreasonable.

---

[4] Ding Yulan. Ergonomics [M]. Beijing: Beijing Institute of Technology Press, 2011.4.

4   Summary of Usability Evaluation

After evaluating the usability of Learn2 from different aspects, a series of pain points are summarized, as shown in Table 12.

To sum up, the user's problems are mainly concentrated in three aspects: item storage, difficulty in turning the desktop, and uncomfortable sitting and standing.

1. Most users think that the structural design of the rack is unreasonable, the space is too small, and it does not meet the needs of item storage.
2. Although the design of the signification design between structures is reasonable, it is still difficult to use and the ease of use is poor. And it is more difficult to learn, and it needs to go through a certain trial, so it is less easy to learn.
3. In addition, quite a number of users said that the space of the product is cramped and they feel uncomfortable when using it. And sitting for a long time, there will be back pain.

Table 12. The summary of pain points.

Items	Pain points	Evaluation			
		Ease of use	Ease of learning	Task match	User satisfaction
Storage	①Shelf utilization is not high.	☆	☆☆☆☆	☆☆	☆
	②Slightly large items such as school bags cannot be properly placed on the shelves.	☆	☆☆☆☆	☆☆	☆
Desktop	①Long grooves and round hole grooves have unclear semantics.	☆☆	☆☆☆	☆	☆☆
	②Desktop rotation is too flexible.	☆☆	☆	☆☆	☆☆
	③No tilt angle is not conducive to reading and electronic product use.	☆☆			☆☆
Chair	①Stool surface can be rotated too much.	☆☆☆	☆☆☆		☆☆
	②The universal wheel is too flexible, and it is easy to hit the foot when moving.	☆☆	☆☆		☆
Ergonomics	①The chair is too high and not deep enough.	☆	☆☆☆☆		☆☆
	②Desk height is slightly lower.	☆	☆☆☆☆		☆☆
	③Sitting for a long time is not breathable.	☆☆☆	☆☆☆☆		☆
	④Improper force when using the chair back handle to push and pull the table and chair.	☆☆	☆☆		☆☆☆

For the subsequent improvement of the design, some necessary pain points were screened out, and corresponding design points were proposed for these pain points, as shown in Table 13. There are three filter criteria:

1. The problem is prominent.
2. Urgent needs of users.
3. Large room for improvement.

Table 13. Pain point selection

Modifiable pain points	Design points
Insufficient shelf space	Shelf structure
The position of the cup groove is unreasonable and the utilization rate is low	Shelf structure
Desk angle is not adjustable	Desktop structure
Unclear semantics of desktop grooves	Signification design of desktop
The grip design of the seat back handle is unreasonable	Chair back handle design
Sitting for long periods of time is not breathable	Optimization of the stool surface

5 Redesign

We redesigned Learn2 seating based on usability evaluation. Actively looking for solutions to the problems we found, and ultimately presenting an improved design. The final redesign display effect is shown in Fig. 10.

Fig. 10. The final redesign of Learn2

As shown in the Fig. 10, the main design points of the redesign are:

1. Shelf structure
2. Desktop structure
3. Ideographs of desktop-related structures
4. Chair back handle design
5. Optimization of the stool surface

5.1 Shelf Structure

The redesign of the shelf mainly includes two parts, as shown in Table 14:

Table 14. The redesign of the shelf.

Redesign	Design point	Evaluation		
		Ease of use		
		Before	After	
	Horizontal storage space	☆	☆☆☆☆☆	
		Task match		
	Shift the position	Before	After	
	of the hole for the	☆☆	☆☆☆☆	
	water cup			

(1) The bottom shelf in the original design was improved from two slopes to one slope and one horizontal storage space.
(2) Shift the position of the hole for the water cup from the center to the front side.

5.2 Desktop Structure

The redesign of the desktop structure includes two parts, as shown in Table 15:

(1) The desktop is improved to a tabletop with adjustable tilt angle.
(2) Design drop-stop baffles for sloping desktop.

Table 15. The redesign of the desktop structure.

Redesign	Design point	Evaluation		
		Ease of use		
		Before	After	
	A tabletop with adjustable tilt angle	☆	☆☆☆☆	
		Ease of learn		
		Before	After	
	Drop-stop baffles for sloping desktop	☆	☆☆☆☆☆	

5.3 Signification Design of Desktop

The redesign of the signification design of desktop mainly includes two parts, as shown in Table 16:

(1) The round hole on the table is a reminder for the force point itself, and then it is designed to be moved to the corner of the table, which is more convenient for force.
(2) Design symbol for the desktop anti-drop bezel, tap to pop out the bezel.

Table 16. The redesign of the signification design of desktop.

Redesign	Design point	Evaluation	
	Move the position of the force point	Ease of use	
		Before	After
		☆	☆☆☆☆
	Symbol for the drop-stop baffles for sloping desktop	Task match	
		Before	After
		☆	☆☆☆☆☆

5.4 Chair Back Handle Design

The redesign of the handle mainly includes two parts, as shown in Table 17:

(1) Shift the position of the handle from the middle of the seat back to the side of the seat back.
(2) Expand the arc of the handle to adapt to the direction of the hand.

Table 17. The redesign of the handle.

	Redesign	Evaluation	
		Move the position and shape of the hole to the side	Expand the arc of the handle
		Ease of use	Task match
Before		☆	☆☆
After		☆☆☆☆	☆☆☆☆☆

5.5 Optimization of the Stool Surface

Table 18. The redesign of the stool surface.

	Redesign	Evaluation
		Make holes in the stool surface
		Ease of use
Before		☆☆
After		☆☆☆☆

The redesign of the stool surface mainly includes one parts, as shown in Table 18: Make holes in the stool surface to make the stool surface breathable.

Promising or Influencing? Theory and Evidence on the Acceptance of Mobile Payment Among the Elderly in China

Ruisi Liu[1], Xueai Li[2], and Junjie Chu[1(✉)]

[1] Ocean University of China, Qingdao 266100, China
chujunjie@ouc.edu.cn
[2] Peking University, Beijing 102627, China

Abstract. Mobile payment has become popular in China recently. However, China's population is aging rapidly at the same time. Therefore, it is necessary to explore factors that can affect the elderly to accept mobile payment. By adding two constructs of trust and social influence, this study proposed an extended TAM, and a questionnaire survey was conducted among the Chinese elderly. Structural equation modeling (SEM) was used to analyze the data. Results show that the model explains 77.3% of the variance in behavioral intention. Besides, perceived usefulness and social influence significantly and positively affect behavioral intention, while trust does not. This result demonstrates that what matters is the usefulness and influence from important others, but not the promise provided by mobile payment platforms. Based on the results, this study provides suggestions for the future development of mobile payment.

Keywords: Technology acceptance model · Mobile payment · The elderly

1 Technology Acceptance Model; Mobile Payment; The Elderly

In recent years, a variety of innovative technologies have made people's life more and more convenient. However, the problem of population aging is also intensifying, and there will be an increasing number of people over 65 in the world population in the coming decades. According to Seventh National Population Census, the number of elderly people over the age of 65 has reached 190 million, accounting for 13.5% of China's total population (National Bureau of Statistics of China 2021). In this context, society has begun to increase the care for the elderly, and technology companies have launched corresponding measures to meet the needs of the elderly, like applications for the elderly. In the academic world, studies have gradually turned to focus on the technology acceptance of the elderly, exploring factors that can help the elderly better adapt to the digital life, so as to provide some design suggestions.

Since the rise of mobile Internet technology, people's lives have undergone earth-shaking changes. Various mobile services are rapidly popularized (like mobile payment, mobile games, mobile food ordering services, etc.), especially mobile payment services, whose market scale keeps expanding. According to the 47th Statistical Report on China's Internet Development, as of December 2020, China had 853 million mobile payment users (CNNIC February 2021). Due to its convenience, security, and speed, mobile payment attracts users of all ages, even the elderly user group. Some recent studies have focused on the adoption of mobile payment by the elderly. For example, Cham et al. (2021) indicated that the elderly's psychological obstacles (e.g., lack of trust, technology anxiety) and risk obstacles may lead to their resistance to mobile payment. In addition, Hanif and Lallie (2021) indicated that the elderly's perceived cyber security risk has a significant influence on their intention to use mobile banking applications. However, research (Li and Jia 2021) also showed that the use of the Internet can improve the mental health of middle-aged and elderly people, and has a greater effect on the mental health of the elderly.

At present, mobile payment is prevalent in China, and the elderly population is gradually increasing. On the one hand, it is an inevitable trend for the elderly to use mobile payment systems. On the other hand, the physical and psychological characteristics of the elderly may hinder their use of mobile payment. In order to better understand the acceptance of mobile payment among the elderly in China and its determinants, this study extended the Technology Acceptance Model (TAM) by adding trust and social influence in the model, and finally provided suggestions for future development of mobile payment based on the research results.

The rest of this paper is organized as follows: Sect. 2 is a literature review on mobile payment, characteristics of the elderly, and TAM. Section 3 presents the research model and research hypotheses. Section 4 presents the research methodology and the analysis results. Section 5 presented discussions of the results and outlines the conclusion.

2   Literature Review

2.1   Mobile Payment

Mobile payment refers to the behavior of users using mobile devices to complete payments. Consumers can use devices like mobile phones to pay for various services or digital and physical goods without cash, checks, or credit cards (Bai 2020). Driven by the Chinese government, telecom operators, third-party payment enterprises, and technological development, the mobile payment market of China has witnessed explosive growth (Zhao et al. 2022). Nowadays, many people can't live without mobile payment in China, and some of them no longer carry and use cash in their daily life.

Studies found that different people have different perceptions about mobile payment. Chen et al. (2021) showed that users who prefer traditional payment methods tend to find mobile payment risky and not suitable for use. While more innovative users find mobile payment convenient, low-risk, and fun. In terms of different countries, Fan et al. (2018) found that payment culture and perceived security had significantly smaller influences on trust in the United States than in China.

2.2   Physical and Psychological Characteristics of the Elderly

The elderly are often characterized by poor sensory perception and cognitive ability. In terms of sensory, the elderly may have blurred vision, deafness, poor ability to touch accurately, and other problems (Bai 2020; Wang 2021). These problems slow them down and make it difficult for them to respond quickly to a large amount of information. In terms of cognitive ability, the brain processing ability of the elderly decreases, and their ability to capture and understand information may decline (Bai 2020; Wang 2021). These may discourage the elderly from using emerging technologies. In addition, some ideas of the elderly themselves may also hinder their acceptance of technologies. With the rapid development of technology, the cognitive styles of the elderly cannot keep up with the changes of the time, which may lead them to refuse to use emerging technologies or be gullible (Bai 2020; Wang 2021).

Some studies on the use of intelligent technology by the elderly have shown the barriers that the elderly may encounter when using technologies. Chen (2021) indicated that older people tend to have a higher level of trust than young people, which may lead to a greater chance of being cheated by false information. In addition, Li (2014) found that in the process of online consumption, being unfamiliar with the operating procedures will affect the elderly's intention to use. Similarly, the elderly may face the same problem when using mobile payment.

2.3   TAM and Its Use in the Context of Mobile Payment

The Technology Acceptance Model (TAM) is proposed by Davis (1989) to explain the decisive factors for the wide acceptance of computers. The most important variables in TAM are perceived usefulness and perceived ease of use. They can affect users' attitude and behavioral intention. TAM has been applied to research in different fields. In order to enhance the explanatory ability of the model, researchers have added some new variables to the original model (e.g., social influence and facilitating conditions), and proposed some adapted models, such as TAM2, UTAUT, and UTAUT2.

With the development of mobile payment technology and the expansion of its market, a number of studies have focused on the adoption of mobile payment by users. Then some research provided a review of those studies on mobile payment adoption. TAM and its adapted model have been widely used. Abdullah et al. (2021) counted the author keywords of the research in the context of mobile payment, and found that TAM appeared nine times, only second to the occurrence of "mobile payment". This suggests that TAM was widely used by researchers to investigate mobile payment adoption. Besides, Pal et al. (2019) demonstrated that UTAUT and TAM are the two most frequently used models in research on mobile payment adoption and usage, and perceived usefulness and perceived ease of use are the most frequently used factors. In addition, Karsen et al. (2019) showed that the five most important factors in the use of mobile payment are perceived ease of use, perceived usefulness, perceived trust, perceived risk, and social influence. Moreover, Pramana (2021) demonstrated that the five most frequently investigated factors in the theoretical model are perceived usefulness, perceived ease of use, risk, trust, and social influence. Similarly, Pal et al. (2019) showed that the five most frequently appearing factors that influence mobile payment adoption and usage are perceived ease of use, perceived usefulness, risk, trust, and cost. Considering the importance of social influence and trust in using mobile payment for the elderly, which is also shown in the studies above, the present study added the two constructs in the original TAM.

Additionally, although there have been a number of studies on user adoption of mobile payment, Pramana (2021) suggested that, in this research context, developing countries in Asia (excluding India) need to be more active. Therefore, this study applied an extended TAM to investigate the elderly's acceptance of mobile payment.

3   Research Hypotheses and Research Model

Based on previous studies, this study extended TAM to explore the factors that influence mobile payment acceptance by the elderly in China. The proposed research model is shown in Fig. 1.

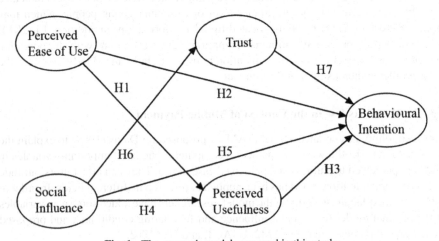

Fig. 1. The research model proposed in this study.

3.1   Perceived Ease of Use and Perceived Usefulness

In TAM, perceived ease of use and perceived usefulness are two main factors affecting users' behavior intention, which are respectively defined as "the degree to which a person believes that using a particular system would be free of effort" and "the degree to which a person believes that using a particular system would enhance his or her job performance" (Davis 1989). In the context of mobile payment, perceived ease of use (Li et al. 2019; Ma et al. 2018; Wiradinata 2018) and perceived usefulness (Li et al. 2019; Wang and Dai 2020; Wiradinata 2018) have been proved to have significant influence on behavioral intention. In addition, perceived ease of use was proved to positively impact perceived usefulness (Li et al. 2019; Ma et al. 2018; Wang and Dai 2020). Similarly, we expect these hypotheses to apply when the elderly in China use mobile payment.

Therefore, we propose the following hypotheses:

H1: Perceived ease of use positively impacts perceived usefulness.
H2: Perceived ease of use positively impacts behavioral intention.
H3: Perceived usefulness positively impacts behavioral intention.

3.2 Social Influence

Venkatesh et al. (2003) defined social influence as "the degree to which an individual perceives that important others believe he or she should use the new system". For the elderly, suggestions or supports from their family members, friends, or people important to them may affect their intention to use mobile payment.

In the context of mobile payment, studies showed that social influence positively influence perceived usefulness (Conci et al. 2009). Besides, studies also showed that social influence positively influence behavioral intention (Al-Saedi et al. 2020; Conci et al. 2009; Mensah 2019; Patil et al. 2020). Besides, de Luna et al. (2019) studied the social influence in form of subjective norms, and indicated that subjective norms positively affect perceived usefulness and intention to use SMS (Short Message Service), QR (Quick Response), and NFC (Near Field Communication) mobile payment systems. Similarly, we expect these hypotheses to apply when the elderly in China use mobile payment.

Therefore, we propose the following hypotheses:

H4: Social influence positively impacts perceived usefulness.
H5: Social influence positively impacts behavioral intention.

3.3 Trust

Trust plays an important role in many scenarios. In the use of the mobile payment, users' trust in mobile payment platforms may affect their adoption of mobile payment. The present study believes that the elderly's trust in mobile payment platforms will affect their intention to use mobile payment, and specifically, the more the elderly think the mobile payment platforms are reliable, the more willing they are to use mobile payment.

Previous studies have proved that trust has a positive and significant effect on users' intention to use mobile payment (Kalinic et al. 2019; Liu et al. 2019; Shao et al. 2019). In terms of the relationship between social influence and trust, Qu et al. (2015) showed that social influence has a positive impact on trust. That is, the more seniors perceive that their important others believe they should use mobile payment, the more they trust mobile payment platforms. Similarly, we expect these hypotheses to apply when the elderly in China use mobile payment.

Therefore, we propose the following hypotheses:

H6: Social influence positively impacts trust.
H7: Trust positively impacts behavioral intention.

4 Methodology

4.1 Data Collection

Mobile payment includes many ways, such as QR Code (Quick Response Code) and NFC (Near Field Communication). In China, the most commonly used payment method is to scan the payment code (QR code) provided by merchants, or provide payment code

(QR code or one-dimension bar code) for merchants to scan, and this payment method mainly relies on two platforms, WeChat and Alipay. According to the Research Report of Mobile Payment Security published by China UnionPay (2021), 96% of respondents pay via QR codes. Therefore, the survey in this study focused on the mobile payment that through the payment code.

This survey was conducted through online questionnaire distribution. Before the formal distribution of the questionnaire, a simulation test on 5 elderly people over the age of 55 was conducted to judge whether the content of the questionnaire is easy for the elderly to understand. The results show that the respondents can understand the meaning of the topic well and complete the questionnaire independently. A total of 436 questionnaires were collected. By screening, we deleted (1) Questionnaires with respondents younger than 55 years old; (2) Questionnaires that took less than 50 s or more than 1,000 s to complete; (3) All but two (or fewer) answers are the same. Finally, 130 valid questionnaires were used.

According to the statistical results, the proportion of men and women who filled in the questionnaire is average, accounting for 44.62% and 55.38% respectively. In addition, the number of respondents aged 55–59 is the largest, accounting for 65.38% of the number of valid questionnaires. The number of respondents with an education level of junior high school or below is the largest, accounting for 45.38% of the number of valid questionnaires. Most respondents have used mobile payment for more than two years, and may be familiar with mobile payment. It is well representative that the elderly with different ages, different gender, different educational background, and different using experience of mobile payment were included in the questionnaire sample.

There are two parts in the questionnaire. The first part investigates the basic information of the respondents, and the second part uses the 7-point Likert scale to investigate the respondents' agreement with different statements. The basic information of the respondents is shown in Table 1. And Table 2 demonstrates the items of the second part and their source.

Table 1. The basic information of the respondents.

Information		Number	Percentage
Gender	Male	58	44.62%
	Female	72	55.38%
Age	55–59	85	65.38%
	60–64	22	16.92%
	65–69	13	10.00%
	70–74	5	3.85%
	Above 75	5	3.85%

(continued)

Table 1. (*continued*)

Information		Number	Percentage
Education	Junior high school or below	59	45.38%
	Senior high school (including specialized secondary school)	55	42.31%
	College (including college degree) or above	16	12.31%
Using experience	Less than half a year	17	13.08%
	Half a year to a year	18	13.85%
	One to two years	21	16.15%
	More than two years	74	56.92%

Table 2. The items of the second part.

Items	Source
Trust TR1 - I think mobile payment platforms are trustworthy TR2 - I think mobile payment platforms are reliable TR3 - I believe mobile payment platforms will keep users' interests in mind	Hanif and Lallie (2021), Khalilzadeh et al. (2017), Patil et al. (2020)
Perceived ease of use PEU1 - The steps of using mobile payment for transactions are simple PEU2 - It would be easy for me to learn how to use mobile payment PEU3 - Becoming skillful at using mobile payment would be easy for me	Davis (1989), Venkatesh et al. (2003)
Perceived usefulness PU1 - Using mobile payment would make my life more convenient PU2 - Using mobile payment saves me time PU3 - Using mobile payment would help me to accomplish payment more quickly	Davis (1989), Venkatesh et al. (2003)
Social influence SI1 - My family and friends think that I should use mobile payment SI2 - People whose opinions I value think that I should use mobile payment SI3 - People who influence me think that I should use mobile payment	Venkatesh et al. (2003)

(*continued*)

Table 2. (*continued*)

Items	Source
Behavioral intention BI1 - I intend to continue using mobile payment in the future BI2 - I will use mobile payment on a regular basis in the future BI3 - I will increase the frequency of using mobile payment in the future	Venkatesh et al. (2003)

4.2 Data Analysis

We used structural equation modeling (SEM) to analyze the data. The data analysis includes two parts: analysis of measurement model and structural model.

Measurement Model. Confirmatory factor analysis (CFA) was used to analyze the measurement model.

Table 3 shows the parameters of significant test and item reliability. As the table shows, all the standardized factor loadings are greater than 0.6, and most of them are greater than 0.7, reaching the recommended standard. In addition, all the R-square exceed 0.5, indicating that the item reliability is good.

Table 4 shows the results of composite reliability, convergent validity, and discriminate validity. The CR (composite reliability) of all the constructs is higher than 0.7, which shows acceptable composite reliability (Hairs et al. 1998). AVE (average variance extracted) of all the constructs is higher than 0.5, indicating a good convergence validity (Fornell and Larcker 1981). In addition, the results demonstrated at the diagonal is the square root of the AVE of each factor, each of them is greater than the other figures (the Pearson correlation coefficients with other constructs) in its row and column.

Table 3. Parameters of significant test and item reliability.

Factor	Items	Estimate	S.E	Est./S.E	P-Value	R-square
Trust (TR)	TR1	0.769	0.064	12.027	***	0.591
	TR2	0.962	0.047	20.563	***	0.925
	TR3	0.668	0.11	6.07	***	0.446
Perceived ease of use (PEU)	PEU1	0.831	0.054	15.415	***	0.691
	PEU2	0.877	0.039	22.531	***	0.769
	PEU3	0.899	0.046	19.48	***	0.808
Perceived usefulness (PU)	PU1	0.913	0.034	26.656	***	0.834
	PU2	0.893	0.028	31.599	***	0.797
	PU3	0.862	0.031	27.783	***	0.743

(*continued*)

Table 3. (*continued*)

Factor	Items	Estimate	S.E	Est./S.E	P-Value	R-square
Social influence (SI)	SI1	0.923	0.032	28.524	***	0.852
	SI2	0.927	0.027	34.935	***	0.859
	SI3	0.772	0.066	11.68	***	0.596
Behavioral intension (BI)	BI1	0.905	0.029	31.636	***	0.819
	BI2	0.855	0.066	12.882	***	0.731
	BI3	0.811	0.039	20.836	***	0.658

**p < 0.001

Table 4. Composite reliability, convergent validity, and discriminate validity.

	CR	AVE	TR	PEU	PU	SI	BI
TR	0.847	0.654	**0.809**				
PEU	0.903	0.756	0.709	**0.869**			
PU	0.919	0.791	0.623	0.782	**0.889**		
SI	0.908	0.769	0.656	0.770	0.843	**0.877**	
BI	0.893	0.736	0.570	0.716	0.848	0.837	**0.858**

Structural Model. The model fitting indices are χ^2/df, CFI, TLI, RMSEA, and SRMR. The model fitting indices in this study are shown in Table 5. All the indices meet the recommended value, indicating that the structural model fits well.

Table 5. Model fit.

	Recommended value	Index	
χ^2/df	$1 < \chi^2$/df < 3	1.143	Matched
CFI	>0.9	0.990	Matched
TLI	>0.9	0.987	Matched
RMSEA	<0.08	0.033	Matched
SRMR	<0.08	0.057	Matched

Table 6 shows the results of the hypotheses. P-value < 0.05 indicates that the hypothesis is supported. There are seven hypotheses in the model, of which five are supported and two are not supported. As the results shows, perceived ease of use positively influences perceived usefulness ($\beta = 0.306$, $p < 0.01$), perceived usefulness positively influences behavioral intention ($\beta = 0.483$, $p < 0.01$), and social influence positively influences perceived usefulness ($\beta = 0.607$, $p < 0.001$), behavioral intention ($\beta = 0.444$, $p < 0.01$), and trust ($\beta = 0.673$, p < 0.001). Therefore, H1, H3, H4, H5, H6 are supported. However, H2 and H7 are not supported. In Fig. 2, the results for the research model were shown. Besides, results showed that the model explains 45.3% of the variance in trust, 75.4% of the variance in perceived usefulness, and 77.3% of the variance in behavioral intention.

Table 6. Hypothesis analysis.

DV	IV	Estimate	S.E	Est./S.E	P-value	R^2	Hypothesis
TR	SI	0.673	0.07	9.631	***	0.453	Support
PU	PEU	0.306	0.091	3.347	0.001	0.754	Support
	SI	0.607	0.085	7.156	***		Support
BI	SI	0.444	0.161	2.766	0.006	0.773	Support
	TR	−0.042	0.062	−0.684	0.494		Not Support
	PEU	0.018	0.088	0.203	0.839		Not Support
	PU	0.483	0.143	3.38	0.001		Support

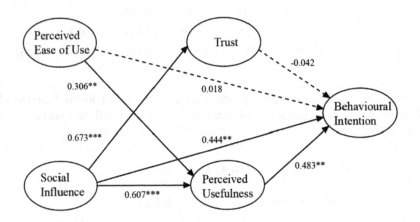

***p < 0.001 **p < 0.01 *p < 0.05.

Fig. 2. Results of the research model.

5   Discussion and Conclusion

5.1   Discussion

By extending TAM, this paper explores the factors that affect behavioral intention of the elderly to use mobile payment.

The results show that social influence is an important factor in mobile payment acceptance by the elderly. Social influence has a significant impact on trust, which is consistent with the previous research results (Qu et al. 2015). This indicates that the positive influence of others will improve the elderly' trust in mobile payment platforms. In addition, social influence also shows a significant impact on perceived usefulness and behavioral intention, which is also consistent with prior research (Conci et al. 2009). This indicates that when people who are important to the elderly think that the elderly should use mobile payment, the elderly can perceive the usefulness of this payment method and are more willing to use it.

Moreover, it is also consistent with previous studies that perceived usefulness has a significant impact on behavioral intention (Li et al. 2019; Wang and Dai 2020; Wiradinata 2018). However, perceived ease of use does not have a significant impact on behavioral intention. Thus, compared with the ease of use, usefulness is more important in future product design. Besides, results also show that perceived ease of use has a positive impact on perceived usefulness. That is, the more seniors find mobile payment easy to use, the more likely they are to find it useful.

Contrary to our expectation, results shows that trust has no significant effect on behavioral intention. In this study, the construct of trust focuses on security, which is a feeling provided by mobile payment platforms. And it is actually a security promise made by the service providers to the user. This promise, according to the results, has no significant relationship with the behavioral intention of the elderly. Hence, promises or commitments from the service providers are useless, that is, appearing credible is useless. But it is the use and recommendations of people around the elderly that are useful.

Therefore, the promotion will not work well through enhancing the trust by design, while the effective way to promote is to tell the elderly that important others are using it and have good comments. It is a feature of Chinese society, which can also explain why the leading products of mobile payment are particularly preferred in China, because of the herd mentality.

5.2 Conclusion

At present, the problem of population aging is becoming more and more serious. Meanwhile, various technologies develop rapidly. Therefore, how to promote the elderly to use innovative technology is a problem that must be solved. The present study investigated factors that impact the Chinese elderly's behavioral intention to use mobile payment through an extended TAM.

Results show that perceived usefulness has a significant effect on behavioral intention, but perceived ease of use does not. This suggests that future design should focus more on improving product usefulness than ease of use.

Moreover, in order to better understand factors that affect the elderly's acceptance of mobile payment, this study added the constructs of trust and social influence into TAM. Results show that social influence has a significant impact on behavioral intention while trust does not have. Through analysis, this study believes that the result may be caused by the prevailing herd mentality of Chinese people. Therefore, designing to enhance trust or security of the products is not a good way to promote, but telling the elderly that people around them are using the products is.

References

Abdullah, K., Khan, M.N., Kostadinova, E.: Determining mobile payment adoption: a systematic literature search and bibliometric analysis. Cogent Bus. Manag. **8**(1) (2021)

Al-Saedi, K., Al-Emran, M., Ramayah, T., Abusham, E.: Developing a general extended UTAUT model for M-payment adoption. Technol. Soc. **62** (2020)

Bai, L.: Research on user experience design based on mobile payment dilemma of the elderly group. Tianjin University of Technology (2020)

Cham, T.H., Cheah, J.H., Cheng, B.L., Lim, X.J.: I am too old for this! Barriers contributing to the non-adoption of mobile payment. Int. J. Bank Mark. (ahead-of-print) (2021)

Chen, B.C., Chen, H., Wang, Y.C.: Cash, credit card, or mobile? Examining customer payment preferences at chain restaurants in Taiwan. J. Foodserv. Bus. Res. (2021)

China Internet Network Information Center (CNNIC): The 47th Statistical Report on China's Internet Development (2021)

China UnionPay: Research Report of Mobile Payment Security (2021)

Chen, Y.: Over-Trust and Vulnerability to Fraud of the Elderly: The Influence of Emotional Arousal on Trust and Trust Learning. Tian Jin Normal University (2021)

Conci, M., Pianesi, F., Zancanaro, M.: Useful, social and enjoyable: mobile phone adoption by older people. In: Gross, T., et al. (eds.) INTERACT 2009. LNCS, vol. 5726, pp. 63–76. Springer, Heidelberg (2009). https://doi.org/10.1007/978-3-642-03655-2_7

Davis, F.D.: Perceived usefulness, perceived ease of use, and user acceptance of information technology. MIS Q. **13**, 319–340 (1989)

de Luna, I.R., Liébana-Cabanillas, F., Sánchez-Fernández, J., Muñoz-Leiva, F.: Mobile payment is not all the same: the adoption of mobile payment systems depending on the technology applied. Technol. Forecast. Soc. Chang. **146**, 931–934 (2019)

Fan, J., Shao, M.X., Li, Y.F., Huang, X.M.: Understanding users' attitude toward mobile payment use. Ind. Manag. Data Syst. **118** (2018)

Fornell, C., Larcker, D.: Structural equation models with unobservable variables and measurement error. J. Mark. Res. (1981)

Hairs, J.F., Anderson, R.E., Tatham, R.L., Black, W.C.: Multivariate Data Analysis. Printice Hall, Englewood Cliffs (1998)

Hanif, Y., Lallie, H.S.: Security factors on the intention to use mobile banking applications in the UK older generation (55+). A Mixed-method study using modified UTAUT and MTAM - with perceived cyber security, risk, and trust. Technol. Soc. **67** (2021)

Kalinic, Z., Marinkovic, V., Molinillo, S., Cabanillas, F.L.: A multi-analytical approach to peer-to-peer mobile payment acceptance prediction. J. Retail. Consum. Serv. **49** (2019)

Karsen, M., Chandra, Y.T., Juwitasary, H.: Technological factors of mobile payment: a systematic literature review. In: 4th International Conference on Computer Science and Computational Intelligence (2019)

Khalilzadeh, J., Ozturk, A.B., Bilgihan, A.: Security-related factors in extended UTAUT model for NFC based mobile payment in the restaurant industry. Comput. Hum. Behav. **70** (2017)

Li, Z.G., Jia, C.C.: The impact of internet use on mental health of middle-aged and elderly people: a test of heterogeneity and mechanism. Jiangsu Soc. Sci. (2021)

Li, J., Wang, J., Wangh, S.Y., Zhou, Y.: Mobile payment with Alipay: an application of extended technology acceptance model. IEEE Access **7** (2019)

Li, Z.Z.: Online Consumer Behavior of Urban Aging Group in China—With the Case of Quanzhou City. Huaqiao University (2014)

Liu, Z.Z., Ben, S.L., Zhang, R.D.: Factors affecting consumers' mobile payment behavior: a meta-analysis. Electron. Commer. Res. **19** (2019)

Ma, L.J., Su, X.Y., Yu, Y., Wang, C., Lin, K.Q., Lin, M.Y.: What drives the use of M-payment? An empirical study about Alipay and WeChat payment (2018)

Mensah, I.K.: Predictors of the continued adoption of WeChat mobile payment. Int. J. E-Bus. Res. **15** (2019)

National Bureau of Statistics of China: Bulletin of the Seventh National Population Census (2021)

Pal, A., De', R., Herath, T., Rao, H.R.: A review of contextual factors affecting mobile payment adoption and use. J. Bank. Financ. Technol. **3** (2019)

Patil, P., Tamilmani, K., Rana, N.P., Raghavan, V.: Understanding consumer adoption of mobile payment in India: extending meta-utaut model with personal innovativeness, anxiety, trust, and grievance redressal. Int. J. Inf. Manag. **54** (2020)

Pramana, E.: The mobile payment adoption: a systematic literature review. In: 2021 3rd East Indonesia Conference on Computer and Information Technology (EIConCIT) (2021)

Qu, Y., Rong, w., Ouyang, Y.X., Chen, H., Xiong, Z.: Social aware mobile payment service popularity analysis: the case of Wechat payment in China. In: Yao, L., Xie, X., Zhang, Q., Yang, L., Zomaya, A., Jin, H. (eds.) APSCC 2015. LNCS, vol. 9464, pp. 289–299. Springer, Cham (2015). https://doi.org/10.1007/978-3-319-26979-5_22

Shao, Z., Zhang, L., Li, X.T., Guo, Y.: Antecedents of trust and continuance intention in mobile payment platforms: the moderating effect of gender. Electron. Commer. Res. Appl. **33** (2019)

Venkatesh, V., Morris, M.G., Davis, G.B., Davis, F.D.: User acceptance of information technology: toward a unified view. MIS Q. **27**, 425–478 (2003)

Wang, L., Dai, X.F.: Exploring factors affecting the adoption of mobile payment at physical stores. Int. J. Mob. Commun. **18** (2020)

Wang, B.: Research on bridging the digital divide between urban and rural elderly. Heilongjiang University (2021)

Wiradinata, T.: Mobile payment services adoption_the role of perceived technology risk (2018)

Zhao, C.K., Wu, Y.Q., Guo, J.H.: Mobile payment and Chinese rural household consumption. China Econ. Rev. **71** (2022)

Applying a New Questionnaire to Evaluate the Usability of Peruvian E-Government Websites

Freddy Paz[✉] (ID)

Pontificia Universidad Católica del Perú, Lima 32, Peru
fpaz@pucp.pe

Abstract. Usability has become an extremely relevant aspect that must be considered in the development of any software product. If usability is not considered, then there is a high probability that its users will reject the application. A software product is destined to fail in a highly competitive environment such as the current one, depending on its capability to be understood, learned, and attractive to its users. For this reason, a set of usability evaluation methods have been developed that allow specialists to systematically determine whether graphical interfaces are usable. Among the methods that exist, one of the most used due to its simplicity and low demand for resources is the usability assessment questionnaire. However, most of the questionnaires that have been designed are intended to be answered by end-users of the application. In contrast to this paradigm, in a previous work, a questionnaire was developed and designed that can be used by specialists in Human-Computer Interaction. This new questionnaire involves a set of 60 items with which it is possible to verify if the interfaces of a software product fulfill aspects that make them usable. In this study, the new questionnaire was employed to evaluate the usability of the main Peruvian E-Government Websites. The intention of this scientific article is to serve as a source for future improvement of the websites and to serve at a methodological level so that specialists can widely use the evaluation instrument and the conduction process that has been carried out in this research.

Keywords: Human-computer interaction · Usability · Heuristic evaluation · E-government · Assessment questionnaire

1 Introduction

Ensuring that a software product is easy to use and intuitive to the degree that it leads to the achievement of its users' goals is a highly relevant aspect today [1]. Software development teams are concerned about the level of usability offered by the interfaces of their products and services. The importance of this quality attribute is because usability could be an aspect that makes the difference in a highly competitive market in which several options are available [2]. Usability refers to the capability of a software product to be used to achieve quantified objectives with effectiveness, efficiency, and satisfaction

M. M. Soares et al. (Eds.): HCII 2022, LNCS 13321, pp. 460–472, 2022.
https://doi.org/10.1007/978-3-031-05897-4_32

in a quantified context of use [3]. In the web domain, if a web system is difficult to use, or not understandable, or the users get lost navigating, then leave the website, and the probabilities that they will use the website again decrease [4]. For this reason, it is important to guarantee a friendly interaction experience and ensure that the design of graphical interfaces is adjusted to the needs of users as well to the context of use, allowing the achievement of their objectives and meeting expectations.

The importance of a software product being usable has led to the development of a set of evaluation methods [5]. These methods allow specialists to determine through an array of well-defined actions if the interfaces are understandable, attractive and if they generate user satisfaction during the interaction with them. According to Fernandez et al. [6], the methods can be classified into (1) testing, (2) inspection, (3) inquiry, (4) analytical modeling, and (5) simulation. Of all the methods that have emerged so far, only a few are the ones that draw the attention of professionals and academics. According to a previous study [7], user tests, heuristic evaluation, and questionnaires are the most used and reported in the literature.

All methods have their advantages and provide relevant results. It is not possible to indicate that one method is better than another. In contrast, the methods complement each other [8]. However, questionnaires are widely recognized and used because they require few resources to be applied. Unlike user tests in which it is required to prepare material, observe the user, analyze their behavior, and process all the collected information, questionnaires become an interesting alternative when time and resources are not enough in a project [9]. In addition to being quick to use, the questionnaires allow specialists to effectively identify users' perceptions concerning certain aspects of the graphical interfaces required for evaluation. Performing a usability assessment with questionnaires only requires that a group of people interact with the software product to be evaluated and afterward request them to answer a set of closed questions regarding their perception of the degree of usability the software product presents. There are several proposals for questionnaires that can be used by specialists and industries to assess usability [10]. However, most of these questionnaires have been designed for end-users and not for specialists in design and Human-Computer Interaction (HCI). The existing approaches establish that the questionnaires must be answered by a large number of participants in a way in which the analysis of the level of usability is possible. However, in a previous research [11], a questionnaire for specialists was elaborated. Unlike common questionnaires where specialists try to collect the perception of users regarding the degree of ease of use, this questionnaire serves as a checklist for those who know about good design principles that graphical interfaces should have.

Electronic government applications are those considered to provide information and services to citizens [12]. Government institutions use these websites as a means to communicate information that is important in the public domain (about government management, data of interest to citizens, news, and events), and likewise to facilitate the population's access to the services provided by the public administration. Given the relevance of these applications, it is important that they are usable and accessible. This research shows the results of carrying out a usability assessment of the main e-government websites in Peru using the new questionnaire proposal for specialists. The objective of this research is to serve as a basis for future usability evaluations, to validate the new questionnaire, and also to demonstrate the level of concern of the Peruvian government to offer its population quality websites. The results of this work can be used to improve the design of electronic government applications and for the development of future proposals.

2 Related Work

Usability evaluation questionnaires are an extremely reliable instrument to determine the perception of the degree of ease of use of a software product quickly and simply [9]. Users are asked to previously interact with the application and subsequently, they can then answer a set of questions about the noticed level of usability. The main purpose of most of the questionnaires that exist registered in the literature is to identify the satisfaction of end-users with respect to the interaction with the software product [10]. However, in a previous study [11], the development of a questionnaire that can be used by specialists was proposed. This new proposal was elaborated on the basis of an evaluation instrument established by Granollers [13]. In this approach, the ten heuristics proposed by Nielsen [14] and the nineteen Tognazzini's principles of interaction design [15] were used. After an exhaustive analysis of both sources of information, it was possible to elaborate a set of 60 specific questions that allow determining if the design fails in certain aspects of usability.

The principles were later examined in writing and wordiness topics and a new version of 60 questions was afterward elaborated [11], oriented to the understanding of HCI specialists. The difference with traditional questionnaire proposals is this instrument is aimed at people with extensive experience in usability evaluations. This new questionnaire represents a checklist that helps testers to quickly perform an inspection considering the most important usability aspects. Unlike the first versions of the questionnaire that involved a YES or NO response, the new version establishes that each question is answered on a scale of 0 to 4 where 0 means the non-consideration of the guideline (strongly disagree) and 4 a total consideration of it in the interface design (strongly agree). Table 1 shows the possible responses along with their associated values. On the other hand, it is important to mention that the questions are grouped into 15 categories [11, 13]: (1) visibility and system state, (2) connection between the system and the real world, metaphor usage, and human objects, (3) user control and freedom, (4) consistency and standards, (5) recognition rather than memory, learning, and anticipation, (6) flexibility and efficiency of use, (7) help users recognize, diagnose and recover from errors, (8) preventing errors, (9), aesthetic and minimalist design, (10) help and documentation, (11) save the state and protect the work, (12) color and readability, (13) autonomy, (14) defaults and (15) latency reduction.

For the total calculation of the percentage of usability of the software product, it is necessary to add all the values obtained according to the answers. This questionnaire allows specialists to indicate if a question does not apply to the software product being evaluated. There are certain aspects of usability that due to the domain and nature of the software cannot be evaluated or inspected or are simply not required to be considered. This must be determined by the specialist who has the option to indicate if the usability aspect that must be analyzed does not apply. The value obtained must be divided by the number of questions that do apply and have been answered with a value from 0 to 4, multiplied by 4. This procedure generates as a result the global percentage of usability of the application and can be averaged with the final values obtained by other specialists who have participated in the evaluation. The equation that allows obtaining the final usability score of a software product is detailed in Fig. 1. Likewise, as an example and extract, Table 2 shows the questions that are part of the *"visibility and system state"* category of the questionnaire.

$$
\frac{\sum_{i=1}^{n} \left(\dfrac{\sum_{j=1}^{m} s_j}{4 * (m - z)} \right)}{n} * 100
$$

where:
- n: is the number of specialists that are participating in the evaluation.
- m: is the total number of usability questions.
- s_j: is the obtained score for question j by the specialist i.
- z: is the number of questions that do not apply for the specialist i.

Fig. 1. The equation used to calculate the final usability value of a software product

Table 1. Likert scale and scores used for the usability questions

Possible response	Value
Strongly disagree	0
Disagree	1
Neither agree nor disagree	2
Agree	3
Strongly agree	4
Does not apply	No value is assigned

The form of usability evaluation proposed in this research is based on the heuristic inspection [5], in which HCI specialists must offer their opinions regarding the compliance of the graphical user interfaces (GUI) with certain design principles. Because of this, the recommended number of specialists who participate in an evaluation with this instrument should be from 3 to 5, since according to some analysis conducted by Nielsen [16], as more specialists are incorporated, the costs increase, and the findings are fewer. Given the expertise of the specialists who participate in an evaluation of this type, it is

Table 2. Usability questions for the category of *"visibility and system state"*

ID	Question
Q01	Does the application provide visible titles that clearly identify the different sections of the system?
Q02	Is it always possible to determine in which section of the system we are?
Q03	Is it possible to determine the actions the system is executing all the time?
Q04	Are the links provided by the system visible, clear, and understandable?
Q05	Is it possible to quickly identify the actions provided by the system?

possible to identify, with a few participants, the most critical aspects of usability that must be corrected in a software product. Those questions whose scores are low must be considered as opportunities for improvement for the inspected application. Likewise, it is possible to analyze the results for each of the categories established in the questionnaire.

3 Settings of the Case Study

This study reports the results of using the questionnaire proposed by Paz and Granollers [11] to assess the usability of the three main electronic government websites in Peru. The importance of this research lies in determining whether the applications offered by the Peruvian government to its citizens are easy to use to the point that they allow to easily identify information of public interest and to appropriately perform public service procedures. According to Siau and Long [17], the development of e-government in a country can be carried out in the following 4 areas:

- **Government-to-citizen (G2C):** whose purpose is to provide services and access to information for citizens. These are initiatives aimed at providing administrative and information services to citizens through Information and Communication Technologies (ICT), that is, from any place that has access and at any time.
- **Government-to-employee (G2E):** that are initiatives to provide services for the professional development of public administration employees.
- **Government-to-business (G2B):** that are initiatives aimed at providing administrative and information services to companies through the Internet.
- **Government-to-government (G2G):** that are initiatives to enhance cooperation and collaboration between governments of different levels and various physical locations.

In this research, the evaluation was focused on G2C-type web applications. Some examples of these government initiatives are those that provide access to information about laws, policies, news, government job offers, web links of interest, and procedures to carry out administrative procedures with government entities. Likewise, these applications are used as means to facilitate transactions between the government and citizens. Some examples involve procedures related to tax payment, fines, public fees, grants, loans, civil registration, social insurance, driver's license among others. The benefits that these initiatives bring to citizens translate into savings in time and money (travel to public offices, waiting at counters) and flexibility, in addition to access to updated information published regularly by the Government.

Considering this aspect as a premise, the following websites were selected:

- **SUNAT** (www.sunat.gob.pe): This is the website of the *National Superintendence of Customs and Tax Administration*. This is the government entity that administers the taxes of the Peruvian national government. In this application, several procedures and services related to taxation can be carried out. In addition, nthe website provides a payment gateway to perform online payments.
- **Migrations** (www.gob.pe/migraciones): This is the website of the *National Super-intendence of Migration*. This is a specialized technical organization attached to the Ministry of the Interior which is responsible for the immigration control of national and foreign citizens, the issuance of travel documents to national and foreign citizens, and the granting of Peruvian nationality. Although this website does not have an embedded payment gateway, it is possible to use www.pagalo.pe to make payments online.
- **SUNARP** (www.gob.pe/sunarp): This is the website of the National Superintendence of Public Registries. This is an organization in charge of registering and publicizing acts, contracts, rights, and entitlements of people in a timely, inclusive, transparent, predictable, and efficient manner. In addition, this website allows making payments online.

These e-government applications were selected based on their importance. These websites incorporate the most frequent procedures carried out by the Peruvian popu-lation. In addition, they are part of the National Plan in which it is established that Electronic Government is promoted through the intensive use of information and com-munication technologies (ICT) facilitating the access of citizens to online public services, organized in a simple, close and consistent way, as well as providing them with access to permanently updated information.

Regarding the procedure that was followed, the specialists were contacted to carry out this inspection remotely. It is possible to mention that all the evaluators who participated in this usability inspection have a similar background since they have carried out and have been involved in multiple inspections both at an academic and industrial level. The number of specialists who participated in this usability evaluation of the main Peruvian electronic government sites was three, given that according to Nielsen studies, it is an appropriate number of professionals to identify the greatest number of usability problems [16]. Table 3 shows the academic degree of each of the evaluators involved in the usability evaluation. Respecting the informed consent protocol, names and identities are kept confidential. For academic and reporting purposes, an identifier has been established for each of the participating specialists.

Table 3. Profile of each of the specialists who participated in the usability inspection

Specialist ID	Last academic degree obtained
S1	Doctor of Engineering Degree - Specialty in Human-Computer Interaction
S2	Master's Degree in Computer Science - Specialty in Software Engineering
S3	Master's Degree in Informatics Engineering

First, the specialists were asked for their consent to be part of this study. All contacted specialists agreed to participate voluntarily and were invited to a virtual meeting. In this meeting, they were asked to interact with one of the selected websites for approximately 20 min. After the specialists became familiar with the website, they were sent a Microsoft Excel file containing all the questions of the usability evaluation questionnaire. They were asked to answer each of the questions on the established Likert scale. Subsequently, the results were collected, and the procedure was repeated for the next website until concluding with the inspection of all the selected applications.

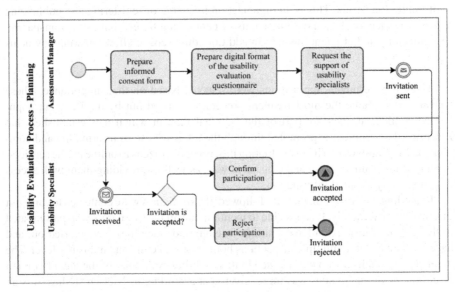

Fig. 2. Usability evaluation planning process

The entire process took about 2 h. Perceptions about the degree of usability of the three selected Peruvian e-government websites were collected. Figures 2 and 3 show in detail the process that was followed to carry out the inspection.

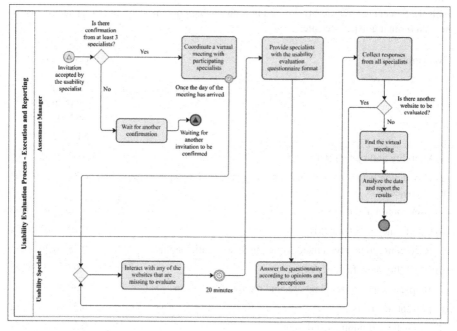

Fig. 3. Usability evaluation process - execution and report phases

4 Analysis and Results

The evaluation was carried out on February 1, 2022. Once the virtual meeting was over in which all the specialists' results were collected, the data was processed, and the information analyzed. The usability results were analyzed for each of the categories established in the evaluation questionnaire [13]. In order to calculate the percentage of usability covered by the application in each evaluation aspect, the formula established in Fig. 1 was used. All the values established by the specialist in each question corresponding to the evaluation criterion were added up and this result was divided by 4 multiplied for the total number of questions of the category minus the number of questions that according to the evaluator did not apply. For example, the first category entitled *"visibility and system state"* has a total of 6 questions. The responses of the first specialist were: strongly agree (4), strongly agree (4), neither agree nor disagree (2), agree (3), and agree (3) for each of the questions in Table 2. In this way, the percentage of usability covered is (4 + 4 + 2 + 3 + 3)/(4 * (5 − 0)) resulting in 0.80.

Table 4. Percentage of usability covered in each evaluation item according to each specialist for the "www.sunat.gob.pe" website

Evaluation item	Percentage of usability covered according to each specialist		
	S1	S2	S3
(1) Visibility and system state	0.90	0.80	0.80
(2) Connection between the system and the real world, metaphor usage, and human objects	0.81	0.75	0.63
(3) User control and freedom	0.75	0.92	1.00
(4) Consistency and standards	0.79	0.67	0.54
(5) Recognition rather than memory, learning, and anticipation	0.75	0.70	0.65
(6) Flexibility and efficiency of use	0.92	1.00	0.75
(7) Help users recognize, diagnose, and recover from errors	0.50	0.67	1.00
(8) Preventing errors	0.58	0.58	0.42
(9) Aesthetic and minimalist design	0.56	0.63	0.31
(10) Help and documentation	0.35	0.40	0.25
(11) Save the state and protect the work	0.50	1.00	1.00
(12) Color and readability	0.63	0.75	0.81
(13) Autonomy	0.58	0.42	0.67
(14) Defaults	1.00	1.00	1.00
(15) Latency reduction	0.75	0.50	0.38
Full degree of usability covered	**0.69**	**0.72**	**0.68**

Likewise, there are some cases where the specialist may contemplate that a question does not apply. This is the case of specialist 1 in the evaluation item of "*user control and freedom*". This category is made up of a total of 3 questions and the answers of this specialist were: strongly agree (4), does not apply (0), and strongly agree (4). In this case, the percentage of usability covered by the application in this category is calculated in this way $(4 + 0 + 4)/(4 * (3 - 1))$ since 1 question did not apply to the evaluator, resulting in 1.00. The results obtained for the "www.sunat.gob.pe" website can be seen in Table 4. Similarly, the results for the "www.gob.pe/migraciones" website are found in Table 5. Finally, the results on the percentage of usability covered by "www.gob.pe/sunarp" are shown in Table 6.

Table 5. Percentage of usability covered in each evaluation item according to each specialist for the "www.gob.pe/migraciones" website

Evaluation item	Percentage of usability covered according to each specialist		
	S1	S2	S3
(1) Visibility and system state	0.75	0.70	0.70
(2) Connection between the system and the real world, metaphor usage, and human objects	0.69	0.88	0.81
(3) User control and freedom	0.25	0.33	0.25
(4) Consistency and standards	0.71	0.75	0.67
(5) Recognition rather than memory, learning, and anticipation	0.55	0.75	0.55
(6) Flexibility and efficiency of use	0.71	0.75	0.63
(7) Help users recognize, diagnose, and recover from errors	0.33	0.58	0.00
(8) Preventing errors	0.50	0.42	0.58
(9) Aesthetic and minimalist design	0.50	0.50	0.56
(10) Help and documentation	0.45	0.35	0.35
(11) Save the state and protect the work	1.00	1.00	0.50
(12) Color and readability	0.81	0.69	0.75
(13) Autonomy	0.50	0.67	0.25
(14) Defaults	1.00	1.00	1.00
(15) Latency reduction	0.75	0.75	0.50
Full degree of usability covered	**0.63**	**0.67**	**0.54**

There are some cases in which none of the questions of a certain evaluation item applied. In these scenarios, since according to the specialists they are aspects that should not be considered in the usability evaluation, the 100% compliance score (1.00) was considered in a way they do not affect the results obtained. Likewise, there have been cases wherein an evaluation item the sum of the scores obtained has been 0. This is because the evaluators have answered with the answer of "strongly disagree" in all the questions that they have considered applicable to the evaluation of the application. In these cases, since it represents a total non-compliance with the evaluation item, a percentage of 0% (0.00) has been assigned. The occurrence of these special scenarios is interesting because they allow to improve the evaluation instrument and determine improvements based on the results.

Table 6. Percentage of usability covered in each evaluation item according to each specialist for the "www.gob.pe/sunarp" website

Evaluation item	Percentage of usability covered according to each specialist		
	S1	S2	S3
(1) Visibility and system state	0.80	0.85	0.75
(2) Connection between the system and the real world, metaphor usage, and human objects	0.81	0.75	0.63
(3) User control and freedom	0.75	0.50	0.58
(4) Consistency and standards	0.75	0.71	0.58
(5) Recognition rather than memory, learning, and anticipation	0.70	0.75	0.65
(6) Flexibility and efficiency of use	0.58	0.63	0.46
(7) Help users recognize, diagnose, and recover from errors	0.25	0.50	0.25
(8) Preventing errors	0.50	0.42	0.33
(9) Aesthetic and minimalist design	0.75	0.50	0.63
(10) Help and documentation	0.45	0.50	0.30
(11) Save the state and protect the work	1.00	1.00	1.00
(12) Color and readability	0.75	0.69	0.50
(13) Autonomy	0.58	0.75	0.50
(14) Defaults	1.00	1.00	1.00
(15) Latency reduction	0.50	0.63	0.38
Full degree of usability covered	**0.68**	**0.68**	**0.57**

The results show that although the level of usability of the websites is acceptable, there are still aspects that can be improved to be considered high-quality web applications. According to the results, the usability level of the website "www.sunat.gob.pe" is 0.70 (70%) considering the values of 0.69, 0.72, and 0.68. The result for the website "www.gob.pe/migraciones" is 0.61 (61%) considering the values of 0.63, 0.67 and 0.54. Finally, for the "www.gob.pe/sunarp" website, the usability level is 0.64 (64%) considering the values of 0.68, 0.68 and 0.57.

Although the final results are between 60% and 70%, it is necessary to consider those aspects where the scores have been rated with low values. It is highly required to improve consistency in the design and use of standards. The analyzed websites usually refer to other platforms and it is important that the subsections maintain the same design style to avoid confusing the end-users. Likewise, it is necessary to improve the error messages and fault tolerance of the systems. In certain sections there is a lot of information that overloads the graphical interface, making it complex. Through an evaluation of the information architecture, it would be possible to restructure the data so that users can quickly identify the information they are looking for as well as the services offered by several government institutions. The evaluation questionnaire has proven to be effective and valid to measure the usability and quantitatively determine the level of ease of use of a set of Peruvian e-government applications.

5 Conclusions and Future Works

Usability is an attribute of software quality that is currently highly relevant in the development of technological products. Designing a graphical interface without considering the context of use and the user's final goals can lead to the failure of the software. In this sense, several methods have emerged that allow specialists to determine if a product is easy to use, understandable in such a way that it leads to the satisfaction and achievement of the objectives of the end-users. One of these methods is the questionnaire that allows quickly and easily to determine the perception of usability of a system. However, most questionnaires are intended to be responded by end-users. In this work, a new proposal for a questionnaire aimed at specialists in Human-Computer Interaction has been tested. For this, the three most representative electronic government websites in Peru were selected. The results showed that although the level of usability of these websites is acceptable, there are many improvement opportunities that government authorities can consider. Based on these results, it is possible to conclude that although some aspects of usability have been considered, there are still efforts that must be made to have applications with a high level of quality in Peru.

The questionnaire has proven to be an effective evaluation instrument to measure the level of usability in quantitative terms. However, it is necessary to take into consideration that the experiment carried out has been conducted in a controlled environment, following a certain procedure. It is still necessary to carry out a greater number of case studies to determine the validity of the evaluation instrument. Likewise, as future work, it is possible to carry out a statistical analysis of reliability in conjunction with the data obtained in the present research. The results can be compared with evaluation scenarios of software products from other domains and other realities. This work has been carried out with the aim of describing a case study that serves as a methodological basis and evidence to achieve a new valid usability evaluation instrument that can be used within the heuristic evaluation process.

Acknowledgments. This research is highly supported by the HCI, Design, User Experience, Accessibility, and Innovation Technology Research Group (HCI-DUXAIT). HCI-DUXAIT is a research group of Pontificia Universidad Católica del Perú (PUCP) – Peru.

References

1. Güncan, D., Onay Durdu, P.: A user-centered behavioral software development model. J. Softw. Evol. Process **33**(2), e2274 (2021). https://doi.org/10.1002/smr.2274
2. Anderson, J., Fleak, F., Garrity, K., Drake, F.: Integrating usability techniques into software development. IEEE Softw. **18**(1), 46–53 (2001). https://doi.org/10.1109/52.903166

3. International Organization for Standardization: ISO/IEC 25010:2011, Systems and software engineering – System and software Quality Requirements and Evaluation (SQuaRE) – System and Software Quality Models. Geneva, Switzerland (2011)

4. Nielsen, J.: Usability 101: Introduction to Usability (2012). https://www.nngroup.com/articles/usability-101-introduction-to-usability/. Accessed 01 Feb 2022

5. Nielsen, J.: Usability inspection methods. In: Proceedings of the SIGCHI Conference on Human Factors in Computing Systems (CHI 1994), pp. 413–414. Association for Computing Machinery (1994).https://doi.org/10.1145/259963.260531

6. Fernandez, A., Insfran, E., Abrahão, S.: Usability evaluation methods for the web: a systematic mapping study. Inf. Softw. Technol. **53**(8), 789–817 (2011). https://doi.org/10.1016/j.infsof.2011.02.007

7. Paz, F., Pow-Sang, J.A.: A systematic mapping review of usability evaluation methods for software development process. Int. J. Softw. Eng. Appl. **10**(1), 165–178 (2016). https://doi.org/10.14257/ijseia.2016.10.1.1

8. Paz, F., Paz, F.A., Villanueva, D., Pow-Sang, J.A.: Heuristic evaluation as a complement to usability testing: a case study in web domain. In: Proceedings of the 12th International Conference on Information Technology - New Generations (ITNG 2015), pp. 546–551. IEEE (2015).https://doi.org/10.1109/ITNG.2015.92

9. Nielsen, J.: Usability Engineering, 1st edn. Morgan Kaufmann, Burlington (1993)

10. Sauro, J., Lewis, J.R.: Quantifying the User Experience: Practical Statistics for User Research, 1st edn. Morgan Kaufmann, Burlington (2012)

11. Paz, F., Granollers, T.: Redesign of a questionnaire to assess the usability of websites. In: Ahram, T., Karwowski, W., Pickl, S., Taiar, R. (eds.) IHSED 2019. AISC, vol. 1026, pp. 423–428. Springer, Cham (2020). https://doi.org/10.1007/978-3-030-27928-8_65

12. Schelin, S.H.: E-government: an overview. In: Garson, G. (eds.) Modern Public Information Technology Systems: Issues and Challenges, pp. 110–126. IGI Global, Hershey (2007). https://doi.org/10.4018/978-1-59904-051-6.ch006

13. Granollers, T.: Usability evaluation with heuristics. new proposal from integrating two trusted sources. In: Marcus, A., Wang, W. (eds.) DUXU 2018. LNCS, vol. 10918, pp. 396–405. Springer, Cham (2018). https://doi.org/10.1007/978-3-319-91797-9_28

14. Nielsen, J.: 10 usability heuristics for user interface design (2020). https://www.nngroup.com/articles/ten-usability-heuristics/. Accessed 10 Feb 2022

15. Tognazzini, B.: First principles of interaction design (revised & expanded) (2014). https://asktog.com/atc/principles-of-interaction-design/. Accessed 10 Feb 2022

16. Nielsen, J.: How to conduct a heuristic evaluation (1994). https://www.nngroup.com/articles/how-to-conduct-a-heuristic-evaluation/. Accessed 10 Feb 2022

17. Siau, K., Long, Y.: Synthesizing e-government stage models - a meta-synthesis based on meta-ethnography approach. Ind. Manag. Data Syst. **105**(4), 443–458 (2005). https://doi.org/10.1108/02635570510592352

Online Virtual Simulation Course Design for VR Glasses Fit Analysis

Meng Qiu, Haining Wang$^{(\boxtimes)}$, Yujia Du, and Yuxin Ju

School of Design, Hunan University, Changsha 410082, China
haining1872@qq.com

Abstract. With the development of the metaverase, virtual reality technology is invading various fields. As a carrier of virtual reality (VR) technology, VR glasses have become a new type of smart wearable devices and are widely used. It's crucial to improve the wearing comfort of VR glasses. Based on the practical requirements for industrial design education, an online course of virtual simulation for students majoring in industrial design was designed and developed. The aim of this course is to test the fit of the VR facial interface to people's face shapes through a virtual simulation experiment, which can be conducted by five 3D Chinese statistical head models generated from 3400 3D Chinese head scans using the principal component analysis (PCA) panel. After the alignment between the facial interface and the headforms, deviation analysis was carried out and the analysis report was generated. The report contains gap analysis texture maps and data including positive max deviation, negative max deviation, positive mean deviation, negative mean deviation, and the standard deviation of the gap distribution. This online course provides a platform for industrial design students to evaluate the fit of a VR facial interface design on Chinese population effectively and can also be used as an accurate reference for the improvement of the wearing comfort for other head worn products such as glasses, headphones and masks.

Keywords: Online virtual simulation course · VR glasses · Facial interface · Fit · Statistical shape models

1 Introduction

Virtual reality technology is making inroads into every sector. Glasses-type wearable computer displays should be designed to improve anthropometric fit for better wearing comfort [1]. Therefore, various industries are working to produce more adaptable VR glasses to make them more appealing to consumers [2]. The core component of VR glasses in contact with the human head and face is the facial interface, which forms a fitting surface around the eyes and face for stable wearing and isolation of external light [3]. When wearing VR glasses, the headband creates upward and backward forces that deform the material of the upholstery for a better fit [4]. Over-compact or over-spaced will result in a poor fit. The facial interface that are not suitable for the user's face shape will cause problems such as local pressure and light leakage, which will affect the

M. M. Soares et al. (Eds.): HCII 2022, LNCS 13321, pp. 473–483, 2022.
https://doi.org/10.1007/978-3-031-05897-4_33

immersive experience of the product [5]. Therefore, wearing comfort can be improved by evaluating the fit of the facial interface.

3D anthropometry is widely used in the industrial design process to address differences between humans with the aim of optimizing product fit, comfort, functionality and safety [6]. Design methods including anthropometric analysis, fit evaluation, and product design need to utilize 3D human scan data in the ergonomic design of wearable products such as helmets and glasses [7]. Accurate 3D body data in digital form is useful for optimizing product comfort and function [8]. Several digital platforms using 3D data-aided design have been established in the past few years. Meunier et al. [9] developed a system to assess helmet wear resistance using a 3D scanner to measure the gap between the helmet and the skull. Ellena et al. [10] proposed a helmet fit assessment system by calculating the gap between the head and helmet using 3D scan data. Luximon et al. [11] designed a software that enables users to design head-related products using head scan data in a CAD environment. Lee et al. [12] produced a dimensional analysis system for head-related product design based on the Civilian American and European Surface Anthropometry Resource (CAESAR) database. Directly assessing the suitability of a digital product model will greatly accelerate the progress of product design [13]. Virtual fit assessment has become a research hotspot from physical media to digital media because it can assess fit and comfort without the need to build physical prototypes [14].

Experimental teaching is an indispensable link to cultivate students' innovative ability and practical ability, which enables students to fully digest and absorb scientific knowledge in observation and experiment [15]. With the rapid development of technology, various online teaching platforms have demonstrated how to use new scientific and technological achievements in experimental teaching to reduce the difficulty of teachers' teaching and improve students' learning efficiency and adaptability. Huang et al. [16] constructed a networked teaching platform for the experimental course of traditional Chinese medicine chemistry. Ma et al. [17] created an electromagnetic network course teaching platform, which provided a wealth of teaching resources for students to learn independently. Compared with traditional teaching methods, this online teaching platform shows great advantages, such as sharing teaching resources, improving students' learning enthusiasm and teaching efficiency.

One of the pedagogical goals of industrial design education is to educate students to use digital design software and to be at the forefront of technological developments in increasingly complex systems [18]. Based on the practical teaching of industrial design education, an online course of virtual simulation for students majoring in industrial design was designed and developed. Since it is important to improve the wearing comfort of VR glasses, the experimental platform took VR glasses as an example to conduct deviation analysis on the adaptability. The purpose of this course is to test the fit of the VR facial interface to people's face shapes by using five 3D Chinese statistical head models generated from the principal component analysis (PCA) panel from Chinese headbase survey, which was developed by Wang et al. [19] and enriched to a sample size of 3400 in 2020. With this training platform, simple and effective simulations can be performed to help design students design VR glasses more efficiently.

2 Running Logic of Online Virtual Simulation Experiment Platform

The virtual fit approach is a suitable method for designing and evaluating ergonomic wearable products in the product development process [20]. In this study, a online virtual simulation experiment platform was built to evaluate the fit of VR glasses, especially for the facial interface. In order to improve the suitability of VR facial interface for Chinese users, and reduce the wearing pressure and light leakage problems, it is necessary to consider the variety of Chinese head shapes. The design is based on a large number of facial measurement from the Chinese headbase database [3]. Three types of information are included in virtual fit analysis of headset shape and size: (1) 3D head scans and facial measurements of Chinese population, (2) correct position of VR glasses on the face, and (3) facial interface, that is, the specific inteface of the VR headset which is in contact with the face. The distance between the facial interface and the 3D head model was analyzed by the platform to guide the ergonomic design of the VR glasses. The virtual fit analysis method and principles used in the experimental platform is presented in the following subsections.

2.1 3D Head Scans and Facial Measurements of Chinese Population

Experiment-related teaching platforms require technical and teaching resources [21]. Multivariate anthropometry captures most of the variation in body shape with limited variables [22]. The PCA method is widely used in the field of anthropometrics, since it is a classic dimensionality reduction method that can simplify and classify complex datasets. The National Institute of Occupational Safety and Health (NIOSH) [23] developed a principal component segmentation method for artificial respirators in the United States. Based on the method, a large number of user groups are classified according to their head shapes. Zhuang et al. [24] used five three-dimensional headforms representing American workers when designing an industrial respirator. Applying PCA panel can classify the measurement data and build the reference headforms for a specific product, which makes it easier to improve the ergonomics design process.

Based on the PCA panel, five 3D Chinese statistical head models, which include long-narrow, large, short-wide, medium and small heads, were generated from 3400 3D Chinese head scans in order to improve the wearing suitability of facial interface and make them more suitable for the Chinese heads and faces.

2.2 Correct Position of VR Glasses on the Face

The VR glasses-wearing position information is important for the analysis of the distance between a specific headset design and different faces. The center of the pupil of the human head is aligned with the center of the lens of the VR glasses, and there is a certain distance between the center of the pupil and the center of the lens (exit pupil distance) when the VR glasses are properly worn. Therefore, in the design of the experimental platform, the user needs to click to select the center point of the lens and the center point of the pupil, which will be assisted by the system to align.

2.3 Facial Interface Selection

The cover, head strap, display and lenses were excluded from the fitting process, as we only aimed to investigate the way that the facial interface fit the participant's face shapes. When performing a fit analysis on the inner surface of the VR glasses, only the portion that is in contact with the face, which is the facial interface, is retained.

2.4 Algorithm Development

The deviation analysis of the facial interface and the human head model in the wearing calibration model group was carried out by calculating the horizontal distance among a number of reference points between the head model and the facial interface, the **gap analysis texture map** and deviation analysis statistics of the face area are obtained.

A new algorithm has been added to the above mentioned measurement software to calculate the distance between the facial interface and the headform. The algorithm can be explained as follows: From the measurement model point to the triangular face of the reference model, the intersection point is formed with the triangular face reference model, and the distance line segment between the measurement model point and the reference model triangular face is the display of spikes. The results are displayed in different colors when the calculated distances are gap and interference respectively. The interference area (blue) in the color map reflects the tight fit area in the real wearing relationship, and the gap area (red) reflects the wearing gap in the real wearing relationship. The green areas are deviation within the threshold value. The detailed algorithm flow is shown in Fig. 1.

3 On-Line Course Design

The aim of this course is to test the fit of the VR facial interface to five 3D Chinese statistical head models through a virtual simulation experiment. The user selects target head model and 3D VR model, and then online deviation analysis was conducted after model processing and facial interface-headform alignment. The report was generated and exported after the analysis was completed.

3.1 Steps for Conducting an Experiment

The main interface of the virtual simulation online course platform is shown in Fig. 2. The user clicks the "Start" button to enter the comfort evaluation simulation experiment.

Step 1: Select the Target Head Mold. Five sizes of reference headforms were adopted in this system, which include: long-narrow, large, short-wide, medium and small heads. The user selects a specific head model to start the VFA (see Fig. 3).

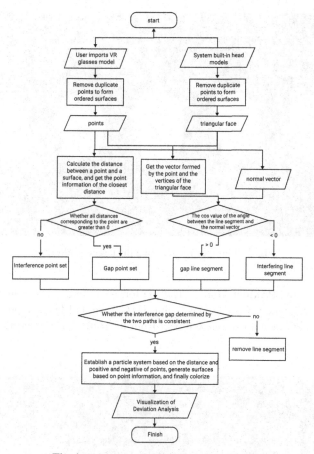

Fig. 1. Algorithm flow of deviation analysis

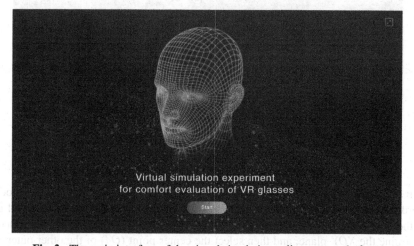

Fig. 2. The main interface of the virtual simulation online course platform

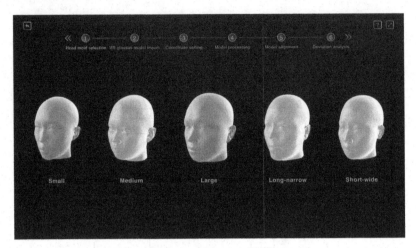

Fig. 3. Interface for selecting the target headform

Step 2: Choose the Product Model. The platform has integrated 3 mainstream VR headset models, namely Google Daydream, HTC Vive and Oculus Quest. Users can choose from them or upload a new model from local files. The interface is shown in Fig. 4.

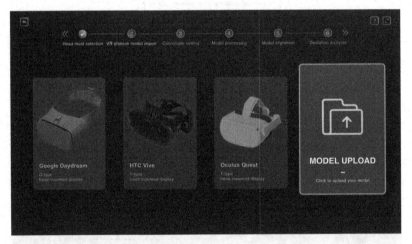

Fig. 4. Interface for importing VR models

Step 3: Rebuild the Product Coordinate System. The steps to rebuild the product coordinate system are as follows: (1) Users first select two lens centers ($O1$ and $O2$) on the inner surface of the product and one lens center ($O3$) on the outer surface to determine the XOY plane, and then select the center point ($O4$) of the other outer surface lens. $O4$ is placed on the XOY plane by default by the system. The midpoint of the $O1$–$O2$ line is calculated as $H1$. The mid-perpendicular line of $O1$–$O2$ on the XOY plane is determined as the x-axis. (2) The user selects the positive direction of the x-axis, and the intersection of the x-axis and $O3$–$O4$ is recorded as $P1$, then the midpoint of $H1$–$P1$ is determined as the origin of coordinates. The parallel line of $O1$–$O2$ through the coordinate origin is taken as the y-axis. (3) The user selects the positive direction of the y-axis. The vertical plane of the XOY plane through the x-axis is determined as the XOZ plane. (4) The user selects the positive direction of the z-axis, and the coordinate system is established (see Fig. 5).

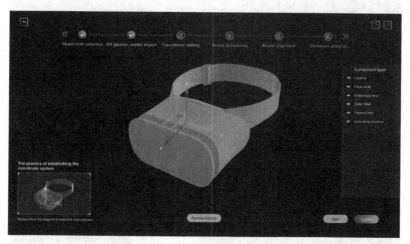

Fig. 5. Rebuild VR glasses coordinate system interface (Color figure online)

Step 4: Select the Inner Surface of the Model as the Measurement Model. When performing a fit analysis on the inner surface of the VR glasses, the facial interface is selected (see Fig. 6).

Step 5: Head Model - VR Glasses Alignment. The users select point 1 "center point of right eye lens of VR helmet" and point 2 "pupil point of right eye of headform". The midpoint of the pupil connection line of the head model with the midpoint of the pupil connection line of the glasses were aligned automatically using the n-points manual registration algorithms (see Error! Reference source not found.). The distance between the center of the lens and the pupil is then automatically adjusted according to the default settings. The exit pupil distance can be adjusted by the user until the interference and gap between the facial interface and the center of the forehead of the headform is close to zero. An interactive UI was designed and developed so that users can adjust the exit pupil distance freely by dragging the slider (see Error! Reference source not found.). The users click the "Confirm" button to start the virtual fit so that the gap between the head and the helmet can be analyzed (Figs. 7 and 8).

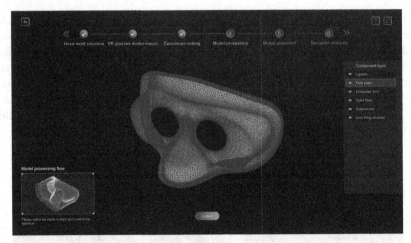

Fig. 6. Interface for selecting VR facial interface

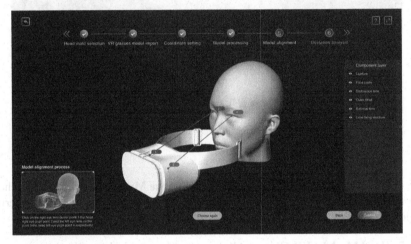

Fig. 7. Head model - VR glasses alignment interface (Color figure online)

Step 6: Deviation Analysis. After model processing and Head model - VR glasses alignment, deviation analysis was conduced and the analysis report was generated. The report contains gap analysis texture maps and data on maximum interference, maximum gap, average interference, average gap, and the standard deviation of the gap distribution. The gap analysis texture map is shown in Error! Reference source not found. The green areas stand for deviation within the threshold value. The deviation analysis results represent the objective spatial relative position of human-machine adaptation. The actual facial interface is deformed when people wear the VR glasses, while the 3D model of facial interface is inserted directly into the 3D headform during virtual fitting (the purple area in Fig. 9). If more detailed subregional analysis is required, users can export the analysis report for viewing.

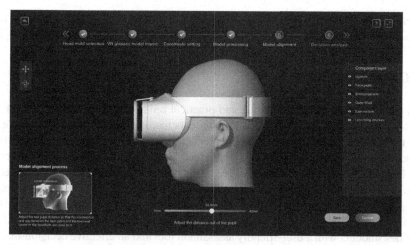

Fig. 8. A slider that controls the exit pupil distance

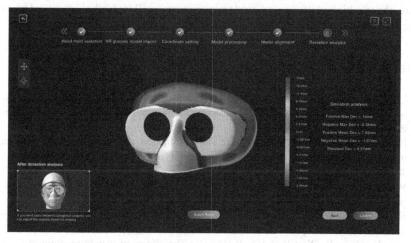

Fig. 9. The interface after the deviation analysis (Color figure online)

3.2 Assessment

The virtual simulation experiment platform is the first online platform in the world that can conduct product fit analysis based on Chinese reference headforms. Five 3D head-forms were provided, enabling design optimization based on quantitative measurements such as the horizontal distance between the VR facial interface and the face surface. Compared with the traditional adaptive design evaluation method for wearable products, the virtual simulation experiment platform established in this study has lighter weight and lower cost. The proposed virtual fitting analysis method effectively reduces the time and cost of prototyping and usability evaluation during VR headset design processes. While virtual fit analysis methods can help designers find ergonomic face patch shapes for a variety of faces, this study did not consider contact pressure and soft tissue deformation when wearing glasses. The validity and applicability of the virtual fitting method need to be further explored.

4   Conclusion

This paper proposes a cost-effective and practical online experiment platform for VR glasses fit, which enables undergraduate students majored in industrial design to evaluate the comfort of VR glasses conveniently. The virtual fitting experimental platform proposed in this study can be applied to product design and evaluation before prototyping. The objective spatial relative position of the human-machine adaptation is reflected through deviation analysis to provide an objective reference for the wearing comfort of VR glasses. The design method developed in this study can be applied to other head worn products. Through the platform's interactive interface, the online teaching platform provides students with a user-friendly assessment tool and an effective decision-making tool for improving the adaptability of VR glasses. It makes the teaching of industrial design more modern, and further improves the quality of education and teaching. In the future, the teaching platform and academic programs will be further improved based on student feedback.

References

1. Chang, J., Moon, S.K., Jung, K., Kim, W., Parkinson, M., Freivalds, A., et al.: Glasses-type wearable computer displays: usability considerations examined with a 3D glasses case study. Ergonomics **61**(5), 1–12 (2018)
2. Farah, M.F., Ramadan, Z.B., Harb, D.H.: The examination of virtual reality at the intersection of consumer experience, shopping journey and physical retailing. J. Retail. Consum. Serv. **48**, 136–143 (2019)
3. Wang, H., Chi, Z., He, R.: Fit improvement of facial interface for VR headset based on principal component analysis panel. J. Mach. Des. **37**(5), 117–124 (2020)
4. Jin, W., He, R.: An exploratory study of fit assessment of the virtual reality glasses. J. Ambient. Intell. Humaniz. Comput. **201**, 1–10 (2021). https://doi.org/10.1007/s12652-021-03335-1
5. Yan, Y., Chen, K., Xie, Y., Song, Y., Liu, Y.: The effects of weight on comfort of virtual reality devices. In: Rebelo, F., Soares, M.M. (eds.) AHFE 2018. AISC, vol. 777, pp. 239–248. Springer, Cham (2019). https://doi.org/10.1007/978-3-319-94706-8_27
6. Pheasant, S., Haslegrave, C.M.: Bodyspace: Anthropometry, Ergonomics and the Design of Work. CRC Press, Boca Raton (2016)
7. Lee, W., Jung, D., Park, S., Kim, H., You, H.: Development of a virtual fit analysis method for an ergonomic design of pilot oxygen mask. Appl. Sci. **11**(12), 5332 (2021)
8. Verwulgen, S., et al.: A new data structure and workflow for using 3D anthropometry in the design of wearable products. Int. J. Ind. Ergon. **64**, 108–117 (2018)
9. Meunier, P., Tack, D., Ricci, A., Bossi, L., Angel, H.: Helmet accommodation analysis using 3D laser scanning. Appl. Ergon. **31**(4), 361–369 (2000)
10. Ellena, T., Subic, A., Mustafa, H., Pang, T.Y.: The helmet fit index–an intelligent tool for fit assessment and design customisation. Appl. Ergon. **55**, 194–207 (2016)
11. Luximon, Y., Ball, R.M., Chow, E.H.: A design and evaluation tool using 3D head templates. Comput. Aided Des. Appl. **13**(2), 153–161 (2016)

12. Lee, W., et al.: A 3D anthropometric sizing analysis system based on North American CAE-SAR 3D scan data for design of head wearable products. Comput. Ind. Eng. **117**, 121–130 (2018)
13. Hwang, H.J., Lee, S.J., Park, E.J., Yoon, H.I.: Assessment of the trueness and tissue surface adaptation of CAD-CAM maxillary denture bases manufactured using digital light processing. J. Prosthet. Dent. **121**(1), 110–117 (2019)
14. Rudolf, A., et al.: New technologies in the development of ergonomic garments for wheelchair users in a virtual environment. Industria Textila **68**(2), 83–94 (2017)
15. Cui, Z., Wang, J.E.: Research of an intelligent experimental teaching platform based on Internet. Procedia Comput. Sci. **107**, 75–79 (2017)
16. Huang, Y., Niu, Q., Yuan, J.: Design of network teaching platform for Chinese medicine chemistry experiment course. Asia Pac. Tradit. Med. **17**, 18–28 (2017)
17. Ma, Q., Jia, G., Li, Z.: Construction and practice of electromagnetic network teaching platform. Educ. Teach. Forum **10**, 1–10 (2018)
18. Aldoy, N., Evans, M.: A review of digital industrial and product design methods in UK higher education. Des. J. **14**(3), 343–368 (2011)
19. Wang, H., Yang, W., Yu, Y., Chen, W., Ball, R.: 3D digital anthropometric study on Chinese head and face. In: Proceedings of 3DBODY, TECH 2018–9th International Conference and Exhibition on 3D Body Scanning and Processing Technologies, pp. 287–295 (2018)
20. Lee, W., Kim, H., Jung, D., Park, S., You, H.: Ergonomic design and evaluation of a pilot oxygen mask. In: Proceedings of the Human Factors and Ergonomics Society Annual Meeting, vol. 57, pp. 1673–1677. SAGE Publications, Los Angeles (2013)
21. Shen, Y., Yu, H.: Multimedia network teaching platform and its application in mechanical design. Int. J. Electr. Eng. Educ. (2021)
22. Jellema, A., Galloin, E., Massé, B., Ruiter, I., Molenbroek, J., Huysmans, T.: 3D anthropometry in ergonomic product design education. In: DS 95: Proceedings of the 21st International Conference on Engineering and Product Design Education (E&PDE 2019). University of Strathclyde, Glasgow (2019)
23. Zhuang, Z., Bradtmiller, B., Shaffer, R.E.: New respirator fit test panels representing the current US civilian work force. J. Occup. Environ. Hyg. **4**(9), 647–659 (2007)
24. Zhuang, Z., Benson, S., Viscusi, D.: Digital 3-D headforms with facial features representative of the current US workforce. Ergonomics **53**(5), 661–671 (2010)

A Systematic Review About Quantitative Metrics for the Usability Evaluation of Retail E-commerce Web Sites Based on Open Source Platforms

Maria Quispe[✉]

Pontificia Universidad Católica del Perú, San Miguel, Lima 32, Peru
maria.quispeq@pucp.edu.pe

Abstract. The fast-growing e-commerce has created a new way to do transactions globally, as a result, more business has to provide online stores to maintain themselves in this new competitive environment. Given that context, it is understandable how much acceptance open-source platforms had received for new businesses, with their lower costs and open community support. Facing this growth in the e-commerce domain, the relevance of usability is even more significant. For this reason, metrics that can be used to determine whether a software product meets the appropriate level of usability are needed. However, the traditional metrics fail to cover all aspects that these open-source platforms. Because of that, this article presents a systematic review to identify metrics that can measure the degree of usability. It also shows the most reported aspects that are needed to measure in e-commerce websites based on open-source platforms.

Keywords: Systematic review · Usability evaluation · Software metrics · E-commerce · Open-source websites · HCI · And Usability metrics

1 Introduction

Nowadays, consumers expect to be able to browse and make purchases online. Because of this, many businesses are jumping online and creating storefronts to compete for sales. In today's world, an online presence is essential for staying competitive especially in the retail domain [14]. However, to launch online successfully needs a strategy encompassing many business aspects. In particular, you can partner up with an e-commerce management services provider who will drive the development of your e-commerce solution and choose the right platform that will meet your business needs [14].

Open source is one of the most popular options. Making use of an open-source platform that can be modified and adapted according to the needs of each company, free of charge with the possibility of having access to a community that is dedicated to contributing to the growth and improvement of the page, has made the quality of open-source increased and above all, it has become one of the most attractive tools on the market [14].

© The Author(s), under exclusive license to Springer Nature Switzerland AG 2022
M. M. Soares et al. (Eds.): HCII 2022, LNCS 13321, pp. 484–503, 2022.
https://doi.org/10.1007/978-3-031-05897-4_34

The current context forces software development teams to consider usability as a significant advantage in a market that is highly competitive such as e-commerce [3]. These usability evaluation techniques can be classified into qualitative or quantitative methods [5]. In this scenario, quantifying the usability can be more advantageous because allow consultants to perform benchmarking [3]. By establishing the usability degree in numerical values companies can determine how far they are from their competitors or notice to which extent they exceed their main referents online [3].

Since open-source e-commerce platforms at present are embedded with new features every day to satisfy user needs, such as real-time processing, sophisticated designs, complex components, and excessive functionality [3], that affect the usability degree of the web applications directly, it becomes important to determine the metrics that are being used and the aspects that have been measured to solve the gap in research.

In this study, the authors present a systematic review to identify the quantitative metrics and measured aspects that are reported in the literature to evaluate the usability of e-commerce websites based on open-source platforms. This article is structured in four parts: Background of the terms used in this paper, the detailed process of the Systematic Literature Review, Report of results obtained, and Conclusions. The review covers a spectrum of five years (from 2017 to 2021), and it is intended for developers, researchers, and designers to be used and serve as a tool to evaluate usability degree in these specific e-commerce websites based on open-source platforms.

2 Background

This section describes the different concepts and definitions that are related to the topic in order to help the reader to better understand the context.

2.1 Usability

According to Jakob Nielsen, it is a quality attribute that assesses how user-friendly user interfaces are [8]. Also, this author defined usability by 5 quality components:

- **Learnability**: How easy it is for users to accomplish basic tasks the first time they encounter the design.
- **Efficiency**: Once users have learned the design, how quickly they can perform tasks.
- **Memorability**: When users return to the design after a period of not using it, how easily they can reestablish proficiency.
- **Errors**: Number of errors made by users, the severity of these errors, and how easily users can recover from the errors.
- **Satisfaction**: How pleasant it is to use the design.

2.2 E-commerce

E-commerce or electronic commerce refers to all online activity that involves distribution, purchase, sale, marketing, and supply of goods, products, or services using the internet as a medium [11]. This form of commerce has become very popular with the rise of the Internet, as well as the growing interest of users to buy online [11].

2.3 Metric

It is a numerical or nominal value assigned to characteristics or attributes of an entity and is calculated from a set of observable data consistent with intuition [12].

2.4 Systematic Literature Review (SLR)

It's a methodological process that allows identifying the latest studies that have been carried out in a scientific area concerning a certain research topic [14].

2.5 Open-Source e-commerce Platforms

An open-source e-commerce platform is a "software application which allows online businesses managing their website, marketing, sales and operations" [14]. Also, all of them provide free access to their project code. Their main benefits are [14]:

- Most of them are free.
- Platforms give the business a customizability opportunity.
- You can scale your online shop anytime.
- Most platforms with open source have developed community support.

3 Conducting the Systematic Literature Review

A systematic literature review (SLR) is a methodological process that allows identifying the latest studies that have been carried out in a scientific area concerning a certain research topic and are published in the literature [7].

The present work was performed following the methodology defined by Kitchenham [7] to carry out an objective search. Two research questions were formulated to guide this SLR and a search string based on the PICOC method (Population, Intervention, Comparison, Output, Context) was developed [7]. The databases used for the primary search were Scopus, IEEE Xplore, and ACM Digital Library.

3.1 Research Questions

The systematic review was conducted with basis on the following research question:

RQ1: What metrics have been reported in the literature during the last five years for the usability evaluation of E-Commerce websites?

RQ2: What aspects are measured in the usability evaluation of e-commerce websites?

In order to structure the research questions and the information search to perform this systematic review, the general concepts based on PICOC were defined. These concepts are Population, Intervention, Comparison, Output, and Context. Given that the purpose of this review was not focused on comparing metrics that are employed for the usability evaluation of software products, the comparison criterion was not considered for the definition of PICOC (Table 1).

Table 1. PICOC criteria defined for systematic review

Criterion	Description
Population	Retail e-commerce websites based on open-source platforms
Intervention	Quantitative metrics to evaluate the usability
Comparison	It does not apply
Output	Case studies where a set of quantitative metrics have been applied for the evaluation of usability degree in retail e-commerce websites based on open-source platforms
Context	Academic context, software industry, and all kinds of empirical studies

3.2 Source Selection

Three recognized databases were selected to perform the search process because they are the most relevant in the area of computer engineering. The selected databases were the following:

- Scopus
- IEEE Xplore
- ACM Digital Library

3.3 Search String

For the elaboration of the search string, five general concepts were proposed taking into consideration the Population and Intervention criteria previously defined. Different terms were established for each general concept (Table 2).

Table 2. Defined terms for the search string

General concepts	Terms
GC1 - usability	Usable
GC2 - quantitative metric	Metric*, measurement
GC3 - evaluation	Quantitative evaluation
GC4 - E-Commerce	e-commerce website, commercial website, web application, transactional website, shopping online, retail, open source platforms, open source*
GC5 - web site	web site*, web

After establishing the search terms, the following basic search strings were defined:
C1: "usability" OR "usable".
C2: "quantitative metric" OR "metric*" OR "measurement".

C3: "evaluation" OR "quantitative evaluation".

C4: "E-Commerce" OR "e-commerce website" OR "commercial website" OR "web application" OR "transactional website" OR "shopping online" OR "retail" OR "open source platforms" OR "open source*".

C5: "web site*" OR "web".

Then, the final search string was the following:

C1 AND C2 AND C3 AND C4 AND C5.

("usability" OR "usable") AND ("quantitative metric" OR "metric*" OR "measurement") AND ("evaluation" OR "quantitative evaluation") AND ("e-commerce" OR "ecommerce" OR "e-commerce website" OR "commercial website" OR "web application" OR "transactional website" OR "shopping online" OR "open source platforms" OR "open source*") AND ("web site*" OR "web").

Finally, the search strings adapted to the syntax used by the search engine of each database were established:

SCOPUS: TITLE-ABS-KEY (("usability" OR "usable") AND ("quantitative metric" OR "metric*" OR "measurement") AND ("evaluation" OR "quantitative evaluation") AND ("e-commerce" OR "e commerce" OR "e-commerce website" OR "commercial website" OR "web application" OR "transactional website" OR "shopping online" OR "open source platforms" OR "open source*" OR "retail") AND ("web site*" OR "web*")).

IEEE Xplore: (("usability" OR "usable") AND ("quantitative metric" OR "metric*" OR "measurement") AND ("evaluation" OR "quantitative evaluation") AND ("e-commerce" OR "ecommerce" OR "e-commerce website" OR "commercial website" OR "web application" OR "transactional website" OR "shopping online" OR "open source platforms" OR "open source*" OR "retail") AND ("web site*" OR "web*")).

ACM Digital Library: ("usability" OR "usable") AND ("quantitative metric" OR "metric*" OR "measurement") AND ("evaluation" OR "quantitative evaluation") AND ("e-commerce" OR "ecommerce" OR "e-commerce website" OR "commercial website" OR "web application" OR "transactional website" OR "shopping online" OR "open source platforms" OR "open source*") AND ("web site*" OR "web").

Only relevant studies whose publication date was since 2017 were considered for this review.

3.4 Inclusion and Exclusion Criteria

The inclusion criteria were the following:

1. The article is written in English.
2. The article presents a case study in which one or some quantitative metrics have been applied for the evaluation of usability degree in retail e-commerce websites.

On the other hand, to determinate which studies will not be considered, the following exclusion criteria were established:

1. Articles not related to evaluating quantitatively the usability of e-commerce websites
2. Studies about usability evaluation of websites for people with disabilities
3. Studies related to the usability evaluation of physical devices
4. The article's publication date wasn't 2017 or later.

3.5 Data Collection

The automated search for this systematic literature review was performed on October 8th, 2021 in the Scopus database and on November 23th, 2021 in the IEE Xplore and ACM Digital Library database.

A total of 192 results were obtained from the three consulted databases. After the inclusion and exclusion criteria were applied, 6 articles were selected as relevant for this review process.

Table 3 shows the number of articles that were found during the search process and Table 4 shows the list of articles selected. This list included one article which year isn't included in the range established previously because this article is mentioned in one of the previews articles mentioned and the information provided is useful for the research.

Table 3. Summary of search results

Database name	Search result	Duplicated papers	Relevant papers
Scopus	92	0	4
IEE Xplore	27	5	3
ACM digital library	404	20	2

Table 4. Details of selected articles

Year	Author(s)	Paper title
2020	Vasconcelos, L. G., Baldochi, L. A., & Santos, R. D. C	An approach to support the construction of adaptive Web applications
2020	Wahyuningrum, T., Kartiko, C., & Wardhana, A. C	Exploring E-Commerce Usability by Heuristic Evaluation as a Complement of System Usability Scale
2019	Diaz, E., Arenas, J. J., Moquillaza, A., & Paz, F	A systematic literature review about quantitative metrics to evaluate the usability of E-commerce web sites

(*continued*)

Table 4. (*continued*)

Year	Author(s)	Paper title
2019	Diaz, E., Flores, S., & Paz, F	Proposal of Usability Metrics to Evaluate E-commerce Websites
2018	Puteri, R. N., & Widyanti, A	E-commerce of Islamic fashion product: usability and user acceptance
2017	Ahmad et al	Utilizing WAMMI Components to Evaluate the Usability of E-commerce Website
2017	Anjos & Gontijo	Usability Tool to Support the Development Process of E- commerce Website
2017	R. Kumar and N. Hasteer	Evaluating usability of a web application: A comparative analysis of open-source tools
2016	Santos et al	Metrics focused on usability ISO 9126 based

4 Report and Analysis of Results

The articles obtained from the systematic literature review help to answer the two research questions defined previously.

4.1 Metrics Used for the Usability Evaluation of E-Commerce Websites

According to the results obtained from the systematic review, a large number of metrics used to evaluate e-commerce websites were identified. However, no study was found in the literature that shows the existence of usability evaluation metrics focused on open-source e-commerce platforms, therefore, answering the question posed, it was shown that currently there is no previous study in this regard. Despite this, the importance of the content of each of the articles obtained by the systematic search should be highlighted since, although they are not focused on open-source e-commerce platforms, the existence of evaluation metrics can be visualized of usability in e-commerce web platforms.

After an analysis of the relevant papers, we were able to determine seventy-nine metrics that are currently reported in the literature during the period 2017–2021 to assess the usability of e-commerce websites. The results are presented in Table 5.

Table 5. List of quantitative metrics reported in the systematic review

ID	Metric	Formula	Aspect
M1	SUS	Sum of all score contributions for the ten items multiplied by 2.5	Satisfaction
M2	Usability index	$(\sum sim(Si, Sj))/QI$ Si represents the sequence of events resulting from the end-user interactions. Sj is the sequence of events of the optimal path. QI is the number of times task and I was performed by end-users	Effectiveness, Efficiency
M3	Loading time	T = Ti where Ti is the loading time of the home page	Accessibility
M4	Help accessibility	X = A/B where A is the number of correct tasks online found and B the total of tasks evaluated	Accessibility
M5	Easy to learn how to perform a task	T = Tf where Tf is the amount of time a user takes until they achieved the desired result in the task performed	Learning
M6	Average time of component use	T = Hu – Hi where Hu is the final time after the component is used and Hi is the initial time of component use	Learning
M7	Average time to master the component	T = Hd – Hi where Hd is the end time after mastering the component, and Hi is the initial time of the test	Learning
M8	Proportion of elements that get the customer's attention (banners, animation, etc.)	X = A/B where A is the number of elements identified by the user and B is the total of elements in the website	Attractive
M9	Operation interface density	X = A where A is the number of functions found in a GUI	Attractive

(continued)

Table 5. (*continued*)

ID	Metric	Formula	Aspect
M10	Attractive interaction	Questionnaire to evaluate the attractiveness of the interface for users after the interaction	Attractive
M11	Appearance and aesthetics of user interfaces	$X = A/B$ is the number of aesthetically pleasing screens for the user and B is the number of screens displayed	Attractive
M12	Categories in help section	$X = A/B$ where A is the number of categories found by the user and B is the total of help categories	Help and documents
M13	Help messages understood	$X = A/B$ where A is the number of messages understood by the customer (successfully proved) and B is the total of help messages consulted	Help and documents
M14	Customer support	$X = N$ where N is equal to 0, if a virtual assistance chat does not exist and equal to 1, if a virtual assistance chat exists	Help and documents
M15	Proportion of filters by category	$X = 1 - A/B$ where A is the number of filters selected by the user and B is the total of filters in the search section	Information search
M16	Proportion of search boxes	$X = A/B$ where A is the number of search boxes showed and B is the number of sections visited	Information search
M17	Proportion of filters to advanced search	$X = A/B$ where A is the number of filters found and B is the total of search filters	Information search
M18	Products related to the search	$X = C$ where C is the number of products related to the search	Information search

(*continued*)

Table 5. (*continued*)

ID	Metric	Formula	Aspect
M19	Help with errors	X = N where N is equal to 0, if the website does not help the user with their errors, and equal to 1 if the website offers help with errors	Quality of error
M20	Error messages by the density of functional elements	X = C where C is the total number of errors that show up due to overload	Quality of error
M21	Proportion of error messages that are correctly understood	X = A/B where A is the number of errors that are understood by users and B is the total number of errors	Quality of error
M22	Correction of the user's entry errors	X = A/B where A is the number of entry errors for which the system provides a suggested correct value and B is the number of entry errors detected	Quality of error
M23	Payment methods	X = A/B where A is the number of payment methods that the user found useless and B is the number of payment methods provided by the website	User's cultural background
M24	Affiliates registration	X = N where N is equal to 0, if the website does not offer to affiliate with Facebook, Gmail or others and equal to 1, if the website offers to affiliate with Facebook, Gmail or others	User's cultural background
M25	Contact information	X = C where C is the number of means to contact with the customer service	Behavior of the after-sale service
M26	Purchase confirmation message	X = N where N is equal to 0, if an email confirmation does not exist and equal to 1, if an email confirmation exists	Behavior of the after-sale service

(*continued*)

Table 5. (*continued*)

ID	Metric	Formula	Aspect
M27	Tracking order	X = N where N is equal to 0, if the user cannot track its order and equal to 1, if the user can track their order	Behavior of the after-sale service
M28	Order options (returns, changes, cancellations)	X = A/B where A is the number of order options that the user found useless and B is the number of order options that the website provides	Behavior of the after-sale service
M29	Design style	X = A/B where A is the number of sections with the same style of design and B is the number of sections navigated by the user	Web design consistency
M30	Simplified product information	If, A < B then X = A/B If, B < A then X = B/A Where A is the number of elements of information by product the user needs and B is the total number of elements of information of a product	Density of the information
M31	Relevant product information	X = A/B where A is the total of aspects that the user wants to know about the product and B is the total of aspects that provides the system about the product	Density of the information
M32	Metaphors understood	X = A/B where A is the number of metaphors understood by the user and B is the number of metaphors consulted to the user	Understanding
M33	Complete description	X = A/B where A is the number of functions that are understood by the user and B is the total of functions	Understanding

(*continued*)

Table 5. (*continued*)

ID	Metric	Formula	Aspect
M34	Demonstration of accessibility	X = A/B where A is the number of satisfactory cases in which the user achieves to watch the demonstration and B is the number of cases in which the user is requested to watch the demonstration	Understanding
M35	Demonstration effectiveness	X = A/B where A is the number of functions correctly performed after the tutorial and B is the total number of demonstration or tutorials reviewed by the user	Understanding
M36	Understandable functions	X = A/B where A is the number of interface functions correctly described by the user and B is the number of functions available in the interface	Understanding
M37	Understandable inputs and outputs	X = A/B where A is the number of input and output data elements that the user understands successfully and B is the number of input and output data elements available from the interface	Understanding
M38	Proportion of exceptions that are correctly understood	X = A/B where A is the number of exceptions that were used correctly and B is the total number of exceptions	Understanding
M39	Proportion of returned values that are correctly understood	X = A/B where A is the number of returned values that are understood by the user and B is the total number of returned values	Understanding
M40	Hover time	X = T where T is the total time of suspension of a component	Understanding

(*continued*)

Table 5. (*continued*)

ID	Metric	Formula	Aspect
M41	Standard iconography	X = C where C is the number of icons identified by the user who do not know their usefulness	Web design standards
M42	Recommended products	X = A/B where A is the number of recommended products satisfactory to the user and B is the number of products that recommend the website	Flexibility and effectiveness
M43	Selected products	X = A/B where A is the number of sections from where is possible to access to the shopping cart and wish list and B is the number of sections visited by the user	Flexibility and effectiveness
M44	Response time	T = Tr where Tr is the response time of the website	Functionality
M45	Proportion of functional elements with the appropriate name	X = A/B where A is the number of functions with a correct name and B is the total number of functions	Functionality
M46	Proportion of functional elements used without errors	X = A/B where A is the number of functions that were used correctly and B is the total number of functions	Functionality
M47	Product information	X = A/B where A is the number of information labels per product that the user finds and B is the total of information labels of a product that the user is looking for	Information
M48	Product quality	X = A/B where A is the number of types of qualification found by the user and B is the total rating types on the website for the product	Information

(*continued*)

Table 5. (*continued*)

ID	Metric	Formula	Aspect
M49	Information about the delivery of the product	X = A/B where A is the amount of the information the user needs and B is the amount of information about the delivery of the product	Information
M50	Product availability	X = N where N is equal to 0, if there is no visibility of the information and equal to 1, if there is a visibility of the information	Information
M51	Hovers	X = A where A is the number of suspensions of a component	Information
M52	Understandable information	X = A/B where A is the number of information labels understood by the user (description, specifications) and B is the number of information labels read by the user	Legibility
M53	Understandable labels	X = A/B where A is the number of information labels understood by the user in all their queries (categories, sections, etc.) and B is the number of information labels read by the user	Legibility
M54	Appearance of wish list	X = A/B where A is the number of times the desired list icon is found in the sections visited and B is the number of sections visited	Minimize memory load
M55	Desired products	X = N where N is equalto0, if there is no list of desired products and equal to 1, if there is a list of desired products	Minimize memory load

(*continued*)

Table 5. (*continued*)

ID	Metric	Formula	Aspect
M56	Recent search	X = A/B where A is the number of recent searches displayed by the website and B is the total of searches made by the user	Minimize memory load
M57	Loading time between the different sections	$T = \Sigma (T_i)$ where T_i is the loading time in each section	Navigability
M58	Proportion of identified product categories	X = A/B where A is the number of categories found by the user and B is the total of categories of the website	Navigability
M59	Operational consistency	(a)X = 1–A/B where A is the number of messages or functions that the user has found inconsistent with what he expected and B is the number of messages or functions (b) Y = N/UOT where N is the number of operations that the user found inconsistent with what was expected and UOT is the user's operating time (during the observation period)	Operability
M60	Correction of error	T = Tc – Ts where Tc is the time to complete the correction of a specified type of errors of the performed task and Ts is the start time of the correction of the errors of the performed task	Operability
M61	Appearance consistency	X = 1 – A/B where A is the number of user interfaces with similar elements but with different appearance and B is the number of user interfaces with similar elements	Operability

(*continued*)

Table 5. (*continued*)

ID	Metric	Formula	Aspect
M62	Number of steps for the purchase process	$X = C$ where C is the number of steps made by customers to make a purchase	Transaction status feedback
M63	Standardized symbology	$X = A/B$ where A is the number of icons consulted by the user in all the sections that fulfill the same functionality and B is the number of icons consulted by the user	Standard symbology
M64	Relative task efficiency	$X = \Sigma(Ti*Ni)/\Sigma(Ti)$ where Ti is the time it takes for the client "i" to complete the task and Ni is equal to 0, if the task is not completed and equal to 1, if the task is completed	Simplicity
M65	Register	$X = A/B$ where A is the amount of information that the user considers necessary and B is the amount of information requested by the website	Simplicity
M66	Proportion of visible offers	$X = A/B$ where A is the number of visible offers and B is the total of offers on the website	Purchase decision
M67	Existing questions	$X = A/B$ where A is the number of questions found by the user and B is the number of questions sought by the user	Purchase decision
M68	Comments	$X = N$ where N is equal to 0, if you are not allowed to comment and equal to 1, if you are allowed to comment	Purchase decision

(*continued*)

Table 5. (*continued*)

ID	Metric	Formula	Aspect
M69	Payments	X = A/B where A is the amount of information regarding the payment found by the user and B is the amount of information regarding the payment necessary for the user	Purchase decision
M70	Purchase time	T = Tc where Tc is the time it takes to complete a transaction	Transaction
M71	Help in the purchase	X = N where N is equal to 0, if there is no guide or purchase tutorial for users and equal to 1, if there is a shopping guide or tutorial	Transaction
M72	Purchase summary	X = N where N is equal to 0, if there is no purchase summary for users and equal to 1, if there is a purchase summary	Transaction
M73	Visibility of the number of customers	X = N where N is equal to 0, if there is no visibility of the information and equal to 1, if there is a visibility of the information	Visibility and clarity of elements and status of the system
M74	Visibility of the system state	X = N where N is equal to 0, if there is no visibility of the information and equal to 1, if there is a visibility of the information	Visibility and clarity of elements and status of the system
M75	Visibility on the status of the purchase in all sections of the purchase process	X = N where N is equal to 0, if there is no visibility of the information and equal to 1, if there is a visibility of the information	Visibility and clarity of elements and status of the system
M76	Binary system	Percentage of the success of the user in completing the task of using the product	Effectiveness
M77	Time of task completion	The task completion time	Efficiency
M78	Frequency of error	The mistakes made by users while using website	Efficiency

(*continued*)

Table 5. (*continued*)

ID	Metric	Formula	Aspect
M79	Questionnaire for User Interaction Satisfaction		User Satisfaction

4.2 Aspects Measured in the Usability Evaluation of E-Commerce Websites

According to the articles resulting from the systematic review, different aspects are measured in the usability evaluation of e-commerce websites. In Table 6, we show new aspects that don't form part of the ISO/IEC 25022:2016 standard.

Table 6. Aspects

ISO/IEC 25022:2016	SLR
Effectiveness	Learning
Efficiency	Attractive
Satisfaction	Information search
Flexibility	Quality of error
	User's cultural background
	Behavior of the after-sale service
	Web design consistency
	Density of the information
	Understanding
	Web design standards
	Functionality
	Information
	Legibility
	Minimize memory load
	Navigability
	Operability
	Transaction status feedback
	Standard symbology
	Simplicity
	Purchase decision
	Transaction
	Visibility and clarity of elements and status of the system

In addition, the literature review allows determining the five most reported aspects to measure in usability evaluation, which are: (1) effectiveness, (2) efficiency, (3) satisfaction, (4) learning, and (5) attractiveness.

5   Conclusions and Future Work

From the systematic review of the literature, we can conclude that there are studies in which several usability evaluation metrics have not only been proposed but also validated in e-commerce web pages.

Following a predefined protocol, 79 quantitative metrics and 27 usability aspects were identified. This work allowed us to determine that: (1) effectiveness, (2) efficiency, (3) satisfaction, (4) learning, and (5) attractiveness are the most reported aspects to measure in usability evaluation according to the literature. Moreover, in this study, we have identified that one of the most used usability evaluation metrics is the metric number 76 (M76), which indicates the percentage of the success of the user in completing the task of using the product. This metric was recalled in most of the articles since it provides very useful information to detect the problems that users have with the GUI of a system and reflect easily the effectiveness of the website.

Even though there weren't any articles or studies found in the literature that propose or evaluate these metrics in retail domain e-commerce websites based on open-source platforms, the list of metrics and aspects that had been identified based on the review can be used as a preliminary approach for the future elaboration of a new set of usability evaluation metrics for e-commerce websites based on open-source platforms.

References

1. Ahmad, A., Hussain, A., Hamid, O., Abdulwahab, W., Sabri, M.: Utilizing WAMMI Components to Evaluate the Usability of E-commerce Website (2020)
2. Anjos, T., Gontijo, L.: Usability Tool to Support the Development Process of e-Commerce Website (2017). https://doi.org/10.1007/978-3-319-58750-9_2
3. Diaz, E., Arenas, J.J., Moquillaza, A., Paz, F.: A Systematic literature review about quantitative metrics to evaluate the usability of e-commerce web sites. In: Karwowski, W., Ahram, T. (eds.) IHSI 2019. AISC, vol. 903, pp. 332–338. Springer, Cham (2019). https://doi.org/10.1007/978-3-030-11051-2_51
4. Diaz, E., Flores, S., Paz, F.: Proposal of usability metrics to evaluate e-commerce websites. In: Marcus, A., Wang, W. (eds.) HCII 2019. LNCS, vol. 11586, pp. 85–95. Springer, Cham (2019). https://doi.org/10.1007/978-3-030-23535-2_6
5. Fernandez, A., Insfran, E., Abrahão, S.: Usability evaluation methods for the web: a systematic mapping study. Inf. Softw. Technol. 53, 789–817 (2011). https://doi.org/10.1016/j.infsof.2011.02.007
6. ISO/IEC 25022:2016 Systems and software engineering – Systems and software quality requirements and evaluation (SQuaRE) – Measurement of quality in use. International Organization for Standardization, Geneva, Switzerland (2016)
7. Kitchenham, B.A.: Systematic review in software engineering: where we are and where we should be going. In: Proceedings of the 2nd International Workshop on Evidential Assessment of Software Technologies, pp. 1–2. ACM, Lund (2012)
8. Nielsen, J.: Usability 101: Introduction to Usability. https://www.nngroup.com/articles/usability-101-introduction-to-usability/. Accessed 23 Nov 2021
9. Puteri, R.N., Widyanti, A.: E-commerce of Islamic fashion product: usability and user acceptance. In: 2018 International Conference on Information Technology Systems and Innovation (ICITSI), 2018, pp. 143–147 (2018). https://doi.org/10.1109/ICITSI.2018.8696004

10. Kumar, R., Hasteer, N.: Evaluating usability of a web application: A comparative analysis of open-source tools. In: 2017 2nd International Conference on Communication and Electronics Systems (ICCES), pp. 350–354 (2017). https://doi.org/10.1109/CESYS.2017.8321296

11. Salesforce Homepage: Ecommerce - What is it, Examples, and Benefits. https://www.salesf orce.com/products/commerce-cloud/resources/what-is-ecommerce/. Accessed 2021/11/23

12. Santos, C., Novais, T., Ferreira, M., Albuquerque, C., de Farias, I.H., Furtado, A.P.C.: Metrics focused on usability ISO 9126 based. In: 2016 11th Iberian Conference on Information Systems and Technologies (CISTI). https://doi.org/10.1109/CISTI.2016.7521437

13. Vasconcelos, L.G., Baldochi, L.A., Santos, R.D.C.: An approach to support the construction of adaptive Web applications. Int. J. Web Inf. Syst. **16**(2), 171–199 (2020). https://doi.org/10.1108/IJWIS-12-2018-0089

14. Vyshnova, J.: 11 Best Open Source e-Commerce Platforms for 2022 https://dinarys.com/blog/10-best-open-source-ecommerce-platforms-for-2018. Accessed 23 Nov 2021

15. Wahyuningrum, T., Kartiko, C., Wardhana, A.C.: Exploring e-commerce usability by heuristic evaluation as a complement of system usability scale. In: 2020 International Conference on Advancement in Data Science, e-Learning and Information Systems, ICADEIS 2020 (2020). https://doi.org/10.1109/ICADEIS49811.2020.9277343

Usability Study of Museum Website Based on Analytic Hierarchy Process: A Case of Foshan Museum Website

Yiteng Sun, Zhelin Li, and Zhen Liu[✉]

School of Design, South China University of Technology, Guangzhou 510006,
People's Republic of China
liuzjames@scut.edu.cn

Abstract. With the development of communication technology and network, museum websites have become an important way for people to appreciate cultural relics and understand the urban culture. The museum website is the forerunner of the physical museum, and the usability of the website greatly affects the user's experience. To systematically study the influencing factors of museum website usability, this paper used the Analytic Hierarchy Process (AHP) to construct a museum website usability evaluation system, and took the Foshan Museum website as the research object, using the classic usability testing method to evaluate the website usability, collected objective performance indicators, behavioral data, and subjective evaluations of participants. A total of 10 university graduate students participated in this experiment. The experimental results showed that the current website of Foshan Museum had problems such as confusion of information structure and lack of key information. The hierarchical structure of the website was optimized using the Hierarchical Task Analysis (HTA) method. Finally, the usability test was repeated, and the improvement of the website usability was verified through data analysis. This study also draws some general conclusions, which provide some reference value for the same type of website optimization in the future.

Keywords: Usability testing · Museum website · Usability design · Analytic hierarchy process · Hierarchical task analysis

1 Introduction

Museums are among the most influential cultural institutions [1], and a study commissioned by the European Union showed that the recruitment of cultural institutions such as museums can help promote social innovation and creativity. As the forerunner of the physical museum, the museum website undertakes the function of displaying the basic information of the museum [2]. Users can get a preliminary understanding of the physical museum through the website; secondly, with the development of communication technology and the network, the museum website has gradually become the exhibition of cultural relics. As one of the main channels of commerce, more and more people tend to choose the form of online cultural relics visit. Studies have shown that the number of visitors to online museums has increased substantially [3]. It can be seen that museum websites are playing an increasingly important role in cultural promotion [4].

The usability, content and other characteristics of the website have a significant impact on the willingness of users to visit the museum again and the entity to visit the museum [5, 6]. However, many website developers currently ignore the needs of the main website visitors and lack principles to guide the development process [7], causing most users to experience problems with it. In addition, the content of museum websites is mixed, the information is complex, and the interactive features vary widely, so there is a huge demand for evaluating such websites. To solve the above problems, this paper takes the website of Foshan Museum as the research object and conducts relevant usability research.

2 Method

First, based on the existing usability research and the characteristics of museum websites, this paper built a usability evaluation system for museum websites and used the Analytic Hierarchy Process (AHP) method to assign weights to different indicators in the system. After that, this paper took the Foshan Museum as an example and used the classic usability testing method to test and evaluate its usability. Finally, through data analysis, we found the inadequacy of website usability and proposed improvement directions for the website. The usability research method used in this paper is shown in Fig. 1.

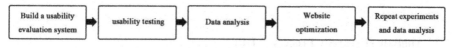

Fig. 1. Method flow map

2.1 Usability

Availability is defined by many scholars, and its connotation and denotation are not the same. In 1993, Nielsen defined usability as the function that users can easily use the system, and he also set the five criteria of usability evaluation as easy to learn, easy to remember, efficacy, less operational errors, and user satisfaction [8]. In 1994, scholar Preece further defined usability as the degree of ease of use, effectiveness, efficiency and security of the system used, as well as the user's attitude towards the operating system [9]. In 2003, Iwarsson et al. considered usability as the user's ability to use a product, interface or system instinctively and efficiently [10]. In 2006, Fengpei et al. believed that usability refers to the extent to which a system, product or service can be effectively, efficiently and satisfactorily implemented by a specific user in a specific environment [11]. The international standard ISO9214 defines usability as the effectiveness of the interaction process, interaction efficiency and user satisfaction when users use the product to complete specific tasks in a specific environment [12].

Some researchers have developed usability assessment methods and used them for website evaluation. For example, Fotakis and Economides proposed a quality assessment framework called MuseumQual [13]. In addition to these, there are the Museum Site Evaluation Framework (MUSEF) [14], Questionnaire For User Interaction Satisfaction (QUIS), and Software Usability Measurement Inventory (SUMI).

WAMMI, developed in 1999 by the Human Factor Research Group (HFRG), is one of the most popular website assessment tools [15]. WAMMI divides the factors of website usability into attractiveness, controllability, efficiency, helpfulness and learnability, and evaluates the above five factors through a 20-standard sentence questionnaire. Combining the cultural characteristics and visiting attributes of museum websites, and referring to WAMMI and other usability theories, this paper defines museum website usability as four dimensions: effectiveness, efficiency, aesthetics, and controllability. The specific definitions are shown in Table 1.

Table 1. Usability index of the Museum Website

Dimension	Symbol	Definition
Effectiveness	C_1	Accuracy and completeness with which users achieve goals
Efficiency	C_2	Resources used to the results achieved
Aesthetics	C_3	Satisfaction with website appearance, layout, text and pictures
Controllability	C_4	The user's perception of the website's operating status

2.2 Analytic Hierarchy Process (AHP)

This paper uses the Analytic Hierarchy Process (AHP) to assign weights to the above four usability dimensions. AHP was first proposed by the famous American operations researcher ALsaaty in 1971 in the 1970s. The method divides the elements related to the target into different levels, and on this basis, qualitative and quantitative analysis of the elements of each level. Analysis, its quantitative indicators come from the comparison between two elements, and finally the weights of different elements can be obtained through calculus. The specific operations are as follows:

(1) Establish a ladder hierarchy model: The usability model of the museum website above is shown in Fig. 2.

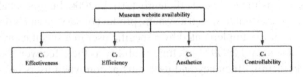

Fig. 2. The usability model of the museum website for Analytic Hierarchy Process.

(2) Construct a judgment matrix: use the comparison scale method to assign the importance of the elements, compare the elements in pairs, and use the numbers from 1 to 9 and their reciprocals to indicate the relative importance of the assessment factors to the risk. The comparison scale is shown in Table 2. Based on consulting relevant experts, the final comparison result is the judgment matrix, as shown in Table 3.

Table 2. Comparison scale description.

Importance scale	Importance description
1	Equal importance of "i" and "j"
3	Weak importance of "i" over "j"
5	Strong importance of "i" over "j"
7	Demonstrated importance of "i" over "j
9	Absolute importance of "i" over
2, 4, 6, 8	Intermediate values

Note: 1, 1/2, 1/3, ..., 1/9 are the results of the inverse comparison of the above two factors

Table 3. Judgment matrix.

	C1	C2	C3	C4
C1	1	3	5	7
C2	1/3	1	3	5
C3	1/5	1/3	1	3
C4	1/7	1/5	1/3	1

(3) Calculate the weight vector, do the consistency check and calculate the weight value: use the geometric mean method to calculate the weight vector Wi of the judgment matrix, which is the weight value Wi after normalization. The formula is shown in (1) (2), and the calculation result is as follows shown in Table 4.

$$W_i = \sqrt[n]{\prod_{j=1}^{n} x_{ij}} \ , \ i,j = 1, 2 \ldots, n \tag{1}$$

$$W_i^n = \frac{W_i}{\sum_{i=1}^{n} W_i} \tag{2}$$

Table 4. Availability weight calculation results.

Item	Feature vector	Weights	Maximum eigenvalue
Effectiveness	2.232	55.789%	4.118
Efficiency	1.053	26.335%	
Aesthetics	0.487	12.187%	
controllability	0.228	5.689%	

To ensure the consistency of the importance before and after the pairwise comparison process, a consistency test is required.

$$CI = \frac{\lambda - n}{n - 1} \tag{3}$$

$$CR = \frac{CI}{RI} \tag{4}$$

Among them, CI is the consistency test index, CR is the consistency ratio, RI is the random consistency index, λ_{max} is the maximum eigenvalue, and n is the matrix dimension. When n = 4, consult the international average random consistency index RI value table, RI = 0.58, CR = 0.039 < 0.1, so the matrix meets the consistency requirements.

2.3 Usability Testing

Process of the Experiment
The experimental process of this paper is: scenario test, questionnaire survey and retrospective interview.

The performance measurement method was used in the scenario test to record the time to complete the task, the number of errors and the number of help. During the test, subjects were encouraged to express their inner thoughts when taking actions, and screen recording was turned on during the test to record the subjects' complete operation process for subsequent analysis and review.

After the scenario test and questionnaire survey, the main tester interviewed the subjects about the usability of the website, and recorded the subjects' answers, as shown in Table 5. The interview is a review and evaluation of the website as a whole. The subjects give personal opinions through the actual use process. The feedback is subjective, direct and highly targeted. These subjective evaluations can provide suggestions for subsequent website optimization.

Table 5. Retrospective interview form.

Question	Answer
Was anything too obtrusive?	
Was anything too well hidden?	
Problems or kudos on the color scheme?	
Easy to read (both font style and size)?	
How did you find the layout of the site?	
How intuitive and helpful is the navigation system?	
What would encourage you to return to this site in the future?	
Name your three favorite things about the site, and your three least favorite	
If you could change one thing on the site, whether it is major or minor, what would be at the top of the to-do list?	

Scenarios Settings

According to the user's habit of visiting museums in real life, the scenario test designs three usage scenarios and corresponding tasks. The difficulty of scenarios and tasks goes from simple to deep, which is similar to the process of users gradually understanding the website when using the website. The roles of each scene are graduate students who need to have an in-depth understanding of Foshan's history and culture.

Scenario 1: You are a graduate student of the School of Design. According to the course arrangement, you are currently conducting research on Foshan culture. To gain a deeper understanding of Foshan culture, you plan to visit the Foshan Museum recently. Before that, you want to know in advance through the website of the Foshan Museum. For the specific location and opening hours of the Foshan Museum, if possible, I would like to check whether the museum has a voice broadcast service. The tasks of Scenario 1 are shown in Table 6.

Table 6. Scenario 1 task sheet.

No	Content
Task 1–1	Find the exact location of the Foshan Museum
Task 1–2	Find the exact opening hours of the Foshan Museum
Task 1–3	Find out if the Foshan Museum has a voice broadcast function

Scenario 2: You are a graduate student of the School of Design. You have two main interests in browsing the Foshan Museum website this time. First, you are very interested in historical celebrities in Foshan, such as Huang Shijun, and want to know his life stories. Second, you love calligraphy, and you want to appreciate the calligraphy

of famous people, such as Zhang Ruitu's cursive handscroll. Return to the main page after browsing. The tasks of Scenario 2 are shown in Table 7.

Table 7. Scenario 2 task sheet.

No.	Content
Task 2–1	Find out about Huang Shijun's life story
Task 2–2	Find Zhang Ruitu's cursive handscroll
Task 2–3	Back to the home page of Foshan Museum

Scenario 3: You are a graduate student of the School of Design. After understanding the culture of Foshan, you finally choose "Foshan's ancestral temple culture" as the main content of the course report. For this purpose, you need to understand the historical origin of the Foshan ancestral temple; and you are writing the direction of the Foshan ancestral temple, you need to check whether the library has related papers. The task table for scenario 3 is shown in Table 8.

Table 8. Scenario 3 task sheet.

No	Content
Task 3–1	Find the historical origin of Foshan Zuo Temple
Task 3–2	Find papers on ancestral temples in Foshan

Usability Scale

After the test of each scenario, the subjects filled out the usability scale and scored various indicators of the website according to the just-completed experimental scenario. After the three scenarios were tested, subjects were required to fill out a total of three usability scales. The scale is modified from WAMMI 20 structured questions, as shown in Table 9. Each question in WAMMI will be represented by the letters A-P below.

The questions in the scale have both positive and negative descriptions. To facilitate the analysis, this paper unifies the correspondence between the scores in the scale and the semantics in the subsequent analysis. 5 points indicate that you are very satisfied with the website on this issue, and 1 point for strong dissatisfaction.

The usability scale scores the website mainly from the aspects of layout design, ease of use, and efficiency, and quantifies the user's evaluation through the usability scale, which is conducive to our subsequent exploration and modification of website deficiencies.

Table 9. Usability scale.

Post-survey user experience	
Characteristics	Statement
C_1 Effectiveness	A. Using this website saves time
	B. I can quickly find what I want on this website
	C. The response speed of this website is too slow
	D. The information organization structure of the website seems to be in line with my logic
C_2 Efficiency	E. The content information on the website is useful
	F. I can easily find what I am looking for on this site
	G. When I click on something on this website, the interface that pops up is not what I want
	H. This site has some redundant features or duplicate content
C_3 Aesthetics	I. The pages on this site are very attractive
	J. The text and pictures on this website are clearly visible
	K. The number of buttons/links on this website is reasonable
	L. This website is easy to use
C_3 Controllability	M. I am aware of the current operating status of the website
	N. I know where I am currently on the site
	O. I can easily go back to the previous website interface
	P. When I use this site, I feel like everything is in control
Participation	Instructions and guidelines for participating in the usability testing were clear
1 Strongly Disagree, 2 Somewhat Disagree, 3 Somewhat Agree, 4 Agree, 5 Strongly Agree	

Participant Sample Description

The participants in the experiment were all from the first-year postgraduates of the School of Design, South China University of Technology, and their ages ranged from 21 to 25 years old. There were 4 males and 4 females, all of whom had museum visiting experience, but they all used the Foshan Museum website.

3   Results

3.1   Performance Results

Task duration, fork in the road, help statistics: The time and forks spent by each subject on each small task were recorded, and the data are shown in Table 10, 11 and 12. The completion time of each task and the number of fork roads taken are recorded in the table. The time measures the efficiency of completing the corresponding task, and the fork roads represent the number of times of being misled. At the same time, the form also recorded whether the subjects needed help. The way to help was to inform the subjects of the location of the interface where the current task was located. Since the subjects were often able to successfully solve the task after one prompt, there was no need to record the number of times of help.

Table 10. Task time and Fork Statistics in Scenario 1.

No.	Total time/s	Time of task 1–1/s	Fork road of task 1–1	Help	Time of task 1–2/s	Fork road of task 1–2	Help	Time of task 1–3/s	Fork road of task 1–3	Help
1	325	65	0		103	3	√	157	4	√
2	207	11	0		75	6	√	121	5	√
3	334	45	0		103	4	√	186	3	√
4	331	36	0		121	3	√	174	3	√
5	347	47	0		134	4	√	166	2	√
6	298	53	0		112	4	√	133	2	√
7	235	24	0		83	2		128	3	
8	371	35	0		187	5	√	149	4	√
Sum	2448	316	0	0	918	31	7	1214	26	7
Average	306	39.5	0		114.7	3.8		151.7	3.25	
Variance	3226	286.2	0		1214	1.5		538.2	1.07	

From the specific data, for the three subtasks in scenario 1, they are all inquiries about the basic information of the venue, but the time of 1–1 is significantly less than that of 1–2 and 1–3. This is because the task goal of 1–1 is It is listed separately in the navigation bar of the website and is very clear. The help rate of tasks 1–2 and 1–3 is very high, because the two task goals of "time and place" do not appear in a conspicuous position, making it difficult for users to find, and the information given is very vague, making it difficult for users to accurate judgment. Therefore, some general information that each museum should have, such as location and opening hours, should be placed in a place that is eye-catching and user habitual—the home page, which is a habit formed by users browsing similar websites. The detailed data are shown in Table 10.

For the three tasks in scenario 2, it is more obvious that the number of forks in tasks 2–2 is large, with an average of 4.4, indicating that there is a problem with the information guidance of the website on the solution of the task, which is caused by the inaccurate classification of the navigation bar. Yes, the classification of content on the website appears to contain and overlap each other, which makes users very confused. Secondly, the help rate of 2–2 is also extremely high. Combined with the analysis of the actual situation of the website, this is because the entrance of this task is difficult to find. The time to complete tasks 2–3 is very short, with an average time of 14.3s, but the

Table 11. Task time and Fork Statistics in Scenario 2

No.	Total time/s	Time of task 2-1/s	Fork road of task 2-1	Help	Time of task 2-2/s	Fork road of task 2-2	Help	Time of Task 2-3/s	Fork road of task 2-3	Help
1	239	31	1		193	5	√	15	3	
2	135	10	0		113	1		12	1	
3	194	30	1		147	6	√	17	1	√
4	214	25	0		179	6	√	10	0	
5	202	29	0		158	3	√	16	2	
6	280	41	1		223	5	√	16	3	√
7	259	36	0		206	4	√	17	2	
8	165	18	0		135	3		12	0	
Sum	1689	220	3	0	1354	33	6	115	12	2
Average	211.1	27.5	0.38		169.2	4.13		14.3	1.5	
Variance	2300	96.8	0.26		1408	2.98		7.1	1.42	

Table 12. Task time and Fork Statistics in Scenario 3

No.	Total time/s	Time of task 3-1/s	Fork road of task 3-1	Need help	Time of task 3-2/s	Fork road of task 3-2	Need help
1	191	65	3		126	1	
2	120	45	0		75	0	
3	175	58	2		117	4	√
4	313	90	0		223	9	√
5	247	72	2		175	4	√
6	292	85	3		207	6	√
7	259	76	2		183	4	
8	170	46	0		124	2	
Sum	1767	537	12	0	1230	30	4
Average	220.8	67.1	1.5		153.7	3.75	
Variance	4491.8	281.2	1.71		2592.2	8.21	

number of forks is abnormally large, with an average of 1.5. Combined with the analysis of the website and tasks 2–3, this is because the website is in this part. The home page return key is set too hidden. The detailed data are shown in Table 11.

For the two tasks in Scenario 3, the classification levels of the two tasks are the same, that is, the third level, and the content of the tasks is similar. However, compared with 3–1, task 3–2, the average duration, the average number of forks, and the total number of assists are significantly higher. This is due to a large amount of content on the website. The task goals of 3–2 are on the third page of the same interface level, while 3–1 is on the first page. Therefore, when the target information cannot be found on one page, the time cost will increase exponentially, and errors will occur. At this time, the search bar at this level is very critical. It is worth noting that users prefer search tools for this level of content, rather than site-wide search tools. The detailed data are shown in Table 12.

3.2 Usability Results

According to the weights of different dimensions calculated in 2–2 in the text, the calculation formula of the total score is as follows:

$$U = \sum_{i=1}^{4} C_i R_i \tag{5}$$

U is the overall usability score of the website, R is the score of a usability dimension, C is the weight value corresponding to the dimension, and i is the dimension index. The score R of the usability evaluation dimension is the average of the four questions under this dimension.

Table 13. Usability scale statistics in Scenario 1.

Post-survey user experience- scenario 1											
Charact-eristics	Sta-	Hong	Zhou	Biao	Wan	Pei	Wu	Jia	Dan	Average	
C1 Effectiveness	A	4	2	4	4	4	1	4	3	3.25	2.31
	B	2	2	1	3	2	1	2	1	1.75	
	C	4	2	2	5	3	3	1	1	2.63	
	D	1	1	1	4	1	2	1	2	1.63	
C2 Efficiency	E	3	2	4	4	2	4	4	3	3.25	2.50
	F	3	3	2	2	3	5	2	1	2.63	
	G	3	1	4	4	2	2	3	3	2.75	
	H	2	1	2	1	1	1	2	1	1.38	
C3 Aesthetics	I	3	4	3	3	2	3	3	3	3.00	3.13
	J	3	3	4	3	2	2	3	3	2.88	
	K	3	3	4	3	3	3	4	2	3.13	
	L	3	4	3	5	4	3	3	3	3.50	

(continued)

Table 13. (*continued*)

Charact-eristics	Sta-	Hong	Zhou	Biao	Wan	Pei	Wu	Jia	Dan	Average	
Post-survey user experience- scenario 1											
C4 Controllability	M	2	2	2	5	2	2	2	2	2.38	3.03
	N	3	3	2	4	3	3	2	3	2.88	
	O	3	3	2	5	4	4	3	3	3.38	
	P	3	4	3	3	5	4	3	3	3.50	
Total score		2.54	2.38	2.38	3.85	2.15	2.31	2.31	2.08	2.5	
Participation		4	4	5	5	5	4	4	4	4.38	

1 = Strongly Disagree, 2 = Somewhat Disagree, 3 = Somewhat Agree, 4 = Agree, 5 = Strongly Agree

For scenario 1, the D. information organization clarity of the website is only 1.63, indicating that the information logic of the website is not reasonable; the average score of B. is only 1.75, indicating that the website users have difficulty finding the target information. Lowered the overall score for site effectiveness. The efficiency of the website is also unsatisfactory, only 2.5 points, of which the average score of item H. is only 1.38, indicating that there is too much interference information on the website, which affects the efficiency of use, which is consistent with the score of item B. The average score of C3 layout design is 3.13, and C4 Controllability is 3.03, which does not arouse users' disgust. The overall satisfaction is 2.5 points < 3 points, and the usability of the website needs to be improved. The final participant score is the subject's score on the clarity of their task. If the score is too low, it means that the subject does not have a good understanding of the experimental content, which will directly lead to invalid experimental data. This situation does not occur in scenario 1. The detailed data are shown in Table 13.

Table 14. Usability scale statistics in Scenario 2.

Charact-eristics	Sta-	Hong	Zhou	Biao	Wan	Pei	Wu	Jia	Dan	Average	
Post-survey user experience- scenario 2											
C1 Effectiveness	A	3	2	3	3	3	2	3	3	2.75	2.38
	B	2	2	3	2	2	3	2	3	2.38	
	C	3	5	3	4	2	3	1	1	2.75	
	D	1	2	2	2	1	2	1	2	1.63	

(*continued*)

Table 14. (*continued*)

Charact-eristics	Sta-	Hong	Zhou	Biao	Wan	Pei	Wu	Jia	Dan	Average	
Post-survey user experience- scenario 2											
C2 Efficiency	E	2	3	3	5	3	3	4	4	3.38	2.81
	F	2	3	3	2	3	4	2	3	2.75	
	G	3	2	3	4	3	2	3	3	2.88	
	H	2	2	3	3	2	3	1	2	2.25	
C3 Aesthetics	I	1	3	2	2	1	2	2	3	2.00	1.91
	J	2	1	3	2	2	1	2	2	1.88	
	K	1	2	1	2	2	1	3	1	1.63	
	L	1	2	2	4	3	1	3	1	2.13	
C4 Controllability	M	2	2	2	5	2	2	2	1	2.25	3.00
	N	3	2	3	3	4	2	3	2	2.75	
	O	3	4	3	5	4	3	3	2	3.38	
	P	4	3	4	3	3	4	3	5	3.63	
Total score		2.17	2.59	2.74	2.99	2.27	2.49	2.10	2.40	2.47	
Participation		4	5	4	5	4	4	4	4	4.25	

1 = Strongly Disagree, 2 = Somewhat Disagree, 3 = Somewhat Agree, 4 = Agree, 5 = Strongly Agree

For scenario 2, the C_3 layout and appearance of the website caused slight discomfort to users, and the average score was only 1.91 points. This is because in the task of this scenario, the subjects entered a sub-site, and the color and layout style of the sub-site was the same as that of the main website. Completely different, which caused strong discomfort for users, and this style inconsistency also led to a decline in users' evaluation of the clarity of D. information structure, because users needed to re-understand the logical structure of the subsite. The efficiency of use did not cause a strong dislike, but it was also rated low in B. Fast information search, with an average score of 1.50, because the entrance of the sub-site was difficult to find. The overall satisfaction is 2.47 points < 3 points, and the usability of the website needs to be improved. In scenario 2, the participants' average score for the task was 4.25, and the subjects were clear about their tasks. The detailed data are shown in Table 14.

Table 15. Usability scale statistics in Scenario 3.

Post-survey user experience- scenario 3

Characteristics	Sta-	Hong	Zhou	Biao	Wan	Pei	Wu	Jia	Dan	Average	
C1 Effectiveness	A	2	3	3	5	4	2	3	4	3.25	2.47
	B	1	2	1	2	1	2	1	2	1.50	
	C	3	3	4	5	2	3	1	2	2.88	
	D	2	1	2	4	2	3	1	3	2.25	
C2 Efficiency	E	1	2	2	3	1	2	1	2	1.75	1.66
	F	1	2	1	1	2	4	2	1	1.75	
	G	2	1	3	2	1	2	2	1	1.75	
	H	2	1	2	1	1	1	2	1	1.38	
C3 Aesthetics	I	4	3	2	2	3	4	2	3	2.88	2.88
	J	2	3	4	3	2	3	2	3	2.75	
	K	4	2	3	2	3	3	2	4	2.88	
	L	4	2	4	3	4	2	2	3	3.00	
C4 Controllability	M	2	3	2	4	3	2	3	2	2.63	2.94
	N	2	3	3	4	2	3	2	3	2.75	
	O	2	4	2	4	3	4	3	4	3.25	
	P	2	4	2	3	5	4	2	3	3.13	
Total Score		2.05	2.15	2.45	3.21	2.13	2.54	1.68	2.43	2.33	
Participation		3	5	5	5	4	4	5	5	4.5	

1 = Strongly Disagree, 2 = Somewhat Disagree, 3 = Somewhat Agree, 4 = Agree, 5 = Strongly Agree

For Scenario 3, the most prominent part of the data is the C2 usage efficiency column, with an average score of only 1.66 points. Users generally believe that the website usage efficiency is not high, and the average score of B. item information quick search is also low. This is due to this task. The target information is on the third page of a certain level, which is deeply hidden, and there is no search bar for this section, which makes users lose patience when browsing. The overall satisfaction is 2.33 points < 3 points, and the usability of the website needs to be improved. In scenario 3, the average score of the participants for the task score was 4.5, and the subjects were clear about their tasks. The detailed data are shown in Table 15.

3.3 Behavioural and Physiological Metrics Results

User Comments: Before and after the scenario test, the subject was asked some basic information and questions about the website, and the responses were recorded. The user experience gave a certain evaluation, here is a summary of the Q&A and comments with reference, as shown in Table 16.

Table 16. User evaluation statistical analysis form.

Comment	Analyze
The appearance matches the impression of the museum website, but I don't like it, it's a bit rigid	The appearance and layout of a museum website do not have to be retro and traditional, especially for a museum in a city, and a modern design may be more appealing to younger users
The look of the site and the overall ambiance strikes me as classy	The overall appearance of the website is very eye-catching in red, and the first impression it gives people is very matching with the museum
Where is the search bar? can't find	The search bar is very important, the search bar on this site is not easy to use, and it is not obvious enough
I don't think this part should be put here	The categorization of content should be clear and precise, without overlapping or inclusion
Looking at the name of this navigation bar, I don't know what's in it, so I didn't click it	The generalization of the content should be precise and clear, not vague or too abstract
There's too much content, I don't want to continue reading	The content cannot fit on one page, and it will be difficult to use when you need to constantly jump to the page to find information
I don't know what is the relationship between these two pages, I just feel that the styles are inconsistent	Some sub-other websites under the website of Foshan Museum should keep the same style, otherwise it will be very abrupt
Navigation bar text is a bit crowded	The text in the navigation bar has no obvious separation symbols, which makes the columns appear a bit cluttered
Can't find this content in the category of the navigation bar?	The navigation bar should be able to cover all the content of the website

Behavior Analysis: During the scenario test, some typical behaviors of users were found through observation, and the main tester recorded and analyzed the typical behaviors, as shown in Table 17. These typical behaviors help in the development and design of the website, and can provide some guidance for it.

Table 17. Statistical analysis table of typical user behavior.

No.	Behaviors	Approximate proportion
1	When users are exposed to unfamiliar websites, their attention is focused on the home page	87.5% of users only used the scroll wheel when they browsed the site for the first time, instead of jumping the page
2	When browsing pages with purpose, users look at the navigation bar first	75% of users move the mouse on the navigation bar first, and then use the scroll wheel when doing a scenario test
3	The homepage navigation bar has priority over other parts of the homepage	There are many categories and sections on the homepage of the website. 75% of users will use the navigation bar first, and then browse other sections of the homepage if they are unsuccessful
4	The user will repeatedly enter the same page to confirm the information	After 75% of users do not find the target information on their estimated page, they will click to enter the page several times for verification and confirmation
5	It is easy for users to confuse the address of the museum, the address of an exhibition and the address of the office	Due to the particularity of the museum website, which contains a variety of addresses, 50% of users will confuse it, and 75% of users need to stay on this information to distinguish
6	When there are several pages of content, more users only browse the first page	62.5% of users will return to the previous level after not finding the target information on the first page; 25% of users will browse the second page
7	When images and captions (titles) exist at the same time, users tend to click on images	87.5% of users will click on the picture to jump to the page when the picture and the caption (title) exist at the same time, and 12.5% will click on the caption (subtitle)
8	Users use the search bar when they encounter a problem, not from the start	75% of users will initially try to find the target information by browsing the page and navigation bar, but fail to use the search bar

4   Website Redesign

4.1   Application of Hierarchical Task Analysis (HTA)

Aiming at the more prominent problems of the Foshan Museum website - the overall information structure of the website is chaotic and the logic is not clear, this paper adopts the hierarchical task analysis method to optimize. Hierarchical task analysis (HTA) is a core ergonomic method based on performance theory [16], which is often used to sort out the hierarchical structure of a system and provide a variety of expressions. The core idea of the Hierarchical Task Analysis method is to decompose a complex task from top to bottom, showing the hierarchical relationship between the tasks, to obtain the corresponding subtasks and corresponding subordinate operations of the task. This method is widely used in a series of applications, interface design and workflow design.

AHP is not a strict procedure, but a general method for analyzing complex systems or tasks. According to the different users and research objects, the results of this method will be different, and the method has a certain degree of subjectivity. The AHP follows three guiding principles:

(1) At the highest level, tasks consist of operations, and operations are defined by goals.
(2) Operations and targets can be decomposed into lower operations and lower targets.
(3) Operation and subordinate operation, there is a hierarchical relationship between the target and the subordinate target.

The general operation steps of the hierarchical task analysis method are shown in Fig. 3.

Fig. 3. Task analysis method flow diagram.

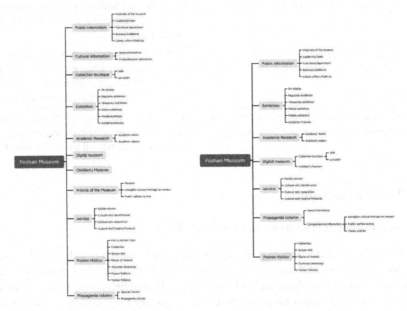

Fig. 4. Before and after comparison of website hierarchy.

The menu tree structure is used as the basis for finding the optimal path for the task, combined with expert opinions, the information architecture of the Buddha Museum website is optimized, and the results are shown in Fig. 4. But the classification and indexing are complex tasks and no single solution can satisfy all needs.

4.2 Website Optimization

Through the above data analysis, behavior analysis and comment summary, we can find some deficiencies in the website of Foshan Museum. Here, we will summarize the common problems, and write the corresponding improvement directions after the corresponding problems, as shown in Table 18, and appendix The upper part of the interface is modified before and after the comparison chart. This optimization is done using Adobe XD. Figure 5, 6 and 7 shows a comparison chart of some improvements on the website.

Table 18. Website problems and design opportunities.

Problems	Optimize
The overall information structure and logic of the website are not clear, and some titles are too general	Reorganized the navbar to remove overlapping and contained sections, and rename the blurry headings
There is no drop-down menu under some headings in the navigation bar	Complete the drop-down menu
The text in the navigation bar is a bit crowded, and the visual division is not clear enough	A horizontal line is used to separate the different columns of the navigation bar
The webpage only has Chinese mode	Add language switch function (English) in the upper right corner
Faced with a blank page, I don't know if it is loading or it has no content itself	Add text prompts to blank pages to remind users of the current status of website pages
Pages with a lot of content should be placed on several pages	Design a search bar tool for this section to quickly find and search content
Basic information about the venue (such as time) is difficult to find and the location can be confusing	Put basic information such as the venue's time and place in a prominent position on the home page
It's hard to understand what's in the picture without a caption or caption	Supplementary image captions in the website
Some pages are inconsistent in style and layout	Unify the style and layout of the subsite with the main site

a) the ancient one   b) the redesign one

Fig. 5. Comparison chart of the basic information page of the web pages.

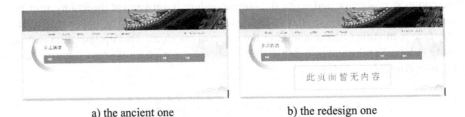

a) the ancient one   b) the redesign one

Fig. 6. Blank page comparison of the web pages.

a) the ancient one   b) the redesign one

Fig. 7. Search tool page comparison of the web pages.

4.3 Optimization Effect Comparison

To quantify the effect of website optimization, this paper asked eight new subjects to repeat the above usability test on the optimized website. Compare the new data obtained with the original data to assess whether the improvements to the web page are effective.

As can be seen from Figs. 8 and 9, in the comparison of the three experimental scenarios, the total duration of each task, the total number of requests for help, and the average number of forks have decreased significantly, which shows that the website is optimized for efficiency and ease of use. There is a boost.

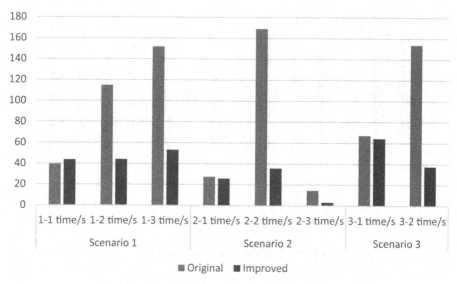

Fig. 8. Fork in the road, help data comparison.

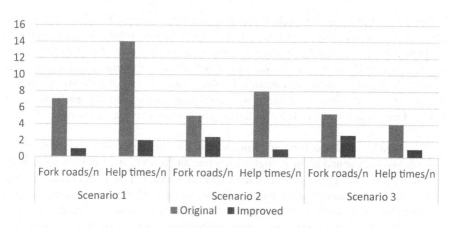

Fig. 9. Task duration comparison.

Through the comparison of the user experience scale data in Fig. 10, it can be found that the website has significantly improved in terms of the navigation bar, ease of use, and efficiency, and this is the case in all three scenarios. The page layout is only significantly improved in Scenario 2, and the changes in Scenarios 1 and 2 are not obvious. This is because the styles of the sub-site and the main website of Scenario 2 and 2 are unified, and the page layout of Scenarios 1 and 2 has no obvious change.

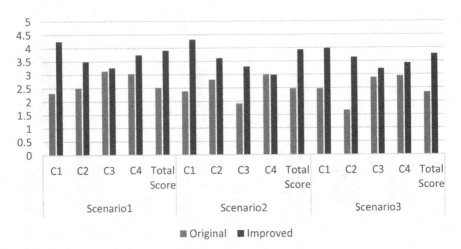

Fig. 10. Usability scale data comparison.

5 Discussion and Conclusions

Combined with previous research, this paper proposes a new usability evaluation system for museum websites, and takes the Foshan Museum website as an example to complete a website optimization iteration. The results of the control experiments show that the optimization results are satisfactory, which also confirms the effectiveness of the usability evaluation system from the side. From the data analysis of the two comparative experiments, some common problems were found, and some general guidelines for the design of museum websites were also found. The conclusions are as follows:

1. The overall logical structure and clear layout of the website are the top priority in user usability. A clear and accurate logical structure and layout can help users solve problems quickly and greatly improve the user experience. On the contrary, the chaotic logical structure makes users into confusion, and the cumbersome interface makes users dazzled and impatient, which in turn affects the overall user experience. The navigation bar is the most concentrated embodiment of the website logic structure, and the content of the home page is also a partial embodiment of the website logic structure.
2. Users will develop usage habits based on the experience of using the website in daily life. For example, when using the campus official website, student users will habitually log in to their student accounts, which is also confirmed on the museum website. Users will habitually think that the opening time and address of the museum should be on the home page. There should be a Chinese-English switching mode. And it is possible to try other different types of website experience on the museum website, so paying attention to the habitual behavior of users is conducive to the development of the website by developers and improves the user experience of the website.

3. A notable behavior of the user is that when the user does not find the required information in his estimated level, the user will repeatedly enter this interface for confirmation. Therefore, when a user enters the same interface multiple times in a short period of time, it is likely to encounter a problem. Developers can identify users who encounter difficulties based on this phenomenon and provide assistance.
4. A search bar is not enough for a massively structured website. Many museum websites now have only one general search bar, and museum websites are complex in content and complex, which greatly reduces the usability of the search bar for difficult to filter search results. So in the sub-level with more content, it is very useful to have a search bar for this section.

The usability testing methods and conclusions of this paper have certain references for website optimization, and it is hoped that the follow-up research can be combined with more examples to verify.

References

1. Poulot, D.: Museu e museologia. Autêntica (2013)
2. Pallud, J., Straub, D.W.: Effective website design for experience-influenced environments: the case of high culture museums. Inf. Manage. **51**, 359–373 (2014)
3. Kabassi, K.: Evaluating websites of museums: state of the art. J. Cult. Herit. **24**, 184–196 (2017)
4. Kabassi, K., Karydis, C., Botonis, A.: AHP, Fuzzy SAW, and Fuzzy WPM for the evaluation of cultural websites. Multimodal Technol. Interact. **4**, 5 (2020)
5. Koo, B.: A study on the usability for museum websites for interactive museum experience. 예술경영연구 **22**, 145–170 (2012)
6. Troyer, O., Leune, C.J.: WSDM: a user centered design method for Web sites. Comput. Netw. ISDN Syst. **30**, 85–94 (1998)
7. Hertzum, M.: A review of museum web sites: in search of user-centred design. Arch. Museum Inform. **12**, 127–138 (1999)
8. Nielsen, J.: Usability Engineering. Usability Engineering (1993)
9. Preece, J., Rogers, Y., Sharp, H., Benyon, D., Holland, S., Carey, T.: Human-computer Interaction Addison-Wesley. Harlow, England, pp. 17–18 (1994)
10. Iwarsson, S., St?Hl, A.: Accessibility, usability and universal design--positioning and definition of concepts describing person-environment relationships. Disabil. Rehabil. **25**, 57–66 (2003)
11. Fengpei, H.: The studies of eye tracking and usability test. In: International Conference on Computer-Aided Industrial Design & Conceptual Design (2006)
12. Jeng, J.: What is usability in the context of the digital library and how can it be measured? Inf. Technol. Librar. **24**, 5 (2013)
13. Fotakis, T., Economides, A.A.: Art, science/technology and history museums on the web. Int. J. Digital Culture Electron. Tour. **1**, 37–63 (2008)
14. Pallas, J., Οικονομίδης, A, Economides, A.: Evaluation of art museums' web sites worldwide. Inf. Serv. Use **28**, 45–57 (2008)
15. Mentes, T.: Assessing the Usability of University Websites (2012)
16. Stanton, N.A.: Hierarchical task analysis: developments, applications, and extensions. Appl. Ergon. **37**, 55–79 (2006)

Cumulative Distortions in Usability Testing: Combined Impact of Web Design, Experiment Conditions, and Type of Task and Upon User States During Internet Use

Alexander V. Yakunin[✉] and Svetlana S. Bodrunova

School of Journalism and Mass Communications, St. Petersburg State University,
7-9 Universitetskaya nab, St. Petersburg 199004, Russia
{a.yakunin,s.bodrunova}@spbu.ru

Abstract. The proposed study examines the simultaneous influence of factors (environment, type of task, and product properties) upon functional user states that critically affect assessor performance during the realization of various online tasks. In addition, test environment format varies as individual vs. group one, to assess whether testing conditions affect the test results. The test uses two types of tasks that, respectively, induce user functional states of anxiety and monotony/fatigue. Differences in product features are represented by two university website layouts with high and low aesthetic quality, as measured by website aesthetic quality index (U-index, our earlier elaboration). We have employed two groups of metrics to measure user performance, directed at both cognitive and emotional components of the user states. For cognitive efficiency, intellectual lability and productivity of cognitive operations were assessed. Emotional stress was measured by four metrics of self-assessment, namely the level of anxiety, fatigue, excitement, and confidence. Two assessor groups were put in conditions of individual vs. group task solving. Within each group, sub-groups were assigned either anxiety-inducing or fatigue-inducing tasks. For each task, subgroups worked with webpages of either high (U-index > 17) or low (U-index < 8) aesthetic quality. As the test results show, group task solving enhances the synchronous impact of website aesthetics and task features upon the user states. Interaction of high-quality design, group environment, and a monotonous task provides for an antagonistic effect: aesthetic layout in a group environment significantly reduces the fatigue rate. Low aesthetic quality in a group environment leads to cumulative effects in combination with any type of task: for monotonous tasks, it contributes to the development of fatigue, while for anxiety-inducing tasks it grows anxiety, and, in both cases, productivity drops.

Keywords: Web usability · Web design · Functional user states · U-index · Cumulative effects in web usability

1 Introduction

The paper is dedicated to exploring the combined impact of factors that affect the results of usability testing. According to the four-factor 'contextual fidelity' model [1, 2], such

© The Author(s), under exclusive license to Springer Nature Switzerland AG 2022
M. M. Soares et al. (Eds.): HCII 2022, LNCS 13321, pp. 526–535, 2022.
https://doi.org/10.1007/978-3-031-05897-4_36

factors as the test conditions, participants' traits, the properties of the tested product, and task features can significantly affect both testing accuracy and final result.

However, today, most studies assess their impact individually and do not address their cumulative impact. Most often, various characteristics within individual factors are investigated. Such studies focus on specific aspects of user behavior, task, product, or the test context and do not attempt to establish a relationship between these factors. For example, testing environment studies look at field vs. laboratory testing efficiency [2, 3], or the impact of remote testing on the overall user experience [4].

Product-focused research examines the impact of usability on objective user productivity [5] and perceived usability [6], as well as the impact of usability on perceived aesthetics. As a rule, in most of these studies, the results indicate a direct relationship between user ratings and performance, on one hand, and the quality of usability, on the other [7, 8].

Just like usability, the impact of the aesthetic quality of a website on the user experience is being actively studied. The effects of web aesthetics can be divided into subjective and objective. Subjective effects are linked to changes in the user's perception of certain qualities of the product, due to the layout aesthetics. The most significant effect here is the relationship between aesthetics and perceived usability, when, as experiments show, a product with higher aesthetic quality is also perceived as more convenient to use.

The influence of product aesthetics on objective criteria of its usability, and, in particular, on user productivity, remains under-investigated, despite a certain number of studies in this area. Here, some contradiction in the research results may be noted. Thus, on the one hand, a positive effect of aesthetics upon user motivation is stated, the increase of which has a positive effect on the overall performance in solving the task [9]. On the other hand, some researchers have found a direct relationship between aesthetic design and performance degradation: the time to complete a task increases as the aesthetic quality of a product grows [10].

In most cases discussed above, studies of product properties are focused on finding patterns of causal relations between a narrow range of its qualitative features of usability or aesthetics and the user states. Obviously, posing research questions this way does not capture the possible multi-dimensional relationship of product properties with the context of testing and the task features.

In studies dedicated to the task features, most often, it is the quantitative characteristics of tasks that become the research focus. E.g., the performance when solving single and dual tasks is compared [6, 7]. However, the qualitative features of tasks and their connection with the testing environment are not specifically considered.

The research on another element of the 'contextual fidelity' model, namely user traits as a factor that affects user performance, is also limited. As part of these studies, problems associated with various effects of the user traits are actively discussed. However, despite the active interest in this topic, most research focuses on single characteristics of experience and their causal relationship with each other - for example, the impact of user incompetence on user motivation and self-efficacy [9, 11, 12]. In particular, within this area, our own research has focused on the relationship between the aesthetic quality of a product, the effectiveness of user actions in solving a problem, and perceived usability [7]. However, here, we need to note that this research sub-field is so scarce and non-systemic that, till today, individual user traits have not been systematized, and users' inborn physical traits (like gender or age) have been distinguished neither from rational mental capacities (like competence, education level, experience etc.) nor from cognitive and emotional states that have temporal character and may change before/after or within the experiment not only as a result of the experiment but also by other reasons. We add to this research area by involving into the DUXU studies the research on complex (dys)functional user states that have cognitive and emotional elements (see below).

The results of such studies show both obvious patterns (high aesthetic quality of a product increases perceived usability) and paradoxical dependencies (high quality design contributes to lower productivity). Resolution of this paradox may lie in non-direct relationship between aesthetic quality of layouting and user performance, as this connection may be conditioned by other factors that affect user experience. However, at the present stage, there is a significant lack of research that would study the effects of the interaction of various testing factors.

The few studies that address this topic focus on the impact of product features on the user—e.g., the effects of design aesthetic quality on user experience when solving a problem. In line with this, our earlier study [13] focused on combined effects of product features (web esthetics) and task features upon assessor performance and satisfaction. However, the induced user states were not investigated. Moreover, how the environment of the experiment would further affect this already non-negligible combination remained an open question. In particular, the impact of social environment upon task fulfillment was not investigated. As it follows from previous studies [14], this factor may significantly affect performance efficiency.

2 Method

2.1 Functional User States in the Context of Usability Testing Factors

Based on this need, we have developed an empirical experiment methodology that can demonstrate combinational effects in the synchronous interaction of various usability testing factors. The proposed study examines the simultaneous influence of three testing factors (environment, type of task, and product properties) upon functional user states that critically affect assessor performance.

As shown in [13], critical changes in users' mental and emotional states while performing complex tasks are best described by functional states theory. The functional state of a user is understood as an integral and simultaneous complex of mental and bodily functions that determine professional performance [4]. (Dys)functional user states consist of cognitive and emotional states that combine and results in definite, specific, and detectable task-related (often task-induced) behavioral changes.

User states may foster or diminish functional productivity. Dysfunctional user states that form due to unfavorable combinations of task performance factors deserve special attention, as they may significantly affect working performance; we hypothesize that they affect performance of online tasks similarly.

According to Leonova [15], the range of possible emotional-behavioral reactions and modes of activity may be limited to several distinct dysfunctional states that vary in their destructive effect upon working performance, from desire to activity shifts to exhaustion to panic to extreme distress. However, the extreme states are very rare for Internet use; much more often, boredom, tiredness of monotonous work, and anxiety are experienced. Thus, we have selected two dysfunctional states – monotony and anxiety – as two opposing user states.

Experiencing these states manifests via the two respective stable sets of features (patterns) that may determine the specifics of user experience. As stated above, they are detectable and, thus, allow for accurately identifying a dysfunctional state that a user encounters via cognitive and emotional markers.

In the dysfunctional state of anxiety, a drop in intellectual lability is accompanied by a violation of concentration due to stressful conditions for performing a task. Also, this state is characterized by an acceleration in the pace of work with a simultaneous increase in errors and the resulting tendency towards an increase in unproductive information processing strategies. The ability to switch attention between different activities also tends to increase, but is characterized by hypersensitivity to distractions and poor self-control. At the same time, the degree of awareness of one's own actions decreases, and emotional stress grows, reaching the level of distress in the extreme values.

In the dysfunctional state of monotony, there is also a drop in intellectual lability, but, in this case, it is due to other reasons. First of all, narrowing of the amount of attention and the decrease in the ability to switch between different tasks, due to increased fatigue, are responsible for this. The overall pace of activity in solving the problem slows down (in particular, making choice is complicated), the efficiency of switching from one type of reaction to another decreases. The level of emotional stress, as a rule, falls, approaching apathy and fatigue at the extreme.

In accordance with these patterns, the test uses two types of tasks. Their differences are determined by how they influence the user functional state: They are a forced task, which contributes to the formation of the state of anxiety, and a monotonous one, which evokes the growth monotony/fatigue. Since the main factor in the functional state of anxiety is the lack of time and information in solving the problem, for its formation it is enough to provide unforeseen changes in the working conditions, e.g., to dramatically complicate the task without prior warning, or to suddenly change the content of the task while reducing the time for solving.

2.2   The Research Hypotheses

Based on the conclusions from the analysis of academic publications and the development of research tasks, we formulated two research questions:

RQ1: How does the combination of task features and web aesthetics affect user performance in terms of formation of anxiety and monotony?

RQ2: How does the group format of tasks solving affect the interaction of factors that form the user states?

RQ3: What are the cumulative effects of the combination of task features, web aesthetics, and testing circumstances?

In accordance with the research questions, we have put forward three hypotheses, on the basis of which we developed the design of the experiment:

H1: In the conditions of group problem solving, the effects that arise due to the simultaneous influence of the website aesthetics and the task features upon the user states will be cumulative, i.e., will intensify;

H2: The interaction of the high aesthetic quality of the website and tasks of both types in the conditions of group testing will lead to a decrease in cognitive efficiency and an increase in emotional stress (anxiety), also in comparison to individual testing;

H3: The interaction of the low aesthetic quality of the website and tasks of both types under conditions of group testing leads to unfavorable emotional states corresponding to the nature of the tasks (an increase in anxiety for a forced task and fatigue for a monotonous one), while cognitive efficiency decreases in both cases, also in comparison with individual task solving.

2.3 Experimental Tasks

In accordance with this, the structure of the forced task to foster anxiety was developed. Thus, each user was asked to find a given piece of content on a website of either high or low aesthetic quality within 10 min. Three minutes after the start of the search, the curator of the experiment announces a change in the purpose of the search and a reduction in time to 5 min, then, another minute later, to 2 min.

For the monotony pattern, an activity with a large number of simple and monotonous movements with little creative component is decisive. To create appropriate conditions, each user was offered a monotonous task: within one hour it was necessary to prepare a full text version of the website of either high or low aesthetic quality (in *.doc format). The exact time of completion of the task (35 min) was not reported.

The main factors in the formation of monotony are, in this case, the uncertainty of the completion time of the task and a significant number of repetitive operations for copying and distributing web content into a Word document.

2.4 Measures and Instruments

The differences in product features are represented by two university website layouts with the high and low aesthetic quality, as measured by the website aesthetic quality index, that one we had elaborated and called U-index [16].

We have employed two groups of metrics to measure user performance. For cognitive efficiency, intellectual lability was assessed as a metric of the productivity of cognitive operations. We have measured this indicator using the test for switching attention known as the 'Gorbov – Schulte table' [17] before and after the experiment. The method implies that the participants pronounce figures from 1 to 25 (on grey squares of the table where grey and red squares are mixed) and from 24 to 1 (on red squares of the table), switching from grey to red and back. The time of task solution and the number of mistakes are fixed and then are rendered into two respective specially elaborated scales proposed by Gorbov and Schulte. The overall lability is measured for each participant individually and calculated as:

$$A = T - C,$$

where T is the scaled metric for the longevity of the test, and C is the scaled metric for the number of errors. The smaller A, the worse the performance is. We have calculated A for each participant before and after the main task completion, thus detecting the drops (if any) of intellectual lability. Then, we have calculated the mean (M) for all the assessors in each sub-group (see below).

Emotional stress was measured by four indicators of self-esteem: In accordance with the method of self-assessment of emotional states proposed in [18], we measured by the 1–10 Likert scales the level of:

- anxiety (the 'calmness/anxiety' scale);
- fatigue (the 'energy/fatigue' scale);
- arousal (the 'excitement/depression' scale);
- confidence of users (the 'self-confidence/helplessness' scale).

And, finally, differences in testing conditions were created by the two formats of the testing environment, namely the individual and the group one.

2.5 Experimental Design and Procedures

The test tasks were performed in two groups, one of which performed the task under the conditions of in-aula group activity, and the second one individually, one by one.

Within each group, sub-groups were assigned either anxiety-inducing or fatigue-inducing tasks. For each task, subgroups worked with webpages of either high (U-index > 17) or low (U-index < 8) aesthetic quality.

Both groups had 16 participants each, with 8 assessors in each sub-group.

3 Results

As the test results show (Table 1), in three cases out of four, the group problem solving enhances the cumulative impact of website aesthetics and task features upon user states.

For the design of low aesthetic quality, the factor of collaborative activity leads to cumulative effects in combination with any type of tasks: with monotonous tasks, the group environment contributes to the development of fatigue, with tasks that cause anxiety, anxiety increases, and, in both cases, productivity decreases. The results are in line with the expectations. In particular, when solving a monotonous task in a group environment, the difference in the values of intellectual lability before and after the experiment is somewhat higher than for an individual test (187/179 vs. 187/176). In assessing the emotional state, a decrease in the indicator on the fatigue scale (that is, *growth* of fatigue) is also observed (7/5.5 for an individual test and 7/5 for a group test).

However, performing the task individually may help neutralize the impact of a group: When solving a task that fosters anxiety, there is a decrease in the indicator of intellectual lability in the group environment (187/174), while, when performing the test individually, productivity remains practically unchanged (187/187.6). Changes in the emotional state also support the trend towards a decrease in the productivity of group work, which is manifested in a more pronounced increase in anxiety for the group test (6.8/5.7 vs. 6.5/5.2).

Table 1. The results of the experiment

Dysfunctional state	Metrics		Individual test				Group test			
			Aesthetic design, mean		Non-aesthetic design, mean		Aesthetic design, mean		Non-aesthetic design, mean	
			Before the task is completed	After completing the task	Before the task is completed	After completing the task	Before the task is completed	After completing the task	Before the task is completed	After completing the task
Monotony	Intellectual lability		187	183	187	179	187	185	187	176
	Emotional state	Anxiety	7	7	7	7	7	7	7	7
		Fatigue	6	5.5	7	5.5	6	6	7	5
		Excitement	7	7	7	7	7	7	7	7
		Confidence	6.85	7	7	7	6,5	6,8	6,7	7
Anxiety	Intellectual lability		187	171	187	187	187	159	187	174
	Emotional state	Anxiety	7	6	6.8	5.7	6.7	5	7	5.7
		Fatigue	6	6	6	6	6	6	6	6
		Excitement	7	7	7	7	7	7	7	7
		Confidence	7	7	7	7	7	7	6	6

For the design of high aesthetic quality, the cumulative impact of group activity is manifested only in combination with the anxiety-forming task. Here, there is a maximum decrease in intellectual lability in both test settings that is observed. The changes are, respectively, 187/159 for the group work and 187/171 for the individual performance. We have observed that group activity enhances the tendency of lability increase to hyperlability. This is accompanied by a synchronous increase in anxiety, if one assesses the users' emotional state (6.85/5.7 for the individual testing vs. 6.7/5 for the group test).

Performing a stressful or monotonous task as part of a group enhances the dysfunctional states associated with it. This allows us to claim the full manifestation of the cumulative effect for the combination of low-quality usability factors, tasks of both types, and a group testing environment. It also indicates a complete confirmation of the **H3** hypothesis and a partial confirmation of the **H1** hypothesis.

However, this effect is not confirmed in all cases. As the results of the experiment show, the dynamics of the formation of dysfunctional states becomes particular in the interaction of high-quality design, group environment, and a monotonous task.

In this case, there is an effect that can be defined as antagonistic: The tendency of decrease in cognitive efficiency, which is evident in the individual test (187/183), is reduced in the group test (187/185). A similar situation is observed in the assessment of the emotional state: The tendency of increase of fatigue true for the individual testing is not confirmed when this type of task is performed in a group. Thus, group testing reverses the negative effects of high-quality design noticed by the previous research.

The effect that occurs under these conditions is aimed at reducing emotional stress and reducing the rate of decline in intellectual lability. Hypothesis **H2**, therefore, is only partially confirmed. The factor of aesthetic impact in the conditions of group testing when solving monotonous tasks becomes more of a compensatory character: It slows down the development of stressful conditions and helps maintain concentration.

4 Conclusion

Our work has demonstrated that factors that affect user performance in solving online tasks have to be assessed in complex, as individual assessment of single factors does not explain the effects discovered by earlier literature. However, combination of factors shows divergent patterns of impact which have greater explanatory power.

A further question posed by the results of the experiment can be formulated as follows: Which of the factors, along with the group testing environment, most contributes to the development of cumulative effects and the unfavorable functional states caused by them? This sets a whole new sub-area of research upon cumulative effects in DUXU.

We have shown that the testing format plays a leading role in usability testing and may critically affect what results the scholars receive from testing user performance. The results of the study confirm its influence on any combination of other factors related to the nature of the task and product usability. Undoubtedly, other factors also turn out to be significant for the productivity and emotional states of users. At the same time, the significance of these factors is unequal. Thus, in the proposed study, the next in importance after the individual/group format is the type of task. In particular, in formation of anxiety, the cumulative effect is observed regardless of the usability/aesthetic quality of the product.

To the greatest extent, it concerns intellectual lability. It looks like that the anxiety factor that determines the nature of such tasks is the most destructive for the cognitive efficiency of the user. In particular, among the negative manifestations of the dysfunctional state of anxiety, researchers name impulsiveness in decision-making, narrowing of the operational memory, an increase in the sensory threshold, and the destruction of productive thinking strategies (combinatorics, finding common and different features in signals, transforming concepts and judgments etc.), which results in heuristic user operations being replaced by template ones. We can confirm this trend by the test results: The depth of decrease in intellectual lability for a forced task differs several times from the indicators for solving a monotonous task, both in individual and group testing settings. The lack of connection between productivity and emotional stress indicators, on one hand, and the quality of usability, on the other, confirms the decisive importance of the specifics of the task itself and the experience that it forms.

And, finally, the difference in test results for the two types of tasks allows us to formulate the second question further research: What could be the reason for the difference in the rate of decline in intellectual lability for a monotonous task?

As can be seen from the results, in the case of a low aesthetic quality (low U-index rate), the group environment contributes to a deeper decrease in intellectual lability than an individual test does. However, for the high aesthetic quality (high U-index rate), the group environment slows down both the development of fatigue and the decrease in intellectual lability.

The reason for this difference may be largely due to the quality of the usability of the product: The higher it is, the stronger the compensatory effect of design on the developing state of monotony. As in the case of anxiety, the negative manifestations of monotony include a drop in the ability to concentrate and self-control, difficulties in updating working memory, and a general decrease in the efficiency of thinking. However, unlike anxiety, these phenomena are caused by fatigue that develops as a result of performing stereotypical actions without clear criteria for their effectiveness. Under these conditions, the speed of reactions slows down and the concentration of attention on the task decreases, although the level of emotional stress increases slightly. Perhaps this increases the sensitivity to distractions – in particular, to the presence of other people in the context of the task. From this point of view, low-quality design is perceived by the user as a source of visual noise, contributing to switching attention to factors that are not related to the task at hand. This demands further research.

Acknowledgements. This research has been supported by the project 'Center for International Media Research' at St. Petersburg State University, project #92564395. The authors are grateful to all the assessors who took part in the study, including the students of School of Journalism and Mass Communications, St. Petersburg State University, Russia.

References

1. Gilal, N.G., Zhang, J., Gilal, F.G.: The four-factor model of product design: scale development and validation. J. Prod. Brand Manag. **27**(6), 684–700 (2018)

2. Madathil, C.K., Greenstein, J.S.: Synchronous remote usability testing: a new approach facilitated by virtual worlds. In Proceedings of SIGCHI Conference on Human Factors in Computing Systems, pp. 2225–2234. ACM (2011)

3. Kjeldskov, J., Skov, M.B., Stage, J.: A longitudinal study of usability in health care: does time heal? Int. J. Med. Inf **79**(6), 135–143 (2008)

4. Leonova, A.B.: The concept of human functional state in Russian applied psychology. Psychol. Russia **2**, 517–538 (2009)

5. Sonderegger, A., Zbinden, G., Uebelbacher, A., Sauer, J.: The influence of product aesthetics and usability over the course of time: a longitudinal field experiment. Ergonomics **55**(7), 713–730 (2012)

6. Sauer, J., Sonderegger, A., Heyden, K., Biller, J., Klotz, J., Uebelbacher, A.: Extra-laboratorial usability tests: an empirical comparison of remote and classical field testing with lab testing. Appl. Ergon. **74**, 85–96 (2019)

7. Sauer, J., Sonderegger, A.: The influence of product aesthetics and user state in usability testing. Behav. Inf. Technol. **30**(6), 787–796 (2011)

8. Tuch, A.N., Roth, S.P., Hornbaek, K., Opwis, K., Bargas-Avila, J.A.: Is beautiful really usable? toward understanding the relation between usability, aesthetics, and affect in HCI. Comput. Hum. Behav. **28**(5), 1596–1607 (2012)

9. Partala, T., Surakka, V.: The effects of affective interventions in human-computer interaction. Interact. Comput. **16**(2), 295–309 (2004)

10. Ben-Bassat, T., Meyer, J., Tractinsky, N.: Economic and subjective measures of the perceived value of aesthetics and usability. ACM Trans. Comput. Human Interact. **13**(2), 210–234 (2006)

11. Jones, F., Harris, P., Waller, H., Coggins, A.: Adherence to an exercise prescription scheme: the role of expectations, self-efficacy, stage of change and psychological well-being. Br. J. Health. Psychol. **10**(3), 359–378 (2005)

12. Klein, J., Moon, Y., Picard, R.W.: This computer responds to user frustration: theory, design, and results. Interact. Comput. **14**(2), 119–140 (2002)

13. Yakunin, A., Bodrunova, S.: Website aesthetics and functional user states as factors of web usability. In: Ahram, T., Taiar, R. (eds.) IHIET 2021. LNNS, vol. 319, pp. 394–401. Springer, Cham (2022). https://doi.org/10.1007/978-3-030-85540-6_51

14. Wiltermuth, S., Heath, C.: Synchrony and cooperation. Psychol. Sci. **20**(1), 1–5 (2009)

15. Leonova, A.B.: Occupational stress, personnel adaptation, and health. In: Spielberger, C.D., Sarason, I.G. (eds.) Stress and Emotion: Anxiety, Anger, and Curiosity, pp. 109–125. Routledge, London (1996)

16. Bodrunova, S.S., Yakunin, A.V.: U-index: an eye-tracking-tested checklist on webpage aesthetics for university web spaces in Russia and the USA. In: Marcus, A., Wang, W. (eds.) DUXU 2017. LNCS, vol. 10288, pp. 219–233. Springer, Cham (2017). https://doi.org/10.1007/978-3-319-58634-2_17

17. Mashin, V.A.: Analysis of heart rate variability based on the graph method. Hum. Physiol. **28**(4), 437–447 (2002)

18. Wessman, A.E., Ricks, D.F.: Mood and Personality. Holt, Rinehart and Winston, New York (1966)

Author Index

Printed in the United States
by Baker & Taylor Publisher Services

Printed in the United States
by Baker & Taylor Publisher Services